Fostering First Gen Success and Inclusion

FOSTERING FIRST GEN SUCCESS AND INCLUSION

A GUIDE FOR LAW SCHOOLS

EDITED BY **BRITTANY L. RAPOSA**

CAROLINA ACADEMIC PRESS
Durham, North Carolina

Library of Congress Cataloging-in-Publication Data
Names: Raposa, Brittany L., editor.
Title: Fostering first gen success and inclusion : a guide for law schools / edited by Brittany L. Raposa.
Description: Durham, North Carolina : Carolina Academic Press, 2025. | Includes bibliographical references.
Identifiers: LCCN 2024057708 | ISBN 9781531023935 (paperback) | ISBN 9781531023942 (ebook)
Subjects: LCSH: Law schools—United States. | Law—Study and teaching—United States. | Law students—United States. | Law students—Vocational guidance—United States.
Classification: LCC KF272 .F67 2025 | DDC 340.071/173—dc23/eng/20241203
LC record available at https://lccn.loc.gov/2024057708

Carolina Academic Press
700 Kent Street
Durham, North Carolina 27701
(919) 489-7486
www.cap-press.com

Printed in the United States of America

Contents

PART V Academic Success, Diversity Initiatives, and the Library

PART VI Supporting First Gen Students in the Classroom

Introduction

From Hardship to the Legal Academy

The Experience of a First-Gen Law Professor

Brittany L. Raposa

I WISH THIS BOOK HAD EXISTED when I was in law school. Being a first-generation law student is *hard.* It feels good to finally put those words in print. Words I think many first-generation law students and graduates could scream. Throughout this book, you will see that a "first-generation" student is typically someone who was the first to graduate from college in their family.[1] I am a first-generation American, high school, college, and law school graduate. My family immigrated to the United States from Portugal and Brazil and were not able to finish high school because they had to work to help support their families. My hands and shoulders carry shadows and realities of years of factory work and economic hardship. The fabric of my identity is woven by individuals who had to work hard to see their family smile, who had to live in fear of being deported, and who were ridiculed for their language and their culture.

Like many of our first-generation students, especially those who are first-generation American, I come from a place where I learned that our futures are not promised to us. A future is constructed day-by-day, through the choices you make. Your future is earned, little by little, through hard work and action. It was expected that I would go to graduate school because, as my family constantly echoed, I wouldn't be able to make any money with a bachelor's degree in English Literature and another in Writing, Rhetoric, and Communications. It had to be law school, they insisted. Why? Lawyers make money, and we never had any, and you can finally have some. Did my family actually know if all lawyers made money? No. Did I know anything about the salary of a lawyer? Another no. I went to law school because it was expected of me, and I had this tremendous need to make them proud. We had nothing, and I had to be someone who gave us something.

My mother and father were both factory workers for over 20 years. My mother worked in a factory making jewelry boxes and my father in one that made electrical supplies. We did not have much money, but we always made it week-by-week. En-

1. If an author in this book intends another definition, you will see that definition provided in their writing.

glish is their additional language, and although they speak it strongly now, they faced many language and cultural barriers to help me academically throughout the years. While they were emotionally supportive, they could not help me with navigating the college application process or the financial aid process, and could not assist me with assignments, readings, or papers. It felt like navigating an entirely new world, while still being responsible for the cultural expectations of another world.

I always questioned whether I would be able to make it through law school. My law school experience is similar to the stories you will read in parts of this book. I went to an affordable, four-tier institution because I simply could not afford to go anywhere else. When I speak about affordability, I do mean money, but I also mean affordability in terms of familial obligations. It was never an option to leave the family I was helping, and would continue to help, throughout law school. I also did not have much knowledge about the advantages of going to other law schools. I took the LSAT, got into the one law school I applied to, and that was it.

I think it's fair to say that I had no idea what I was doing when I got to law school. I remember orientation so vividly. We had to read a civil procedure case about subject matter jurisdiction and had a mock class. I read the case about 20 times before this orientation class, and not one part of me understood it. I looked up so many words in a dictionary and I took notes on the case I was reading. I tried everything in my power and pulled an all-nighter to try to understand what was happening in this case, and I just couldn't. I graduated *magna cum laude* in college, so I constantly asked myself, what's wrong with me? Although I felt defeated, after much debate, I showed up to orientation and attended the mock class. The professor asked for volunteers, and there was a sea of hands raised. Everyone seemed to know the answers. Everyone seemed to know what was going on. If you can envision a human physically shrinking in their seat in a room filled with people in suits, that would be what I was feeling on the inside. My immediate thought was that there was no place for me in law school. I didn't see myself as someone who contribute positively to the legal profession, and how could I, if I had no idea what was going on in our first class and everyone else did? If only I had been told that the characteristics I bring through my identity would be an asset, it would have made this first experience much easier.

I eventually figured out law school, through many tears, late nights, and losing a bit of myself. Gone were the days where I spent time with friends or socialized. I taught myself how to learn and to study. It took countless weeks and trials and errors, but something eventually just clicked. I did all of this while maintaining a job in retail and in my law library to help my family. Not many people in my class worked, so I didn't talk about it. I did not want to be seen as the person who was different more than I already felt. Throughout my journey, I realized a lot that I didn't know. I didn't know that money could make opportunities swing open. I didn't know that if you came from a lower-ranked undergraduate institution, you wouldn't be taken as seriously and predicted to fail classes and the bar exam. I didn't know that being a first-generation student was at times synonymous with being "at-risk." I didn't know that the traditional structure and pedagogy of law school was intended to at times make us feel humiliated and incompetent instead of brilliant and brave.

At some points throughout my journey, there was this overbearing sense of hopelessness. The type of hopelessness from knowing too little and feeling too much and not knowing how to move forward. Hopelessness was then followed by this overwhelming desire to *not* have to have everything figured out. I wished I could turn off the part of my brain that needed to perfectly succeed and to make my family proud because I was *the first*. I wish I had someone there to tell me that I was still just human. Just a small thing that must find its way like everyone else in this enormous world. Instead, it just felt like I had to be okay because there was no other option. No one in my family understood this process, or what law school and the stress of it alone could do to your mental health. The answer was always to "just study" or to "stop being dramatic." My pain was never more valuable than my potential.

However, as I alluded to, I got through law school successfully. I had the support of an amazing mentor in law school,[2] and the support of some other students I found who were also first-generation students. I realized, at the end of my law school journey, that I wasn't just a statistic or an at-risk prediction. I wasn't a burden. I brought with me hard work, grit, and unique perspectives that my peers did not have. From difficulty, my confidence has grown. From anger, stemmed purpose. One of my purposes, I truly believe, is to help first-generation law students, and one way to do that is through this book.

Despite the difficulties I had, I recognize the immense privilege I had in law school. I am a cis-gender, heterosexual woman, with white skin. I speak English as my first language, and while it was difficult, I was able to sustain enough income to make it through law school and beyond. I've met many students who do not have these privileges. Students who are brilliant but face multiple barriers. Students who are capable, but the law school system and how it's built is designed to bring them challenges. Once we add layers to someone's identity as a first-generation student, the more susceptible they are to experiencing more layers of hardship. Our students have likely been mocked, insulted, threatened, questioned, and told, either through words or actions, that they are nothing and do not belong. Our students have experienced trauma outside and inside our law school buildings based on their identities. Our first-generation students deserve to feel safe and free, and I hope this book paves the way to assisting law schools in helping them feel just that.

Why should you read this book? More and more first-generation students are applying and getting admitted into law school. However, many institutions and individuals are beginning to acknowledge that law schools must do more than just

2. I am indebted to Professor Jim Freeley. I don't think I could have made it without your guidance and support, and a simple line in this book is insufficient to show my gratitude, but I thank you always.

admit first-generation students — we must support them.[3] Further, studies demonstrate that first-generation students have more difficulty finding jobs after law school compared to their peers.[4] Although first-generation college students bring with them to law school incredible skill and unique experiences, they often lack the social, cultural, and financial capital that others have. First-generation law students also bring diversity to law schools.[5] The purpose of this book is not to stress the importance of having diversity within our law school buildings — this book assumes that you, the reader, already value and know the reasons why diversity is critical in law schools and in the legal profession.

In 2021, I conducted a survey throughout those working in law schools, which included both faculty and staff.[6] The question I posed called for a simple yes or no answer, and the question was: "Are you aware of the unique difficulties first-generation college students face in law school?" When looking at the results, 67% of responders answered "no" to this question. I'm not sure if I should have been, but I was incredibly surprised at the results of my survey. I have heard some of my colleagues indicate that they didn't know much about first-generation students, but I was ignorant to the fact that perhaps it was a law school-wide issue. Consequently, this book answers the questions of *who*, *why*, and *how* as it pertains to supporting our first-generation law students.

First, this book will share the stories of first-generation students to illustrate the unique hardships that these students face in law school to demonstrate *why* we need specific programming and initiatives to help these students. This book is written through many different experiences and perspectives to give you, the reader, a large picture of what our first-generation students have been faced with, and what they continue to be faced with. Second, this book will describe *who* our first-generation law students are, and the different identities and the diversity they bring to our law school. The book will go through the unique challenges of our first-generation students of color, our first-generation students in the LGBTQ+ community, our disabled first-generation students, our indigenous first-generation students, and beyond. Finally, this book will explain *how*. This book will take you through each part of a student's journey, through admissions to bar exam preparation, and explain how to create programming and how to support our first-generation law students.

---

3. *Law Schools Must Do More to Retain First-Generation Students*, Bloomberg Law, https://news.bloomberglaw.com/us-law-week/law-schools-must-do-more-to-retain-first-generation-students (Feb. 15, 2022).

4. Debra Cassens Weiss, *First-Generation College Grads Find Fewer Jobs After Law School Than Their Peers, New NALP Data Says*, ABA J., https://www.abajournal.com/news/article/first-generation-college-grads-find-fewer-jobs-after-law-school-than-their-peers-nalp-says (Oct. 20, 2021).

5. *See* Michelle Silverthorn, *First-Generation Lawyers: The Next Diversity Frontier*, Legal Mgmt., April 2018, at 11, 12.

6. Survey on file with author. There were 207 responses to the survey, spanning 42 different law schools, all over the United States.

The authors in this book are incredible, and many are former first-generation students themselves. I continue to be inspired by our authors and their commitment to their students and those committed to strengthening law schools. Some of our authors are law professors and law school staff who come from a variety of institutions across the United States and have diverse backgrounds and perspectives. Other authors are lawyers or work in other legal careers, and they bring valuable insight and experience to this book. The focus of this book is to explain the unique challenges many of our first-generation students face, and to present you with tools and resources that you can bring to your law schools to support your students.

How should you approach this book? In my opinion, everyone should read the portions of this book that describe the first-generation law student experience, which is presented in Chapters 1 and 2. It's important to listen to the first-generation law student experience and to see how our students are impacted by our institutions. Then, the book should be utilized in the area you work in with your institution. You will find that the book is broken down by different sections of the law school experience. The book shows how to support first-generation law students in the following spaces:

1. Pre-orientation and orientation programming;
2. Academic success departments, diversity offices, and the library;
3. The doctrinal classrooms;
4. Legal research and writing classrooms;
5. Career development, experiential education, and financial aid offices; and
6. Bar exam support.

There is something in this book for every member of the law school community.

Why am I putting together this book? The answer to this question is probably the simplest — it does not already exist, and it is very much needed. Although I and many authors in this book were able to achieve great success in law school despite the challenges we faced, many current students do not have the means nor the resources to do so. When thinking about supporting first-generation law students at my institution, I conducted a lot of research, and unfortunately there was not much. There are books and resources written to a student audience with tips for first-generation law students. No body of work existed for law school faculty and staff where they could search for ideas on how to create or strengthen first-generation programming in law schools, apart from a few law review articles.[7] As a former first-generation student, I wanted to put this book together to help future first-gen-

---

7. *See* Jaqueline M. O'Bryant & Katharine, *First-Generation Students in Law School: A Proven Success Model*, 70 Ark. L. Rev. 913 (2018); Tomiko Brown-Nagin, *Rethinking Proxies for Disadvantage in Higher Education: A First Generation Students' Project*, 2014 U. Chi. Legal F. 433 (2014); SpearIt, *Not for Free: Exploring the Collateral Costs of Diversity in Legal Education*, 48 U. Pac. L. Rev. 887 (2017).

eration students who experienced difficulties like I did, and to help first-generation students who were different from me and may have experienced even more challenges than I did. More importantly, as a law professor, I see how first-generation students struggle, and they made my passion for this book burn brighter and brighter as each semester passed. Having these students in our law schools is an incredible thing, to have been there with them and to help them, and to see how fantastic they can be in the world.

Most say students, like people, grow and develop linearly. However, I find that for first-generation students, it is cyclic. **Students grow up, but first-generation students grow around; we strengthen around the place that brings us hardship, but our vulnerable core is never gone**. What makes us vulnerable will always exist, and law schools need to be able to manage and deal with this type of learning and growth for our first-generation students. Being a first-generation student inspired me to be a law teacher. I learned how to learn, so I want to teach students how to learn. I know the emotions that can come with being the first at this, so I want to teach students how to handle those emotions. I succeeded, and I want nothing more than to help all our first-generation law students succeed.

This book would not be possible without the caring and talented contributing authors who wrote pieces for this book. I'm truly inspired by their passion and their words, and I hope you will be, too. Their care for law students is infectious, and I have no doubt that their ideas and passion will assist you in building a better law school.

I would also like to thank my family, my partner, my friends, and my law school colleagues for always believing that I could belong in any space I wanted to, such as this one. Finally, I would not be able to do this without the inspiration and lessons I've learned from my students. They have truly made me a better teacher and a better advocate. This book is for all my students who, along the way, were told they could not do this, and a little bit for the younger girl in me who didn't believe at times she could do it either. It is my hope that one day, someone can finally say, "I'm happy this book existed when I was in law school."

PART I The First Gen Law Student Experience

One

Speaking from Experience

Profiling the First Gen Perspective to Foster Inclusion in Legal Education

Amy Vaughan-Thomas*

IMAGINE IT IS YOUR FIRST DAY OF LAW SCHOOL. A moment that you've anticipated with excitement and trepidation. You are optimistic about making an impact on the world, instituting social justice reform, and envision your future filled with success. You've looked forward to this moment for months, but you are the first in your family to pursue an advanced education and know little about what to expect. As you walk onto the campus, you see towering stone buildings all around you, with statutes and busts of historical figures throughout the campus green. You enter the law school building and pass through a hall filled with oil painting portraits of old White men that, to you, look like the wizards' portraits in Hogwarts from the *Harry Potter* movies. You laugh to yourself, imagining that one will start speaking to you. Little do you know that you are about to enter a world filled with mystery, much like young Harry. You settle into your seat in a large, cold lecture hall. You notice that everyone else has a laptop and the expensive new textbook for the course. Meanwhile you sit with a recycled notepad and a used book, falling apart at the seams. Your professor strolls through the door, right on time, wearing a tailored black suit, a tie, and glasses. He opens his book, calls your name, and tells you to debrief the case. You have no idea where to begin and fumble over your words. Your professor quickly calls on someone else and moves on with the discussion, while you're left wondering how things started off so wrong.

While the theory of law promotes equality and justice, the system training the minds of lawyers is riddled with inequity. That inequity weighs heavily on the first-generation law student experience, and is detrimental to the progress of the profession. Before this book's contributors explain methods to better serve and cultivate the first-generation law student experience, it is vital that the readers place themselves in the shoes of first-generation students. This essay seeks to introduce and immerse the reader in four firsthand, first-generation law student experiences to help the reader understand perspective and grapple with the inequities of each

* University of Massachusetts School of Law—Dartmouth.

experience. For those unfamiliar with the term, first-generation law students are also first-generation professionals, meaning they have little professional exposure. Many first-generation students have parents who did not attend college, although that isn't always true. But the common thread among all first-generation students is that they have not had anyone in their near family attend law school.[1]

The four individuals chosen to share their experiences represent a mix of first-generation law students throughout the country. Their names were changed to protect anonymity and to encourage a frank and open discussion. While some individuals were the first members in their family to attend any form of post-secondary institution, others had family members who completed college but not an advanced degree. This feature is an important starting point in understanding the first-generation law student perspective. The entire experience—from beginning the application through graduation and the bar exam—is new. However, the challenges and lessons learned along the way are unique for each person, and thus one should avoid overgeneralizing persons identifying as first-generation before getting to know each story. Appreciating the differences in each story promotes well-rounded programming. Examine these four experiences, not from a narrow lens but from a broad view, recognizing that these narratives make up only a small portion of a much larger picture.

I. Rachel Reflects on The Myth of Law School Rankings and Calls for Better Programming

Rachel classifies herself as a first-generation law student because she is a woman who comes from a blue-collar family and is the first person in her family to go to an undergraduate university and law school.

When Rachel started to consider law school, she knew that there was a ranking list, and she knew that she needed to take the LSAT when she researched the application process. However, she didn't understand what the LSAT meant and how different the LSAT was in comparison to other standardized tests she took in her life. She took the LSAT without having studied, and didn't understand what her score meant in the context of the application process. She did not understand that she should have taken the exam again—she took the exam once and began to apply to law schools. She never knew that the LSAT was a factor that had influence in receiving scholarships.

1. Interview by Michelle Silverthorn, Diversity and Education Director for the Illinois Supreme Court Commission on Professionalism, with Sally Olson, Chief Diversity Office at Sidley Austin LLP; Michelle Jackson, Director of Alumni Advising at Northwestern Law, *First Generation Lawyers: The Next Diversity Frontier*, 37 Legal Mgmt. No. 4, 11 (April 2018).

Rachel had very little familiarity with the law and did not speak to others about her decision to go to law school. Her impression was that being a lawyer was a career in which she could make a lot of money.

She also did not have a strategy for applying to law schools. Instead, Rachel chose to apply to schools that sent her marketing material. She applied to many schools but did not research what each school had to offer. She was accepted into most of the schools and for her selection process she decided to use the ranking list.

Her selection process was solely based on the rank of the school on the list. She narrowed down her decision-making process to two schools. Her two choices were between a top-50-ranked law school offering her no financial assistance, and a top-100-ranked law school offering her a full scholarship.

Rachel didn't consider the financial cost this decision would have on the rest of her life, and she did not have anyone in her family or mentors telling her otherwise. All Rachel believed was that she needed to attend the highest ranked school possible because that is what she saw in the movies. She chose the top 50 school despite having already borrowed financial aid to afford undergrad and without regard for the additional cost for law school. Upon entering law school, Rachel borrowed the full amount awarded.

Throughout the process, Rachel did not have any financial counseling.

From the first day of law school, Rachel quickly learned that she was a part of a highly competitive program and worked hard to improve her grades after a challenging first quarter.

Many times, Rachel felt that she didn't belong. Her law school had a lot of legacy students and a lot of students with wealth. She felt disadvantaged because the legacy students had connections to the law, were well versed in the law, and came into law school having studied in pre-law programs. She also felt financial strains that many of the wealthy students didn't experience. Due to these financial constraints, Rachel needed to work during law school so that she could afford to pay her bills. She also needed some additional spending money on top of the money she borrowed. In total, excluding her undergraduate borrowing and credit cards, Rachel finished law school with $250,000 of student loan debt—some of which was federal borrowing and some of which was private lending. Today, her student loans are over $400,000 because of the interest on these loans.

Rachel also reflected on her learning experience in law school, stating that it took her longer to "get it" in comparison to the multi-generation legacy students. In terms of "getting it," Rachel quickly recognized that she was behind on reading comprehension as she had never read so much information in one sitting to prepare for one class. She did not understand how to properly case brief and, instead, took word-for-word notes on the cases without proper case brief structure. While reading, she frequently stumbled over unfamiliar legal language in her readings, found it difficult to identify the parties involved in the case, and could not distinguish between a rule and a holding for quite some time. To her, it felt as if the rule should be explicitly defined for the reader in each case, and she had trouble understanding how to synthesize a rule from case law. The struggles with reading and briefing were exacerbated by the classroom dynamic and the use of the Socratic Method. She often was so anxious about being called on that she did not learn or hear significant portions of the lecture because she was grappling with her anxiety. She was fortunate to surround herself with a small group of similarly situated students and they worked together to navigate these challenges because no professors took time to explain how to navigate the learning process.

Rachel felt that many of her legacy student colleagues had much better context for the expected work product. Some of her colleagues wrote briefs "as if they had written on the same topic before."[2] Their exposure to the concepts gave them an advantage when it came to the use of their time and their learning process. This is a prime example of what she means when she says it took her longer to "get it."

Another example of her learning challenges was her experience in mock trial. The rigor of this curriculum, the demand of the program, and the White-male-dominated lecture discussion made the program incredibly intimidating. While she doesn't think that the professors saw the first-generation students any differently, the students themselves felt unwelcome in this environment.

The class composition was about 95% White students. Rachel's small group of friends was a majority of the diverse student body. Her friends became her main support system, and each person helped the other to foster their success.

In reflecting on her time in law school, Rachel believes her school could have implemented three specific resources for first-generation law students. First, she would have benefited substantially from a pre-law course introducing basic concepts like case briefing and note taking in law school. The course also could explain the structure of law school—for example, an explanation of what law review means in comparison to moot court.

The mentor program could also be improved to specifically cater to first-generation law students. Mentors could have been a student or a professor—someone to speak to about, for example, basic legal terms: "What is a case brief? What is a supplement? How do I use a supplement? What is an outline?"[3] There was no academic success program to assist students in need, and she relied on her own academic resourcefulness to forge her path to success.

Finally, financial counseling prior to law school and during law school is essential so that students understand how the decisions they make impact the rest of their life.

Rachel views her strengths as a first-generation law student in her ability to manage time, to manage multiple responsibilities, and to adapt to new environments.

2. Interview with alias Rachel Black, Licensed Attorney, via Zoom (November 8, 2022).
3. *Id.*

While she faced many challenges as a first-generation law student, she promotes the value of first-generation law students as employees. She emphasizes that improvements to programming during law school promote access to the profession and are essential to diversity initiatives.

II. Deborah Persevered in Silence and Now Emphasizes the Need for True Allies

Deborah knew she wanted to go to law school, but she also knew she needed to be close to home. She valued her ability to assist her immigrant family and made law school a priority as she saw it as a means to elevate her socioeconomic status. She identifies as a first-generation law student because she comes from an immigrant family and was the first person in her family to obtain an advanced degree.

In applying for law school, Deborah knew very little about the process. She knew she had to take the LSAT to apply, but did minimum preparation. She purchased a book online, did some practice from the book, and took the exam. When she received her LSAT score, no one told her the importance of the score or what it meant in relation to pursuing a law degree. She didn't know that there was a ranking process, or that there was any information that she should research when applying to law school. For example, she did not know anything about the bar exam—other than what she heard in the movies—so she never looked at any school's bar pass rate. The only factors she considered were affordability and location.

Deborah framed affordability as anything that would put her in less than $100,000 debt. The reason affordability was a large part of her decision was because she took loans for undergrad, including private debt her family withdrew to afford her first year of undergraduate because they were unaware of the financial aid process. She wanted to make sure she put herself in a position where she would be able to pay this back. However, despite her financial awareness, Deborah borrowed the maximum amount during law school because she needed to contribute funds to support her family.

Deborah decided to only apply to one law school. She never considered any other law school, and never knew anything about scholarships throughout her application process. She didn't know that schools would offer scholarships and when the one school she applied to did offer her a scholarship, she turned the scholarship down out of fear that she may not satisfy the requirements of the scholarship while in law school.

Upon entering law school, Deborah realized very quickly that her law school didn't acknowledge the experience of first-generation students. While the atmosphere of the school and classroom experience was not "cutthroat,"[4] she hid in her

4. Interview with alias Deborah Strong, Licensed Attorney, via Zoom (November 11, 2022).

class and, at times, felt as if she didn't belong. For example, her faculty advisor told her that she "wouldn't make it because of where she came from and her background." This experience was quite isolating, and further pushed Deborah to hide among her colleagues.

In addition to this specific example, Deborah noted that there was only one faculty member who identified as diverse, and no faculty members spoke about or identified as first-generation professionals. Her experience as a first-generation law student was lonesome because she felt that she didn't relate on a professional level with her majority white faculty.

Many of her multi-generation colleagues spoke up quite frequently in class and were quite confident in their abilities. In answering questions, they would often mention their experiences with the law and the connections of their family members. This often rattled her confidence. Deborah also found it difficult to connect with other first-generation students because it was an unspoken topic. In forging friendships, Deborah did not create friendships with other first-generation or diverse students because most were dismissed after the first semester. The dismissals further heightened her fear that she didn't belong and that she would be kicked out.

In attempting to forge a bond with the diverse faculty member, Deborah quickly learned that while outwardly a person may appear an ally, that may not always be the case. This faculty member was supportive of Deborah until Deborah was unwilling to participate in a specific workshop held by this faculty member. After that occasion, this faculty member outwardly rejected Deborah and spoke about Deborah to her colleagues. This further increased Deborah's isolation from the community, and still haunts her because she felt betrayed by the one person who was purportedly representative of the diverse students at the school. Deborah feels this faculty interaction, in comparison to the previous interaction with her faculty advisor, was much more devastating because she didn't have anyone who was a part of the law school space that would support her. Deborah emphasized that negative interactions with diverse and "allied"[5] faculty members are far more harmful long-term to the psyche of first-generation law students than negative experiences with non-diverse, non-ally faculty members.

The isolation of the law school experience was not solely limited to interactions with students and faculty. Deborah didn't receive any financial counseling, and did not know to ask for such counseling. She also didn't reach out for any academic assistance. Further, Deborah didn't know about the internship process, and was not counseled to seek an internship after her first year of law school. All the while, Deborah placed lot of pressure on herself to do well and experienced challenges with mental health. She didn't speak to anyone at the school about these challenges, and

5. *Id.*

sought resources outside of the school because she did not want to give anyone at the school reason to believe that she wouldn't make it.

In reflection, Deborah wishes her school provided more resources and support for first-generation students to avoid isolation. For example, sessions specifically tailored to first-generation students related to classroom basics like reading, case briefing, and note taking, as well as career counseling for first-generation students explaining what law internships look like and why they are important. Most persons today who are part of legal education and academia are not first-generation students because of the hierarchy embedded in the system, and she emphasizes the need for institutions to consider alternative traits, like diverse exposure and professional backgrounds, besides merely law school pedigree and publishing rates in the faculty hiring process.

As a first-generation student, Deborah finds that her experience has led to a better ability to understand varying perspectives, instilled grit, and led to increased social and emotional intelligence that some of her multi-generational colleagues lack. While she hopes for improvements for future first-generation students, she is appreciative of her experience and feels privileged to be part of the legal community.

III. Daniel Had a Strong Mentor and an Awareness of the Legal Process, Which Contributed to Sound Decision Making

As the oldest grandchild in a large immigrant family from Mexico, Daniel was the first person in his immediate and extended family to complete an undergraduate degree and go to law school. His family owned a successful small business as Daniel was growing up and, at one time in his life, his family needed the assistance of a lawyer. This was Daniel's first experience meeting a lawyer and he was quickly motivated to become a lawyer. Daniel liked that the attorney was helping people and admired how the attorney carried himself professionally.

This attorney offered Daniel an opportunity to shadow him and work within his law office assisting with administrative duties. Daniel embraced this opportunity, and worked with the attorney for three summers during high school, and his first year in college. Daniel became very familiar with the legal process from this experience.

When he decided to apply to law school, Daniel found that the LSAT and application process was the most challenging. From his experiences in applying to college on his own, he knew that he needed to do research to better understand the law school application process. In researching, he learned about LSAT prep programs, enrolled in a prep program, and even extended his plan to take the LSAT so that he had more time to prepare for the exam.

Upon receiving his LSAT score, Daniel used a predictor website to determine his likelihood of success in applications to law schools across the country. This gave Daniel a better idea of the schools where he could receive admittance. In narrowing down the schools in his application process, Daniel considered the location in comparison to his family's home, the cost of attendance, and the class size, as well as strong bar pass rates.

Unlike other first-generation students, Daniel knew to make these considerations because he did a lot of research in his undergraduate application process. Daniel also knew about the importance of the bar exam because of his experiences working for the attorney. While he knew about the bar exam based on pop culture references, he found that his experience with the lawyer put the bar exam in greater context. He relied on his work with the lawyer and his professors in undergraduate to inform his decision making in the application process.

Daniel chose to attend his law school based on the location of the school, the culture of the city, the high scholarship he was awarded, the class sizes, and the success of the law school on the bar exam. While the ranking of the school was not strong, he knew that the strong bar passage rate would make a difference in his overall success as a first-time taker.

Daniel enjoyed his time in law school. He appreciated the small sections and the practical structure of the curriculum. The school marketed to a diverse student body, and he felt included as part of that student body. However, he does feel that the experience could have been more diverse—there could have been more students that looked like him and shared in his experiences.

In starting law school, he felt slightly disadvantaged in comparison to his multi-generation colleagues. Some of his colleagues had a strong legal lexicon and were more comfortable in the classroom at the start. While he felt comfortable with some language that he had learned about while working for the lawyer, he felt weak in other aspects. For example, he knew the meanings of *motion*, *deposition*, and *summary judgment*. But he was still unfamiliar with case briefs, IRAC, and note taking.

Daniel surrounded himself with close friends who were also first-generation and diverse students. This helped normalize his experience and gave him a group to rely on throughout his time in law school. His law school offered many clubs for students like La Raza and the Entertainment and Sports Law societies, but he did not find there were specific resources offered to first-generation students.

In working with faculty members, some were more approachable than others. Faculty interactions inside and outside the classroom left an impression on his experience. During his first week of law school, his professor wrote on his first assessment, "You should really reconsider if law school is for you."[6] This experience left

6. Interview with alias Daniel Cruz, Licensed Attorney, via Zoom (November 11, 2022).

Daniel heartbroken and contributed to Daniel's imposter syndrome. As a result, he avoided that faculty member for his three years in law school.

Throughout his time in law school, Daniel felt pressure to do well for his family and was aware of the pressure to succeed as the first person in his family to attend law school. When attending family events, many family members would ask him about his schooling, his internship experience, and the awaiting results of the bar exam. Everyone in his family and extended family knew that Daniel was waiting for the bar results, which created a high amount of emotional pressure.

In reflecting on his experience, he wishes his program would have adjusted curriculum to assist students from the start as opposed to later academic intervention programs that only assisted after the students didn't perform well. He also wishes tutoring programs were better structured to explain to students why they didn't understand a problem, as opposed to showing the students how to write the problem without any further explanation.

While law school was at times frustrating, demanding, and daunting, Daniel is grateful for the experience. Daniel finds his experience as a first-generation law student contributed to his tenacity as a professional, and gave him the ability to solve problems on his own. He is now able to guide and give back to other family members who want to pursue advanced education and values his ability to do so.

IV. Kelly's Experience as a First Gen Student and the Importance of Recognizing the Intersectionality of Identities

Kelly identifies herself as a first-generation student, not because she is the first person in her family to go to an undergraduate institution, but because she is the first in her family, in quite a long time, to complete her undergraduate and J.D. sequentially at a young age. She has extended family members who were social workers, engineers, dentists, economists, and nurses, but she was the first in her family to go to college at 18, finish her degree, and go to graduate school. There is some unknown about her family history but as far as she knows, she was the first person in her family to go to law school.

In her immediate family, there was no one to advise her on debt or attending an in-state versus out-of-state institution. She decided to meet with a pre-law advisor during college. The pre-law advisor spent significant time with Kelly assisting her in reworking her personal statement. Kelly's pre-law advisor helped Kelly explain her personal connection to understanding the legal system and the power that comes with being an attorney. Kelly felt tension between telling the truth in her statement and exploiting her truths for some kind of gain. Drafting the personal statement was an uncomfortable part of the application experience. Her pre-law advisor worked with Kelly to uncover her realities, truths, and honesty in her personal statement, for which Kelly will always be grateful.

Kelly found a way to afford a preparation course for the LSAT, but her first LSAT outcome was not as expected. She decided to take the LSAT a second time after having read a resource book on applying to law school, and felt more confident after reading that resource. Kelly applied to four law schools because she received her second LSAT score late, and the applications were costly.

Kelly was accepted into two law schools and waitlisted in two others. One of those acceptances was her top choice and this school also awarded her the best scholarship. Kelly sought advice from her pre-law advisor, who advised her that she "needed to go to the best law school" and that she shouldn't attend her top choice because of a lack of resources at the institution and the rankings. Kelly disagreed and chose to attend her top choice.

The small structure of the institution allowed the school to implement a mentoring program for each student early on in the law school experience. The mentoring program at the law school paired an upper division student with an incoming student. Kelly happened to know her mentor from a previous connection, and she found that this connection in law school helped her save money by receiving passed-down textbooks. She also was able to discuss common experiences with the same professor.

The institution had a lot to offer their law students that could not be detailed or accounted for in the ranking. The institution promoted access to the profession for students, kept the cost of attendance low, and offered diverse programming to assist students to become attorneys.

Kelly had several Black professors at her school, and did not face concerns speaking out in class in comparison to the fears she had in other White instructor courses. Her class composition was diverse (the class population was not majority White), which helped create a comfortable atmosphere to learn and challenge hierarchal structures embedded within the law.

There was not an outright Academic Success Department on campus, but there were shadow intervention support classes for students not performing as well. If you weren't a student who needed the additional support, you didn't seek any additional resources or engage with these supports. There was shame around needing support, because there was a strict bell curve with mandatory Ds and Cali Awards with the top performer's names posted. While this created stigma, there was no imposter syndrome at this institution because there was not an underrepresented group at the institution.

Black lawyers were the majority on faculty and in the class, and this allowed the structure of the curriculum to tackle stereotype threat and improve and prepare Black students to be Black lawyers. There were many conversations about taking and passing the bar exam that pushed the academic success mindset. The small class sizes also allowed faculty to work closely with students and assist students in their learning.

As a student who performed well in law school, Kelly noted that many persons assumed she was not a first-generation law student. She overlays this as a class and socioeconomic stereotype. Many students who perform well in law school are presumed to come from generational professionals but that is not always the case.

There was no specific programming for first-generation students; identifying multi-generation students versus first-generation came from observation. Wealthier students lived close to campus in expensive apartments, and some students had family members who were governors, senators, astronauts, and doctors. Kelly finds that this was a wonderful experience as a Black woman. Prior to law school, she notes how she was only exposed to a limited depiction of what it meant to be Black in America. However, once at her law school, she was enlightened to the beauty of diversity within the Black community—students from historic lineage, varying political beliefs, gender identities, and sexual orientations are a few examples.

Kelly explains that "first-generation is often used as proxy for socio-economic status and class."[7] These were not necessarily conversations that she had thought about before entering law school. The self-consciousness that was more about socioeconomic class at the time felt synonymous with being first-generation. Today she wants others to understand that being first-generation is not monolithic. There is a quite a bit of diversity within the group of first-generation students. There may be first-gen law students who are from a lower economic class, and there could be others who are wealthy but could be the first generation to attend law school. While both of these types of students are self-conscious, approaching first-generation students and creating programming should be intentional when considering intersectionality of backgrounds and identities.

One particular improvement Kelly recommends is critically rethinking the financial aid process and the timing for refund checks because many low-income, first-generation students are continuously disadvantaged by the distribution and lending process. In reflecting on her experience, Kelly emphasizes the need for institutions to create a sense of belonging within the school by displaying images of lawyers from all communities, teaching students to embrace struggle, talking about current issues in society in a legal context, and continuously celebrating first-generation student victories.

---

7. Interview with alias Kelly Sampson, Licensed Attorney, via Zoom (December 7, 2022).

V. Let These Experiences Leave a Lasting Impression and Create Space for Change

While Rachel, Deborah, Daniel, and Kelly's experiences are similar, each story depicts various aspects of first-generation law student challenges. Financial concerns, a sense of belonging, socioeconomic status, and access to mentors are key characteristics impacting the first-generation experience. Many first-generation students crave a sense of belonging in an education system that has historically marginalized this group. Most important, early guidance for first-generation students is a necessity for the success of this cohort.

As you carry these experiences with you through the remainder of this book, understand that the first-generation experience is not a one-size-fits-all approach. Once you identify students who are first-generation within your institution, create resources that will assist in developing each first-generation student's learning process and professional identity. Create a community that fosters diversity and cultivates inexperience as an opportunity, rather than viewing a lack of exposure as a detriment. Look for ways to reinvigorate a sense of belonging by diversifying leadership and inviting diverse public speakers to create a platform for new voices in the legal community. Finally, remember where you fit into the puzzle when working with first-generation students and make small adjustments to your role to better cater to this important group.

Ask yourself, "What is one example of a time when I presumed all students understood a "process," "procedure," or "expectation" in law school?" Write down your answer. As you proceed throughout the remainder of this book, carry these stories with you and reflect on your own presumptions. By the end of this book, rethink your presumption and craft an answer to avoid this in the future. Understanding and remembering these experiences are the first steps on the path toward fostering a better first-generation experience.

Two

Many Firsts, One Goal

Three Black Women's Stories of Navigating Many "First" Experiences on Their Journey Through Law School

Yasmin Blackburn,* Sonia L. Canzater,** and Meron Wondwosen***

> *What is often called exceptional ability is nothing more than persistent endeavor.*
>
> —Pauli Murray

IN 1872, CHARLOTTE E. RAY GRADUATED from Howard University School of Law, becoming the first Black woman to earn a law degree in the United States. She would continue the streak of "firsts" by becoming the first woman to gain admission to the District of Columbia bar, as well as "the first Black woman lawyer in the nation's history."[1] Despite the fact that she was "one of the first women to argue a case

* Yasmin Blackburn is a Senior Associate and Director of HR at Kidambi & Associates, P.C. in Trumbull, Connecticut. Yasmin's favorite cases are "the unwinnable ones" where the underdog comes out on top. Yasmin serves as the Chair of the Diversity Equity and Inclusion Committees for the American Immigration Lawyer's Association and the Girl Scouts of Connecticut, where she is also a board member. Yasmin earned her J.D. at Temple University Beasley School of Law. She also holds a BA and MA from Iowa State University.

** Sonia Canzater is the Associate Director of the Center for HIV and Infectious Disease Policy at the O'Neill Institute for National and Global Health Law at Georgetown University Law Center. Sonia is also an Adjunct Professor of Law at the Law Center, teaching the Health Equity and Social Justice Seminar. Sonia is the proud daughter of immigrant parents from Panama, and is the first in her family to earn a terminal degree. She holds a J.D. and Master of Public Health from the University of South Carolina, and a BA in Anthropology from Temple University.

*** Meron Wondwosen is co-founder of and serves as counsel for Young Doctors Project, a multi-generational mentoring, education and pipeline to careers in medicine program for high school boys in Southeast, Washington, D.C. Meron has written several reports to the United Nations on the state of human rights in the United States and Ethiopia. Meron is the proud daughter of Ethiopian immigrants and is the first member of her family to earn a law degree in the United States. Meron holds two Bachelor of Arts degrees in Political Science and French from Iowa State University and a Juris Doctor, cum laude, from Howard University School of Law.

1. Rebels in Law: Voices in History of Black Women Lawyers 9 (John Clay Smith ed., 2000).

before the District of Columbia Supreme Court"[2] and had some measure of success, including successfully representing a Black woman in a divorce case in 1875,[3] Ms. Ray was forced to shutter her practice due to the prevailing racism and sexism in society and in the law.

Ms. Ray's story is relevant to the experience of Black women law students today, many of whom are the "first generation" to graduate college, first in their families to attend a law school and become among only 4.7 % of lawyers who are Black[4] to join this "most conservative of all professions."[5] Further, her experience is instructive because of her exit from the legal profession due to structural racism and sexism.

Yet in breaking the barrier, graduating, and becoming a member of the bar, Ms. Ray exemplified this "persistent endeavor" on the part of Black women to obtain a legal education. In 2020, Black students represented only 8% of entering first-year law students,[6] demonstrating that systemic barriers such as racism and sexism loom even in admittance to law school. And entering law school is simply the first step.

A study by the Center for Women in Law and the NALP Foundation released in 2020 found that among those surveyed, Black women (at 38%) were "most likely to have seriously considered leaving law school,"[7] making them the most likely of the groups surveyed to contemplate ending their legal studies. Considering the barriers Black women face in society are often replicated in law schools, the study isn't surprising. Consistent with those findings, the authors argue that pivotal to the success of Black women lawyers is a positive and affirming experience in law school that can include, *inter alia*, choosing a school to fit their specific needs, solidifying peer support, finding a mentor, garnering institutional support, understanding their goals in attending law school, and mapping their career paths.

This chapter explores how three Black women, who as first-generation law students, navigated the diverse terrain of three law schools—a northeastern predominantly white institution (PWI), an HBCU (Historically Black Colleges and Universities), and a southern PWI—to graduate successfully and secure careers in different professional paths. Their journeys as law students can provide a guide for law schools to support first-generation students. The authors' research as well as their lived experiences provide pivotal insight, considering the state of Black women in law schools and the legal profession.

---

2. Women in American History: A Social, Political, and Cultural Encyclopedia and Document Collection 346 (Peg A. Lamphier & Rosanne Welch eds., 2017).

3. *Supra*.

4. American Bar Association, *2021 ABA Profile of the Legal Profession*, https://www.abalegalprofile.com/demographics/.

5. Rebels in Law: Voices in History of Black Women Lawyers, *supra* note 1.

6. American Bar Association, *supra* note 4.

7. NALP Foundation for Law Career Rsch. & Ctr. for Women in the Law, Women of Color: A Study of Law School Experiences 18 (2020).

Just Grateful to Be Here? Yasmin's PWI Law School Experience

My journey to law school started with a treasured acceptance and a quip from a gay, male student who had just found out he did not get into any of the law schools to which he applied. "I wish I was a black woman, maybe I would have gotten into law school too. Being gay simply wasn't enough." That was the first time I experienced imposter syndrome.[8/9] *A feeling that despite my years of service in student government, my volunteer work, and service on various boards on campus, my undergraduate, double-majored degree earned with honors, and my graduate degree, I was a fraud. I was only accepted to law school because of my race, color, and gender?*[10]

I am a second-generation American and the first in my family to go to law school. It was predetermined. I was verbose, argumentative, and well-read. I thought I was a shoo-in. I knew I was intelligent and figured that was all that was necessary to be a lawyer. However, in that first moment of "acceptance," I simply got a sneer for all that I had accomplished. Self-doubt about why I was accepted to Temple Law and what I would be able to do while there started to creep in and caused me to put a pause on my attendance. Many of my friends and family members do not know that I was supposed to start law school three years before I finally matriculated in 2000. According to the ABA, "first generation law school students or non-college family members may find themselves explaining to those family members the many structural differences that exist between what they witnessed in undergrad and the expectations of law school...These similar differences are quite significant and indeed account for much of the anxiety that many, including non-first-generation law school students, experience."[11]

The legal profession is an anomaly. From the Socratic method to the dreaded curve, the bar exam and everything in between, the study of the law is something people speak about without truly conveying the nuances of each aspect of the experience. First-generation law students are not privy to the necessity for networking, talking to professors, and the value of shared experiences. According to Maggie Wilder in *Helping First-Generation Lawyers Thrive*, "[t]here is a huge knowledge and resource gap—particularly when it comes to networking. As a first-generation pro-

---

8. Ruchika Tulshyan & Jodi-Ann Burey, *Stop Telling Women They Have Imposter Syndrome.* HARV. BUS. REV., February 11, 2021.

9. Abigail Abrams, *Impostor Syndrome—The Idea That You've Only Succeeded Due to Luck, and Not Because of Your Talent or Qualifications*, TIME, https://time.com/5312483/how-to-deal-with-impostor-syndrome/ 06/20/2018.

10. Sheryl Nance-Nash, *Why Imposter Syndrome Hits Women and Women of Colour Harder*, BBC, https://www.bbc.com/worklife/article/20200724-why-imposter-syndrome-hits-women-and-women-of-colour-harder. 07/27/2020.

11. JD Advising, *How to Overcome Challenges as a First-Generation Law Student*, https://abaforlawstudents.com/2021/08/25/first-generation-law-student-challenges/. 08/25/2021

fessional, you are unlikely to have family ties or connections to the legal field, so you have to work to build those on your own."[12] This is probably the most important lesson I needed to learn before my first day of law school. Without this knowledge, I started law school on the wrong foot—doubting myself and my capabilities and ill-prepared for what lay ahead.

Keep Coming Back

I had a new outfit, lots of pens, and a notebook full of loose-leaf. I read and reread all the materials sent to us, especially the financial documentation, but somehow missed that we had a reading assignment due. I showed up to class after our orientation expecting an introduction to the law. What I encountered was a class of probably 150 people with their carefully highlighted and sidenote-filled pages splayed out in front of them. I sat praying the professor wouldn't call on me. I listened to the hushed chatter around me and realized a lot of the people in my classes had some background in this experience. Most were not like me. They had friends or family members who attended the school or who were already attorneys and could tell them about the process and set up expectations.

Again, I wondered if I made the right decision. I felt like a fraud. Who misses the first assignment? Imposter syndrome began to creep in again, but I was afraid to go home and afraid to fail. So, I faked it. I pretended I belonged until I was able to put the pieces together and force myself to belong no matter how tenuous that belonging felt. According to the *Harvard Business Review*, "the label of imposter syndrome is a heavy load to bear. 'Imposter' brings a tinge of criminal fraudulence to the feeling of simply being unsure or anxious about joining a new team or learning a new skill." At the time, I was unable to give myself the grace to accept that learning the law was a new skill. It was a new way of thinking and looking at the world. I didn't know what I didn't know. Today, when I speak to people about the law and what to expect from the law school experience, I tell them to expect a rebranding of sorts. A complete reworking of your perspective.

That perspective is not limited to thought. It extended to life experiences. For the first time, I truly understood the difference between the haves and the have-nots. Temple University is in Philadelphia, Pennsylvania, where the Declaration of Independence and the Constitution were signed. It is the cradle of possibilities, right? Unfortunately, Temple University is also surrounded by poverty and a lack of opportunity. The inhabitants of the community see an institution right next door that should make the American dream that much more attainable, but they likely cannot afford the tuition and/or have not been afforded the educational groundwork to qualify for admission. Recent data provided by the Philadelphia School District

---

12. Grover E. Cleveland, *Helping First-Generation Lawyers Thrive*, ABA Law Practice Today, 4/13/2018, https://www.lawpracticetoday.org/article/helping-first-generation-lawyehttps://abaforlawstudents.com/2021/08/25/first-generation-law-student-challenges/.rs/.

shows that just 22% of twelfth-grade students achieved college readiness benchmarks on either the SAT or the ACT for the 2018–2019 school year.[13] For me, the law school symbolized access to opportunities. According to Nicole P. Dyszlewski in the *Roger Williams University Law Review*, "the implications were that not only were women attorneys excluded from places and experiences, but that they were also excluded from opportunity. These missed opportunities could have real, long-lasting, and serious consequences."[14] I was determined to use the opportunities to stomp out imposter syndrome and forge my own path.

Finding My Tribe

About two days into my law school experience, I received a legal writing assignment and went to the library as instructed to begin my research. Much to my chagrin, all the books, periodicals, and basically all of the literature I needed were gone. I stood in the middle of the first floor of the library dumbfounded. Nothing? There were three legal writing classes, and we were all working on the same assignment, so I expected to have to wait for items to become available. I expected to have to research and write my brief in parts. I did not expect items that could not leave the library to be missing. I did not expect the library to be bereft of everything I needed to complete the assignment due in less than 48 hours. A lifelong friend found me that day. She walked up and began to talk to me. She was a second-year law student and not much further along in her law school journey than I, but she guided me through those missing periodicals and the sinking feeling, once again, that I did not belong in that building. That I had bitten off more than I could chew. She explained the "hazing" or "trial by fire" indoctrination into the practice of law that was a part of this process and how to navigate it successfully. She also introduced me to other people who looked like me and had succeeded—other 2Ls and 3Ls.

Seeing people who looked like me, quasi role models if you will, in the same space that I occupied went a long way toward helping me to overcome imposter syndrome and find a sense of belonging. My first encounter was with Joanne Epps. She was a beautiful, Black woman who commanded our criminal law classroom. Next came Phoebe Haddon and her husband, Frank M. McClellan. There were a few others, and seeing them in the space helped me to feel a sense of belonging. "The lack of role models for marginalized communities has a major impact on making people feel like they do—or don't—belong in these corporate environments. Without this representation, there's no "signal of the possibility of advancement... [or] how they managed

---

13. School District of Philadelphia, District Performance Office, *District Scorecard*, 5/16/2022, https://www.philasd.org/performance/programsservices/school-progress-reports/district-scorecard/#AG1_college_career.

14. Lack of access to opportunities stymies the progression of women in the legal field. Nicole P. Dyszlewski, *Boldly Marching Through Closed Doors: The Experiences of the Earliest Female Attorneys in Their Own Words*, Roger Williams L. Rev., Summer 2020.

the realities of stereotype, stigma and oppression in order to advance."[15] Once I found my tribe, I was able to find my stride. Law school was doable and attainable. I just needed some people who looked like me to find comfort.

You Can Have It All

At the beginning of my second year of law school, I found out I was pregnant with my first child. I was panicked and terrified, but with the assurances of some third-year law students who had been in my shoes, I was confident I could finish without missing a beat. The support and encouragement I received both inside and outside of the school were phenomenal. I had a very supportive and loving family. My fiancé, although stationed in the military abroad, was excited and ready for the task, and I had jumped over the hump of being a first-year law student and felt like I had a rhythm. As has happened to me many times since finding out about my firstborn's impending entrance into this world, I realized that LIFE is going to happen no matter how inconvenient it is. Life and the law are going to interrupt the bar exam, court dates, the carefully planned vacation—and how and when you pivot will determine your success. So, I pivoted. I had applied and been accepted into a study abroad program in Tokyo that would run for the second and third trimesters of my first pregnancy. Eek! I had applied and been accepted into one of our law reviews. Eek! Eek! I had applied and been accepted to teach undergraduate classes on our main campus. Eek! I had applied to work for several large firms in preparation for THE 2L summer, which is also when my baby was due (at that time, I had been on several second interviews). Eek! There were no guidebooks on my situation. There were but so many encouraging words I could hear from my family and supporters. I had too many competing and compelling interests and emergencies to wing it. I had to make lists and lay out the next two years of my life like I was drafting my response to a law school exam: determine the issue, explain and explore the rules, apply the rules to the situation, and come to a conclusion or course of action.

Mary Esten, who at the time was Assistant Dean for Admissions, Financial Aid and Student Affairs, listened to my ever-growing list of challenges and helped me to map out my next steps. She told me it could be done and because I trusted her I believed her. Professor Phoebe Haddon, a Black woman married to another Black law school professor, told me that a child was not the worst thing that could happen in the world and in fact that this time might be the best time to do it because once I started my career it would be exceptionally hard. I needed to hear that from another woman of color—in fact, I needed to see another woman of color who had children and was still successful. The male members of the law school were equally as encouraging and supportive and that helped because I worried most about how male members of the profession would view me.

15. Sheryl Nance-Nash, quoting Thema Bryant-Davis, *supra*.

At the very beginning of my last year in law school, my world went topsy-turvy: my fiancé was abroad, I had a three-month-old baby, I taught undergraduate classes two days out of the week, I had two off-site clinicals, and a family member died. My whole family went home to Panama to attend the funeral. I had a newborn, a densely packed schedule, and no childcare. Other parents at Temple brought their children to classes, so I packed up my baby and did the same. Acceptance of my baby was markedly different. Approximately 10 minutes into one of my first classes, I was verbally attacked by one of my classmates for having a baby. He charged up approximately 30 steps and pushed his face into mine. I was engrossed in taking notes, so to say I was stunned into acknowledgment would be mild. What followed was unnerving. I was admonished for not being serious about my legal education and for taking the space of someone more serious and more deserving. I was berated repeatedly for having the audacity to think it was acceptable to bring a baby into the hallowed halls of a law school classroom. My first instinct was to protect my daughter, who by then had been awoken by the violent screaming inches from her face. Another classmate ran over and took her out of the classroom. The professor, startled out of her lecture, tried to regain control of the class. This type of occurrence, the attack, was an anomaly. How did I know this? Two of my friends also had babies. They were third-year law students. One was Black and one was white. My Black friend was pregnant in the building but only brought her baby to school sporadically. My white friend brought her baby boy to school and he often played outside of the classrooms between classes, or in classes when she was unable to secure child care. We watched him take his first steps and speak his first words in the basement of the law school. A few of the male students brought their babies with them to class from time to time and some brought their older children. Seeing all of this over the two years before I had my daughter made me believe I was allowed to have a baby in the building as well.

My newborn baby and her presence in the law school became a thing. A living breathing thing that moved past the walls of the law school into the greater legal community and then into the newspapers of one of the largest cities in America. There were lines drawn, people picked sides, and the administration promised to protect my rights in the building. But I wasn't protected. I never felt safe in the building again and I was crystal-clear about one thing: I was attacked because I was a Black woman and a mother and therefore subject to open hostility.

As explained by Leigh Abramson, "[m]any infer that having a child makes a woman less serious about work."[16] But that is simply not true. "A woman who can generate a stellar brief in time to make it to her daughter's afternoon soccer game is less profitable than an associate who takes all night to complete the same task. 'Moms

---

16. Leigh McMullan Abramson, *Parents in Law: Is It Possible to Be Both an Attorney and a Committed Mom or Dad?*, The Atlantic, last modified September 17, 2015, https://www.theatlantic.com/business/archive/2015/09/mom-dad-parent-lawyer/405742/.

are probably the most efficient workers in the marketplace.'"[17] The pressure on women in law to decide whether or not to bear children is a heavy burden. Nicole Dyszlewski references a quote from the Honorable Mary M. Lisi, stating "the result of this pressure [described in this article's previous section] was a tendency to overdo it... to work relentlessly just to prove that women could be good lawyers and have families too."[18] I chose my family.

Having my daughter taught me to find and celebrate success in different forms. I studied abroad for six months of my pregnancy and learned so much about another culture and another area of the law. At the end of my law school experience, I had the most beautiful baby girl and a wealth of experiences to draw from. I learned that I did not have to work at a large law firm to feel productive or successful. And unfortunately, I learned that, to many, law school and the practice of law is reserved for people who don't look like me, but I no longer ascribe to those notions. I know I belong and I strive to make sure other little brown girls know the same. For current law school faculty reading this piece, think about what would have made a difference in your survival: advice offered to someone who is struggling OR who you know has very difficult decisions to make, abandonment of the Socratic method in times when a more human touch is warranted, investing more (whatever that is) in the BLSA, LaLSA, APLSA (or the equivalent on your campus), financial counseling, support specifically for first-gen law students, and child care and other resources for older students and students with families—the *non*traditional students, if you will. All or some of these things would have been helpful to me in my law school journey and to others I've spoken with who had less-than-stellar experiences.

Old School Girl, New School Experience: Sonia's Story of Attending Law School as a Nontraditional Student

Finding My Calling

March 23, 2010 ,was a turning point for health care and for my life. It was the day that the Patient Protection and Affordable Care Act (ACA) was signed into law. Whatever one's personal opinions about that law, my experience both as a public health professional and daughter who navigated years of bureaucracy and expense through my mother's unsuccessful battle with breast cancer told me that it was a milestone event. It embodied so many of the reasons why I went into public health and wanted to work to improve health care equity and access for all people in the United States. I had completed a master's in public health five years prior and knew that my academic journey was not quite finished. However, I did not know what the

17. Abramson, *supra* quoting Erin Clary Giglia.
18. Dyszlewski, *supra* at 363.

next step should be. The passage of the ACA made me want to learn more about the laws that govern health in this country. I began researching health law and public health law and found a range of professional opportunities there.

But going to law school at 34 years old? I recalled the stress my friends who went to law school directly out of college described. I recalled not hearing from or seeing them for the better part of those three years because of how demanding law school was, not including the time needed to study for the bar exam once they graduated. I knew of people who had taken the bar as many as five times without ever passing. How could I possibly take on such a burden? I was a military spouse with a husband stationed in another state while my daughter and I stayed in South Carolina to give her stability while she finished school. We owned a house. I already had plenty of student loan debt and we had my daughter's college expenses looming only five years on the horizon. I could not be like some of my friends who went to law school right after undergrad and were broke the entire time or moved back home with their parents. I had real bills. I did not have those options. *What was I thinking?!*

Finding a Way

Nontraditional students like me must weigh many considerations when thinking about attending law school. We have financial and time demands of caring for a family that must be added to the time needed to dedicate to classes and studying. For us, not only does our time management need to be impeccable, but we need to get buy-in from those who depend on us to also be willing to make the sacrifices needed for us to succeed. I shared my desire to apply with my husband and daughter and was transparent that I would not be as available as they were used to, and that financial and time constraints could make all our lives stressful throughout this process. Luckily, they responded with overwhelming support.

I also needed to rally my village around me and ask my friends and family for extra support that I knew I would need while I was in school. This was humbling for me because I am not comfortable asking for help, and I felt exposed telling people my plans, because there was a high probability that I would not get into law school anyway, which for me would be humiliating.

One Shot

Oftentimes for those K-JD students applying to law school straight out of college, they can apply to many different schools across the country to increase their chances of acceptance and accomplishing their goal of earning a law degree. This also increases their odds of receiving full or partial scholarships to pay for school. For many nontraditional students who are balancing family obligations, we do not have that luxury. My family had already made many sacrifices, and my daughter was thrilled to be soon attending one of the most acclaimed high schools in the state. If I were to attend law school, it would have to be locally. If I were in a large city like my hometown of Brooklyn, New York, this would not be a problem as there are several law schools in the area. In Columbia, South Carolina, however, there was only one law school and one of the two law schools in the entire state. On top of that, the University of South Carolina School of Law did not offer a part-time or evening law school program. It is strictly a full-time day program, which meant that I would have to quit my full-time job. These were daunting considerations for me and my family. My husband and I took a long time crunching the numbers and weighing the options to find a way to make it work. I had heard from friends who went to law, medical, or dental school about their six-figure debt from their student loans. What I did not know was that a large part of that debt was because student loans are available to also cover living expenses while you attend these programs. That is not a concept that exists for undergraduate student loans. While this was not ideal because it meant that I would graduate with six-figure student loan debt higher than my mortgage, it was comforting to know that I had a safety net of income since I could no longer work.

Applying Myself

In the summer of 2011, I began the process of applying to law school, and by "began the process" I mean I called my lawyer friends and asked them how to apply to law school. Thus began my climb up the whirlwind learning curve of the law school experience. I had not taken a standardized test in years and opted to take the LSAT "cold" with little preparation other than a brief review of a study guide, in order to get a baseline score.

On test day I was in the waiting room with a slew of people at least 10 years younger than me. Many of them knew each other as they were still undergraduates at the university where the test was held. I listened to their chatter as they discussed the target grade that they "needed to get" to get into the *T 14* law schools they wanted to attend, and how anything below a certain score may relegate them to only qualifying for a *tier 3* law school. They discussed how many schools they were applying to, the varied alumni they knew at many of these schools, area law firms, or currently on the bench—including their own parents and grandparents. As they spoke in this strange language of *Ts, Tiers, GPAs,* and *connections,* I realized that there was a whole community and knowledge base to this law school experience of which I was not a part. They were well-versed in the requisites and standards for many law schools, yet I could not tell you about the requirements for the one and only law school to which I was applying. At first, I felt intimidated. I felt woefully underprepared for this process. But I quickly proceeded to take mental notes of the things they said, resources they referenced, and was determined to join their world.

My score from that cold LSAT was underwhelming but promising. Now that I had done my due diligence and knew what qualifications I needed for the University of South Carolina School of Law, I signed up for an LSAT prep course to achieve my target score. There I was again, in a room full of people much younger than me taking this course taught by a brilliant woman who was also younger than me. Nevertheless, I persisted.

I took the LSAT three times to achieve a score that I thought gave me a fighting chance, albeit not much of a fight. I grew more concerned about my prospects of acceptance. I recalled hearing those younger students lament about the onus put on how high their GPA and LSAT scores needed to be. The average GPAs and LSAT scores of many law school entering classes I reviewed certainly exceeded my numbers, and once again I started to doubt this decision.

But I had a master's degree. I started my own consulting business. Shouldn't that count in my favor more than my 13-year-old college GPA? Well, I was going to MAKE IT COUNT! I had too many people invested in this mission to feel defeated. I needed the committee to value my life and professional experience just as much as those score numbers. I also needed to unequivocally convey to the USC Law acceptance committee just how imperative it was that I be accepted to their school. Rather than dwell on shortcomings, I used my personal statement to highlight my attributes. I told them about my family, my professional background, my desire to study the law, and why USC Law was the school I *needed* to attend to realize my professional goals while also taking care of my family. I laid it all out there.

It is easy for nontraditional students to feel alienated by not seeming to fit the conventional expectations of a law school applicant. But that is exactly what makes us nontraditional. We bring a diversity of insight that a 22-year-old straight out of undergrad just cannot offer. Plus, I worked hard on those achievements, so why would I ever view them as encumbrances rather than opportunities to champion myself?

As more people are reexamining their professional goals and starting new careers later in life, law school administrators should think through ways to improve messaging and outreach to nontraditional students. These students are often intimidated by the process of returning to school, and can be easily overwhelmed and defeated by it. Resources targeting prospective students like myself with information on how we can finance and realistically pursue a law degree would have saved me a lot of time and angst.

The Waiting Game

During the relentless two months between submitting my application and getting a decision, I picked up a few extra part time jobs (now commonly known as "side hustles,") in order to build up my savings so that my family would have a bit of a safety net for when I had to stop working altogether. My husband and I also cut costs where we could so that we could eliminate some other debts. The process was helpful for us as it made us take a careful look at our expenditures and spending habits and find new ways to save money.

Receiving that acceptance letter was surreal. I was elated, but my thoughts quickly shifted to what lay ahead. The months-long application process had evoked so many emotions and led me to challenge myself in ways I never thought possible. Did I have enough resolve to make it through another three years?

"That Was 1L of a Year!"

My preparation to start my 1L year was a flurry of creating strategies to organize as much of my life as possible and decrease my chances of falling behind in school. I felt self-conscious of the perception of nontraditional students being frazzled and less prepared, and I was determined not to fit that stereotype. I learned in that LSAT waiting room the importance of being part of the community, so I signed up for every social media group and email list available to stay informed. Thanks to the guidance of my supportive attorney-friend Yasmin—my fellow co-author of this chapter—I had purchased all of my books weeks before and completed my first day assignments. All I had left to do was wrap my brain around three years of classes with classmates and even some professors who were younger than me. I had a very conscious desire to downplay my age as much as possible. Luckily, much of my worry around my age making me stand out was unwarranted, as I met several other nontraditional students on my first day of orientation. It was also made clear rather quickly that our shared struggles trying to navigate this new experience as 1Ls transcended many of the barriers I thought the age difference with my classmates would create. The beauty of the structure that most law schools follow of creating cohorts for their 1L students so you attend all of the same classes together truly helps you build a sense of camaraderie with your peers rather quickly. Many of us knew no one else at the school, so we looked out for one another when we needed study help or just a moment to vent to someone who could relate.

These relationships would prove invaluable to me as we got further into the semester. A typical day for me in my first year of law school started with classes from 8:00 a.m. until about 3:00 p.m. Once classes ended and many of my classmates were retreating to the library to do our daily readings and to prep for the following day, I was walking to the parking garage to head back to my side of town so I could pick up my daughter from school or attend one of her games or school programs that often would not end until 8:00 or 9:00 p.m. Once the event was over and I got her back home and settled, I would get back in my car and do the 25-minute drive back to the law library so that I could do my reading and prep for the following day. I knew if I stayed home, I would get distracted by wanting to spend time with her or doing things around the house and the schoolwork would fall to the wayside. I would arrive back at the law school just in time to hold the door open for most of my classmates as they were walking out after completing their work for the day, while I was just getting started. Those nights would easily last until 1:00–2:00 a.m., when I would get back in my car and drive home so I could make sure that I was there to get my daughter to school in the morning, take a shower, and do it all over again. When some of my classmates learned of my schedule, they would help by sharing notes or giving me a heads-up about tricky parts of the readings. Looking back, I know I would not have made it through that first year without this support from my peers.

While I do not think nontraditional students should get any special concessions, I do think administrators can do more to consider the needs of all of their students with different life demands. At a law school like mine that did not have a part-time program tailored for unconventional students, there was often little regard given, for example, around the timing of some school events that precluded my participation because of family commitments. Also, students who have been away from the collegiate world for a while are not as familiar with some of the technology and terminology used in current academia, so providing a forum for these students to come up to speed on these concepts without having to suffer embarrassment in front of their peers would be a great way to promote a greater sense of inclusion among these students. When I was an undergraduate, there were no *online learning platforms* to use; I didn't even own a computer in college. It takes a little more time for nontraditional students to adjust, so some support and grace for us through that process can go a long way to ensuring our success.

Growing and Thriving

The journey of personal growth that I undertook just to allow myself to apply to law school really did benefit me in unexpected ways. I think sometimes we become stagnant and resigned to aspects of our personality and behavior and don't really push back against them. I had to enter many different, uncomfortable places and step out of many different comfort zones as part of this journey. Once I truly took in the scope of commitment that law school was going to be and committed myself to it, I realized that part of the process was also going to be letting go of some of the default behaviors and personality characteristics that I had just let persist even though I knew that they were detrimental—for example, not asking for help. Not asking for help covers a broad swath of scenarios. For me, one of those scenarios is an unwillingness to ask clarifying questions or to admit that I do not know something. Following our first week of classes and assignments, I felt myself becoming overwhelmed and confused. I tried looking things up myself after class to avoid raising my hand, but I was lost. I was now faced with a new challenge of exposing my vulnerability and raising my hand in class whenever I had a question. I had to also find the confidence to say "professor, I am not sure what my question is, but I'm lost." Twenty-two-year-old Sonia fresh out of college would not dream of sounding weak in front of her peers, but 34-year-old Sonia knew very well that type of pride would be my downfall.

While initially I was self-conscious about being a nontraditional student in law school, over the three years I came to embrace my role as a "more seasoned" classmate. I came to realize that insecurities around my age also led me to alienate my classmates and hold their youth against them by perceiving them as being fundamentally unrelatable to me. I was able to see things in my younger classmates, especially the ones with whom I had become close friends, that I recognized as being in myself when I was a student at their age. I used those insights to offer them advice from my own lived experiences. I was also able to overcome feeling intimidated or embarrassed at being a student the same age or even older than some of my very accomplished law professors. Over time I used us being contemporaries as an opportunity to relate to my professors and have evolved my relationships with many of my professors into friendships after graduation.

Law school is not for the faint of heart. One has to wholly commit to the discomfort that is required to see this through. I am very grateful not only for the degree that came out of my three years in law school, but for the person I became by embarking on this journey. This experience showed me how many times in my past I let insecurities or concerns about other people's opinions about me or my abilities dictate my decisions. It awakened in me a sense of humility and self-confidence I never thought possible.

A Lawyer...Is a Social Engineer: Meron's HBCU Law School Experience

Some 23 years ago, the acceptance package arrived on an early spring morning. Adorning the exterior of the papers was an elaborately decorated cloth wrap with an African mask. Frederick Douglass' words, etched on the cover page, greeted me: "if there is no struggle, there is no progress." I was graduating from a PWI where we battled daily for dignity and for some progress. The contents of the envelope represented an escape hatch, a passport announcing: Welcome to the Mecca: Howard University School of Law.

The arrival of the welcome packet and what I knew of Howard University had already imbued me with a colloquial sense of belonging—I would be among a group of students, faculty, and staff who have a shared experience, a similar socio-political outlook on the world—at least more similar than the ones I found at the midwestern PWI from where I had recently graduated. Beyond that, this welcoming, first denoted through the aesthetic of the acceptance packet, touched on a critical concept in education known as "belonging."[19] A 2020 law school student survey report[20] posited that a "lack of belonging can have negative academic and professional consequenc-

---

19. As described by psychologists, school belonging can be understood as the degree of liking and acceptance felt by students, the respect they felt, and the support they received to participate. This in turn fostered feelings of value and inclusion as an essential part of the school community. See Kelly-Ann Allen, Margaret L. Kern, Dianne Vella-Brodrick, John Hattie & Lea E. Waters, *What Schools Need to Know About Fostering School Belonging: A Meta-analysis*, 30 Educ. Psych. Rev. 1 (2018).

20. Indiana University's Center for Postsecondary Research, *The 2020 Law School Survey of Student Engagement (LSSSE) Diversity and Inclusion Survey*, September 29, 2020, https://lssse.indiana.edu/wp-content/uploads/2020/09/Diversity-and-Exclusion-Final-9.29.20.pdf.

es"[21] and concluded that belonging is a "predominant factor for law school academic success."[22]

As institutions educating Black students, HBCU law schools[23] contribute to the sense of belonging and do so on a level deeper than mere aesthetics. At Howard Law, for example, Black law students have tangible examples of how our predecessors have contributed to the legal discipline and can envision where we would fit into the profession. In my experience, both theoretically and practically, my law school worked to demystify the law and render the profession and the discipline accessible to another generation of Black law students. In choosing Howard Law, I sought to be part of this experiment and noted history. Since its inception and by necessity, Howard Law has served as a disruptor of the status quo—particularly in how it educates and trains Black law students. I entered the halls of the law school as a novice with perhaps a peripheral understanding of how I may fit within this profession. And while I faced academic rigors at Howard Law as I would have at any other law school, absent from my concerns were questions regarding my place in the law school or the value of my contributions. My experience at Howard eradicated imposter syndrome by providing examples where Black women lawyers contributed to the discipline and in many ways helped shape it. Further, my education at an HBCU law school included traditional legal instruction as well as preparation for the realities of an American workforce, including how to tackle structural racism and sexism.

That education, one that merged legal theories with practical advice tailored to Black law students, is of value and it is an area where PWI law schools have faltered. In fact, the 2020 LSSSE survey report posited that law students of color may recognize that "their schools have equipped them with neither the information nor the skills they need to confront discrimination or harassment after graduation."[24] HBCU law schools such as Howard are uniquely positioned to address this issue. A major theme of my experience in law school is resilience followed by success because of a supportive scholastic environment. This included the presence of the notion of belonging, the absence of questions regarding Black students' intellect and capability, and tangible institutional support for students from professors and administrators. It also meant robust student activities and organizations, helmed by Black students, providing an additional avenue of camaraderie and leadership. What I experienced at Howard was a culture rooted in acknowledging and tackling the deep inequities faced by Black students and other students of color upon their entry into law school.

---

21. Indiana University's Center for Postsecondary Research, *supra* at 10.

22. Jenipher Jones Bonino, *As They Are: The Power of Belonging*, LSAC Blog (Oct. 28, 2021), https://www.lsac.org/blog/they-are-power-belonging#cit4.

23. There are six HBCU law schools: Florida Agricultural & Mechanical University College of Law, Howard University School of Law, North Carolina Central University School of Law, Southern University Law Center, Texas Southern University Thurgood Marshall School of Law, and The University of the District of Columbia David A. Clarke School of Law.

24. Indiana University's Center for Postsecondary Research, *supra* note 20, at 15.

A. To Slay a Ghost in the Room

The protective nature of attending an HBCU was not as evident to me at first glance, perhaps because I, a Black woman, an Ethiopian immigrant, and the first generation of my family to attend law school, expected to be supported in this environment. While learning to discern the difference between *dicta* and the holding in briefing cases is an expected part of the first-year experience, Black students in law school, as in other educational environments, face additional barriers. One such impediment is stereotype threat, which posits that a particular person's ability to perform is negatively impacted by being aware of negative stereotypes toward their particular social group.[25] In his book *Whistling Vivaldi: How Stereotypes Affect Us and What We Can Do*, psychologist Claude Steele discusses the extra burden caused by stereotype threat.[26] He notes that in addition to learning the lessons of your class, you are also tasked with conquering the negative stereotype, which he described as attempting to slay a ghost.[27] Some have argued[28] that "law school is the perfect proving ground for stereotype threat."[29] By attending an HBCU law school, I was able to remove this additional burden and multitasking. Here, the presumption is that I, as a Black student, belong, my intellect is affirmed, and my presence is welcomed and supported. In fact, Black students' arrival at my alma mater wasn't merely happenstance; the conventional wisdom at this particular HBCU law school was that we earned our place and deserved to be supported. On my end, attending an HBCU law school removed the burden of stereotype threat. Hence there were no ghosts to slay, only cases to brief. Rather than entertaining questions about my or other Black students' perceived deficiencies, I focused on my studies and extracurricular activities.

---

25. An example used to explain this phenomenon is that before taking a math test, women in a room were told that women aren't expected to perform as well in math. As a self-fulfilling prophecy, those women, therefore, perform worse than a group of women who were not told about women's supposed math deficiencies. See *infra* note 26 and note 27. The idea is that instead of focusing on taking the test, these women would be consumed not simply by performing well on this test but in addition by this other secondary responsibility—to discount and disprove the stereotype.

26. Claude Steele, Whistling Vivaldi: How Stereotypes Affect Us and What We Can Do (2011).

27. Steele, *supra* note 26, at 111.

28. Russell A. McClain, *Helping Our Students Reach Their Full Potential: The Insidious Consequences of Stereotype Threat*, 17 Rutgers Race & L. Rev. 1 (2016).

29. McClain, *supra* at 40. (discussing that the design of law schools "foster the growth of stereotype threat for minorities." As support for their conclusion, they provide the following seven points: "(1) enroll minority students who identify highly with scholarly achievement and who have a strong personal investment in succeeding in a particular academic endeavor; provide a type of material that is difficult to comprehend and challenging to master, even for high-achieving students; (3) Provide a volume of material that pushes to the limit every student's capacity to maintain focus; (4) Place minority students in classes every day where their intelligence is evaluated, actually or apparently, by their professors and classmates; (5) Provide minority students with as few role models as possible, i.e., keep low a school's percentage of minority professors; (6) Isolate minority students, keeping them from participating in integrated study groups and other voluntary activities; and (7) Provide little to no feedback to students during the semester."

In retrospect, it was the sense of belonging as well as the lack of energy and brain-power expended to combat stereotype threat that allowed me to dust myself off even after a few stumbles during the first few weeks and go on to become among the top graduates of my class.

B. Into the Fray: The First Few Weeks as a 1L

The room, bustling with students finding their seats a few moments ago, was now eerily silent as the professor peered at me from above his smudged bifocals. He had started at the end of the alphabet, upending social norms and nudging my last name from where it comfortably sat for the entirety of my educational journey. He asked me to stand and proceeded with a barrage of questions on a case I hadn't read, evoking a scene not too dissimilar to a firing squad.

Arriving to class unprepared was a cardinal sin at any institution. In law school, it may herald a shaky start at best and at worst, a stillborn legal career. I had fumbled that first day of law school in Civil Procedure, the first class of my law school career. It was death by the Socratic Method. While I was embarrassed, I would return to the same class the next day and begin anew. I would go on to earn the highest grade in the class and years later, I was the only one who remembered the incident. My professor, an African American man who didn't allow that first impression to color his view of my abilities, was my biggest champion. He provided support, challenged me, and offered me a second chance. Black students, like others, fumble and falter, yet we are rarely provided the opportunity to redeem ourselves—a part of school and life that is afforded to others.

I often reflect on how that experience would have been handled at a different law school—such as a PWI, one that was not invested in my success. At such a school, not only would my lack of preparation be questioned (a valid criticism and appropriate response) but it would also be accompanied by questions about my innate ability (an undeserved yet realistic outcome). Thus, my stumble would have been confirmation of a preexisting bias: Black students and Black women students are not as smart as white ones and therefore don't belong in law school. This may be further reinforced by a "professor [who is] ... less willing to work through a difficult issue with a student in class or in office hours because of the implicitly biased judgment that minority students are not as capable as whites of success in law school."[30] In addition, at a PWI my first day fumble may have also impacted my relationships with other students, particularly white ones, as "biases of white students can have a negative impact"[31] including, for example, exclusion from group activities such as study groups.

---

30. McClain, *supra* at 43.
31. McClain, *supra*.

And yet, at my HBCU law school, my grave error committed in the first few weeks of law school did not have a deleterious effect on my experience and on my academic standing. The sense of belonging, the absence of stereotype threat and the presence of supportive professors resulted in the opposite. My stumbles did not mar the remainder of my law school journey and would not even survive the first semester. I, on the other hand, would go on to join law review and become an articles editor, join a powerhouse study group, become part of a moot court team, and graduate at the top of my class.

C. Unique Space of HBCU Law Schools

Except for Harvard Law School, my alma mater Howard Law graduates the largest number of Black lawyers in the country. Thus, in yet another aspect, I chose a law school that holds a special place in the discipline and has an awesome responsibility in educating Black attorneys. The importance of African American presence within the legal profession is not merely a matter of representation—although that is a concern detailed in many reports and articles. Rather, Black lawyers' participation in the profession has a profound impact for at least two reasons. The first is practical: African American lawyers are more likely to indicate an interest in serving their community post-graduation. Second, Black lawyers advance cases, practices, and theories that make the profession more equitable and contribute to building a more just society.[32] In this regard, Black lawyers remind the profession of its promise and its burdens: that the law is not inherently impartial and those of us from communities traditionally marginalized and penalized by the law have a vested stake in its development. Finding a law school that embodies this duality, which often mirrors the experiences of African Americans, was critical to my decision to attend and succeed at Howard Law.

D. Look to Your Left, Look to Your Right: Fostering Cooperation

At this HBCU law school, the oft-quoted tale that begins "look to your left, look to your right, three years from now, only one of you will still be here" was anathema. The competition was certainly there but Howard Law, at least in the early aughts, fostered a different environment. Here, the school sought to train students according to the credo of one of the institution's giants: that Howard-educated lawyers are social engineers and not parasites on society. This approach seems counter to the profession's philosophy, which breeds and supports a competitive, cutthroat atmosphere that can be daunting to many. During the late 1990s, the *Hunger Games*-esque atmosphere that existed at other law schools was discouraged at Howard Law. It appeared that HBCUs were aware of the underrepresentation of Black students in these fields and recognized that such an approach does not serve the mission of the school or

32. Three tangible examples are Charles Hamilton Houston, Pauli Murray, and Kimberlé Crenshaw.

the profession. In line with that philosophy, my experience at Howard Law offered a different perspective—one of cooperation. That culture began at a pinning ceremony, where incoming students are matched with a mentor. It is imperative to understand that cooperation, where students were not pitted against each other, did not mean nor did it beget mediocrity. Such an approach elicited a student body at Howard Law that was exceptionally creative, compassionate, and strived to excel. This philosophy was also exemplified in the support offered to students.

E. Institutional Support

There are several examples of institutional support offered at my law school, including an exemplary and highly competitive career counseling center. However, one of the foundational experiences of my law school years was a course titled "Legal Methods," which was offered to 1Ls as a means to acquire "fundamental skills in legal research, analysis, and writing." In addition to the traditional instruction, our professor also imparted important lessons aimed at acclimating students to law school. Here, not only were the mysteries of the Socratic Method imparted, but our professor, a Black woman who was a graduate of Howard Law, offered a rare and necessary glimpse behind the curtain. For example, this professor was known for her view espousing that we, Black students, should dress conservatively. In one incident when I was a student, I had asked for her advice on my resume. After she meticulously reviewed my resume and provided me with edits and comments, she slowly arched her brows at my nail polish, and cautioned me: "you should certainly remove that nail polish before your interview at the law firm." Although I might not have agreed with her advice, I still appreciated the level of care and attention to the smallest detail.

In addition to seemingly mundane yet necessary topics such as the appropriate attire for my interview, the course covered ethics, as well as advice for those seeking assistance in procuring clerkships. Importantly, the professor also responded to questions students may have felt uncomfortable asking at a PWI. Substantively her course was pivotal in demystifying the profession and providing Black women attorneys with role models, which at times proved elusive at PWIs. Fundamentally, the course, in line with the philosophy of the law school, offered a unique space where I could learn legal doctrine and discuss cases from my perspective as a Black woman. Here, my viewpoint was not the exception or the outlier, but rather the prevailing sentiment.

F. What PWI Law Schools Can Learn from HBCU Law Schools

In terms of institutional support for Black students at PWI law schools, much can be done to build programs that foster the "belonging" I experienced at my HBCU law school. I will offer a few examples. To begin, PWI law schools committed to creating and sustaining such an environment must adopt a philosophy and an action plan aimed at rooting out anti-Blackness. For example, a law school where professors can espouse racist theories and are allowed to remain as faculty cannot seriously commit to creating a welcoming and supportive environment. Creating a sense of belonging must include a diverse faculty who are invested in the success of the student body, including its Black members. Further, as previously noted, students of color graduate from law schools and find they are unprepared for the realities of a profession still struggling with institutional racism and sexism. PWI law schools must be committed to dismantling these barriers and thus must work to develop programs committed to producing Black students who are capable of meeting the academic rigors of the discipline and who are trained to identify and confront discrimination in the profession. This latter part of the commitment can include creating a mentoring pipeline with second- and third-year law students as well as established Black attorneys and judges. PWI law schools, as training grounds for the discipline, must also be prepared to call on the profession to meaningfully support Black lawyers and other lawyers of color who challenge discrimination and racism.

Further, PWI law schools could provide tangible and sustainable support for existing programs or work to establish programs aimed at supporting Black students. For example, PWI law schools can provide financial assistance to Black students not only upon entry into law school, but also provide the opportunity to students to obtain scholarships based on academic success once they are in law school. Considering that financial hardships are yet another barrier to retaining Black students, law schools should consider establishing or increasing the funding of scholarships that reward Black students who demonstrate academic excellence once they have entered law school. In addition, PWI law schools should generously fund Black-led organizations, such as Black American Law Student Association (BALSA), which serve Black students and ensure they receive institutional backing for their programming. Two other areas where institutional support can be impactful include law reviews and career counseling. Since joining a law journal is a prestigious and rewarding experience, PWI could provide support for establishing or supporting law reviews at their institutions that are focused on race. Such an endeavor would support legal scholarship by and for Black students and other students of color. Finally, career counseling services at PWI law schools must provide meaningful assistance for Black students who are seeking summer internships, clerkships, and employment post-graduation.

These are only a few examples based on my experiences, but they highlight that the work to instill "belonging" in law schools must be done at an institutional level with financial commitments and action rooted in eradicating systemic barriers.

G. Peer Support

Even in an institution where my outlook on the world is shared by other students, peer support and camaraderie are still essential parts of the law school experience. This is also why stereotype threat and lack of belonging can be impediments to Black law students. Finding a cohort, whether as part of a study group, an affinity group, or a student organization such as a law journal, participation with fellow students in activities outside of the classroom is integral to a well-rounded experience in law school. While my grades and classwork were paramount, I was engaged in other activities, including International Moot Court, the law student newspaper, and the BALSA. I was also invited to join law review and became an articles editor of *Howard Law Journal*. Juggling these various activities was a challenge, but I was determined to ensure that my law school experience included more than my grades. In addition, these organizations helped dispel the isolation that often burdens law students and resulted in friendships that endured well past graduation day.

Finally, I developed a network of peer support among fellow student organizers. Law school can afford students an incredible opportunity to support the local community and become engaged in the issues that impact marginalized communities. At a minimum, law schools should ensure that their students are at least aware of the needs or issues of importance to those in the communities surrounding the law school. On my end, student organizing at Howard Law meant I was engaging in work around curbing police brutality, planning protests at the Supreme Court against the death penalty, and supporting policies protecting voting rights as well as expanding the franchise to those who were formerly incarcerated. Organizing around these issues helped ground the theories I was studying in the reality faced by marginalized communities. This view of lawyers, that our roles should include "solving problems of… local communities" and we should be working in "bettering conditions of the underprivileged citizens"[33] is the guiding mission of my alma mater and has had a profound impact on my career. In this manner, my community organizing at Howard Law solidified my sense of belonging and enveloped me into the organizing tradition of the school.

My time in law school was enriching and challenging and my experiences have shaped my career trajectory. To be clear, attending law school is a difficult endeavor and choosing an HBCU is not a panacea and my experience should not be read as a blanket endorsement. HBCUs, similar to other schools, have many areas where they must continue to innovate and challenge the legal education system. However, by removing barriers such as stereotype threat and instilling a sense of belonging, Howard Law allowed me excel academically and to flourish in an environment that acknowledged and affirmed my race and gender.

---

33. Steven D. Jamar, *Brown @ 50: Fulfilling The Promise*, (2004), http://law.howard.edu/brownat50/BrownBios/BioCharlesHHouston.html.

Three

The Hidden Curriculum of Culture

Getting from Young, Scrappy, and Hungry to the Room Where It Happens

Randolph M. Fiedler,* Raj N. Shah,** Andrew B. Talai,*** and Brittany Paloma Fiedler†

> *Let me tell you what I wish I'd known when I was young and dreamed of glory....*
>
> —George Washington, as portrayed in *Hamilton*[1]

I. Introduction[2]

FOR MANY, GETTING TO LAW SCHOOL *is* the accomplishment. Navigating the labyrinth to law school—undergraduate admissions, the LSAT, and then law school admissions—is the goal achieved. But in fact, this accomplishment, while worthy, is not the end of the road. Being admitted to law school, by itself, gives students little idea of what being a lawyer is or what kind of law they will want to practice.

* Randolph M. Fiedler is a Las Vegas public defender representing death row inmates in their state and federal post-conviction proceedings. He was the Vice President of the Nevada Coalition Against the Death Penalty and a past president of Nevada Attorneys for Criminal Justice.

** Raj N. Shah is a Los Angeles public defender representing death row inmates in their state and federal post-conviction proceedings.

*** Andrew B. Talai is a Los Angeles public defender representing indigent clients in their federal criminal appeals.

† Brittany Paloma Fiedler is a Teaching and Learning Librarian and Assistant Professor at the University of Nevada, Las Vegas, where she provides information literacy instruction, research support, and co-curricular outreach opportunities for students.

1. *History Has Its Eyes on You*, HAMILTON (ORIGINAL BROADWAY CAST RECORDING) (Atlantic 2015) (hereinafter HAMILTON).

2. The views expressed in this section reflect the opinions solely of the authors.

Law schools often don't help. The emphasis on doctrine, through teaching appellate decisions, suggests that the beginning, middle, and end of the profession is knowing the rules of law and applying them to a set of given facts. This focus implicitly instructs, "learn the law and success will follow." The competitive nature of law school adds, "Well, learn better than your classmates, and *then* success will follow." This, the students understand, is a profession built on meritocracy, and knowing the law is how your merit will be evaluated.

First-generation students are easy marks for this mythos. After all, these are high-achieving students; they've already overcome much, met success, and found their way to Great Law School. Many have read the relevant year's *U.S. News & World Report*; they know their school's august ranking; they see the high (impressively high!) percentage of graduates who will secure full-time employment. They think, "Surely, I, who have already done so much, will be of the many people who land a full-time, long-term bar passage required job. I got here and the rest will work itself out."

But there is a hidden curriculum to law school, and more specifically to the process of gaining employment after graduation. Locking down that first job requires more than good grades. Further, many first-generation students—like the authors of this chapter—enter law school not knowing the many unwritten rules that govern getting that first post-law school job. Unfortunately, it can be very difficult to know what you don't know, especially if you don't know that you don't know (*not* a Donald Rumsfeld reference). This chapter seeks to help first-generation law students by exploring the concept of the "hidden curriculum," and offering counsel (pun intended) about some of the unwritten rules for obtaining employment after graduation.

The chapter proceeds in four parts. First, we provide an overview of the term "hidden curriculum," and how the concept might help law students and administrators think about law school. In the next three parts, the article discusses three examples of the hidden curriculum as they relate to finding that elusive post-graduation job: (1) creating realistic career goals, (2) finding mentors, and (3) accessing pre-professional and post-graduate opportunities, like externships, law review, and clerkships.

II. The Hidden Curriculum

The "hidden curriculum" refers to "the tacit rules of educational practice."[3] The phrase is primarily used by scholars of education to "describe a process and set of everyday practices that, while remaining unacknowledged and unexamined, nonetheless serve to maintain the status quo or support a dominant worldview."[4]

---

3. Rachel Gable, The Hidden Curriculum: First Generation Students at Legacy Universities ix (2021).

4. *Id.*

Professor Molly Townes O'Brien contrasts the hidden curriculum with the official curriculum and the operational curriculum. The official curriculum "usually set out in the course syllabus and in various law school policy documents, is the formal substance of the course."[5] The operational curriculum "may diverge from the official curriculum intentionally (as when a teacher decides to discuss a topic not included in the syllabus) or unintentionally (as when, for example, a teacher gives up on trying to find evidence of critical thinking in exam answers and awards points to answers that simply regurgitate rules.)."[6] In contrast, the hidden curriculum "encompasses the conceptual assumptions and implicit norms that underpin both the official and operational curricula."[7]

In the context of education generally, the term is used to critique these unacknowledged practices with the hope of helping universities improve. Studying these practices can also be educational for students by making them aware of the "unwritten rules and unspoken expectations," like "how to cultivate relationships, advocate for themselves, and pursue opportunities that... more advantaged peers have learned from college-educated parents and mentors."[8] First-generation students, who don't necessarily have access to friends and family with experience navigating these hidden norms, have a disadvantage in higher education.

In the law school context, scholars have noted how "most law schools heavily favor the study of legal doctrine in a classroom setting over other so-called more applied, and often experiential, approaches to preparing lawyers."[9] Professor David M. Moss notes the irony of a law professor extolling "the benefits of team work, brainstorming, collaborative inquiry, effective communication, and problem solving.... from the front of an auditorium-style classroom, where students voices are only acknowledged on a limited basis."[10] Or, to take another example, Professor O'Brien explains how law school curriculum "has historically been oriented towards adversarial process."[11]

Eileen N. Wagner provides an illustrative example in the first-year experience of "briefing cases."[12] Law professors exalt the process of outlining a case as a fundamentally important learning exercise. Less savvy students spend a great deal of time on

---

5. Molly Townes O'Brien, *Facing Down the Gladiators: Addressing Law School's Hidden Adversarial Curriculum*, 37 MONASH U. L. REV. 43, 44 (2011).

6. *Id.* at 44–45.

7. *Id.* at 45.

8. Marcia Chatelain, We *Must Help First-Generation Students Master Academe's "Hidden Curriculum,"* CHRON. HIGHER EDUC. (Oct. 21, 2018), https://www.chronicle.com/article/we-must-help-first-generation-students-master-academes-hidden-curriculum/.

9. David M. Moss, *The Hidden Curriculum of Legal Education: Toward a Holistic Model for Reform*, 2013 J. DISP. RESOL. 19, 21 (2013).

10. *Id.*

11. O'Brien, *supra* n.3, at 45.

12. Eileen N. Wagner, *Do as I Say, but Watch What I Do: Rooting Out Law School's Hidden Curriculum*, 19 STUDENT LAW. 46, 47 (1991).

these briefs, only to find that there is little direct connection between doing the briefs and performing well on the exam.[13] The formal curriculum dictates outlines; the hidden curriculum dictates "a certain pragmatism about getting an education" that focuses solely on mastering the law school exam.[14]

Getting a job after graduation is another example of the hidden curriculum. Both the formal and operational curricula of law school suggest that the path to a post-graduation job is simple: get good grades because as long as your class rank is high enough, you'll get a job. But for most law students, finding that job will involve substantially more than simply having a high GPA. The formal curriculum requires "brains," but the hidden curriculum requires "polish."[15] First-generation law school students will need both if they don't want to throw away their shot.[16] The following sections attempt to unpack various aspects of this hidden curriculum for first-generation law students.

III. Crafting Realistic Goals

Forming realistic career goals can be a particular challenge for first-generation law students, who are eager to "prove that [they're] worth more than anyone bargained for."[17] Consider "international human rights law." One of the authors (who we'll politely leave unidentified) did an undergraduate major in philosophy, wrote his senior thesis about Albert Camus, took a couple of classes on Chinese politics, and concluded, after scouring the internet, that he wanted to be an "international human rights lawyer focusing on China." Because no one in his family had ever practiced law, this author had no idea what an "international human rights lawyer focusing on China" did every day, nor could he name a single person who was an "international human rights lawyer focusing on China." He took Chinese language courses but was not even conversational. He looked at which law schools had a good "international law" program and applied there. He assumed the rest of his career path would work itself out in law school.

What he found soon after starting school was that international law was not at all what he imagined it to be (although, honestly, none of "law" was what he imagined it to be) and that very few people in the world practice international law. Most importantly, he discovered that being an "international human rights lawyer focusing on China" was not the kind of career aspiration that was helpful for a law student, because that is not a job a new graduate can get hired for (at least, practically speaking). In short, this author's career aspirations were unrealistic. His experience illus-

13. *Id.* at 47.
14. *Id.* at 48.
15. *My Shot*, HAMILTON.
16. *Id.*
17. *Aaron Burr*, HAMILTON.

trates an aspect of the hidden curriculum unknown to many first-generation students: how to set realistic career goals.

Admittedly, there is a danger in labeling any career aspiration as "unrealistic." The ambition that fosters a very-difficult-to-achieve-career-aspiration is the same ambition that drives first-generation students to get into law school. So, there is a balance: ambition acknowledging constraint. But this then poses the question: how do you find this balance?

First, first-generation students need to think critically about how to define their goals. Students need to define for themselves a post-graduate job that is consistent with their ambition, but also achievable. Marc Effron, a business talent consultant, suggests determining a "From/To," wherein you identify where you are, and where you want to go.[18] "The from/to is two brief statements—one describing where you are today and one describing your next big (not your ultimate) destination."[19] These statements need to accurately assess both the starting point and ending point. A good one for our would-be human rights lawyer might look like this:

- From a law student with little professional experience to a lawyer whose daily practice involves working on issues of civil rights.

This statement both identifies the law student's current weakness as a candidate and indicates a next step that can be achieved in a number of different ways. Formulating such a statement requires the student to think critically about *why* he wants to be an international human rights lawyer and realize that what he actually wants is to do civil rights work.

Such self-reflection may be difficult. As Effron points out, "To get an accurate from/to, you'll need to check your ego at the door and ask some trusted superiors and colleagues for their extremely candid view of your origin and destination."[20] But, however difficult, our would-be human rights lawyer would have benefited by learning earlier on that his original aspiration was unrealistic, which would have helped him craft a more realistic goal (e.g., being a public defender, which is the achievable goal he eventually pursued).

Ron Carucci, another business consultant, suggests thinking about goals within three dimensions: performance ambition, growth ambition, and achievement ambition.[21] The questions he suggests for each dimension are helpful in crafting an effective from/to statement:

- What goals can I realistically attain through my own efforts?

---

18. Marc Effron, *A Simple Way to Map Out Your Career Ambitions*, HARV. BUS. REV. (Nov. 30, 2018), available at https://hbr.org/2018/11/a-simple-way-to-map-out-your-career-ambitions.

19. *Id.*

20. *Id.*; *see also Meet Me Inside*, HAMILTON.

21. Ron Carucci, *How Ambitious Should You Be?*, HARV. BUS. REV. (Apr. 13, 2020), available at https://hbr.org/2020/04/how-ambitious-should-you-be.

- What skill or knowledge will I need to improve or acquire?
- What rewards do I hope to gain as a result of my efforts?[22]

Unsurprisingly, first-generation law students will not be equipped to answer some (or even all) of these questions on their own and may not know anyone who can help them find answers. Fortunately, there is another resource that can help them: informational interviews.

An informational interview is "an informal conversation you can have with someone working in an area of interest to you."[23] The purpose of an informational interview is not to ask for a job or find job interviews, but to learn more about a field and the mechanics of finding a job in that field.[24] As Rebecca Knight, a business journalist, explains, the goal is "to grasp the reality of the industry and job so you can begin to decide if it's right for you."[25] Informational interviews are so someone in the field can "offer you some free advice."[26] She suggests the following questions (which have been modified for the legal profession):

- How did you get into this practice?
- What do you enjoy about it?
- What's not so great about it?
- What's changing in the practice?
- What kinds of people do well in this practice?
- What are the worst parts of your job?
- What didn't you know before you got into this practice that you wish someone had told you?[27]

These informational interviews can help first-generation students formulate from/to statements, answer some of the questions posed by Carucci, and thereby determine their post-graduation goals.

Where can law students find practitioners to interview, you ask? Luckily, they have many options. Law schools are well-equipped to give students opportunities and guidance on how to connect with practitioners. For instance, as discussed in the next section, many law schools have an extensive alumni network and can offer connections for law students. However, law students will also encounter practicing

22. *See id.*

23. University of California, Berkeley, Informational Interviewing, available at https://career.berkeley.edu/Info/InfoInterview.

24. *Id.*

25. Rebecca Knight, *How to Get the Most Out of an Informational Interview*, HARV. BUS. REV. (Feb. 26, 2016), *available at* https://hbr.org/2016/02/how-to-get-the-most-out-of-an-informational-interview.

26. *Aaron Burr*, HAMILTON.

27. Knight, *supra* n.28.

lawyers through off-campus work experiences, most of whom will be accustomed to being asked for informational interviews or advice. Finally, law students should feel comfortable reaching out through email or social media to ask practicing lawyers for a 30-minute phone call or coffee chat.

IV. Finding a Mentor

For any up-and-coming law student, a mentor—defined here as a legal practitioner committed to helping a student flourish—can be a godsend. At their best, mentors educate and advise; they help mentees navigate what is often an intimidating and scary industry; they connect mentees with helpful resources and expand their professional networks; they serve as references and help promote mentees to employers; and they are a lifelong source of wisdom, support, and even friendship. One student's reminiscences underscore this point: "'My mentors were invaluable for helping me to understand and navigate the public interest community. These relationships were essential for making connections that helped me to build the bridge from law school to my career.'"[28]

Mentors are especially important for first-generation law students because of the hidden curriculum that permeates law school. Mentors can educate first-generation law students about the unspoken norms that are common knowledge to students with relatives practicing in the field. They can impart advice on matters ranging from the mundane (e.g., social expectations at a law office, dress codes, how to format a cover letter and résumé) to the profound (e.g., how to craft a legal memo and how best to present ideas to colleagues and superiors). In short, mentors can enlighten first-generation students to all the things they don't know they don't know.

But paradoxically, the very *process* of finding a good legal mentor—someone who can educate you about the hidden curriculum of law—is *itself* a part of the hidden curriculum. Mentors don't just fall from the sky; they are not George Washington plucking Alexander Hamilton from the battlefield:[29] "developing a mentorship requires student initiative to seek out and build relationships."[30] Unsurprisingly, the process of building and maintaining a relationship with a professional mentor can be as unfamiliar and counterintuitive to a first-generation student as other aspects of the hidden curriculum of law.

The modern law school does little to help. Law schools, as has already been mentioned, are structured around teaching legal reasoning: the goal of law school is to

---

28. Catherine Albiston et al., *Making Public Interest Lawyers in a Time of Crisis: An Evidence-Based Approach*, 34 Geo. J. Legal Ethics 223, 267 (2021).

29. *See Right Hand Man*, Hamilton.

30. Albiston et al, *supra* n.24, at 278.

teach students how to "think like lawyers."[31] While there is certainly nothing wrong with this mission, it does little to help students build long-lasting and enriching mentor-mentee relationships.

This is not to say that law schools do not help students *meet* practitioners. You would be hard-pressed to find a law school that doesn't host networking events of various kinds (e.g., job fairs, mixers, and happy hours) designed to connect students with different sorts of practitioners and recruiters. And some schools go even further still and connect students with alumni who have volunteered to serve as "mentors."[32]

Unfortunately, it is the experience of the authors of this chapter that such connections usually do not produce sustained mentor-mentee relationships. It's easy to see why from a practitioner's perspective. If you were an overworked lawyer with limited time and attention, who would you take an active interest in mentoring? Whose success would you be invested in? A random student out of the many you ran into at a mixer? A random student out of the many you shook hands with at a job fair? A random student out of the many you caught drinks with at some happy hour? No, no, and no! The shared problem in each of these instances is the lack of anything creating a lasting, individualized bond between a prospective mentor and mentee.

This problem is equally true of law schools' efforts to pair students and alumni. The experience of one of the authors of this chapter illustrates this point. This author—let's call him Mentee—was paired with a different alumni "mentor" for each of his three years in law school. He exchanged emails with all three and even personally met one. But he quickly found these relationships lacked any depth or lasting engagement; he and his prospective mentors very quickly fell out of touch. And years later, when Mentee himself became an alumnus and volunteered to "mentor" law students, he encountered similar results: a few conversations that soon petered out.

Now, this is not to say that making connections with different legal practitioners is not important, or that law schools are on the wrong track in arranging such connections. A professional network is composed of more than just mentors; there is certainly value in knowing a range of people within the legal industry. For instance, networking can allow students a chance to engage in the informational interviews mentioned in the previous section. This is all to say that a sustained mentor-mentee relationship requires more than networking alone.

So what is the secret? How can law students find a reliable and dedicated mentor (as it were, the Washington to their Hamilton)? The shared experience of all the

---

31. Wilson Huhn, The Five Types of Legal Argument 12 (1st ed. 2002) ("The purpose of legal education is to teach students 'how to think like lawyers.'"); *see also* Nancy B. Rapoport, *Is "Thinking Like a Lawyer" Really What We Want to Teach?*, 1 J. Ass'n Legal Writing Directors 91, 91 (2002).

32. *See, e.g.*, University of California, Los Angeles, *Stay Connected to UCLA Law*, https://law.ucla.edu/alumni-giving/ways-connect/volunteer-opportunities; Berkeley, University of California, Student Guidelines for Mentorships, https://www.law.berkeley.edu/careers/for-students/public-interest/public-interest-careers/student-guidelines-for-mentorships/.

authors is this: the best way for students to build a meaningful relationship with a legal practitioner is to work on a shared project (or better yet, a series of projects) together and for the students to prove they are exceptionally hard-working, enthusiastic, and diligent. It is essential that they work longer hours, write like they're running out of time, and crank out the highest-quality work product possible. On top of that, they should volunteer to take on assignments (*especially* tedious ones) whenever possible. This is a surefire way for students to earn recognition, respect, and to foster a mentor's emotional investment in their success—the critical ingredients for a lasting mentor-mentee relationship.

To illustrate this point, let's return to Mentee's story. During his second year of law school, Mentee externed with a government agency and developed a passion for its work. He began repeatedly volunteering for assignments from his supervisor and tried to show genuine enthusiasm and gratitude for the work opportunities he received. He worked diligently, put in long hours, and paid attention to every last detail. Over a summer of such work, he impressed and developed a rapport with his supervisor. That supervisor went on to be a constant source of advice and support all the way up to the present day; he also went to bat for Mentee when he applied for jobs after law school, strongly recommending him for employment to both judges and lawyers alike. Stories such as this demonstrate the broader point: you build stronger connections from, as it were, fighting alongside someone in the trenches than from casual networking.

So, what does this all boil down to in practical terms? Work experiences—not networking—are the key to finding mentors who will help students succeed in the long term. Notably, these experiences need not be limited to work in a law office. Students could achieve the same results if they were to work with a practitioner through a law school clinic, extern for a judge, or work on a research project with a law professor. The key point is to pursue work experiences that allow them to prove their worth and dedication to a legal practitioner on an individualized basis. Law schools can help by facilitating these relationships and by making sure students understand that finding such mentors is one of the most important goals of these working relationships. The more such experiences students accrue and the more dedication they demonstrate, the more mentors they will acquire. *This* is the hidden curriculum of finding good mentors—something all the authors, as first-generation students, had to discover for themselves.

V. Pre-Professional/Post-Graduate Options

Apart from not knowing how to set realistic career goals and find mentors, first-generation law students can also be oblivious to the world of pre-professional and post-graduate opportunities. They know the goal is to get a legal job, but they are unaware of the pre-professional and post-graduate opportunities that can help them get that legal job, such as externships, law review, and clerkships. They might also not realize the process begins early—during their first year in law school, when students typically start preparing to apply for competitive summer positions that will impact their job prospects. The idea of meritocracy makes it easy to go in thinking: "I got good grades in college, I'm probably going to get good grades in law school, and things will fall into place."

There is, unfortunately, much more required to succeed. And first-generation law students often don't have anyone to show them the ropes. Their parents and relatives are, by definition, outsiders to the legal profession—they can't be expected to know about judicial externships, joining law review, or serving as a law clerk. They might not even have any social connections to anyone with a professional job requiring post-graduate education. Nor is it guaranteed that first-generation students will have participated in pre-law programs during undergrad, or that their college professors will be familiar with the legal profession and be able to offer specific guidance.

This was true for one of the authors, who we will affectionately refer to as Promising Law Student. That's what he was, but he also probably wouldn't have fared well if left to his own devices. He was still relatively young starting law school and so he imagined that he'd go home that first summer, reconnect with family, and hang out with old friends. He presumed that, like high schoolers and undergrads, law students would get time off until the next year started. Luckily, Promising Law Student ran into an advisor at his career development office who sent him down a better path. She was probably just doing her job, but the authors of this chapter like to think she realized that first-generation students needed people like her—someone with practical experience, who had lived through the process of getting a legal job, and who could "fan t[heir] spark into a flame."[33] This section will explore the experiences of Promising Law Student, to illustrate the importance of judicial externships, law review, and clerkships to employment prospects after law school.

Judicial Externships. Law students are expected to begin working long before they pass the bar exam. These pre-professional experiences, which typically begin during first-year summer, are critical steps in the process of securing full-time employment after graduation. A "judicial externship" is one example. It provides an opportunity to work at a court and get to know the judge and their law clerks. Although the position is unpaid, it's more than just making copies or getting coffee. An extern may have the unique opportunity—as a law student—to review briefs, prepare memos, revise opinions, attend oral arguments, and be privy to internal deliberations. Externs get to learn how judges think, how they decide important cases, and which arguments they find persuasive.[34]

---

33. *My Shot*, HAMILTON.

34. For more information on how judges think and write, *see, e.g.*, RICHARD A. POSNER, HOW JUDGES THINK (2010); ROSS GUBERMAN, POINT TAKEN: HOW TO WRITE LIKE THE WORLD'S BEST JUDGES (2015).

At the recommendation of his career advisor, Promising Law Student did an externship with a federal appellate judge. He didn't know where to begin, but his career advisor gave him a blueprint. To apply for an externship, he prepared a cover letter, a resume, a copy of his first-semester transcript, and list of references. His career advisor then reviewed his application materials and provided detailed feedback. (The author had not yet developed a discerning legal eye, so his resume still had embarrassing typos that might have drawn scorn.) The career advisor also provided a list of federal appellate judges and their chambers' addresses, taught Promising Law Student how to set up a mail merge, and gave him the confidence to prepare and send out hundreds of unsolicited paper applications to judges across the country. He received numerous responses, and while the vast majority were rejections, a couple of federal judges were willing to take him on.

Although there is usually a formal interview process, that wasn't the case for Promising Law Student: if he could get there on his own dime, the job was his. So he accepted an externship in a different state, in an entirely different region of the country, in a place where he had no family, friends, or any other connections. He flew out, rented a car, and lived out of a hotel for the next few months—surviving mostly on hotel breakfast and fast food. His rental car was dingy, his suit was too big, and he was lonely. But he was "non-stop."[35] He put in the long hours, got to know the law clerks and the judge, added value with thorough research and clear writing, and even traveled to attend an oral argument. He asked questions about how the law clerks got their positions and how he might one day follow in their footsteps. This judicial externship was important because it was his first real exposure to a previously hidden world and the people who inhabited it. It was his first foray into "the room where it happens,"[36] and he was finally starting to understand what it took to succeed.

Law Review. Law students are also expected to pursue certain pre-professional opportunities alongside their coursework. This can mean participating in a clinic or a practicum, or entering moot court or appellate advocacy competitions, but the primary and most well-known example is "law review."

Before he started law school, Promising Law Student had never heard of a "law review" or any other type of legal journal. He had been aware of academic articles in college, but always thought they were peer reviewed—by and for other professors. Journal articles were stodgy, inaccessible reading assignments. And students were relegated to the role of audience, or at most involved as research assistants who gathered source material. But again, thanks to a helpful nudge from his career advisor, Promising Law Student discovered the world of legal academia. Most law schools have a flagship academic journal (called the "Law Review"), which publishes articles by legal scholars and practitioners on various topics. The journal is generally run by students, although there is often some professorial supervision. The students may

35. *Non-Stop*, HAMILTON.

36. *The Room Where It Happens*, HAMILTON.

get academic credit for their work, but it's mostly considered a prestigious extracurricular opportunity.

Some law reviews select their members using a grade cut-off system (students can "walk on" to law review if their class rank is high enough), while others require everyone to participate in a selection competition (students have to "write on" to law review). The competition usually occurs during first-year summer, and it is a test of the student's editing ability, citation skills, attention to detail, and various other criteria. If a student makes the cut, his or her first year on law review mostly consists of general editing. But the second year on law review is usually much more specialized; for example, a student may get elected to a senior position on the editorial board and take on responsibility for running the journal and publishing articles.

Students aiming to join the law review should consider their journal's specific walk-on and/or write-on procedures and their class standing after first year, and should also be realistic about whether law review is something that would interest and excite them. Promising Law Student's school required students to write on to secure a spot, regardless of grades. Although the competition is like a take-home exam, undergraduate education and the first year of law school might not be enough to guarantee success. Of course, you don't know what you don't know, but it is worth it to spend time studying legal citation manuals, brushing up on grammar, and reviewing a few issues of your school's law review. Promising Law Student devoutly studied, and was selected to join the law review, eventually becoming an editorial board member. This was a major time commitment (in addition to coursework), but it forced him to refine core skills that would come in handy later while clerking and practicing as a lawyer: citation, issue spotting, assessing credibility and merit, managing large amounts of information, and editing the work of others.

Clerkships. Many recent law graduates go directly into a law firm or a public interest organization, but a lucky few serve as judicial law clerks in the federal court system. If an externship is like the minor league, then a "clerkship" is the majors. Law clerks are full-time, paid employees of the federal judiciary. They work side-by-side with a federal judge, helping him or her carry out the business of the court. A clerkship ordinarily lasts for one term (usually a year or two), but career positions are also available for more experienced attorneys. The job generally entails reviewing briefs, drafting bench memoranda, attending court proceedings, and drafting opinions and orders. It's considered one of the most prestigious positions in the legal profession for recent graduates—a credential that bolsters future employment prospects and follows an attorney for the rest of his or her career.

But clerking has a deeper value: it exposes young attorneys to new areas of the law, helps them learn firsthand the difference between good and bad legal writing and oral advocacy, and forces them to develop research and writing skills at an accelerated pace (they, too, "write like [they're] running out of time"[37]). It also gives them

---

37. *Non-Stop*, HAMILTON.

invaluable insight into judicial decision making. Young lawyers become intimately familiar with how judges think about and resolve complex legal issues—lessons that provide a head start when practicing and a foundation for continued growth.[38]

Many law students begin applying for clerkships during their second year of law school. But Promising Law Student decided to wait until his final year in law school: after speaking to his career advisor, he realized that he could bolster his chances by taking things slowly and presenting the best version of his application. He focused on crafting his application materials, boosting his grades, and accumulating other markers of achievement (e.g., publishing a student note on law review). This meant that he would have a gap year between graduation and clerking. But that was okay: Promising Law Student learned that some judges prefer to hire clerks with at least a year of post-graduate experience—i.e., working at a "real job" where attorneys put in long hours and take on serious responsibility. The idea is that, by hiring experienced candidates, there will be fewer hiccups at the outset and law clerks will be able to hit the ground running.

The process of applying for clerkships is a lot like applying for judicial externships, though somewhat more streamlined and accessible. There is an online system called OSCAR,[39] which allows candidates to search for and electronically apply to judges of their choosing. Candidates needn't send random paper applications to every judge in the nation; instead, they should send tailored electronic applications to specific judges of interest or judges sitting in regions of interest. Students will typically need to upload a cover letter, a resume, a grade sheet, a list of references, and one or two writing samples. They will also need letters of recommendation from professors or supervisors, those who know the candidate well and are willing to advocate on his or her behalf.[40]

Promising Law Student opted to apply for federal appellate clerkships first. These are more competitive and less widely available than federal district court clerkships. His initial strategy was to apply to the same court at which he externed, thereby leveraging his experience and establishing some connection to the region. He also applied to his home circuit because he knew that he ultimately wanted to return

---

38. For more information on the role of a judicial law clerk, *see, e.g.*, LAW CLERK HANDBOOK: A HANDBOOK FOR LAW CLERKS TO FEDERAL JUDGES (3d ed. 2019); JENNIFER L. SHEPPARD, IN CHAMBERS: A GUIDE FOR JUDICIAL CLERKS & EXTERNS (2012); MARY L. DUNNEWOLD ET AL., JUDICIAL CLERKSHIPS: A PRACTICAL GUIDE (8th ed. 2010); Abner J. Mikva, *Judicial Clerkships: A Judge's View*, 36 J. LEGAL EDUC. 150 (1986).

39. Online System for Clerkship Application and Review ("OSCAR"), https://oscar.uscourts.gov/.

40. For more information on applying for clerkships, *see, e.g.*, DEBRA M. STRAUSS, BEHIND THE BENCH: THE GUIDE TO JUDICIAL CLERKSHIPS (2d ed. 2016); Ruggero J. Aldisert et al., *Rat Race: Insider Advice on Landing Judicial Clerkships*, 110 PENN ST. L. REV. 835 (2005); Georgetown Law, *Judicial Clerkship Manual* (last updated Jan. 15, 2020), https://www.law.georgetown.edu/wp-content/uploads/2020/05/Judicial-Clerkships-Manual-20-01-15.pdf.

there. Nonetheless, Promising Law Student was willing to apply widely and accept the first clerkship offer that he received, even if it was in a distant state.

But he didn't hear back for quite some time (which caused him to feel nervous and apprehensive). He started to wonder whether he was ever going to get a clerkship, if his applications were flawed, or if he just wasn't good enough. It didn't help that many of his classmates (including his law review colleagues) were visibly rejoicing about the clerkships they did receive. Of course, Promising Law Student's story has a happy ending: he did eventually receive an interview. He prepared by talking to former law clerks, and he then received an offer, too.

The experience of Promising Law Student reflects some important but not obvious points about these opportunities: finding them takes longer and starts sooner than might be obvious to a first-generation student; preparing for them requires work and knowledge that first-generation students are likely to not have; so, compensating for that gap requires getting assistance and advice from more experienced or knowledgeable people.

VI. Conclusion

First-generation law students, as a class, get "a lot farther by working a lot harder by being a lot smarter by being [] self-starter[s]."[41] These virtues should not be overlooked in offering advice and guidance to these students. But neither should these virtues cloud that the process of going from law student to lawyer includes information unwritten, processes unknown, and customs unfamiliar; the law, after all, is not just a profession, but a culture. And, as students finish their studies and practice law, we can (and should) help them "rise to the top." There are a million things our first-generation students have not done, "[b]ut just you wait, just you wait."[42]

41. *Alexander Hamilton*, HAMILTON.
42. *Id.*

Four

Overcoming Imposter Syndrome as a BIPOC First Gen Law Student

Helping BIPOC First Gen Law Students Embrace their Belonging to Focus on What Matters to Excel in Law School

R. Allyce Bailey, Esquire*

I. Introduction

IMPOSTER SYNDROME IS LOOSELY DEFINED AS "doubting your abilities and feeling like a fraud," and it disproportionately affects minorities.[1] As a former BIPOC (Black, Indigenous, and people of color) first-generation law student, I know firsthand that I and many similarly situated law students of color struggle from the outset of law school wondering if they even belong. This chapter endeavors to assist educational administrators with identifying and addressing imposter syndrome in their BIPOC students, and to provide guidance to compile resources to assist minority law students with the issues unique to their personal matriculation experience.

* R. Allyce Bailey, Esquire, is a civil litigator and communications professional practicing in Columbia, South Carolina. Bailey dedicates this written work to her husband, attorney Tyler D. Bailey, and their two adored sons, Tyler Jr. and David Christian.

1. Ruchika Tulshyan & Jodi-Ann Burey, *Stop Telling Women They Have Imposter Syndrome*, Harv. Bus. Rev. (2021), https://hbr.org/2021/02/stop-telling-women-they-have-imposter-syndrome#:~:text=Imposter%20syndrome%20is%20loosely%20defined,they're%20deserving%20of%20accolades. (last visited Jan 13, 2022).

II. What Is Impostor Syndrome?

Imposter syndrome is loosely defined as "doubting your abilities and feeling like a fraud."[2] It is the idea that one has only succeeded due to luck, and not because of their talent or qualifications.[3] Individuals who struggle to own or internalize their own success are said to be exhibiting traits of impostor syndrome.[4]

Researchers typically divide impostor syndrome into five categories,[5] including:

- The Perfectionist—individuals consistently holding themselves to the highest standards;
- The Natural Genius—individuals able to clearly see others' success, but struggle to recognize and accept their own success;
- The Expert—individuals who feel they lack the skills and experience for certain jobs or tasks despite clear credentials contradicting this notion;
- The Individualist—individuals who fear asking for help and prefer working alone;
- The Superwoman/man—individuals who often see overworking themselves as the solution to proving their value.

Some commons signs of impostor syndrome include but are not limited to:

- Difficulty assessing one's own competence and skill set;
- An inability to accept credit for personal success;
- Hypercritical evaluation of one's performance;
- Fear of failing to meet expectations;
- Perfectionist traits and overachieving mentality; and
- Self-sabotage and self-doubt.[6]

Law school is ripe for revelation of impostor syndrome, as research shows that approximately 25 to 30 percent of high performers suffer from impostor syndrome, with competitive environments often serving as the breeding grounds for impostor syndrome.[7] Even celebrities and public figures like Tom Hanks, Michelle

---

2. *Id.*

3. Abigail Abrams, *Yes, Impostor Syndrome Is Real: Here's How to Deal with It*, TIME (2018), https://time.com/5312483/how-to-deal-with-impostor-syndrome/ (last visited Jan 13, 2022).

4. *Id.*

5. Vanessa Van Edwards is Lead Investigator at Science of People. She is the bestselling author of *Captivate: The Science of Succeeding with People* (2017), and *The 5 Types of Imposter Syndrome (And How to Overcome It!)* (2021), https://www.scienceofpeople.com/impostor-syndrome/ (last visited May 6, 2022).

6. Jaruwan Sakulku, *The Impostor Phenomenon*, 6 J. BEHAV. SCI. 73–92.

7. *Imposter syndrome*, PSYCH. TODAY, https://www.psychologytoday.com/us/basics/imposter-syndrome (last visited May 6, 2022).

Obama, and Maya Angelou have publicly disclosed their experiences with impostor syndrome.[8]

A. My Personal Impostor Syndrome Experience

I completed both my bachelor's degree and juris doctor with academic scholarships. From high school, I was president of numerous honor societies, had won several awards, and held countless leadership positions even in law school. Despite these "successes," *every single day* of law school up until I received notification that I had successfully passed the bar, I wondered if I would actually make it to the finish line.

I entered law school as the first in my family to pursue any type of graduate degree. I did not know a single lawyer personally except the ones that performed my parents' divorce when I was a child. That was also the only time I had the opportunity to see a lawyer's office or a courtroom. Despite my dream of becoming a lawyer, the idea that I could be one of the actors in the legal scenario seemed aspirational. I consistently wondered if I had merely skated through life and whether this law school dream would ever materialize.

B. Results of Minority Law Student Survey

I compiled a survey that was sent to minority students at both predominantly white institutions and historically Black law schools, the results support the conclusion that impostor syndrome overwhelmingly plagues minority law students.[9]

The students were asked the following questions:

- Are you a first-generation law student?
- Were you a first-generation college student?
- Do you ever exhibit the signs of impostor syndrome?
- Have you ever questioned whether your success was attributed to anything other than your ability, i.e., attributing your success to sheer luck or simply having good contacts?
- Do you worry about meeting expectations?

---

8. Vanessa Van Edwards is Lead Investigator at Science of People. She is the bestselling author of *Captivate: The Science of Succeeding with People* (2017), and *The 5 Types of Imposter Syndrome (And How to Overcome It!)* (2021), https://www.scienceofpeople.com/impostor-syndrome/ (last visited May 6, 2022).

9. Minority Impostor Syndrome Survey, R. Allyce Bailey—Survey Monkey. Law schools surveyed included Southern University Law Center, Florida A&M University School of Law, Charleston School of Law, the University of South Carolina School of Law, and the National Bar Association Law Student Division; 26 students responded to the survey.

- Have you ever doubted or do you doubt your ability to succeed in law school?
- Do you ever feel like you do not belong in law school?
- Have you ever felt like your majority classmates knew more about how to succeed in law school than you?
- With what minority group do you identify?

Survey takers included minorities self-identifying as Black/African-American, Latina/o, Native American, Hindu Indian, and one student also noting that they fell into the disabled and queer category.

- Over 96% of the students were the first in their family to attend law school.
- Over 92% admitted to exhibiting impostor syndrome.
- Over 80% questioned whether their success was attributed to anything other than their ability, i.e., attributing their success to sheer luck or simply having good contacts.
- Over 92% worry about meeting expectations.
- 96% doubted their ability to succeed in law school.
- Almost 90% of the students believed their white counterparts knew more about how to succeed in law school than they d*id.*

The results of this survey confirm for me that my hypothesis, that BIPOC students are disproportionately plagued by impostor syndrome, is an unfortunate reality. The survey results confirm a direct correlation between being the first in their families to embark upon the ambitious endeavor of becoming a lawyer, and overwhelming feelings of self-doubt.

C. Statistics on Minorities and Impostor Syndrome

In my opinion, the systemic issues of our day will go unresolved until the majority bears just as much concern for issues that affect minority communities as if they were a part of that class. Accordingly, an understanding of the origin of BIPOC impostor syndrome is critical to developing the emotional intelligence necessary to draw both a sympathetic and empathetic response to the issue. Sympathy shows that you see the issue and are sorry for that person's experience.[10] A sincerely *empathetic* response, however, captures that while you may never walk a mile in a BIPOC student's shoes, you have a genuine understanding of the issues they are facing.[11]

10. Words at play—Sympathy Empathy Difference, Merriam-Webster, https://www.merriam-webster.com/words-at-play (last visited Jan 13, 2022).

11. *Id.*

Statistics, data, and research support that impostor syndrome overwhelmingly affects minorities in general but particularly minorities in fields dominated by the majority.[12] With minorities comprising a dismal less than 1% of Fortune 500 executives, less than 5% of American lawyers, and less than 5% of American doctors, it is not surprising that most minorities in these settings struggle on a daily basis to not only find colleagues to whom they can relate, but also often lack a mirror image of success at the top of the ranks they are seeking to climb.

It has been said that "[a] sense of belonging fosters confidence."[13] Fundamental to impostor syndrome is the feeling that one does not belong.[14] Thus, minorities in majority-dominated situations often unfoundedly lack confidence in, or at the very least question, their ability to succeed in a particular arena.[15] Notably, implicit bias causes us to feel most comfortable around those we see and identify as being "like us"[16]—a place of comfort BIPOC students struggle to find among the majority each day. Consequently, an emphasis on diversity, or lack thereof, can have a direct effect on the retention and success of BIPOC students.

> The more people who look or sound like you, the more confident you feel. And conversely, the fewer people who look or sound like you, it can and does for many people impact their confidence. We're more likely to experience im-

---

12. *Exploring Impostor Syndrome from a Black Perspective*, Maryville Online (2021), https://online.maryville.edu/blog/impostor-syndrome-black-perspective/ (last visited Jan 13, 2022); Darreonna Davis, *Why Black and Latina Women Are More Likely to Struggle with Impostor Syndrome—And How to Overcome It*, CNBC (2021), https://www.cnbc.com/2021/08/04/why-black-and-latinx-women-struggle-more-with-impostor-syndrome.html (last visited Jan 13, 2022).

13. Abigail Abrams, *Yes, Impostor Syndrome Is Real: Here's How to Deal With It*, Time (2018), https://time.com/5312483/how-to-deal-with-impostor-syndrome/ (last visited Jan 13, 2022).

14. Margaret Crable, *How to Overcome Impostor Syndrome in College and Beyond*, USC News (2021), https://news.usc.edu/trojan-family/college-impostor-syndrome-usc-support-mental-health (last visited Jan 13, 2022); Vanessa Van Edwards, *The 5 Types of Imposter Syndrome (And How to Overcome It!)* (2021), https://www.scienceofpeople.com/impostor-syndrome (last visited Jan 13, 2022); Kirsten Weir, *Feel Like a Fraud?* Am. Psych. Ass'n, https://www.apa.org/gradpsych/2013/11/fraud (last visited Jan 13, 2022).

15. *Exploring Impostor Syndrome from a Black Perspective*, Maryville Online (2021), https://online.maryville.edu/blog/impostor-syndrome-black-perspective/ (last visited Jan 13, 2022); *97% of Medical Students Experience Imposter Syndrome, Survey Finds*, Healio (2021), https://www.healio.com/news/primary-care/20210924/97-of-medical-students-experience-imposter-syndrome-survey-finds (last visited Jan 20, 2022); Sheryl Nance-Nash, *Why Imposter Syndrome Hits Women and Women of Colour Harder*, BBC Worklife (2020), https://www.bbc.com/worklife/article/20200724-why-imposter-syndrome-hits-women-and-women-of-colour-harder (last visited Jan 20, 2022).

16. Kathleen Woodhouse, *Council Post: Implicit Bias—Is It Really?* Forbes (2017), https://www.forbes.com/sites/forbescoachescouncil/2017/12/19/implicit-bias-is-it-really/#68e8a33459ce (last visited Apr 13, 2020); R. Allyce Bailey, *Bias Within Bias: How Washington General Rule 37 Addresses Disguised Racial Discrimination in Jury Selection and a Blueprint for Rule 37's Nationwide Implementation In All American Courtrooms*, 14 L. J. Soc. Just. 55 (2021).

poster syndrome if we don't see many examples of people who look like us or share our background who are clearly succeeding in our field.[17]

From elementary schools, BIPOC children are taught they have to run twice as fast, jump twice as high, and be twice as smart just to get the same chances their majority counterparts receive while exerting half the effort.[18] A mantra that many scoffed at for generations as an exaggeration of the Black community, but now data supports that Black employees are often scrutinized at greater lengths than white employees, and I would hypothesize the same is likely true in the realm of academia.[19]

There are often headlines marking the first Black editor-in-chief of the law review at X predominantly White institution or the first Black CEO or C-suite executive of ABC multibillion-dollar corporation, because minorities are often the first to integrate certain scenarios, often the first in their families to embark upon particular endeavors.[20] This compounds the pressure, whether founded or unfounded, to outperform their similarly situated majority counterparts in order to be taken seriously or even considered for the same opportunities.[21] This is demonstrated in overpreparation, spending too much time on a task and not billing all of the time for it in fear of seeming incompetent, etc.[22] This is also supported by the results of my survey, in

---

17. Abigail Abrams, *Yes, Impostor Syndrome Is Real: Here's How to Deal With It*, TIME (2018), https://time.com/5312483/how-to-deal-with-impostor-syndrome/ (last visited Jan 13, 2022).

18. Gillian B. White, *Black Workers Really Do Need to Be Twice as Good*, THE ATLANTIC (2018), https://www.theatlantic.com/business/archive/2015/10/why-black-workers-really-do-need-to-be-twice-as-good/409276/ (last visited Jan 13, 2022).

19. *Id.*

20. Phil Wahba, *Only 19: The Lack of Black CEOs in the History of the Fortune 500*, FORTUNE (2021), https://fortune.com/longform/fortune-500-black-ceos-business-history/ (last visited Jan 13, 2022); Fox Butterfield, *First Black Elected to Head Harvard Law Review*, N.Y. TIMES, February 6, 1990; Liz Mineo, *Harvard Law Review President Sees Leadership as a Learning Experience*, HARV. GAZETTE (2018), https://news.harvard.edu/gazette/story/2018/11/harvard-law-review-president-sees-leadership-as-a-learning-experience/ (last visited Jan 13, 2022); Alex Resnak, *Jeannine Holmes Becomes Georgia State's First Black Law Review Editor*, GEORGIA ST. NEWS HUB (2021), https://news.gsu.edu/2021/03/09/jeannine-holmes-j-d-22-becomes-georgia-states-first-black-law-review-editor/#:~:text=College%20of%20Law%20student%20Jeannine,chief%20of%20the%20Law%20Review (last visited Jan 13, 2022); Mike Fox, *Virginia Law Review Names First Black Editor-in-Chief*, University of Virginia School of Law (2021), https://www.law.virginia.edu/news/202102/virginia-law-review-names-first-black-editor-chief (last visited Jan 13, 2022); Campaign US Staff, *CMO 50: Bozoma Saint John*, CAMPAIGN US (2021), https://www.campaignlive.com/article/cmo-50-bozoma-saint-john/1718225 (last visited Jan 13, 2022).

21. Vanessa Nepomuceno, Taking Action: *The Imposter Syndrome and Graduate Minority Students*, AM. SOC. PHARMACOGNOSY (2021), https://www.pharmacognosy.us/taking-action-the-imposter-syndrome-and-graduate-minority-students/ (last visited Jan 13, 2022).

22. Danielle Page, *How Impostor Syndrome Is Holding You Back at Work*, NBCNews.com (2017), https://www.nbcnews.com/better/health/how-impostor-syndrome-holding-you-back-work-ncna814231 (last visited Jan 20, 2022); Julia Carpenter, *How to Get Over Your Impostor Syndrome*, CNNMONEY (2017), https://money.cnn.com/2017/08/15/pf/impostor-syndrome-productivity/index.html (last visited Jan 20, 2022).

which 92% cited worrying about meeting expectations, and 96% doubted their ability to succeed in law school.[23]

Despite schools and businesses bearing well-meaning intentions as they boast their diversity and inclusion statements, the lack of true inclusion leaves minorities often feeling as if those diversity initiatives are merely obligatory boxes to check. Institutions often boast that diversity is an important tenet of their school's operational structure, but the institution's *culture* fails to support this notion with tangible evidence or systems in place to support the unique challenges many BIPOC students face. Examples of failures to truly embed diversity efforts into institutional culture can include but are not limited to lack of diverse staff at both the faculty and administrative level, failure to acknowledge social issues and urgent current events affecting BIPOC students, and failure to recognize and acknowledge holidays and historic events important to BIPOC communities.

As uncomfortable as the reflection and evaluation may be, if institutions are going to change to become more embracing of diversity at their core, that change likely starts with recalling the initial foundation and objectives of the institution, and assessing whether BIPOC students were contemplated at the institution's inception. "It is the strain of trying to thrive in a system that was never designed to include them let alone be conducive to their success."[24] Diversity is inviting the minority to the party, but inclusion is allowing them the opportunity to dance.[25] In actuality, that looks like developing systems and processes with more than just the majority in mind. First-generation BIPOC law students face a particularly unique set of challenges during matriculation, whether it is being the first in their family to pursue higher education, lacking mentors of which to ask simple questions like what classes to take or what supplies to purchase; having additional out-of-class responsibilities like caring for family members or raising children as a single parent; or not being able to afford to attend school full time without also working to ensure their economic survival, which places additional demands on their time needed to devote to their studies.

---

23. Minority Impostor Syndrome Survey, R. Allyce Bailey—Survey Monkey.

24. Ruchika Tulshyan & Jodi-Ann Burey, *Stop Telling Women They Have Imposter Syndrome*, Harv. Bus. Rev. (2021), https://hbr.org/2021/02/stop-telling-women-they-have-imposter-syndrome#:~:text=Imposter%20syndrome%20is%20loosely%20defined,they're%20deserving%20of%20accolades. (last visited Jan 13, 2022).

25. Janet Cho, *Diversity Is Being Invited to the Party and Asked to Dance*, Cleveland (2016), https://www.cleveland.com/business/2016/05/diversity_is_being_invited_to.html (last visited Jan 13, 2022); Ludmila N. Praslova, *Dancing with Diversity: From Inclusion Illusion to Authentic Belonging*, Blog.SHRM.org (2020), https://blog.shrm.org/blog/dancing-with-diversity-from-inclusion-illusion-to-authentic-belonging (last visited Jan 13, 2022).

III. "You Belong. Period." — What Law Schools Can Do to Help BIPOC First Gen Law Students Overcome Impostor Syndrome in Matriculation

> Imposter syndrome is aggravated by bias and microaggressions, negatively reinforcing what a student is already thinking of themselves. It is critical for advisors, faculty, and staff to educate themselves, assess their bias, and work to cultivate a better learning and working environment for all.[26]

If impostor syndrome is fueled by a lack of sense of belonging, fostering a genuine sense of belonging would appear to be the necessary antidote. Emphasis on diversity efforts being genuine in nature is critical to ensuring minorities do not feel as if entities' diversity efforts are lip service rather than being rooted in sincerity. The *Merriam-Webster Dictionary* defines genuine as "sincerely and honestly felt or experienced."[27] In order to overcome an atmosphere that breeds impostor syndrome, diversity initiatives must be both sincerely and honestly felt and experienced by the minorities the efforts are endeavoring to benefit, as well as being sincerely and honestly desired by those implementing the programs. The following are several initiatives law schools can implement to foster genuine inclusiveness for their BIPOC students.

A. Safe Spaces

In talking to students and law clerks I have worked with, I have learned the vital importance of BIPOC students having genuine safe spaces. From how to address a superior's consistent microaggressions to how to address natural hairstyles or name discrimination in the on-campus interview process, BIPOC students logically feel most comfortable discussing these vulnerable and sensitive issues with people they genuinely believe will not judge them or who can genuinely relate to the matter. Law schools must hire diverse staff so that there are sufficient faculty members to serve as mentors to the students of color. Law schools should also make a pointed effort to establish BIPOC alumni councils the members of which can be called upon to mentor current students so that students have both an on- and off-campus BIPOC mentor with whom they can relate and confer. If the issue a student is having is with a current faculty member, having an off-campus mentor as a safe space is crucial to helping the BIPOC student navigate difficult situations of first impression during an already stressful season in their lives.

---

26. Samyukta Mullangi & Reshma Jagsi, *Imposter Syndrome: Treat the Cause, Not the Symptom*, JAMA, 2019.

27. *Genuine*, definition and meaning, Merriam-Webster, https://www.merriam-webster.com/dictionary/genuine (last visited Jan 13, 2022).

B. Support BIPOC Organizations

Law schools can foster an inclusive environment by allowing students to charter organizations for diverse students. Organizations like Black Law Students Association, and the law student divisions of the National Bar Association, National Asian Pacific American Bar Association, and Hispanic National Bar Association allow students to commune and recharge with their counterparts and are often the spaces in which students feel most secure. Additionally, law schools should make their facilities available to minority community organizations. Allowing the local NAACP or Urban League chapter to use a conference room to host a town hall represents to BIPOC students that the school's administrators care about issues that affect their community.

C. Take a Stand

When news headlines present issues that affect minority communities, these issues often weigh on BIPOC students. Many BIPOC students carried the weight of George Floyd's death into the classroom that week. Issuing statements on behalf of the institution in support of minority communities shows solidarity and an empathetic response to the issues they face. Most importantly, the statement should not simply show remorse, but should provide some call to action for the local community to get involved to make some meaningful change regarding the issues or provide some tangible plan of action the institution plans to implement to address similar issues on their campus.

D. Genuinely Celebrate Diverse Culture

Law schools can work to genuinely celebrate diverse cultures by planning law school events, the school's organizational structure, etc., with BIPOC students in mind. The creation of a Cultural Inclusion Council could be the key to convening students of different backgrounds to share the issues and events that are significant to their respective culture to ensure that diversity efforts are conducted sensitively, respectfully, and with authenticity.

Institutions can start with recognition of holidays and events significant to minorities' culture. For instance, hosting a Juneteenth Block Party could be a great showing of solidarity. Recently, Juneteenth has become more widely recognized to commemorate the day Black American slaves on plantations learned of the signing of the Emancipation Proclamation and their resulting freedom. In addition to celebrating the Fourth of July, Black Americans nationwide have taken to hosting similar gatherings in honor of Juneteenth. Additionally, the holiday season is an excellent time to recognize not only Christmas, but Hanukkah and Kwanzaa as well.

E. Primers on Subject Matter for Exposure

Lacking the legal professional role model that many of their majority counterparts have prior to entering law school, first-generation BIPOC law students may not have the general exposure to the concepts and issues presented by law school classes.

For instance, I was once in a professional setting, and to make conversation, a "superior" suggested we discuss our world travels and the most exotic destinations to which we had ever traveled. I did not come from a family that could afford to take lavish vacations when I was a child; I worked two jobs all throughout college and took double loads so I could graduate early; and worked tirelessly to bill countless hours as a young lawyer to support my family depending on me back home. At the time of this conversation, I had not yet reached a point at which I would have many exciting trips to add to that conversation. The person meant well and had no idea the privileged tone the conversation presented, but it is from this same place of ignorance that law school hypotheticals are often written, and law school classes are presented.

There have also been reports of professors exhibiting bias or even blatant racism in the drafting or wording of their exam questions, like the University of Illinois-Chicago School of Law professor's use of the "n-word" in a law school exam or the Georgetown Law professor who was recorded on video noting her lower grades as usually belonging to students of color.[28]

It is critical that law professors take note that there are varying backgrounds presented by their class roster, and work to teach in a way that levels the playing field for all.

I participated in a program called "Pre-Law" at my law school. About one month before the start of our 1L orientation, a select number of admittees of the incoming class were invited to participate in the program that simulated several first-year courses. For approximately three weeks, the group sat through actual law school lectures (with required reading), experienced the Socratic method, and even took mock final exams, which were graded and provided us feedback on our areas for

28. Stephanie Francis Ward, *Exam Question Wasn't Only Offensive Behavior of UIC Law Professor, According to Internal Investigation*, A.B.A. J. (2021), https://www.abajournal.com/web/article/exam-question-wasnt-only-offensive-behavior-of-uic-law-professor-according-to-internal-investigation (last visited Jan 13, 2022); Eugene Volokh, *The Law School Acknowledges That the Racial and Gender References on the Examination Were Deeply Offensive*, Reason.com (2021), https://reason.com/volokh/2021/01/15/tenured-law-prof-apparently-suspended-for-racial-harassment-lawsuit-problem-on-a-civil-procedure-exam/ (last visited Jan 13, 2022); Janhvi Bhojwani & Nicole Acevedo, *Georgetown Law Professor Resigns Over 'Insensitive Remarks' About Black Students*, NBCNews.com (2021), https://www.nbcnews.com/news/education/georgetown-law-professor-resigns-over-insensitive-remarks-about-black-students-n1261034 (last visited Jan 13, 2022).

improvement. The program was invaluable for someone like me whose only experience with the law was during my parents' divorce when I was child.

Like me, there are numerous other students who could benefit from assistance with the broad understanding of the subject matter of the first-year law courses, particularly for those first-year law students who are not liberal arts or business majors who may have had some cursory introduction to some legal concepts in some of their upper-level undergraduate courses like business law for business majors or the typical constitutional law class many political science majors take.

Even if a school does not have the time or resources for a full-fledged mock law school program, an expanded orientation session specifically for first-generation BIPOC students that generally explains the basis of each class's subject matter, the concepts and themes that will be discussed, and how that information will be tested could be critical to a student's successful matriculation.

A bonus to additional academic help for BIPOC first-generation law students would be a legal writing workshop. As a Bachelor of English with a concentration in Professional Writing, I was dismayed when my legal writing professor bled over my first legal writing assignment with his red pen. Even the best writers must transition to the unique style that legal writing requires. The ability to write concisely and to organize one's thoughts also in grammatical form under time constraints is often a hurdle in passing law school exams and eventually the bar exam. Thus, first-generation law students could benefit from additional assistance in crafting their legal writing style.

F. Provide a Learning Style Assessment

Reprogramming our minds with positive self-talk to counter the lies of impostor syndrome is an integral part of overcoming impostor syndrome. However, there are also practical steps administrators can take to assist students with convincing themselves that they have the tools to succeed in law school even when their subconscious disagrees. Every student has individual strengths and areas of opportunity. Forcing every student to try to learn the same way may leave a very capable student feeling like a fish trying to climb a tree. With varying learning styles such as visual, auditory, reading/writing, and kinesthetic,[29] helping a student identify their strongest retention method and learning style can equip them to better understand and retain the information taught in law school classes, which will in turn work to counter their impostor syndrome as they see their marked success.

---

29. *4 Types of Learning Styles: How Do Students Learn Best?*, Bay Atlantic Univ. (2021), https://bau.edu/blog/types-of-learning-styles/ (last visited Jan. 13, 2022).

IV. Encourage the Adoption of Positive Habits

A. Do What Has Worked Thus Far

Whenever I am mentoring law students and they solicit study tips to succeed in law school, my number one advice is "Don't reinvent the wheel." I remind students that it is no mistake that they have successfully matriculated through high school, college, and the standardized tests necessary to enter law school. Whatever study habits they implemented in their academic career thus far are likely the methods they should continue using in law school. If a student was used to studying in a group setting, law school is not the time to go it alone. If a student is accustomed to doing their best studying in the library, law school is not the time to try to study at home or at a busy coffee shop.

B. Time Management

Emphasize the importance of time management. Law school has been described as a "jealous mistress," to which you will have to devote significant amounts of time.[30] Teaching students early how to prioritize their time can give them the edge so they feel in control and more confident in their abilities.

C. Personal Life Incorporation

Overcoming impostor syndrome really hinges on developing confidence in one's abilities. With its endless competitiveness for the highest grades and best clerkships, law school can leave students feeling inadequate. Another way to help students overcome impostor syndrome is by encouraging students to continue incorporating aspects of their personal life throughout their law school matriculation. For instance, winning a medal for a marathon, mastering a new dish in a cooking class, leveling up on a new martial arts belt, or winning an award for one's garden produce can help a student realize that their value and self-worth is not defined by their law school rank and that they have so much more to offer the world than a perfectly crafted IRAC response.

D. Focus on Tested Concepts

While only the professor knows exactly what they plan to place on a law school exam, law students with relatives or connections to law school will often at least understand what the most tested concepts are. This allows those students to focus their valuable study time and not waste time memorizing or focusing on case law or concepts that professors rarely cover. Administrators can assist first-generation law

30. "The law is a jealous mistress and requires long and constant courtship. It is not to be won by trifling favors, but by lavish homage." Statement made in 1929 by United States Supreme Court Justice Joseph Story.

students by providing insight into how to ace a particular professor's class. Providing the disclaimer that all concepts are testable and of course are fair game, but sharing some of the professor's past hypotheticals or old exams; highlighting the topics often tested on the bar exam from certain subjects; and encouraging students to focus their memorization and study efforts on the concepts most likely to be tested while not neglecting the other material could be incredibly helpful.

V. Leveling the Playing Field with Resources

Statistics show that BIPOC students are disproportionately affected by unique challenges outside of the classroom like food insecurity, transportation issues, lack of family support, and childcare issues. [31] For instance, a 2018 study performed by researchers at Temple University found that 36% of their first-generation students were food insecure, with projections for that statistic to increase to 42% for the following year.[32] Additionally, research shows that transportation issues pose a number of challenges for BIPOC students as due to cost, distance, and unreliability of public transportation routes.[33] Parenthood also poses unique challenges for matriculating students, as 53% of student parents fail to complete their degree programs after six years.[34] Thus, it is likely these challenges also continue to plague students at the

31. Karen Collias, *First-Generation College Students Among Those Affected by Food Insecurity*, Knowledge Without Borders (2018), https://knowwithoutborders.org/first-generation-college-students-among-those-affected-by-food-insecurity/ (last visited Jan 13, 2022); *Food Insecurity During College Years Linked to Lower Graduation Rate*, Johns Hopkins Bloomberg Sch. Pub. Health, https://publichealth.jhu.edu/2021/food-insecurity-during-college-years-linked-to-lower-graduation-rate#:~:text=While%2076%20percent%20of%20students,insecure%20first%2Dgeneration%20students%20graduated. (last visited Jan 13, 2022); Charlotte West, *A Surprising Reason Preventing Some Students from Finishing College: Lack of Transportation*, Wash. Post (2021), https://www.washingtonpost.com/education/2021/12/10/college-students-transportation-struggles/ (last visited Jan 13, 2022); Troy Markowitz, *The Barriers to Success and Upward Mobility for First Generation Students and How to Fix the Problem*, Forbes (2021), https://www.forbes.com/sites/troymarkowitz/2017/08/08/the-barriers-to-success-and-upward-mobility-for-first-generation-students-and-how-to-fix-the-problem/?sh=16c8bc3e1cb3 (last visited Jan 13, 2022); *College Students with Children Are Common and Face Many Challenges in Completing Higher Education*, Inst. for Women's Pol'y Rsch. (2013), https://files.eric.ed.gov/fulltext/ED556715.pdf.

32. Karen Collias, *First-Generation College Students Among Those Affected by Food Insecurity*, Knowledge Without Borders (2018), https://knowwithoutborders.org/first-generation-college-students-among-those-affected-by-food-insecurity/ (last visited Jan 13, 2022).

33. Charlotte West, *A Surprising Reason Preventing Some Students from Finishing College: Lack of Transportation*, Wash. Post (2021), https://www.washingtonpost.com/education/2021/12/10/college-students-transportation-struggles/ (last visited Jan 13, 2022); Derek V. Price & Drew Curtis, Overcoming Transportation Barriers to Improve Postsecondary Student Success, https://www.dvp-praxis.org/wp-content/uploads/2018/02/Kresge-Higher-Education-and-Transportation-Brief.pdf (last visited May 6, 2022).

34. *College Students with Children Are Common and Face Many Challenges in Completing Higher Education*, Inst. for Women's Pol'y Rsch. (2013), https://files.eric.ed.gov/fulltext/ED556715.pdf.

graduate level. Accordingly, helping BIPOC first-generation law students overcome their imposter syndrome can be addressed by leveling the playing field by providing resources to address some of these unique challenges that undoubtedly make law school more difficult.

My undergraduate institution, Northwestern State University, has in recent years started a student food bank. The food bank looks just like a typical grocery store or convenience store and any students are welcome to take whatever essential items they need. Law schools could mimic this model and provide a confidential food bank by allowing students to inform their faculty advisor of their desire to receive such services and a discreet exchange of the needed items could be arranged.

Administrators also are likely familiar with the communities in which their schools exist. Accordingly, compiling a transportation guide of public transportation and childcare options that operate during school and library hours could be very beneficial for students who lack personal or reliable transportation or childcare.

The exorbitant cost of academic textbooks can pose an additional financial burden on law students. Encouraging upperclassmen to donate their books or supplies perhaps for extra credit, a gift card, or some other valuable incentive to start a textbook and supply bank for incoming students could be beneficial.

Conclusion

Implicit bias, the comfort we find in maintaining historic norms, and established but often antiquated institutional infrastructure prevent the implementation of diversity efforts from occurring by happenstance. Helping BIPOC students overcome imposter syndrome and other barriers impacting their success in law school requires deliberate effort and action on the part of law schools. These action plans are not just necessary to benefit BIPOC students, but are critical to the success and longevity of our law schools. In order to reach that success, law schools must cultivate environments that provide the necessary elements to allow BIPOC students to not merely enter and survive law school, but to successfully matriculate and thrive.

PART II Fostering Inclusion in All Law School Spaces

Five

Cultivating and Encouraging BIPOC First Gen Law Students

Krishnee Coley* and Kia Vernon**

IN FEBRUARY 2014, ATTORNEY PAULETTE BROWN MADE HISTORY by becoming the first African American woman to be nominated to become president of the American Bar Association.[1] As the first African American woman—and only the third African American—to lead the organization founded in 1878, she not only understood the magnitude of her nomination, but also the responsibility it bestowed upon her as a woman of color.[2] Her primary goal was "to create systemic and sustained change in the legal profession."[3] A May 2015 *Washington Post* article forecast the gargantuan challenge she faced once her term officially began. As the title succinctly provided, "Law is the least diverse profession in the world. And lawyers aren't doing enough to change that."[4] While "[e]ighty-eight percent of lawyers are white... 81 percent of architects and engineers are white; 78 percent of accountants are white; and 72 percent of physicians and surgeons are white."[5]

During her one-year term, Attorney Brown created the Diversity & Inclusion 360 Commission, which established four working groups to assess diversity, equity, and

* Associate Professor of Law, Legal Practice and Director of Academic Success Program, University of Richmond School of Law.

** Associate Dean of Academic Success and Professor of Law, North Carolina Central University School of Law.

1. James Podgers, *Paulette Brown Will Be the First Woman of Color to Serve as ABA President*, A.B.A. J. (May 1, 2014, 7:30 AM), https://www.abajournal.com/magazine/article/paulette_brown_will_be_the_first_woman_of_color_to_serve_as_aba_president.

2. *Id.*

3. Richard D. Harvey et al., *2020 ABA Model Diversity Survey* at 3, ABA Comm'n on Racial & Ethnic Diversity in the Profession [https://www.americanbar.org/content/dam/aba/administrative/racial_ethnic_diversity/aba/credp_2020_mds_report.pdf] (last visited April 29, 2022).

4. Deborah L. Rhode, *Law Is the Least Diverse Profession in the Nation. And Lawyers Aren't Doing Enough to Change That*, Wash. Post (May 27, 2015) https://www.washingtonpost.com/posteverything/wp/2015/05/27/law-is-the-least-diverse-profession-in-the-nation-and-lawyers-arent-doing-enough-to-change-that/.

5. *Id.*

inclusion in the legal profession.[6] One of the working groups, the Economic Case Working Group, drafted Resolution 113, to increase diversity in the legal profession and reduce implicit bias in the legal profession.[7] The Resolution was adopted by the House of Delegates in 2016.[8] In 2015, when Attorney Brown first began her tenure, there were 1,160,000 employed lawyers in the United States.[9] Of these, 4.6% were Black or African American, 4.8% were Asian, and 5.1% were Hispanic or Latino. Six years later, employment figures reflect little progress. In 2021, there were 1,085,000 employed lawyers in the United States; 5.4% were Black or African American, 4.7% were Asian, and 6.9% were Hispanic or Latino.[10]

Recent events have once again drawn attention to the lack of minorities in the profession and the impact it has on society. In August 2021, after a summer of seemingly endless killings of black and brown people by police officers, there was a renewed focus on systemic racism and the implicit biases that are pervasive in our society, especially in the justice system. In response, the American Bar Association passed a Member Diversity, Education, and Inclusion Plan to "strengthen and increase full and equal participation in the Association by all members."[11] The plan advances numerous goals and objectives, including encouraging ABA entities "to develop, partner with, or co-sponsor pipeline programs targeted to college and K-12 students designed to advance diversity, equity, and inclusion in the legal profession."[12]

It is apparent that there is still much work that needs to be done to diversify the legal profession. Forming commissions, passing resolutions, and expecting the change to come from within the profession has produced few results. Law schools must recruit, admit, and retain more students from historically underrepresented backgrounds. Although the solution appears to be simple, it is quite complex. First, significant work needs to be done to encourage BIPOC students, especially BIPOC first-generation students, to explore careers in the legal profession. Second, BIPOC first-generation students must be supported throughout the law school application process. Finally, once BIPOC first-generation students are admitted, law schools must recognize their uniqueness and provide programs to ensure they are successful in law school and in their legal careers.

---

6. *ABA Model Diversity Survey*, ABA Comm'n on Racial & Ethnic Diversity in the Profession, https://www.americanbar.org/groups/diversity/DiversityCommission/model-diversity-survey/ (last visited May 4, 2022).

7. *Id.*

8. *Id.*

9. U.S. Bureau of Labor Statistics, *Characteristics of the Employed, Table 11: Employed Persons by Detailed Occupation, Sex, Race, and Hispanic or Latino Ethnicity*, U.S. Dept. of Labor, https://www.bls.gov/cps/aa2015/ cpsaat11.htm (last visited May 4, 2022).

10. *Id.*

11. *Diversity and Inclusion Resources*, Am. Bar Ass'n, https://www.americanbar.org/groups/diversity/resources/ (last visited on May 2, 2022).

12. *Id.*

I. Cultivating BIPOC First Gen Students

An integral component of a plan to increase diversity in the legal profession is programming and resources to encourage BIPOC first-generation students to explore careers in law. The ABA Council for Diversity in the Legal Profession and the Law School Admissions Council (LSAC) created the Pipeline Diversity Directory, which includes programs, scholarships, internships, and LSAT programs that are available for minority students.[13] AccessLex Institute also maintains a Diversity Pipeline Program Directory "to help prospective law students and pre-law advisors identify pipeline programs serving college students and/or college graduates from historically underrepresented groups with information and resources premised on aiding their successful matriculation into law school and the legal profession."[14] These are both great resources for BIPOC students interested in attending law school who are highly motivated, or who have access to information from robust pre-law programs or other sources. However, for many BIPOC first-generation students, these resources remain elusive.

In a recent meeting of BIPOC first-generation students,[15] many expressed frustration about how difficult it was to access information about law school. One BIPOC first-generation student stated that she was so clueless about the law school admissions process that she did not know that she had to first take the LSAT to apply. Another student, a daughter of immigrants, discussed how helpful it would have been to simply talk to someone about the process. While there were pre-law programs at the PWI she attended, she was too intimidated to be in a room that was full of children whose parents were lawyers. She did not have anyone within her inner circle who could answer any of her questions. Another student, who is also the daughter of immigrants, agreed. Although she decided that she wanted to attend law school as a child after witnessing first-hand how the lack of access to legal assistance negatively impacted her parents who were facing foreclosure, she had no idea where to even start. Although all three eventually made it to law school, they delayed applying for several years because they lacked confidence and thought it was too difficult to get into law school.

BIPOC first-generation students who attended PWIs shared troubling stories of being discouraged from attending law school by pre-law advisors. One student was

---

13. *ABA National Pipeline Directory*, AM. BAR ASS'N, https://www.americanbar.org/content/dam/aba/administrative/diversity-inclusion-center/pipeline-directory12-17.pdf (last visited on May 2, 2022).

14. *AccessLex Institute Diversity Pipeline Program Directory*, ACCESSLEX INST., https://www.accesslex.org/ accesslex-diversity-pipeline-program-directory (last visited n May 2, 2022).

15. BIPOC first-generation students in attendance were all current students at North Carolina Central University School of Law, a historically black institution. Most students present attended predominantly white undergraduate institutions. What was most surprising was that despite being at an HBCU law school with a majority of students who identified as BIPOC, these students nonetheless expressed thoughts of feeling alone and isolated due their status as first-generation students.

told by her pre-law advisor that she was not smart enough to attend law school; thus, the advisor refused to help her. She attempted to navigate the process on her own and even worked two jobs to pay for a commercial LSAT preparation course. She was so discouraged after taking the LSAT the first time that she took several years off before attempting to take the exam again. Unfortunately, her story was not unique. Another student shared a similar experience of being discouraged from taking the LSAT by a pre-law advisor, which affected her preparation and performance on the exam. She shared that it led to an extreme case of imposter syndrome, which still affects her in law school.

In contrast, students who completed their undergraduate degrees at HBCUs indicated that the resources and programs by pre-law advisors at their institutions were extremely helpful in educating them about law school. These students were also first-generation students, but did not experience the same level of anxiety, as most students in their pre-law undergraduate program were similarly situated. Students without access to any pre-law advisors indicated that they acquired information by using online search engines and forums, which at times proved to be incorrect or outdated and was unnecessarily time-consuming. Thus, pre-law advisors are valuable resources for BIPOC students. However, pre-law programs specifically designed for BIPOC first-generation students would provide them with a safe space to access valuable information and ask questions. Schools with pre-law programs should also provide training to ensure that all students, regardless of color or ethnicity, should be given access to critical information and encouraged—never discouraged—to pursue careers in law.

Several of the BIPOC first-generation students surveyed entered law school after serving as a guardian *ad litem*[16] or working as a paralegal. Prior to this exposure into the legal system, the students had never thought about becoming a lawyer but were encouraged to consider it by others who observed their passion, commitment, and work ethic. These programs can serve as a conduit for law school and should be explored to further diversify the profession. As one student stated, she never imagined that she could be an attorney until someone reassured her and told her, "You can get there from here." Accordingly, community college programs as well as outreach within other legal careers would help to facilitate more BIPOC first-generation students entering the legal profession.

Another way to educate and encourage BIPOC first-generation students to explore legal careers is through attorney outreach. A recurring frustration for BIPOC

16. While the role of a Guardian ad Litem (GAL) varies depending on the state, in North Carolina, a GAL is a trained community volunteer who is appointed by a district court judge to investigate and determine the needs of abused and neglected children petitioned into the court system by the Department of Social Services. The GAL advocates for the best interests of children in court. https://www.nccourts.gov/programs/guardian-ad-litem/about-guardian-ad-litem-gal#:~:text=Equips%20community%20volunteers%20to%20serve,their%20best%20interests%20in%20court. (last visited on May 4, 2022).

first-generation students is the inability to learn more about the legal profession prior to entering law school. Not only do BIPOC first-generation students not have anyone in their families who attended college, much less law school, many indicated that they had never known anyone who was an attorney and had little reference—apart from television—of the role of an attorney, much less how to become one. A study by the National Native American Bar Association (NNABA) reinforces the import of attorney role models. "Many Native American attorneys report that their decision to pursue legal education was strongly influenced by personal interaction and the persuasion of family, mentors, lawyers or other professionals," it concluded.[17] It further provided that "[c]ommunity and social network influence must remain a strong and central component in the pipeline that will produce future law students and legal professionals."[18]

Attorney outreach serves several functions. It provides BIPOC first-generation students with an opportunity to learn about the legal profession and what it entails. BIPOC first-generation students can gain valuable experience from attorneys and receive relevant information about how to overcome some of the barriers to attending and succeeding in law school, such as the law school admissions process, considerations for selecting law schools to attend, and how to be successful in law school.[19] Additionally, it provides encouragement and motivation, especially when BIPOC first-generation students can listen to the experiences of successful BIPOC attorneys who were also first-generation students.

These recommendations will provide invaluable assistance to BIPOC first-generation students who already have an interest in attending law school. A greater issue is how to attract BIPOC students who have not previously explored the possibility of entering the legal profession. While lawyers surveyed in the general lawyer population indicated that "a challenging and rewarding career and financial security"[20] were the primary reasons they chose to attend law school, BIPOC first-generation students often decide to attend law school as a result of a personal experience with the judicial system or witnessing a close friend or family member's involvement with the judicial system.[21] ABA and attorney outreach should include programs that encourage students, especially BIPOC first-generation students, to consider careers in law. Law schools can also help through summer programs and community outreach. One example of a summer program and community outreach is a Legal Eagle Law

---

17. Mary Smith, *Native American Attorneys Systematically Excluded in Legal Profession*, at 18 (Oct. 1, 2014), https://www.nativeamericanbar.org/wp-content/uploads/2014/01/2015-02-11-final-NNABA_report_pp6.pdf.

18. *Id.*

19. *Id.* at 19.

20. *Id.* at 21.

21. In our discussion with our BIPOC first-generation students, all cited personal legal issues or experiences with the judicial system, or legal issues experienced by family members, as the reasons they decided to attend law school.

Camp held at North Carolina Central University School of Law in partnership with Durham Public Schools. The week-long camp provides rising seventh through tenth graders an opportunity to receive an overview of the legal system, learn more about the legal profession, and participate in a mock trial. Pro bono opportunities within the law school also provide law students with the opportunity to partner with local courts and organizations for community outreach.[22]

II. Preparing BIPOC First Gen Students for Law School

Another key component to a plan to increase diversity in the legal profession is to ensure BIPOC first-generation students are supported throughout the law school application process. Even though LSAC has dedicated resources on its website regarding applying to law school,[23] many BIPOC first-generation students in the meeting expressed a desire to also have someone to guide them through the process. One student shared that while he followed the application checklist and made sure his application contained the necessary components, he realized after the fact that the quality of his application was poor. He admitted that he thought he could bolster his application by securing letters of recommendation from "big wigs" in his community instead of focusing on the quality of his writing for his personal statement. Another BIPOC first-generation student did not have a knowledgeable advisor or mentor to read his application and offer feedback prior to him submitting it.

Even the BIPOC first-generation students who decided early on that they wanted to apply to law school admitted that they had the bare minimum of understanding of what was required due to lack of exposure to the legal field. One student agonized over choosing the correct major in college believing that he had to study political science. This same student expressed regret over not knowing how to network and to meet with admissions officers because he missed out on critical information that would have helped him during the application process, such as the LSAC fee waiver. Based on his experiences, the student feels as if the legal field is a closed-off world for the BIPOC first-generation community. On the opposite end of the spectrum, a couple of BIPOC first-generation students who attended PWI undergraduate institutions stated they had access to support during the application process, but they were strongly discouraged from applying to HBCU law schools. One of the students had to research HBCU law schools on her own once she informed her pre-law advisor that she was not interested in attending a PWI law school. Both were accepted

---

22. Students at North Carolina Central University School of Law have also participated in Teen Court programs and a Street Law class that teaches students in Durham Public Schools about the legal system and legal careers.

23. *See, e.g.*, *Steps to Apply: JD Programs*, Law School Admission Council, https://www.lsac.org/jd-applicants/steps-apply-jd-programs (last visited May 4, 2022).

into a PWI law school, which they declined because they sought an environment where they would be supported and nurtured. They further encourage other BIPOC first-generation students to select a law school that helps them to grow and thrive.

Several BIPOC first-generation students also shared stories of how they persisted despite not being admitted during their first attempt. One woman, who is a nontraditional student, decided to apply to law school after working in the social services field for almost a decade. She shared that she was initially denied when she applied for law school, but it was a follow-up conversation with a law school admissions officer that directed her to valuable resources, such as AccessLex Institute Lex Scholars, to improve her next application. Several others chimed in with the same experience of receiving helpful advice directly from a law school after an unsuccessful attempt. Some students were still too intimidated to speak to someone in the legal field, so they turned to the internet instead for tips on applying to law school after receiving an initial denial. There was one student in the meeting who acknowledged not knowing how complex the application process was and only spent one day preparing her application materials. She was one who relied solely on the internet when she prepared her applications after postponing her efforts for several years before reapplying. It is concerning that the majority of the students in the meeting learned by trial and error and had to apply to law school multiple times before being admitted. Moreover, these stories do not take into account the number of BIPOC first-generation applicants who were afraid to follow up after initially being denied acceptance, and thus they did not receive the benefit of learning about application preparation support.

The recurring theme among the BIPOC first-generation students who recounted their law school application process was the desire to have individualized assistance or access to people in the legal profession who could assist them. Moreover, they were not familiar with numerous resources and programs that could have assisted them with the application process beyond generic internet searches. Below is a non-exhaustive list of the pre-law programs and resources to assist future BIPOC first-generation law school applicants with the application process:

Pre-Law Programs[24]

- **Council on Legal Education Opportunity Inc. (CLEO)**, founded in 1968, started with a mission of increasing the number of Black and low-income students in law school by enrolling them in a pre-law summer institute designed to prepare them for success in law school. CLEO has added programming including CLEO ASAP, Achieving Success in the Application Process, which is a two-day seminar to help prospective law school appli-

24. We encourage law schools to add these resources to their admissions page as a resource for prospective BIPOC first-generation law students. We also encourage undergraduate institutions to provide this information to their pre-law advisors to share with their advisees.

cants navigate the admission process. Many of the participants in CLEO programs identify as first-generation law students.[25]

- **SEO Law (Sponsors for Educational Opportunity)**
  - **Catalyst by SEO Law**—This is a free, nine-month program that provides resources to historically underrepresented students interested in applying to law school. SEO Law offers both a four-month Spring LSAT Program and a five-month Admissions Consulting Program. The admissions consulting program includes workshops, attorney mentors, roundtable discussions with law school admissions officers, as well as customized guidance and review of application materials.[26]
  - **SEO Law Fellowship Program**—This program provides historically underrepresented students a 10-week, paid summer experience prior to law school, which includes two weeks of career and academic development and an eight-week internship at a corporate law firm in numerous cities across the country. Fellows receive ongoing support and mentorship during law school.[27]
- **LSAC Prelaw Undergraduate Scholars (PLUS) Programs**— LSAC partners with law schools across the country to host college students, with a focus on students from groups historically underrepresented in the legal profession. The programs provide assistance with the law school admissions process, offer insight into the law school experience, and guidance on legal careers. There is no cost to participants to attend the program and each participant is eligible to receive a $1,000 stipend and a LSAC fee waiver after completing the program.[28]
- **AccessLex Institute** has several areas of focus, including diversity programs for law school prospects, and it has an online database of diversity pipeline programs.[29] AccessLex also offers multiple programs in support of minority law school applicants, including the LexScholars Post-Baccalaureate Program. This program is a partnership with 10 law schools that guarantee first-generation and minority law school applicants deferred admission and scholarships. The participants must agree to spend a year working to im-

---

25. *Pre-Law Programs, CLEOinc*, https://cleoinc.org/pre-law-programs/ (last visited May 4, 2022).

26. *SEO Law Catalyst*, SEO Law, https://www.seo-usa.org/law/our-program/catalyst/ (last visited May 4, 2022).

27. *Apply to SEO Law Programs*, SEO Law, https://www.seo-usa.org/law/our-program/apply /(last visited May 4, 2022).

28. *LSAC Prelaw Undergraduate Scholars(PLUS) Programs*, Law School Admission Council, https://www.lsac.org/discover-law/diversity-law-school/prelaw-undergraduate-scholars-plus -programs (last visited May 4, 2022).

29. *AccessLex Diversity Pipeline Program Directory*, AccessLex Inst., https://www.accesslex .org/accesslex-diversity-pipeline-program-directory (last visited May 4, 2022).

prove their LSAT scores and preparing for law school by completing online foundational law courses to build critical thinking and analytical skills.[30] The students will also participate in curriculum coaching and financial counseling. Once they successfully complete the program, the students will receive a stipend of $3,000 from AccessLex Institute and the partner law schools will offer a scholarship of up to 20% of tuition.[31]

- **The American Bar Association** offers the Legal Opportunity Scholarship. The scholarship is intended to encourage racial and ethnic minority students to apply to and attend law school. This scholarship grants the students $15,000 of financial aid over three years.[32] The ABA website also houses a link to the National Pipeline Diversity Initiatives Directory.[33]
- **Practicing Attorneys for Law Students Program, Inc. (PALS)** was founded in 1984 to assist minority law students in the New York City area with career and professional development services and employment opportunities with major law firms. PALS services are available to students at 13 law schools in the New York Metropolitan area. Programs offered include a summer civil rights fellowship, mentoring, skills workshops, and networking opportunities.[34]
- The **Playing Field Project** is a nonprofit organization founded in 2020 with a mission to provide financial support to low-income BIPOC law students. The Project's financial assistance covers LSAT and pre-law school prep programs, as well as law school application assistance.[35] The Project also recently partnered with Leg Up Legal, a mentoring program and platform for prospective law students to further support low-income BIPOC prospective law students.[36]

---

30. Amanda Robert, *New Program Guarantees Diverse Student Admission to Law School*, A.B.A. J. (Nov. 29, 2021, 10:28 AM CDT), https://www.abajournal.com/news/article/new-program-guarantees-diverse-students-admission-to-law-school.

31. Karen Sloan, *New Law School Diversity Program Has a Twist: Guaranteed Admission*, Reuters (Nov. 29, 2021, 6:24 AM EST), https://www.reuters.com/legal/legalindustry/new-law-school-diversity-program-has-twist-guaranteed-admission-2021-11-29/

32. *Legal Opportunity Scholarship*, Am. Bar Ass'n, https://www.americanbar.org/groups/diversity/diversity_pipeline/projects_initiatives/legal_opportunity_scholarship/ (last visited May 4, 2022).

33. *National Pipeline Diversity Initiatives Directory*, Am. Bar Ass'n, https://www.americanbar.org/groups/diversity/diversity_pipeline/projects_initiatives/pipeline_diversity_directory/ (last visited May 4, 2022).

34. *See, e.g.*, PALS, https://www.palsprogram.org/about-us/our-history (last visited May 4, 2022).

35. *Leg Up Legal Partners with the Playing Field Project to Provide Mentorship to Low-Income BIPOC Students*, Leg Up Legal (Jan. 13, 2021, 4:30 PM CST), https://www.leguplegal.com/playing-field-project-partnership.

36. *Id.*

- **LAW*Bound*** is a pre-law program with a goal to increase the number of Latinx students in law school. The program provides its members with mentoring, networking, and outreach activities to help students overcome barriers to the law school admissions process. Students who are members of the program continue to receive support after acceptance into law school to bar admission ("wrap-around program").[37]
- **Prelaw Summer Institute for American Indians and Alaska Natives (PLSI)** is an eight-week law school prep program for American Indian and Alaska Native students. The goal of the program is to prepare the students for the rigors of law school through intensive instruction in the law, analysis, writing, and research. Students who participate in PLSI also develop mentoring relationships with a national network of Native lawyers.[38]

III. Nurturing BIPOC First Gen Students in Law School

Gaining admission into law school is, in and of itself, a huge accomplishment. However, BIPOC first-generation students need further support, encouragement, and assistance to ensure their growth in law school and, ultimately, in the practice of law. Law school is undeniably challenging for all law students. First-generation, and especially BIPOC first-generation, students are presented with additional challenges in law school. As one BIPOC first-generation student described, law school is like a secret society. This makes it especially difficult for BIPOC first-generation students to navigate the first year in law school. Among the many challenges, BIPOC first-generation students encounter unfamiliar language, struggle with imposter syndrome, experience financial and family issues, and encounter mental health challenges.[39]

Studies reveal that BIPOC students are disproportionately represented in attrition numbers. Although the studies do not provide attrition statistics for first-generation students or BIPOC first-generation students, the large disparity in attrition rates between white students and BIPOC students alone is cause for alarm. According to a 2018 study of law school attrition rates, in 2016, the "[first year] non-transfer attrition rate of white students was 5 percent, but… the [first year] non-transfer at-

---

37. *LAWBound*, Latino Justice, https://www.latinojustice.org/en/lawbound (last visited May 4, 2022).

38. *PLSI*, American Indian Law Center Inc., https://www.ailc-inc.org/plsi/ (last visited May 4, 2022).

39. *See also* Nicole P. Kabalkin, *Addressing Barriers to College Completion for BIPOC First Generation Students: Recommendations to Improve Students' Sense of Belonging and College Persistence Outcomes* (2021). *Doctorate in Social Work (DSW) Dissertations*. 157, https://repository.upenn.edu/edissertations_sp2/157 (last visited May 4, 2022), for a discussion of barriers facing BIPOC first-generation students in college.

trition rate was nearly 9 percent for Hispanic law students and 11 percent for black students."[40] The first-year non-transfer attrition rate for Native Hawaiian students was 11.8 percent, and the first-year non-transfer attrition rate for American Indian students was 13 percent.[41] More surprisingly, attrition rates were consistent across all ABA-approved law schools, regardless of whether the law school was a public or private law school or a low LSAT median or high LSAT median school.[42] As one law review author said it best, "These numbers should be a wake-up call to law schools that admitting a diverse class is not enough. Law schools have an obligation to also assess what happens to students once they matriculate."[43]

Another recent study reflects that the non-transfer attrition rates for BIPOC students has continued to rise. In 2018, "53% of first-year academic attrition was by students of color. In contrast, according to 2017 admission data, 34% of admitted 1Ls were students of color."[44] In summary, "legal education is losing students of color at a rate nearly 19% higher than it is attracting them."[45] While the majority of attrition is attributable to scholastic performance, students who do not feel supported or comfortable at their institutions struggle emotionally, mentally, and academically. Therefore, law schools must create an environment for BIPOC first-generation students that acknowledges the unique challenges these students encounter throughout their law school experience and provide mechanisms to support and assist them. This is true regardless of whether the students attend PWI or HBCU law schools.

Law students of color also encounter different challenges due to their law school environment. In 2020, the Law School Survey of Student Engagement (LSSSE) surveyed over 13,000 law students from 68 law schools. "Almost a quarter (21%) of law students who are Black, Latinx, or Native American, and almost a third (32%) of first-generation students (students whose parents did not finish high school) said they 'do not feel comfortable being [themselves] at [their] institution,' compared to just 12% of White students."[46] Additionally, "25% of Black students said their law schools do 'very little' to prevent students from being stigmatized based on characteristics like race/ethnicity, gender, religion, and sexual orientation [compared to] 9.3% of White students."[47] Programming that provides BIPOC first-generation stu-

---

40. Kylie Thomas & Tiffane Cochran, *ABA Data Reveals Minority Students Are Disproportionately Represented in Attrition Figures*, AccessLex Inst. (Sept. 18, 2018), https://www.accesslex.org/xblog/aba-data-reveals-minority-students-are-disproportionately-represented-in-attrition-figures.

41. *Id.*

42. *Id.*

43. Allie Robbins, *Preventing Attrition: Critical Interventions to Close the Racial Gap in Not Transfer-Attrition*, 26 Widener L. Rev. 143, 146 (2019).

44. *Id.* at 145.

45. *Id.*

46. *Diversity and Inclusion, LSSSE Annual Survey 2020*, at 10. https://lssse.indiana.edu/wp-content/uploads/2020/09/Diversity-and-Exclusion-Final-9.29.20.pdf (last visited May 4, 2022).

47. *Id.*

dents with an environment that fosters a sense of community within it would alleviate some of the issues presented in the student engagement survey.

Although the intent of this chapter was to research organizations and programming specifically for BIPOC first-generation students, research quickly showed that while there were many programs specifically designed for first-generation students, few law schools advertised programs specifically for BIPOC first-generation students. While BIPOC first-generation students can certainly benefit from the programming for all first-generation law students, not all first-generation law students are the same. BIPOC first-generation law students have different challenges, and thus, would gain invaluable benefits from programs designed to embrace and celebrate their differences and provide additional opportunities for them to grow and thrive.

Many BIPOC first-generation students arrive on campus without a strong system of support from family and friends. Others have family support, but due to the lack of familiarity with the rigorous law school environment and the pressures that are associated with the first-year law experience, their support system does not know how to best support them. Thus, programs for BIPOC first-generation students should be geared toward providing essential support as they begin the crucial first semester of law school. An informal mixer for BIPOC first-generation students would be a great way to allow students to meet other BIPOC first-generation students, to create a support group and sense of community as the semester begins. It is also beneficial—especially for the first meetings—to have different programming for separate groups within the BIPOC first-generation community.[48] Similar to first-generation students, all BIPOC first-generation students are not equal. Recognizing the diversity that exists within the BIPOC first-generation community will help to ensure that all groups feel welcome and supported during the critical first weeks of law school.

Mentoring groups within the law school community and alumni network are also extremely beneficial. BIPOC first-generation students often feel more comfortable talking to students with similar backgrounds and experiences. As one BIPOC first-generation student stated, talking to upperclassmen who had similar anxieties and frustrations as a first-year student, allowed them to feel that they were not alone. Additionally, fostering these relationships in law school provides students with a built-in support system once they transition to legal practice. BIPOC first-generation students also found mentoring programs with alumni very beneficial. Alumni who were also BIPOC first-generation students are eager to assist entering BIPOC first-generation students and provide assistance as needed throughout their law school matriculation.

One challenge in law schools is student engagement. Surprisingly, BIPOC first-generation students acknowledged their lack of participation in events hosted

48. For example, NCCU School of Law programs for and outreach to male POC students and female POC students.

for all students, even though they were intended to provide them with access to networking opportunities and additional support. An example provided was a networking event hosted by the local bar association. BIPOC first-generation students expressed that they felt unprepared to attend the events, so they decided to forego the opportunities altogether rather than risking ridicule for not knowing what to say or how to act. Utilizing alumni to provide BIPOC first-generation students with additional opportunities to practice networking skills or learn how to interact with others during the events would enable them to be more active and prepared during the law school events. Another consideration is ensuring that BIPOC first-generation services have appropriate interview attire. As BIPOC first-generation students, many do not know the proper dress for interviews, and may not have the financial means to purchase them. Career services programs can employ alumni and faculty to provide professional attire sessions and help secure funds or vouchers for those who need financial assistance.

Most importantly, BIPOC first-generation students expressed appreciation for opportunities to be heard. After a focus group to discuss BIPOC first-generation experiences, students were grateful for an opportunity to share with other BIPOC first-generation students and learn that they were not alone. As a result, the students suggested a monthly informal meeting to meet with law school faculty and/or staff to simply ask questions about law school or just discuss their experiences. This would require a minimum amount of effort, but provide BIPOC first-generation students with an inestimable benefit as they continued to navigate the law school experience.

IV. First Gen Programming

While we did not identify any law schools that offer BIPOC-specific first-generation support, many law schools do offer resources, programs, and/or student-led support organizations for first-generation students. Below is a summary of law school programs for first-generation law students:

- **Boston University School of Law**—First Generation Professionals (FGP) is a group for students who identify as first generation. The group offers community building and support via mentorship, professional development, and networking opportunities.[49]
- **Campbell Law**—created a virtual program for First Generation Law Students in Spring 2021 called the First Gen Blueprint. The program is "designed to help remove barriers, close knowledge gaps and inspire future

49. *See, e.g., Law Student Organizations*, Boston University School of Law, https://www.bu.edu/law/.admissions/student-life/student-organizations/ (last visited May 9, 2022).

students, who are the first in their immediate family to attend law school."[50] The self-paced program takes approximately six hours to complete and includes information on LSAT preparation, financial assistance, mental health resources, and exploration of the first-year experience as shared by members of the legal profession and current first-generation students. Also, the program aims to instill confidence in first-generation students and promote a strong work ethic for their future careers.

- **Chicago-Kent College of Law**—the First Generation Law Student Association (FGLSA) was founded in 2020. During its first year, the group held networking and panel events with first-generation judges and attorneys as guest speakers. During the second year of operation, FGLSA added an alumni mentorship program and started a pipeline program for undergraduates interested in the legal profession.[51]
- **DePaul College of Law**—First Generation Law Student Organization (First Gen) is a group for students who come from low-income/working-class backgrounds and those who identify as first generation. The goal of the group is to provide the First Gen students with financial, social, and academic support.[52]
- **Duke Law**—First Generation Professionals (1GP) offers mentoring, networking, professional development, and practical experiences for students who are the first in their family to graduate from college. 1GP sponsors various programs, including lunch with professors, financial planning, professional etiquette, and a law firm visit.[53]
- **Elon University School of Law**—hosted a national, virtual event, "The National Alliance of First Generation Law School Students," in April 2021 for first-generation law school candidates and current students. Elon University's First-Generation Student Support Services collaborated with its law faculty and their Alliance of Legal Pioneers and Supporters for networking and support sessions. Participants were also able to share common experiences and learn about resources available to support them in their law school journey. The event organizers stated this as a "first step toward the creation

---

50. Kerry Branon, *Campbell Law Launches Virtual Initiative to Help First-gen Law Students Succeed* (Mar. 17, 2021), https://news.campbell.edu/articles/campbell-law-launches-virtual-initiative-to-help-first-gen-law-students-succeed/.

51. Dawn Young & Ricardo Santiago, *Looking at the Challenges Facing First-Generation Law Students and (How to Address Them)*, https://abaforlawstudents.com/2021/10/14/the-challenges-facing-first-generation-law-students/ (last visited May 9, 2022).

52. *See, e.g., Student Organizations*, DePaul College of Law, https://law.depaul.edu/student-resources/student-activities/student-organizations/Pages/default.aspx (last visited May 9, 2022).

53. *See, e.g., Student Organizations—First Generation Professionals*, Duke Law, https://law.duke.edu/life/orgs/#fgp (last visited May 9, 2022).

of a new National Alliance of First-Generation Law School Students with resources and data on related issues managed at Elon Law."[54]

- **FIU Law**—In 2020, Law Dean Antony Page made a $200,000 planned gift to FIU to establish a scholarship for first generation law students.[55]
- **Harvard Law**—First Class was launched in late 2017 as a support and advocacy group for first-generation college and/or low-income students. The goal of First Class is to provide a community environment by hosting social events such as an annual welcome dinner as well as monthly dinners, supporting group members with career development, and advocating for programming tailored for first-generation students.[56]
- **Loyola University Chicago**—First Generation Law Students (FGLS) is a newly chartered organization created to provide personal, professional, and academic support for its first-generation students.[57]
- **New England Law | Boston**—First Generation Students Program provides life skills workshops, networking and scholarship opportunities, and one-on-one advising. The school also provides monthly group sessions co-facilitated by a faculty member and licensed clinical social worker to support student mental health and wellness.[58]
- **New York University School of Law**—First Generation Professionals is a student-led organization that supports the transition into law school through mentorship, career advising, and social activities.[59] NYU also offers full-tuition funding via the AnBryce Scholarship Program for first-gen students.[60]
- **Nova Southeastern University School of Law**—First Generation Professionals Legal Society provides social support to students who are the first in

54. Eric Townsend, *Elon Hosts National Conversation for First-Generation Law Students* (Apr. 20, 2021), https://www.elon.edu/u/news/2021/04/20/elon-hosts-national-conversation-for-first-generation-law-students/.

55. Clara-Meretan Kiah, *FIU Dean Creates Scholarship for First-Generation Students* (Aug. 20, 2020), https://news.fiu.edu/2020/fiu-law-dean-creates-scholarship-for-first-generation-students.

56. Elaine McArdle, *First Class* (Feb. 6, 2020), https://today.law.harvard.edu/feature/first-class/.

57. *See, e.g.*, *Student Life—First Generation Law Students*, Loyola University School of Law, https://www.luc.edu/law/studentlife/organizations/firstgenerationlawstudents/ (last visited May 9, 2022).

58. *See, e.g.*, *Student Life—First Generation Students*, New England Law Boston, https://www.nesl.edu/student-life/first-generation-students (last visited May 9, 2022).

59. *See, e.g.*, *Student Groups—First Generation Professionals*, NYU Law, https://www.law.nyu.edu/ studentorganizations/first-generation-professionals (last visited May 9, 2022).

60. *See, e.g.*, *AnBryce Scholarship Program*, NYU Law, https://www.law.nyu.edu/financialaid/jdscholarships/anbryce (last visited May 9, 2022).

their family to attend professional school. The group also aims to serve the surrounding community in addition to the student body.[61]

- **Roger Williams University School of Law**—The school hosted a pre-orientation program in August 2022 to help acclimate BIPOC and first-generation law students to law school.[62]
- **Stanford Law School**—First Generation and Low-Income Professionals (FLI) is a student-led group that offers support and a safe space to assist students with their transition into law school. Programs offered for first-gen and low-income students include academic support, social activities, career advising, and mentorship.[63]
- **Suffolk University Law School**—First-generation incoming students who start at Suffolk Law are eligible for at least $20,000 in a*id.* Eligibility is based on students who are first-generation college students who received their undergraduate degree from one of the 25 schools listed on Suffolk Law's website. The school also has a First-Generation Law Student Association which provides student support via mentoring, networking, and academic support.[64]
- **Syracuse University College of Law**—The First Generation Law Student Association (FGLSA) strives to build a community of support by connecting students who face similar obstacles prior to and during law school. The FGLSA offers support via mentoring and networking experiences with current and former Syracuse Law first-generation students.[65]
- **University of California, Berkeley School of Law**—First Generation Professionals (FGP) offers support to students from similar working-class backgrounds. Berkeley Law also invites first-generation law students to apply for the Berkeley Law Opportunity Scholarship for three years of guaranteed funding for tuition and fees (approximately $180,000). FGP programming

---

61. *See, e.g., First Generation Professionals Legal Society*, NOVA SOUTHEASTERN UNIVERSITY SHEPARD BROAD COLLEGE OF LAW, https://www.law.nova.edu/current-students/orgs/fgpls/index.html (last visited May 9, 2022).

62. *See, e.g., Pre-Orientation Program for BIPOC and First-Generation Students*, ROGER WILLIAMS UNIVERSITY SCHOOL OF LAW, https://law.rwu.edu/admission/accepted-students/jump-start (last visited May 9, 2022).

63. *See, e.g., Stanford Law First-Generation and Low-Income Professionals*, Stanford Law, https://law.stanford.edu/flip/ (last visited May 10, 2022).

64. *Guaranteed $20,000 to Students who are First in Family to Graduate College*, SUFFOLK UNIVERSITY LAW SCHOOL, https://www.suffolk.edu/law/about/diversity-inclusion/first-generation-college-student-scholarship (last visited Oct. 14, 2021).

65. *See, e.g., Student Organizations—First Generation Law Students Association*, SYRACUSE UNIVERSITY COLLEGE OF LAW, http://law.syr.edu/student-affairs/student-organizations/ (last visited May 9, 2022).

includes career and academic support, networking, and mentoring via a "buddy system" which pairs 2Ls and 3Ls with first-year students.[66]

- **University of Cincinnati College of Law**—First Generation Law Students (FGLS) provides support and programming to first-generation students to help them adapt and transition to law school, as well as help them prepare for future legal careers.[67]
- **University of Georgia School of Law**—First Generation Student Association (FGSA) is a student-led organization that provides resources and support for issues commonly faced by first-generation students in law school in areas such as academic, social, financial, and emotional. The group builds community via outreach, mentoring, and service.[68] The law school also offers a scholarship to support first-gen students.[69]
- **University of South Carolina School of Law**—First Generation Law Student Association offers support to students both inside and outside of the classroom, to help them thrive at the law school. The group also mentors undergraduates at the University of South Carolina via their law school pipeline program. [70]
- **University of Southern California Gould School of Law**—First Generation Professionals is a student-led group that is open to first-generation students. The group provides a supportive community via networking opportunities, mentoring, and social activities.[71]
- **University of St. Thomas-Minnesota School of Law**—The First-Generation Law Student Association is a support group for first-generation students. The association promotes an "active dialogue surrounding first-generation

---

66. *See, e.g., Entering Student Scholarships and Gift Aid—Berkeley Law Opportunity Scholarship*, Berkeley Law, https://www.law.berkeley.edu/admissions/jd/financial-aid/types-of-aid/scholarships/entering-student-scholarships/berkeley-law-opportunity-scholarship/ (last visited May 10, 2022).

67. *See, e.g., Student Organizations—First Generation Law Students*, University of Cincinnati College of Law https://law.uc.edu/student-life/experiences/student-organizations.html (last visited May 10, 2022).

68. *See, e.g., First-Generation Student Association*, University of Georgia School of Law, https://www.law. uga.edu/fgsa (last visited May 10, 2022).

69. *See, e.g., Authentic Scholarships*, University of Georgia School of Law, https://www.law.uga.edu/ authentic-scholarships (last visited May 10, 2022).

70. *See, e.g., Student Organizations—First Generation Law Student Association*, University of South Carolina School of Law, https://sc.edu/study/colleges_schools/law/student_life/student_organizations/index.php (last visited May 10, 2022).

71. *See, e.g., Student Organizations—First Generation Professionals*, University of Southern California Gould School of Law, https://gould.usc.edu/students/organizations/ (last visited May 10, 2022).

challenges such as acclimating to the law school experience, navigating the legal landscape, and finding fulfilling post-graduate employment."[72]

- **Wake Forest School of Law**—First Generation Law Students (FGLS) offers social support and professional skills development for first-generation students, as well as those who come from working-class or low-income backgrounds. The goal of the group is to provide an inclusive environment.[73]
- **William & Mary Law School**—First Generation Student Alliance strives to provide resources and support for first-generation students within their academic, professional, and social lives. The group facilitates service to others via a mentorship program. The group also "plays a strong role in the Why We Can't Wait equity and inclusion agenda at William & Mary to promote justice and equity not only in the Law School community but throughout the world."[74]
- **Yale Law School**—First Generation Professionals (FGP) is a student-led group that supports students from lower-income or working-class backgrounds and first generation. Programs include social events, faculty mixers, faculty mentors, and professional development. The group hosts events that connect FGP with other student groups as well as FGP-only events. FGP also advocates for school policies that take into consideration the needs of the group members.[75]

General Resources and Programs:

- The **Diversity Scholarship Foundation** provides opportunities for underrepresented minorities in the legal profession and the nonprofit hosted its inaugural First-Generation Mentor/Mentee program in Chicago in 2021. The program paired first-generation attorneys and judges with first-generation law students.[76]

---

72. *See, e.g., Law School Organizations—First Generation Law Student Association*, University of St. Thomas-Minnesota https://stthomas.campuslabs.com/engage/organization/fglsa (last visited May 10, 2022).

73. *See, e.g., Student Organizations—First Generation Law Students*, Wake Forest Law, http://studentlife. law.wfu.edu/organizations/#57 (last visited May 10, 2022).

74. David F. Morrill, *William & Mary Law School 1Ls Support First Generation Students with New Alliance*, William & Mary Law School (Apr. 20, 2021), https://law.wm.edu/news/stories/2021/william-mary-law-school-1ls-support-first-generation-students-with-new-alliance.php.

75. *See, e.g., Yale Law First Generation Professionals*, Yale Law School, https://yaleconnect.yale.edu/fgp/home/ (last visited May 10, 2022).

76. *See, e.g., Diversity Scholarship Foundation—First Generation Mentor/Mentee Program*, Diversity Scholarship Foundation, NFP, https://diversitychicago.org/event/the-dsfs-first-generation-mentor-mentee-program-reception/ (last visited May 10, 2022).

- The **American Constitution Society** hosted virtual panel discussions in February 2021 and January 2022[77] to help first-generation and BIPOC law students learn about the judicial clerkship process. The panels provided information on the application process, the need for diversity, and the daily experiences of clerks.[78]
- The **Massachusetts SJC Standing Committee on Lawyer Well-Being** advocates for law students from underrepresented or historically excluded backgrounds. The Committee published a list of "Public and/or Non-Profit Resources Addressing Diversity, Equity and Inclusion in the Massachusetts Legal Profession."[79] The list, last updated during the summer of 2021, predominantly references Massachusetts and New England area resources, it contains some national organizations that offer resources to black, native American Indian, and Asian-Pacific students.[80]

V. Conclusion

In a recent article, past ABA president Paulette Brown reflected on her presidency and the legacy she left behind. Reflecting on her accomplishments and the progress that has been made on diversity, equity, and inclusion in the profession she stated, "People are coming to understand that, you get your best talent and you get your best results, when you are more inclusive."[81] She acknowledged that a lot of work still needs to be done, but is hopeful that there will be more progress in the future.[82] Only through investing in BIPOC first-generation students will the legal profession fulfill the dream of Attorney Brown and those who have come after her. Diversification of the profession is not only possible, but imperative, and BIPOC first-generation students are critical to accomplishing this goal.

---

77. *See, e.g.*, *Navigating the Clerkship Process for First-Generation & BIPOC Law Students*, Am. Const. Soc., https://www.acslaw.org/event/navigating-the-clerkship-process-for-first-generation-bipoc-law-students-2/ (last visited May 10, 2022).

78. *Id.*

79. Rachel Casper, *BIPOC Mental Health Month 2021: Reflections in the Legal Profession*, Lawyers Concerned for Lawyers (July 29, 2021), https://www.lclma.org/2021/07/29/bipoc-mental-health-month-2021-reflections-in-the-legal-profession/.

80. Lawyer Well-Being Massachusetts, *Public and/or Non-Profit Resources Addressing Diversity, Equity and Inclusion in the Massachusetts Legal Profession*, https://static1.squarespace.com/static/5e6d105ff4b7d15cf766c1e1/t/60cba2ab6c5781220a786fb8/1623958187391/DEI+Resources+Chart+%28Updated+June+17%2C+2021%29.pdf (last visited May 4, 2022).

81. Todd Nelson, *Q & A: Past ABA President Paulette Brown*, Minn. Law., Apr. 23, 2021, https://minn lawyer.com/2021/04/23/qa-past-aba-president-paulette-brown/.

82. *Id.*

Six

Exploring Double Consciousness, Altering White Spaces, and Removing the White Gaze in Law School

Supporting First Gen Black Law Students

Marcelius L. Braxton, J.D., M.A.*

BLACK LAW STUDENTS, ESPECIALLY FIRST-GENERATION, at predominantly white institutions (PWIs) in the United States are forced to navigate the duality of two worlds, which W.E.B. Du Bois described as "double consciousness." In an article for *The Atlantic*, he wrote that Black people in America are:

> born with a veil, and gifted with second-sight in this American world,—a world which yields him no self-consciousness, but only lets him see himself through the revelation of the other world. It is a peculiar sensation, this double-consciousness, this sense of always looking at one's self through the eyes of others, of measuring one's soul by the tape of a world that looks on in amused contempt and pity. One feels his two-ness,—an American, a Negro; two souls, two thoughts, two unreconciled strivings; two warring ideals in one dark body, whose dogged strength alone keeps it from being torn asunder.[1]

Du Bois described double consciousness as "warring," where Black people in America navigate two types of ideals, their Blackness and the Eurocentric view of Americanness, while existing in one body. Being Black in America also means being forced not only to evaluate and measure oneself based on norms of white America,

* Marcelius L. Braxton is the Director of the Center for Social Change and Belonging and an Affiliate Associate Teaching Professor of African Studies and Philosophy at Penn State.

1. W.E.B. Du Bois, *Strivings of the Negro People*, The Atlantic (August 1897), *available at* https://www.theatlantic.com/magazine/archive/1897/08/strivings-of-the-negro-people/305446. (Du Bois talks about double consciousness through the context of being Black and American. While the focus of double consciousness centers the Black American experience, this chapter will be inclusive of all Black law students in the United States, some of whom might not identify as Black Americans and may have experiences that differ from a Black American experience. Their inclusion is to acknowledge that they, by virtue of being a Black law student in the United States, may also have their own unique experience navigating their Blackness and the Eurocentric view of Americanness.)

but also to be aware that the norms were set by those who view Black people through the lens of hate and/or condescension.

This double consciousness is ever present at the law school level, especially at PWIs. Law schools construct their own double consciousness for Black law students, which is further exacerbated for first-generation Black law students. First-generation Black law students already face many of the same issues and concerns that most first-generation law students face, whether that relates to finances, academics, careers, or social/emotional issues. But additionally, they navigate a law school experience that was built to harm and exclude them without the benefit of witnessing and receiving support from a previous generation that successfully navigated this path of being Black and in the field of law.

In this chapter, I will articulate the institutional barriers Black law students face in law school and the legal process because of the bar examination, accreditation, and the LSAT, and how this can cause Black law students to grapple with the sensation of double consciousness. This sensation of "looking at oneself through the eyes of others" and "measuring one's soul by the tape of a world that looks on in amused contempt and pity" is exacerbated due to the presence of white space and the white gaze that is embedded in law school. Finally, I will recommend that in order to support Black law students, particularly Black first-generation law students, law schools must substantively change their spaces in order to encourage the elimination of the white gaze.

I. Bar Exam and Accreditation

In order to understand the barriers that Black law students face, it is first important to understand the barriers that exist with respect to becoming a Black lawyer. The bar exam is a requirement in almost every state in order to be admitted to practice law as an attorney, and it directly serves as a barrier for law graduates of color, especially Black law graduates. In 2020, the bar examination pass rate for white candidates was 87.65% while it was lower for all others. The pass rates were 79.92% for Asian candidates, 78.02% for Native American candidates, 77.5% for Hawaiian candidates, 75.59% for Hispanic candidates, and 66.28% for Black candidates.[2] So, of the 2,328 Black candidates who took the bar exam in 2020, *785 (33.72%) candidates did not pass.*[3] White women had the highest first-time pass rate (88.11%) while Black men had the lowest first-time pass rate (62.55%).[4] Teachers of law have acknowledged that the bar exam can be harmful to the law school curriculum, can

2. Stephanie Francis Ward, *New ABA Data Parses Out Bar Exam Pass Rates by Race and Ethnicity*, A.B.A. J. (June 22, 2021), available at https://www.abajournal.com/news/article/new-aba-data-parses-out-bar-exam-pass-rates-by-ethnicity.

3. *Id.*

4. *Id.*

serve as a barrier for diversity, and doesn't measure one's ability to practice law.[5] However, the bar exam is still administered today despite the knowledge of whom it harms and the barriers it creates. And this is largely the case because the American Bar Association (ABA), which started in 1878 and is the largest voluntary association of lawyers in the world[6], from its inception, was committed to putting barriers in place to exclude Black people from becoming attorneys.

The first bar exam was conducted orally in Delaware in 1763. There were no written bar exams until 1855 in Massachusetts.[7] For most of the nineteenth century, there were minimal standards to be admitted to the bar. Most examinations were completed orally and administered by a local court, and candidates were frequently admitted regardless of training or ability.[8] State boards with state jurisdictions did not begin until the 1880s in New Hampshire. It wasn't until 1931 that every state (except Indiana) had a state board that administered mostly written bar exams.[9]

In the early twentieth century, the ABA played a significant role in making it more difficult to be admitted to the bar. The ABA expressed concern about bar admission standards that varied based on states, and the ABA's Section on Legal Education helped to found the Association of American Law Schools in 1900. They also assisted in founding the National Conference of Bar Examiners (NCBE) in 1931. The NCBE aimed to upgrade questions, encouraged questions with hypothetical factors that required analysis, and pressed for written examinations that required essay answers. The Multistate Bar Exam (MBE), which was a six-hour multiple-choice exam that could be given by every state, was developed in the 1970s,[10] and the Multistate Professional Responsibility Exam (MPRE), which is a 50-question, two-hour multiple-choice exam, was introduced in 1980.[11] Today, most state bars require applicants to complete the MPRE, the MBE, the Multistate Essay Examination (MEE), which is comprised of multiple 30-minute essay questions covering a variety of topics, and the Multistate Performance Test (MPT), which is two 90-minute tasks meant to test whether the applicant can apply legal skills to realistic situations.[12]

Without a doubt, the ABA played a large role in making admission to the bar more difficult, which has influenced how law schools are accredited and how the law school admissions process occurs. Professor George Shepherd, in his article "No African-American Lawyers Allowed: The Inefficient Racism of the ABA's Accredita-

5. *See* Society of American Law Teachers, *Statement on the Bar Exam*, 52 J. LEGAL EDUC. 446 (2002).

6. See American Bar Association, https://www.americanbar.org/ (last visited Jan 18, 2022).

7. Jessica Williams, *Abolish the Bar Exam*, CALIF. L. REV. BLOG (Oct. 2020), https://www.californialawreview.org/abolish-the-bar-exam/.

8. Margo Melli, *Passing the Bar, A Brief History of the Bar Exam Standards*, 21 U. WIS. L. SCH. F. GARGOYLE 1, 3 (1990), https://media.law.wisc.edu/m/ywq4n/gargoyle_21_1_2.pdf.

9. *Id.* at 4.

10. *Id.*

11. *Id.* at 5.

12. Williams, *supra* note 7.

tion of Law Schools,"[13] contended that the ABA's decisions were based in large part to exclude minoritized racial and ethnic populations. Shepherd pointed out that "the bar exam and accreditation were the ABA's new line of defense against minorities that the ABA erected after overt discrimination began to fail."[14] While being a lawyer was accessible for white men, there were only 795 Black lawyers by 1910, which represented 0.7% of lawyers. And the ABA formally excluded Black lawyers from joining their organization until 1943.[15] However, this overt discrimination began to fail for two reasons. First, potential Black applicants sued to be admitted to state law schools, and the Supreme Court ruled that state-run schools couldn't completely exclude Black people. This led to states either creating "separate but equal" schools or integrating their schools. Second, for-profit part-time law schools started to open in the early 1900s. These schools had lower tuition and lower academic requirements, allowing Black people to utilize the schools as opportunities to become lawyers. The number of Black lawyers doubled from 1900 to 1940.[16] As Black people gained more opportunity to become lawyers, Shepherd points out that the ABA started constructing more barriers.

Two barriers the ABA put into place were lowering the bar exam passage rate and imposing accreditation requirements, both of which harmed minoritized racial and ethnic populations. Requirements were put into place that eliminated for-profit law schools. And the ABA put accreditation requirements into place for schools that required undergraduate degrees, expensive buildings/libraries, full-time professors, and specific standardized test scores and grades, where lower test scores or grades would result in no accreditation from the ABA.[17] The ABA worked with federal and state governments to only issue law licenses to ABA accredited schools. In 1923, no state required these modifications, but 15 years later, nearly half of the states required ABA accreditation.[18] ABA advocates were also able to convince states to require postsecondary education prior to law school. In 1927, only one state required two years of undergraduate education, but 15 years later, almost every state required it although lawyers in the previous system were exempt from this requirement. Through 1950, more than half of practicing lawyers had no college education.[19]

---

13. George B. Shepherd, *No African American Lawyers Allowed: The Inefficient Racism of the ABA's Accreditation of Law Schools*, 53 J. Legal Educ. 103–156 (March 2003).

14. *Id.* at 110.

15. Shepherd, *supra* note 13, at 109; Richard L. Abel, American Lawyers 99–100 (New York, 1989)

16. Shepherd, *supra* note 13, at 109–10; Abel *supra* note 15, at 99–100; Robert Stevens, Law School: Legal Education in America from the 1850s to the 1980s 74 (1983).

17. Shepherd, *supra* note 13, at 110; *see also* George B. Shepherd & William G. Shepherd, *Scholarly Restraints? ABA Accreditation and Legal Education*, 19 Cardozo L. Rev. 2120–22, 2126–51 (1998).

18. Shepherd, *supra* note 13, at 112; Abel, *supra* note 15, at 42, 55.

19. Shepherd, *supra* note 13, at 112; Stevens, *supra* note 16, at 209; Abel, *supra* note 15, at 49.

Notably, the ABA followed the model of the American Medical Association, which implemented an accreditation process that cut the number of medical schools that existed in 1900 in half by 1920. As a result, this reduced the number of Black physicians. There were fewer Black physicians practicing medicine in 1950 than there were in 1900.[20] Accreditation resulted in the reduction of law schools serving Black students, and other schools were forced to raise requirements, which limited the entry of many Black students. Shepherd observed that "like the AMA before it, the ABA used accreditation to exclude blacks just as effectively as earlier generations had used direct racial discrimination. Only in 1970, after affirmative action began, did the proportion of black lawyers again achieve its level of 1940."[21]

Shepherd noted further that the accreditation process makes schools emphasize high undergraduate grades, high bar passage rates, and high LSAT scores because without them, the school risks not being granted accreditation. He noted in the early 2000s that although the ABA did not explicitly deny accreditation based on LSAT scores, no ABA-accredited law school had an average LSAT score below 142. ABA-accredited law schools usually required average LSAT scores of 143, and the ABA often denied accreditation to law schools that admitted students below 140.[22]

II. LSAT

Because the LSAT plays such a large role in the accreditation process and whether Black students receive entry into law school, it's important to examine how the LSAT might harm Black applicants in the law school process. In his article, "Test Bias and the Prediction of Grades in Law School," Robert Linn proposed a definition of test bias, which is that bias exists if the average test score of one population is greater than another. He used this definition with the assumption that populations don't differ on the characteristic it aims to measure, so any differences in scores would be a result of bias or imperfection. By this definition, almost any standardized/aptitude test could be shown to be biased.[23]

Linn also pointed out that many professionals do not necessarily believe that differences mean bias but that groups might differ on the characteristic being measured, and the test is a reflection of that difference. However, he noted that test scores are often loaded with a "surplus meaning" and are used to infer differences about inherent ability or personal worth of individuals or groups. He stated that "[n]o

---

20. Shepherd, *supra* note 13, at 112; Stevens, *supra* note 16, at 218.

21. Shepherd, *supra* note 13, at 113; Abel, *supra* note 15, at 101.

22. Shepherd, *supra* note 13, at 114; *see* American Bar Association, *Statistics*, https://www.americanbar.org/groups/legal_education/resources/statistics/ (last visited Jan 18, 2022). Statistics will be shown based on the 25th, 50th, and 75th percentile, which can be used to get a general idea of where scores are today.

23. Robert L. Linn, *Test Bias and the Prediction of Grades in Law School*, 27 J. LEGAL EDUC. 296 (1975).

claim should be made that the LSAT measures an individual's 'inherent ability' or 'mental capacity.'"[24]

Linn acknowledged that one might make the claim that the LSAT is useful as an indicator of how one might perform in law school, specifically the first year, and that it is influenced by background and educational experiences. So, as many groups have been denied opportunities for so long, it would be expected that those groups might have a lower average score on the LSAT.[25]

LaTasha Hill, in her article "Less Talk, More Action: How Law Schools Can Counteract Racial Bias of LSAT Scores in the Admissions Process," examined the LSAT score gap that exists based on race/ethnicity and pushed back on the idea that the LSAT is not a reflection of bias, noting several studies.[26] She referenced a 1981 study that points out that the LSAT gap exists even when minoritized racial and ethnic college graduates are matched with similarly situated white college graduates. The study compared minoritized racial and ethnic applicants with white applicants from the same undergraduate institution and with similar GPAs (+/- 0.1 GPA point). Even with that control, Black, Latino, and Indigenous applicants scored 110, 97, and 78 points lower respectively (former LSAT scale was from 200–800) than white applicants.[27] She also referenced a study by William Kidder that analyzed applicants from 15 colleges/universities from 1996–1998 who applied to Boalt Hall Law School (University of California, Berkeley).[28] Kidder matched Black, Latino, Indigenous, and Asian Pacific American applicants with white applicants who had the same undergraduate GPA from the same colleges during the same time period. He also created subgroups for the Asian Pacific category (Chinese, Japanese, Filipino, Korean, Southeast Asian, etc.). He found that even with the same college performance, Black, Latino, Indigenous, and Asian Pacific American applicants scored 9.2, 6.8, 4.0, and 2.5 points lower respectively than their white counterparts. Kidder even accounted for college majors and found a race/ethnicity gap for students with similar performance in college and the same major.[29] Kidder concluded that "heavy reliance on standardized tests does, in fact, penalize underrepresented minority applicants."[30]

In his article, "Official Elitism or Institutional Self Interest—10 Reasons Why UCDavis Should Abandon the LSAT (and Why Other Good Law Schools Should

---

24. *Id.*

25. *Id.*

26. LaTasha Hill, *Less Talk, More Action: How Law Schools Can Counteract Racial Bias of LSAT Scores in the Admissions Process*, 19 U. Md. L.J. Race, Religion, Gender & Class 313–338 (2019).

27. Hill, *supra* note 26, at 323; David M. White, *The Requirement of Race-Conscious Evaluation of LSAT Scores for Equitable Law School Admissions*, 12 Berkeley La Raza L.J. 405 (2001).

28. Hill, *supra* note 26, at 323.; William C. Kidder, *Does the LSAT Mirror or Magnify Racial and Ethnic Differences in Educational Attainment?: A Study of Equally Achieving "Elite" College Students*, 89 Calif. L. Rev. 1058 (2001).

29. Kidder, *supra* note 28, at 1074.

30. *Id.* at 1100.

Follow Suit),"[31] Richard Delgado suggested some flaws with an overreliance on the LSAT. He indicated that standardized testing originated in the twentieth century as a way for eugenicists to "demonstrate the intellectual superiority of northern European whites."[32] They were used during World War I for job assignments and to label individuals as unfit, and high marks were given to those of "Nordic stock" while low marks (intelligence and morality) were given to Slavs, Mediterraneans, and Black people.[33]

Delgado argued that, in addition to being based on notions of white supremacy, standardized tests are also often poorly written.[34] He noted that the LSAT "only requires verbal and reasoning fluency, not the ability to command probability, scientific reasoning, humanistic thought, historical thought, or knowledge of human motivation and psychology—all skills important for lawyers."[35] Delgado also pointed out that the LSAT is completed under time constraints, which favors certain individuals, and also that there are multiple intelligences and intellectual tasks that are required for lawyers but aren't measured in the LSAT.[36] He included "empathy, communication skills, common sense, reasoning by analogy, synthetic reasoning, and the ability to make order out of situations that are ambiguous, complex, and uncertain."[37] He compared using the LSAT as a measure for law school fitness to "picking basketball players based on a trial of foul shots."[38]

Delgado indicated that standardized test scores are correlated with income, social class, and race, and he pointed out that except for minoritized racial and ethnic populations, admissions decisions don't change when you consider test scores.[39] And, when test scores weren't considered, more minoritized racial and ethnic ap-

---

31. Richard Delgado, *Official Elitism or Institutional Self Interest? 10 Reasons Why UC-Davis Should Abandon the LSAT (and Why Other Good Law Schools Should Follow Suit)*, 34 UC Davis L. Rev. 593–614 (2009).

32. Delgado, *supra* note 31, at 595; Jean Stefancic & Richard Delgado, No Mercy: How Conversative Think Tanks and Foundations Changed America's Social Agenda 35 (1996); Richard Delgado, *Ten Arguments Against Affirmative Action—How Valid?*, 50 Ala. L. Rev. 135, 143–44 (1998).

33. Delgado, *supra* note 31, at 595.

34. *Id.* at 598.

35. Delgado, *supra* note 31, at 598; Susan Sturm & Lani Guinier, *The Future of Affirmative Action: Reclaiming the Innovative Ideal*, 84 Calif. L. Rev. 953, 976 (1996).

36. Delgado, *supra* note 31, at 598.

37. Delgado, *supra* note 31 at 598; Peter Sacks, Standardized Minds: The High Price of America's Testing Culture and What We Can Do to Change It 221 (1999); Sturm & Guinier, *supra* note 35 at 976.

38. Delgado, *supra* note 31 at 598; Douglas Lederman. *Persistent Racial Gap in SAT Scores Fuels Affirmatlve-Action Debate*, Chron. Higher Educ., Oct. 30, 1998, at A36.

39. Delgado, *supra* note 31 at 603–604; William Kidder, *Portia Denied: Unmasking Gender Bias on the LSAT and Its Relationship to Racial Diversity in Legal Education*, 12 Yale J.L. & Feminism 1, 10 (2000).

plicants were admitted.[40] Delgado posited that test struggles for minoritized racial and ethnic populations can exist due to lack of school resources, poverty, and lack of test prep access, but struggles can also occur because standardized tests often include knowledge that is more common in middle/upper class white communities.[41] He stated that "the Multi-State Bar Exam (MBE) and LSAT questions emphasize business and property concepts, not civil rights, minority history, or literature," and some LSAT passages were disparaging to noted figures like W.E.B. Du Bois, Cesar Chavez, and Harriet Tubman.[42] Additionally, some LSAT questions assume legal knowledge,[43] and this would be particularly harmful for first-generation law students.

III. White Spaces and White Gaze

The impact of and failure to address the inequities of the bar exam and the LSAT created law schools that are de facto white spaces. In *The White Space*, Elijah Anderson detailed how many spaces (including universities) are often segregated and create settings called "the white space" where Black people "are typically absent, not expected, or marginalized when present."[44] He noted that when Black people are present in white spaces, they note the presence and proportion of white people, look around for other Black people with whom to commune/bond, or possibly adjust their comfort level. And if they see a space as "too white," Black people could become uneasy and view the space as "off limits."[45] Anderson also highlighted that spaces that white people see as "diverse" might be viewed by Black people as homogenous and privileged.[46]

Anderson also stated that while "white people usually avoid Black spaces, Black people are required to navigate the white space as a condition of their existence."[47] He noted that there are situations where a Black person enters a white space, and others try to figure out who that person is or why they are present. And this often

---

40. Delgado, *supra* note 31 at 604; Daria Roithmayr, *Barriers to Entry: A Market Lock-In Model of Discrimination*, 86 VA. L. REV. 762–3 (2000).

41. Delgado, *supra* note 31 at 605; Clarence Page, *Schools Must Give All Students Chance to Succeed*, CINCINNATI POST, Aug. 6, 1999, at 21A.

42. Delgado, *supra* note 31 at 605; *Sex and Race Differences on Standardized Tests: Before the Subcomm on Civil and Constitutional Rights of the House Comm.* on the Judiciary, 100th Cong., 1st Sess. 298 (1987).

43. Delgado, *supra* note 31 at 605; see Colloquy, *Affirmative Action and Standardized Testing*, 4 TEX. HISP. J.L. & POL'Y 89–90 (1998).

44. Elijah Anderson, *The White Space*, 1 SOC. RACE & ETHNICITY 10 (2015).

45. *Id.*

46. Anderson, *supra* note 44, at 10; Ronald L. Jackson, *White Space, White Privilege: Mapping Discursive Inquiry Into the Self*, 85 Q. J. SPEECH 38–54 (1999).

47. Anderson, *supra* note 44 at 11.

leads to stereotypes about that individual.[48] Anderson described a common situation:

> ... whites and others often stigmatize anonymous Black persons by associating them with the putative danger, crime, and poverty of the iconic ghetto, typically leaving Blacks with much to prove before being able to establish trusting relations with them. Accordingly, the most easily tolerated black person in the white space is often one who is "in his place"—that is, one who is working as a janitor or a service person or one who has been vouched for by white people in good standing. Such a person may be believed to be less likely to disturb the implicit racial order—whites as dominant and blacks as subordinate.[49]

As a result of this situation, Black people are often forced to "perform" by showing they are different from perceived stereotypes or prove themselves in ways that would not be asked of white people. This could include things such as the manner of talking or dressing, or it could be having to produce identification in situations where white people would not need to do so. And acceptance from white people might be gained if a Black person passes the test or "passes inspection" although they might be forced to pass that test repeatedly.[50] Anderson also noted that societal progress has made it so it might be more believable that a Black person belongs in a particular place, but he described a "cognitive dissonance" where white people might become confused, disturbed, or outraged by that Black person's presence, resulting in attempts to put Black people back in their place.[51]

Black first-generation law students at PWIs are forced to navigate these white spaces, and they often do not have the benefit of those who preceded them to help them with this navigation. Many first-generation law students deal with "imposter syndrome," but the issues for a Black first-generation law student could be exacerbated by having to enter a white space like a predominantly white law school. Black first-generation law students might view this white space as uncomfortable or off-limits. Additionally, they might be seen as "out of place" by white individuals because they are the first in their family to attend law school and could be seen as disturbing the racial order even more than other Black students.

Along with navigating white spaces, first-generation Black students must also endure the nuances of the white gaze, a concept popularized by Toni Morrison. White gaze describes the assumption that the reader or observer is white as well as the consciousness (or self-consciousness) that impacts one's thinking and writing.[52]

---

48. *Id.* at 13.
49. *Id.*
50. *Id.*
51. *Id.* at 14.
52. L.J. Alonge, *Writing Past the White Gaze as a Black Author*, NPR (2017), https://www.npr.org/sections/codeswitch/2017/03/04/515790514/writing-past-the-white-gaze-as-a-black-author (last visited Jan 18, 2022).

Morrison said, "What happens to the writerly imagination of a black author who is at some level always conscious of representing one's race to, or in spite of, a race of readers that understands itself to be 'universal' or race-free?"[53] LJ Alonge described the impact of the white gaze, saying "stories you know to be true and interesting somehow become distorted and unfamiliar." Alonge described trying to write scenes and worry about playing into narratives of "Black criminality" or fueling ideas about "Black-on-Black violence"[54] He remarked that:

> It's no secret that the stories we tell are important—they give shape to our experiences, they document our humanity, they cultivate our sense of possibility—but I realize now that I'd underestimated the mental work that "telling your story" actually takes, the kind of sustained effort needed to resist everything this country tells you about how marginalized or unimportant you are without the white gaze.[55]

Morrison and others talked about the white gaze from a writer's perspective, but it also applies for a Black first-generation law student, who is forced to navigate law school knowing that it is a white space and an institution built upon whiteness while being fully aware of that in their thinking, writing, and responses. Adding this pressure onto the normal difficulties associated with being a first-generation law student means that the white gaze could prevent Black first-generation law students from sharing their experiences, contributing meaningfully inside and outside of class, and pursuing endeavors that they value.

In *The Mark of Oppression: Explorations in the Personality of the American Negro*, Kardiner and Ovessey wrote about the experience of Black Americans in which they are:

> constantly receiving an unpleasant image of himself from the behavior of others to him. This is the subjective impact of social discrimination, and it sounds as though its effects ought to be localized and limited in influence. This is not the case. It seems to be an ever-present and unrelieved irritant. Its influence is not alone due to the fact that it is painful in its intensity, but also because the individual, in order to maintain internal balance and protect himself from being overwhelmed by it, must initiate restitutive maneuvers in order to keep functioning-all quite automatic and unconscious.[56]

First-generation Black law students are already receiving this constant, unpleasant image of themselves, and it could become worse during the law school process. They are forced to take a biased exam (LSAT) to gain entrance into institutions that

53. *Id.*
54. *Id.*
55. *Id.*
56. A. Kardiner & L. Ovessey, The Mark of Oppression: Explorations in the Personality of the American Negro 302–3 (1972)

have been curated by the American Bar Association to either exclude or present additional barriers for entry into the field. And these barriers have created white spaces that prevent Black law students from bringing their true selves to that space, forcing them to maintain balance and protect themselves socially and emotionally to function and make it through law school.

Kardiner and Ovessey also noted that there's more than simply maintaining balance. They stated that:

> In addition to maintaining an internal balance, the individual must continue to maintain a social facade and some kind of adaptation to the offending stimuli so that he can preserve some social effectiveness. All of this requires a constant preoccupation, notwithstanding the fact that these adaptational processes all take place on a low order of awareness.[57]

If Black first-generation law students are forced to consider the barriers of entry into law school and the legal field, navigate white spaces caused by these barriers, and worry about bringing themselves fully into the social experience of law school because of the white gaze, this could create preoccupation that negatively impacts academic, social, and career success.

IV. Altering the White Space and Eliminating the White Gaze

As we think about how to alter white spaces and eliminate the white gaze, we first need to address the legal industry's reliance on standardized testing. As mentioned, many of those who teach law recognize that the bar exam can harm law school curriculum, serve as a barrier for diversity, and doesn't measure one's ability to practice law. Combine that with the racist history and context of the bar exam, and our priority should be to eliminate the bar exam. As long as the bar exam exists, the legal field will continue to perpetuate barriers for entry into law school and contend with the resulting disparities in employment outcomes[58] for law graduates based on socioeconomics, race, ethnicity, ability, family identity, and more.

In addition to eliminating the bar exam, law schools must address and deemphasize the LSAT. As has been highlighted, standardized tests were historically used to perpetuate white supremacy, and the LSAT is an exam that exhibits racial biases even when controlled for other factors. Additionally, Delgado pointed out that the LSAT does not test many of the skills that are important for lawyers, favors certain

57. *Id.* at 303.

58. Press Release, NALP Reports Employment Outcomes for First-Generation College Students Fall Below Those of Their Peers, and Disparities in Outcomes by Race/Ethnicity Persist (2021), https://www.nalp.org/uploads/PressReleases/NALPPressReleaseJobsandJDs_20October2021.pdf (last visited Jan 18, 2022).

individuals with its constraints, does not consider multiple forms of intelligence, and is correlated with income, social class, and race, which can be especially harmful for Black first-generation law students. Given what we know about how the LSAT works and how it serves as a barrier of entry, the ABA should examine how it values the LSAT, and law schools should consider eliminating the LSAT as a requirement for entry or deemphasizing its importance.

In addition to addressing the barriers of entry into the legal profession and law schools, it is imperative that law schools address their climate, culture, and curriculum to eliminate white spaces and the white gaze. In her article, "Do Not 'Decolonize' . . . If You Are Not Decolonizing: Progressive Language and Planning Beyond a Hollow Academic Rebranding," Dr. Nayantara Sheoran Appleton suggested that we need to address power structures in the following ways:

1. Diversify your syllabus and curriculum
2. Digress from the canon
3. Decenter knowledge and knowledge production
4. Devalue hierarchies
5. Disinvest from citational power structures
6. Diminish some voices and opinions in meetings, while magnifying others[59]

Dr. Appleton's ideas apply well to law schools. She emphasized the need to hire permanent faculty to magnify voices and concerns of marginalized communities and that we need to be intentional about changing the hiring criteria and committees to accomplish this goal. She also suggested that these hires need to be faculty who are willing to challenge, and it is imperative that faculty are listened to.[60]

Law schools need to be intentional in their hiring, and they also need to be transparent. They should articulate what they're looking for in a hire, and they should also provide opportunities to train and prepare students to join academia. Law schools should identify promising law students and expose them to what academia is like. Law schools can also create paid programs/fellowships for post-graduation where students get the opportunity to teach, research, and work with an experienced professor. Black first-generation students would benefit from this intentionality related to hiring and establishing a pipeline of applicants, and they should also be given space to offer feedback about what works and what does not work while law schools provide a plan for accountability showing that they've listened to this feedback. This

---

59. Nayantara Sheoran Appleton, Do Not 'Decolonize' . . . If You Are Not Decolonizing: Progressive Language and Planning Beyond a Hollow Academic Rebranding, Critical Ethnic Studies Blog (February 4, 2019), http://www.criticalethnicstudiesjournal.org/blog/2019/1/21/do-not-decolonize-if-you-are-not-decolonizing-alternate-language-to-navigate-desires-for-progressive-academia-6y5sg.

60. *Id.*

accountability has to be taken on by everyone in the law school, including administration, faculty, and other staff.

Dr. Appleton also suggested that as we re-examine class design, syllabi, and curriculum, there's value in adding a question mark to the end of class titles, creating syllabi and curricula that are unique and innovative, and being willing to look beyond the canon and be inter/multi/anti-disciplinary. She also emphasized the need to create physical and intellectual space for marginalized students.[61] Law schools have an opportunity to examine the classroom space, what is taught, and how it is assessed. Professors should teach the law, but it's also important to examine who created the law, why they created the law, who the law included, and who the law excluded. This allows space to analyze the law on every level and elevate the voices of those who were and continue to be minimized. It also allows for a shifting of norms and values, where we don't assume that certain laws or procedures are important or valuable simply because of who created them and when they created them. Law professors should also seek out and embed in their courses the works and voices of those who don't fit the traditional and limiting law structure.

In addition to creating classroom spaces where every student should be challenged and forced to question defaults and norms, spaces, and communities outside of the classroom need to be created to address issues or struggles that minoritized or marginalized students may face. Some of these spaces will need to be made up exclusively of the minoritized population in order to have the freedom to vent, connect, relax, and receive the sort of internal support and validation from those who are part of the collective experience. At the same time, law schools have a responsibility to build trust, engage with students, and create spaces that center the experiences of those who have been minoritized so that schools can validate student experiences, receive feedback from students, and also actively work to eliminate and eradicate the issues that impact those students. If students are forced to navigate an environment that is discriminatory, filled with microaggressions, or is hostile or willing to ignore their experience, their classroom success will be inhibited. Making the law school environment physically, emotionally, and intellectually safe and comfortable for all students is a commitment every law school needs to make to all students.

Most of all, law schools can be proactive in altering white spaces and eliminating the white gaze by examining how they need to construct and protect spaces (inside and outside of the classroom) that acknowledge power, oppression, and hierarchy without shying away from the fact that law schools often reinforce power, oppression, and hierarchy. Law schools can simultaneously teach students to operate within the power structure, put in mechanisms to push back against that power structure, advocate for changes to that power structure, and place responsibility on the entire community to advocate and fight for changes to the structure and to produce

---

61. *Id.*

equity. Law schools can begin this process by providing a concrete set of considerations to which the entire community should adhere when a situation or structure is questioned:

1. Is this situation or structure fair? Does it prioritize one group over another whether intentionally or unintentionally? How long has this situation or structure existed, and what is the current and historical harm and impact?
2. If the situation or structure is unfair, how can I use my abilities, privileges, or circumstances to challenge this unfairness? How can I make others aware of this inequity and push them to also challenge this unfairness?
3. What needs to be done in order to make this situation and structure fair? Is there work already being done to fight this inequity, and have I listened to those doing that work and those who might be directly impacted by these inequities?
4. If I can't change this situation or structure right now, what can I do to advocate for change later, and what can I do to support those who have been harmed?

And, when thinking about spaces, law schools need to provide physical spaces for students to feel comfortable and also intellectual spaces where students can express their opinions, discuss their thoughts, and make suggestions with the knowledge that they will be valued.

To help guide the construction of these spaces, law schools need to adopt an equity framework that actively acknowledges and dismantles spaces in the school that have become "white spaces" due to policies, procedures, and structural racism. For law schools to adopt an equity framework, they must reject culturally incompetent behaviors, which are reactive, in favor of cultural proficiency behaviors, which are transformative.[62] Culturally incompetent behaviors often reflect a mandated equality, where the focus is on others being the problem and about tolerating others. It views diversity as a problem that needs to be solved, and it expects assimilation.[63] Culturally proficient behaviors focus on the collective and view diversity and inclusion as goals. They prioritize adapting to meet the needs of others and examining existing policies, procedures, and practices.[64]

A culturally proficient equity framework in law schools needs to emphasize a shift in how to think about intent. For too long, law schools have settled for thinking about policies, procedures, and practices in terms of the present. That means that

62. Kikanza Nuri-Robins, Delores B. Lindsey, Raymond D. Terrell & Randall B. Lindsey, Cultural Proficiency: Tools for School Leaders, https://defendinged.org/wp-content/uploads/2021/08/Document_2021-02-09_162747-1.pdf (last visited Jan 17, 2022).

63. *Id.*

64. *Id.*

schools have focused on whether their decisions actively or presently intend to discriminate. In many cases, their decisions don't intend to discriminate in the present, but do not account for the harm and discrimination that occurred in the past. Instead, the equity framework should have proactive thinking; where, when any policy, procedure, or practice is considered or questioned, law schools need to ask if they intend to produce equity and/or how they intend to produce equity. If schools cannot detail if and how they intend to produce equity, they should not incorporate or maintain that policy, procedure, or practice. This equity framework should consider the following model for thinking about intent:

1. How are/will you (or we) consider and factor in the impact of years of discrimination (racism, sexism, ableism, etc.), white supremacy, anti-Blackness, and other historical context that has led to and perpetuated inequity?
2. Have any repairs/reparations been put into place to address the barriers that exist, and what is the tangible positive or negative impact that has occurred or might occur because of this policy, procedure, or practice?
3. Have you (or we) decided to put this policy, procedure, or practice in place with the intent of producing, maintaining, or sustaining equity, and are your decisions guided by some level of proof and/or evidence?

This framework transitions from thinking about intent as a stand-alone consideration and makes us consider historical context, intent versus impact, and other systemic barriers that can be used to alter white spaces and eliminate the white gaze. For example, if law schools asked if the LSAT or bar exam intend to discriminate in the present context, they might be able to answer that they do not. However, as has been highlighted above, when considering the impact, historical context, barriers, and ways to produce equity, law schools that truly intend to produce equity would need to reexamine their practices and requirements in order to support students.

V. Conclusion

The experience of Black first-generation law students is often one of forced double consciousness that W.E.B. DuBois used to describe the Black experience. The law school experience is defined by historical and racist structures and barriers that were put in place through the bar exam, accreditation, and LSAT. These harmful structures and barriers lead to law schools becoming white spaces that can feel off-limits or limiting. In turn, the white gaze becomes even more amplified and ingrained in the law school space.

Toni Morrison once said, "If you took the gaze of the white male—or even the white female, but certainly the male—out of the world, it was freedom! You could think anything, go anywhere, imagine anything... there was no longer the problem of looking through the master's gaze."[65] Black first-generation law students have to face the potential barriers and difficulties of being Black and first-generation in law school, and it is imperative that we collectively work to eliminate structural inequities and white spaces that uphold and encourage the white gaze. And as the legal community takes ownership of removing barriers, the legal community will benefit from strong Black first-generation law student voices. Our work will only be complete when Black first-generation law students feel free to enter spaces where they feel comfortable using their voices because they have been elevated, valued, respected, and honored.

65. Toni Morrison & Nikki Giovanni, Toni Morrison: The Last Interview and Other Conversations 133 (2020).

Seven

Supporting First Gen Intersectional Identities by Creating Space for the LGBTQIA+ Community

Jeffrey A. Dodge*[/1]

FIRST-GEN STUDENTS WHO ALSO IDENTIFY AS MEMBERS OF THE LGBTQIA+ COMMUNITY carry varied intersectional experiences with them to law school. Some may have difficult relationships with loved ones, leaving them completely unsupported in their endeavors. Others may be struggling to come to terms with their identities and where they see themselves personally and professionally. Many others may be motivated to pursue law school due to traumatic challenges to their identity by family, religion, and the rule of law. These experiences and many more are not just unique to every individual, but also thematic to the inequality and otherness associated with being LGBTQIA+.

Law schools value the diversity first-gen LGBTQIA+ students bring to their student body and, in principle, seek to support them by fostering equitable and inclusive cultures. These efforts ideally create belonging in law schools that have traditionally evaded both first-gen and LGBTQIA+ identities. Establishing a culture that truly creates belonging in these spaces requires intentional effort both in and out of the classroom; the recruitment and retention of culturally competent faculty and staff; resources and programming oriented to the needs of first gen LGBTQIA+ students; and a strong, actionable commitment to the experiences of all students with minoritized identities. Each academic and administrative area touches on and forms a culture that shapes the experiences of the students navigating them.

This chapter seeks to provide a foundational understanding of LGBTQIA+ identities by first defining terms around sex, gender, and sexuality. Establishing an inclusive culture for first gen LGBTQIA+ students begins with leaning into and being comfortable with how to speak about the community. Even in spaces that value di-

* Associate Dean for Academic & Student Services, Assistant Professor of Law and Joseph H. Goldstein Faculty Scholar, Penn State Dickinson Law.

1. Special thanks to Aria Plants '23 and Lucille Sherman '24, two of my research assistants from Penn State Dickinson Law, for their assistance with this essay. Their thorough and expeditious support made the project possible.

versity there exists overt and covert bias around the unknown. Making these identities, including the terminology and their ways of being, more known removes some of the potential discomfort with inclusive practices. The second part of this chapter will briefly connect the LGBTQIA+ lived experience to the rule of law. There exists a tenuous, sometimes rocky relationship between this community and power. Like many other minoritized identities, the existence of so many legal questions around LGBTQIA+ identities, expression, and rights strike at the very humanity and freedoms privileged others enjoy. First-gen LGBTQIA+ law students are not just navigating educational spaces unavailable to their ancestors but are pursuing degrees in a profession that has excluded them and proved an unreliable ally to their very existence. The last part of this chapter will offer law schools a sampling of best practices to establish a culture of inclusion that supports first-gen LGBTQIA+ students. This includes insights on the varied operations at a law school ranging from marketing to employee recruitment and retention and career services to the curriculum. This non-exhaustive compilation of ideas is meant to help law schools enhance from what higher education scholars Drs. Brandon Wolfe and Paulette Dilworth call the diversity "Three Fs" of food, festivals, and famous people to the "Three Es" of education, engagement, and empowerment.[2]

I. LGBTQIA+ Terminology

The first step in creating equity and inclusion for first gen LGBTQIA+ students is to understand their identities and use proper terminology.

As a start, *sex* refers to the biological and physiological characteristics that society uses in designating someone male, female, or intersex. Sex is established at birth and is often assigned by a doctor based on an infant's genitals. In contrast, gender is formed after birth and refers to social roles, behaviors, activities, and attributes that a given society considers "appropriate" for men and women. In navigating life, a person may have been assigned a sex at birth, but find they identify more with the lived experiences of a different gender. This formation of one's gender identity is about a person's self-conception as male, female, genderqueer, or something else. How one chooses to act on their gender identity is called gender expression, which is how a person's behavior and attributes message their gender to society. Society can perceive a person as masculine, feminine, or androgynous based on the clothing, hairstyles, and other physical and behavioral manifestations that someone uses to express themselves.

2. Brandon Wolfe & Paulette Dilworth, *Breaking the Cycle to Heal: How Campus Leadership Can Center Diversity, Equity, and Inclusion*, INSIGHT INTO DIVERSITY (Nov. Sept. 17, 2020), https://www.insightintodiversity.com/breaking-the-cycle-to-heal-how-campus-leadership-can-center-diversity-equity-and-inclusion/.

The interconnection between sex, gender, gender identity, and gender expression are things everyone carries with them. For some, their female sex assignment matches their gender as a woman, and they choose to represent that through their gender identity and expression. These folks are referred to as cisgender because their gender corresponds to their sex. Transgender folks are generally nonbinary or gender nonconforming and do not experience their gender as exclusively the sex of male or female. They may also experience no gender, agender, both like a man and woman, bigender, or other ranges of gender-fluid identities and expressions. Trans folks often exhibit personal gradations of masculine and feminine behaviors and many, but not all, elect to use gender neutral pronouns like they/them. Some of these individuals may even identify as transgender as well as their gender identity, like trans men and trans women.

While connected, sexual orientation stands separately from gender. A person's sexual orientation describes their attraction to others, be that physical, romantic, emotional, and/or some other form, or the lack of attraction to others at all. Some of these identities include lesbian, gay, bisexual, and asexual, among others. Understanding the distinction between gender and sexual orientation is critical to appreciating the diversity of the LGBTQIA+ community. People carry both identities with them and bring the needs of each to the spaces they navigate, like law school.

II. Law and LGBTQIA+ Identities

Like many who carry minoritized identities in the world, LGBTQIA+ people, both individually and as a group, have a historically difficult relationship with systems of political power and the law. Centuries of laws have sought to regulate, criminalize, and erase the LGBTQIA+ community. From 1290's Ecclesiastic Law in England outlawing sodomy and characterizing it as an offense to God[3] to 2022's "Don't Say Gay" law in Florida banning instruction on sexual orientation and gender identity in kindergarten to third grade,[4] religious and civil legal authorities alike have been in centuries-long coordination around these efforts. Knowing this, even seeking to enter the profession where law is developed, enforced, and challenged should be seen as both an act of protest and vulnerability for LGBTQIA+ students. Adding a first-gen identity to that experience adds a potentially frightening, but brave dynamic to their endeavor.

To contextualize LGBTQIA+ students' experience with the law further, a first-year law student coming directly from undergrad today has been alive to personally feel the impact of several major legal issues. During their lifetime *Bowers v. Hardwick*[5] finally decriminalized sodomy laws; California's Proposition 8 and similar

3. David F. Greenberg, The Construction of Homosexuality (1988).
4. Fla. Stat. 1001.42 (2022).
5. Bowers v. Hardwick, 478 U.S. 186 (1986).

state initiatives elsewhere banned same-sex marriage; "Don't Ask, Don't Tell" prevented out LGBTQIA+ people from serving in the military[6]; *Obergefell v Hodges* made marriage equality the law of the land[7]; and a baker did not legally have to make a wedding cake for a same-sex marriage because it infringed on his freedom of speech and religion rights in *Masterpiece Cakeshop, Ltd. v. Colorado Civil Rights Commission.*[8] For members of the transgender community, the rule of law has validated their murder through the adoption of trans panic defenses in the 1960s,[9] prohibited gender-affirming medical care for trans youth,[10] and structurally ignored the trans community's disproportionate violent victimization.[11]

This non-exhaustive summary of legal questions around the humanity and dignity of LGBTQIA+ people in society is traumatizing. These students grew up in environments where surrounding adults debated these issues, expressed joy or disappointment at each decision, and invested money, time, and votes behind their beliefs. These are the experiences that LGBTQIA+ people bring to the study of law, each heightened in their challenge when also doing so as a first gen student facing some form of imposter syndrome.

III. Best Practices

The good news is that supporting first-gen LGBTQIA+ law students is possible, but only through intentional implementation of best practices in academic and administrative operations. The material below details a number of those practices broken down by law school functions.

Institutional Identity and Branding

Law schools have several important ways to message their values around diversity, equity, inclusion, and belonging. Websites, publications, and social media are some of the most accessible ways a law school can demonstrate these commitments both in words and images. Ensuring that the marketing team is aware of the desired inclusion might lead to changes like the use of gender-neutral language, images that

---

6. Defense Directive 1304.26.

7. Obergefell v. Hodges, 576 U.S. 644 (2015).

8. Masterpiece Cakeshop, Ltd. v. Colorado Civil Rights Commission, 584 U.S. ___ (2018).

9. Christy Mallory, Brad Sears & Luis A. Vasquez, *Banning the Use of Gay and Trans Panic Defenses*, UCLA School of Law Williams Inst. (April 2021), https://williamsinstitute.law.ucla.edu/publications/model-leg-gay-trans-panic/.

10. Kerith J. Conron, Kathryn K. O'Neill, Luis A. Vazquez & Christy Mallory, *Prohibiting Gender-Affirming Medical Care for Youth*, UCLA School of Law Williams Inst. (March 2022), https://williamsinstitute.law.ucla.edu/publications/bans-trans-youth-health-care/.

11. Rachel Dowd, *Transgender People Over Four Times More Likely Than Cisgender People to be Victims of Violent Crime*, UCLA School of Law Williams Inst. (March 23, 2021), https://williamsinstitute.law.ucla.edu/press/ncvs-trans-press-release/.

show nonbinary or gender non-conforming community members, featuring first-gen LGBTQIA+ stories, and working collaboratively with the LGBTQIA+ community to ensure the messaging accurately reflects their experiences. These documented experiences also need to be authentic as first-gen LGBTQIA+ students are especially vulnerable—they need safety and community support resources available.

Law schools that seek to offer comprehensive support to first-gen LGBTQIA+ students can use the Law School Admissions Council's LGBTQ+ Guide to Law Schools Survey[12] and the LGBTQ+ Bar's Law School Campus Climate Survey[13] as barometers for their efforts. These survey instruments ask law schools important questions that many LGBTQIA+ students need answers to when making an enrollment decision. Participating in these survey efforts is a baseline expectation, and the information collected gives institutions some direction for ways to improve. Additionally, The LGBTQ+ Bar offers a best practice guide[14] that is instructive on ways to strengthen an inclusive campus climate.

Representation matters for both first gen and LGBTQIA+ students. Seeing and reading about themselves is an important way establish that presence.

Admissions and Financial Aid

Many institutions share the same strategic goal in their admissions operations: recruit the most students with the highest median LSAT score and undergraduate grade point average possible. Some institutions incorporate into that goal the prioritization of a diverse student body, while others expect diversity through inertia plus a little more. Whatever the institution's strategy, the admissions office is the starting point for living the value of diversity. Without making the enrollment of a diverse student body an uncompromising goal of the law school, a culture of equity, inclusion, and belonging for those with minoritized identities reads shallow. To be successful, students need peer support that provides shared lived experiences.

To achieve diversity in the student body, institutions should move away from seeing diversification as in tension with the volume and quality goals. While *U.S. News & World Report* rankings compel institutions to play into this paradigm, an inclusive culture students are proud of can pierce the marketing noise and ring authentically to highly qualified candidates. Tools like diversity-focused scholarships can attract first-gen LGBTQIA+ applicants seeking an institution that will support their whole person. Connecting those applicants with current students who feel

12. Law School Admissions Council, *LGBTQ+ Guide to Law Schools Survey* (2022), https://www.lsac.org/discover-law/diversity-law-school/lgbtq-law-school/lgbtq-guide-law-schools.

13. The LGBTQ+ Bar, *Law School Campus Climate Survey* (2022), https://lgbtqbar.org/climate-survey/climate-survey-2022/.

14. The LGBTQ+ Bar, LGBTQ+ *Best Practices for Law Schools: A Guide to Institutional Equity* (Nov. 2020), http://lgbtqbar.org/wp-content/uploads/sites/6/sites/8/2020/10/Law-School-Best-Practices-Guide.pdf.

supported and belong at the institution helps advance the message. Schools may also consider targeted marketing campaigns and recruitment programs focused on first-gen applicants. This community may need different information and even the deconstructing of the mythology around law school. LGBTQIA+ applicants could also have questions that are specific to their identity so invite space for one-on-one follow-up conversations or connect them to administrators charged with diversity duties. The diversity a law school seeks may not be in regional proximity to the applicant, and so make sure to offer these opportunities both in-person and virtually. As a bonus, virtual options also help reduce the cost of enrolling in law school, a key consideration for many first-gen and LGBTQIA+ applicants.

Academic, Professional, and Student Services

A key motivation for student services and academic support professionals is helping students realize their greatest potential in law school. Law students bring their whole self to their academic pursuits and experience ups and downs along the way. Recognizing the interplay between how an institution supports a student personally, financially, professionally, and academically is especially critical for students who hold intersectional identities.

In the student services area, law schools should focus on efforts that support equity and engage the community in inclusive practices. First-gen LGBTQIA+ students would benefit from having resources that address food and financial insecurity concerns. Food pantries, professional clothing closets, and textbook lending libraries are obvious initiatives in this area. Schools should also consider whether any funds are available to help students when life circumstances create financial hardship that impacts their academic success, mental health, and more.

Good mental health and overall wellness is a critical requirement for success in law school. Many first-gen LGBTQIA+ students carry trauma and insecurity from their past that can manifest itself consequentially under the stress of law school. Imposter syndrome is a common result and can paralyze students from asking questions, seeking resources, and recognizing problems. Law schools should normalize discussions around mental health and offer resources that address the needs of their students. Incorporating these discussions into mandatory programs on academic success and professional identity development is critical. Law school support professionals also need to be willing to offer compassion and empathy when they themselves may not understand a student's struggle. In greater measure, such a culture needs to develop further in classroom environments to be truly effective.

At many institutions, student organizations contribute greatly to the overall co-curricular experience. Institutions should provide leadership training, faculty and staff advisors, and administrative support to student organizations. Such efforts show institutional recognition of peer-to-peer connection as an integral component of the student experience. For first-gen LGBTQIA+ students, knowing others with a shared identity is more critical than any support offered by the law school.

On the academic support side, it seems fair to consider first-gen LGBTQIA+ students in need of special assistance from the start of their legal education. Reaching out individually to set up introductory meetings pierces the potential intimidation and cultural stigmatization associated with the academic support office. Following up by monitoring these students' performance on mid-semester assessments in their first semester shows both interest in their success and provides an honest assessment of their needs. Establishing trusted relationships with first gen LGBTQIA+ will allow for more honest discussions about academic, financial, and personal planning for bar exam success. This can manifest into effective advising on course selections that prepare students for the bar exam, financial planning for licensing, exam, and commercial bar preparation course fees, and personal counseling on wellness in law school and beyond. These students rely on the honest, but supportive assessment of academic support professionals to navigate the known and unknown steps in their journey to becoming lawyers. Paying special attention to first gen LGBTQIA+ students from the beginning of their academic journey is critical to removing barriers and unlocking success.

The final piece in the co-curricular area is the professional development of first-gen LGBTQIA+ students through career services. For first-gen students, preparing a resume and cover letter can be extremely intimidating. This might also be the first time that the student is thinking about their professional identity more broadly in terms of physical appearance and attire, networking, and online presence. A student's LGBTQIA+ identity further complicates things as they are navigating spaces where people like them are minimally represented. Considerations like putting involvement in LGBTQIA+ organizations on their resume, wearing clothing that expresses a non-conforming gender identity, and pursuing opportunities with employers who have unpublished non-discrimination policies and health care benefits are things career services should be able to counsel on in an affirming way. LGBTQIA+ students are also likely to worry more about interview questions and networking events that could expose their minoritized identity and have seemingly consequential impacts on their professional opportunities. While some of these fears are unfounded, the truth is that members of this community are understandably unsure of who their allies are, both at the law school and in the legal profession. To combat this uncertainty, LGBTQIA+ students should be made aware of affinity bar associations and relevant sections of legal organizations that offer mentors and resources. For example, the LGBTQ+ Bar organizes the annual Lavender Law Conference & Career Fair. Offering financial support to students who want to attend this national event would demonstrate a law school's commitment to their professional success. Additionally, the National Association for Law Placement, Inc. (NALP) offers resources for these students, including a list of professional and legal organizations that work on relevant causes and articles and research on LGBTQ lawyers. As career counselors support first-gen LGBTQIA+ students, it is critical to not assume that these students want to pursue civil rights on behalf of the community. These students will have the varied interests of any other population on campus and their identity may be one aspect of themselves that is completely unrelated to their professional goals. Harnessing the opportunities offered within all fields of law and the diversity initiatives of each is a broad responsibility of career services professionals. First-gen LGBTQIA+ students will benefit from the communication of those resources.

Employees and Facilities

The mythology of law school passes down the idea that the experience, especially the first year, is demoralizing and overwhelming. Does it need to be? Much of the culture around law school was developed to keep people out, often those with minoritized identities. As law schools diversify and seek to create equitable and inclusive places where all students belong, schools must engage in deep reflection on how employees and the physical spaces they occupy at the institution impact the student experience.

Like in the student body, representation matters. First-gen LGBTQIA+ students will gravitate to faculty and staff that have shared identities and life experiences. Students will naturally feel more comfortable asking questions of someone who has been through what they are going through. Law schools should be mindful in faculty and staff hiring of their out representation of the LGBTQIA+ community. Like other forms of diversity, these identities enhance an institution in immeasurable ways. The presence of LGBTQIA+ persons in faculty meetings, behind a classroom podium, leading an administrative department, or counseling a student adds to the inclusive experience, and models an existence in the legal profession that is unreplicated by others outside the community. In fact, a complete lack of out LGBTQIA+ employees can have the harmful effect of messaging to students that the law school is not a safe space for them. These same employees should also be supported through an equitable work environment that acknowledges that bias exists in responses to teaching evaluations, the LSSSE and in other places where the community is asked for performance feedback. Additionally, trainings for all employees that promote the desired culture ensure that diversity in the community is supported. Recruiting a diverse workforce is only step one, keeping them and building a culture where they belong is the real work.

The two foundational contributors to the operation of a law school are its employees and facilities. The latter defines so much of what people do and where. Community connection space is an important way for students to meet each other and find others like them. Common spaces, such as open seating areas, cafes, and lounges are important to protect. If space is available, offices for student organizations create safe spaces for affinity groups, which signals their importance to the community. Finally, law schools should ensure there are dedicated gender inclusive restrooms for community use. These are often single-occupancy restrooms with signage that represents their use by anyone. It is important to select signage that does not undermine the goal of the restroom by reenforcing the gender binary. Restrooms are, sadly, a legal battleground in the K-12 environment, but they do not need to be for law schools. In fact, there are many people outside the LGBTQIA+ community who would benefit from these single-occupancy spaces too, including folks who are pregnant, have special medical needs, or simply need additional privacy. If the institution provides menstrual hygiene products, be sure they are in all restrooms. There are people assigned female at birth who identify as men that need these resources. Facility functions can send unintentional messages about a law school's inclusion of the LGBTQIA+ community. Listen to students when they share concerns and trust that their lived experiences are helping the institution improve.

Curriculum and Teaching

The curriculum and learning experience available at a law school is, in the end, why a student enrolls. There was something about the institution and its offerings that drew the student to send in a seat deposit and make the commitment. Once a first-gen LGBTQIA+ student arrives on campus, it is important to have a curriculum and academic resources that may interest them. Similarly, the learning experience in the classroom must reflect the inclusive values projected by the law school.

In the curriculum, there are many ways for first-gen LGBTQIA+ students to feel seen and supported. The obvious suggestions are stand-alone upper-level courses on gender and sexuality law. The natural extensions of that are the incorporation of legal issues that intersect with LGBTQIA+ identities in other courses. Bold as it may be to assert, every area of law intersects with the inequality of minoritized identities in some way. Covering cases and topics that engage critical thinking around these intersections will enhance first-gen LGBTQIA+ student learning and message an openness to safe dialogues on the topic. Similarly, with the rise of experiential learning comes increased staffing and relationship building for internship opportunities. A law school that does not offer a clinic in gender, sexuality, and the law might consider strategic discussions with LGBTQIA+ nonprofit organizations seeking increased legal assistance capacity. The COVID-19 pandemic has unlocked virtual internships in ways that have never been available before, so the organizations no longer need to be regionally proximate. Additionally, law schools can consider supporting pro bono efforts, like transgender name-change clinics, to provide interested students a way to support the LGBTQIA+ community. Materials through the law library that supplement the learning and research in these areas are also needed. First-gen LGBTQIA+ students will know if these resources are unavailable or insufficient, especially if they are engaged in seminar papers, work as research assistants, or perform other coursework in the field.

Navigating LGBTQIA+ identities can be tricky and even uncomfortable for law school faculty who are unfamiliar. It is important for faculty to be aware of the terminology to establish an inclusive learning environment and avoid unintentionally offending students. The following tips are good starting points for enhancing inclusivity in the classroom:

1. Ask folks what they want to be called and what prefix and pronouns to use. Listen for clues. Law schools often have this information through the admissions process, but if it is not available, consider collecting it. Ideally, there would be an institutional process to collect and distribute this information in advance of each semester. Some institutions, like Penn State Dickinson, even collect audio recordings of students saying their name to make available to faculty.
2. Model the practice of not assuming pronouns by introducing yourself with your prefix and pronouns. This practice allows students, when they participate in class, to share that information with their classmates. Such a practice is effective at the start of the semester as the class dynamic is established and fades as the class gets to know each other.
3. Share resources for navigating institutional policies pertaining to changing names or gender markers within systems; offer an opportunity to indicate such. In a class syllabus and the Student Handbook, identify the processes to make formal changes to their name and gender. While many course management systems, like Canvas, allow for informal changes, a recognition of the formal policies shows support for students who may be in transition.
4. Listen to and validate the lived experiences of students in the class. Course material in the law can evoke a range of reactions and responses, usually a mix of legal, personal, academic, and political. Offer support to first-gen LGBTQIA+ and other minoritized identifying students who bravely share some of their lived experiences in the classroom. A faculty member's response can define for that person and the community they are part of whether or not to engage in the future.
5. Avoid projecting gender by not saying things like ma'am, sir, ladies, gentlemen, guys, etc. Use first names, folks, or other non-gendered terms instead. Law school faculty often feel the need to use prefixes and last names in a classroom. Addressing students as such comes with a gendered prefix that may not reflect their identity. While there are additional prefixes beyond derivations of Mr. and Ms. available, a more inclusive practice is using first names.

6. When working with LGBTQIA+ students, do not publicly insert their gender identity or sexuality in class conversations without their advance permission. Even the most out person has comfort levels that may be impacted by a formalistic learning environment.
7. If relevant in a reading for the day, acknowledge when gender identity and sexuality is a relevant factor in a case. First-gen LGBTQIA+ students welcome opportunities to know more about the community's legal history, especially if part of a larger historical context.
8. Acknowledge current events that may be impacting members of minoritized communities. Regional, national, and international events that negatively impact the LGBTQIA+ community impact students individually. When faculty acknowledge injustice in the day's headlines students feel seen and supported. The matter may need only a few words to accomplish this goal. Silence is equally heard by students and left to possible negative interpretation. To be clear, not all events need recognition, but it is safe to assume that if the nation or the community's attention is captured, then students are being impacted.

Alumni Relations and Development

The end of the rainbow experience for first-gen LGBTQIA+ law students is in the alumni relations and development area. Professionals in this area might consider how best to harness alumni diversity to add value to the student experience. Working with student organizations, career services, and faculty to connect current students with LGBTQIA+ alumni through panels, mentorship, and guest lectures can enhance the student experience. These opportunities also give students a model of what is looks like to be good friend to the law school after they graduate.

Alumni and development professionals seek to both friend-raise and fundraise with graduates of their institutions. An inclusive student experience increases the likelihood of both goals in the future. An institution can keep their first-gen LGBTQIA+ graduates engaged after law school by continuing to make the affiliation professionally valuable. Hosting continuing legal education workshops on timely topics, creating in-person and virtual networking opportunities, and proudly sharing the diverse accomplishments of their alumni are some of the ways to achieve these goals. Where capacity and interest exist, an alumni association chapter or series of programming may also make sense.

As the circle of life cycles further away from the law school, LGBTQIA+ alumni have traditionally had more expendable income to support philanthropic causes of interest. Development officers should consider ways to translate the unique challenges and experiences of first-gen LGBTQIA+ alumni toward meeting institutional goals. Scholarships focused on recruiting a diverse student body, funds to advance research on gender and sexuality legal issues, and basic needs and wellness support for students all seem like potentially ripe areas for financial support from this community. Financially supporting future generations of students like themselves offers an institution a compelling pitch in areas that can never have enough resources.

IV. Final Thoughts

Writing this chapter was cathartic for me in many ways. As a first-gen college and law student who identifies as gay, I had a difficult time with every step in the process. I navigated each new process and space fueled by the possibility of a realized dream but overwhelmed by the unknown before me. In retrospect, it is miraculous that I made it as far as I have without the knowledge and financial means that comes with families who generationally achieve higher levels of education.

My identity as a cisgender gay man plays an interesting role in this story. I came out in college to just my friends and it wasn't until I told my parents I was moving to New York for law school that I came out to them. This was a necessity as I had been selected for an inaugural fellowship in LGBT Civil Rights at Hofstra Law School. While the timing wasn't ideal, acknowledging I was gay to my family was a scary thought. Many in my extended family were extremely religious and their church did not welcome LGBTQIA+ people. All relationship models and family members around me also appeared to be heterosexual, leaving no idea of what love would look like as I aged. The only family member I knew was gay, my uncle, was shunned by his father. He lived in Hawaii with his partner and died of AIDS when I was a child. We never got to meet. Aside from his experience, I had no context for how I would be received by my family, if I would be supported further in life, or what my personal and professional future entailed. All of these open questions left me vulnerable, unsure, and feeling like an imposter in my own life.

My story is not that uncommon from the first-gen LGBTQIA+ students enrolling in our law schools today. My hope is that each of them is met by law schools that are increasingly equipped to meet their needs and that this chapter provides a roadmap of considerations to advance that goal.

Eight

Lawyering While Chinese

Yi Song*

I. The Other Side of the Ocean

I WAS BORN AND RAISED IN BEIJING, CHINA, the capital city with a population of 22 million in a country of 1.4 billion. There were no lawyers in my family, nor as a child did I know anyone who had ever been to the United States. America, the country on the *dayang bian* or "the other side of the ocean" remained distant and irrelevant to me until I was a teenager. I was drawn to a TV program called *yizhipian yuandi* or "the garden of foreign films." The movies and TV shows are predominantly American.

Watching American movies and TV had a positive impact on my language acquisition. In eighth grade I miraculously topped all the English exam rankings all semester. But then I devoted more time to studying English simply to maintain my winning streak. In my formative years, English was to me what a favorite rock band or sports team is to most kids. Studying English soon became a commitment, an obsession, a purpose. When I was in secondary school, children are taught British accent in China. Learning American English on my own became an act of rebellion in my adolescence. Years later I watched the late-night show host asking French actors to read simple and silly sentences in French because "everything sounds better in French." That is how American English sounded to my teenage ears.

Coming of age in the late 1990s and early 2000s, the only two American TV lawyers I knew were Elle Woods from *Legally Blonde* and Ally McBeal from her eponymous show. Elle, a Fashion Merchandising major at the fictional California University Los Angeles ends up at Harvard Law School just to prove herself to her boyfriend who broke up with her because he needs "to marry a Jackie, not a Marilyn." Ally, a Boston lawyer who sometimes hallucinates and sees unicorns and dancing babies works in a fictional law firm alongside her childhood sweetheart. These improbable characters were my introduction to the glamorous, eccentric, and often misconstrued worlds of law in America. In hindsight, I realize I was drawn to them

---

* Yi Song is the Executive Director and Adjunct Professor of Law of the International and Graduate Programs at Georgetown University Law Center.

because they are both misfits in their own ways. They end up forging their own paths on their journeys through law school and law firms.

Through the ups and downs in Elle and Ally's lives, I inhabited their worlds, felt their hopes and concerns, and experienced their dreams and sufferings. Before long, I found myself imagining a new life as if my "real" life was going to happen somewhere far away, and its soundtrack would be in English. I did not know when that life would begin or what it would entail. I did know that when it began I would know because I would not need to imagine it anymore.

Certain narratives precede and predict life events. Before long, I found myself landing in a U.S. law school. My early adjustment included embarrassing missteps navigating daily life. Grocery shopping was a challenge without vocabulary such as "cilantro" and "spatula" to locate what I needed to make an edible meal. I showed up at my professor's house party too early, panicking about what to say in the professor's vast living room where I heard my own words echo. More existential questions include searching for a new voice to accompany the new "me" in the new milieu. I sounded "weird" in English, too high-pitched yet overly restrained, eager to express myself yet intimidated to do so.

I arrived at law school in the heyday of Facebook. Seeing their FB posts, I could not help but compare myself to some of my fellow law students who seemed to manage to attend fun events, explore the city, and socialize with like-minded multilingual lawyers. If my days at law school were to appear in a (postmodern) film, the majority of the footage would be one long shot of me sitting behind a desk with a poker face. I was hyper-stressed about the bar exam and my precarious career prospects. The only activities I signed up for were those with career-minded buzz words such as "bar review" in the description. (As it turned out, that "bar review" entailed was getting together to drink in bars near the law school.)

II. My English Is Not Very Good

According to data from the Institute of International Education (IIE), about 1.1 million international students were enrolled in U.S. universities in the 2019/2020 academic year, and 35% of these international students were from China.

Even before I arrived in law school in the U.S., I was aware of the stark differences between the classroom cultures in the U.S. and China. A professor at my college in China described the differences vividly. When asked whether anyone has any questions, Chinese students show their intellectual superiority by remaining silent. The assumption is that if one asks too many questions, it reveals that one has not been working hard enough to understand the course materials. American students bombard the instructor with questions based on the assumption that active engagement is a way of showing that they genuinely care about the subject matter and about learning.

However, even knowing this trick does not mean that one can navigate the dynamics with ease. I distinctly remember the horror of being cold-called in class. No matter how well I prepared for class, if and when called upon, I would feel slightly embarrassed by wasting everyone's time and struggling to search for the right words in a language that felt less endearing to me in this context. It can be challenging to articulate complex legal issues in one's native language, let alone in a second or third language.

It is some solace to know that cold-calling and the Socratic method are daunting to almost anyone, including native speakers. Justice Neil Gorsuch of the U.S. Supreme Court remembered that he was "scared to death" as a 1L. He was on stage with five other Supreme Court Justices for an event to commemorate the 200th anniversary of Harvard Law School. The Justices were asked what their law school experience was like as a first-year law student. After Justice Gorsuch revealed that he had been terrified, he was further pressed: "how long does that stay with you?" Justice Gorsuch replied: "I will let you know."

Studies[1] show that lack of language proficiency can make international students feel isolated and excluded from their environment in law school. The perceived identity as being "international" due to the language hurdles can reinforce the distance students feel in the interactions with peers and faculty members. Linguistic assistance for those who need it is imperative to improve students' overall experience at law school.

My students often say, "My English is not very good." We come to law school to learn how to think like a lawyer. For many international students, the first question is: Should I think like a lawyer in English or in my native language?

How students process and approach the coursework is directly influenced by their language and their legal training. Bai Rui, a current law student, struggled in class when she just began as a fresh law student in the U.S. "It took me weeks, if not months, to realize that the problem is I was wired to think in these vague terms that the Chinese language often employs. The English language seems to be much more specific than Chinese. I'm also getting used to the common law system. The professor was discussing specific fact patterns. I was trying to summarize the class discussion into one or two rules, as we do in China, a civil law country. Instead all I have in my notes are random fact patterns. At some point I lost track of what the professor was trying to get at. When I asked other (American) students questions, they asked me instead: 'what do you mean specifically?' That's when I realize the fundamental differences between Chinese and English. I will not be able to understand the content in English fully if I continue to think in Chinese."

---

1. Swethaa S. Ballakrishnen & Carole Silver, *A New Minority? International JD Students in US Law Schools*, Law & Soc. Inquiry, vol. 44, no. 3, pp. 647–678 (2019), https://doi.org/10.1017/lsi.2018.12.

"Cathy," a current law student, confessed that she has not solved the issues of notetaking. "Should I take notes in Chinese or in English? If I take notes in English, I don't often understand my own notes when I review them after class. I understand every word but the essence of the complex legal arguments escapes me. I feel like I can only grasp the essence of the content in Chinese by translating the professor's speech to myself consecutively, and by the time I have done that, I have missed other important points. Reading and writing in English takes longer as well because I need to translate the materials, if not in writing, at least in my mind in order to understand them."

There is a gap between comprehension and speaking when the students answer questions in a second language. To speak or not to speak in class becomes a question that calls for careful calculation. Mengyao He, a recent law school graduate, said that "Even when I know the answer to the professor's questions, I hesitate to answer because I do not know what his next question is. I don't know whether I am able to organize my thoughts quickly enough and articulate in real time. I don't want to waste everybody's time and have the whole class watch me struggle. The only time I volunteer to answer questions is when I am fairly certain that the question requires a single-phrase answer."

Mengyao previews the literature in Chinese to familiarize herself with any subject matter. "It helps me understand the professors better in class. If the professor is talking about a specific person, an event or using an acronym, or a cultural reference, I would be lost without further explanation."

"Zachary," a current law student, takes marginal notes and writes outlines in Chinese. "It may not be the best way to improve my English but it is the most efficient way for me to navigate the materials in a second language. I enjoy taking the oral communication class in law school, where the students are made to discuss complex legal questions and form their thoughts in English. I receive comments and guidance from trained linguists. The practice and training are crucial to improving my English."

A study[2] shows that international students who are less willing to communicate in English, due to fear of negative evaluations, attribute their concerns to Americans' bias. Thus, they tend to avoid generally interacting with Americans. This avoidance impedes their learning and disrupts smoother transitioning into U.S. universities, while also limiting both the international students' and Americans' opportunities to enrich their respective educational experience.

Not all faculty are required to be country-specific experts. However, less engaging or poorly informed discussion can be discouraging to students who would otherwise be willing to participate in class discussions. Students expect course materials

2. I-Ching Wang, Janet N. Ahn, Hyojin J. Kim & Xiaodong Lin-Siegler, *Why Do International Students Avoid Communicating with Americans?* J. Int'l Students, vol. 7, no. 3, pp. 555–582 (2017). Https://files.eric.ed.gov/fulltext/EJ1140259.pdf.

to be up to date to inspire in-depth discussion. "Stephanie," a current law student, took a course on international human rights. "I feel like the professor's view on China was biased. When I offered to point out his errors on the criminal procedure timeline in China, my opinion was acknowledged yet brushed off. I saw the looks in the eyes of a few classmates. They looked unconvinced, even condescending. There was no meaningful discussion from a comparative law perspective. It is not like I was deliberately silenced but it was disheartening to see my perspective dismissed. I don't know if I would bother to speak up next time since no one seems to care anyway."

Faculty at law schools should be aware of the diversity of the class, not only in racial, ethnic, gender, and socioeconomic, but also linguistic terms. Speak slowly and clearly. Over-explain everything. Use Blackboard. Provide written outlines, notes, and lists of terms. Explain everything related to American culture (especially sports analogies) and the law school classroom culture. Spell out all the acronyms. Be mindful of the presence of non-native speakers. Create opportunities for students to interact in class. Update the curriculum to accommodate and reflect the diversity in the classroom. This extra attention to clarity helps all students, of course, even native speakers.

III. They Are Watching Us

When I came to the U.S. for law school, Beijing hosted the 2008 Summer Olympic Games. It was a time of tremendous pride for China and especially so for a native Beijinger. It was arguably the most hopeful time in the U.S.-China Relations. President George W. Bush attended the opening ceremony to cheer on Team USA. He attended the U.S. Men's Basketball game against China with his father, former President George H.W. Bush, who had been the first chief envoy in the U.S. liaison office in Beijing in the 1970s. The younger President Bush stated that "in the long run, America better remain engaged with China and understand that we can have a co-operative and constructive, yet candid, relationship."[3]

Yet today even the most optimistic China watcher would agree that the optimism is a thing of the past. When Beijing hosted the Winter Olympics in 2022, the U.S. announced a diplomatic boycott and sent no officials. Now, Chinese students must live with the consequences of the deteriorating U.S.-China relations. They are caught between a Chinese government that demands political loyalty and a U.S. government and American public holding increasingly negative views about China.

The Carter Center's "U.S.-China Perception Monitor"[4] conducted a poll of approximately 3,400 internet users in China regarding their views of the U.S. Sixty-two

---

3. Elaine Quijano, *Bush Mixes Diplomacy, Sports in Beijing*, CNN (Aug. 11, 2008). Https://www.cnn.com/2008/POLITICS/08/11/bush.olympics/index.html.

4. U.S.-China Reception Monitor, *The Pulse: Chinese Public Opinion*, Carter Ctr. and RIWI (2021) Https://uscnpm.org/the-pulse/.

percent of participants held a negative view of the U.S. Likewise, a recent Pew Research Center survey[5] found that an astounding 89% of American adults consider China as a "competitor or enemy" of the U.S.

Besides this general change in public attitudes, Chinese students are under increasingly direct pressure to conform with the views and ideology of the Chinese Communist Party (CCP), amidst a shifting legal environment on speech control. The Hong Kong National Security Law enacted on June 30, 2020, allows China to pursue and prosecute people outside China who participate in "sedition, subversion, terrorism and colluding with a foreign country." The law has brought new risks to Chinese students in the classrooms on U.S. campuses.

During the Covid-19 pandemic, Zhihao Kong, a graduate student at Purdue University in Indiana, posted an open letter praising the heroism of students killed on Tiananmen Square in 1989. The topic is considered politically sensitive and censored from the Chinese internet. A few days later, his parents called Kong from China, crying: "They told us to make you stop or we are all in trouble."[6] Kong realized that it does not matter where he is physically. His words and actions have been watched.

Students from China whom I spoke with have largely reported that they self-censor on social media such as WeChat and Weibo. WeChat (Weixin 微信) is one of the most popular social media apps in China, with 1.15 billion monthly active users globally. The number of monthly active users of Weibo, the Chinese equivalent of Twitter, is around 566 million.

"Chloe," a current law student, admitted that she turned off her phone while attending a human rights seminar in law school. She was afraid of being "listened" to via her Chinese social media app. She is careful not to leave any records in writing discussing politically sensitive topics on WeChat. The WeChat public account, in which Medium-like posts can be shared and circulated by millions, now will reveal the users' locations through IP address tracing.[7] Chloe intends to return to China to work in the public sector or state-owned enterprises upon completing her studies in the U.S., and thus does not want to risk her career prospects by a casual mistake during law school.

Chloe's concerns are not unfounded. China has an expansive system of censorship, including surveillance and restrictions on the internet, applications, and media outlets. Internet platforms operating in China are subject to content controls. Yet

---

5. Pew Research Center, *Most Americans Support Tough Stance Toward China on Human Rights, Economic Issues* (2021), https://www.pewresearch.org/global/2021/03/04/most-americans-support-tough-stance-toward-china-on-human-rights-economic-issues/.

6. Sebastian Rotella, *Even on U.S. Campuses, China Cracks Down on Students Who Speak Out*, ProPublica (Nov. 30, 2021), https://www.propublica.org/article/even-on-us-campuses-china-cracks-down-on-students-who-speak-out.

7. Eduardo Baptista, *Tencent's WeChat to Reveal User Locations on Public Account Posts*, Reuters (April 29, 2022). https://www.reuters.com/technology/tencents-wechat-reveal-user-locations-platform-posts-2022-04-29/.

what content is subject to censorship is only vaguely defined by the law. It is prohibited to post content that "disrupts social order and stability," but since no one can be sure what this means, users tend to err on the side of caution. Studies[8] have found that content and data from users outside China are used to refine the censorship algorithms operating in China. Chinese citizens and those who have close personal ties to China in law school—including students, faculty, and staff—are subject to additional risks.

Other students believe that CCP speech control has little impact on them on neutral topics, even when the discussion is perceived as criticism of China. "Zachary" took a comparative law course in which the professor discussed the monopoly power of China's state-owned enterprises. "The professor's view may be portrayed as criticism by some in China. I think the professor was correct in stating that the executive branch in China is too powerful, as opposed to the U.S. or Europe, though it makes me feel like that he singled out China in this regard. It does not affect how I participate in the class discussion. Even in China, it is not like you live in George Orwell's 1984."

Nevertheless, China's techno-authoritarianism is having a significant impact on the ways Chinese students choose to interact with faculty and peers on U.S. campuses. There is a growing list of topics deemed politically sensitive by Beijing. Sometimes the term "China" itself is politically sensitive.

Jiayu Liu, a current law student, believes that the process of self-censorship is like the proverbial boiling frog. "At some point, I am no longer certain whether I lost interest in certain topics or I no longer dare to speak up. For example, I realize that, in the U.S., Taiwan is listed alongside with China, as if it is independent from China. Though I hold the view that Taiwan is part of China, I am not interested in getting into an argument with someone who believes otherwise."

Chloe was initially interested in attending a welcome event hosted by an Asian legal studies group on campus. No politically sensitive topics were to be discussed. In fact, no topics would be discussed whatsoever; it was simply a meet-and-greet event for the students and faculty in Asian legal studies. However, she saw on the email that students from "Taiwan" and "Hong Kong" were invited too. Chloe was immediately offended by what she saw as the "separatists' attempt" at suggesting that Taiwan and Hong Kong are not part of China. She had conducted due diligence on the organizers as an excellent lawyer would. One faculty director who organized the event is a human rights expert on China. That raised a red flag for her. "I don't know what ulterior motive he [the faculty director] has." She did not want to risk appearing in the wrong place at the wrong time. She did not attend the event nor did any of the students she knew from the People's Republic of China. Law schools should

8. Jeffrey Knockel, Christopher Parsons, Lotus Ruan, Ruohan Xiong, Jedidiah Crandall & Ron Deibert, *We Chat, They Watch. How International Users Unwittingly Build Up WeChat's Chinese Censorship Apparatus*, University of Toronto, Citizen Lab Report (2020).

think of ways to avoid triggering concerns and unintentionally putting PRC students in this kind of dilemma. At the same time, the law school administration should avoid weighing in on the status of Taiwan directly or indirectly.

"Politically sensitive" topics used to mean discussing certain subject matters, but now the area of sensitivity includes interactions with certain groups and/or individuals who have expertise on politically sensitive topics, including professors teaching at institutions PRC students attend. The shifting and vague boundaries of what is deemed "politically sensitive" by China fuels students' paranoia. A recent report[9] revealed that China can discover the identities of people behind certain social media accounts and trace users' families on the mainland. The authorities can threaten family members in China or even detain account holders when they return to China to compel online critics to delete sensitive posts. What is considered "off limits," indeed? If certain individuals are deemed "sensitive," what about people who work with them, such as faculty and staff who appear in the same webinars? What about their colleagues and research assistants?

I happen to be good friends with the organizer of the event that Chloe did not dare to attend. One day, I was having coffee with him on campus. Chloe and a few of her friends walked by. Our eyes met and we waved. When she and her friends saw whom I was having coffee with. I noticed a distinct change in their looks. They were talking to each other as they walked by. For a moment, even I was wondering whether they would "ghost" me from now on because I was interacting with a "separatist" whose his organization sent an email welcoming students from Taiwan and Hong Kong instead of "Taipei, China" and "Hong Kong, China."

Zachary, who was not concerned about classroom criticism of China's state-owned enterprises, had a similar reaction regarding setting boundaries for what is politically sensitive. He planned to select a neutral course on investment in Asia. The course itself did not involve any topics deemed politically sensitive by China. However, when Zachary looked into the background of the instructor, he found out that a Chinese mouthpiece media outlet had condemned the instructor for his views regarding China's human rights record. Zachary dropped the class. "I have no interest in getting involved in politically controversial topics. Personally, I respect the professor's view, though I disagree with him. I have nothing against the professor personally, though he is 'blacklisted' by [CCP mouthpiece media outlet]. Taking the course does not seem to be worth the risk."

Despite all the efforts to protect freedom of speech on campuses, the reports[10] on China's digital surveillance on Chinese students by algorithms and informants has a

---

9. Muyi Xiao, Paul Mozur & Gray Beltran, *Buying Influence: How China Manipulates Facebook and Twitter*, N.Y. Times (Dec. 20, 2021), https://www.nytimes.com/interactive/2021/12/20/technology/china-facebook-twitter-influence-manipulation.html.

10. Nazpari Sotoudeh & Erica Stefano, *Free Speech Risky as China Keeps Close Tabs on Its Overseas Students*, Eurasianet (Sep. 29, 2021), https://eurasianet.org/free-speech-risky-as-china-keeps-close-tabs-on-its-overseas-students.

significant chilling effect on students' speech. Chuangchuang Chen, a law student at St. John's University in New York, said: "If there are more than three or four Chinese students in the same class, you are scared to talk. A Chinese student is definitely seen in good favor by the Chinese government for reporting someone.... It is real: the fear of being constantly watched, of being at risk."

Dr. Avery Goldstein, a professor at the University of Pennsylvania, sent out his syllabus to enrolled students to alert them of possibly sensitive information. "We have to leave it up to the students whether they enroll, because it is ultimately their lives that are going to be affected," he sa*id.* "I will make it clear that there is nothing I can do to protect them."[11]

Law schools should acknowledge the problem and give discretion to students, faculty, and staff to define their own comfort level to participate in activities deemed politically sensitive by the CCP. There is a delicate balance between protecting academic freedom and the safety of its own students.[12] Besides working to protect student data security on an institutional level, law school courses that cover China sensitive materials should come with a warning label that allows students to make their own informed decisions about their risk tolerance and exposure.

There are also ways that universities can protect students taking controversial courses; for example, using codes instead of names on registration and students' work to protect their identities, introducing blind grading and anonymous online chats; and avoiding open discussion of PRC hot-button issues in forums where PRC students might identify each other. Classes should be recorded rarely, and never when students are to discuss these topics in class to allow faculty and students to express their views freely. Access to class recordings should be limited to registered members of the class, and viewable only by streaming—not downloadable in a format that could be leaked. Where class participation is usually an element of students' grades, students should be able to opt out without penalty when politically sensitive matters are discussed. Other seminars, including public lectures, should not be recorded in a way that allows identification of audience members, either in the lecture hall or on a Zoom screen.

In general, there are a variety of technological or administrative ways in which universities and professor could greatly improve safety and encourage participation of PRC students without compromising course content. On most campuses, we have barely begun to implement these changes, but consideration of our students from China necessitates it.

---

11. Lucy Craymer, *China's National-Security Law Reaches Into Harvard, Princeton Classrooms*, Wall Street J. (Aug. 19, 2020), https://www.wsj.com/articles/chinas-national-security-law-reaches-into-harvard-princeton-classrooms-11597829402.

12. Dititar D. Gueorguiev, Xiaobo Lv, Kerry Ratigan, Meg Rithmire & Ropy Reuex, *How to Teach China This Fall*, ChinaFile (Aug. 20, 2021), https://www.chinafile.com/reporting-opinion/viewpoint/how-teach-china-fall.

IV. That Could Be Me

On November 9, 2021, before 2:00 p.m., University of Chicago graduate Shaoxiong "Dennis" Zheng was walking home in Hyde Park, an affluent neighborhood inhabited by many doctors and professors,[13] when a masked man approached him. The man was later identified as 18-year-old Alton Spann. According to two witnesses, there was a brief struggle before Spann shot Zheng in the chest, ran back to a car, and drove away. Zheng was taken to University of Chicago Medical Center minutes later, but pronounced dead at 2:13 p.m. The gunman sold Zheng's personal belongings, including his laptop and iPhone purchased at a cellphone store for about $100. Chicago Police Superintendent David Brown said: "Just let that sink in. A hundred dollars for Mr. Zheng's life and his family's grief."

The Chinese social media mourned Zheng as yet another student murdered in a senseless crime in the U.S. Two days before Zheng was murdered in Chicago, his mother in Leshan, Sichuan, received a fifty-seventh birthday present[14] sent by her son. Since Zheng had first left home for college at the University of Hong Kong, he called his mother every evening at 10:30 to say goodnight. On November 10, 2021, the call never came. Zheng was not only a straight A student throughout his school years; he excelled at piano, Chinese calligraphy, and ping pong. His best childhood friend posted memories of Zheng on WeChat. He liked to play Mahjong and often won among friends and relatives due to his expertise in statistics. The post went viral.

Another widely circulated post on Chinese social media includes detailed instructions on how to "survive in a place like Chicago." It was penned by a professor from the University of Chicago who had lived in Hyde Park for more than 30 years: "You must bring cash at all times when you go out. When you encounter an armed robbery, give them everything they want, including your cash, mobile phone, laptop, wallets, and car keys, as long as it spares your life. Robbers are only interested in property. Your life means nothing to them."

According to Gun Violence Archive,[15] the number of gun violence deaths in the U.S. have been increasing in recent years: there are 39,578 gun violence deaths in 2019, 43,670 in 2020, and 45,004 in 2021. A survey[16] conducted during the Covid-19 pandemic among 22,519 undergraduate students and 7,690 graduate and professional students by University of California Berkeley's Center for Studies in Higher Edu-

13. Sylvia Goodman & Katherine Rosenberg-Douglas, *"I Arrived A Few Minutes Too Late," Says Doctor Who Tried to Save International Student Killed in Hyde Park*, CHI. TRIB. (Nov. 10, 2021), https://www.chicagotribune.com/news/breaking/ct-university-chicago-graduate-killed-hyde-park-20211110-jcqptf2mpjhszjjlblzygsocdq-story.html.

14. Zai Ren Jian Living, *After the Gunshot in Chicago, Zheng's Mother Decided to Bring Son Home Despite the Covid Risk* (Nov. 14, 2021), https://mp.weixin.qq.com/s/QZ4AxGHO5b3GY7doobVpUw.

15. Gun Violence Archive (May 13, 2022), https://www.gunviolencearchive.org/.

16. SERU Covid-19 Survey (July 2020), https://cshe.berkeley.edu/seru/about-seru/seru-surveys/seru-covid-survey-reports.

cation found that international students' gravest concerns were not about academics or remote learning, but rather with the larger environment—immigration, health, and safety.

Zheng was the third University of Chicago student killed in 2021. Since his death, the University of Chicago expanded safety measures including more shuttle bus services and free Lyft rides through the day.

Mengyao He, who graduated from law school in 2021, moved to Chicago upon graduation. "I came to the U.S. with the assumption that Chicago is a dangerous place. I have followed social media influencers on WeChat and get the daily anecdotes about shootings and robbery in Chicago. It then occurred to me that not all of Chicago is dangerous, though some parts can be. I became jaded after a while. The daily updates of local crimes and shooting just becomes a number. Zheng's murder changed that assumption. Now in the back of my mind I think that even in a traditionally safe neighborhood, safety is not absolute. "

The opinions of the Chinese students seem to be divided on the safety issues. In a law school with prominent homeless populations nearby, many students expressed concerns about personal safety while walking to their homes just blocks away. Their encounters include being approached for money or food, whistled at, and verbally harassed. Some comply and give whatever is asked. Others do not engage and are otherwise left alone.

One student who has seemed to find peace with her surroundings commented: "The homeless are harmless. Just don't engage. You will be fine." Others have developed their own assessment system: "If I see someone walking with a coffee or a dog, I know that person is fine." Still many believe that expanded safety measures provided by law school can be helpful such as safety training, free ridesharing services, and free frequent shuttle bus services to nearby residential areas and public transportation locations. A student commented: "Though I don't live in Chicago, my parents are still really worried about my safety after Shaoxiong Zheng's murder. That could be any of us. That could be me."

Americans, and even Chinese who have lived in the U.S. for some time, become accustomed to news about gun violence. University administrators, faculty, and others engaged in student affairs should be aware that stories such as Zheng's can become viral news events in China while barely meriting a paragraph in the U.S. newspapers. Concrete measures to enhance student safety are a must. In addition, though, it is important to understand that students from China are often psychologically affected by news of such violence in ways different from U.S. native students, especially when a Chinese student is the victim. Given, too, that Chinese media and social media discussions often lack sensitivity about American social issues, Chinese, like other international students, also need help navigating the codes by which Americans discuss and distinguish issues involving race, homelessness, and crime in our communities.

V. The Pandemic That Changed Everything

The Covid-19 pandemic and ever-contentious U.S.-China relations present challenges to students even before they arrive in the U.S. Limited flights, travel restrictions, drastic quarantine requirements upon returning to China, and even the very decision to pursue education in the U.S. are subject to questioning in these unusual times.

Zachary recalled that the mainstream attitude toward the U.S. was overwhelmingly positive before 2013, the year President Xi Jinping took office. "America was the country all about freedom, democracy, openness. Then, after 2013, the collective consciousness about America just went downhill. Around 2019 when I was in college, a law degree here [from the U.S.] was still valuable; it is a stepping stone to a prosperous career in international law firms in China, though I have given up on America nor do I want to stay in America upon graduation."

Weize Yuan, a current law student from China, recalled, "Before I came to the U.S. the news about the country was almost exclusively negative, especially regarding the case numbers in the Covid-19 pandemic. The news pitches the U.S. against China, as if they were the only two countries in the world."

Some of Weize's relatives in China questioned her decision to study in the U.S. at the worst possible time with surging Covid cases and deaths, an alarming number of anti-Asian hate incidents and crimes, and U.S.-China relations at the lowest point in some time. "They asked me: 'What made you so obsessed with the U.S. to put yourself through that?'" Weize understands their fears, but points out that "[m]y parents support my decision to pursue my studies in the U.S. They both have studied and lived in Germany. Education exchanges enriched their life experiences. I have friends and relatives who live in the California. I can see their lives seem calm and normal, unlike what the news has portrayed in China,"

In March 2020, Washington, D.C., was in a pandemic lockdown. "Cathy," a current doctoral student, visited the law school campus to retrieve her belongings. At the time, the CDC had not recommended that the public wear masks. Knowing how Covid spread like wildfire in China, she arrived on campus in a mask. She bumped into an unmasked student in the library. The person looked up and took a dramatic leap away from her. She confessed that "I was startled by his reaction. He was probably startled by me and my mask. It made me feel like I was the problem."

Coincidentally, "Amanda," a current law student, went to the grocery store in the early days of lockdown. She was wearing a mask when most shoppers were not. When she was in the cashier line, a woman before her saw her wearing a mask. The woman turned around and demanded Amanda to move further away from her because she was "standing too close." Amanda was confused and ashamed, as she was being hyper-conscious about social distancing. She was not sure whether the demand was due to the fact that she was wearing a mask or that she was Asian.

The Chinese and East Asian experience with SARS in 2003 led to early and widespread mask-wearing by East Asians everywhere during the Covid-19 outbreak, but in early days of the pandemic this sensible practice could be stigmatizing in the U.S. Students sought guidance on mask-wearing during the early days of the pandemic from the public health officials and the law school but there was none. Mask wearing is clearly effective in Covid-19 transmission reduction. In early April 2020, studies showed substantial reductions in transmission when masks were worn. A Chinese study[17] reported on an infected traveler who took two long bus rides. He began coughing on the first ride, then bought a face mask before boarding a minibus. Five passengers on the first ride were infected, and no one on the second. Another study detected no viral particles in aerosol or droplets from the infected subjects wearing surgical masks. Chinese students, with access to this kind of information not available to most Americans, took masking seriously from the beginning.

A survey[18] conducted during the Covid-19 pandemic revealed that about half of students who experienced behavior they perceived as discriminatory said it affected their mental health. Nearly a third said it interfered with their relationship with American peers or friends. Chinese students reported experiencing isolation and heightened anxiety as the Anti-Asian violence surged in the U.S. and as former President Trump repeatedly used racialized terms for Covid-19.

In this kind of social and political climate, law schools should voice their support for and solidarity with Asian students and conduct outreach to offer support groups and counseling services, validate their personal experiences, and build conversations among students who experience or might experience discrimination.[19] It is vitally important to offer training on the concept of race and racism in American society to the international students, and also to integrate anti-AAPI racism more fully in existing materials and training programs already offered on campuses. It may empower the students to approach institutional racism with political activism; Indeed, the opportunity to do so might offer them a more complete American experience.

---

17. Ye Shen, Changwei Li & Hongjun Dong, *Community Outbreak Investigation of SARS-CoV-2 Transmission Among Bus Riders in Eastern China*, JAMA Intern. Med., 180(12) (2020), pp. 1665–1671.

18. SERU Covid-19 Survey (July 2020), https://cshe.berkeley.edu/seru/about-seru/seru-surveys/seru-covid-survey-reports.

19. Xiaofeng Wan, *How Can Universities in the US Tackle Anti-Asian Racism?*, Univ. World News (Oct. 30, 2021), https://www.universityworldnews.com/post.php?story=20211025095928462.

VI. Mental Wellness and the Nation of One Child

China is the only country in the world that had a one-child policy that lasted nearly four decades, starting in the late 1970s and not officially ended until 2016. The controversial policy was originally enacted to address the rapid growth rate of the population. While not universally applied to all PRC citizens, moderately well-off urban Han Chinese couples, whose children make up the bulk of Chinese students studying in the U.S., had generally been restricted to only one child. Being the only child in such families as the result of national policy poses unique circumstances affecting students' mental wellness.

Growing up as an only child myself, I was acutely aware of the multigenerational expectation placed on me. It goes without saying that I am the only hope for the entire family, even if my parents have never put it in so many words. Chinese children are born into a competitive world. Students today used the term *neijuan*, or involution, to describe their living conditions, where intense competition produced diminishing returns. As the New Yorker staff writer Peter Hessler puts it: the only child was "spoiled mostly in the sense of having been provided every possible opportunity to do more work. This is typical in Chinese families: extra resources are dedicated to education."[20]

Looking back at my law school journey, it seems amazing that I did not have a mental breakdown while adjusting to a new life, trying to study, taking the bar exam, looking for internships and jobs, maintaining my visa status, moving multiple times, not to mention being far away from my family and support system. The competition of my early years may have prepared me. Another reason may be that the Chinese fatalism serves as a protective factor. I relied on the notion that as long as I give it my best, fate will take care of the rest. I did not grow up in a religious household, yet that belief system, which I share with many of my compatriots, resembles religion in many ways. It provides a worldview to assist someone to integrate and make sense of what is happening to her.

As we begin the third year of pandemic living, the U.S. finds itself undergoing a mental health crisis.[21] A recent study[22] shows that 85% of international students experienced moderate-to-high perceived stress, 12% had moderate-to-severe symptoms of anxiety and depression, and 18% had moderate-to-severe symptoms of in-

---

20. Peter Hessley, *A Teacher in China Learns the Limits of Free Expression*, New Yorker (May 9, 2022), https://www.newyorker.com/magazine/2022/05/16/a-teacher-in-china-learns-the-limits-of-free-expression.

21. Tara Parker-Pope, Christina Caron & Mónica Cordero Sancho, *Why 1,320 Therapists Are Worried About Mental Health in America Right Now*, N.Y. Times (Dec. 16, 2021), https://www.nytimes.com/interactive/2021/12/16/well/mental-health-crisis-america-covid.html

22. A.Y. Lai, L. Lee, M.P. Wang, Y. Feng, T.T. Lai, L.M. Ho, V.S. Lam, M.S. Ip & T.H. Lam, *Mental Health Impacts of the COVID-19 Pandemic on International University Students, Related Stressors, and Coping Strategies*, Frontiers in Psychiatry, 11, 584240 (2020), https://doi.org/10.3389/fpsyt.2020.584240.

somnia. Those who stayed in the U.S. had significantly higher Covid-19-related stress, due to concerns over personal health and lack of social support.

For international students, stress is related to personal health, availability of reliable Covid-19-related information, academics, personal attainment, uncertainties about their academic program, changes in the learning format, and lack of social support. Resilience, positive thinking, and exercise were predictors of less severe mental health impacts.

International students, perhaps living far away from home for the first time, are immersed in a new language and new culture. We not only "think" in language, we "feel" in language. Research revealed that the American approach to mental health has shaped the world's understanding of the human psyche. Counseling or having a therapist popularized by American culture almost becomes a status symbol. How a culture thinks about mental wellness influences the diseases and treatments themselves.[23]

A significant part of the law school journey is self-discovery. Bai Rui was stressed out the most when she could not meet her own expectations. "I understand that for most of my peers in class, English is their first language. We are not competing on a level playing field. A big part of my stress derives from the fact that I was disappointed at myself because I was almost always behind in my reading assignments. I would be less stressed if I were able to finish all the reading, since even if I still couldn't understand everything taught in class, at least I could tell myself that I gave my best. At some point I came to peace with myself that sometimes it is just impossible to finish everything on my to-do list. That realization makes me forgive myself. When I really can't take in any more reading, I take my bike out for an hour. I used to think that is an hour wasted. Now I know that exercise just helps me de-stress and focus on my studies better."

Some students seemed to gravitate toward church groups as a coping mechanism during the pandemic. Yudi Ruan went into lockdown with her fiancé in California at the beginning of the pandemic. All her classes went virtual. She did not see other people for many days (if not weeks) in a row. Ruan grew up in Guangdong Province. Her mother had taken her to a Christian church a couple of times in her childhood. The calming experience left an impression on her. During the pandemic, Ruan found herself looking into local church support groups. She found one nearby that welcomed her with open arms. "We went hiking. I mostly talked to them about my concerns: taking a challenging class, stressing about finals and the job hunt. My church friends chatted with me as if we were old friends. I was a transplant to California. I don't even live here full time. Yet because of our common belief, they accepted me whole-heartedly."

---

23. E. Watters, Crazy Like Us, The Globalization of American Psyche (2010).

Whether or not one turns to faith for peace of mind during the pandemic is a personal decision. The reality paints a more nuanced picture. "Wendy" participated in a few dinners hosted by local church groups. "They seem to be genuine and kind people. They offer us free meals. The kindness from strangers means a lot when you are thousands of miles away from home. After a few gatherings though, I started to wonder, in my Chinese mentality: 'What do they want from me? Can I still go to the dinners in good conscience without accepting their faith?' After talking to a few (American) friends who are Christians, I understand that their caring for one another in the community should not be conditioned on anything. If the only reason they offer us free meals is to try to convert us, they are not completely truthful to their Christian values. Knowing that makes me feel relieved that I don't have to be converted to attend the events. I don't want to be a free rider either, because I don't think I will be converted to any religion. I don't think I need an external belief system to validate who I am. Whether or not I believe in God has nothing to do with whether I'm able to take on further challenges in life."

Zachary is enrolled in a law school that provides free counseling to all students. He is aware of the mental well-being services the law school offers, though he has not attended any counseling sessions. "People would not broadcast to the world after they have seen a therapist. It does not mean that the services are not valuable. People of my generation (born in the 1990s) are much more accepting to mental health support, perhaps due to the raised awareness on Chinese social media. China has advanced to the point where its development is not only evaluated in economic terms; the social, psychological, and mental development is also being recognized. Everyone is increasingly viewed as an individual holistically, not just as a 'tiny screw that holds society together.'"

Still, a public stigma about mental health remains in China—something that is worth remembering when offering such services to Chinese students on American campuses. Studies[24] found that most people in the PRC were not familiar with the causes, treatments, and prevention of mental health issues. A survey[25] conducted among 350 higher education institutions across the U.S. reveals that acculturative stress negatively affects Chinese international students' quality of life, irrespective of their academic standing. Nevertheless, despite the clear stress many Chinese students in the U.S. are experiencing, universities should not assume that Chinese students will self-diagnose and actively seek assistance as readily as their American peers will.

---

24. H. Yin, K.J. Wardenaar, G. Xu, H. Tian & R.A. Schoevers, *Mental Health Stigma and Mental Health Knowledge in Chinese Population: A Cross-Sectional Study*, BMC PSYCHIATRY, 20(1), 323 (2020), https://doi.org/10.1186/s12888-020-02705-x.

25. Z. Su, D. McDonnell, F. Shi, B. Liang, X Li, J. Wen, Y. Cai, Y-T Xiang & L. Yang, *Chinese International Students in the United States: The Interplay of Students' Acculturative Stress, Academic Standing, and Quality of Life*, FRONT. PSYCHOL. 12:625863 (2021), doi: 10.3389/fpsyg.2021.625863.

"Scarlett," a current law student, confessed that she was unlikely to seek counseling even if it is free of charge, not because of the social stigma, but because of the language barrier. "I would have trouble describing how I feel or why I feel what I feel in English. Struggling to talk about my emotions with a stranger in a second language would just stress me out more. I would rather go out with friends for a nice meal."

As more law schools begin to form a wellness culture to normalize discussions and actions around the mental, physical, and spiritual care of students, it would be helpful to have multilingual and multicultural counselors on board to address the wellness needs of international students, especially those in large cohorts such as students from PRC. During the ongoing Covid-19 pandemic and after, the law schools should address the stress and trauma of "otherism"[26] experienced by students of color, including Chinese students. Resources such as mental wellness counseling and training, wellness workshops, and meditation groups are helpful to international as well as local students. The shift to focus on wellness begins with faculty and staff in legal education, who are modelers of wellness as well as educators of law.

All the above issues may seem complicated and difficult to address, but the common denominator to addressing all of them is the willingness and compassion to learn more about Chinese students' experience and cultivate awareness of their background and the linguistic, cultural, and political environment they inhabit on campus and in their lives more broadly.

---

26. Janet Thompson Jackson, *Legal Education Needs a Wellness Reckoning*, Bloomberg Law (Apr. 7, 2021), https://news.bloomberglaw.com/us-law-week/legal-education-needs-a-wellness-reckoning.

Nine

Where Are Our Hispanic Lawyers?

How We Can Respect, Recruit, and Retain Law Students of Hispanic Descent

Christopher Doval, Simon Gugerli, and Angela Lohman

I. Hispanic Demographics and Identity

CURRENTLY, PEOPLE WHO IDENTIFY AS HISPANIC constitute 18.5% of the overall U.S. population.[1] By 2030, the Bureau of Labor Statistics projects people of Hispanic descent to account for 21.2% of the labor force.[2] As of 2020, the Hispanic presence in all legal fields accounts for 8.3% of the total U.S. legal workforce. Of the 1,882,000 people employed in the industry, the Hispanic presence is minuscule: Lawyers (5.8%), judicial workers (6.2%), paralegals, and legal assistants (15.1%), and all other legal support staff (17.2%).[3] On the other side of the spectrum, according to a survey from 2007, 1-in-27 (4%) people of Hispanic descent were under some form of corrections control, such as probation, parole, prison, or jail. Additionally, the share of inmates of Hispanic descent in state, federal, and local prisons and jails has increased from 16% in 2000 to 20% in 2008. Regardless of which doors the Hispanic population walks through when entering a courtroom in the United States, there is a huge disparity of representation.

This chapter will discuss the many barriers that prevent first-generation students of Hispanic descent from successfully enrolling in and completing law school, leading to these small numbers in the profession. Further, this chapter will expound on the opportunities for law schools to garner the attention of these potential Juris Doctoral candidates.

Over the past decade, the high school dropout rate for people of Hispanic descent has decreased dramatically from 32% in 2000 to 12% in 2014 among those ages 18 to

1. *U.S. Census Bureau QuickFacts*, www.census.gov/quickfacts/fact/table/US/RHI725219.

2. Kevin Dubina, *Hispanics in the Labor Force: 5 Facts*, U.S. Department of Labor Blog (Sept. 15, 2021), blog.dol.gov/2021/09/15/hispanics-in-the-labor-force-5-facts.

3. U.S. Bureau of Labor Statistics, *2020 Annual Averages* (Jan. 22, 2021), www.bls.gov/cps/cpsaat11.htm.

24. Although marginally higher than their white, black, and Asian counterparts, this is a dramatic improvement. Additionally, people of Hispanic descent are making big inroads in college enrollment. In 2014, 35% of people of Hispanic descent ages 18 to 24 were enrolled in a two-year or four-year college, up from 22% in 1993.

Despite the increase in attendance at undergraduate schools, people of Hispanic descent still lag behind other groups in obtaining a four-year degree. As of 2014, of those between the ages of 25 and 29, only 15% had obtained a bachelor's degree or higher. This gap is partly because people of Hispanic descent are less likely than others to enroll in a four-year college, attend an academically selective college, and enroll full-time.

In response to changing demographics, the White House has offered new criteria for federal funding for universities. If a university can show that 25% of its undergraduate population is Hispanic, it may garner the title of Hispanic-Serving Institution (HSI) and receive exclusive federal funding. In the fall of 2018, across the 411 HSIs located in 24 states and Puerto Rico, 4.1 million students were enrolled in HSIs, and nearly half were students of Hispanic descent. While the title of HSI does not require that these universities be exemplars in supporting this target population, these universities have learned to support and produce graduates now potentially ready for law school.[4]

This target demographic has multiple hurdles to overcome in higher education, but law schools have many opportunities to support them. It should be acknowledged that students of Hispanic descent are more likely than other racial or ethnic groups to be first-generation students.[5] Further, those who enroll graduate less often with a degree, whether an associate's or doctoral degree. The Hispanic share of degrees earned has dropped to 23.8% for associate's degrees, 14.2% for bachelor's degrees, 9.5% for master's degrees, and 7.5% for doctoral degrees. In contrast, their white counterparts earn over 50% of all degrees in the United States. [6]

This degree disparity begins to explain the lack of people of Hispanic descent in the courtroom, whether attorneys or the judiciary, and may illuminate the larger number of paralegals and support staff that find their way into the legal field.

Educators have been working for decades to address the achievement gap between people of Hispanic descent and other students. And now, due to the changing face of higher education, many law schools have noticed and begun to market toward and put in place programs that support the unique needs of this demographic.

---

4. White House Initiative on Advancing Educational Equity, Excellence and Economic Opportunity for Hispanics, *Celebrating Hispanic-Serving Institutions* (2020), https://sites.ed.gov/hispanic-initiative/2020/10/celebrating-hispanic-serving-institutions/ (last visited May 12, 2022).

5. *Latino Students* PNPI (Sept. 19, 2021), pnpi.org/latino-students/.

6. *Id.*

II. Lawyers of Hispanic Descent and Future Generations

Despite the growing population of people of Hispanic descent in the United States and the growing number of attendees in higher education, the lack of Hispanic presence results in a shallow understanding of a diverse population with unique challenges. For instance, much of the research regarding the Hispanic experience in higher education focuses on presenting for a wider, often whiter, audience the story of an individual or examples of students of Hispanic descent as they struggle through applying, attending, and graduating from alien and inaccessible university systems.

What does the current incoming lawyer of Hispanic descent look like? According to the American Bar Association, for the graduating class of 2020, there were approximately 34,162 graduates; out of those graduates, 29,531 of them decided to take the bar exam. People of Hispanic descent achieved a 76% passage rate for first-time takers out of 3,638 graduates, which was topped by their white counterparts at 87%, out of 19,453 graduates. Thus, this creates a further gap in the legal field between white and non-white admitted lawyers.[7]

This widely underrepresented demographic and its missing cultural contribution to law schools and the legal field have the unfortunate effect of producing few tangible or accessible exemplars with whom candidates of Hispanic descent may idealize or identify. Further, this leads to legal professionals and their respective institutions without a Hispanic voice with which to connect to and better understand the needs and qualities of these communities. A hurdle that is difficult for law schools to overcome without sensitivity and Hispanic flag-bearing faculty or administration.

III. How the United States Frames the Hispanic Population

In 1976, the U.S. Congress, in its first effort to collect and analyze data on a specific ethnic group, mandated that government entities and agencies record the number of "Americans of Spanish origin or descent" that they served.[8] This would be the early definition for what the United States would call "Hispanic or Latino"—Hispanic being the term used predominantly on the east coast of the United States to

7. American Bar Association, *Summary Bar Pass Data: Race, Ethnicity, and Gender 2020 and 2021 Bar Passage Questionnaire*, https://www.americanbar.org/content/dam/aba/administrative/legal_education_and_admissions_to_the_bar/statistics/20210621-bpq-national-summary-data-race-ethnicity-gender.pdf.

8. H.J. Res. 92–94th Congress (1975-1976): *Joint Resolution Relating to the Publication of Economic and Social Statistics for Americans of Spanish Origin or Descent*, H.J. Res. 92, 94th Cong. (1976), https://www.congress.gov/bill/94th-congress/house-joint-resolution/92.

describe this demographic and Latino for those on the west coast.[9] Ultimately, the term encompassed "A person of Mexican, Puerto Rican, Cuban, Central or South American or other Spanish culture or origin, regardless of race."[10] This definition has grown to include Portugal, Brazil, and former Spanish territories like the Philippines—much more extensive than the initial 20 Spanish-speaking nations it had previously included.

A. How Does the Hispanic Population Identify?

Despite the above definitions, the U.S. Census depends entirely on how respondents self-identify, a standard intended to "reflect a social definition of race and ethnicity recognized in this country" that does not "conform to any biological, anthropological, or genetic criteria."[11]

And so, how do Hispanics self-identify? While it is common practice for people of Hispanic descent to self-identify with their nation of origin, as in "I am Cuban, because my family came from Cuba," despite generations of American citizenship. According to the Pew Research Center, among adults with Hispanic origins, 61% prefer the term Hispanic to describe their overall population, whereas 29% prefer Latino and 4% Latinx. Of those who are third generation or more born in the United States, 72% prefer Hispanic.[12] Regardless, there also appears to be a generational decline for immigrants to self-identify as Hispanic. As early as the second and third generations, American-born people of Hispanic descent begin to identify as American.[13] For law schools to target these demographics more effectively, an approach that combines numerous nationalities into one term, LatinX, would be misguided.

B. Latin, Latin American, Latine over LatinX

Over the past decade, the term Latinx has emerged as a gender-neutral and pan-ethnic label for people of Hispanic descent. Despite its use by news and entertainment outlets, corporations, local governments, and universities, only about one-fourth of people of Hispanic descent in the United States have even heard of the la-

9. Revisions to the Standards for the Classification of Federal Data on Race and Ethnicity, 62 FR 58782.

10. OMB Directive 15, *Race and Ethnic Standards for Federal Statistics and Administrative Reporting*, wonder.cdc.gov/wonder/help/populations/bridged-race/directive15.html.

11. U.S. Census Bureau, *Frequently Asked Questions (FAQs) About Hispanic Origin* (Dec. 3, 2021), www.census.gov/topics/population/hispanic-origin/about/faq.html.

12. Luis Noe-Bustamante, Lauren Mora & Mark Hugo Lopez, *About One-in-Four U.S. Hispanics Have Heard of Latinx, But Just 3% Use It*, Pew Research Center's Hispanic Trends Project (2021), https://www.pewresearch.org/hispanic/2020/08/11/about-one-in-four-u-s-hispanics-have-heard-of-latinx-but-just-3-use-it/ (last visited May 12, 2022).

13. Mark Hugo Lopez, Ana Gonzalez-Barrera & Gustavo López, *Hispanic Identity Fades Across Generations as Immigrant Connections Fall Away*, Pew Rsch. Ctr., December 20, 2017, https://www.pewresearch.org/hispanic/2017/12/20/hispanic-identity-fades-across-generations-as-immigrant-connections-fall-away/.

bel, while 3% of them actually use it.[14] As the world moves toward gender-neutral language, the addition of Latinx to the Spanish language, for some, is a challenge to the traditional male and female constructions inherent in the language, and is considered presumptuous.

As discussed, the terms used for identifying the Hispanic community in the United States are primarily constructs of how Americans describe and conjoin many nations of Spanish speakers. Critics argue that Latinx crosses a line of Anglicizing the Spanish language and is culturally offensive.[15] While languages develop over time, critics suggest that Spanish does not need to be fixed from the outside, but rather a solution will be born of the community and should not be imposed upon the culture.

How we self-identify is an issue of belonging, and to describe a student with a foreign term does not facilitate that belonging. Further, it is culturally insensitive to create terms or labels that collect over 20 different nations and cultures together, many of which have had few interactions over centuries.

Not to undercut the value of a gender-neutral term, the term Latine has origins in Argentina; others simply suggest Latin or Latin American are appropriate terms without a major imposition on the language and culture.[16]

Nonetheless, beyond Hispanic and Latin, people of Hispanic descent have not come to embrace other terms. Due to the inevitable continued use of Latinx outside of the Hispanic community, a more appropriate or respectful use would entail a Spanish pronunciation, as in Latin[equis].

C. Diversity Among the Hispanic Community

For those who are not of Hispanic descent, trying to identify, recruit, and support this broad demographic has considerable difficulties. How might we begin to distinguish these cultures?

According to Professor Geert Hofstede, culture is "the collective programming of the mind distinguishing the members of one group or category of people from others."[17] Through extensive research, Hofstede devised a six-dimension model that distinguishes countries, not individuals, based on independent preferences for one

---

14. Luis Noe-Bustamante, *Latinx Used by Just 3% of U.S. Hispanics. About One-in-Four Have Heard of It*, Pew Rsch. Ctr. (Aug. 11, 2020), www.pewresearch.org/hispanic/2020/08/11/about-one-in-four-u-s-hispanics-have-heard-of-latinx-but-just-3-use-it/.

15. Giancarlo Sopo, *Progressives, Hispanics Are Not 'Latinx.' Stop Trying to Anglicize Our Spanish Language*, USA Today (Oct. 25, 2019), www.usatoday.com/story/opinion/2019/10/25/latinx-race-progressives-hispanic-latinos-column/4082760002/.

16. Evan Odegard Pereira, *For Most Latinos, Latinx Does Not Mark the Spot*, N.Y. Times (June 15, 2021), www.nytimes.com/2021/06/15/learning/for-most-latinos-latinx-does-not-mark-the-spot.html.

17. National Culture, Hofstede Insights (2019), https://www.hofstede-insights.com/models/national-culture/ (last visited May 12, 2022).

state of affairs over another and means of comparing them. These are not stereotypes or caricatures, but quantified distinctions. The six dimensions are Individualism versus Collectivism, Indulgence versus Self-restraint, Uncertainty Avoidance, Long Term Orientation, Masculinity versus Femineity (task orientation versus person orientation), and Power Distance (strength of social hierarchy).

The table below provides a landscape of the cultural distinctions of all the Hispanic nations Hofstede was able to study and how they compare with each other and the United States. It would be misguided to apply recruiting and retention strategies toward people of Hispanic descent that fail to address their unique cultural distinctions or to assume American practices would suffice. For example, people who are from the United States, according to Hofstede, are highly individualistic (91), a giant departure from cultures that are Hispanic (6–51). A recruitment approach based on responsibility to the community would be more effective than one focused on personal success or prestige. Further, as discussed, people of Hispanic descent lack mentors in the legal field, have poor experiences interacting with law enforcement, and have a variety of other concerns this chapter will address. An approach that assumes a low level of Uncertainty Avoidance, as in the United States (46), will get little traction from cultures that are Hispanic (a majority over 70). Exposure to mentors, cost-effective access to counsel, legal education during high school, matriculation support for higher education, application fee waivers, and knowledge of, and easy access to, scholarship opportunities are all more effective recruitment strategies with long-term results.

	Individualism	Indulgence	Long-Term Orientation	Masculinity	Power Distance	Uncertainty Avoidance
United States	**91**	**68**	**26**	**62**	**40**	**46**
Argentina	46	62	20	56	49	86
Bolivia	10	46	25	42	78	87
Chile	23	68	31	28	63	86
Colombia	13	83	13	64	67	80
Dominican Republic	30	54	13	65	65	45
Ecuador	8	-	-	63	78	67
El Salvador	19	89	20	40	66	94
Guatemala	6	-	-	37	95	98

	Individualism	Indulgence	Long-Term Orientation	Masculinity	Power Distance	Uncertainty Avoidance
Honduras	20	-	-	40	80	50
Mexico	30	97	24	69	81	82
Panama	11	-	-	44	95	86
Paraguay	12	56	20	40	70	85
Peru	16	46	25	42	64	87
Puerto Rico	27	90	0	56	68	38
Spain	51	44	48	42	57	86
Uruguay	36	53	26	38	61	98
Venezuela	12	100	16	73	81	76
Brazil	38	59	44	49	69	76
Portugal	27	33	28	31	63	99

IV. Barriers to Matriculation

The predominant barriers to matriculation into law school stem from cultural bias and systemic inequalities. Due to the lack of presence of people of Hispanic descent in legal institutions, they often fail to address this demographic's concerns proactively. The purpose of this chapter is to provide perspective and educate in that regard. The remaining systemic issues, whether inherent in LSAC or in law schools, need to be addressed holistically, and no one is better suited to implement change than law schools themselves through strategic investment and restructuring.

As a strong step in the correct direction, the LSAC PLUS program was formed to allow members of underrepresented communities to gain insight into the inner workings of law schools as well as their admission process. The program is free to participants, and they receive an additional stipend of $1,000. 2,700 students have completed the program since 2002.[18]

---

18. *LSAC PLUS Program Gives First-Gen Law Candidate a Window into Law School*, Law School Admission Council (2021), https://www.lsac.org/blog/lsac-plus-program-gives-first-gen-law-candidate-window-law-school#:~:text=The%20LSAC%20PLUS%20Program%20is,during%20the%20COVID%2D19%20pandemic (last visited Apr 28, 2022).

A. The Role of Language

People who are of Hispanic descent who are bilingual are on average more economically and educationally successful than those who only speak Spanish. Almost three-fourths of people who are of Hispanic descent and bilingual have finished high school, whereas only 30% of adults who speak only Spanish have finished high school. Employers in the United States highly prize the ability to speak English proficiently; therefore, the combination of their English proficiency with an educational advantage puts people of Hispanic descent and bilinguals far ahead in the U.S. job market, resulting in higher household incomes than their counterparts.

Consequently, if this bilingual skill is not refined properly, it can negatively impact student comprehension levels, especially in educational settings. For instance, based on a 2008 report from the U.S. Department of Education's National State Assessment Score Database, there is a significant difference in comprehension for "English language learners" (ELL). In Texas, 22% of eighth-grader ELL students scored at or above the proficient level on their math assessment, compared with 44% of black eighth-graders. Furthermore, in both elementary and middle school grades, ELL students are less likely than white students to score at or above the proficient level in mathematics. For example, 45% of ELL third-graders scored at or above the proficient level on their math assessment, compared with 78% of white third-graders in Florida.[19]

The public education system in the United States is predominantly delivered in an English format with limited support for those who learn English as a second language. Although some support is provided through funding, students whose language is not primarily English tend to struggle with understanding complex topics. This is not due to intelligence, or the lack thereof, but simply because certain students cannot comprehend the topic as quickly because it is not in their native language.[20]

For recruitment purposes alone, it is imperative that law schools understand that they are missing a large talent pool of Spanish speakers whose access to legal education is only impeded due to language constraints and an English-biased education system. Is it the job of law schools to teach English? Perhaps not, but strategic investment in early intervention English as a Second Language (ESL) programs and creating a language-driven talent funnel could have long-term payoffs for the school and community. Moreover, bilingual attorneys are more rare than they should be and are highly sought after in a variety of fields. For those who are fortunate enough to be bilingual, translation services and a culturally sensitive writing support staff can help retain talent that struggles with English nuance and vocabulary.

---

19. *The Role of Schools in the English Language Learner Achievement Gap*, Pew Research Center's Hispanic Trends Project (2020), https://www.pewresearch.org/hispanic/2008/06/26/the-role-of-schools-in-the-english-language-learner-achievement-gap/ (last visited Apr 28, 2022).

20. *Id.*

B. Family

Language, however, is not the only factor to consider as a barrier to higher education. Family is one of the most important and fundamental concepts to humans worldwide; however, it means even more in Hispanic culture. Family is beyond fundamental for people of Hispanic descent. According to a survey in 2009, a large majority of people of Hispanic descent (84%) agree that relatives are more important than friends.[21] The view that relatives are more important is held by all nationalities of Hispanic descent, further cementing the belief that family is important above all else.

With this emphasis on family, it is easy to see why, among people of Hispanic descent, 48% are in a three-generation household, 47% are in a two-generation household, and 4% are in a skipped-generation household. But having a multigenerational household does not simply mean that it is easier to see relatives. According to a separate Pew Research survey taken in 2005, it was found that a majority of the public (56%) considers it a "family responsibility" for adult children to take into their home an elderly parent who wants to live with them, thus pressuring the younger adult to assume both physical and financial responsibility for the parent.[22]

This added responsibility burdens the younger generation to go immediately into the workforce to support the family, despite the fact that the median full-time salary for college graduates, ages 25 to 37, is about $24,700 more annually than employed young adults holding only a high school diploma. The immediate lure of a steady income is more appealing to a younger head of household responsible for another generation than incurring debt for four years and pursuing career goals.[23] Without an income safety net, it becomes exponentially more difficult for people of Hispanic descent to branch out and get advanced degrees without the support of their families.[24] Even with financial assistance, a student would still have to pay close to $10,000 out of pocket to attend college, while there would be one less person available to support the older generation[25]—not to mention the guilt of abandoning

---

21. *Between Two Worlds: How Young Latinos Come of Age in America*, Pew Research Center's Hispanic Trends Project (2020), https://www.pewresearch.org/hispanic/2009/12/11/between-two-worlds-how-young-latinos-come-of-age-in-america/ (last visited Apr 28, 2022).

22. *The Return of the Multi-Generational Family Household*, Pew Research Center's Social & Demographic Trends Project (2020), https://www.pewresearch.org/social-trends/2010/03/18/the-return-of-the-multi-generational-family-household/%C2%A0 (last visited Apr 28, 2022).

23. Drew DeSilver, *10 Facts About American Workers*, Pew Rsch. Ctr. (2021), https://www.pewresearch.org/fact-tank/2019/08/29/facts-about-american-workers/ (last visited Apr 28, 2022).

24. Rakesh Kochhar, *Latinos' Incomes Higher Than Before Great Recession, but U.S.-Born Latinos Yet to Recover*, Pew Research Center's Hispanic Trends Project (2020), https://www.pewresearch.org/hispanic/2019/03/07/latinos-incomes-higher-than-before-great-recession-but-u-s-born-latinos-yet-to-recover/%C2%A0 (last visited Apr 28, 2022).

25. *Is College Worth It? Chapter 5: The Monetary Value of a College Education*, Pew Research Center's Social & Demographic Trends Project (2019), https://www.pewresearch.org/social-trends/2011/05/15/chapter-5-the-monetary-value-of-a-college-education/ (last visited Apr 28, 2022).

your family in need or the betrayal one's family might feel for the student prioritizing their education over familial responsibilities. Any support for students of Hispanic descent must take their families into consideration.

C. Prior Academic Preparation

For a large number of people of Hispanic descent, their academic outcomes and potential for law school are directly tied to the zip code of their public schooling. A 2020 study conducted by The Century Foundation called for the redistribution of funds among school districts to support children living in poverty, specifically children of Hispanic descent who were put at a disadvantage compared with their white peers. As discovered, "districts with high concentrations of Latino and black students were far more likely to be underfunded than majority-white districts." This funding gap was established to be, on average, more than $5,000 per student when comparing a district that was predominantly Hispanic versus a predominantly white district.[26] Further, a report by Edbuild revealed a fundamental disparity in funding between minority school districts and white school districts. The study outlined that school districts serving predominantly black and brown neighborhoods received roughly $23 billion less in funding compared to their white counterparts.[27] This is a systemic issue that culminates in the economic discrimination against minority citizens and should be a consideration for long-term recruitment and retainment efforts by law schools.

D. Application Process and the LSAT

Applying to law school is no simple feat for anyone, but it is easier to consider and effectively address with privilege or legacy. The Law School Admission Council (LSAC) outlines a process of application that makes considerable assumptions of potential candidates and places several barriers in front of them.[28] Without a mentor or a legacy, potential candidates of Hispanic descent may be confronted by an immovable object.

Non-English or bilingual speakers can struggle to apply for law schools as applications are predominantly in English, with rare instances where translations are available. In an effort to mitigate this issue, law schools are now making their web-

---

26. Laura Meckler, *Study Finds Black and Latino Students Face Significant "Funding Gap,"* Wash. Post (2020), https://www.washingtonpost.com/education/study-finds-black-and-latino-students-face-significant-funding-gap/2020/07/21/712f376a-caca-11ea-b0e3-d55bda07d66a_story.html (last visited Apr 28, 2022).

27. Dana Givens, *Report: White School Districts Receive $23 Billion More in Funding Than Black Districts*, Black Enterprise (2020), https://www.blackenterprise.com/education-report-white-school-districts-receive-23-billion-more-in-funding-than-black-districts/ (last visited Apr 28, 2022).

28. The Law School Admission Council (LSAC), https://www.lsac.org/ (last visited May 13, 2022).

sites available in other languages. This, however, is a very limited feature and is mainly available only on the main pages of law schools.

Despite the increasing demand for bilingual attorneys, the LSAT is mainly provided in English, thus making it difficult for non-English speakers to compete for the attention of prestigious law schools. Although the LSAT is available in Spanish, people of Hispanic descent and other Spanish speakers may only take this version of the test in Puerto Rico and can only report the scores to one of the three ABA-accredited law schools in Puerto Rico. These schools include the Inter-American University School of Law, Pontifical Catholic University of Puerto Rico School of Law, and University of Puerto Rico School of Law. The LSAC will not release scores to schools outside of Puerto Rico,[29] thus making it impossible for any non-English Spanish speaker to have access to other law schools. Additionally, forcing every Spanish LSAT test-taker to apply to the same three schools limits the number of applicants they can accept, making it even more difficult to attend law school. This systemic hurdle lends to the real-world dilemma that law firms and legal departments are actively seeking attorneys who speak foreign languages.[30]

Beyond a language barrier, people of Hispanic descent often suffer from a technology gap; lack of computer ownership and access to high-speed internet. Currently, the majority of law school applications are completed online, and the LSAT must now be completed on a personally owned laptop. According to a Pew Research Study conducted in 2021, "Eight-in-ten White adults report owning a desktop or laptop computer, compared with 69% of Black adults and 67% of Hispanic adults. Eight-in-ten white adults also report having a broadband connection at home, while a smaller number of black and Hispanic adults say the same—71% and 65%." This results in applicants with varying degrees of tech-savviness and anxiety.

This lack of adequate technology places applicants of Hispanic descent at a significant disadvantage considering that the LSAT is timed and no additional significant accommodations are provided for technical issues. This issue then leads to higher stress during testing and lower scores among test-takers of Hispanic descent.[31]

Ultimately, lower test scores lead to a further lack of diversity among top tier law schools, the importance of those schools accepting these students, and putting in place supports to overcome this long list of hurdles once matriculated. Upon graduation, a poor test score, a lack of school recognition, and the competitive nature of

---

29. *LSAT en Español*, LAW SCHOOL ADMISSION COUNCIL, https://www.lsac.org/lsat/register-lsat/lsat-en-espanol (last visited May 13, 2022).

30. Jennifer Borum Bechet, *The Language of Law: The Demand for Bilingual Attorneys in Corporate Law Departments*, MINORITY CORP. COUNSEL ASS'N (2006), https://www.mcca.com/mcca-article/the-language-of-law-the-demand-for-bilingual-attorneys/ (last visited Apr 28, 2022).

31. Sara Atske & Andrew Perrin, *Home Broadband Adoption, Computer Ownership Vary by Race, Ethnicity in the U.S.*, PEW RSCH. CTR. (2022), https://www.pewresearch.org/fact-tank/2021/07/16/home-broadband-adoption-computer-ownership-vary-by-race-ethnicity-in-the-u-s/ (last visited Apr 28, 2022).

the market leave many of these candidates with fewer options for employment from the beginning of their careers.[32]

E. Expense

Law students have forever griped about the numerous fees and costs associated with not just a legal education but attempting to obtain one. The LSAT application fees and preparation course fees may be waived, but many students are unaware of these waivers.[33]

In addition to the nickel-and-diming, candidates of Hispanic descent see less aid from law schools than their white counterparts. Starting in the mid- to late 2000s, law schools began diverting money from need-based aid and investing it into merit-based aid, utilizing LSAT scores to decide who deserves the money, therefore ensuring only the test-takers with the highest scores would receive aid to attend law school. The Law School Survey of Student Engagement (LSSE) Reports conducted by the Indiana University Center for Post-Secondary Research showed that 90%of those with an LSAT of 165 or above received a merit scholarship, in comparison to 57% of those who scored between 151 to 155 and only 16% of respondents with a score of 140 or below.[34] The average LSAT score from a test-taker of Hispanic descent in 2020 was 146.[35]

F. Undocumented Applicants

Undocumented immigrants are by far some of the most restricted groups of people in the United States. They have severely limited circumstances to live their lives, to the point that, according to interviews conducted by the American Psychological Association, being undocumented feels like being in an "invisible prison." Aside from the trauma associated with living in this environment, many undocumented immigrants feel like they can never aspire to anything—resulting in a lack of care and dedication to their education. If these students pursue higher education, they experience severe anxiety about being discovered, lack of ability to identify with classmates, and impostor syndrome (to say the least), all of which lead to negative educational outcomes. Identifying these students early and providing support is es-

---

32. Marisa Manzi & Nina Totenberg, *"Already Behind": Diversifying the Legal Profession Starts Before the LSAT*, NPR (2020), https://www.npr.org/2020/12/22/944434661/already-behind-diversifying-the-legal-profession-starts-before-the-lsat (last visited Apr 28, 2022).

33. *Id.*

34. Catherine Morris, *Blacks, Hispanics Losing Out on LSAT-Based Financial Aid*, Diverse (2017), https://www.diverseeducation.com/students/article/15099947/blacks-hispanics-losing-out-on-lsat-based-financial-aid (last visited Apr 28, 2022).

35. Marisa Manzi & Nina Totenberg, *"Already Behind": Diversifying the Legal Profession Starts Before the LSAT*, NPR (2020), https://www.npr.org/2020/12/22/944434661/already-behind-diversifying-the-legal-profession-starts-before-the-lsat (last visited Apr 28, 2022).

sential for a group of students that will eventually become more prevalent in higher education.[36]

V. Barriers to Success in Law School

A. Academic Skills Supports

Upon admission into a nationally ranked law school, first-generation law students of Hispanic descent continue to encounter obstacles. In public and private law schools, Hispanic law students made up 11.6% of first-year enrollment but 15.9% of first-year dropouts.[37]

Many law schools have recognized that marginalized communities have been struggling to succeed in their coursework and have begun to put the necessary programs in place to aid these students. Syracuse University, like many others, has put in place programs to identify students of promise and put them through rigorous preparatory programs like Orange Edge. Students are required to complete a tuition-free, intensive summer program in legal methodology and legal writing. Not only are students prepared for their first semester of schooling with a boot camp on all first year-subjects, but students build bonds and network early with faculty and their cohort.[38]

B. Maximizing Resources

According to a *National Jurist* article, which utilized data from a recent study by the National Association for Law Placement (NALP), the author found that first-generation students had a harder time finding legal positions compared to their peers. In total, first-generation students "lagged 11 percentage points behind those graduates who had a parent who held a Juris Doctorate in getting bar-passage required jobs."[39] Perspective and experience from mentors lead non-first-generation students to utilize more resources and support from their university. For instance, "only 18% of first-generation college students enrolled in law school were members of a law

36. *Undocumented Americans: What Is It Like to Grow Up as an Undocumented Youth in America?* Am. Psych. Ass'n (2013), https://www.apa.org/topics/immigration-refugees/undocumented-video%C2%A0 (last visited Apr 28, 2022).

37. Kylie Thomas & Tiffany Cochran, ABA Data Reveals Minority Students Are Disproportionately Represented in Attrition Figures, AccessLex (2018), https://www.accesslex.org/xblog/aba-data-reveals-minority-students-are-disproportionately-represented-in-attrition-figures (last visited Apr 28, 2022).

38. Syracuse University College of Law, https://law.syracuse.edu/admissions/j-d-admissions/orange-edge/.

39. Mike Stetz, *First-Generation Grads Face Uphill Battle in Career Opportunities*, Nat'l Jurist (2022), https://nationaljurist.com/national-jurist-magazine/first-generation-grads-face-uphill-battle-career-opportunities (last visited Apr 28, 2022).

journal, while 27% of their non-first-generation counterparts were members."[40] This lack of experience does not just translate to performance during law school, but also affects the ability of first-generation students to land jobs post-graduation.

Even the soft skills of first-generation students are stifled without mentorship. For instance, "[t]here is a huge knowledge and resource gap—particularly when it comes to networking."[41] The awareness to pursue or effectively pursue work experience during law school or the seasons between semesters is a space where first-generation law students fall behind their peers.

Generations of lawyers of Hispanic descent can attest to the value of student organizations like the Latino Law Students Association (LaLSA) and the Black Law Students Association (BaLSA) for their camaraderie, motivational support, student mentorship, and academic support.[42] While there are nationally organized versions of these student organizations, many chapters seem to stand alone on the backs of the students who bond over their common experiences. Folding these communities into the infrastructure of student life at law schools demonstrates university commitment to something that students have mostly developed. Further, enrollment gaps may lead these organizations to disappear for years at a time when there is a limited membership.

C. Faculty Mentors

The lack of visible, accessible, and tangible legal exemplars poses for people of Hispanic descent a significant barrier to entering and succeeding in the legal field. The value of having a mentor who shares a cultural identity and physical appearance with their students often goes underappreciated. Of the full-time teaching faculty in today's law schools, 82.7% of males and 75.9% of females are Caucasian.[43]

While many law schools undoubtedly claim and likely do prioritize the recruitment of minority faculty to promote a diverse faculty population, the reality is that diverse faculties rarely exist. Men and women of Hispanic descent make up a fraction of the student-facing full-time teaching (4.3% and 4.6%), skills (3.3% and 5.6%), writing (3.3% and 5.6%), and library (3.6% and 4.1%) positions at law schools.[44]

It should not be surprising that few lawyers of Hispanic descent climb the legal ladder into the professoriate. The recurrent nature of the cultural and institutional

---

40. Jacqueline M. O'Bryant & Katharine T. Schaffzin, *First-Generation Students in Law School: A Proven Success Model*, 70 Ark. L. Rev. 913 (2018).

41. Grover E. Cleveland, *Helping First-Generation Lawyers Thrive*, ABA Law Practice Today (2018), https://www.lawpracticetoday.org/article/helping-first-generation-lawyers/ (last visited Apr 28, 2022).

42. NLLSA, https://www.nllsa.org/ (last visited May 13, 2022).

43. *Recruitment & Retention of Minority Law Faculty Members*, Ass'n Am. Law Schools (2021), https://www.aals.org/about/handbook/good-practices/minority-law-faculty-members/ (last visited Apr 28, 2022).

44. *Id.*

struggle of these potential juris doctor candidates lends to their long-term absence in the faculty hiring pool. Without a diverse faculty to promote minority talent, the professoriate will remain cyclically culturally and racially skewed.

Qualifications and academic preparedness aside, if people of Hispanic descent constitute 12.8% of all students in ABA-accredited law schools, it would appear that this large demographic has been overlooked for legal research, publication, and leadership opportunities.[45] Yes, hiring and recruiting talent should continue to be a priority, but law schools as a whole would benefit from practices meant to promote training and scholarship of students of Hispanic descent early in their legal careers. While faculty are best equipped to identify talented students, the administration needs to ensure that students of Hispanic descent are afforded all the same opportunities as their non-Hispanic counterparts; cultural awareness and sensitivity training need to be incentivized and made a priority for professional development internally. Otherwise, these students will continue to be invisible and move through our classrooms without fulfilling their potential.

The Association of American Law Schools' handbook has a wealth of best practices for the recruitment and retention of minority legal faculty. Many of which address the same issues regarding people of Hispanic descent, like social isolation from non-minority colleagues and students, being overlooked for opportunities, and not having an equal voice.[46]

VI. In Closing

Supporting first-generation students of Hispanic descent begins with respect and understanding of the cultural diversity and systemic issues that underlie people of these various cultures. As Americans and their institutions take considerable pride in the cultural identities associated with their states of residence, so should we understand that our immigrants of Hispanic descent come with the same multitude of backgrounds. In the United States, these communities have been incorrectly thrown together, labeled, and neglected. The existence of this growing, misrepresented, and under-supported American population creates an opportunity for law schools to reflect on long-standing practices that have made the legal profession culturally and racially stale, and change for growth and inclusivity. We must not fail them in their primary and secondary schooling through direct investment and out of our own social responsibility to our communities. We must put in place proactive practices and supports that create equity beyond equality for the underrepresented.

---

45. *2018 Law School Diversity Report: JD Enrollment by Race & Ethnicity*, ENJURIS, https://www.enjuris.com/students/law-school-race-2018.html (last visited Apr 28, 2022).

46. *Recruitment & Retention of Minority Law Faculty Members*, ASS'N AM. LAW SCHOOLS (2021), https://www.aals.org/about/handbook/good-practices/minority-law-faculty-members/ (last visited Apr 28, 2022).

This chapter has illuminated key areas of understanding and support that are needed for people of Hispanic descent—all of which are for the betterment of our legal system, our legal community, and our lawyers.

¡Carajo!

PART III Pre-Law, Undergraduate Education, and Admissions Considerations

Ten

Why Do Law Schools Need to Understand the Special Needs of First Gen *Pre*-Law Students?

Rebecca Flanagan*

FIRST-GENERATION PRE-LAW STUDENTS ARE AN OVERLOOKED GROUP. There is very little written about first-generation law students, and there is virtually no research on first-generation *pre*-law students.[1] While there are affinity groups for students of color, such as the National Black Pre-Law Conference and Law Fair[2] and underrepresented ethnicities, such as the National Hispanic Pre-Law Conference and Law Fair,[3] first-generation pre-law students, who often have multiple, intersecting identities, are often neglected.[4] They face challenges that go unnoticed because first-generation prelaw students can be invisible; their status is not readily visible, unlike skin color or ethnicity. In a law school admissions atmosphere of rivalry and competition, where cultural, social, and professional capital are the currency of the realm, many first-generation pre-law students do not want to advertise an identity perceived as weaker or underprepared. This leads first-generation students to enter law school feeling like imposters, and that they "will soon be exposed as a fraud."[5]

This chapter will focus on the specific and overlooked challenges specific to first-generation college students and post-graduates interested in pursuing a legal

* Associate Professor/Director of Teaching & Learning Methods, UMass Law.

1. Aaron N. Taylor, *Robin Hood in Reverse: How Law School Scholarships Compound Inequality*, 47 J.L. & EDUC. 41, at 69 (2018).

2. National Black Pre-Law Conference and Law Fair, https://blackprelawconference.org (last visited May 8, 2022).

3. The National Hispanic Pre-Law Conference and Law Fair, https://hispanicprelawconference.org (last visited May 8, 2022).

4. LAW SCH. SURVEY OF STUDENT ENGAGEMENT, *Looking Ahead: Assessment in Legal Education Annual Results* 2014 8 (2014), https://lssse.indiana.edu/wp-content/uploads/2016/01/LSSSE_2014_AnnualReport.pdf (last visited May 8, 2022). 48% of first-generation law students identify as Hispanic, 43% identify as Black, and 25% identify as Asian.

5. John Goodyear, *Traveling Down an Unpaved Road: My Experience as a First-Generation College Graduate*, 89 J. KAN. BAR ASS'N 66 (2020).

career.[6] However, there is virtually no research on first-generation pre-law students, but we can extrapolate from the significant volume of research on first-generation post-secondary students, a group that includes first-generation students interested in pursuing a law degree. Their challenges begin with lack of outreach, targeted support, and guidance on their college campuses, where pre-law assistance is often hidden within other programs. The challenges for post-graduates looking for guidance during the admissions process can be even more daunting, where many face the challenge without the institutional support of their alma mater. While one of the most substantial hurdles to attending law school is success on an admissions exam, either the Law School Admission Test (LSAT) or now, the Graduate Record Exam (GRE), students without a network of professionals within their family can struggle to understand the preparation and cost to take the test. First-generation pre-law students frequently lack the family network helpful when looking for pre-law internships that often lead to post-law school employment opportunities.[7] The chapter will close with a roadmap for law schools looking to attract and retain first-generation law students; how to reach them at the start of their journey, how to keep them motivated and focused on success, and how to alleviate common fears that derail first-generation law students from enrolling or graduating from law school.

The Pre-Law Landscape: Unique Challenges for First Gen Students

When a student or graduate wants information on law school or legal careers, where do they start? For almost everyone, the internet is the beginning of their search. Like all internet searches, an array of helpful and not-so-helpful information, including sponsored ads and solicitations from law schools, are delivered.[8] The internet is excellent at delivering information, but less helpful as a sorting-and-filtering mechanism, separating sales and disinformation from sound advice and objective information. The internet is particularly poor at the personal, experience-based questions that are at the heart of pre-law preparation. What do I need to do to get into law school? When should I apply to law school? What does it mean to

---

6. While undergraduates focused on attending law school are frequently referred to as pre-law, I will use this term for both college students and post-graduates hoping to attend law school.

7. *New Findings on Disparities in Employment Outcomes Based on Level of Parental Education*, NAT'L ASS'N FOR LAW PLACEMENT, https://www.nalp.org/1121research (last visited May 8, 2022) ("The employment rate was almost 5 percentage points higher (92.8% vs. 88.0%) and the rate of employment in bar passage required/anticipated jobs was more than 11 points greater (84.3% vs. 73.2%) for continuing-generation JD students in comparison to first-generation college students.").

8. An internet search "applying to law school" presents a sponsored advertisement for a local law school, LSAC guidance, five law-school sponsored articles on applying to law school, a link to *U.S. News and World Report* rankings, and a YouTube advertisement for an obscure LSAT preparation company. GOOGLE, https://www.google.com/search?q=applying+to+law+school, (last visited May 8, 2022).

be a "good" law school? Is it important to go to a good law school? Is law school like undergrad? Can I take out loans? When do I need to start repaying those loans? Why is *U.S. News and World Report* so important to law schools? Questions that seem straightforward to students with friends and family who have completed post-secondary education are complex and confusing to first-generation pre-law students without knowledgeable support. From the start of the process, information asymmetry is a cause of confusion and delay for students without an experienced guide to the admissions process.

For students and graduates with access to campus when not in class, the next step in the process is to find the pre-law office, or pre-law advisor, on their campus. Many, if not most, colleges and universities provide some post-graduate career and professional advising. These offices are usually open to graduates as well as students, but due to the logistical hurdles of returning to campus after graduation, it is much more challenging for post-graduates to seek on-campus support. Finding the pre-law office or advisor is the first logistical hurdle for current students and graduates; it requires students to know that the office exists, where to find it on campus, who the office is open to, and how to make an appointment. An internet search may lead to a webpage with helpful advice and directions for seeking one-on-one guidance, or it may lead to a link and a name, with no other information.

The advising organizations that focus on pre-law students, the six regional associations of pre-law advisors, meet almost every year, and the national organization overseeing the regional bodies, the Pre-Law Advisors National Council, or PLANC, meets every four years, to discuss concerns specific to pre-law advisors.[9] The six regional associations, as well as PLANC, have a long history of collaboration and partnership with the bodies that regulate (ABA), support (CLEO and AccessLex), measure (NALP), and provide testing and credentialing (LSAC) for law schools.[10] These partnerships help provide pre-law advisors with the knowledge about legal education and legal careers that inform fruitful conversations with pre-law students. Despite the wealth of experience and training provided by advising organizations, from NACADA to the regional associations of pre-law advisors, there is much that is unknown about the current state of pre-law advising.[11] Per administrators at LSAC and officers of PLANC, there is no national accounting of pre-law offices, so no organization is collecting statistics on the availability or composition of pre-law advising at colleges and universities.[12]

---

9. PLANC, *About PLANC*, www.planc.org (last visited May 8, 2022).

10. *Id.*

11. *See* PLANC, *Resources*, http://www.planc.org/planc_resources (last visited May 8, 2022) (linking to a number of outside organizations, but only two links to information provided by PLANC).

12. Email to PLANC president Sandy Self, 7/20/2020, on file with the author; email to LSAC Senior Vice President for Schools and Institutions, Vivian Bowden, 7/1/2020, email on file with author. Neither organization collects information on pre-law advisors on a national level.

However, even among pre-law advising associations, there are no recommended or required credentials or degrees.[13] A pre-law advisor can be a career counselor with a master's degree in higher education or educational leadership, a professor in political science or history who earned a Ph.D., not a J.D., or a lawyer with a J.D. that wanted to exit practice.[14] There is also no standard location for pre-law advising offices. Many pre-law advising offices are housed with career counseling offices[15]; however, others are independent,[16] or housed within specialized departments, such as enrichment programs[17] or political science or history departments.[18] The lack of standardization allows for flexibility within colleges and universities, but it also creates confusion for students and graduates. When the pre-law advisor is also a career counselor, it's difficult to know if their job is to find you a job within legal-related fields, or whether they can help you with the law school admissions process. When the pre-law advisor is also a political science professor, it is hard for an English (or Engineering, Nursing, or History) major to know if advising is open to them or only students within the Political Science department. There are officially no recommended pre-law majors,[19] pre-law offices are located all over campuses, and pre-law advisors can be lawyers, career counselors, academic advisors, or professors. There is no home for pre-law, unlike pre-med, which is usually within a bio-sciences department.[20] For students and graduates without the support of a knowledgeable

---

13. PLANC, *The Roles and Responsibilities of Pre-Law Advisors*, https://tinyurl.com/4ubw82bm (last visited May 8, 2022).

14. A look at the credentials of the PLANC Board finds many board members with Juris Doctor degrees, but also a master's degree in marketing, a master's degree in college student development, and a Master of Education in Higher and PostSecondary Education. http://www.planc.org/leadership (last visited May 8, 2022).

15. *See Pre-Law*, Northeastern University (May 8, 2022). https://careers.northeastern.edu/article/pre-law/; *Pre-Law Advising*, Tufts University, https://careers.tufts.edu/channels/pre-law-advising/ (last visited May 8, 2022)., *Career Services Schedule a Pre-Law Advising Appointment*, University of Pennsylvania, https://careerservices.upenn.edu/schedule-a-pre-law-advising-appointment/ (last visited May 8, 2022); *Pre-Law Advising Career Services*, Loyola University Chicago, https://www.luc.edu/prelaw/ (last visited May 8, 2022).

16. *See Pre-Law Advising*, Brown University, https://www.brown.edu/academics/college/advising/law-school/ (last visited May 8, 2022).

17. *See Enrichment Programs*, University of Connecticut, https://enrichment.uconn.edu/our-programs/; *Pre-Law Advising Office*, University of Connecticut, https://prelaw.uconn.edu (last visited May 8, 2022).

18. *See Political Science Pre-Law Office*, Southern Connecticut State University, https://inside.southernct.edu/political-science/pre-law-program (last visited May 8, 2022); *Pre-Law Information for Political Science Majors*, University of Missouri-St. Louis, https://www.umsl.edu/~polisci/Undergraduate%20Program/prelaw_adv3.html (last visited May 8, 2022); *Undergraduate Pre-Law*, Assumption University, https://www.assumption.edu/undergraduate/pre-law (last visited May 8, 2022).

19. *See Pre-Law Applying to Law School*, Am. Bar Ass'n, https://www.americanbar.org/groups/legal_education/resources/pre_law/ (last visited May 8, 2022).

20. *10 Things to Do to Prepare for Applying to Medical School*, Ass'n Am. Med. Coll., https://students-residents.aamc.org/preparing-medical-school/10-things-do-prepare-applying-medical-school (linking to National Association of Advisors for Health Professions, which provides assistance for students who do not have a pre-med advisor on their campus) (last visited May 8, 2022).

friend or family member, the search for preliminary guidance on legal careers is the first challenge.

Pre-law advising straddles the boundaries of several departments on undergraduate campuses, and is also governed by National Academic Advising Association, or NACADA. as well as PLANC and regional pre-law associations. NACADAs focus on academic advising overlaps with pre-law advising that takes place within academic departments, as well as advising that has an academic component.[21] Academic advising is a much broader field than pre-law advising, and the NACADA core values of "respect, professionalism, inclusivity, empowerment, integrity, commitment, and caring" reflect their larger numbers and wide range of services to undergraduate students.[22] NACADA does set out core competencies for academic advising, but does not specify what education or training is required for advising.[23] NACADA recommends "an earned graduate or professional degree in a field relevant to the position they hold or must possess an appropriate combination of educational credentials and related work experience."[24] However, even within academic advising, only two-thirds of advisors who responded to a survey by NACADA indicated that a master's degree was the most common degree earned among college advisors.[25] While pre-law advisors belong to the larger family of academic advisors, there is little guidance within NACADA that would support requirements for training, professional development, or education for advising that straddles more than one department on campus.

Regardless of where an applicant seeks pre-law advising assistance, the next step is assessing when to attend law school and how to prepare their application. The process of selecting law schools and applying for admission is costly in both time and money. The LSAT or GRE, application fees, and costs associated with visiting law schools and attending law school fairs can run into the hundreds, if not thousands, of dollars. Financial challenges are why many first-generation college students drop out of college, and additional costs associated with preparation for law school contribute to the financial strain of higher education.[26] Applying to one law

---

21. Ruth Darling, *The Academic Advisor*, 64 J. GEN. ED. 90, 91 (2015).

22. *Core Values*, NACADA, https://nacada.ksu.edu/Portals/0/Resources/Pillars/Core%20Values%20Handout.pdf (last visited May 8, 2022).

23. *Core Competencies*, NACADA, https://nacada.ksu.edu/Portals/0/Resources/Pillars/Abridged%20NACADA%20Academic%20Advising%20Core%20Competencies%20Guide.pdf (last visited May 8, 2022).

24. Mark A. Taylor, *Professional Advisor Credentials, Career Ladders, and Salaries*, NACADA CLEARINGHOUSE OF ACADEMIC ADVISING RESOURCES, http://www.nacada.ksu.edu/Resources/Clearinghouse/View-Articles/Professional-Advisor-Credentials-Career-Ladders-and-Salaries.aspx (last visited May 8, 2022).

25. *Id.*

26. Judith J. Andrews, *How Am I Going to Pay for That?!: First-Generation University Students and Their Financial Concerns* 34 (2013) (Ph.D. dissertation, U. of Minnesota) (ProQuest); Hugh T. Ferguson, *First-Generation Students Struggle with Finances, Unsafe Environments, Online Learning Amid Pandemic, New Report Finds*, NAT'L ASS'N STUDENT FIN. AID ADMIN. (Aug. 17, 2020), https://www.nasfaa.org/news-item/22961/First-Generation_Students_Struggle_With_Finances_Unsafe_Environments_Online_Learning_Amid_Pandemic_New_Report_Finds.

school can cost $400 or more, accounting for individual law school application fees, costs to take the LSAT or GRE, and the required registration with the Credential Assembly Service (CAS), which supplies transcripts, letters of recommendation, and test scores to admissions offices. The LSAC offers fee waivers for LSAT and CAS, but only if the applicant is earning between 150 and 350% of the federal poverty guidelines.[27] The application for a LSAC fee waiver requires no less than 10 forms from the IRS, as well as supporting documentation proving citizenship, and documentation of maximum asset and cash balances in bank accounts.[28] If an applicant can prove financial need to the LSAC, they may receive application fee waivers from individual law schools, either through the LSAC Candidate Referral Service, or directly from the law school. This process trades time for money; while applying for fee waivers may allow a low-income applicant to apply to law school, it takes considerable time to gather required documentation and wait for approval. For first-generation applicants who must work through their undergraduate career, this may be an impossible trade-off; give up unavailable free time to collect and submit tens of documents, or give up money they do not have in order to apply.

Preparing for the LSAT or, now, GRE, presents time *and* money problems, instead of time *or* money problems. The barriers to thorough LSAT or, now, GRE, preparation are myriad and complicated.[29] Standardized test preparation is not one-and-done, or even three-and-done, but a three- to six-month process requiring time, money, and substantial effort.[30] Test preparation is a type of shadow education, or educational activity outside the formal channels of the educational system designed to improve a student's chances of success in a chosen system.[31] The effects of standardized test preparation are difficult to disentangle from other confounding variables, the benefits of shadow education in the form of test prep "emanate from the overlapping and reinforcing character of tangible resources (i.e., income) and knowledge and efficacy (i.e., parental education)."[32] Students whose parents understand the college admissions process know that "to get into elite colleges, one must

27. *Fee Waivers for the LSAT & Credential Assembly Service (CAS)*, LSAC, https://www.lsac.org/lsat/register-lsat/lsat-cas-fees/fee-waivers-lsat-credential-assembly-service-cas (last visited May 8, 2022).

28. *Id.*

29. See Raeshanda Wilson, *Predicting Graduate School Success: A Critical Race Analysis of the Graduate Record Examination* 1,70 (May 2020) (Ph.D. dissertation, Kennesaw State University) (Digital Commons); Stephanie Francis Ward, *With GRE Restrictions Lifted for Law Schools, Some Urge Caution*, A.B.A. J. (Dec. 16, 2021), https://www.abajournal.com/web/article/with-gre-restrictions-lifted-for-law-schools-some-urge-caution; Rachel Margiewicz, *The New Role of the GRE in Law School Admissions*, Nat'l Jurist (Aug. 9, 2019), https://nationaljurist.com/prelaw/new-role-gre-law-school-admissions.

30. Donald E. Powers, *Relations of Test Item Characteristics to Test Preparation/Test Practice Effects: A Quantitative Summary*, 100 Psychol. Bull. 67, 67 (1986).

31. Claudia Buchman et al., *Shadow Education, American Style: Test Preparation, the SAT and College Enrollment*, 89 Soc. Forces 435, 436 (2010).

32. *Id.* at 438.

train for standardized tests with the intensity of an athlete," while students from less affluent families do not know that test prep begins young and continues until they receive the requisite exceptional scores.[33] Shadow education, specifically test preparation, "flourishes in educational systems where high-stakes testing serves as a gatekeeper to future educational opportunities."[34] The standardized test knowledge gap does not close during college. One first-generation immigrant noted that "[t]he first time I took the LSAT, I had no idea what I was doing."[35] Leonard Baynes, the primary founder of the award-winning Ronald H. Brown Prep Program for College Students, has noted:

> The LSAT is the biggest challenge for pipeline programs.... The students often have unrealistic expectations of the LSAT. First, they think the LSAT percentile is a percentage.... In reality, the LSAT is a zero-sum game in which some people taking the test are destined to be on the top and some of the bottom. They can maximize and improve their performance, but it is constricted by this zero-sum game.[36]

Students without familial guidance must rely on institutional support to prepare for the LSAT or GRE, so the challenge of LSAT preparation is threaded into pre-law advising and preparation. If a first-generation pre-law student can find a pre-law advisor on their campus, they rely on that advisor for accurate and complete advice on how to prepare for the LSAT or GRE.[37]

Law school admissions was not always so complicated. At the turn of the twentieth century, just as law schools were ascendant and the law practice apprenticeship was receding, law school admissions was simpler. The explicitly anti-immigrant, racist, and anti-Semitic roots of the institutionalization of legal education led to a series of reforms, amongst them, admissions standards and the LSAT.[38] After World War I, "legal politicians found that the legal profession was a means by which Jews, immigrants, and city-dwellers might undermine an American way of life." The foreigner and the immigrant, who could not be admitted to Yale or Harvard Law, found their way to night and part-time law schools unaffiliated with a larger university,

---

33. Dylan Hernandez, *How I Learned to Take The SATs Like a Rich Kid*, N.Y. Times (April 10, 2017), https://www.nytimes.com/2017/04/10/opinion/how-i-learned-to-take-the-sat-like-a-rich-kid.html?smid=url-share.

34. Buchman et al., *supra* note 31, at 439.

35. Nayram S. Gasu, *How Reddit Helped Me Excel on the LSAT and Get into Law School* 56, N.Y. St. B.J., (Sept. 2018) https://archive.nysba.org/Journal/2018/Sep/How_Reddit_Helped_Me_Excel_on_the_LSAT_and_Get_Into_Law_School/.

36. Dorothy H. Evensen & Carla D. Pratt eds., The End of the Pipeline: A Journey of Recognition for African Americans Entering the Legal Profession, 269 (2012).

37. Robert Stevens, Law School: Legal education in America from the 1950s to 1980s, 37, 112 (1983).

38. *Id.* at 99–100.

known as "proprietary" schools.[39] These law schools threatened the "professional pride" of the bench and bar.[40]

Along with changes in admissions criteria, the 1920s saw the development of the admissions aptitude test.[41] The history and development of the LSAT helps explain why the test is so challenging for first-generation pre-law students; it was a "predictive tool of first-year success"[42] of "white male veterans" returning from World War II.[43] The test was designed to measure the aptitude (although the creators were loath to use that word)[44] of a homogenous group of men with similar formative experiences, which is the opposite of the diversity of gender, experience, race, ethnicity, and education represented by applicants to law school in the last 40 years. The LSAT's birth dates to 1947, when the deans of the law schools we now recognize as some of the most prestigious in the country—Boston University, Harvard, Columbia, Michigan, New York University, Northwestern, Yale, Rutgers, and Syracuse—met to discuss the creation of an admissions test to help them decide on "those borderline on college record and from unknown colleges."[45] The "democratizing forces" that followed World War II also began a democratizing process within law school admissions. While admissions officials found it easy to evaluate the applications of white males with Ivy league credentials and family pedigrees, they found it more challenging to evaluate the applications of immigrant, working class veterans who used the newly created GI Bill to enroll in the "unknown colleges" without the established prestige well-known universities.[46] While these democratizing forces opened law schools to white males who previously would not have considered law school, admissions remained largely limited to white males for several more decades.[47] While the LSAT does not explicitly discriminate against any group, it was tested and normed against the narrow slice of the population considered for admission post-World War II, a slice that now represents less than 50% of incoming classes.

As an admissions test, the LSAT was designed to measure general aptitude on broad intellectual skills.[48] Those skills have been controversial and debated over time, with several different iterations of the test.[49] Today, the test measures reading comprehension, logical reasoning, and analytical reasoning (the dreaded logic

39. *Id.* at 35, 113.

40. *Id.* at 101.

41. Thomas O. White, *LSAC/LSAS: A Brief History*, 34 J. Legal Educ. 369, 369 (1984).

42. William P. LaPiana, *Merit and Diversity: The Origins of the Law School Admissions Test*, 48 St. Louis. L.J. 955, 974 (2003–2004).

43. *Id.* at 962.

44. *Id.* at 968.

45. *Id.* at 967.

46. *Id.*

47. *Legal Education*, A.B.A. Profile of the Legal Profession, https://www.abalegalprofile.com/women.html (last visited November 16, 2024.

48. LaPiana, *supra* note 42, at 968–967.

49. *Id.* at 970, 973, 979.

games section, which will remain a part of the test until 2023).[50] Information on how to prepare for the LSAT is not common knowledge or intuitive.[51] As an aptitude test, there are no specific college courses that teach these skills, although some majors have been found to do better on the LSAT than others, perhaps reflecting a greater emphasis on critical thinking and analytical reasoning. Preparation outside of prescribed college courses, in the form of time-intensive and costly commercial test preparation services, is the key to higher scores on the LSAT. The LSAT has predictive value, especially for time-limited, in-class final exams[52] and it has been speculated that its predictive value is in test-taking speed, and repeated, sustained practice increases this speediness.[53] Without help from someone familiar with the marathon-like process of studying for the LSAT, it would be difficult to know what to study, how long to study, and where to focus additional attention, such as speed.

Test prep programs make a difference.[54] Test prep programs, such as Princeton Review and Kaplan, are also expensive.[55] Commercial test prep programs, unlike pre-law advisors, have the advantage of being everywhere (posters on dorm bulletin boards, ads on student union digital displays, flyers posted on car windows in parking lots), and having student representatives at all the places students are likely to congregate. Being ubiquitous on most college campuses doesn't make test prep programs accessible; a first-generation student noted "LSAT courses cost around $1000. While that $1000 course could get me a 170+ score and thus probably a full ride to law school...I simply did not have the money, so I could not make that investment."[56] Research on first-generation college and law students and student debt suggests that the lower levels of family wealth contribute to greater levels of student

---

50. Kelly Rossman-McKinney, *MI AG Nessel Recognizes Work of Angelo Binno in Overhaul of LSAT's Accessibility Through Settlement of Years-Long Lawsuit* (Oct. 8, 2019), https://www.michigan.gov/ag/0,4534,7-359-92297_47203-509444--,00.html (last visited May 8, 2022).

51. Andrea A. Curcio, Gregory Todd Jones & Tanya M. Washington, *Does Practice Make Perfect? An Empirical Examination of the Impact of Practice Essays on Essay Exam Performance*, 35 Fla. St. U. L. Rev. 271, 285 (2008).

52. William D. Henderson, *The LSAT, Law School Exams, and Meritocracy: The Surprising and Undertheorized Role of Test-Taking Speed*, 82 Tex. L. Rev. 975 (2004).

53. Curcio et al., *supra* note 51, at 285–286.

54. Michael J. Higdon, *A Place in the Academy: Law Faculty Hiring and Socioeconomic Bias*, 87 St. John's L. Rev. 171, 189 (2013) (When it comes to standardized tests, like the LSAT, students from higher socioeconomic backgrounds "are more likely to afford private high schools, tutors, test prep courses, and other prerequisites that usually translate into higher test scores.")

55. *See* Princeton Review, https://www.princetonreview.com/law/lsat-test-prep (last visited May 8, 2022) (pricing ranges from $799 for an online, self-paced course, to $3649, for a course that guarantees a score above 165); Kaplan Test Prep, https://www.kaptest.com/lsat (last visited May 8, 2022) (pricing ranges from $1200 for a live, online course to $2399 for tutoring and a live, online course).

56. *Id.* at 16, 56.

loan debt;[57] if a student is struggling to pay for college, it is unlikely they will be able to budget for a $1000 LSAT prep course.[58]

This challenge of preparing to apply to law school has become more labyrinthine—but possibly less challenging—with the addition of the GRE, or Graduate Record Exam. As of November 19, 2021, the Council of the American Bar Association Section of Legal Education and Admission to the Bar allows law schools to accept GRE scores from applicants in lieu of the LSAT.[59] However, if an applicant submits both an LSAT score and a GRE score, it is rumored only the LSAT score is what will be reported, or will "count" when the law school reports their median LSAT to the ABA and *U.S. News and World Report*.[60] This makes the decision to take the LSAT or GRE fraught; before taking either test, the potential applicant must weigh whether they will do better on the LSAT or GRE, because taking the LSAT will nullify a potentially higher GRE score. They are likely to get this information from extensive test prep, which, as a first-generation applicant, they are less likely to access or afford.

However, for applicants who know the LSAT is the primary obstacle to their admission to the law school of their choice, the addition of the GRE may be perceived as a sea change.[61] The decision by the ABA to allow all law schools to use the GRE as an admissions test may be particularly helpful to first-generation students who are unsure of their path, or want to pursue a law degree as well as another post-graduate degree. The GRE is standard entrance exam for many, if not most, master's and Ph.D. programs, meaning that students who are undecided about their path will only need to prepare for and pay for one admissions test. The pervasive presence of the GRE makes test prep materials easier to find, and they are usually available in most academic departments that have post-graduate programs. An additional benefit of using the GRE is its similarity to the SAT. For applicants who have taken the SAT in high school, the format of the GRE will be familiar; both consist of verbal reasoning, quantitative reasoning, and analytical writing sections.[62] One of the benefits of removing the unknown, such as a format of the LSAT, can itself help first-generation

57. Jacqueline M. O'Bryant & Katharine Traylor Schaffzin, *First-Generation Students in Law School: A Proven Success Model*, 70 Ark. L. Rev. 913, 917 (2018).

58. Stevens, *supra* note 37, at 3, 11.

59. *Summary of Actions of the Section's Council at its Public Meeting* Nov. 19, 2021, Council of the ABA Section of Legal Education and Admissions to the Bar (last visited May 8, 2022) https://www.americanbar.org/content/dam/aba/administrative/legal_education_and_admissions_to_the_bar/council_reports_and_resolutions/nov21/21-nov-legal-ed-summary-of-council-meeting.pdf.

60. Ward, *supra* note 29.

61. Rachelle Veikune, *Access to Legal Education for Minorities Increases Access to Justice for Underserved Populations*, J. Kan. Bar Ass'n, March 2016, at 14.

62. Margiewicz, *supra* note 29; Shelly Quance, *What You Need to Know about the Difference Between the SAT and the GRE*, The Summit Ahead: A Blog for Future Graduate Students, Jan. 18, 2017, https://blog.graduateadmissions.wvu.edu/the-summit-ahead/what-you-need-to-know-about-the-difference-between-the-sat-and-the-gre (guidance provided by the West Virginia University Graduate Admissions Office).

test-takers who struggle with anxiety on tests. Another benefit of the GRE is flexibility; the GRE is offered more often than the LSAT, making it easier to access.[63] The GRE is offered at both home, 24 hours a day, if the test-taker has the right equipment, or at test centers with a wide availability of test times; there are no specific dates that the GRE is offered.[64] Since time is one of the resources in short supply for many first-generation applicants, especially those with family commitments and work responsibilities,[65] the flexibility offered by the GRE is a significant advantage.

Admissions tests of any kind will be a barrier to admission for students who do not come from families with knowledge of the test. These challenges—of prior knowledge of the test, of how to study, of how to pay for the test—are not insurmountable, and law schools can help first-generation students with the LSAT and GRE preparation process. First, law schools can view themselves as partners with undergraduate universities. Many law schools already partner with undergraduate universities, through three-plus-three programs, honors admissions programs, or close relationships because they belong to the same university system.[66] Law schools can also leverage the expertise in affiliated schools of education, psychology departments with expertise in psychometric evaluation, along with the pre-law office, to create programs that meet first-generation pre-law students where they are—in college.

Law schools are ideal partners with undergraduate pre-law offices seeking additional support for applicants because most law schools are already experts at preparing their graduates for a high-stakes standardized test—the bar exam. Law schools can leverage their knowledge and skills in this area to offer assistance to pre-law students preparing for the LSAT and the GRE. Many of the test-taking skills needed to master the multiple-choice questions on the Uniform Bar Exam are the same skills necessary to succeed on the LSAT and GRE. We know there is overlap between people who score well on the LSAT and people who pass the bar exam.[67]

---

63. Karen Sloan, *Should Law Schools Embrace the GRE? New Report Urges Caution*, REUTERS, Oct. 5, 2021, https://www.reuters.com/legal/legalindustry/should-law-schools-fully-embrace-gre-new-report-urges-caution-2021-10-05/.

64. *GRE General Test Locations and Dates: Choose When and Where to Test*, ETS, https://www.ets.org/gre/revised_general/register/locations_dates/ (last visited May 8, 2022).

65. *See* Kara Balemian and Jing Feng, *First-Generation Students: College Aspirations, Preparedness and Challenges*, COLLEGE BOARD 47 (2013), https://files.eric.ed.gov/fulltext/ED563393.pdf.

66. *See 3+3 Accelerated Programs*, ASS'N AM. LAW SCHOOLS, https://www.aals.org/news/33-accelerated-programs/ (last visited May 8, 2022); Honors to Law, UNIVERSITY OF AKRON, https://www.uakron.edu/law/admissions/honors-to-law, (last visited May 8, 2022); *Special Program in Law*, UNIVERSITY OF CONNECTICUT, https://admissions.uconn.edu/apply/first-year/special-programs/law/ (last visited May 8, 2022); *South Carolina Honors College*, UNIVERSITY OF SOUTH CAROLINA, https://sc.edu/study/colleges_schools/honors_college/study/prepare_for_professions/pre-law/index.php (last visited May 8, 2022).

67. Keith A. Kaufman, V. Holland LaSalle-Ricci, Carol R. Glass & Diane B. Arnkoff, *Passing the Bar Exam: Psychological, Educational, and Demographic Predictors of Success*, 57 J. LEGAL EDUC. 205, 206 (2007). ("Similarly, Wightman found that LGPA and LSAT scores were the strongest predictors of bar exam passage for all groups examined.")

While this correlation can be related to many things, the most reasonable explanation is that the skills necessary to do well on the LSAT transfer to the bar exam. The most notable skill is one already mentioned—speed.[68] Success on the bar exam, like the LSAT, is strongly associated with reading and answering multiple-choice questions quickly and accurately.[69] Law schools can leverage existing assets to build pre-admissions programs as robust as their post-graduate bar support programs. Equity needs to start before admissions, and continue through bar passage. So the skills taught in the third-year bar prep courses that have become ubiquitous at almost all law schools can be taught to pre-law students preparing for the LSAT. An additional benefit to law schools is better bar pass numbers. Preliminary research from *New York Times* journalist Jay Caspian Kang suggests that students who do more test prep earlier in their academic career do better on standardized tests.[70] First-generation law students cannot pass the bar if they are never admitted to law school due to low LSAT or GRE scores.

Law schools can also leverage the skills and knowledge of their own students to offer LSAT and GRE test prep to potential applicants. Using current students, either through work-study or traditional employment, provides first-generation students with potential mentors. This would also give first-generation students familiarity with law school culture. Like first-generation applicants, time is what is in short supply for both bar prep professionals and law students. Test prep courses offered by a law school need not be offered in person or at an undergraduate campus. With advances in online learning brought about by the pandemic, law schools can create synchronous, asynchronous, or hybrid online LSAT prep courses that can be offered to undergraduate universities outside their immediate area.[71] Bar prep professionals are in-house experts at high-stakes test prep. Asking bar prep professionals to design LSAT and GRE test-prep courses is a one-time expenditure of costs and resources with a potentially significant payoff. High-scoring students can teach test prep courses. This has the added benefit of providing resources to resource-strapped students, while connecting potential applicants to representatives of the law school who can answer their questions about law school while preparing them for the LSAT or GRE. Bringing LSAT and GRE preparation in-house helps ameliorate the information asymmetry and cost barriers that stymie the advancement of first-generation and low-income law school applicants.

While law schools would do well to partner with undergraduate universities, they also need to look beyond the walls of nearby undergraduate colleges, LSAC forums,

---

68. Henderson, *supra* note 52, at 975.

69. Kaufman et al., *supra* note 67, at 206.

70. Jay Caspian Kang, *Why SAT Test Prep Doesn't Help Who You Might Think It Helps*, N.Y. Times, Sept. 9, 2021, https://www.nytimes.com/2021/09/09/opinion/sat-standardized-tests-ucs.html?smid=url-share.

71. *See* Max Huffman, *Online Learning Grows Up—and Heads to Law School*, 49 Ind. L. Rev. 57, 65 (2015).

CLEO, and pre-law fairs to recruit and prepare first-generation law school applicants. The same barriers that confound first-generation applicants from seeking help on campus—logistics, time, location—can stymie first-generation applicants looking for extracurricular help. Information asymmetry still complicates efforts by students who do not know where to look for help on campus; they are similarly unlikely to know where to know about outside sources of assistance, because they would learn about those sources from on-campus pre-law offices they cannot find or access. Many first-generation students are also low-income,[72] and the challenge to attending pre-law school fairs, LSAC forums, and CLEO events is financial; time to explore law school options is time away from work, earning money to support themselves and their families.[73] First-generation pre-law students are also more likely to have dependents;[74] pre-law fairs and LSAC forums generally do not offer childcare and are not child-friendly environments, which makes attending events outside of school hours very difficult.[75] LSAC forums are usually in large cities,[76] in conference or hotel ballrooms, which can be too far to travel or cost-prohibitive. Missing out on events for pre-law students cuts these potential applicants off from connecting with law schools with programs that can meet some of their needs. Many admissions professionals can offer fee waivers to students who attend LSAC forums or on-campus pre-law fairs, making the financially prohibitive process of applying to law schools manageable. LSAC forums also offer on-site pre-law advice, workshops on managing finances, and help with fee waivers, all designed to make the process more accessible for applicants without adequate familial support or resources.[77]

To reach more first-generation pre-law students, law schools need to begin thinking outside the traditional methods of outreach and marketing. The lack of research on first-generation pre-law students makes this particularly challenging.[78] While we can extrapolate from the substantial body of research on all first-generation college students, this research does not help law school admissions understand the specific, and perhaps unique, barriers facing first-generation pre-law students. Law schools need specific research on where they can meet first-generation pre-law students where they are, and how to overcome family and financial barriers to attending informational forums and fairs. Law schools also need more information on the perceived barriers to preparing for and applying to law school. Without adequate infor-

---

72. *See generally* Elliott Ingersoll et al., *Spiritual and Religious Support for Underrepresented First-Generation, Low-Income (UFGLI) Students*, 12 Religions 548, 549–550 (2021).

73. *Id.* at 549.

74. *Id.*

75. *2022–2023 LSAC Law School Forums*, LSAC, https://www.lsac.org/lawschoolforums (last visited May 15, 2022).

76. *Id.*

77. *2021–22 LSAC Law School Forums On-Demand Workshops*, LSAC, https://www.lsac.org/lawschoolforums/on-demand-workshops (last visited May 15, 2022).

78. Kayla Molina, *First-Gen Students Face Unique Challenges*, 48 Student Law. 19, 20 (2019–2020).

mation on the specific challenges and needs of first-generation pre-law students, law schools are left with a spaghetti-on-the-wall strategy that they warn first-year law students not to employ on exams; throw some ideas up on the wall, and see what sticks. With more research on the needs of first-generation pre-law students, law school admissions teams can make informed choices that meet the unique needs of first-generation applicants.

Outreach to pre-law students should recognize that first-generation pre-law students come with personal, cultural, and financial considerations that are different from continuing-generation students. The first consideration is family. First-generation undergraduate students are more likely to be older when they begin college and more likely to have dependents when they attend college.[79] The decision to attend law school is life-changing; the decision to move your family is life-altering for not just the student but the dependents they support or, in the alternate, the ability to move your family to attend law school may not be possible. The calculus surrounding law school choice is different, more complicated, and more emotionally challenging when it involves more than one person.

The financial implications of attending law school are also different for many first-generation pre-law students. Many first-generation pre-law students work through their undergraduate years in order to provide for their family; sometimes this is a cultural expectation, sometimes this is a financial necessity.[80] These considerations can change the landscape of the law school search. If the applicant cannot move because they need to keep a job or cannot leave their family of origin, the law school search is geographically limited. This may not be an issue in large cities with multiple options for law school attendance, but this can be a challenge for first-generation applicants in smaller cities.

Law schools can also meet the needs of students with family concerns with innovative solutions that are not commonplace among law schools, but are available to graduate students in many other programs. One of the challenges for applicants with families—and especially single mothers—looking to attend law school is child care. Child care is an expense that can rival the expense of law school tuition at many state schools.[81] Many large universities have child labs staffed by early education students, offering affordable child care for faculty and graduate students. Opening up spots in on-campus child labs, or on-campus child care facilities, with the potential for subsidized child care, would allow first-generation students, and students with families, to have a safe and reliable place to send their children while they are studying.

---

79. Ingersoll, *supra* note 72, at 549.

80. Danielle R. Adams, *The Relationship Between Financial Strain, Perceived Stress, Psychological Symptoms, and Academic and Social Integration in Undergraduate Students*, 64 J. Amer. Coll. Health 362, 362 (2016).

81. Jason De Parle, *When Child Care Costs Twice as Much as the Mortgage*, N.Y. Times, Oct. 9, 2021, https://www.nytimes.com/2021/10/09/us/politics/child-care-costs-wages-legislation.html?smid=url-share.

Few law schools offer law student housing. Another way to attract and support first-generation law students is offering apartments or family housing at or near campus. Many large research universities provide on-campus housing to doctoral students; offering the same housing to law students would mean increasing the availability of such housing, but would not present a new responsibility for universities. For first-generation applicants with families, balancing law school study with caring for dependents is incredibly challenging; doing so when commuting a distance to law school is an untenable balance for many. Offering reasonably priced housing relieves the burden of a commute to law school. Keeping law students on or near campus encourages students to be engaged in the law school community, including extracurricular opportunities, such as moot court and law review, which enhance resumes and help graduates find jobs. Providing on-campus housing is not an insurmountable goal for law schools, but it does represent an opportunity to attract and retain first-generation law students who would otherwise struggle with family responsibilities while studying law.

How We Can Help: Pipeline Programs

Outreach needs to begin in the community and at colleges. Evidenced by the number of first-generation law school aspirants versus the number of first-generation students who enroll, law schools are not doing enough to support interested first-generation pre-law students through the preparation and application process, from undergraduate education through matriculation. Many of the ideas to support first-generation students are not new or revolutionary; programs to support first-generation applicants can leverage existing expertise and expand programs that work. Law schools need to remove the silos within their own programming. Admissions needs to work with bar prep to create programs that can help students on the LSAT; admissions and ASP can work together to create pre-law academic preparation programs; doctrinal or podium professors need to be engaged with mentoring students who do not have the familial support, or cultural or social capital that facilitates professional success. All these programs have one barrier—cost—that needs to be addressed by creative administrative teams that reach out to enterprises willing to support their mission to engage with first-generation and other underrepresented populations.

As Professor Emeritus Michael Olivas has noted, the path to law school is not so much a pipeline as a river, with tributaries feeding the river at all points, supporting a broader ecosystem that works together to flow to its destination.[82] Law schools need to support the tributaries that feed the river, not just expect the river to lead to admissions without their active assistance. Law schools can meet the unique needs of first-generation students with admissions programs tailored to the needs of

82. Pratt and Evenson, *supra* note 36.

first-generation students. Conditional admissions programs, alternative testing programs, and expanded part-time programs can attract and, critically, retain first-generation law students who may not have the resources or support to prepare for or finance legal education. The University of Memphis Tennessee Institute for Pre-Law (TIP) is one example of a conditional admission program with positive outcomes for its enrollees. TIP is an "admission-by-performance program for Tennessee and border county residents." TIP simulates the first year of law school in a four-week course taught by law school professors.[83] Students who successfully complete the program are admitted to the University of Memphis.[84] Similar to TIP, Florida International University School of Law's (FIU) PATH program, sponsored by AccessLex, represents another law school partnership designed to increase "enrollment of low-income, first-generation, minority and other traditionally underrepresented groups into law school."[85] The program, like TIP, is taught by full-time law school faculty, as well as members of the Academic Excellence team, and provides "exposure to traditional law school experience supplemented by a range of opportunities including academic enrichment and critical skills development, intensive LSAT preparation, personalized counseling throughout the application process, and individualized mentoring by a member of the bench or bar."[86] Offered online, there are two different "pathways"—one for undergraduate students in their sophomore or junior year, and a second "pathway" for college seniors applying to law school. FIU's PATH is offered to students without cost, through the sponsorship of AccessLex. FIU's PATH program was recently awarded the Association of American Law Schools (AALS) Programmatic Change-Maker Award, awarded to "programs that have created structural and systemic change to increase access to legal education and diversify the legal profession."[87]

In addition to conditional admissions programs like TIP and PATH, law schools can offer more targeted programs designed to prepare for or substitute for the LSAT or GRE. The University of Arizona Law School's JDNext program is an example of a prospective alternative testing program, as well as an example of a law school-testing company collaboration. JDNext is a fully online pre-law school summer course that introduces "the kind of doctrinal concepts and legal skills students will encounter at law school through guided analysis of case law and legal hypotheticals."[88]

---

83. *TN Institute for Pre-Law*, University of Memphis Cecil C. Humphreys School of Law, https://www.memphis.edu/law/about/tip.php (last visited May 15, 2022).

84. *Id.*

85. *FIU Law Path (Pre-law Program)*, Florida International University College of Law, https://law.fiu.edu/admissions/jd/fiu-law-path-pre-law-program/ (last visited May 15, 2022).

86. *Id.*

87. *FIU Path to the Legal Profession earns Association of American Law Schools' Programmatic Change-Maker Award*, Florida International University College of Law, https://law.fiu.edu/2021/10/19/fiu-path-to-the-legal-profession-earns-association-of-american-law-schools-programmatic-change-maker-award/ (last visited May 15, 2022).

88. JDNext, https://jd-next.org (last visited May 15, 2022).

As a partnership between University of Arizona Rogers College of Law and Educational Testing Service (ETS), JDNext is a part of a research study on alternative testing programs. ETS funding allows this program to be free to students who enroll through a partner law school.[89] While research is still being conducted on the success of the program, JDNext has the potential to replace high-stakes testing with a short-form law school course for first-generation students who experience test anxiety and for students who want to combine law school academic preparation with the admissions process.

The one resource shared by conditional admissions and traditional pipeline programs is the active engagement with Academic Support Programs or ASPs. ASPs are well-situated to provide support before admission to law school as well as their traditional role supporting students during law school. Support provided before admission has benefits to ASPs as well as students. The origins of ASP's are in serving less-advantaged populations at a time when law schools were just beginning to expand enrollment beyond white men.[90] ASPs are familiar with the non-academic challenges that cause academic challenges for many first-generation students—imposter syndrome and fear of failure leading to fear of asking for much-needed help, lack of social and cultural capital creating misunderstanding in the classroom, and the isolation from family and friends who cannot understand the unique, and sometimes overwhelming, pressures of law school study. With their origins in serving less-advantaged populations, ASPs are well-situated to work with pre-law advisors and admissions professionals to expand outreach and early academic assistance to first-generation applicants. In fact, many ASPs have been working in this area for years without adequate recognition. ASPs are the primary administrators, and frequently the instructors, in summer pre-orientation programs, such as the University of North Carolina's LEAP program.[91] These programs have already been designed by ASP professionals, and they know what types of programs provide benefits to students, and which ones do not.[92]

Whether through traditional pipeline programs or informal relationship-focused outreach to undergraduate pre-law programs, ASPs can reduce their caseload by supporting students before they reach law school. Involving ASPs earlier in students' academic careers, by preparing first-generation students for the challenges before law school, they can help them move through law school with less stress and fewer academic issues. Pre-law intervention is the proverbial ounce of prevention, pound of cure. Early support to first-generation students can mean less intensive academic

89. JDNext FAQ, https://jd-next.org/enroll/ (last visited May 15, 2022).

90. Ellen Yankiver Suni, *Academic Support at the Crossroads: From Minority Retention to Bar Prep and Beyond—Will Academic Support Change Legal Education or Itself Be Fundamentally Changed?*, 73 UMKC L. Rev. 497, 498 (2004).

91. *Legal Education Advancement Program (LEAP)*, UNC School of Law, https://law.unc.edu/academics/academic-excellence-program/1l/ (last visited May 15, 2022).

92. *See* O'Bryant and Traylor Schaffzin, *supra* note 57, at 928.

support later in their law school career. By capturing their target audience through LSAT prep courses, outreach to pre-law programs, on-campus and online pre-law prep programs in the form of conditional admissions, pipelines, and pre-orientation programs, ASPs can create durable trust networks that are essential for academic and personal success.[93] Trust involves "a willingness to assume risk and open oneself up to the possibility of gain as well as loss," and as an individual or organization "proves trustworthy, the choice to trust again seems more rational and to involve less risk."[94] By building trust between first-generation students and the professionals trained to support their academic success before they matriculate, the decision to seek help before academic disappointment becomes rational instead of risky.[95] Some of the particular challenges faced by first-generation law students, such as imposter syndrome, can prevent first-generation students from seeking academic assistance for fear they will be "found out" by their classmates. An existing relationship with ASP transforms a risky choice to seek academic assistance into a routine opportunity to chit chat with a trusted professional, opening doors for ASP to provide substantive support. This allows first-generation students to seek help with deepening feelings of inadequacy and intellectual fraudulence that are a part of imposter syndrome.[96] ASPs can also support the success of first-generation law students by supporting a growth mindset that attributes success to their personal effort, instead of external sources, such as family connections or luck.[97] ASPs can provide first-generation students with the tools to succeed, which are often perceived by students without the social or cultural capital that comes from family connections as products of family wealth or luck.[98]

Trust networks extend to bar preparation. Building relationships with first-generation students through undergraduate LSAT or GRE preparation serves a dual purpose—to provide immediate assistance with the admissions test while also forming a relationship with professionals they will see again when they prepare for another high-stakes standardized test, the bar exam. By acclimating students to test preparation before they even begin law school, they are introduced to the basic concepts they will need again during their last semester of law school when they take a final-semester bar prep class. Most importantly, LSAT success breeds trust in bar professionals to help them. Trust, as well as a mindset of perseverance, provide the foundation required to strengthen academic skills and substantive knowledge.

---

93. Julie R. Posselt, *Trust Networks: A New Perspective on Pedigree and the Ambiguities in Admissions*, 41 REV. HIGHER ED. 497, X (2018).

94. *Id.* at 500.

95. *Id.*

96. Gill Corkingdale, *Overcoming Imposter Syndrome*, HARV. BUS. REV., May 7, 2008, https://hbr.org/2008/05/overcoming-imposter-syndrome.

97. See generally CAROL S. DWECK, MINDSET: THE NEW PSYCHOLOGY OF SUCCESS (2007).

98. Sarah E.O. Schwartz et. al., *"I'm Having a Little Struggle With This, Can You Help Me Out?": Examining Impacts and Processes of a Social Capital Intervention for First-Generation College Students*, 61 AM. J. CMTY. PSYCH. 166, 168 (2018).

Asking ASP and bar prep professionals to take on more responsibility is not without impediments. The most prominent worry would be that already stretched-thin bar prep staff and faculty do not have the time, or adequate staffing, to learn the differences between the LSAT and the bar exam, and teach another course. However, the vast wealth of materials already produced on LSAT study, some by the same companies that produce bar prep study materials, requires less time-intensive learning and study than designing a semester-long bar prep class or summer bar prep program. The LSAT is also a shorter, much less complicated test than the bar, but the fundamental test-taking skills, particularly speed,[99] are required for both tests. By preparing students to read and respond to multiple choice questions quickly and accurately on the LSAT, we are preparing the same students, as law school graduates, to finish each multi-state bar multiple choice question in 1.8 minutes, or 1 minute and 50 seconds, and do so for 200 questions.[100] The skills overlap can free up time in bar prep for more focus on essay writing and multistate performance test skills, which are more challenging, and more time-intensive, than mastering multiple-choice skills.

Conclusion: Bringing Out a Welcome Mat: Understanding First Gen Fears in Order to Attract First Gen Law Students

Attracting first-generation pre-law students may begin with a river, but during and after orientation, that river flows right into the Academic Support office. A healthy river requires many tributaries, flowing from mountains, springs, and rainwater. Like a river, law schools need to support their underserved tributaries—pre-law offices, non-traditional methods of outreach, pipeline, and conditional admissions programs—that produce first-generation law school applicants. Law schools have the means, through ASP and bar prep, to partner with undergraduate universities to provide the preparation that is often unavailable or inaccessible to first-generation students. By building trust networks before matriculation, law schools can use one of the more powerful tools of academic and personal success—a support network of knowledgeable professionals who students can rely on if they do not have professional networks within their family. When students have a well-developed trust network, first-generation students can open up about the obstacles that can undermine success.

Alleviating the fears of current first-generation students is the intersection of academic support and student services; because apprehension, anxiety, and feeling like

99. Henderson, *supra* note 52, at 975.

100. Diane Curtis, *The LSAT and the Reproduction of Hierarchy*, 41 W. New Eng. L. Rev. 307, 319 (2019).

you don't belong have an impact on academic performance. Financial challenges, imposter syndrome, and fear of the unknown—these fears are both rational and wise. There are resources to address these fears.

Cultural capital can be provided to students through relationships. Fear of the unknown is less of an impediment when there is a trust network in place to ask questions without shame. Financial challenges can present more thorny problems, but supportive relationships within the law school can provide options first-generation students may not discover on their own.

For many first-generation law students, students loans are a significant fear. The fear stems from many sources. For some it is rooted in cultural differences; others are afraid of adding to the already substantial student loan debt they owe from their undergraduate education; some are rooted in fears flamed by the recession of 2008 and the raft of articles criticizing law schools after enrolling more students than they could place in jobs.[101]

Cultural differences around student loans and carrying debt are an often-overlooked source of anxiety for first-generation students, especially students from immigrant families. While I was the Director of Academic Support at a prior law school, I had a student living with many family members and trying to attend law school. She came from a culture where loans of any type were often predatory, and usually controlled by criminal enterprises; missing a loan payment could mean physical harm to the debtor or their family. She was trying to succeed, although her living situation left her with no time or place to study. She was often asked to care for her younger nieces and nephews who lived with her. In a cramped house, she had no space to study because she shared a room with multiple younger family members. Because she was the first in her family to go to college, and no one in her family had attended graduate school in the United States or in her country of origin, no one in her family understood why she was struggling. When she tried to explain to her family that she needed more time and dedicated space to read, they could not understand because she had always succeeded while juggling family needs, a part-time job, and living in the multigenerational, multifamily home. None of her academic struggles were the result of academic unpreparedness, or a lack of effort. She needed to adjust her living situation, which would require her to take out student loans, something she was terrified to do, based on her family's lived experience.

To help her succeed, we needed someone with an intimate understanding of her cultural heritage as well as knowledge of her country of origin to explain the differences between student loans in the United States and the loans in her country of

---

101. Lincoln Caplan, *An Existential Crisis for Law Schools*, N.Y. Times (July 14, 2012) https://www.nytimes.com/2012/07/15/opinion/sunday/an-existential-crisis-for-law-schools.html?searchResultPosition=4; Editorial, The Law School Debt Crisis, N.Y. Times (Oct. 24, 2015), https://www.nytimes.com/2015/10/25/opinion/sunday/the-law-school-debt-crisis.html?searchResultPosition=8.

origin. It is critical that the conversation was with someone who understood and respected her heritage and experience, and did not demean or belittle her country of origin. One of the gaps in outreach to first-generation students is respect; first-generation immigrant students come from families and cultures with as rich, wise, and deep as the cultures of students who have generations of post-secondary educational attainment. In addition to discussing her loan options, we explored additional scholarships, grants, and post-graduate loan forgiveness programs she might not have been aware of that would reduce her total loan burden, while allowing her to move into housing that would give her the space to study. The goal of the conversations was to give her options and allow her to make her own choices. When given all the information, she was able to make an informed decision without the fear that had limited her choices earlier in her law school career.

ASP, bar prep, relationships, and support cannot provide answers to all the questions and challenges faced by first-generation students, but some of the most powerful tools in the ASP toolbox are tools we employ on a daily basis. Listen. Be the safe space for students in, as law school has been called, the cauldron of competition. It is key to remember that first-generation law students cannot go home and commiserate with family members or friends who have shared this experience. A study of law school graduates found their parents had graduated from college at three times the rate of parents nationally.[102] Imposter syndrome that begins during the preparation and application phase only intensifies in the first year of law school. For first-generation students struggling with imposter syndrome, intersecting identities, and financial stress, providing a supportive shoulder and acting as a cheering section can provide a substitute for the social and family capital they do not have.

One of the most helpful things Academic Support professionals can do is make themselves available and visible. First-generation students should not face the same struggles many of them face when looking for help from pre-law advisors. Searching for help is hardest when you are already in distress. By forging relationships with first-generation students before they matriculate, it builds trust and confidence that ASP is a source of assistance, instead of shame.

You don't need to be a first-generation law school graduate to make academic support a safe space for first-generation students. If you were a first-generation law student, share your story. Show first-generation students they do belong in law school; they are not alone in their fears. If you were not a first-generation law student, ask alumni who were to come and share their law school experiences.

---

102. Taylor, *supra* note 1, at 62.

Eleven

Elevating First Gen Law Students through Undergraduate Legal Programs

Laken Gilbert Albrink, Kelly E. Collinsworth, and Dianna Murphy*

> *I wanted to thank you for everything you have done to prepare me for law school. Coming from MSU as a paralegal undergrad major is proving to be very helpful. I am seeing that I have an edge over many of my classmates and even got a 13/15 on my first memo assignment (the highest grade was a 14 and the lowest was 8.5). That was our closed memo, and we are currently working on our first open memo. Research and writing are definitely the most important classes in undergrad for anyone wanting to attend law school (although they seem daunting then). I am so appreciative of the opportunity I had to get practice in research and writing! In research I have got A's on all my assignments and spend about 1/3 of the time as my fellow classmates. This helps because I can spend that time on other classes and get an advantage.... In KLEO, I got the highest grade on the mock exam (mostly, I think, because I knew how to organize it with Issue, Rule, Reasoning, Conclusion, etc.)....*
>
> —Email to Professor Murphy from 1L Laken Gilbert, October 12, 2012

HARRY POTTER AND HERMIONE GRANGER simultaneously entered Hogwarts School of Witchcraft and Wizardry. Harry, living beneath stairs and lacking parental support, had no previous exposure to Wizardry and lacked confidence in his abilities to succeed in an environment for which he had no prior context. Hermione, though a Muggle (born of non-magic parents) with no previous exposure to Wizardry, prepared for school the summer before by reading all of her textbooks. Her perfor-

* Laken Gilbert Albrink is an Assistant Professor of Legal Writing at the University of Kentucky J. David Rosenberg College of Law, a 2012 graduate of the Morehead State University Legal Studies program, and a first-generation law student. Kelly Collinsworth was an Associate Professor of Legal Studies at MSU and is currently Director of Bar Support at Southern Illinois University Simmons Law School. Dianna Murphy was Associate Dean at Morehead State University and formerly the Program Coordinator of the Legal Studies Program.

mance in class outshined even the students who had grown up in Wizarding families. Although Harry was eventually able to succeed through natural talent and support of his professors and friends, Hermione was always a step ahead. While Harry Potter is a fictional universe, its lessons in preparation of students rings true. First-generation students often feel a step behind students who grew up around the law and lawyers. However, first-gen students often excel beyond legacy students, especially after they become familiar with the language of law. The undergraduate Legal Studies program at Morehead State University (hereinafter MSU) graduates a large number of students who are both first-generation college students and future law students. These students have been extremely successful in law school and report feeling a step ahead of other students, especially during their first semester of law school. Like Hermione, these students have "read ahead."

Section I of this chapter looks at first-generation college students in MSU's Legal Studies program and their admission rates and first-year success in law school and identifies components in the program that bridged their success. In Section II, co-author Laken Gilbert Albrink, a graduate of the Legal Studies program and now Legal Writing professor, provides a personal account of her first-generation law school experience. Finally, Section III recommends ways that undergraduate institutions can replicate components from MSU's Legal Studies program to support success of first-generation students.

Section I: The Legal Studies Program

The Legal Studies program at MSU is an American Bar Association-approved program designed to prepare students with the career competencies to work as a professional paralegal. Those competencies qualify the paralegal to perform specifically delegated substantive legal work for which an attorney is responsible. Substantive legal work includes, but is not limited to, performing legal research and document review and rendering an opinion to the attorney. The program offers a Bachelor of Arts major[1] with a required 36 credit hours of Legal Studies courses and a Bachelor of Arts Area major[2] with a required 48 credit hours of Legal Studies courses.

While the program prepares students to work as paralegals, students graduating from the Legal Studies program at MSU have experienced great success in their applications to law school and degree completion. Since 2010, the program has had nearly a 100 percent acceptance rate of seniors who applied to law school, and a high number are awarded scholarships. Since 2017, at least 30 legal studies students were

1. Undergraduate Catalog, Morehead State University, https://moreheadstate.smartcatalogiq.com/2021-2022/Undergraduate-Catalog/Caudill-College-of-Arts-Humanities-and-Social-Sciences/School-of-Humanities-and-Social-Sciences/History-Philosophy-Politics-Global-Studies-and-Legal-Studies/Legal-Studies/Legal-Studies-Major-Bachelor-of-Arts (last visited May 11, 2022).

2. *Id.*

accepted to almost 30 separate law schools, including four "top 25" schools. During this period, these students collectively were offered about $2 million in law school scholarships. According to the Law School Survey of Student Engagement (LSSE), first-generation students worry more than non-first-generation students about the ability to pay for law school and living expenses, including "21% who expressed "very much" concern, compared to just 11% of students who have at least one parent with a college degree."[3]

Additionally, the program's students successfully complete law school. In the last 10 years, only two Legal Studies students, out of more than 40 students, did not complete law school after matriculation, which is better than the national attrition rate.[4] Interestingly, one of those Legal Studies students who graduated from law school became an assistant professor in the Legal Studies program at Morehead State before transitioning to teach law school.

These students' successes are particularly impressive considering the demographic makeup of students in the program and at MSU. MSU is a regional public university located in Appalachian Kentucky. There are 22 counties in the MSU Service Region.[5] Of those, 17 counties are ranked as "distressed" by the Appalachian Regional Commission. Economically distressed counties are among the bottom 10 percent of the nation's counties.[6] As a point of reference, for fiscal year 2022, 81 counties in the *entire* country are designated as distressed. Forty-eight percent of economically distressed counties in Appalachia are in Kentucky. Ninety-four percent of undergraduate students at MSU receive financial a*id.*[7]

While universities have only recently begun to officially track first-generation college student enrollment, every year at graduation, MSU asks first-generation students to stand up during commencement. It is always amazing to see more than half of students standing year after year. In programmatic feedback from 31 legal studies/law school graduates who graduated from MSU between 2012–2019, over *60 percent* of respondents were first-generation college students. According to the Law School Survey of Student Engagement (LSSE), the national rate for first-generation college students attending law school is 27%.[8]

---

3. Law School Survey of Student Engagement, https://lssse.indiana.edu/annual-results/, last visited Jan. 19, 2022).

4. Stephanie Francis Ward, *Is Sweet Spot for Avoiding Academic Attrition at Law Schools a Median LSAT of at Least 150?* A.B.A. J., https://www.abajournal.com/news/article/sweet_spot_nontransfer_attrition_law_schools_LSAT_median (last visited Jan. 20, 2022).

5. MSU Service Region, https://www.moreheadstate.edu/about-msu/strategic-plan/msu-service-region (last visited Jan. 18, 2022).

6. *Distressed Designation and County Economic Status Classification System,* Appalachian Regional Commission, https://www.arc.gov/distressed-designation-and-county-economic-status-classification-system/ (last visited Jan. 20, 2022).

7. *Supra*, note 4. Https://www.moreheadstate.edu/about-msu/at-a-glance.

8. Law School Survey of Student Engagement, Looking Ahead: Assessment in Legal Education 8, 10 (2014), http://lssse.indiana.edu/wp-content/uploads/2016/01/LSSSE_2014_AnnualReport.pdf [hereinafter *Looking Ahead*}

Students in the Legal Studies program report that the skills they learned in undergrad carried into law school and that the program contributed to their success. The courses that comprise the major are all taught by practicing attorney faculty. The core curriculum for the program looks very similar to that of the first year of law school, but with the additional requirements of Trial Practice, an internship, and a capstone course (*See* Figure A for curriculum).[9] Students in the major learn how to perform electronic legal research for primary and secondary sources, as well as print research in the library's law collection. They learn to draft motions, orders, affidavits, client letters, and memorandums. They learn the Rules of Professional Conduct. They negotiate and draft contracts. Every student in the major learns to do a title search and opinion. Every student in the major completes a mock trial. They also learn legal procedures for filing documents, calculating time deadlines, and recording billable time for clients.

Figure A

Legal Studies Major Requirements

LGS 210	Introduction to Law and Ethics	3
LGS 321	Legal Research and Writing I	3
LGS 325	Pretrial Practice	3
LGS 332	Property Law	3
LGS 334	Torts, Personal Injury Litigation and Insurance Law	3
LGS 335	Contracts and the Uniform Commercial Code	3
LGS 340	Criminal Law and Procedure	3
LGS 421	Legal Research and Writing II	3
LGS 425	Trial Practice	3
LGS 490	Legal Studies Internship I	3–6
LGS 499C	Senior Paralegal Practice Seminar	3
		Subtotal: 33

9. Undergraduate Catalog, Morehead State University, https://moreheadstate.smartcatalogiq.com/2021-2022/Undergraduate-Catalog/Caudill-College-of-Arts-Humanities-and-Social-Sciences/School-of-Humanities-and-Social-Sciences/History-Philosophy-Politics-Global-Studies-and-Legal-Studies/Legal-Studies/Legal-Studies-Major-Bachelor-of-Arts (last visited Jan. 18, 2022).

Electives

Choose six hours from the following approved electives (at least three hours must be from courses with an LGS prefix):

LGS 305	Legal Reasoning	1–3
LGS 333	Family Law	3
LGS 336	Employment Law	3
LGS 337	Corporate Law	3
LGS 345	Debtor/Creditor Relations	3
LGS 355	Administrative Law	3
LGS 360	Special Legal Topics	1–3
LGS 370	History of American Law	3
LGS 380	Global Legal Perspectives	1–3
LGS 390	Legal Studies Experiential Learning Lab	1
LGS 400	Law and Society Seminar	3
LGS 436	Wills, Trusts, and Estates	3
LGS 476	Special Problems in Legal Studies	1–3
LGS 495	Legal Studies Internship II	1–3
POLS 321	Constitutional Law: Governmental Powers	3
POLS 322	Courts and Civil Liberties	3
POLS 324	Environmental Law and Policy	3
POLS 329	Comparative Constitutional Law and Politics	3

Subtotal: 6

Additionally, every student is required to complete a 120-hour internship under the supervision of a licensed attorney. In this internship, students are expected to perform legal work at the level of a paralegal graduate. The students are not just observers or runners; they are working in the legal profession, interacting on a professional level with practicing attorneys and other legal professionals. Their performance is evaluated by supervising attorneys. An example of the criteria for evaluation is located in Appendix A. Data from these evaluations are used as part of the program's yearly assessment of programmatic goals. The students' achievements and preparedness for working with the legal profession are demonstrated by the program's 2018–2019 goal assessments that are measured by these evaluations,[10] which are shown in Figure B:

10. *See* Legal Studies BA (2019–2020), Weave Assessment Finding, on file with authors.

Figure B

Goal	Target	Finding
Students will demonstrate proficient knowledge of the rules of civil procedure.	Each student evaluated will receive a score of 4.0 on a 5.0 scale for the assessment statement, "Exhibits a basic understanding of legal procedures" on their Internship Evaluations.	All 21 students who completed an internship during this time period met the target of receiving a 4.0 or above on the internship evaluation assessment, "Exhibits a basic understanding of legal procedures for the assessment, specifically: 15 scored 5.0 and 6 scored a 4.0
Students will demonstrate achievement of proficient career skills on internship evaluations and success in their legal careers.	Ninety percent (90%) of interns will earn a minimum average score of 4.0 on a 5.0 scale after the areas of legal knowledge and skills are averaged for each student internship evaluation.	Of the 21 students completing the internship 95% scored an average of 4.0 or above on the 21 categories of assessment, specifically: 20 scored 4.0 or above; 1 scored 3.75. 16 students scored 4.8 or above. None scored below a 3 on all individual assessments.
Students will demonstrate professionalism in dress, communications with co-workers, and others.	Ninety percent (90%) of students completing their internship in the current cycle will receive a 3.0 or higher on each criterion of the professionalism section of the internship evaluations completed by the on-site supervisor.	One hundred (100%) of the 20 students scored 5.0.
Students will demonstrate effective use of technology skills relevant to the practice of law.	During this period ninety percent (90%) of student interns will earn a score of 3.0 or higher on a 5.0 scale on the evaluation of the statement, "The student demonstrated adequate skill in using law office technology." Internship Evaluations will be sent, collected, and calculated, by the program coordinator.	Of the 14 students who were evaluated, 13 scored 5.0 and 1 scored 4.0 on the assessment of their skill in using law office technology.

In addition to these required courses, students have the opportunity to take classes in a variety of legal specialty subjects where they learn practical skills such as how to use bankruptcy software to complete a Chapter 7 bankruptcy filing, how to draft and perfect a mechanic's lien, how to calculate child support, and how to draft a mediation statement, mediate, and then draft a Settlement Agreement in a divorce. Students can help actual clients with the necessary paperwork for a divorce filing through the pro se divorce clinic offered in conjunction with the local Legal Aid office and supervised by licensed program faculty. Also, the program offers students the opportunity to travel abroad through the Global Legal Perspectives course. In that course, Legal Studies faculty, often in conjunction with faculty from other disciplines, look at legal systems in different countries and then travel to those countries for one to two weeks. Many of the students who travel with the class have never been on a plane, much less left the country.

While the program is designed to prepare students for a career as a paralegal, the skill sets needed to perform paralegal work are essential skills for attorneys. The Kentucky Supreme Court defines a paralegal as:

> A person under the supervision and direction of a licensed lawyer, who may apply knowledge of law and legal procedures in rendering direct assistance to lawyers engaged in legal research; design, develop or plan modifications or new procedures, techniques, services, processes or applications; prepare or interpret legal documents and write detailed procedures for practicing in certain fields of law; select, compile and use technical information from such references as digests, encyclopedias or practice manuals; and analyze and follow procedural problems that involve independent decisions.[11]

Learning these skills before law school, while developing relationships with attorney faculty and their internship supervisors, contributes to the students' successes in law school. In a 2019 program survey, law school graduates of the legal studies program provided feedback on their law school preparedness. The results are shown below in Figure C (following page):

11. Kentucky Supreme Court Rule 3.700—Provisions relating to Paralegals.

Figure C

	STRONGLY AGREE	AGREE	SOMEWHAT AGREE	DISAGREE	STRONGLY DISAGREE
The law school advising and assistance that I received from the legal professors helped me to obtain admission to law school.	71.43% 15	23.81% 5	4.76% 1	0.00% 0	0.00% 0
The legal courses at MSU contributed to my success as a first year law student	66.67% 14	19.05% 4	14.29% 3	0.00% 0	0.00% 0
As a result of my legal studies at MSU, I was better prepared for law school than were most of the other incoming first year students.	66.67% 14	14.29% 3	14.29% 3	4.76% 1	0.00% 0
The classes at Morehead State are similar to those in Law School.	4.76% 1	28.57% 6	47.62% 10	14.29% 3	4.76% 1
I was able to learn skills at Morehead State that I have carried into Law School.	75.00% 15	20.00% 4	5.00% 1	0.00% 0	0.00% 0
Law School has prepared me for working in the legal field.	45.00% 9	25.00% 5	25.00% 5	0.00% 0	5.00% 1

The survey results show that the program contributed to student success and that the skills they learned in the program were carried into law school. The curriculum provided practice in applying concepts to real-world professional legal tasks in class, in clinics, and in internships. It advanced the development of critical thinking skills through real-world application with real consequences. While the respondents in this survey were not all first-generation law students (60% of the students in the program are first generation), we can surmise that the program helps first-generation law students to be successful. However, how specifically this "reading ahead" and exposure to the law and lawyers contributes to first-generation students' successes is better described from a first-generation graduate's own perspective.

Section II: A First-Gen College Legal Studies Grad / Now Legal Studies Professor's Perspective

It was a culture shock to attend university despite it being only 25 miles from my home. The initial shock was even greater with law school, even though it was, likewise, less than two hours from my hometown. However, having a degree in Legal Studies gave me the confidence to feel like I fit in. Being a first-generation college graduate posed many challenges academically, financially, culturally, socially, and emotionally in undergrad and law school. Graduating from the Morehead State University Legal Studies program mitigated many challenges for me that I observed other first-generation students face in law school.

Since becoming Program Coordinator of Legal Studies at Morehead State University and transitioning to Assistant Professor of Legal Writing at the University of Kentucky J. David Rosenberg College of Law, I have had the pleasure of working with students who face many of the same difficulties that I faced. Maslow's Hierarchy of Needs depicts human needs within a five-tier pyramid model[12] (See Figure D, following page). First, there are physiological needs, including eating, sleeping, drinking, and rest. Second, there is safety. We look for ways to feel safe and secure. The next level is love and belonging and feeling as though we belong to a particular group. At the fourth stage, we look for self-esteem to set us apart from others in our respective group. Motivation to perform and compete is now at its highest. Only if we meet our physical needs, feel safe, feel part of a group, and feel special within that group, can we reach the fifth stage of self-actualization where we can motivate ourselves to go beyond our individual selves and reach our full potential.

12. Saul McLeod, *Maslow's Hierarchy of Needs*, updated December 29, 2020, https://www.simplypsychology.org/maslow.html.

Figure D

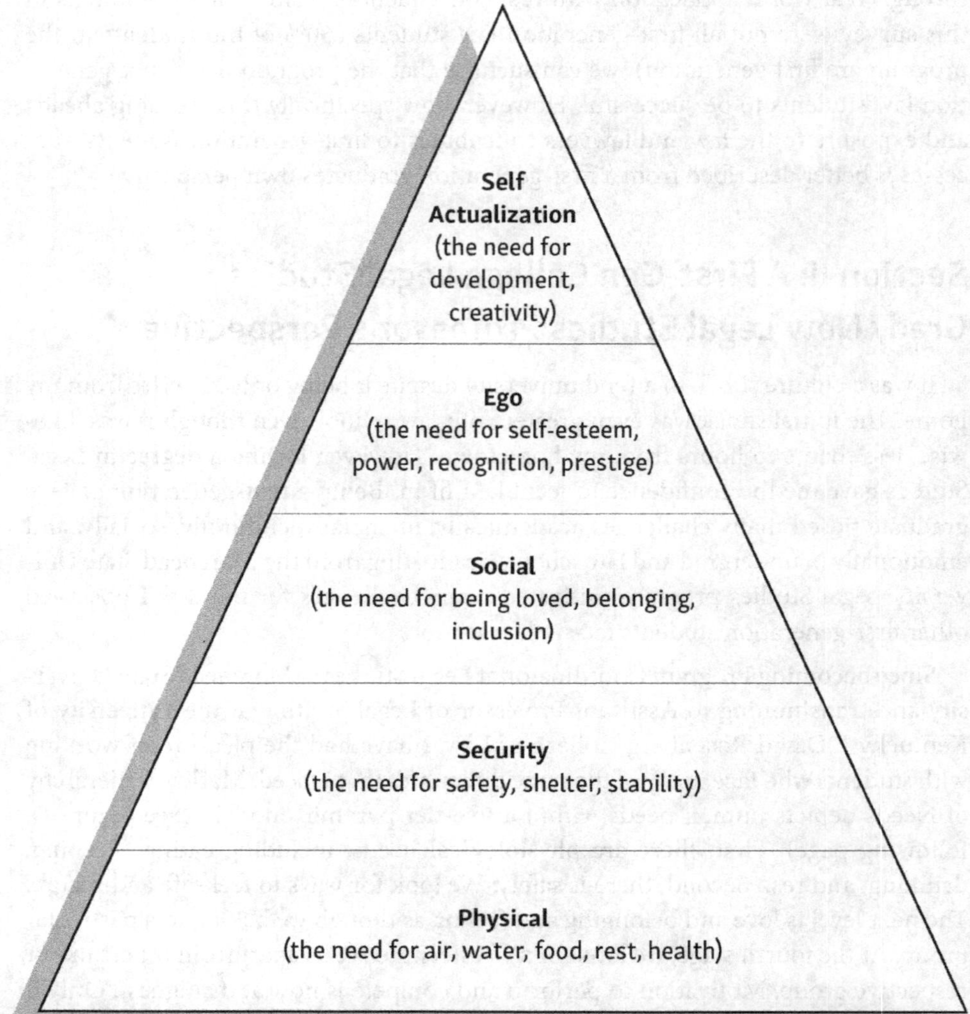

Maslow's hierarchy of needs informs us that we must create a law school environment that ensures every student is able to achieve self-actualization. First-generation students often struggle to meet needs throughout the levels of Maslow's hierarchy and may not have the support systems or resources in place to shelter them against pitfalls and struggles. My own experience confirms this.

Background

I grew up in rural northeastern Kentucky. I lived in a home riddled with addiction, abuse, poverty, and untreated mental health issues with a mother, stepfather, and four younger half-siblings. I was frequently truant in middle and high school, often spending that time working. Growing up, I witnessed many criminal activities, illicit substances, and experienced childhood abuse, caregiver incarceration, and more. In accordance with Maslow's hierarchy, my physical and safety needs were often unmet. I also struggled to obtain a sense of belonging. Growing up, I felt isolated, did not have many friends, and felt culturally and socially disconnected from my peers. I grew up with an Adverse Childhood Experience (ACE) score of 8, arguably 9, out of 10.[13] The higher the ACE's score, the greater the statistical indicators of risk of disease, social, and emotional problems.[14]

Despite academic success not being a priority in my family and being behind in high school due to truancy, I was able to graduate with the help of high school counselors. I enrolled at Morehead State University, majoring in pre-engineering. My first semester was rough. I was commuting from home and working. I struggled with online class components and completed online assignments in the parking lot late after work due to unstable internet at home. After a rough semester with a 2.0 GPA and after taking a general education class in legal studies, I switched my major to Legal Studies. Once I switched to legal studies, I found a passion for academics that kept me motivated, eventually landing a 3.409 GPA overall.

Despite the support of faculty and friends at MSU, I still struggled with meeting basic needs. Seemingly small barriers can become mountains for a student without the support most often afforded non-first-gen students. I lived in at least eight different places over four years, all with different family members, friends, or roommates (none of which were on campus). I had extensive car problems, dealt with childhood trauma, had a protective order entered against my stepfather and testified at a criminal trial, and worked (sometimes full time) at Dairy Queen almost 27 miles from the university. I missed significant class time because I fled the house I was renting due to my stepfather knowing its location prior to trial and not wanting to be found on campus. I struggled financially and relied heavily on federal grants and loans.[15]

I struggled with time management, eating healthy, getting enough sleep, maintaining healthy boundaries, self-care, and prioritizing mental health. It became difficult to achieve self-actualization when these basic needs were not being met. None of these life skills were things I was taught as a child. I also had lower expectations for my grades and postsecondary education and thought I needed to focus more on my immediate jobs. I always felt like I did not quite fit in at school but going to

---

13. Center on the Developing Child, *Take the ACE Test—and Learn What it Does and Doesn't Mean*, Harvard University, https://developingchild.harvard.edu/media-coverage/take-the-ace-quiz-and-learn-what-it-does-and-doesnt-mean/#:~:text=An%20ACE%20score%20is%20a,health%20problems%20later%20in%20life (last visited Jan. 20, 2022)

14. *What Does Your Ace Score Mean?*, Stop Abuse Campaign, https://stopabusecampaign.org/take-your-ace-test/what-does-your-ace-score-mean/ (last visited Jan. 20, 2022).

15. As of the date of this draft, I owe $145,596.14 total in student loans ($120,381.01 in principal, $25,215.13 in interest) and am hoping for public loan forgiveness.

school made me not quite fit in at home. Away from school I would find myself minimizing my achievements. There was also extreme guilt about leaving siblings behind in a tumultuous situation

Fortunately, having a legal studies degree helped me, because through the rigorous academic content I developed strong academic skills. I had professors who I trusted and from whom I was able to seek guidance. Specifically, I remember being able to talk to my professors during our study abroad trip about my anxiety about my impending testimony at my stepfather's criminal trial. Legal studies made me view my family's legal issues in a more mature manner. Likewise, my family's legal issues made me view the legal system through the lens that access to justice is not equitable. This infused my passion to pursue law as a career.

I also studied abroad twice, in Asia and in Europe. I worked on political campaigns. I was Student Government Member of the Year, Outstanding Undergraduate in Paralegal Studies, and Kentucky Young Democrat of the Year. I graduated college within four years and was accepted to the University of Kentucky College of Law.

Having faculty who have been to law school teach legal studies courses benefited me greatly with acquiring the confidence to apply for law school, navigating the law school admissions process, making law school material easier to understand, becoming familiar with professionalism in the field, and obtaining mentors I continue to seek guidance from.

Deciding to apply to law school was incredibly intimidating, especially since obtaining a bachelor's degree had seemed like a pipe dream not that long ago. Applying to law school can be a daunting experience for any student, but particularly for those without family who have experience with higher education. However, because I had attorney faculty, I was able to seek advice and guidance during the process. I received help with practice LSATs, LSAT tips, and critiques of my law school applications. Both of my legal studies professors (and co-authors) wrote my letters of recommendation. This was certainly enhanced by the small faculty-student ratio in legal studies and the high level of involvement faculty have with students in and out of class. They also helped me to negotiate a scholarship for law school when I was not offered one upon admission.

As a Law Student

While meeting my basic needs such as transportation, money for food and gas, and housing was still problematic, I found that I was able to perform much better than I expected. I obtained a 3.520 grade point average for my first year of law school with "A" grades in Legal Research and Writing, Contracts II, Property Law, and Torts (A-). Despite being at the lower tier of the admissions index, I achieved the "best brief for appellant" for my writing class section.

I found that having had two semesters of legal research and writing prior to attending law school was perhaps my strongest advantage both in my legal research and writing course and in conveying clear exam responses. I entered law school able to find primary and secondary authorities using print and electronic resources (such as Westlaw and LexisNexis) and Shepardize. I could readily cite authorities, write objective and persuasive memoranda, draft pleadings, client letters, and more. I spent less time looking up unfamiliar words than my classmates did and was able to understand procedural history much easier. I was less anxious about being called on via the Socratic method because I could efficiently read and accurately understand the cases.

Having had professors who actively practiced law helped expose me to practical legal assignments to which my peers were not exposed. Seeing practical application of theoretical principles helped me better understand the theoretical material taught in law school. Having familiarity with terms such as the *mailbox rule*, *parol evidence* (and how to properly pronounce it), *unconscionable*, *anticipatory repudiation*, and *contract of adhesion*, was extremely helpful.

Likewise, I was able to craft stronger policy arguments when called on because I had classes in undergrad where we discussed the policy and dichotomies of legal interests. Having had conversations about the interests of each party helped me better understand and articulate case discussions in law school. One of my fondest law school memories was being called on in Contracts to discuss a case on unconscionable contract provisions. The parties willingly entered into the contract, and I was tasked with explaining why the court would not uphold the contract. I was able to articulate that sometimes provisions are just so unfair the courts should not enforce them even if entered into willingly. Being a legal studies major and a first-generation college graduate gave me a perspective not shared by most of my classmates, specifically, that the courts have a role in protecting the vulnerable among us from predatory practices.

More importantly, I was able to complete research and writing assignments much more quickly than my peers, which allowed me time to focus more on personal matters, as my family home burned my first year of law school. It was also financially advantageous that I kept many of the textbooks I used in the legal studies program. As a first-generation college graduate in law school, I had a difficult time affording extra study materials such as hornbooks and outlines. While there were some accessible through the law library, they were often in use by other students. It was extremely helpful to refer to my legal studies textbooks when creating law school outlines. I could see the forest while also figuring out where all the trees were supposed to go.

Another benefit of my Legal Studies background was that I did not feel forced to take bar topic classes during law school since I had already taken many of those topics in undergrad. Instead, I was able to pursue study in areas for which I had more interest and passion, such as a sex crimes seminar, women and the law, ADR, negotiations, and children and the law. This was advantageous as these courses supported much of my professional work since law school. My legal studies professors were also pivotal in helping me negotiate a lower bar exam prep course fee, which I did not know was possible, and I ended up spending much less than most of my peers.

Getting law clerk positions was much easier because of my Legal Studies experience. While in undergrad, my Administrative Law adjunct professor was an attorney with the Kentucky Office of Attorney General. He helped me secure an internship with the Office of the Attorney General, Division of Consumer Protection. At that time, that office did not accept undergraduate students for internships but made an exception. That internship was critical to my long-term success. In most (if not all) of my job interviews thereafter, that internship experience was a point of discussion. I even ended up working for my internship supervisor after I graduated law school. The work I did in the Division of Consumer Protection gave me important talking points for internship/clerkship interviews. Again, I was able to witness how legal concepts learned in class were used in practice through both my internship experience and the anecdotal discussions my practicing attorney-professors provided.

For example, the Kentucky Rules of Civil Procedure Rule 7.01 provides:

> There shall be a complaint and an answer; a reply to counterclaim denominated as such; an answer to a cross-claim, if the answer contains a cross-claim; a third-party complaint, if leave is given under Rule 14 to summon a person who was not an original party; and a third-party answer, if a third-party complaint is served. No other pleading shall be allowed, except that the court may order a reply to an answer or a third-party answer.

Reading this rule indicates the definition of pleading is limited to those documents explicitly listed in the rule. When tasked with organizing the pleadings of a case, I was extremely confused, because there were many more documents than those listed to be organized. I was able to reach out to my professor and learn that "pleading" is often used in practice to describe any document filed with the court requiring service to the other party(ies). That type of knowledge is invaluable and only derived from connections with people who have practiced law.

As an Attorney and Professor

First-generation students often cannot afford many of the supports to move up Maslow's hierarchy to self-actualization. My Legal Studies program elevated my sense that I "belonged." It is easier to meet your physiological needs if you can spend less time studying and more time acquiring food/housing. Law school was like working a puzzle, and my legal studies degree had given me the opportunity to see the picture before I started working on that puzzle. I was able to allocate some time from law school studies to attend to basic needs.

While being a first-gen student was incredibly difficult for a number of reasons, my experiences also give me a perspective when practicing law and teaching that many do not have. I can relate to my clients, because I understand the struggles they have to get off work, get filing fees together, and bring kids to appointments because they cannot afford a sitter. I appreciate and support the need for social justice and recognize the hurdles that impede access to justice. These skills are critical for the legal profession.

As a professor, I continue to incorporate the skills training that I found so important for my law school success. While teaching at Morehead State, I created and taught a negotiations course. I supervised the Pro Se Divorce Clinic and student staff. And, in 2021, I won first place in the American Association for Paralegal Education (AAfPE) National Teaching Competition for my lecture titled "Applying Statues." I supervised the internships for the Legal Studies program and shared anecdotes about my experience and offered myself as a resource like my professors were for me. I conducted class in a trauma-informed manner and leaned into the topics that impact our students and their families, such as consumer protection and domestic relations, and I provided resource links, like the consumer complaint form at the Office of the Attorney General. I proactively reach out to students who seem to be struggling and provide resources like the University's financial resources for students struggling with transportation or food insecurity.

I continue to be very transparent and communicative about class expectations, but I strive to encourage and include student input and routinely ask them what they need from me to be successful. In undergraduate teaching, for example, I was flexible with policies that could disproportionately impact students, such as method of submitting assignments. I incorporated activities during class time rather than outside of class to reduce the burden on students who work or take care of family. For example, I took the pro se divorce clinic class to the University suit bank to find professional clothes as a course requirement. In property law, where students must complete a title search during the county clerk's business hours, I dedicated class time to the project and was present in the clerk's office to guide students. For some classes, I created an optional class group text so students could text me and each other questions without anyone's numbers being disclosed. Finally, I used a quiz website where students (optionally) answer questions in class as a competition. This gave me live feedback on whether they learned the course objectives for that class session and they simultaneously got excited about competing against each other.

Maslow's hierarchy of needs and my life experience tell me that students cannot learn and reach their potential without having basic needs met. As professors, we have to meet our students where they are and help them learn. I am very honest with my students about my background, because it is important for them to see someone who has faced similar struggles represented in the legal field. Sometimes, professors may need to connect students with university and community resources for their needs to be sufficiently met. Once those needs are met, professors can help students achieve success both in the class and out. For example, in the Legal Studies program, I provided opportunities to expand students' self-actualization through undergraduate research fellowships, clinical opportunities, and internships.

Section III: Incorporating Successful Practices at Your University

Students from the Legal Studies program are successful applying for and performing in law school because they have developed legal reasoning skills and had broad exposure to the legal profession. While adding an entire Legal Studies program for undergraduate students may not be possible for your institution, certainly some of the key components could be added.

First-gen students need a way into the profession, and they need support to get there and be successful. At the undergraduate level, universities could offer legal research and writing courses as an avenue to foster critical thinking through legal reasoning.[16] This will develop career skills while demonstrating to students that they can do the work, thereby increasing students' sense of confidence. The MSU Legal Studies program consistently receives feedback from our law school grads that it takes about one-third of the time to complete their legal research in law school because of having taken Legal Research and Writing in undergrad. This develops and hones critical thinking and writing skills and introduces legal concepts and terminology. "Reading ahead" leaves them more time to allocate to their other courses, activities, family concerns, and employment.

It is important that the legal courses be taught by attorney professors who can uniquely bridge the student to the profession. Attorney faculty serve as a key access point to the profession. They provide consistent professional interaction with students and can connect students with career-relevant, high-impact practices, such as legal internships and service learning through participation in pro bono or pro se clinics.

While most undergraduate institutions provide prelaw advising, first-generation college students are less likely to interact with faculty prelaw advisors.[17] Institutions need to invest in effective prelaw advising which is accomplished by appointing attorney faculty as active prelaw advisors. These faculty speak law school; they have been through the admissions process and know what to expect. But they also need to be highly visible to students. They need to speak to first-year classes; provide

16. A sample Course Unit Description from MSU's Legal Research & Writing I course is provided in Appendix B.

17. *See First-Generation Students in Law School: A Proven Success Model*, 70 ARK. L. REV. 913, 946–947 (2013).

LSAT study sessions, LSAT prep materials, and simulated LSAT testing; provide orientation on the law school application process; and they need to provide feedback to students on personal statements. They also need to develop relationships with law schools and regularly invite law school admissions representatives to campus. They must ensure that these and other co-curricular events are advertised on social media, in online platforms, and direct emails to advisees. These events incorporate opportunities for faculty and students to interact. Providing a space for attorney faculty to talk with students about their struggles increases students' identification with attorneys. Graduates from the Legal Studies program continue to contact their attorney professors from the program for guidance, support, and mentoring.

Establishing a prelaw internship program would also provide opportunities for students to connect with attorneys in the profession and to become more comfortable with the legal world. However, to be worthwhile, the program would need to have established worksites where students could be placed since it would be difficult, if not impossible, for first-gen students to make these connections on their own. It would also be important for students to have had some practical legal classes, minimally a legal research and writing course, before engaging in the internship. Otherwise, a student's participation may be limited to that of an observer, which, while having some value, likely does not provide the confidence boost and support that truly benefits the students.

Finally, paying for law school, and imagining how to pay for necessities when you are not expected to work during the first year of law school, is a major obstacle for first-generation students. Newly proposed revisions to ABA Standard 507[18] would require law schools to provide financial aid and debt information to their admitted students. Previously, schools had been required to only provide debt counseling before a student secured their loan, which usually meant some type of financial aid seminar at Law School Orientation prior to the student signing their financial aid promissory note. By that time, it is really too late for the information to be useful. And for the prelaw student deciding whether they should even apply to law school, even this new standard will not be sufficient. Providing financial aid and budget planning for prelaw students is essential. That can be easily instituted by prelaw advisors by encouraging their students to engage with the AccessLex Institute Max Prelaw web page.[19] This easily accessible, free resource provides learning modules for prelaw students in a variety of topics.

One of the major hurdles that an institution would have to overcome in implementing either a Legal Studies program, or even the more minimal suggestions listed in this section, would be the hiring of practicing attorney faculty. There is a long history of members of the academy viewing academic lawyers as not belonging and

---

18. ABA Final Recommendations: Standards 205, 303, 507, and 508, https://taxprof.typepad.com/files/aba-council.pdf.

19. https://www.accesslex.org/max-pre-law.

considering law an unacademic discipline.[20] Allocating available faculty lines to licensed attorneys may face backlash. And even a Ph.D./J.D. will not ensure credentials that are aligned with student learner outcomes of skills-based training, connections for legal internships, and hands-on service learning unless the Ph.D./J.D. also has a law license and has practiced law beyond a judicial clerkship. In most states, supervising students participating in high-impact practices, specifically legal internships and clinics, requires supervision by a licensed attorney. The Legal Studies program at MSU requires its attorney faculty members to have a minimum of five years as a practicing attorney with experience supervising paralegals. Additionally, the attorney professors should be full-time faculty members, rather than adjuncts, so that students have consistent access to the attorney professor and the attorney professor is committed to the program.

In addition to providing experienced, practicing attorneys, the university needs to provide release time from teaching duties for prelaw advising and funding support for high-impact practices, such as establishing experiential clinics in conjunction with local legal aid providers. These high-impact practices are essential for retention, particularly in relation to first-generation students who do not have ready access to the profession.[21]

Section IV: Conclusion

In the setting of an undergraduate legal studies program, there is no reason we cannot encourage every student, regardless of their circumstances and experiences, to meet their potential and follow their passions. We can help them advance, learn, develop new skills, and gain the confidence they need to be successful in law school and in legal practice. We can help them "read ahead" like Hermione Granger so that they are prepared for that next step. For students who do not have the benefit of an undergraduate legal studies program, Law Schools can provide preadmission support, encouragement, and opportunities to engage with law classes and legal professionals with whom they can identify. After all, any one of them may go on to save the world, or at least some small piece of it, one day.

---

20. *See, e.g.*, Gene Shreve, *Is Law an Academic Discipline? Forays into Academic Culture*, 68 Clev. St. L. Rev. 217 (2020).

21. *See, e.g.*, Theresa Conefrey, *Supporting First-Generation Students' Adjustment to College with High-Impact Practices*, J. Coll. Student Retention: Rsch, Theory & Practice, 2021; 23(1):139-160. https://www.researchgate.net/publication/328622318_Supporting_First-Generation_Students'_Adjustment_to_College_With_High-Impact_Practices.

Appendix A: Student Internship Evaluation Form

Student's Name:

On a scale between 1 and 5 inclusive (1=inadequate, 3=satisfactory, 5=excellent), please evaluate the student's performance in each area below. Please use N/A if you were unable to adequately evaluate the student in a particular area. Thank you.

ATTITUDE Scale (1–5)

ATTITUDE	Scale (1–5)
Mature Attitude	
Pleasant and courteous	
Tactful and considerate	
Professional demeanor with clients	
Professional demeanor with co-workers	
Handles constructive instruction in a professional manner	
Appropriately attired for office	

SKILLS AND WORK HABITS

SKILLS AND WORK HABITS	Scale (1–5)
Completes work in a timely manner	
Meets deadlines for assigned work	
Understands the task assigned	
Completed work is relevant to the assigned task	
Is reliable	
Exhibits initiative	
Exhibits mature judgment	
Is resourceful in gathering information	
Communicates effectively with supervisor	
Is able to effectively summarize information	
Organizes information appropriately	

continued

continued

LEGAL KNOWLEDGE Scale (1–5)

Exhibits a basic knowledge of legal procedures	
Exhibits familiarity with filing/recording methods	
Exhibits effective interviewing techniques	
Exhibits an understanding of fact-gathering methods	
Is able to perform basic legal research	
Coherently analyzes research and information	
Skill level drafting routine documents and pleadings	
Skill level drafting correspondence	
Skill level summarizing depositions	
Effective use of office technology	
Overall GRADE:	

(A=excellent, B=good, C=satisfactory, D=below average, E=not satisfactory)

Appendix B: Sample Unit Description for Legal Research and Writing I

Unit I: Sources of Law

This course will serve as a comprehensive introduction to several important aspects of the legal system and the practice of law.

Objectives:

1. Sources of law. In other words, where "the law" comes from.
2. How the law is made and how it is recorded.
3. How the law is applied to legal disputes and concerns.
4. How to find law relevant to a specific legal dispute or concern.
5. How to interpret law that you find.
6. How to write to others in the legal profession about the law.

UNIT 1 will focus on the basics. Consider it a refresher on American civics. We will review the U.S. Constitution and how it works, we will discuss how the three branches of government interact, and we will familiarize ourselves with the various state and federal court systems in the United States.

Unit II: Statutory Law

The unit reviews how to locate and interpret federal or state law, including statutes and regulations. Instruction will include how to locate laws using secondary sources, citations, and indexes. Basic rules of statutory interpretation will be reviewed.

Objectives:

1. Locate statutes relevant to a given fact pattern or issue using legal citations and electronic and paper indexes.
2. Identify the relevant statutes of an Act. Describe basic rules of statutory interpretation.
3. Identify the prevailing law when two or more laws conflict with one another.
4. Locate case law using annotations and other secondary sources.
5. Demonstrate how secondary sources can be used to better understand laws.

Unit III: Case Law

The unit reviews how to locate a court opinion using proper legal citations. We will learn how to correctly analyze court decisions and use those decisions as precedent to predict the outcome of new fact patterns. And we will learn to summarize our case analysis in the form of a case brief or memorandum.

Objectives:

1. Use citations to locate court opinions.
2. Identify the parts of a court opinion.
3. Analyze the issue and holding of an opinion.
4. Identify the rule of law in an opinion and the key facts used by the court in its reasoning.
5. Accurately summarize a case opinion in the form of a written or oral case brief.
6. Apply case precedent to logically predict how the court would resolve new facts.

Unit IV: Synthesizing Legal Research

In this unit, students use electronic research methods to locate relevant law and precedent. Students will analyze multiple cases to identify common fact patterns. Students will synthesize these patterns to extract and articulate a common rule of law. The rule of law will be applied to a new fact situation to predict how the court may rule. The prediction will be supported by comparing and contrasting the new facts with those of the fact pattern synthesized from the reported cases.

Objectives:

1. Locate relevant case law and authority for a given issue.
2. Analyze cases to identify common patterns.
3. Analyze the pattern to extract and articulate a rule of law that explains the pattern.
4. Apply the rule of law to new facts to predict the outcome and support the prediction by comparing and contrasting the synthesized fact pattern, or reason, with new facts.

Unit V: Final Memo

PART IV Pre-Orientation and Orientation Programming

Twelve

Why Do Law Schools Need Early Programming?

Melissa A. Hale*

"IF YOU BUILD IT, THEY WILL COME." It's a cliché quote, but in this instance it's true. Building summer programming, either pre-orientation or as a compliment to orientation, will help attract first-generation students to your law school. This chapter will focus on the benefits of admitting more first-generations students, and what types of first-generation programming law schools can implement to attract and support those students.

Diversity, or Lack Thereof, in the Legal Profession

Historically, the legal profession has been lacking in diversity, and that remains true today. As of Jan. 1, 2024, there were 1,322,649 active lawyers in the U.S., an increase of 3.2% in the past decade.[1] While white lawyers no longer drive that growth (which has changed since 2020), they are still being overrepresented in the legal profession compared to the U.S. population. The representation of non-Hispanic white lawyers in the profession dropped 10% in the last decade, but non-Hispanic white lawyers still make up 78% of the profession, in comparison to 58.4% of U.S. residents that are non-Hispanic white people. Recent gains among people of color has outpaced the slow increase in female lawyers over the past decade. The percentage of lawyers of color almost doubled in the last decade, growing 11% (12% in 2014 vs. 23% in 2024), while the percentage of female lawyers increased only 5% during that same time period (36% in 2014 vs. 41% in 2024). The story is less promising when broken out by race and ethnicity. Just 5% of all lawyers are Black, the same percentage as 10 years ago, while 13.7% of the U.S. population is Black. Comparably,

* Melissa is the Associate Director of Curriculum at Helix Bar Review. Prior to that she was the Director of Academic Success at Loyola University Chicago, and has been working in academic support for 15 years, focusing on supporting first generation students. She is also the author of "A First Generation's Guide to Law School" and "The Ultimate Guide to the UBE." This chapter was written by Melissa as an individual and the views expressed are her own, and do not represent the views of Helix Bar Review.

1. ABA Profile of the Legal Profession 2024, https://www.americanbar.org/news/profile-legal-profession/demographics/ (last visited Jan. 29, 2025).

6% of all lawyers are Hispanic, up from 4% a decade earlier, although 19.5% of the U.S. population.[2]

The legal profession has taken measures to gatekeep within the profession for centuries. As soon as the legal profession started adopting regulatory efforts, those efforts showed evidence of bias against women, people of color, immigrants, Catholics—frankly, anyone who was not a white Protestant man.[3] I would even go further and say that these regulatory efforts excluded anyone that wasn't a *wealthy* white Protestant man.

During the eighteenth century, law schools didn't exist, meaning that to become a lawyer, one had to seek out and complete an apprenticeship with another lawyer. This meant gatekeeping was endemic, because there was no way to become a lawyer without knowing one. Legal education, or the advent of law schools, started in the 1800s, and by 1860, all but two states had established a bar exam.[4] Initially this exam was oral and informal, which still perpetuated a system of exclusion since it typically meant that you still had to know a lawyer to become part of the profession.[5] As law schools became more common and the law became a course of graduate study, the ABA pushed for a law degree to be a mandatory part of bar admission.[6] Graduation from an ABA-accredited law school was a prerequisite for sitting for the bar exam in all but a few states by 1941, and remains that way today.[7] The bar exam is still gatekeeping the profession, and by doing so, making it harder for the legal profession to become more diverse. Standardized tests create systems where the more privilege one has, the easier it becomes to succeed on the test. Systematic disadvantages, starting in early childhood, work to decrease the scores of students from disadvantaged backgrounds.[8] For example, if a test-taker is hungry, working full-time, or lacks adequate housing, these things can make it harder to be successful on the bar exam.[9] Moreover, specialized prep courses for standardized exams are expensive, so more privileged students tend to do better.[10] "High stake exams, from kindergarten through the bar, solidify the position of well-to-do elites."[11]

---

2. *Id.*
3. Lisa Lerman et al., Ethical Problems in the Practice of Law 18 (5th ed. 2020).
4. *Id.* at 18.
5. *Id.* at 19.
6. *Id.*
7. *Id.*
8. Claudia Angelos, Mary Lu Bilek, Carol L. Chomsky, Andrea A. Curcio, Marsha Griggs, Joan W. Howarth, Eileen Kaufman, Deborah Jones Merritt, Patricia E. Salkin & Judith Welch Wegner, *Licensing Lawyers in a Pandemic: Proving Competence*, Harvard Law Review Blog (April 7, 2020), https://blog.harvardlawreview.org/licensing-lawyers-in-a-pandemic-proving-competence/; Oday Yousif Jr., *Commentary: The Bar Exam Is Stained with Inequality and Racism. It Needs to Be Abolished*, San Diego Union-Trib. (Dec. 7, 2020).
9. *Id.*
10. *Id.*
11. *Id.*

The history of legal education therefore is undeniably one of a profession that effectively excluded anyone not white, male, and wealthy. In fact, Alexis de Tocqueville once observed;

> In America there are no nobles or literaly men, and the people are apt to mistrust the wealthy; lawyers consequently form the highest political class and most cultivated portion of scoeity. They have therefore nothing to gain by innovation, which address a conservative interest to their natural taste for public order. If I were asked where I place the American aristocracy, I should reply without hestitation that it is not among the rich, who are united by no common tie, but that it occupies the judicial bench and the bar.[12]

Unfortunately—but equally undeniably—many of these exclusions still exist today. Our profession is still fighting to maintain the status quo, even if it doesn't fully recognize that it is doing so.

The legal system, and law school itself, is structured to be more difficult for those who did not grow up with privilege. This is because law school is historically difficult and time-consuming, meaning that without generational wealth, it can be a challenge to even attend, much less thrive. In order to create diversity within the legal profession, which benefits society as a whole, we need to increase diversity within our law schools. The American Bar Association is now supporting diversity endeavors by adopting Standard 211, which requires an "Equal Opportunity Effort," demanding that law schools affirmatively seek out and provide special help to minority students.[13]

However, it is not enough to simply increase the number of underrepresented students at the point of admission; law schools must provide admitted students with the tools to thrive and belong.

Who Is a First Gen Student, and Why Do They Benefit Diversity?

A good way to increase diversity is to attract first-generation students, which is a group that is often overlooked when discussing diversity.[14] There is significant intersectionality between first-generation students and historically underrepresented BIPOC students. So, attracting more first-generation students to law schools will

---

12. ALEXIS DE TOCQUEVILLE, DEMOCRACY IN AMERICA 307, Chapter XVI: Causes Mitigation Tyranny in the United States Part 1, 1831.

13. American Bar Association, *Legal Education Standards*, https://www.americanbar.org/content/dam/aba/publications/misc/legal_education/Standards/2013_2014_standards_chapter2.pdf (last visited Oct. 28, 2022).

14. Jacqueline M. O'Bryant & Katharine Traylor Schaffzin, *First-Generation Students In Law School: A Proven Success Model*, 70 ARK. L. REV. 913, 914 (2018).

help increase the diversity of the school, and eventually the profession. According to the Law School Survey of Student Engagement, or LSSSE, 27.5% of law students are first generation, meaning neither parent nor guardian holds a bachelor's degree.[15] Of this percentage, 54.4% of first-generation students are white.[16] However, 40.4% of Black or African American students, 52.1% of Mexican or Mexican American, 31.3% of Puerto Rican, and 41.4% of Native American students identify as first-generation.[17]

According to The Center for First-generation Student Success, a first-generation student is one whose parents or legal guardians have not completed bachelor's degrees—they are the first in their families to attend a four-year school and graduate.[18] In the past decade, high school graduates whose parents did not attend a four-year university are beginning to enter undergraduate institutions at a high rate. This means that many first-generation students are also entering graduate school.[19]

Attracting first-generation students isn't just great for diversity, but it's great for the school and the profession! This is because first-generation students bring with them diversity of background. Essentially, diversity of thought is always a good thing, especially for a profession that works to advocate for others. We need lawyers to represent diverse clients, and often clients feel more comfortable with attorneys who have a familiar background.

What Deficits and Strengths Do First Gen Students Bring to the Table?

In all professions and cultures there are unwritten rules and norms, generally learned over a considerable amount of time. These rules are not usually stated in any explicit way, but are picked up by watching those around us. For first-generation students, even after having made it through a four-year undergraduate course, they still may not have mastered all the unwritten rules and norms, and then they enter law school, which has even more unwritten norms! This means that most first-generation students come to law school with considerable hurdles: lower access to finances, lower social capital (i.e., fewer networking connections), lack of exposure to professional norms and, finally, hurdles related to academic preparation, especially when so much of the language used in law school might be brand-new to them. Most first-generation students themselves come to law school with concerns surrounding

---

15. Law School Survey on Student Engagement, LSSSE Survey Tool 2024, https://lssse.indiana.edu/about-lssse-surveys/ 1 (last visited Jan. 29, 2025).

16. *Id.*

17. *Id.*

18. *FAQ: First-Gen Definition*, Center for First-generation Success, https://firstgen.naspa.org/why-first-gen/students/are-you-a-first-generation-student(Last visited Oct. 28, 2022).

19. Steven Foster et al., *Closing the Law School Gap: A Collaborative Effort to Address Educational Inequities Through Free, Asynchronous Tools* , 14 J. Marshall L.J. 116, 123 (2021).

academic success, their career path, building a professional network, finances, and family obligations.[20]

One of the biggest challenges of first-generation law students is entering their first year with a lack of resources, and often bearing an "achievement gap." The "achievement gap" refers to the disparity in academic performance—grades, standardized test scores, dropout rates, college-completion rates, even course selection and long-term success—between groups of students. In this instance, we are referring to the gap between students who have had parents complete some form of higher education and those that have not. The Close the Gap Foundation refers to this as "the opportunity gap" instead of the achievement gap, and specifically states that it is "the way that uncontrollable life factors like race, language, economic, and family situations can contribute to lower rates of success in educational achievement, career prospects, and other life aspirations."[21]

This is true even for first-generation students who were high achievers in the past—they simply have not been exposed to the language of the law or the norms of the profession. This puts them at a disadvantage compared with their peers, even before they enter orientation. In addition, many students know that they are at a disadvantage, and therefore may also enter law school with a severe case of imposter syndrome,[22] furthering their disadvantage. When students enter with imposter syndrome, they will persist with feelings of doubt, creating an even larger achievement gap between them and their peers, even if they are objectively performing well.[23]

In addition, to improve legal education, "belonging must enter the conversation."[24] Creating a sense of belonging is important for the success and retention of students.[25] "A sense of belonging is linked to positive academic outcomes, such as increased academic motivation, engagement, intent to persist, and achievement."[26]

While it's true that all students may face challenges and question their sense of belonging during law school, law students from disadvantaged social back-

---

20. *Id.* at 124.

21. *Opportunity Gap*, Close the Gap Foundation, https://www.closethegapfoundation.org/glossary/opportunity-gap?gclid=Cj0KCQjwspKUBhCvARIsAB2IYuscRgwXvBQgnHlxQtXJ34Bw4m8g4X_HdMdS_csWATPxgPN0dzuk6eUaAuwKEALw_wcB (last visited May 18, 2022).

22. *Imposter syndrome* is defined as a psychological pattern in which an individual doubts their skills, talents, or accomplishments and has a persistent internalized fear of being exposed as a "fraud." Joe Langford & Pauline Rose Clance, *The Imposter Phenomenon: Recent Research Findings Regarding Dynamics, Personality, and Family Patterns and Their Implications for Treatment*, Psychotherapy, Vol 30 #3, Fall 1993, https://paulineroseclance.com/pdf/-Langford.pdf.

23. Foster et al., 14 J. Marshall L.J. 116 at 125.

24. Elizabeth Bodamer, *Do I Belong Here? Examining Perceived Experience of Bias, Stereotype Concerns, and Sense of Belonging in U.S. Law Schools*, 69 J. Legal Educ .455, 456 (2020).

25. *Id.*

26. *Id.*

grounds—such as first-generation students—may wonder if they truly belong.[27] When students face difficulties in the first week of law school, such as any difficulty reading cases, or struggling with the Socratic method, they tend to interpret these difficulties as evidence that they do not belong, and in turn, this can become a self-fulfilling prophecy.[28] "When students worry that they may not belong in law school, they are more likely to experience anxiety that can interfere with learning and are less likely to reach out to faculty, join study groups, seek out friends, or succeed in the law school environment over time."[29]

Because of this, law schools and legal educators need to help combat this achievement gap, and foster a sense of belonging, long before the first-generation students enter orientation. This is because with proper nurturing, certain so-called disadvantages can be reinterpreted as differences rather than shortcomings.[30]

To start, it is far more likely that first-generation students will be providing care for a dependent, either a parent or a child. In fact, 11.3% of first-generation students care for a dependent more than 35 hours per week, as compared to only 5.2% of non-first-generation students.[31] In addition, first-generation students typically end up working more hours, either in legal or non-legal jobs, than their non-first-generation counterparts.

More time-consuming obligations like working for pay and caregiving lead to less time for study, and as a result, the grades of first-generation students trend lower than non-first-generation students.

In the LSSSE survey, 11,7% of non-first-generation students receive As, and 19.7% receive A-s, whereas for first-generation students, only 8.8% receive As, and 14.4% receive A-s.[32] While this might not seem like a staggering gap, without networking and family connections, first-generation students have to rely more heavily on grades for job prospects.

For first-generation students, job placement can be an issue as well. According to the National Association for Law Placement (NALP), law school graduates with at least one parent with a J.D. parent have about a 5% higher employment rate than

27. Victor D. Quintanilla, LSSSE Website, *Guest Post: A LSSSE Collaboration on the Role of Belonging in Law School Experience and Performance*, Jan 25, 2019 (https://lssse.indiana.edu/blog/role-of-belonging-in-law-school-experience-and-performance/)

28. *Id.*

29. *Id.*

30. Kenneth Oldfield, *Humble and Hopeful: Welcoming First-Generation Poor and Working-Class Students to College* (February 14, 2007), About Campus, January–February 2007, available at SSRN: https://ssrn.com/abstract=3018703

31. Law School Survey on Student Engagement, LSSSE Survey Tool 2024, https://lssse.indiana.edu/about-lssse-surveys/ 1 (Last visited Jan. 29, 2025).

32. *Id.*

their first-generation counterparts.[33] They are also 11% more likely to be employed in jobs that require bar passage.[34] Unfortunately, the bad news for first-generation students doesn't stop there. Law school graduates with lawyers for parents are 62.7% more likely to get a job in private practice, and more likely—by 13.6%—to get a clerkship.[35] In addition, lawyers who have parents, and even grandparents, as lawyers end up with higher median salaries than first-generation students..[36] This is true even when compared to students who had parents with four-year degrees but were not lawyers. Specifically, the median salary for students with parents who also had a J.D. was $13,000 higher while students whose parents had a college education were $8,000 higher. [37]

According to NALP's executive director James Leipold:

> Social capital here would include things like networks of relationships, understanding of professional norms, confidence and comfort interacting in a professional setting, but also can include things like wardrobe. Students with a parent who went to law school bring more familiarity with those unspoken rules and norms of the legal profession with them than do students whose parents are not lawyers, and certainly more than students whose parents have not attended college.[38]

However, this is not all bad news. Law schools can, *and should*, help to fix these deficits. According to Professor Victor Quintanilla, citing research done using LSSSE data:

> [W]orries about belonging are endemic to law school. That's the bad news. And, in my opinion, that's why many fall to the wayside. It's not because of LSAT scores or a lack of motivation. It's just darn difficult to succeed when you don't feel like you are a part of something, that you belong within the community, that you are welcome and embraced as vital law school participants.[39]

Prof. Quintanilla further explains that the quality of a student's relationships with other students, faculty, and administrators significantly predicts one's sense of be-

---

33. *NALP Reports Employment Outcomes for First-Generation College Students Fall Below Those of Their Peers, and Disparities in Outcomes by Race/Ethnicity Persist*, NALP Press Release, October 20, 2021, https://www.nalp.org/uploads/PressReleases/NALPPressReleaseJobsandJDs_20October2021.pdf (last visited Jan 19th, 2022)

34. *Id.*

35. *Id.*

36. *Id.*

37. *Id.*

38. Mike Stetz, *First-Generation Grads Face Uphill Battle in Career Opportunities*, NAT'L JURIST, November 2, 2021, https://nationaljurist.com/national-jurist-magazine/first-generation-grads-face-uphill-battle-career-opportunities last visited January 16th, 2022).

39. Scott Johns, *The Importance of Relationships in Enhancing Belonging and Academic Achievement*, Law School Academic Support Blog, Aug. 29, 2019, https://lawprofessors.typepad.com/academic_support/2019/08/on-belonging.html.

longing, and the strength of belong can predict academic performance. This is true even when controlling for and accounting for traditional academic predictors such as LSAT Scores.[40] To quote Prof. Quintanilla, "law school belonging is a critical predictor of social and academic success among law students."[41] This is great news because law schools can help students foster a sense of belonging, and this can first happen before a first-generation law students begins their first law school class.

Why Create a Summer Program?

First, as an institution, if you invite diverse and first-generation students to your school, you have to be able to support them, from admission until bar passage and beyond. It's not enough to merely diversify at admissions, but rather there needs to be a welcoming environment for first-generation students.[42]

A summer, or pre-orientation program, is often necessary to make first-generation students feel like they "got the memo." It's often the case that students and faculty who are not first-generation are often surprised about the knowledge they take for granted. Kenneth Oldfield reflects on this, stating "I think more and more about how much easier college would have been had I known at the start what most of my privileged cohorts took for granted."[43]

Students who do not feel welcome at a college do not avail themselves of the many opportunities and resources that are available. Campus life is often more stressful for those students than for their peers. "Students who delay integrating into the larger college community also have less access to social support from their peers and from the college as a whole—support that proves crucial to success both in college and in the labor market upon graduation[44]"

According to Oldfield, "For first-generation poor and working-class college students, surviving the social challenges of higher learning can be at least as demanding as achieving a high grade point average."[45] Research has shown that when students have a sense of belonging, they have greater academic success.[46] Specifically aca-

---

40. *Id.*

41. *Id.* (Quintanilla et al., in prep).

42. Kenneth Oldfield, *Humble and Hopeful: Welcoming First-Generation Poor and Working-Class Students to College* (February 14, 2007), About Campus, January–February 2007, available at SSRN: https://ssrn.com/abstract=3018703

43. *Id.*

44. Anthony Abraham Jack, The Privileged Poor: How Elite Colleges Are Failing Disadvantaged Students (2019).

45. Kenneth Oldfield, *Humble and Hopeful: Welcoming First-Generation Poor and Working-Class Students to College* (February 14, 2007), About Campus, January–February 2007, available at SSRN: https://ssrn.com/abstract=3018703.

46. Myra Laldin, *The Psychology of Belonging (And Why It Matters)*, Feb 11, 2016, (https ://www.learningandthebrain.com/blog/psychology-of-belonging/ last visited January 17, 2022).

demic outcomes, such as motivation, dropout rates, and academic performance correlated with feelings of belonging.[47] This is mostly because when students feel they don't belong in an environment, the cognitive energy that should be used on academic endeavors gets shifted to being used to scan for threats.[48] Essentially, a feeling of not belonging can lead to stereotype threat, which in turn can lead to having negative cognitive impacts, whereas a student's self-reported level of school belonging has a positive correlation on academic achievement.[49] However, even if students arrive with worries about their own success, an early intervention that mitigates any doubt as to whether the student belongs can lead to higher academic achievement.[50]

Studies have also shown that a sense of belonging predicts better persistence and mental health.[51] Sadly, first-generation students at four-year institutions report lower feelings of belonging than their non-first-generation counterparts.[52]

Given that belonging is such an integral part of both academic success and mental well-being and, in my observations, alumni support, creating summer programs seems an obvious way to begin to foster belonging immediately. In fact, depending on how the summer program is organized, it can start to foster a sense of belonging at the point of admission. As soon as I receive word from the admissions office, I send students a welcome letter, and include things like a law school glossary. My goal is to make them feel like they belong as soon as they have officially chosen our school.

Another reason to start programming in the summer is because it's a fantastic opportunity for students to interact with faculty and administrators in a less stressful environment. Often students don't seek out help when they need it because they don't know who to reach out to or who to trust. It is critical that students view their professors and administrators as approachable humans. Carol Lunberg states that "[d]isadvantages can be lessened when faculty and student affairs professionals share their capital with first-generation students."[53] I find this to be especially true with law students. Personally, I am very upfront about the fact that I was a first-generation law student, and had no idea what a tort was, nor did I know what the bar exam was, or anything about getting a summer associateship. I advise my school's first-generation law student group, and often gather other faculty and administra-

---

47. *Id.*
48. *Id.*
49. *Id.*
50. *Id.*
51. Maitheryi Gopalan & Shannon T. Brady, *College Students' Sense of Belonging: A National Perspective*, Educ. Researcher, vol. 49, no. 2, Mar. 2020, pp. 134–137, https://doi.org/10.3102/0013189X19897622.
52. *Id.*
53. Carol A. Lunberg, *A Bleacher-Seat View of Cultural Capital: How Bad Is a Dented Bat?* About Campus, 11(6) 8–12 (2007), https://doi.org/10.1002/abc.189.

tors to share similar stories. I also share my capital with them, knowing very well what they are going through. This is because first-generation students often don't know what they don't know.

In her article titled *A Bleacher-Seat View of Cultural Capital: How Bad Is a Dented Bat?*, Carol A. Lunberg shares a story about baseball and a dented bat.[54] Her son played baseball, but neither she nor her husband had ever played, nor were they very knowledgeable about the game. Her son's bat was "deemed unworthy to be used in the game" because of a dent, disqualifying the bat.[55] She explains that even though it was only a problem with the equipment, her son felt like he had been disqualified, or committed some egregious offense.[56] She also explains how the rule may have been written, or explained somewhere, but not being a "baseball family," she really hadn't known about the rule.[57] Thankfully, a teammate's dad, from very much a "baseball family," was there to help explain and clarify the rule to her and her son.[58] But she explains that the most important thing that his parent did was explain, through words and demeanor, that the bat issue was not a major offense.[59] She explains that this is exactly how we share cultural capital with our students. As she teaches English, she uses commas as an example; she deducts points for a misplaced comma, but it's a small offense—she is not disqualifying the student, so to speak.[60]

We, as educators, need to communicate these unwritten rules to students, since it is an entirely new world for them. They don't have parents or friends to help them make sense of law school, or whether something is a major or minor offense. I refer to this as giving students "the memo." Meaning, during law school, my bar exam experience, and early in my career (and sometimes even now) I feel like I missed "the memo" that explained law school and the legal profession, and how it all works. I strive to give my students "the memo" and summer and orientation programming can do this.

Laura Rendon, a professor of Higher Education at the University of Texas at San Antonio, studied first-generation students. She found that they need another person to validate their experience, and believe they are capable of success.[61] This inspires the students to keep going, even when things get tough. It's important to remember that first-generation students don't have that family member, or likely a family friend, who has been through law school and can relate. In fact, by definition, they don't have a family member who has been through any higher education, so their experiences are completely foreign to their families. My mother and grand-

54. *Id*
55. *Id.*
56. *Id.*
57. *Id.*
58. *Id.*
59. *Id.*
60. *Id.*
61. *Id.*

mother have always been my biggest cheerleaders. They support me no matter what, and I appreciate that. However, grandma had an eighth-grade education, and my mother has a high school diploma. They couldn't understand why I couldn't immediately practice law after graduation, or why I needed to take an expensive bar prep course to prepare for an exam. In their minds, I'm smart, and never needed test prep before, so why now? I had no one that really understood my life. In fact, even now—after over a decade in this field—my mother, even though she is proud, still doesn't always completely understand my job. However, that's okay because throughout my career I've developed multiple relationships with people who also do my job, so they completely understand my world. I was also lucky enough to have professors and early professional mentors that helped validate my experiences, and help me navigate my way.

We need to be that support for our students. The following sections of this chapter will go into greater detail about what to include in any first-generation program. However, when planning your programming, there are a few important things to keep in mind.

Financial Burdens

When programming for first-generation students, keep cost in mind. Many schools have designed summer classes to give students a head start on law school.[62] The classes usually include a focus on skills such as reading and briefing cases.[63] Although this is a great idea in theory, and does offer opportunities for first-generation students to become acquainted with the language of law, there are drawbacks to using this approach. Often these classes are for law school credit, and thus cost money. Because they are offered over the summer, financial aid and scholarships are not yet available,[64] meaning that students have to pay, on average, $1,000–$3,000 for such courses. For many first-generation students, this is money that they are unable to spend. In addition, these courses are typically offered on campus, meaning that the students have to be on campus one to two months earlier than class begins. Both

---

62. A large number of law schools are choosing to implement summer programs that are classes, and thus cost tuition money. To name only a few: The University of the District of Columbia David A. Clarke School of Law *Jump Start* (3 credits), Loyola University Chicago School of Law *Introduction to the Case Study Method and the Basics of Legal Writing* (2 credits), Samford University Cumberland School of Law *Legal Process* (2 credits) and *Public Law Process* (3 credits) There are other pipeline programs that are not classes, so will not cost tuition, but require students to be on campus or in a certain location for the summer. The cost for these varies from program to program if there is a cost.

63. *See, e.g.*, Summer Law Institute, CUNY School of Law, https://www.law.cuny.edu/academics/support/professional-skills-center/summer-law-institute/, last visited June 1, 2021.

64. FAFSA is only available to those enrolled at least part time, so this would not apply to a pre-1L summer. 2021 Federal Student Aid Handbook, chapter 1, enrollment status, https://fsapartners.ed.gov/knowledge-center/fsa-handbook/2020-2021/vol1/ch1-school-determined-requirements#pid_1002532

of these realities create barriers to first-generation students, who typically do not have the financial resources or the ability to move to campus months early. This means that the students most in need are the students least likely to be able to take advantage of the summer programs.

The solution needs to be a resource that is free to students, and if a program spans the entire semester, should have significant remote or online capabilities.

Timing

Also keep timing in mind. When can your students be on campus? This overlaps significantly with financial burdens. Will a remote option be more successful? It is often more difficult for first-generation students to move to campus more than a few days early, whether it be family obligations, cost, or work schedules. This often means that even if they have a way to pay for a summer course, if it means being out of work or in a different city all summer, it's simply not possible. One solution is to have asynchronous and synchronous online components. Students can benefit from prerecorded videos done by faculty or administration discussing core concepts such as vocabulary or how to read a case. You can also supplement what your school is doing with programming from CALI or LSAC.[65] This can supplement an in-person component where students can have their first opportunity to meet and interact with other students, faculty, and administrators.

Timing the course prior to orientation can also help students normalize the fact that this is a struggle, and that they are not alone. Using resources mentioned above, such as CALI or LSAC, can help students recognize that their struggles—not knowing certain vocabulary, or how to read a case—is a common law student problem, and it's not specific to them or to their school.

Content and Accessibility

As mentioned above, first-generation students lack the cultural capital that their non-first-generation peers have. This shows up in everything from not knowing how to network, or how to navigate a networking reception, to simply not having the appropriate vocabulary.

Programs geared toward first-generation students can close the gaps if they include components like a basic vocabulary lesson, or an introduction to common law. Even stepping back and explaining what a case is, and why we read them, is important. Also, remember that first-generation students are not going to know certain abbreviations, like "1L" or "Con Law" or "Hypo." This sounds minor, but it can be alienating and further compound feelings of imposter syndrome. I start any programming by giving students a glossary of legal terms and abbreviations, and admit

65. CALI has lessons and podcasts, some geared specifically toward first-generation students, https://cali.org/category/2l-3l-upper-level-lesson-topics/law-school-success and LSAC has "Law School Success," which schools can use to supplement their own programming, https://www.lsac.org/Law-School-Success.

to them that when I entered orientation, I had no idea what a tort was, wondering to myself whether it involved chocolate cake. I also admit that I had no concept of what a clerkship was, or many of the abbreviations frequently used by professors and fellow students. I share this with them so they feel less alone. I remind them that they are not the only one, and if they have questions about terminology, it's likely shared by at least some of their classmates.

It's also a good idea to use a broad cross-section of the school. Many summer programs rely heavily on academic support professionals. This is understandable, given that it is typically the academic support professionals who are best suited to teach things like reading and briefing. However, you want to make students feel welcome by the entire community. First-year faculty can mingle during a lunch break, or host a roundtable discussion about class preparation and their expectations. Career services can do a presentation on networking or job searches. I also try to bring in first-generation faculty and administrators to discuss their own first-generation experiences.

While it is important to help students with core skills such as critical reading, case briefing, and what to expect on exams, it is even more important to leave them with the feeling that they belong, and are welcome, and will be able to thrive. When deciding which information to include, you want to be cognizant of not overwhelming them. Think of each component with the goal of introducing them to the concept, not a deep dive into mastery of the concept. For example, I find that telling them what the bar exam is, and that they will have to study for it after graduation is sufficient. A brief overview of when it is, when to start registering, and the fact that they will likely have to be aware of costs. I then tell them not to worry, as I will be providing them with more information by the end of their second year. I want them to know that it's coming, have a general understanding of what it is, but not overwhelm them with the level of detail I provide to my 2L and 3L students—it's way too soon! Similarly, I have brought in our librarian to speak briefly—20 minutes maximum—about case names and citations. This is not meant to be a legal research course over the summer, and in fact, our librarian tells them that they will receive more information as they take legal research. The idea is to introduce them to the concept, so they feel less out of place as these concepts are introduced. Keep in mind we are only trying to close the gap in knowledge between our first-generation students and those with parents who have experience in higher education. This means the programming doesn't need to cover everything, but merely needs to allow students to feel that they are starting at the same point as their peers.

What About External or Third-Party Programs?

While it is important that incoming students feel welcomed into your specific community, external or third-party bridge programs can be a helpful tool in your toolkit—although it is important to review what the program actually covers and how students respond to it.

There is evidence that online programming, properly and intentionally structured, can have a positive impact on students' sense of belonging and thus, theoretically, support stronger academic outcomes.[66] You should review the syllabus for any third-party bridge program to make sure it addresses the issue of belonging, not just by telling students, "You belong here," but by using active learning and reflection techniques designed to actually have an impact.

Another advantage of third-party bridge programs is that the organizations developing them often have more resources to be able to devote to program development. Many bridge programs are run by academic support professionals, who tend to be busy in the summers helping graduates prepare for the bar exam. That being said, you should make sure that any bridge program covers the full array of academic skills such that your academic support professional is satisfied with the curriculum.

It is also possible to creatively integrate third-party bridge programs with your own faculty, staff, and administration. For example, members of the law school community, including peer mentors, can take the program along with the incoming students and host discussion sessions. It is important to integrate third-party programming on some level so that students connect it with your school and your desire to welcome them to your community.

Finally, if you choose an external program, you should make sure the cost is covered for incoming students. Remember that even if the program is set at a lower cost, that is a hurdle for many first-generation students.

Conclusion

Early programming for first-generation students is key to fostering their sense of belonging, which in turn increases their chances of academic and long-term success. It is incredibly important that schools create such programming for the summer, or provide already existing programs to incoming students.

---

66. Victor D. Quintanilla et al., *Evaluating Productive Mindset Interventions that Promote Excellence on California's Bar Exam*, prepared for the California Bar Exam (2020), https://www.calbar.ca.gov/Portals/0/documents/reports/Mindsets-in-Legal-Education-Executive-Summary.pdf.

Thirteen

Pre-Orientation and Orientation Programming

Opening the Doors to Law School

Petina Benigno,* Jean-Pierre Bonnet-Laboy,**
and Belinda Dantley***

I. Genesis of Our First Gen Pre-Orientation Programming

LEARNING ABOUT THE HISTORY OF ACADEMIC SUPPORT PROGRAMS has motivated our team at Saint Louis University School of Law ("SLU Law") to create programs that target specific groups of students and has encouraged the Office of Inclusion and Diversity Education to work closely with the Academic Resource Center. Our main goal is to dismantle the traditional approaches of how law school operates and shed light on the unique needs of our first-generation students. Our broader goal is to expose the existing hierarchies in legal education and redefine them to foster inclusivity. Attending equally to everyone's interests reproduces inequality. It is no longer acceptable to believe that legal education should be one-size-fits-all. Inequities persist and redistributing access and opportunity should be a goal that law schools have.[1] Thus, we take an equity approach to our programming to level the playing field for our first-generation students.

Unifying the Office of Diversity, Equity and Inclusion and the Academic Resource Center to create first-generation programming was a natural fit. At SLU Law, our offices share similar goals—to educate the whole student while taking into consideration the unique needs of students' learning styles and personal circumstances. Thus, our offices naturally collaborated in our first-generation programming, which

* Assistant Director of Academic and Bar Exam Success, Saint Louis University School of Law.
** Assistant Director for Diversity and Inclusion, Saint Louis University School of Law.
*** Assistant Dean for Diversity, Equity and Inclusion, Saint Louis University School of Law.

1. Paul Gorski, *Avoiding Racial Equity Detours,* ASCD (2019), https://www.ascd.org/el/articles/avoiding-racial-equity-detours (last visited Jan 29, 2022).

ultimately has the goal of leveraging the skills first-generation law students bring with them to law school while also hedging the unique challenges they face in comparison to their non-first-generation peers.

The Office of Diversity, Equity and Inclusion at SLU Law provides development and coordination of diversity, cross-cultural and inclusion awareness, and outreach and retention programs for SLU Law.[2] Belinda Dantley, the Assistant Dean for Diversity, Equity and Inclusion, collaborates with faculty, staff, students, alumni, and the Saint Louis community to enhance recruitment, retention, and mentoring of diverse constituencies within the School of Law.[3] JP Bonnet, the Assistant Director for Diversity and Inclusion, formulates programming for students of all backgrounds to enhance their knowledge of diversity and inclusion strategy and creates relationships and mentors students at all stages of their law school career. Overall, Belinda and JP's work in the Office of Diversity, Equity, and Inclusion creates a diverse learning environment at SLU Law to help students sharpen their critical thinking and analytical skills, while preparing students to succeed in an increasingly diverse and interconnected world.[4] Their work helps to break down stereotypes and reduce bias in the law school and in the legal field, and ultimately welcomes students of all backgrounds into SLU Law.[5]

The Academic Resource Center at SLU Law is designed to assist our students with the support they need to be successful during law school and in their future legal careers.[6] Comprised of both academic support and bar exam preparation, the Academic Resource Center provides resources and assistance from before incoming students begin orientation, continuing through the students' bar exam preparation.[7] Professor Antonia Miceli is the Director of Academic Support and Bar Exam Preparation, and Professor Petina Benigno is the Assistant Director of Academic Support and Bar Exam Preparation at SLU Law. Together, these two professors teach classes for each grade level of law school, including a class for the entire 1L class, lead bar preparation programming, and assist in the creation and implementation of pre-orientation and orientation programming. Building relationships and establishing trust among students is important to the underlying foundation of the Academic Resource Center's mission of meeting students where they are to support the whole student and is expounded by the fact that the professors in the Academic Resource

---

2. Office of Diversity, Equity and Inclusion, Saint Louis University School of Law, https://www.slu.edu/law/student-services/inclusion-diversity-education/index.php.

3. *Id.*

4. U.S. Dep't of Education, Office of Planning, Evaluation and Policy Development, Advancing Diversity and Inclusion in Higher Education: Key Data Highlights Focusing on Race and Ethnicity and Promising Practices (2016), https://www2.ed.gov/rschstat/research/pubs/advancing-diversity-inclusion.pdf.

5. *Id.*

6. Academic Resource Center, Saint Louis University School of Law, https://www.slu.edu/law/academics/academic-resource-center/index.php.

7. *Id.*

Center begin those relationships with students from before the student enters law school, continuing through the students' journey to the bar exam through each year of law school.

Combining the professionals and the experiences of the Academic Resource Center and the Office of Diversity, Equity and Inclusion allows our team to bring multiple perspectives to our programming to cater to the unique needs of incoming 1L students attending SLU Law. Belinda, JP, and Tina each graduated from SLU Law and are each first-generation students, allowing not only a sense of empathy but also an established rapport with the students, since we can emphasize to students that we have been in their shoes, albeit an increasing number of years ago.

SLU Law is a globally connected Jesuit law school in the heart of downtown Saint Louis, Missouri. SLU Law education is rooted in the Jesuit mission of academic excellence and to teach the whole student, mind, body, and spirit.[8] There is a particular emphasis on social justice in the community, and that social justice mission extends to the programming we provide at SLU Law.[9] Thus, our first-generation pre-orientation programming has its purpose rooted in our goal to meet the student where they are in their educational journey, regardless of where they grew up and what resources have been afforded to them thus far. Further, our social justice mission is exhibited in our first-generation pre-orientation programming because the lessons students learn enable them to break down barriers that would otherwise stall their growth or stamina as they enter their first semester of law school. Our hope is that with our first-generation pre-orientation programming, along with our orientation programming and resources in the law student's first semester, the first-generation students dive into the legal concepts that affect bar passage and into other mission-driven learning opportunities, allowing them to accomplish more in their law school career.

In our introductory planning discussions between the Academic Resource Center and the Office of Diversity, Equity and Inclusion on pre-orientation programming, we discovered that we did not have a way to know which students to target our messaging to. SLU Law had not tracked data on first-generation student status, but in preparation for the 2021 admissions cycle, we worked with our Office of Admissions to include a space on the SLU Law application for students to report their first-generation status. Seventy-six percent of the 2021 incoming class identified themselves as first-generation students. This number confirmed our need for programming tailored to these students. This has helped us discover how many students identify as first-generation students, whom to specifically message our programming, and gives us data points for participation rates for first-generation students

8. *Learning Outcomes and Performance Criteria*, Saint Louis University School of Law, https://www.slu.edu/law/academics/learning-outcomes.php.

9. *Id.*

versus those who participate who may not identify as first generation and are seeking additional knowledge.

Targeted programming for specific groups of students has origins in law school academic support programs. Academic support programs grew out of support for the influx of "minority students," as they were referred to in the 1960s on, usually beginning by working with the Black Law Students Associations. During this time there was an influx of minority students entering law school as the legal profession had a desire to diversify. Models that academic support programs took on challenged the traditional "sage on the stage" model of law school and moved to motivate students to engage in the learning process and for professors to be "guides on the side." Traditional legal pedagogy makes the assumption that students already have the skill to move from reading and understanding the pertinent points of a case to problem solving and higher-level legal analysis. Johnson, Johnson, and Smith articulated the characteristics that define faculty teaching under the current paradigm:

transferring knowledge and skills from faculty to students;

filling "passive" students with knowledge and skills;

classifying and sorting students into categories;

maintaining a competitive organizational structure;

conducting education within a context of impersonal relationships; and

assuming anyone with expertise in law can teach without training.

Venallia Randal elaborates, under the Socratic method, law students read cases and the faculty engages them in a question-and-answer exchange regarding those cases. The near-exclusive use of the Socratic method places the faculty at the center of the classroom.

Academic support programs sought to show students the steps to being successful by guiding students on how to have ownership over their academic success and contribute to the classroom experience, enabling them to be lifelong learners of the law. In order to do this, it is important for students to know exactly what it is that they need to know or what they need to do in order to excel in law school. This was especially helpful to students who did not come from legal backgrounds and elite schools, and those who were often left out of traditional law school environments. It is important to note that prior education, experiences, background, learning styles, race, gender, class, culture, religion, and sexual orientation are relevant to learning.

Academic support programs started to address the reality that more and more students do not have these backgrounds, and that they needed to be taught certain skills more explicitly during law school for them to share the same success. It is important for law schools to create programs or courses that work with students to help them develop skills for success, understanding growth mindset versus fixed mindset principles.

Academic support programs were widely successful for the cohort of students they were designated for—minority students. There were also perceptions that these programs were making law school easier for some students and giving them an unfair advantage over other students. Then law schools gradually began to insist these programs be made available to all students.[10] As the programs shifted to broader bases, they became less focused on meeting the needs of the very students the programs were set up to address.[11] It's time for academic support programs to get back to their roots and create programming for students of color, marginalized students, and students that don't have legal professionals in their family—first-generation students.

We seek to meet the needs of students from various backgrounds to ensure that they are engaged in the learning process, feel part of the law school community, and meet their academic and professional goals. We have provided methodologies, techniques, and skills to help our law students develop feelings of self-worth, successful participation, and belonging. Our pre-orientation programming meets these students' needs before students start their first day of law school, which fosters relationships with us as program leaders and with the law school itself, making them engaged with their success throughout law school.

II. Defining Goals to Steer Your Programming

Taking a page from inclusive learning strategies, we intentionally created specific goals and objectives for our programming. Those goals included:

- Instilling a sense of empowerment in our students before they entered law school;
- Providing a buffer to the knowledge gap for students entering the legal profession;
- Providing resources to our students and their families;
- Providing networking opportunities;
- Creating community-building activities for students.

These goals not only help steer us when creating ideas for programming, but also are the most aligned with helping first-generation students.

Our pre-orientation program is titled "First Generation Workshop," and is SLU Law's way to engage and participate in modules, lessons, and community building before they enter their first semester of law school. Students have access to the pro-

---

10. *See generally* Ellen Suni, *Academic Support at the Crossroads: From Minority Retention to Bar Prep and Beyond—Will Academic Support Change Legal Education or Itself Be Fundamentally Changed?*, 73 UMKC L. Rev. 497 (2004).

11. *See generally id.*

gram and are able to engage with the materials starting in early July. As a broad overview, the Workshop includes a series of modules with short, engaging videos on the topic of mental states that first-generation students may feel when in law school, such as isolation, imposter syndrome, and stereotype threat. Additionally, participants watch videos of current and former students who identify as first generation as they describe their experiences transitioning into law school with tips on how to be successful. We include additional information on what to do before, during, and after class as part of their introduction to the Academic Resource Center. We give resources that reference the culture of law school: how the law school classroom environment is set up to test oral analytical skills and their assessment and grade comes in the form of one written exam at the end of the semester; that grades are based not just on the understanding of concepts, but application of the law; and the law school curve, as many first-generation students do not have exposure to this concept in previous educational experiences. In the spirit of collaborating with the entire law school community, we created a "You Belong"[12] video, showing current students, staff, and faculty say "you belong" at Saint Louis University School of Law with a short message to the incoming first-generation students. In summation of the program, we host a live, synchronous Zoom session for the students who utilized the First Generation Workshop resources to ask questions, talk about what they learned, and further build community.

III. SLU Law's First Gen Pre-Orientation Programming, "First Generation Workshop"

A. Emotional Barriers and Mental States

As we began to break down the areas of support we wished to provide to our students, we began to look intently at how law school impacts students outside of the classroom. With the increasing enrollment of first-generation students, there is a prevalent knowledge gap when it comes to dealing with the emotions and mental states that are frequently encountered by first-year law students. Thus, we started our First Generation Workshop with modules focused on emotions and mental states. As all members of our working group were first-generation law students, and we reflected on the mental states and emotional barriers that had the deepest impact on us throughout our own journeys. Imposter syndrome, stereotype threat, and isolation were the three main barriers that became the foundation for our online modules. While these mental states can influence all students, first-generation students

12. Saint Louis University School of Law, *You Belong* (2020) https://drive.google.com/file/d/1JvyglPPNM_-oxWIIR7EbkXfpOSmyTFGj/view.

find themselves even more susceptible to the impact of these mental states.[13] The goal of these modules was to not only provide students with definitions of feelings they may find themselves experiencing throughout law school, but to also provide supportive methods to combat those feelings. This is where our animated videos would be supplemented by blog posts and articles to help provide additional resources and information on overcoming these barriers.

1. Imposter Syndrome

Imposter syndrome has become one of the more frequently studied mental states when it comes to first-generation students at the collegiate level; however, the effects of imposter syndrome still can have hefty effects on first-generation law students. The definition we operated with for imposter syndrome was the feelings of inadequacy that persist despite evidence of success.[14] We then felt it prudent to provide contextual examples of how this mental state can manifest itself with law students. We stated that people experiencing imposter syndrome tend to chronically doubt themselves and their ability despite tangible accomplishments, and they tend to consider themselves to be intellectually fraudulent, even though they had the intellectual ability to be accepted into law school just as their classmates d*id.* Next, we provided different phrases that those experiencing and how to shift perspectives to a more productive mental state. For example, one of the most common situations where first-generation students will feel imposter syndrome is after completing their first week of classes. With the massive influx of new information and terminology, students dealing with imposter syndrome will often call themselves "fakes" or "frauds." This overstimulation caused by the first week of law school often sends students into this spiral of self-doubt, convincing themselves that they have deceived admissions teams and professors into thinking they are deserving of their space. We then provided students with multiple steps to address these emotions: Recognizing these feelings, reframing your self-worth with an emphasis on kindness, and asking for help. As we closed out the module, we found it important to note that imposter syndrome can manifest itself differently for everyone, but that students shouldn't feel alone in their struggles.

This particular mental state was one that we found vital to tackle at the beginning of our module set. There was a need for our research to lead us to the origins of imposter syndrome to be effective in our creation of this module. Psychologist Pauline Rose Clance and Suzanne Imes were the originators of the concept in their 1978 study, which focused on high-achieving women.[15] Clance and Imes stated that "[d]

---

13. Gill Corkindale, *Overcoming Imposter Syndrome*, HARV. BUS. REV. (2019), https://hbr.org/2008/05/overcoming-imposter-syndrome (last visited Jan 7, 2022).

14. *Id.*

15. Ruchika Tulshyan & Jodi-Ann Burey, *Stop Telling Women They Have Imposter Syndrome*, HARV. BUS. REV. (2021), https://hbr.org/2021/02/stop-telling-women-they-have-imposter-syndrome (last visited Dec 19, 2021).

espite outstanding academic and professional accomplishments, women who experience the imposter phenomenon persist in believing they are not really bright and have fooled anyone who thinks otherwise." *Id.* However, it is estimated that 70% of people will experience at least one episode of this imposter phenomenon in their lives.[16] Research has shown that first-generation college students are more likely to experience imposter syndrome than other students, and since their families do not have a full understanding of the demands of higher education, they may not benefit from strong family emotional support.[17] Extending this same research to first-generation students, we found it prudent to provide this support prior to their orientation process as a way to begin providing information and resources to better understand imposter syndrome prior to the information overload that occurs during orientation. The animated modules and accompanying resource articles were intentionally created and selected to reinforce the notion that imposter syndrome is not an individual character fault, but rather a natural response to societal pressure.[18] Students were able to learn through our lessons and resources methods to help combat imposter syndrome such as mental reframing, seeking outside help and affirmation, and self-kindness to provide a few examples. We believe that while imposter syndrome will be an ongoing barrier, the module we have prepared for students will allow them to adequately overcome imposter syndrome when it does present itself.

2. Stereotype Threat

The next mental state that we tackled was the phenomenon of stereotype threat. This mental state is one that isn't as recognized socially as imposter syndrome is, but we felt that stereotype threat posed just as large an impact on first-generation students. Stereotype threat is the psychological effect that negative group stereotypes can have on members of a stereotype group.[19] These effects can impact both conscious and unconscious student behavior and performance in the classroom. In creating this module, we took a more step-by-step explanatory approach to our animated module because this mental state is less often discussed when it comes to preparing for law school. We began with the definition as we did with our other modules, but then dove into a discussion of the process in which stereotype threat plays out in the real-world application through priming. Students were also given insight into how stereotype threat can manifest in their work by slowing their cognitive functions and abilities. Each portion of the animated module was designed to not just provide information on this mental barrier, but to show its direct implication on how it can impact them as law students. The students were then provided

16. Jaruwan Sakulku & James Alexander, *The Imposter Phenomenon*, 6 Int'l J. Behav. Sci. 73–92 (2011).

17. Bridgette J. Peteet, LaTrice Montgomery & Jerren C. Weekes, *Predictors of Imposter Phenomenon Among Talented Ethnic Minority Undergraduate Students*, 84 J. Negro Educ. 1–22 (2015).

18. John Amaechi, The Promises of Giants, Chapter 1, 10 (2021).

19. Russell A. McClain, Helping Our Students Reach Their Full Potential: The Insidious Consequences of Stereotype Threat (2016).

with three techniques to help combat the feeling of stereotype threat. The accompanying piece to the animated video was a law journal article as opposed to the blog post style that was used with the imposter syndrome module. With stereotype threat likely being a newer phenomenon for students, we thought by providing a more analytical approach, students would be able to gain more in-depth knowledge on how this mental barrier affects law students.

This module served as an introduction of the theory of stereotype threat to most of our students, even though most students have experienced some form of stereotype threat without having a proper name or definition of the experience. Over the last 20 years, the depth of study into the power of stereotype threat has increased tremendously.[20] As a professional school, each of our classes are filled with some of the most high-achieving students from across the country. The intensity of law school is of no surprise to those who apply to law school. This extreme level of difficulty in pursuing a law degree leaves students more likely to feel the effects of negative group stereotypes and, additionally, the greater the consequences the students will feel if they do not succeed, thus confirming some negative stereotypes.[21] The impact negative group stereotypes have on the ability of students' brains to process information can have dire consequences when it comes to our students' ability to succeed.[22] However, we were able to use the work of McClain to provide us with avenues to help our students overcome these consequences, while also utilizing one of our own methodologies as well. The first avenue is the use of explicit discussion surrounding stereotype threat. Research shows that by engaging students in explicit discussion of stereotypes and informing individuals about the effect of negative group stereotypes can actually buffer the impact on students' performance.[23] The second avenue provided by McClain that we employed was implementing more effective feedback. In providing feedback, the best form of feedback often both holds students to a high standard and affirms students that this higher standard is achievable.[24] We then utilized the mantra of our own Academic Resource Center educating students on employing a growth mindset during their law school journey. Growth mindset is the belief that intelligence and ability are not stagnant and are skills to be sharpened and developed over time. By focusing on these three techniques, we were able to provide effective methods, backed by research, to help our students recognize and overcome stereotype threat.

---

20. *Id.* at 12.

21. *Id.* at 20.

22. *Id.* at 21.

23. Michael Johns, Toni Schmader & Andy Martens, *Knowing Is Half the Battle: Teaching Stereotype Threat as a Means of Improving Women's Math Performance*, 16 Psych. Sci. 175–179, (2005).

24. Geoffrey Cohen, Claude Steele & Lee Ross, *The Mentor's Dilemma: Providing Critical Feedback Across the Racial Divide*, 25 Personality & Soc. Psych. Bull. 1302–1318 (1999).

3. Isolation

The final mental state we dedicated our modules to was isolation. While it may seem a broad category to tackle, there is a particular context to the nature of isolation in law school that we found important to inform students about. The difficulty and uniqueness of the law school journey can be demoralizing, exhausting, and uncomfortable. When students step into the new world of law school with language and methods of instruction they seldom see prior to getting to law school, they can find themselves questioning whether they are the only ones who struggle with this new normal. We sought to create this module with a more optimistic tone and to reinforce the notion of law school being a difficult and arduous journey for all those who have gone through it, including the faculty and staff who are there to teach and assist our students. We also wanted to begin the discussion of how stress and the competitive nature of law school can amplify feelings of isolation students could experience. The perceived high stakes of grades cause extreme pressure on students and thus increase stress levels. It is with this heightened stress level that students fall into a cycle of pushing themselves to work harder, longer, and faster to try to keep up with their classmates for the scarce resource of grades on the law school curve. This cycle causes students to push away their family and friends, further sending them into isolation and creating uphill battles for students to make meaningful connections with their peers. We used the modules to emphasize the importance of taking the time early in their law school journey to make these meaningful connections. We also wanted to highlight the role that student organizations can play in combating isolation in law school. Joining a group of like-minded people helps provide a community and can refocus students on what ideals brought them to law school in the first place. The next tool for combating isolation was time management. Much like making time for studying and class, carving out time for social engagement is vital to preventing disconnection from your peers and isolation from loved ones. The final helpful tool we provided for students was the use of mentorship to fight isolation. By seeking out a mentor with experience of going through law school, students can have someone to help guide them through the difficulties that are commonly associated with law school. Mentors can reinforce the notion that law students are not alone in their struggles and can prove to be excellent resources for students who find themselves beginning to isolate themselves. This module was designed to not only provide students with tools to combat isolation in law school, but also to serve as a reminder that our offices are here for our students and that all students within our community belong here.

It is a well-known fact that law school has a particularly stressful effect on its students. Nearly 44% of law students will experience clinically elevated levels of psychological distress.[25] This distress is the foundation for many of the mental health

---

25. Benjamin et al., *The Role of Legal Education in Producing Psychological Distress Among Law Students and Lawyers*, Am. Bar Found. Rsch. J. 225–252 (1986).

issues and barriers that law schools and lawyers find themselves confronting. As students begin their first year of school, students have shown that as the year progresses, students' contact with support systems will drastically decrease.[26] Since first-year law students are particularly susceptible to this distress, we found it imperative to provide this module with an overtone of optimism and positivity. Our research led us to find that using an optimistic explanatory style can be an accurate predictor of resilience and higher motivation levels.[27] The negativity associated with isolation can cause students to narrowly focus their minds on the stressors of law school and serve to only further deepen their isolation from their peers and loved ones.[28] By structuring our three tools to combat isolation with positive and optimistic messaging, we are able to broaden students' possibilities for actions that will lead to their academic success.[29] The focus on time management to routinely make time for social engagements stems from the overwhelming benefits that creating and maintaining a time management routine can provide. These benefits are decreased hopelessness, lower anxiety, and greater optimism about their future and success.[30] Finding community and peer connection is a cornerstone in dealing with isolation in law school. Seeking out like-minded peer mentors can aid in new students' acclimation to the new surroundings. These peer interactions provide not only social benefits, but also offer academic and career-related support and guidance for students.[31] We found that mentorship in the context of isolation in law would be a pertinent tool to provide to our students. Mentors can provide not only both academic and emotional support, but also are linked to increased likelihood of student retention and success in career advancement opportunities.[32] This module was key to the success of our program's goal of giving our students the right information to prepare for the journey ahead of them and to prevent them from falling into isolative habits.

B. Before, During, and After Class

After the discussion of the various mental states that a first-generation student might face in law school, the second part of the online, asynchronous program includes a set of modules describing what a first-year law student can and should do to be successful in their law school classes.

---

26. Todd Peterson & Elizabeth Waters Peterson, *Stemming the Tide of Law Student Depression: What Law Schools Need to Learn from the Science of Positive Psychology*, GW LAW FACULTY PUBLICATIONS & OTHER WORKS, 871, 1–93, 4 (2008).

27. *Id.*at 51-52.

28. Barbara L. Fredrickson, *What Good Are Positive Emotions?*, 2 REV. GEN. PSYCH. 300, 303 (1998).

29. *Id.*

30. Christine Bartholomew, *Time: An Empirical Analysis of Law Student Time Management Deficiencies*, 81 U. CINCINNATI L. REV. 933 (2013).

31. Meera E. Deo & Kimberly A. Griffin, *The Social Capital Benefits of Peer Mentoring in Law School*, 38 OHIO N. U. L. REV. 305, 320 (2011).

32. *Id.* at 311.

Students who were raised around lawyers or who are in close contact with a relative who attended law school have the opportunity to gain cultural capital, or knowledge and skills, that can help make law school a more familiar and comfortable environment and transition. Parents or family members who have not attended law school are not able to effectively advise their first-generation family member on how to succeed in law school, including how to prepare for classes, how classes and understanding the material are different from undergraduate studies, and how to prepare effectively after class to prepare for final exams. Thus, we created three separate modules with content on how to effectively prepare for class, what to expect during a law school class, and what is required after class to be successful.

1. Before Class

To introduce our "Before Class" virtual module, we affirmed our incoming students' successes thus far—we acknowledged that each one of them is a successful student, as they have been accepted into law school and been successful in their undergraduate or other graduate degree programs. Yet law school is different from any other degree program to which the students were accustomed. Our "Before Class" module discussed the difference between a textbook and a casebook. Unlike textbooks, casebooks often do not contain definitions or lay out terms clearly, but rather contain judicial opinions. Unlike some undergraduate programs, the information is not given to the student in a clear form, but rather the student must discern the information that the professor wants, creating an expectation of a higher level of thinking.

Further, students must come to class prepared, and part of that entails researching a word or phrase that the student is unfamiliar with. We shared library resources, Westlaw, Lexis, and free *Black's Law Dictionary* sources for their access. Professors conduct classes presuming the student knows what these words mean. We encouraged students to be curious about their reading, but also cognizant of their identities when reading cases.

We acknowledged that, when a student reads case law as a first-generation student, they may garner different feelings from some of their peers. Cases are written by judges who understand legal terms, and they are written in esoteric language that can potentially exclude others from the profession. The esoteric language and sentence formulation will take time to get used to. Importantly, case law includes outdated terms, some very explicit and direct. In other instances, students should expect to encounter cases where offensive language is present to describe people or situations; we include a specific example of a case that uses the terms "master" and "servant" to describe an agency relationship. We acknowledge that this will cause discomfort in students (while also acknowledging that some of their peers will turn a blind eye to such terms and will not be affected). We encourage students to be patient with themselves—legal history and the language used is uncomfortable, and students need to take care of themselves first when faced with an uncomfortable text or case.

In the "Before Class" module, we introduced the students to the "reasonable person." We shared that the law is objective and uses a standard often termed as a reasonable person standard. However, we shared that the reasonable person may "think" or "reason" differently from the first-generation student reader, because the reasonable person standard has, for centuries, been the perspective of a white male. If a first-generation student reader is a person of color, or a woman, or does not identify as heterosexual, reading cases with this standard may make these students feel as though their opinions or diversity of experiences are not valid because they are not seen in the underlying understanding of what is objective and what is reasonable. Further, sometimes case outcomes are unfair or biased, and yet they can be perfectly legal. The injustices students may see in the outcomes of cases can make one feel disoriented or dispirited at times. At this point, we reference the emotions and mental states modules and confirm to the student that when they are faced with this uncomfortable reading or situation, their feelings and thoughts are valid. We emphasize the power of community when facing uncomfortable language in cases or uncomfortable conversations in the law context. Connecting with one of us as faculty members, connecting with their peers in their class, and connecting with upper-class students who experienced similar situations and overcame will be a way for the student to feel that their beliefs are valid and to feel that sense of belonging.

The fact that the first-generation student can see these injustices gives them a leg up as an advocate for their future clients and their future goals as a lawyer. We encouraged students to remember that their unique experiences and perspectives will make them that much better of a lawyer.

2. During Class

After our "Before Class" module, we discussed what first-generation law students should expect during their class period with their professors. We stressed that in undergrad or other graduate degree programs, sometimes classes are structured to where you learn the material during class time. That is not the case with law school classes—law students should not go to class to learn the law, but rather class time is focused on practicing what you learned on your own at home. This is a different structure of learning that is foreign to most before coming to law school, namely first-generation students with no one to tell them differently.

We gave insight into what this structure might look like, acknowledging that professors each have their own norms. Generally, professors give a detailed syllabus at the beginning of the semester that lists the expectations and readings for the entire semester's class. It is the student's responsibility to stay up to task with the reading. The American Bar Association recommends two hours of studying and reading outside of the classroom for each hour that the student spends inside the classroom, and we informed students that this is a minimum they should expect to spend on their classes.

We also introduced the concept of synthesis to the students in the "During Class" module. When reading cases and preparing for class, students should think not only of the facts of that case and their discernment of the rule and the holding, but also how that case relates to others the student has read throughout the semester in that particular class. We encouraged students to ask themselves why this case is important, what are the related issues, and what are the potential counter arguments, since their job as a law student, and later as a lawyer, will be to spot the issues or the trouble areas and to be able to explain the reason for the law they choose to use in their analysis. Even if the student may not be ready to grasp the idea of synthesis and the bigger picture of what their task will be on exams at the time, we have found it important to allow students insight into these expectations before they enter class so they can be more prepared.

Further, we introduced the concept of the Socratic method that professors often use in law school classes. This approach to in-class instruction is unique to law school, and likely a concept that a first-generation law student would not know about from a family member before experiencing it. Further, making students aware of what the final exam might look like now is important so that they can pay close attention to how and why the professor is spending so much time on a particular concept or hypothetical. When in class, students should pay attention to the questions the professor asks, because it shows how the professor is thinking about the cases and legal principles. These questions from the professor are the way the professors are teaching students how they should be looking at these cases, and in turn are the sorts of questions that students should be asking while reading these cases. Training this way during class to read cases this way is then how students should approach their exams. Instruct students to pay attention to what and how the professor asks questions in class about the cases that they read. Explain that students need to train their brain to operate in this way to best set them up for success on the final exam. Again, even if students may not be ready to grasp these ideas and do not yet have experience with law school classes, it is important to allow students insight into these expectations before they enter class so they can be more prepared.

3. After Class

During the semester, one particular gap between first-generation students and those who are not first generation is the after-class synthesis and the time management that comes along with fitting the after-class work into one's schedule. We see this in the additional burdens that first-generation students often face, including the need to work to support themselves or their families, the familial commitments that are not easily delegated to others, and the propensity to live off campus or further from it. All of these things take additional time capital that is not spent on their studies. Therefore, we stressed that balance is crucial to success in law school and discussed the schedule and timeline of a law school semester, breaking the semester up into four quadrants.

1. The first quadrant, the first few weeks of classes, will entail a lot of reading, organizing notes, and finding a preferred note-taking method, thinking about creating outlines, and finding supplements to assist with class understanding.
2. The second quadrant entails beginning to study for midterms, if their classes have a midterm, taking those midterms, and oftentimes balancing a Legal Research and Writing paper assignment in that mix.
3. The third quadrant entails continuing to keep up with readings and to home in on outlining.
4. The last quadrant entails focusing on practice problems and learning from examples to prepare for final exams.

After zooming out to a higher level of understanding of the progression of a law school semester, we could then focus on more details of resources to assist with each quadrant. We emphasized the importance of the after-class synthesis routine, including synthesizing cases to find commonalities or nuances in legal rules. We discussed a technique called the "purple blurb," which is a note-taking technique that enables students to give a short and succinct summary of the themes of the cases they read or the themes of the class, making the font purple (or any other favorite color!) so that when the student goes to outline or synthesize their class notes, they have a structure already in place. This note-taking technique has stuck with our first-generation students, and in advising sessions we often hear students state how helpful this technique has been for their note taking, and the term is somewhat of a unifying nomenclature that unites some of the first-generation students.

Oftentimes, first-generation students have a lower propensity to seek out or know where to seek out support when needed. Thus, we introduced students to the many resources available to them to help with their after-class review, namely the resources offered within the Academic Resource Center and the Law School Library. We introduced students to supplements, or study aids or hornbooks as they are sometimes called. These supplements can help students learn the information needed from cases they discuss in their classes, and they follow the topics of law throughout the semester, but they are written in easier-to-understand terms. Supplements help distill the law and make the connections between the cases and boil down the cases into easy-to-understand chunks. We added that supplements are to be used in addition to casebooks, but this can come with an added expense for the student. We emphasize to students that we have hundreds of supplements available in print and online for students to use at no additional cost.

Our how-to guide of approaching law school classes proved helpful for students. One tangential benefit of these modules was the opportunity for the students to become familiar with what the Academic Resource Center can help students with, and the fact that we already gave them information invited the students to follow up with us and ask questions. This established an ongoing relationship with students and took a burden off of them to understand what the Academic Resource Center's professors can assist them with.

C. Programming Modality

Our First-Generation Workshop was hosted on The West Education Network ("TWEN") learning management system. TWEN is one of the most commonly used learning management systems used at SLU Law, so one of our primary reasons for hosting the First-Generation Workshop on TWEN was to familiarize students with this platform.

We considered recording ourselves showing PowerPoint presentations or more traditional approaches to classroom instruction, but we ultimately decided to utilize a platform called Powtoon to create cartoon-inspired videos with us narrating a voiceover of the content and substance of the information. We created these animated videos in an attempt to hold the attention of students that might otherwise wane with a traditional online lecture. The videos are intentionally short, no longer than seven minutes, to hold students' attention and create incentive to follow through with the entire video. The videos are asynchronous, which allows students to complete the modules at any time, creating accessibility to those who work or have family obligations.

The only synchronous part of our First Generation Workshop is an online Zoom meeting, where we hold a space for students to congregate online to ask questions on the content of the modules or any other questions about law school that they have at the time. This Workshop has been hosted in July, which is around the time students receive their first semester schedule and some book lists. Current first-generation Faculty Fellows also participated in the Zoom meeting, which allowed students to have a successful student's perspective on what they themselves were about to embark on. We found that many members of the first-year class participated in the Zoom meeting, even students who did not affiliate as first-generation students. The students found benefit in meeting us albeit online and meeting other first-generation students like themselves, all fostering our goal of community building.

The first iteration of our First Generation Workshop was an online, module-based Workshop with a follow-up session on Zoom that invited students to join to talk about what they learned and discovered in the modules with each other. The COVID-19 pandemic necessitated our use of the online, module-based Workshop with the associated Zoom session, but we found that this modality fostered participation from a broader set of students who would not have been able to participate if we held the Workshop in-person during the day due to their locations out of state or work commitments. We have decided that we will continue the First Generation Workshop as an online, asynchronous model in the future, even if the opportunity arises to transform it to an in-person synchronous Workshop, because of the number of students who are able to participate in its current modality.

D. Community Building

As previously discussed, these modules were done online to more effectively disseminate this information during the COVID-19 pandemic. This left us with the difficult task of trying to begin the community-building process with no availability to gather in person. In the first year of our pre-orientation program, we had thought it best to create an entire week dedicated to our program rollout. While we had created all of these modules jam-packed with information and resources, there was an evident lack of interaction where students could come together to process together as a group. In the first year of our program, we held an open discussion session that was available to all program participants. This was designed to give our students access to not only the creators of these modules, but also provide a space for other first-generation students to get to know one another prior to their orientation. Granted, this took place after a recruitment cycle that relied heavily on Zoom meetings and events to engage incoming law students as they prepared for their law school journey. In our first year of this program, the discussion session did have a few visitors, but due to the open-ended design there was a negative correlation between design and attendance. Students seemed to feel intimidated to openly discuss the mental state modules in a setting where they had not established connections with their peers or their professors.

In our preparations for the second iteration of the program, we knew a key piece to change would have to be our community engagement event. We found that similar to our isolation module, we needed our incoming students to feel a sense of belonging and community, not only with each other, but with our upper-division students as well. This led to us collaborating with one of our student organizations, First Generation Society, to host a panel-style discussion via Zoom for our incoming students to have the opportunity to ask questions of and learn from upper-division first-generation students. The panel consisted of four upper-division first-generation students from diverse backgrounds and the moderator was another first-generation student. Our goal with this panel was to reinforce the lessons learned throughout the online modules with real-life experiences and examples from current law students who are actively dealing with the same mental obstacles. We were pleased to see our attendance in the revamped event triple from what it was from the year before. Students were actively engaged in the discussion and many students reached out to our panelists after the event for advice and mentorship. In pivoting our approach to community building from year to year, we were able to see a significant increase in both attendance and participation during the events.

There was one aspect of community building programming that we did carry over from the previous year. As previously mentioned, imposter syndrome can create serious doubts for students on whether they truly belong in law school. As a way to explicitly address this mental state, we put together a video featuring numerous members of faculty, staff, and students who identified as first-generation law students. Each member of our community featured was able to craft their own brief video message, all with the unifying theme that each of our incoming students belongs here as a member of our community. These messages served to show that on day one of their law school experience, these incoming students will have a built-in community that is ready and willing to support them throughout their time in law school.

The transition for many first-generation law students can be exceedingly difficult due to not only having to deal with the foreign language of law, but in many cases uprooting their lives to begin law school. There was an extra layer added to these struggles as we had to adjust to the impact the COVID-19 pandemic had on our student community. There were 3L students who were only on campus for one semester before the transition to remote who were desperate to return to the community aspect, they had received during their first semester of law school. Then, there were our 2L students who never had the opportunity to experience what a law school community should be as they had to begin their time virtually with no opportunity for any quality in-person interaction. Finally, we had our newest group of students coming into law school with a blank slate and no real sense of the benefit a community-oriented law school can offer. With the vast experience our programming committee had, as all of us were first-generation law students, we knew we had to cater our programming around a central event to bring all of these students together. Our programming was to serve as their introduction to our law school community, thus we had to ensure we provided a way for the interests of all three groups to be able to connect with each other to begin forming bonds prior to the school year. While our initial focus in the creation of our programming was to serve incoming students during their pre-orientation period, we found that we could have a direct impact on all of our first-generation students by fostering a community where our students can find support from not only our staff and faculty, but from their peers as well.

1. Faculty Fellows

The Academic Resource Center and the Office of Diversity, Equity and Inclusion are afforded the ability to hire current law students to serve as Faculty Fellows. Faculty Fellows assist with research, curriculum building, and program and content creation; Faculty Fellows allow a student perspective when creating curriculum and content to fine-tune where the students have need, as well as allowing the Faculty Fellow to learn and research on a particular area of interest. The Academic Resource Center has specifically sought out students who identify as first-generation students to hire as Faculty Fellows. These Faculty Fellows are aware of the unique challenges they came into law school with as first-generation students and seek to work with our offices to assist current and future first-generation students in mitigating that learning curve. Our Faculty Fellows participate in events with prospective students and with incoming 1L students to start the peer mentoring relationship.

Our Faculty Fellows serve not only as stewards for our offices, but also offer a sense of credibility and camaraderie with current students as mentors who share with students the resources that our offices offer and what has helped them in their law school journey.

E. Resources for Students' Families

Another goal of the First Generation Workshop is to help educate students' families so that the families can support their students even more. Often, law students may not be familiar with the timeline and progression of the law school semester, and unsurprisingly their families are not either. One of the hurdles first-generation students face is potential lack of support or misunderstanding of what the student is experiencing and pressure to explain and educate what the student is going through during the semester. To alleviate some of this pressure, we provided a letter that students could choose to give to their family members about one month into the first semester. The letter describes the stressors students might face and describes the law school timeline to give the family an idea of what the students might be going through. We gave this information to facilitate some of the conversation about responsibilities at school that would take them away from family events. This is a resource for families to get a better understanding of why their loved one would not be available like they may have been in the past. We have since expanded this family resource guide to include law school lingo and definitions that they may hear from their student, a description of the 1L classes, and descriptions of the various offices in the law school that are available to support students. This has been created with the assistance of first-generation students so that we can gain further insight into what information can be helpful for their families. We believe that the more families know about the law school process, the better able they will be to support their students.

First-generation students may lack a familial support system throughout their educational career, including upon making the decision to attend law school and as they assimilate to the demands of law school. Particularly in law school settings, this insufficient support can stem from conflicting values and expectations between family members and students; family members may expect students to contribute to the family while enrolled in classes, while first-generation students may feel the need to focus on their studies full-time to meet the demands set by the school, which may be compounded by the students' feeling that they are not learning and absorbing as much knowledge as their peers.[33]

As part of our pre-orientation programming, we provide a Family Resource Guide to our first-generation students; we let the students make the choice to share the Family Resource Guide with their family if they choose. This resource allows the student to share knowledge of their upcoming law school journey, particularly their

---

33. Jacqueline M. O'Bryant & Katharine T. Schaffzin, *First-Generation Students in Law School: A Proven Success Model*, 70 Ark. L. Rev. 913 at 920 (2018).

first-year experience, with their family. The resource releases a burden on the student to have to explain to their family the particulars of their first-year experience by giving them a packet containing helpful information in one place.

The Family Resource Guide contains a letter from our offices, introducing the reader to our offices' resources. The letter expresses gratitude to the family for entrusting SLU Law with their loved one's education and growth and ends with a note of encouragement of continued family support for their loved one.

The first substantive content in the Family Resource Guide is a list of SLU Law offices that support the student, including the Office of Student Services, the Office of Career Services, the Office of Diversity, Equity and Inclusion, and the Academic Resource Center. The names and titles of the people within the offices are listed so that family members know who the student can seek out for support. Additional resources listed are the Missouri Lawyer Assistance Program and the SLU University Counseling Center contact information. Counseling services are often requested by students and the Missouri Lawyer Assistance Program offers counseling for lawyers, law students, and students' family members. We included this information so that the students' family members can familiarize themselves with the people that the student will encounter often and so that the family member can know how and by whom the student is being supported.

Next, the Family Resource Guide includes the 1L academic calendar, including semester start dates, the last day of the semester, information on the exam period dates, and any scheduled days off. Further, we included a screen capture of a typical full-time day 1L's anticipated schedule. The screen capture shows a picture of a week in Google Calendar with time slots filled in for the 1L student's class time, time spent preparing for class, time spent synthesizing class notes and outlining, and time blocked for eating meals, possible extracurricular activities, and travel time to and from school. This allows the family member to visualize how much time is consumed by law school. This will hopefully allow the family member to understand the student's bandwidth for additional family demands and show them that the student could use support with household tasks, meals, or moral support to meet the demanding schedule.

After the sample student schedule, we include course descriptions for the 1L classes. This serves as a reference point for family members to come back to when the student discusses their classes and the content of their classes.

The next section in the Family Resource Guide is titled "First Year Experiences." This section informs the family member about the law school curve and the particular emphasis that is put on GPA in the first year. Further, there is an explanation of mid-term exams and final exams. We describe how law school exams tend to be different from undergraduate exams, in that oftentimes the final exam constitutes a majority of the students' grades, adding pressure to succeed on the exams. We also note that our law school's semester ends the week of the Thanksgiving holiday, and exams begin the week after the Thanksgiving holiday. We note that students may not be as present or present at all for the holiday, and we encourage the family member to be patient and understanding with their student's study schedule.

We include a section on "Supporting Your 1L." This section suggests ways to support their student, particularly in anticipation of what the student may need if the student is not able to express their needs to their families. We encourage family members to be patient with their student and be understanding of their schedule; further, we encourage both student and family member to listen and communicate; we encourage the family member to express to their student that they are proud of them, and to be encouraging through a process that may alter the student's confidence.

We end our Family Resource Guide with a "Law School Glossary." Law school comes with a jargon familiar to those only with experience of the language, and this glossary will aid in families' understanding of concepts and words that their student may use in conversation. This will also hopefully pique the families' interest in learning about a specific topic or word, which may facilitate conversation between the family and the student. The act of a family member reaching out to inquire and communicate with the student will hopefully make the student feel supported when they know that the family member is interested and invested in the student's learning.

The Faculty Resource Guide was created in large part by our Faculty Fellows. We gave some guidance on the content, but the delivery, tone, and substance were created by these current students. These first-generation Faculty Fellows were best suited to know firsthand what resources and information would benefit their own families as they were entering into law school.

IV. Lessons Learned

A. Explaining the Importance of Targeted Programming

Similar to the backlash against the targeted programming of early Academic Support Professionals, targeted first-generation programs may receive some hesitancy. There are people who will not understand the importance of programs provided to targeted groups of students. The perception may be that targeted programming excludes other students from receiving information. There may be pushback to first-generation programming by some members of the community who believe in catering to all students equally. In these situations, it is important to explain equality versus equity. It is important to explain that our students come to us with unique needs and different barriers to accessing a legal education. Every student does not need the same type or the same amount of support.

B. Outside Speakers

Early in the spring semester, we invited an outside speaker to talk with our students, particularly to our 1L students. We chose this time to bring in a speaker to reinforce study skills messaging because 1Ls had just received their first semester grades, and many students found they did not perform as well as they would have liked. The speaker was a lawyer who found success after struggling in undergrad and now is a law school motivational speaker. She talked to students about studying, the time it takes to be successful, supplements, practice tests, and networking—things that they have heard from us before, but that the students needed to hear again. She also provided activities to help them practice visualization, strategic planning, and the power of positivity. The students were very receptive to the words of this outside speaker, and her ideas and way of presenting study tips resonated with them.

At first, we debated the pros and cons of bringing in an outside speaker, because we did not want to diminish our credibility or have the students consider us less of an expert since they were hearing information from someone other than us. Ultimately, we came to the decision that the students have repeatedly heard things from us as academic support professors, and it would resonate differently with them to hear it from someone else. Similarly, we want doctrinal professors to reiterate the same messages we are giving students when it comes to study skills and retaining the information. Hearing the same message from multiple sources allows adult learners to retain the information better, improving their engagement with the information and increasing their motivation to learn. We spoke to a student about our thoughts on this to get a student perspective, and she shared with us that bringing in an outside speaker actually reinforced what we have been saying to students and did not minimize us as experts. It is important to note that as an Academic Support Professional you need to give the information to your students first so that when they hear things from someone else, it reinforces your own messaging.

C. Collaboration

One reason for the success of our first-generation programming is our efforts to collaborate with others. For example, we included our Office of Admissions at Saint Louis University School of Law, which acts as the primary liaison between the incoming students and us, from the start. The Office of Admissions informs us what questions the incoming students are asking so that we can tailor our programming even more to the needs of the first-generation students and helps us identify who might benefit from our programming. Since the incoming students have heard of who we are and the programming and resources we offer, we have found they are more comfortable approaching us and utilizing the resources of our offices. Additionally, the Office of Admissions has recently added a field on the School of Law application for incoming students to identify as not only first-generation college students but also first-generation law students. This data will help us in reaching out to students who identify as first generation so that they are aware of the resources available to them. Since we have established this relationship with our Office of Admissions, we plan to coordinate to expand our first-generation programming through pipeline work for first-generation students.

Saint Louis University School of Law is fortunate to have a student organization focused on first-generation law students named First Chair Society. We sought to incorporate First Chair Society into our planning but needed to be aware of not adding additional burdens on the students. One lesson we learned is that we should have incorporated them into our discussions earlier to let them know we were planning this targeted programming. A communication line for student input is crucial so that we can learn how best to meet their current needs. We ultimately found a balance of communicating with students and receiving their input and sharing with the students that we as faculty and administration are taking on the task of providing resources. So far, we have collaborated on a panel event with First Chair Society to bring in alumni to speak to their members. This event further established our relationship with that group of first-generation students. First generation programming and first-generation student groups are amazing selling points for an institution. The groups of students entering law school today want to know the types of support schools will offer them once they are students. Diversity and inclusion efforts are important to incoming students, and they want to know what institutions are doing to show that these efforts are important to them as well.

From the beginning, we knew that we wanted to expand our programming beyond the 1L year and collaborate across the law school departments that serve our students, including the Office of Student Services, the Office of Career Services, and the Office of Admissions. Finding ways to integrate our first-generation programming into other law school departments is important for the program to gain traction and exposure to students. When we initially presented our ideas and goals for future programming and collaboration to other law school departments, it came across in a way that seemed final to those other departments. This ultimately proved unsuccessful because the other departments did not feel as though they had the capacity to collaborate with us and were not as invested in the ideas because they did not participate in the planning and idea creation. To avoid this roadblock, we suggest including other departments in the planning phase or let them know this is an idea and not a full plan. We also hope to seek faculty involvement and further staff involvement in our programs. We know that many faculty and staff members are first generation themselves, so it will be more impactful to people we bring into our first-generation network within Saint Louis University School of Law. We know that many hands make light work and will continue to find ways to collaborate with other law school departments to present as many resources as possible to our first-generation students.

V. Conclusion

Saint Louis University School of Law's goal is to produce well-rounded and culturally competent professionals who will respectfully serve their diverse communities. As part of our Jesuit tradition, Saint Louis University remains faithful to the value of promoting justice and the dignity of all human beings. Our mission compels us not only to train lawyers for others, but to address the gap in access to justice faced by underrepresented communities. While our faculty and staff are available to all students, we recognize that law students are not merely getting an education, but entering a profession with its own unique language and culture. For those who are the first in their family to go to law school, it can be particularly challenging. Thus, our first-generation programming through our Office of Inclusion and Diversity Education and Academic Resource Center seeks to bridge gaps for incoming First-Generation students to help them thrive during their time in law school and in their legal career, and ultimately helps us meet our institution's goals of improving access to a legal education.

Fourteen

1L Evening / First Gen Students

Theory & Strategies for the First Four Weeks

Laura Mott*

I. Introduction

> *What sets night students apart, in addition to going [to law school] at night, is their absolute, unshakeable determination to be lawyers.*[1]

> *First-generation college students bring with them... work ethics that position them well to grit and grind their way through the challenges of law school.*[2]

LEGAL EDUCATION CONTINUES TO MAKE STRIDES towards exploding the normative three-year "traditional" J.D. model by implementing more flexibly scheduled programs. This development unequivocally provides access to potential law students who do not have the option of attending a full-time program and works to enrich the profession. This essay will explore early academic achievement methods for first generation students enrolled in "nontraditionally scheduled" J.D. programs. Universally, these programs generally allot four to five years to complete the 83 required

---

* Assistant Professor of Law, Lincoln Memorial University School of Law. Previously, the author served as the first Director of the Academic Skills Center for the 1L Evening Program at CUNY School of Law, the 2022–23 Chair of the AALS Section on Part Time Division Programs, and designed & taught the first academic support component for the New York Legal Education Opportunity program. This short essay is dedicated to my evening law students.

1. Jill Switzer, *What is it About Night Law Students?* Above The Law, January 25, 2017, *available at* https://abovethelaw.com/2017/01/what-is-it-about-night-law-students/. (remarking that "[w]hat sets night law students apart, in addition to going at night, is their absolute, unshakable determination to be lawyers. It's not their default choice. If they can survive night law school, the demands that it places on them, and the bar exam, then they can survive the rough and tumble of practice.").

2. Jacqueline M. O'Bryant & Katharine T. Schaffzin, *First-Generation Students in Law School: A Proven Success Model*, 70 Ark. L. Rev. 913, 914 (2018).

credits for graduation.[3] The discussion will leave behind prescriptive norms of the three-year full-time model to focus on academic success for nontraditionally scheduled students, as further opening access barriers to the profession.[4]

As the above quotes illustrate, this piece exists at the intersection of overlapping descriptors. The first is first generation law students. The second is the status as a part-time, hybrid, evening, or weekend (nontraditionally scheduled) law students. This short essay presents theory, AALS survey data, and concrete planning recommendations that fit somewhat squarely in this overlap, and which experience has proven can advance the academic achievement of first-generation evening/weekend students.

A. Law Student Learning

Various factors effect law student learning and may intersect with first generation students' experience in higher education.[5]

One potential consideration that may affect first-generation law student experience and achievement is the theory of "cultural mismatch." As explained by researchers, the theory of "cultural mismatch" in the context of higher education and first-generation students posits that a "cultural norm" that "pervade[s] American university settings... is universities' focus on middle-class norms of independence as the culturally appropriate way to be a college student... however, these same norms create a *cultural mismatch* for first-generation students, who prior to college are likely to have regulated their behavior according to working-class norms of interdependence, such as connecting to others and being attentive to others' needs."[6]

---

3. *See* ABA Standards and Rules of Procedure for Approval of Law Schools 2021–2022, American Bar Association (2021) at 22–23. Standard 311(a) states that "[a] law school shall require, as a condition for graduation, successful completion of a course of study of not fewer than 83 credit hours. Standard 311(b) states that "... the course of study for the J.D. program be completed no earlier than 24 months and, except in extraordinary circumstances, no later than 84 months after a student has commenced law study... ".

4. Many states have "access to justice" directives from Federal and State court systems, as well as from the DOJ; providing quality legal education–and appropriately-scaled academic support to part-time, evening and weekend Divisions–falls firmly within those directives. *See* Office of Access to Justice, *Mission, available at* https://www.justice.gov/atj.

5. Tomiko Brown-Nagin, *Rethinking Proxies for Disadvantage in Higher Education: A First Generation Students' Project*, 2014 U. Chi. Legal F. 433, 436 (2014) (generally positing that "[f]avorable treatment of first-generation, Pell Grant-eligible status ... [group initiatives], colleges can simultaneously tackle social problems related to income, race, and place...").

6. Nicole M. Stephens et al., *Unseen Disadvantage: How American Universities' Focus on Independence Undermines the Academic Performance of First-Generation College Students*, 102 J. Personality & Soc. Psychol. 1178, 1180 (2012), as cited in Jacqueline M. O'Bryant & Katharine T. Schaffzin, infra note 14 at 922, (emphasis added.)

This is echoed in the history of legal education; at inception, law schools restricted admission to Ivy-pedigreed men; the profession was homogeneous.[7],[8] It was not until the late 1960s and early 1970s that law schools, as a result of the civil rights movement and subsequent higher education affirmative action policies, began to admit more diverse students.[9] This moment *also* marked the first time U.S. law schools saw large numbers of first-generation student enrollment.[10] The trend continued.[11] These statistics bear focus because of the proven negative effects that stereotype threat, implicit bias, and fixed versus growth mindset have on students of color.[12]

Lastly, financial responsibilities are a continuing reality for first-generation students, who are statistically more likely to have to work during law school to support themselves and their families, especially during the first year of law school.[13] This

---

7. Mark T. Flahive, *The Origins of the American Law School*, 64 AMER. BAR ASSOC. J. 1868 at 1871 (1978). In providing a history of the evolution of the American law school, Flahive relates that the first law school was formed around 1794 and admitted only male students from elite Ivy League colleges. These men graduated after two years and served in an apprenticeship for a year. From its earliest inception, U.S. legal education was a short track.

8. JOAN HOWARTH, SHAPING THE BAR, THE FUTURE OF ATTORNEY LICENSING, STANFORD UNIVERSITY PRESS 17 (2023) *citing* JEROLD S. AUERBACH, UNEQUAL JUSTICE: LAWYERS AND SOCIAL CHANGE IN MODERN AMERICA 19 (1976).

9. *See* Russell McClain, *Bottled At The Source, Recapturing the Essence of Academic Support as a Primary Tool of Educational Equity for Minority Law Students*, 18 U. MD. L.J. RACE RELIG. GENDER & CLASS 139, 141–143 (2018) (discussing generally the civil-rights-era enrollment of law students of color, the connection to affirmative action policies of law schools, and tools which evolved to academically support those students over time.).

10. Tomiko Brown-Nagin, *supra* note 6 at 442–43, citing Victor B. Saenz, et al, *First in my Family: A Profile of First-Generation College Students at Four-Year Institutions Since 1971* at 10 (Cooperative Institutional Research Program May 2007), *at* http://www.heri.ucla.edu/PDFs/pubs/TFS/Special/Monographs/FirstInMyFamily.pdf (last visited May 15, 2022) (stating that "[i]n 1971, the overwhelming majority of black students who matriculated to college entered as first-generation college students [as compared to 38.5 percent of freshmen overall. In that same year...69.9 percent [of Latinx students] were first-generation college students."].

11. LAW SCHOOL SURVEY OF STUDENT ENGAGEMENT, LOOKING AHEAD: ASSESSMENT IN LEGAL EDUCATION at 10 (2014). (2014), *available at* http://lssse.indiana.edu/wpcontent/uploads/2016/01/LSSSE_2014_AnnualReport.pdf [https://perma.cc/W3AX-8YVT] (stating that "...larger proportions of Hispanic students (48%) and black/African-American students (43%) are first generation [law] students.")

12. *See generally*, McClain, *supra* note 10 (describing the disparate classroom dynamics and other struggles these psychological elements present in the law school learning process for students of color, emphasizing importance of academic support strategies that center these psychological effects.)

13. Jacqueline M. O'Bryant & Katharine T. Schaffzin, *First-Generation Students in Law School: A ProvenSuccess Model*, 70 ARK. L. REV. 913 (2018), citing Law Sch. Survey of Student Engagement, supra note 12 at 10–11 ("The 2014 LSSE reported that time spent working for pay among first-generation college students was the 'most pronounced' during the first year of law school, when 'first-generation students report spending 40% more time [working for pay.]'") To the author's knowledge, at the time of submission, similar studies have not been gathered for students enrolled in part-time, evening, or weekend J.D. programs, but if data were similar, the trend in consequences for part-time students would likely be as well.

means less time for studying–specifically the kind of studying that law school requires–deep work, with long periods of uninterrupted concentration and focus–to tackle cognitively demanding reading, processing, and distilling. If the requirement of a steady income has resulted in a student's selection of a nontraditionally scheduled law program, a lack of study time is certainly a factor that evening, part-time, and weekend program academic skills planning should account for as well.

Cumulatively, these factors suggests an imperative on professors and administrators as we help educate and prepare first generation students to achieve the career paths, mobility, and goals they have for themselves as they enter law school. Making nontraditionally scheduled J.D. programs responsive to the needs of the first-generation student populations they serve requires thoughtful and intentional deliberation.

B. "Reasonably comparable opportunities"[14]

There exists an implicit idea–baked into the very operational framework law schools exist within–that a three-year J.D. program is the "ideal" or "optimal" way to deliver a legal education.[15] There are reasons for this, certainly; however, this timeline fails to account for realities that students encounter regarding financial limitations, family care needs, and other barriers to full-time schooling–realities that render such a compressed timeline impossible. Therefore, the ABA allows for the

---

14. ABA Standards and Rules of Procedure, *supra* note 4 at 24. Standard 312. Reasonably Comparable Opportunities. A law school providing more than one enrollment or scheduling option shall ensure that all students have reasonably comparable opportunities for access to the law school's program of legal education, courses taught by full-time faculty, student services, co-curricular programs, and other educational benefits. Identical opportunities are not required.

15. It is interesting to explore the origins of this requirement. *See* Livia Gershon, *The Origins of American Law Schools: When Did Law Schools Become A Fixture In the Training of Elite Americans?* JSTOR Daily, December 30, 2014, *available at* https://daily.jstor.org/america-runs-law-schools/. Gershon, citing to Mark T. Flahive, *The Origins of the American Law School*, 64 Amer. Bar Assoc. J. 12, pp. 1868–1871 (December 1978) (relating that before the Revolutionary War, one became a lawyer through an apprenticeship system, rather than through a school. The apprenticeships for prospective attorneys lasted three years and ended in an oral bar exam. During the Revolutionary war, apprenticeships became limited, as hosts were otherwise engaged. *Id.* After that, the law school was born out of necessity to train more aspiring lawyers than there were practicing attorneys for them to apprentice with. Law schools consisting of students from Ivy League undergraduate degrees, many of whom later went on to hold political office in the new Federal government.) Today, the United States Department of Education (USDOE) recognizes the Council of the American Bar Association as an accrediting agency for Juris Doctor law programs, and most U.S. jurisdictions require a J.D. from an ABA-approved law school to sit for the bar exam. See ABA Standards and Rules of Procedure at v. ABA-accredited schools overwhelmingly offer mainly three-year J.D. programs; other iterations typically have much lower enrollment.

83-credit requirement to be satisfied over a longer period of time,[16] as long as such programs provide "reasonably comparable opportunities" as a three-year program.[17]

Both theoretical and practical frameworks exist to support an argument that certain legal education structural norms may no longer wholly serve the students we educate, nor the profession into which they enter. As an example, the U.S. is currently experiencing a seismic crisis in representation for indigent and low-income petitioners and criminal defendants, made worse by COVID.[18] Holistically maximizing both full time and nontraditionally schedule students' chances for success in law school and on the bar exam will enable more attorneys to go into practice, robustly serving those clients and communities. The positioning of our nontraditionally scheduled students remains in conflict with traditional models.

So if empowering first generation part-time evening and weekend students to earn law degrees, pass the bar, and practice law is required to increase access to the profession and serve clients who would otherwise go unrepresented, the only question that remains is how to look at the full-time law school curriculum through the four-year lens, craft a plan that works, and then provide students not just with "reasonably comparable" opportunities, but with finely-tuned academic support and curricular planning to allow them to be successful in the program not just in their first year, but for the duration.

How do we create these new models with well-thought-out support to ensure that students have the maximum time possible to learn, metabolize, practice, and rest? Every program, certainly, is different, but there may be some best practices. One of the main guiding principles behind these practices is to help students avoid "triage mode" with their assignments and exams by equipping them early.

---

16. Standard 311(b) states that "...the course of study for the J.D. program be completed no earlier than 24 months and, except in extraordinary circumstances, no later than 84 months after a student has commenced law study...".

17. ABA Standards and Rules of Procedure, *supra* note 4 at 24. Standard 312. Reasonably Comparable Opportunities. "A law school providing more than one enrollment or scheduling option shall ensure that all students have reasonably comparable opportunities for access to the law school's program of legal education, courses taught by full-time faculty, student services, co-curricular programs, and other educational benefits. Identical opportunities are not required."

18. *See, e.g.* Scott Merrill, *N.H. Supreme Court Task Force Addresses Shortage of Public Defenders*, November 15, 2021, available at https://www.concordmonitor.com/N-H-Supreme-Court-Task-Force-Addresses-Shortage-of-Public-Defenders-43524510 (describing the difficult hiring conditions in the state as due to the fact that "... the pay rates for private practice far and away outstrip public defender pay scales.") Similar issues were reported in Montana and Oregon, where a legal director of the ACLU described events as "the system... buckling before our eyes." Gillian Flaccus, *Pandemic Pushes Oregon's Public Defender System To The Brink*, May 10, 2022, *available at* https://apnews.com/article/covid-health-crime-pandemics-9f479097d57a34907af8629808c46d8c.

C. "Triage Mode", Chronobiology, and How it Affects Evening Student Learning

Reducing or eliminating "triage mode" is an elusive but worthy goal when it comes to supporting evening and weekend students.

What does "triage mode" mean? As academic support faculty will know, many students entering law school see final exams and legal writing assignments as *final products*, rather than as a *process.* In many cases, this perception is a predictable holdover from new law students' prior undergraduate experiences, where grades are mostly earned not by demonstrating mastery of legal analysis and extended-time-frame skill development, but rather from assignments and exams which evaluate mastery of ability to research, write, memorize and regurgitate on a short timeline.

Although "triage" may sound like cramming, what makes the habit different is its longer-term timeline. Students will begin the semester quite focused on one task until its due date; then they pivot to the next task, leaving the first completely behind, siloed. This not only taxes their endurance, but it impedes their ability to transfer skills across their classes.

Triage mindset can be compounded for evening/weekend students who have even less time than day students available to spend with the material. Therefore, it can often be the case that evening 1L students develop the habit of "triaging" assignments for deadlines–even more so than students in full-time day programs. This is exacerbated at least once if not more for each individual student each semester, when life issues come up that cannot be ignored. These disruptions can set students even further into triage.

In any case, such triaging can set into motion a repeating, detrimental cycle which might persist through successive semesters. If sustained, such habits can cause chronic lack of doctrinal absorption, under-application of academic skill sets, and lack of substantive transition into "thinking like a lawyer." This can lead to incomplete/unsound foundational skills, creating a resistance to the cross-curricular nature of the paradigm of legal analysis, and potentially affect bar skill development.

For evening students, chronobiology likely plays a part in retention as well.[19] It can be more difficult to pay attention at night to a dense lecture after a long day at work or caretaking for children or family members, depending on a student's "chronotype", how their circadian rhythms are attuned, and what that means for how tired they become in the evening.[20] Although a deeper discussion of the science on chro-

19. Sandra J. Kuhlman, et al. *Introduction To Chronobiology*, Cold Spring Harbor Perspect. Biol. 10:a033613 (2018) (stating that "[a]s a consequence of the Earth's rotation about its axis approximately every 24 [hours], most organisms on this planet are subjected to predictable fluctuations of light and temperature. A diverse range of species, from cyanobacteria to humans, evolved endogenous biological clocks that allow for the anticipation of these daily variations. Thus, our internal physiology and function is fundamentally intertwined with this geophysical cycle.")

20. *See generally* Bonny L. Tavares, Rebecca L. Scalio, *Teaching After Dark*: Part-Time Evening Students and the First-Year Legal Research and Writing Classroom, 17 Legal Writing: J. Legal

notype is beyond the scope of this essay, recent studies have shown negative academic effects of mismatched chronotype and class times.[21] There are certainly teaching techniques that have been noted as universally useful in pushing back on the effects of fatigue/chronobiology.[22] These tools all help in efforts to head off triaging.

Ultimately, breaking this "triage mode" mentality benefits from all-hands-on-deck planning by academic affairs and other departments, as well as setting up expectations for good habits early. The most important time to help put steps in place to serve nontraditionally scheduled J.D. students throughout law school–particularly first-generation students–is during the first few weeks of law school classes.

II. Nontraditionally Scheduled 1L Academic Skills Programming[23]

Academic support faculty often wear many hats. Planning, designing, and teaching are among those roles, which positions this cohort of faculty well to lead the way in support for nontraditionally scheduled students. Certainly, building the scaffolding to achieve multiple goals (skill-building, doctrinal reinforcement and study piv-

---

WRITING INST. 65, 109 (2011) (analyzing lack of attention and how to cope: "An additional physiological factor that may particularly impact an evening student's ability to absorb information is time-of-day energy levels.")

21. Benjamin L. Smarr & Aaron E. Schirmer, *3.4 million real-work learning management system logins reveal the majority of students experience social jet lag correlated with decreased performance,* Scientific Reports 8:4793 (2018) DOI:10.1038/s41598-018-23044-8. This study extrapolated chronotype from learning management system login times ("[s]tudent LMS logins showed signs that they contain circadian rhythm information, and social disruptions thereof," at 2,) and then assessed student performance on a range of different variables. Based on their findings (one being "increasing amplitude correlating strongly with decreased academic performance, especially in late chronotypes," at 5*)*, the researchers concluded that "[i]t therefore seems reasonable to advocate that circadian rhythms... should be considered in school and class scheduling by institutions as well as by individuals. Universities might want to provide chrono-counseling to students about the importance of chronotype and daily stability to academic achievement." *Id.* at 7.

22. *See* Tavares and Scalio, *supra* note 21 at 107, *citing* Robin A. Boyle & Rita Dunn, *Teaching Law Students Through Individual Learning Styles*, 62 ALB. L. REV. 213, 234 (1998) (suggesting that "[s]tudents can also be advised to take advantage of the technological learning tools provided by the instructor during their chronobiological highs. For example, during their peak times, students could listen to class pod-casts or review PowerPoint slides."). See also Richart Freishtat, To Lecture or Not To Lecture . . . How About Maybe? In Berkeley Center for Teaching and Learning Blog, available at https://teaching.berkeley.edu/news/lecture-or-not-lecture-how-about-maybe-0 (stating that "[u]ltimately, it's about keeping the lecture flexible and not pre-programmed. It's about customizing it for the class, and for these students.").

23. Insights drawn from Evening program at CUNY School of Law, where total student body is 42% first generation college students. See Press Release, January 22, 2025, CUNY Law Leads Nation in Training Diverse Cohorts of Lawyers, *available at* https://www.law.cuny.edu/newsroom_post/cuny-law-takes-top-diversity-ranking-three-years-running/. Many first generation students opt to enroll in the Evening program and continue working full-time jobs during the day to support themselves and their families.

ot points) with a evening, part-time, or hybrid 1L cohort is a task which changes each year and is influenced by changing enrollment numbers, remote learning considerations, and student need. Nonetheless, foundational principles remain.

This section focuses on implementing those foundational principles during that critical period of time which runs from pre-Orientation through the first two weeks of classes—a "littoral zone" of Evening law school experience. During this time, students acclimate to new, often extreme time demands on their schedule, and are guided through a level of detailed future study planning that many may be unaccustomed to. This all occurs against the backdrop of learning to detangle frustratingly circuitous case language, connecting this language with categories in case briefs, adjusting to different teaching styles, and preparing for getting called on during class. The switch from pre-law programs into "the real thing" can feel daunting.

Over the years of working intensively on building the Evening program's capacity to help students adjust during this time, some practices have stood out as effective.[24] This section will highlight those as a resource for law schools with Evening, Weekend, Hybrid, or Part-Time programs at each stage of the timeline during this critical four-week period. Along the way, the narrative will demonstrate how learning science reasoning and methodologies are woven into the design and implementation of these techniques.

If you are reading this, perhaps your institution has one or more nontraditional J.D. programs (i.e. part-time, evening, or weekend); you might be fine-tuning such, or building a new program. It therefore seems advisable to provide a note of encouragement: *Make the investment in your part-time, evening, and/or weekend students.* Work with your Department, your Dean, your central university to *make the investment in your students in nontraditional J.D. programs.* The legal profession needs them.

III. Part-Time/Evening/Hybrid Pre-law Summer Programs

Resourcing in a nontraditional J.D. program should ideally be evident to students upon the class's first contact with the law school. So called "front-end" investment can have a salutary "first impression" effect on the group learning environment, as well as providing a more seamless springboard into law school. And it all starts with pre-law programs.

24. Many of these strategies have been workshopped with the invaluable collaboration and Evening co-teaching expertise of Professor Asima Chaudhary at the City University of New York School of Law.

While it is not a new concept for schools to host pre-law programs for incoming 1Ls, there are several reasons why this is a critical step for schools with nontraditional J.D. programs to take.

There are a few components that seem to make these initiatives very beneficial for first-gen evening students, each of which are discussed below.

In 2021, the Association of American Law Schools (AALS) Division for Part-Time Programs piloted what was possibly the first-ever national survey of non-full-time law programs at U.S. law schools.[25] Of 44 law schools who responded to the survey and affirmed that they had either a part-time, evening, or weekend program at their law school, 35 confirmed that their enrollment was 60 evening students or less. The relatively small number of students in most programs leads to the first recommendation: a robust evening summer or late-summer program open to all. This might be different from–or in addition to–the traditionally offered several-day Orientation.

A. A dedicated learning community

If possible, consider opening some subset of pre-Orientation classes to all incoming nontraditionally scheduled 1Ls. This socioemotionally responsive step can go measures and miles towards building community and ameliorating traces of "cultural mismatch."[26] Building community is of critical importance for the gelling and thriving of a part-time, evening, or weekend higher education program, especially because of the common lack of interaction with day program students.[27] With the cohesion of community comes peace and ease of mind for many students who are the first in their families to attend college or law school. Cross-socialization fosters *interdependence*, and also helps to provide opportunities for students to form study groups, which are often critical to first-semester success. This was especially true during the COVID public health crisis, which rendered the format of academic programming fluid into the future. When multiple variables are up in the air, it can help to know that one has a dedicated learning community.

---

25. This survey was conducted in the Fall-Winter of 2021 via distribution to all U.S. law schools on various list serves, including those for Deans, Student Affairs professionals, and Academic Skills faculty. Results were redistributed and used to formulate robust AALS Section programming highlighting strengths, best practices, and strategies to hone nontraditionally scheduled J.D. programs. Survey data on file with author.

26. *See generally* Stephens et al, *supra* note 7.

27. Sarah B. Zahl, *The Impact of Community for Part-Time Doctoral Students: How Relationships In the Academic Department Affect Student Persistence.* 10 International Journal of Doctoral Studies 301 (2015), available at http://ijds.org/Volume10/IJDSv10p301/-321Zahl0672.pdf (stating the results of this study as: "[p]ositive relationships with peers and faculty served as a source of encouragement and supported persistence, particularly during challenging semesters and later phases of the doctoral program. However, it was often difficult for the participants to develop and/or maintain relationships, due to limited proximity, limited access to faculty, and changing cohorts. Participants did not consider full-time doctoral students to be part of their community, due to perceived differences between part-time and full-time students.").

B. Series of anonymously scored skills-based exercises

It is also recommended that these programs offer a low-stakes environment for students to acquire and practice different methods of performing basic law school skills. This might be in the form of writing tasks or multiple choice questions; ideally any testing or evaluative format they will experience. Once the semester begins, things begin to "count"; this often induces anxiety and can also trigger "overperformance" by students. To avoid implicit bias and stereotype threat, the pre-law weeks are good opportunities to do anonymous grading and comments, as well.

C. Time Management Training

Ideally, begin talking with evening, part-time, weekend, or hybrid students about time. Isolating periods of "deep work" time is challenging; students with full-time employment or other responsibilities on top of law school will inevitably have fundamentally less time to study and internalize skills. Guiding them through the process of creating a detailed calendar with dates mapped in can help with this process, either now or after the semester begins.

D. Extended time off before the semester

Consider leaving more time for nontraditionally scheduled students to rest and recuperate after any pre-law programming than you might for full time students; this on-ramp may need to be longer to allow for a mentally transition.

IV. Academic Skills Classes—The First Two Weeks[28]

Of course, academic skills classes will tackle the largest issues first. Once the nuts and bolts of case reading and briefing, etc. are discussed and somewhat demystified, however, it may be beneficial to discuss with nontraditionally students the more long-game aspect of their journey through their first year of law school.

A large piece of this–and perhaps for evening, part-time, or weekend students, the piece that deserves the most attention at the beginning–is time mapping. For all students, including first generation students, the importance of walking through a detailed schedule of how the first few weeks and months of school will look is critical to their success.[29] Most come from undergraduate programs for which regurgitation of information was sufficient and triaging would lead to success; this is now quite a different exercise which requires a longer lead time on study.

28. These recommendations stem from a curricular model which presumes students have a stable schedule throughout the semester with periodic assignments and exams.

29. O'Bryant & Schaffzin, *supra* note 3 (stating that "[p]arents who have not attended college often do not possess the information needed to effectively advise their first-generation children on succeeding in college.") In this context, this information would consist of the mandate to take time off from work around major due dates or exams.

Generally this is best done in the second week of school, or whenever all syllabi and dates through midterms are set. Here is a step-by-step guide to this lesson plan.[30]

Step 1: Obtain all student assignment due dates from each class all part-time/evening/hybrid 1L students are enrolled in. This includes legal writing, midterms, ungraded assignments, reflection memos, other writing assignments, anything that the students must turn in, or any exams.[31]

Step 2: Place all due dates onto a calendar (preferably one with blocks for each day, and places to enter tasks for each weekend day, including the percentage of how much each assignment is worth.

Step 3: Using the syllabi from each class, map out, together with the students, dates on which to have certain parts of their outlines complete.

Step 4: Map in dates on which to do practice exams or problems.

Step 5: Suggest days which might be good ones to take off from work (if possible) or do half-days.

One reason for such a heavy focus on calendaring up front is that as time begins to move more quickly, due dates come up more quickly. This pre-planning can help to foreground the importance of time management and help to avoid triage so common in part-time/hybrid/evening programs.

V. Conclusion

As discussed at the beginning of the essay, the history of the first generation 4-year J.D. student trajectory is quite divergent from the genesis of the traditional three-year program. And notably, in the context of undergraduate college attendance, it has been observed that for first generation students, an obligation to work and attend school part-time "undermines students' ability to focus on academics and is a risk factor in the failure to graduate from college."[32]

---

30. This process is based on a brilliant overall time management exercise by Professor Haley Meade.

31. Connecting with the Academic Affairs department here may be beneficial; they may (or may be receptive) to managing dates for the first-year evening students to ensure adequate space to study, outline, and practice between exams.

32. Brown-Nagin, *supra* note 6 *at* 483–484 , citing Jennifer Engle and Vincent Tinto, *Moving Beyond Access: College Success For Low Income, First-Generation Students* *20 (The Pell Institute 2008), *available at* http://files.eric.ed.gov/fulltext/ED504448.pdf (last visited May 15, 2022) (stating "[f]irst-generation students from impoverished backgrounds confront pervasive economic hardships that present especially dire challenges in an era of rapidly-rising college costs. These students lack parents or other family members who can afford to provide financial support for full-time study. Consequently, these students frequently make a logical but educationally ill-advised choice: they enroll in college on a part-time basis and work to support themselves. The obligation to work undermines students' ability to focus on academics and is a risk factor in the failure to graduate from college.)

Indisputably, law school is a highly cognitively-demanding daily exercise, where classroom performance—note-taking and professor-student colloquy—is a much more active process than in undergraduate classes. It requires a high level of focus in order to process the material and understand how the law applies to the facts. Further, the trajectory of a law school course can often mirror practice—rule synthesis, an application to facts, recommendations about a party's success with a legal claim.

This makes what has been discussed *infra.* even more important for part-time, evening, and weekend programming. Thoughtful scheduling and programming in the first four weeks is critical to evening/weekend student success. Unlike undergraduate programs, which have more classes offered at more times, and therefore can be more tailored to a part-time schedule, law school three-year programs are designed to offer a specific set of classes and are restricted under ABA standards as far as how long students can take to finish their law degree. The rigidity of these requirements, as well as the–rightfully–pre-requisite heavy upper level curriculum (consisting of live client clinical practice) further restricts such scheduling.

Implied in a conversation of "how things are" is a suggestion of "how things might be." There may be a future where bar admission will look different; law practice is also stretching towards the future in many ways. J.D. programming options are following suit. Crafting evening/weekend academic skills programming to meet and exceed "reasonably comparable opportunities" for our first-generation students who enroll in these programs will serve students, law schools, and the future of the practice of law.

Fifteen

Orientation and Beyond

Unhiding the Hidden Curriculum Helps Level the Playing Field for First Gen Law Students

Tania Shah* and Mary Basik**

Introduction

THERE IS NO UNIVERSAL STANDARD DEFINITION OF *FIRST-GENERATION* used in the context of legal education.[1] First-generation undergraduate students are defined as the first in their families to earn a baccalaureate college degree.[2] However, this definition seems insufficient in the law school context. The legal profession has its own culture, customs, and language. For students entering law school, this legal insider knowledge is the hidden curriculum, neither written nor spoken, and it is inaccessible to first-generation students. However, the hidden curriculum is not only inaccessible to students who are the first in their families to attend a four-year college, but since the hidden curriculum is specific to legal culture, it is also inaccessible to students who are the first in their families to attend law school. For these reasons, we assert that in the legal education context the *first-generation* definition should include students who are the first in their families to attend law school. The ABA uses a similar definition. According to the ABA, "...a first-generation law student is a student who does not have a familial relationship to the legal field. While there is no explicit definition, the phrase usually refers to those who are the first to attend law school in

* Director of the Academic Success Program and Associate Professor of Law, Western State College of Law.

** Assistant Dean for Academic Skills, UC Irvine School of Law.

1. Dawn Young & Ricardo Santiago, *Looking at the Challenges Facing First-Generation Law Students (And How to Address Them)*, ABA FOR LAW STUDENTS: STUDENT LAWYER (October 14, 2021), https://abaforlawstudents.com/2021/10/14/the-challenges-facing-first-generation-law-students/.

2. 20 U.S.C.A. § 1070a-11(h)(3) (West).

their immediate family."[3] Broadly defining *first-generation* to include those lacking access to insider information about law school, and specifically legal culture, allows us to better target first-generation-focused programming to all who may benefit.

Law school is well known as a challenging, arduous, and competitive academic endeavor. While possessing drive and having a keen intellect are required, there is more to being a successful law student with promising career prospects than these traits alone. Lawyers on the "inside" know the culture, understand the customs, and utilize the appropriate terminology. Students fortunate enough to have lawyers "in the know" within their close familial circle have access to a private tour guide to help them navigate this unfamiliar terrain. Students whose personal networks include those who are legally savvy can acclimate to the demands of law school more quickly, which provides a substantial advantage in a highly competitive environment. Students who do not know of the hidden curriculum, because they lack access to those who are legally savvy in their personal networks, are at a competitive disadvantage, which poses predictable difficulties and creates additional anxiety. This disadvantage persists throughout law school and follows them into their careers. We assert that this disadvantage can be ameliorated with law school programming designed to make the hidden curriculum transparent and accessible for all students.

First-generation focused programming is becoming more common in law school pre-orientation programs, which is a positive development. However, first-generation-focused programming should also be incorporated into orientation programming and provided contemporaneously on appropriate topics throughout law school. The challenges imposed by the hidden curriculum of legal culture does not end at orientation, but rather persists and intensifies as students navigate through law school and career planning. For example, a recent study by the National Association for Law Placement (NALP) found that first-generation students fared worse in landing jobs compared to their peers, lagging 11 percentage points behind those graduates who had a parent who held a J.D. in getting bar-passage required jobs.[4]

While it may appear we are making a lot of assumptions in this chapter about first-generation law students, we also know that it is essential to *not* make assumptions about what law students know about law school.[5] The assumptions we make about what our students already know, which is most often based on each educator's own personal experience, penalizes students from first-generation backgrounds. This is especially true since most teaching in the legal academy do not come from first-generation backgrounds. It simply does not occur to many professors that students do not know information that was common knowledge to them.

---

3. Mary Ann C. Krisa, *How to Overcome Challenges as a First-Generation Law Student*, ABA for Law Students (August 25, 2001), https://abaforlawstudents.com/2021/08/25/first-generation-law-student-challenges/.

4. *Jobs & JDs: Employment and Salaries of New Law Graduates, Class of 2019*, Nat'l Ass'n for Law Placement (2021).

5. *Id.*

We advocate for the integration of first-generation legal culture focused programming into general orientation programming and throughout law school to help level the playing field. As educators, we cannot manufacture legally savvy personal networks for our incoming students, but we can transparently provide explicit guidance in the hidden curriculum students could access if they did have such a network. Transparency is the first step toward equity.

Schools may opt to provide first-generation programming only to students who self-identify, and/or such programming can be specifically labelled as pertinent to first-generation students, and/or designed as optional sessions. Another alternative, which we use at UC Irvine Law School, is to provide first-generation focused programming for all students. We use this approach to intentionally and explicitly communicate that we not only support our first-generation students, but we value and celebrate their presence. Each law school should determine its own needs and goals for incorporating first-generation focused programming and can choose from the following suggestions as to which will best meet the needs of their students.

Part 1: Provide Transparency About How the First Gen Experience Impacts Law Students

An important part of our job as educators is to foster a feeling of belonging in the law school environment and the larger legal profession for our first-generation students. A large part of accomplishing this is to share with our students the insider information that will allow them to more confidently feel that they also belong in this esteemed profession.

First-generation-focused programming should start with transparently explaining why first-generation issues are important and worthy of inclusion. It is imperative that law schools have a continued commitment to supporting first-generation students beyond orientation. We should endeavor to teach students essential law school coping skills, help them obtain mentors, navigate the job search process, and share each other's stories of challenges and successes.[6] For law schools that have not done so yet, first-generation concerns when planning professional development programs and activities should be paramount.[7]

PROGRAMMATIC APPLICATION

Starting with orientation, law schools can telegraph our support for our first-generation students. Schools should candidly discuss and celebrate first-generation students to communicate a message of inclusion and highlight the value placed on

---

6. Michelle Silverthorn, *First Generation Lawyers: The Next Diversity Frontier*, 2 Civility (Feb. 14, 2022), https://www.2civility.org/first-generation-lawyers-diversity-frontier/.

7. *Id.*

the importance of diversity for the student body, and the larger goal that the legal profession reflect the communities which it serves. A mission statement is not a solution in and of itself, but it does communicate the importance and commitment to these principles. Pedagogical commitments of law schools must continually underscore the importance of programs for diverse student bodies in law schools, especially people of color, immigrants, children of immigrants, and first-generation students.[8] Orientation is a starting place to encourage and empower students to be confident in their judgement, decisions, and actions in law school, with their professors and in the profession generally. It should not be the responsibility of any one department to ensure there are programs fostering inclusion, but law schools should employ creative strategies that require the collaboration of faculty, staff, and students to create an entire atmosphere of belonging and collegiality for all students. Since we are encouraging transparency in the first-generation experience, this would be a good time to provide guided questions in small groups to all law students asking them to explain some of their feelings surrounding starting law school. We can encourage students to tell us about themselves and ask targeted questions to flesh out different experiences. This will eliminate alienating certain students while students explain their experiences. Students can be asked about what in their background has helped them prepare for law school (family, education, friends, support) and a legal career. We can also ask them what shapes any anxiety they may or may not have about law school.

Transparently Explain Imposter Syndrome to All Students

Feelings of imposter syndrome are prevalent with law students. First-generation law students are particularly susceptible to imposter syndrome.[9] While imposter syndrome[10] is not felt *exclusively* by first-generation students, it is likely felt by virtually *all* first-generation law students.

PROGRAMMATIC APPLICATION

Given its pervasiveness, the psychological phenomenon of imposter syndrome, as discussed in detail earlier in this book, should be introduced at orientation. This explanation will be helpful for all students, but especially those from the first generation. Discovering they are not alone and that feeling like they don't belong is the norm can be comforting. We can help students realize that imposter syndrome is

8. Peter A. Joy, *Challenges to Legal Education, Clinical Legal Education, and Clinical Scholarship*, 26 Clinical L. Rev. 237, 261 (2019).

9. Debra Austin, *Windmills of Your Mind: Understanding the Neurobiology of Emotion*, 54 Wake Forest L. Rev. 931, 948–49 (2019).

10. *Imposter Syndrome? 8 Tactics to Combat Anx*iety, American Bar Association: Your ABA (Oct. 2018), https://www.americanbar.org/news/abanews/publications/youraba/2018/october-2018/tell-yourself-_yet--and-other-tips-for-overcoming-impostor-syndr/.

common and completely understandable given the uniqueness of law study. It is an external discomfort born from inexperience, not a lack of ability, which fuels self-defeating critical thoughts. Transparency about imposter syndrome provides students with a non-internally focused explanation for their unease.

In addition to explaining imposter syndrome, engaging in a hands-on activity can assist students in internalizing the message. Without having students look up the definition of "imposter syndrome," have students define what this phrase means to them. Usually in their own subjective definitions, the student may reveal some of their own feelings. This can be coupled with a think, pair, and share[11] on the definitions or other group activity.

Students can provide an example of a famous person or someone they know who has admitted to experiencing imposter syndrome and assess how that person feels about themself compared to a more realistic external view. For example, Supreme Court Justice Sonia Sotomayor has admitted to struggling with imposter syndrome.[12]

Another activity is to expose students to narratives of older students and/or alumni from a variety of backgrounds admitting to feelings of imposter syndrome. After comparing those experiences to their own, ask the students to take the position of benefactor to other aspiring law students coming from their own background and using what they have learned from those narratives, ask them to advise those students how to overcome any feelings of imposter syndrome.[13] The goal of the exercise is that the students will internalize their own advice.

Transparently Explain a Growth Mindset

Adopting a growth mindset is important to all students, but it is particularly important to a first-generation law student navigating uncharted and unfamiliar territory. According to Dr. Carol Dweck, our underlying beliefs about learning and intelligence can be broken into two categories: either a "fixed mindset" or a "growth mindset." A fixed mindset can negatively impact all aspects of a student's life. Dr. Dweck states:

> Believing your qualities are carved in stone-the *fixed* mindset-creates an urgency to prove yourself over and over. If you only have a certain amount of intelligence, a certain personality, and a certain moral character-well then, you'd better prove you have a healthy dose of them.

---

11. Think, pair, and share is a collaborative learning strategy where students solve problems together.

12. *Supra* note 11.

13. This exercise is inspired by the California Bar Strategies and Stories Program, Victor Quintanilla et al., *Evaluating Productive Mindset Interventions that Promote Excellence on California's Bar Exam*, MINDSETS IN LEGAL EDUCATION (2021).

> . . .
>
> I have seen so many people with this one consuming goal of proving themselves in the classroom, in their careers, and in their relationships. Every situation calls for a confirmation of their intelligence, personality, or character.
>
> . . .
>
> [The] *growth mindset* is based on the belief that your basic qualities are things you can cultivate through your efforts, your strategies, and help from others. Although people may differ in every which way-in their talents and aptitudes, interests, or temperaments-everyone can change and grow through application and experience.[14]

As stated above, in certain instances, a student's sense of being an "underdog" in the legal profession has also led them to exercise high levels of initiative and grit.[15] However, first-generation law students do not have an extra reservoir of grit and perseverance that they should be required to tap into above and beyond their classmates.[16] We need to recognize that unique burden without dismissing.[17]

So what can we do for the *entering* law students right at the beginning of their law school journey? First, the mindset that a first-generation lawyer is professionally undesirable must be eradicated.[18] While it is imperative to talk to first-generation students about the importance of being resilient, working hard, and finding people to advocate for them during their legal education, it is even more imperative to foster a growth mindset by the unique experiences they bring with them to law school that their peers may not.[19] Studies reveal that first-generation college students demonstrate proactivity, goal direction, optimism, and reflexivity.[20] These qualities that first-generation students already possess are well situated to support a growth mindset, and it is up to our law schools to take some steps to recognize, appreciate, and capitalize on those qualities.[21]

---

14. Carol S. Dweck, Mindset: The New Psychology of Success 6–7, 12 (2016).
15. *Id.*
16. K.G. Molina, *Welcome to Law School, First-Generation Students*, Above the Law (Aug. 20, 2019, 10:48 AM), https://abovethelaw.com/2019/08/welcome-to-law-school-first-generation-students/.
17. *Id.*
18. *Supra* note 6.
19. Camille deJorna, *Lessons Learned in Law School: A First-Generation Journey to Balance and Success*, Law School Admission Council (Mar. 15, 2019), https://www.lsac.org/blog/lessons-learned-law-school-first-generation-journey-balance-and-success.
20. Jacqueline M. O'Bryant & Katharine T. Schaffzin, *First-Generation Students in Law School: A Proven Success Model*, 70 Ark. L. Rev. 913, 924 (2018).
21. *Id.*

Programmatic Application

We should not expect students to leave orientation saying, "okay, now I have a growth mindset" simply because we explain to them what it is; providing an exercise can help students internalize the message.

If we teach our students to put the word "yet" after what they believe is a fixed mindset trait, we can begin to teach students how to develop a growth mindset. "I do not know what I am doing" should be switched to "I do not know what I am doing *yet*." "I do not think I will understand contracts" should be "I do not understand contracts *yet*." It is the promise of growth, not that growth will happen immediately.

After students have practiced with the term "yet" to see the mindset shift, additional examples could be presented where students are asked to take a fixed mindset phrase and change it to a growth mindset phrase by rephrasing the concept entirely. Examples of some fixed mindset phrases to give students:

"I am bad at this."

"I can't do this."

"I am afraid of being criticized."

"This is too hard for me."

"I am just not that smart."

See what students come up with in groups or on their own to rephrase these statements into those exhibiting a growth mindset. Here are some suggested examples of growth mindset rephrased counterparts:

"What might I be missing?"

"I am going to figure out how to do this."

"I like getting constructive feedback."

"This may take some time for me to understand."

"I will learn how to do this."

Students may also be directed to participate in a growth mindset/belonging exercise that helps to align law school success with traits the students already possess.

1. Have students briefly write about a difficult undergraduate project or work task that they performed well on or made them proud.
2. Students are then asked to identify three characteristics/traits they possess that helped them perform well on the project/task.
3. Students are then asked how they feel about starting law school.
4. Students are asked to identify steps they can take in the first few months of law school that will increase their feelings of belonging in the law school community and how they can help others increase feelings of belonging.

5. In a group discussion, the moderator helps identify the characteristics related to law school success, reinforcing the strengths students already possess that contribute (growth mindset, resilience, etc.) and bringing out the individual belonging of each student.[22]

Part 2: Practical Programming That Explicitly and Transparently Incorporates Information About Legal Customs and Culture

The unconscious assumptions educators make about what our students know when entering law school unintentionally provides an advantage to students who have access to a legally savvy network. We queried our first-generation students about how they felt when entering law school and if they felt they lacked any important information. In response, our first-generation students described a lack of familiarity with "legal culture," which led to discomfort, doubt, and feelings of not belonging in law school. More specifically, first-generation students thought their classmates had inside information on how to navigate law school and the legal field, while the first-generation students were left to figure out on their own how legal culture worked. The first-generation students were reluctant to ask questions and admit not knowing information that they perceived their fellow students already knew. While it is debatable if most of their fellow students came to law school familiar with legal culture and customs, certainly some students had that advantage. While another student might attribute their lack of information to being a novice in the legal field, a first-generation student can interpret their lack of knowledge as confirmation of their feelings of not belonging in the legal field. Providing explicit instruction on topics of "legal culture" levels the playing field, and thus no students are unfairly advantaged by having access to insider information that a first-generation law student may lack.

Language/Terminology

Learning the law is much like learning another language and law school has its own vocabulary. Unfamiliarity with legal terminology and vocabulary is one area that predictably makes first-generation students feel inadequate. No one wants to mispronounce a word or admit they do not know what a word means, especially when they think everyone else knows. The fear of being embarrassed or revealing an inadequacy or incompetence is a strong motivator with the unintended consequence of inhibiting student development. While many of the words in the law are idiosyn-

22. This exercise is inspired by the work of Laura Riley & Nickey Woods, Address at the AASE Diversity Conference (Oct. 14, 2021).

cratic and unfamiliar to all law students, once again, first-generation students have less ability to gauge this truism without access to a legally savvy personal network.

PROGRAMMATIC APPLICATION

While *Black's Law Dictionary* is an excellent resource for legal terms, it is also helpful to provide a glossary of legal colloquial terms to share with students at orientation. The very act of providing such a document normalizes the concept that it is acceptable and expected that students do not yet know legal terminology. The list should include commonly used terms and acronyms that students will encounter in class, during case reading, while studying, in extracurricular settings, and those related to professional and career development.

Our colleague Melissa Hale[23] created a helpful document she shares with her first-year students called "Words First Year Law Students Should Know." At UC Irvine Law School we share a list with our students that was created in collaboration with the First-Generation Professionals student group. Similar lists can be personalized to capture the idiosyncrasies and preferences at each institution. It is also helpful to include colloquialisms commonly used in law school that first-generation students may be less familiar with, such as the term "red herring." During orientation, students can engage in exercises exposing them to where and how they will encounter some of the terms and provide opportunities to practice them.

Professionalism

First-generation law students bring with them rich life experiences, interdependent life skills, and unfailing work ethics that position them well for the grit necessary to succeed in law school. But they may also often lack the social, cultural, and financial capital that students coming from more traditional backgrounds utilize to pursue academic success.[24] Some first-generation law students also experience challenges overcoming deficits in exposure to social and cultural norms.[25] Some may have a lack of acculturation to expectations in professional settings, a lack of familiarity with terminology, or lack of exposure to certain environments.[26] As legal educators, it is our job to help first-generation law students learn and adapt to the standards of professionalism expected in the practice of law. Explicit instruction on professionalism should be an important focus starting from the first day of orientation and continuing throughout their entire time in law school.

---

23. Melissa Hale is the Director of Academic Success and Bar Programs at Loyola University School of Law in Chicago.

24. *Supra* note 22, at 914.

25. *Supra* note 1.

26. *Id.*

PROGRAMMATIC APPLICATION

Messaging centered around professionalism can be delicate and must be approached sensitively to avoid coming across as condescending. One option is that law schools may wish to employ third-party companies as unbiased objective consultants. Students may feel more comfortable and receptive to receiving sensitive content from those they will not see regularly among the faculty and staff at their school. Companies such as this exist, for example PracticePro,[27] which helps law students bridge the gap between law school and law practice, and Paradigm One.[28] Paradigm One is a Black-owned and woman-owned consulting company, with a mission to empower students to fit well in the professional atmosphere through the teaching of etiquette and soft skills. However, even if law schools choose to present this information themselves, it must be done in such a way as to empower law students to feel comfortable and confident throughout the process. This is discussed more fully below within the various contexts presented.

Email Etiquette and Management

Email is our primary source of professional communication, which makes mastering email an essential skill for law students. Being an effective email communicator can provide students with a competitive edge in an industry where professionalism is highly valued. The essential skills of email etiquette and effective email management are not routinely taught in undergraduate education. It is a mistake to presume all entering law students have already learned these skills or will intuitively learn them without explicit instruction. Law school instruction should include teaching students how to craft effective, timely, and professional emails. In addition, most students need guidance in managing and prioritizing the large volume of emails they can expect to receive as a professional in the legal field. Students will have ample opportunity to practice and perfect their emailing skills while still in law school.

PROGRAMMATIC APPLICATION

Email instruction can be addressed in orientation, or during early fall of the 1L year. The pedagogical technique of "making the student the grader" works well to teach email etiquette. One way to communicate effective email techniques is to introduce sample emails to various recipients, such as a professor or prospective employer, that students can analyze and appropriately revise. This exercise can be done individually, but it works well as a group exercise.

Provide students with several types of email examples that use (or do not use) proper subject lines, greetings, grammar, purpose statements, tone, and closings.

---

27. PracticePro, www.practicepro.cc (last visited May 13, 2022).
28. Paradigm One, www.paradigm1consulting.com (last visited May 13, 2022).

Students can analyze the samples to determine what features are effective or ineffective about the email, and what might have been done differently to communicate better. The email examples can run the gamut from hilarious and casual, to emails that are appropriately polite, but too passive in tone given the content. Students can be instructed to revise the sample emails to better communicate the intended message. After revising, students can be further tasked with producing their own email guidelines using specific prompts to create thorough, well-rounded guidelines. The student-created guidelines should be based on the goal of the communication while considering administrative details such as recommended timeliness of email responses and content considerations. Prompts can also consider other factors, such as who is the intended recipient (professors versus prospective employers, for example). Students can be given specific prompts for creating their guidelines, such as what are guidelines "to sound professional and respectful," "to be direct and to the point," and "for appropriate subject headings," etc. Though these exercises make for fun live group work, they could be assigned as an asynchronous module. To take it to the next level, ask the students to craft a "model email" about assorted topics and choose a few volunteers to share those emails with the whole group.

Interacting with Professors

First-generation students especially can benefit from instruction on how to appropriately interact with law professors, especially since the law school environment is typically more formal than most undergraduate experiences. Students may erroneously interpret a professor's friendliness and approachability as a signal that the professor can be addressed casually and treated like a friend. On the other end of the spectrum, movies like *The Paper Chase* can terrify students at the very thought of interacting with their professors. Lecturing students on interacting appropriately with their professors may come off as condescending if the topic is not approached with the right amount of sensitivity and empathy. While all schools are different, some common topics pursuant to interacting with professors are listed below.

Titles

Students should always call professors by their correct title (usually "professor last name") unless their professor indicates otherwise. The same rule applies to those in administrative roles. When in doubt, students should default to a more formal form of address. This should be clearly explained in orientation since students may come from an undergraduate institution with less formal customs.

The Syllabus

Students should be directed that the law school syllabus is a crucial instructional document that should be read over *numerous* times. Since law students are expected to research and think critically, law professors get especially frustrated with students who ask questions about information contained in the syllabus. There are t-shirts, mugs, and a whole collection of paraphernalia out there with the phrase, "It's in the

Syllabus," and some professors even have quizzes on what is in their syllabus. Students should be instructed to always check their syllabus before asking their professors routine questions about assignment due dates, office hour times, expectations, and grading protocols.

Communication Preferences

It is helpful if professors provide clear guidance on their communication preferences; however, in their absence, advise students to ask their professors how they would best like to be contacted about questions, concerns, office hours, etc. In the absence of an emergency, students should then honor those preferences. For example, I have a 24-hour turnaround time on emails, a policy for urgent matters, and recommend to students that if I do not respond within 48 hours they should email me again because it may have gotten lost, buried, or misplaced.

Being polite, professional, and appreciative are good practices for one entering the legal profession. Students should be taught to thank professors after each class, which is a good way to start building a relationship with professors and introduces students to the idea of thoughtfully managing how they interact with the professionals they will encounter in practice, such as senior partners and judges.

Office Hours

Guidance on interacting directly with professors is helpful for all students, but it is especially helpful for first-generation students who may have less experience interacting directly with highly educated authority figures. Students can alleviate anxiety about interacting during office hours by coming prepared with a specific question(s). When students wish to review their performance on an assignment or exam with their professor, they should be directed to phrase their questions to focus on their desire to make improvements, rather than what can be interpreted as arguing about their score. Suggestions of this type should lead to more productive and helpful interactions with their professors.

PROGRAMMATIC APPLICATION

Role-playing is an effective technique to demonstrate effective and appropriate interaction with professors. This role-playing can be expanded to cover specific scenarios above, such as asking questions during office hours and asking professors about their communication preferences.

Appropriate Attire

Appropriate attire is another subject that can be difficult to broach without sounding patronizing, so it must be handled sensitively. Some students may bristle at what they consider outdated notions of professional attire. Nonetheless, many first-generation students privately express confusion and unease over what to wear in various legal settings. All students want to be confidently dressed appropriately for the occasion or event they attend. Getting it right can be complicated because terms like "business casual" have different meanings in different contexts. Attire that is appropriate business casual for a big law firm would seem overdressed for work at a local public interest advocacy group. The goal in addressing this topic is not to tell students what to wear, but to expose them to the norms, which allows them to make informed choices about how they wish to be perceived by others in legal settings.

PROGRAMMATIC APPLICATION

As students get closer to interacting with prospective employers, these issues can be addressed in a workshop. This type of presentation works particularly well in collaboration with upper-level students. Providing students with a visual "look book" with multiple examples of clothing that would be appropriate for various occasions they may encounter is particularly helpful and appreciated.

Peer Mentors/Peer Tutors

Many law schools have a peer-mentoring or tutoring program in which successful law students tutor their 1L peers. To increase the comfort level for students utilizing these services, we suggest that the vetting process for peer mentors and/or tutors include selecting students from a wide range of backgrounds so all students, and particularly first-generation students, can interact with successful students coming from similar backgrounds. This type of representation, visibility, and support goes a long way toward demonstrating the high value an institution places on the success of their first-generation students. This also helps ensure that this valuable resource is well utilized by 1L students.

PROGRAMMATIC APPLICATION

In addition to providing the standard information about the peer tutor/mentor's availability and legal scholastic background, tutors should provide a biography about themselves and their personal background. This allows students to feel more comfortable about the person they are working with as a peer mentor or tutor and ensures they can select a mentor and/or tutor who can relate to and empathize with the challenges that can arise for first-generation students. Peer mentors and/or tutors must be properly trained and supervised. Part of that training should include instruction on imposter syndrome, stereotype threat, and other issues that are pertinent to working with first-generation students. In addition, confidentiality is extremely important and ensuring that peer mentors and tutors hold any private information strictly confidential is paramount to the integrity of the program.

Supplemental Resources

All law schools provide their students with a variety of on-campus resources, such as academic support, career advising services, law school secondary source supplements, and more. Data from the 2014 *Law School Survey of Student Engagement (LSSSE)*[29] suggests that first-generation students often lack the time to engage these resources. Schools have different approaches to providing students with supplements. Nonetheless, law schools can educate students on the value of the resources available and that many available resources are ultimately time saving instead of time-consuming. Professors may identify their preferred supplements and other secondary sources in their syllabus.

PROGRAMMATIC APPLICATION

There are many different systems that law schools may employ to provide supplements for students. One example from Western State University School of Law involved a collaboration between the library and ASP department, which resulted in the creation of a joint academic resource list for law students and bar takers. This comprehensive list included all resources available, where they were located, and most importantly, highlighted resources recommended by certain professors. The list included clickable links and discount codes when available. This resource packet was sent out to the students and housed on a new ASP-Library TWEN page where students could easily access the list and all free electronic resources. Further, the ASP department collected as many hard copies of these resources as possible, ranging from free samples from publishers and donations from previous students to items from our own offices. In collaboration with the library, we combined these resources with the library resources, having all supplements housed together and available for reserve checkout.

Making Mistakes and Accepting Feedback

In law school, students learn by doing. During the law school process students make mistakes and receive feedback on their performance, which is a normal part of the learning process. However, as noted earlier, first-generation law students have a high incidence of imposter syndrome. One of the effects of imposter syndrome is that sufferers tend to underestimate and undervalue their own performance.[30] The anxiety spiral of the 1L comes from the increasing challenges of law school capped with a high-stakes exam at the end of the semester. A fixed mindset will diminish confidence. Instead, we should be transparent in explaining the process of assess-

29. Indiana University Center for Postsecondary Research, *Looking Ahead: Assessment in Legal Education, Law School Survey of Student Engagement* (2014), https://lssse.indiana.edu/wp-content/uploads/2016/01/LSSSE_2014_AnnualReport.pdf.

30. Christyne J. Vachon, *Tiaras, Queen Bees, Imposters and the Board Room: Lean in & Women in Corporate Governance*, 9 J. Bus. Tech. L. 279, 290 (2014).

ment and that mistakes are always common at first. Mistakes and the stress that comes from these mistakes can be a useful motivator for students to adopt a growth mindset. Students should be reminded about their sense of purpose (i.e., why they are going to law school in the first place).

PROGRAMMATIC APPLICATION

A useful exercise could be to have students write a reflective essay or short answer using the experience of making mistakes to help others. Their essay could essentially be a "Letter to a Future 1L."[31]

Law School Timeline Pursuant to Bar Licensure Process

Law schools primarily prepare students to become licensed practicing attorneys. First-generation students are often unclear about the requirements and timeline of the bar licensure process, while other students can obtain this information informally through their law-savvy personal network. Though first-generation students have typically heard about the bar exam, they may have only heard horror stories and know few specifics. Providing accurate, timely information on the bar licensure process and timeline alleviates stress and the feeling of not belonging that comes with lacking access to this key and potentially stressful information.

PROGRAMMATIC APPLICATION

Starting with orientation and continuing throughout their time at law school, schools should provide guidance on the bar licensure process and timeline. In addition to taking and passing a bar exam post-graduation, other components of the bar licensure process must occur well before graduation. Students may need to register as a law student as a 1L. Students should be warned that commercial bar preparation companies heavily market to 1L students with special "deals" to manufacture urgency to entice the uninformed to unnecessarily commit early to a bar prep company. Students need to pass the Multistate Professional Responsibility Exam (MPRE) in most jurisdictions.[32] Students should be advised to take it in their 2L year so preparing for the MPRE does not interfere with bar preparation. Students should be advised that those seeking a testing accommodation for the bar exam may need to plan well in advance and provide updated medical information. Almost all jurisdictions require a determination of moral character and fitness to practice law before bar passers can be sworn in.[33]

---

31. See *supra* note 15.

32. National Conference of Bar Examiners, *Multistate Professional Responsibility Examination*, https://www.ncbex.org/exams/mpre/ (last visited May 14, 2022).

33. National Conference of Bar Examiners, *Character and Fitness*, https://www.ncbex.org/character-and-fitness (last visited May 14, 2022).

The specific information we provide to the students at UC Irvine Law School starts with a brief bar licensure overview and timeline at 1L orientation. We use this introduction to plant the seed about bar licensure and the relationship between the bar exam and their 1L courses, but keep the information brief, so it is not overwhelming. Midway through their first year we provide a much more detailed chart with information outlining the subjects that are bar tested, the courses we offer and when they should plan to take them, the preferred timeline for bar-associated tasks such as taking the MPRE, and all associated bar licensure-related fees. It is important for all students, but particularly students from more meager financial means, to know well in advance about the fees and costs associated with taking a bar exam, including the cost associated with their inability to work while studying for the exam. Prior to their 3L year, students are provided with a chart that includes the information above and adds a detailed 3L timeline of important things to do, along with a guide to supplemental bar resources.

Law School Timeline Pursuant to Career Goals

Career Services Offices can be a great equalizer by providing an overview of the legal career process and the greater context of why the career search process operates as it does. Many first-generation students are caught unaware by how many important tasks must be attended to during their first year of law school, especially pursuant to laying the groundwork for their future careers. Many students go to law school without having a well-formed idea of what it is that lawyers do, and this is especially true for first-generation students. There is substantial variety in available legal careers, and many options may be unfamiliar to students.

The groundwork for a legal career search is laid in the first year of law school. This early start may leave may first-generation students, who are not in the know, stuck at the starting gate while well-connected students are already halfway around the racetrack. Students with a legally savvy network will receive advice about the importance of first-semester grades and getting the jump on securing 1L summer work, which can place a first-generation student at a distinct competitive disadvantage.

PROGRAMMATIC APPLICATION

The Career Services Office and their role should be introduced during orientation. Career planning information should be transparent with an overview handout of the timeline detailing the process provided to all students at orientation. Similar with the approach used with bar licensure, at UC Irvine Law School we keep the information provided at orientation brief and build on it at other appropriate times throughout the 1L year. In addition, starting in 1L year students meet with career counselors. We inform students of the role that practical experience such as internships, clinics, externships, and pro bono work can play in their career plans. At UC Irvine Law School, all students must participate in a clinical experience and most students participate significantly in providing pro bono work. Therefore, an experiential focus is built into our curriculum and our students are well known in the legal community for their practical training and experience. Prior to December of 1L year, we inform students of the importance of a summer job in their ultimate job search. Such positions are competitive, often unpaid, and are essentially a ten-week job interview. Students must be notified of this in advance to properly prepare them for the financial implications. First-generation students may come from backgrounds that prioritize working and earning wages, instead of spending time on these type of "volunteer" pursuits that are an essential and expected part of the standard process for securing a good job in law post-graduation. At Western State University, we work with the Career Services Offices to not only make a presentation during orientation, but they also spend an entire required class session teaching students the specifics of resume-writing, cover-letter writing, and the application timelines for jobs, internships, and externships. Whatever model is used, early exposure to the Career Services Office allows students to best utilize this key resource, which is especially important for first-generation students who do not come to law school with a ready-made legal network they can tap into for job networking and placement assistance.

A Note on Law School Accommodations

All law schools should ensure that they have accommodations aimed at providing equal access to the law school experience. Reasonable accommodations do not simply encompass exams and other test-taking accommodations, but programs and resources that are designed to meet the needs of first-generation students. These accommodations may include adjusting the student's course load from full-time to part-time for students who must work, working with students on their class schedules, providing access to note-takers and tutors, as well as access to mental health and wellness counselors.

Conclusion

Our goal in writing this chapter as a small part of a greater collection of works addressing first-generation inclusion in law school was to both explore research-backed studies surrounding first-generation law students and to provide practical solutions that may be incorporated in an orientation or pre-orientation program and built upon throughout the law school experience. In the process of writing this chapter, we took a close look not only at other schools, but also at the students and administrations at our own schools. We found that regardless of the school "tier," the issues facing first-generation students are essentially all the same. The goals and programming referenced in this chapter are simply a sampling of what schools may do to increase first-generation inclusion and help unhide the hidden curriculum, and can be utilized at all law schools. The goals and programming ideas are not exhaustive and, at the same time, all need not be incorporated into orientation or pre-orientation. As we stated in our introduction, each law school should determine its own needs and goals for incorporating first-generation focused programming and may choose to incorporate some, all, or none of the suggestions above. We hope that this is just the start of addressing inclusion surrounding a diverse and dynamic growing population of first-generation law students. We thank the author of this book, Brittany Raposa, for giving us the opportunity to explore such an important topic.

Appendix

Academic Skills Program | Bar Licensure Planning Guide | UCI Law

1L (~16-17 units/semester)		2L (~13-14 units/semester)	3L (~13-14 units/semester)
Required Courses	**1L Recommendations**	**2L Recommendations**	**3L Recommendations**
• Civil Procedure • Constitutional Law • Contracts • Criminal Law • Torts • Legal Profession • Lawyering Skills 1 & 2	• Explore areas of interest • Participate thoughtfully in extracurriculars (student organizations, pro bono projects, etc.) • Follow Career Development Office (CDO) guidance and timelines to develop career opportunities	Take bar-tested electives, leaving no more than a few minor subjects untaken before intensive bar study during the 10+ weeks immediately before the bar exam. It is difficult to learn more than a few minor subjects anew during intensive bar study. See chart below. • Take skill development courses	 • Take LAW bar prep course(s) • Complete Early Bar Prep (EBP) workshops as needed to brush up on or learn anew weak bar-tested topics

Other Graduation Requirements

- Race and Indigeneity (1L, 2L, or 3L)
- Upper-Level Writing (2L or 3L)
- Core Clinic (2L or 3L as assigned)
- 86 units to graduate, with 68 units from "regularly scheduled law school classes"
- Maximum of 8 self-selected S/U units (recommended to refrain from taking bar-tested subjects S/U)

Cal. Bar-Tested Electives	Uniform Bar Exam (UBE)-Tested Electives
• Criminal Procedure*	• Criminal Procedure*
• Evidence*	• Evidence*
• Real Property*	• Real Property*
• Business Associations—Agency, Partnership, Corporations	• Business Associations—Agency, Partnership, Corporations
• Professional Responsibility (Cal. & ABA rules)**	• Conflict of Laws
• Community Property	• Family Law
• Remedies	• Secured Transactions
• Wills & Trusts	• Estates (including Wills) & Trusts

*Highly recommended because these subjects (along with the 1L subjects of Civil Procedure, Constitutional Law, Contracts, Criminal Law, and Torts) are tested in minute detail on the bar exam in almost all jurisdictions, both on the Multistate Bar (MBE), or the multiple-choice portion, and on the essay portion.

**Professional Responsibility (PR) rules are covered in your Legal Profession course and are tested on the Multistate Professional Responsibility Exam (MPRE), which is a separate exam you must also pass for bar licensure in almost all jurisdictions. On the California bar exam, PR is the most important and heavily tested subject, and it is tested differently on the bar exam than on the MPRE, so plan to revisit and review this important topic in 3L spring.

Academic Skills Program | Bar Licensure Planning Guide | UCI Law

Becoming a Lawyer: Important and Timely Things To Do

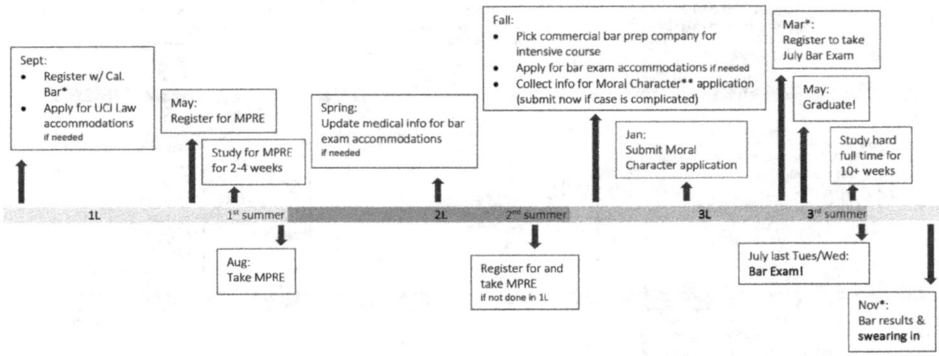

*Bar admissions rules vary by jurisdiction, so check directly with your intended jurisdiction and at ncbex.org for details. This chart reflects information for California.

**A typical Moral Character determination takes 8-10 months to process. A complicated case will take longer, such as where there is a criminal conviction or where other ethical issue(s) are implicated.

- The MPRE is offered three times a year in August, November, and March, with registration two months before the testing date (and accommodations applications four months before testing date). Almost all jurisdictions require passage, though each state sets its own passing score. It is advisable to take the MPRE early and during the summer.
- Bar licensure costs and fees can exceed $4,000-$5,000, and some of these expenses are not covered by financial aid. It is also not advisable to work during the 10-11 weeks of intensive bar study in the 10+ weeks immediately before the bar exam, so plan accordingly.
- The bar exam is offered twice a year on the last Tuesday and Wednesday of February and July. The dates on this chart reflect taking a July bar exam.

For additional and more detailed information on bar licensure, please see the ASP Canvas page for your graduating class/intended bar exam date.

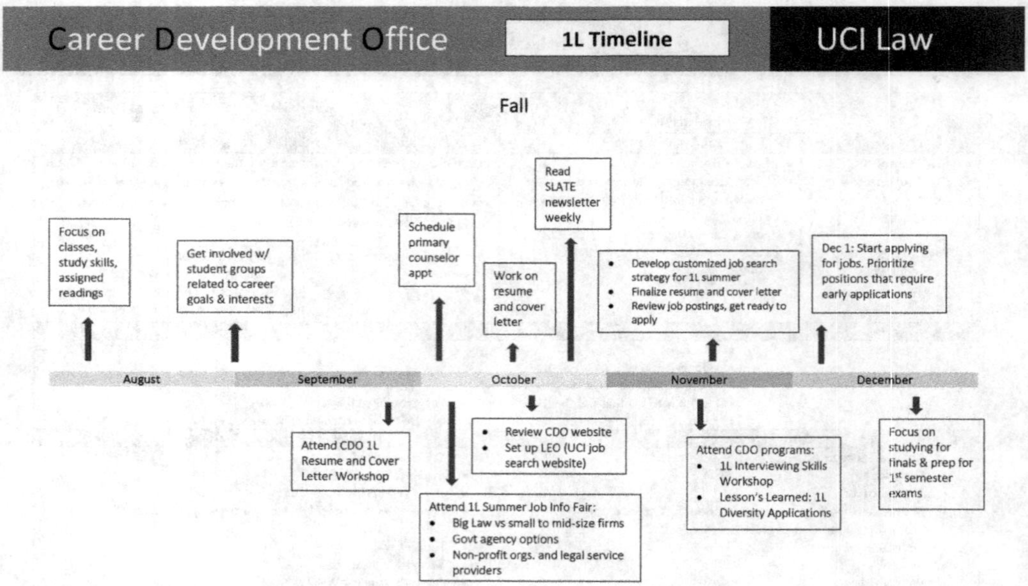

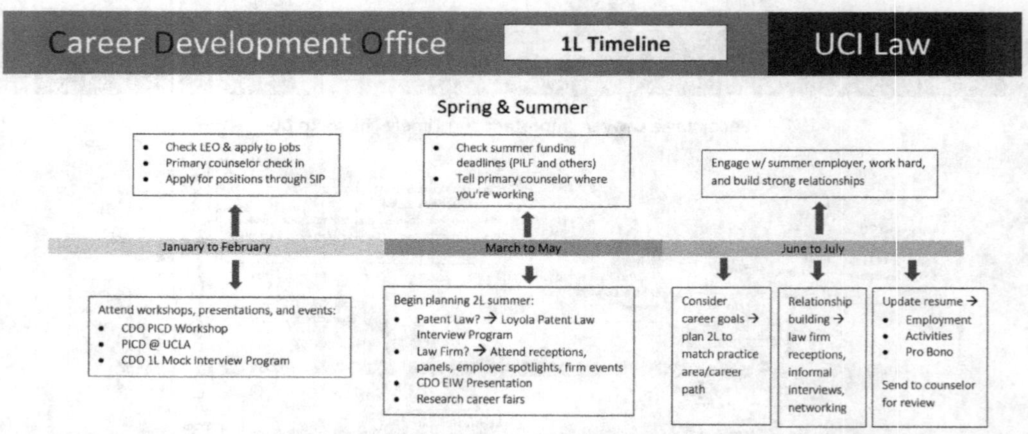

Hiring Timelines by Sector after 1L year	
Private practice	• Big Law firms hire 2 years in advance of graduation, primarily through Early Interview Week (EIW), which typically occurs in late-July after your 1L year • Small to mid-sized firms hire for 2L summer in fall or spring of 2L year and for post-grad positions in fall or spring of 3L year*
Government Agencies	• Federal and State government agencies begin hiring for 2L summer in fall of 2L year and continue into spring of 2L year • Federal government agencies hire for post-grad positions through Honors Programs, which begin accepting applications in August of 3L year • The California Attorney General's Office also hires through an Honors Program later in fall of 3L year • Other California state agencies may hire 3Ls for post grad positions throughout 3L year

Public Interest	• For 2L summer, public interest organizations accept applications in fall of 2L year, but the majority hire in spring of 2L year
	• Post-graduate public interest fellowship applications open during 2L summer
	   ▪ Project based fellowships, like Skadden and Equal Justice Works, have September application deadlines
	   ▪ Organizational based fellowships have application deadlines starting in fall of 3L year
	• Public interest organizations may begin hiring for post-grad positions in the fall, but the majority hire once you have passed the bar and are a licensed attorney*

Judicial Clerkships	• Students begin applying for federal judicial clerkships in June of 2L summer and continue to apply throughout 3L year • Applications for state court clerkships vary by state

*These hiring timelines are based on need and will change regionally.

Sample Orientation Schedule

First-generation focused programming is incorporated for all and noted here in italics.

We provide a glossary of legal terms.

Introduction

- Law School—The Big Picture *(Includes highlighting our core value of promoting equity, diversity, inclusion, and belonging.)*
- How Law School Is Different
- What Successful Law Students Do *(Includes a discussion of imposter syndrome, stereotype threat, growth mindset, and the varied traits they already possess that will lead to success.)*
- Legal Culture *(Includes instruction on professionalism, email etiquette, and legal customs.)*

Legal Foundation and What to Do Before Class

- Introduction to the U.S. Legal System
- Case Method and Socratic Method
- Introduction to the ASP Study Plan
- Case Reading

What to Do Before and During Class

- Mock Class #1
- How to Prepare Before Class (reading and briefing)
- What to Do During Class (note taking)

What To Do During and After Class

- Mock Class #2
- What to Do After Class
- Science-Based Study Strategies
- Introduction to Outlining

What to Do After Class and Looking Further Ahead

- Preview of Law School Exams
- What to Do After Class
- Building Relationships with Professors *(Includes legal customs and professionalism.)*
- Getting Ready for First Day of Classes
- Looking Further Ahead (*Includes highlighting the varied traits they already possess that will lead to their success.)*

Sixteen

Opening the Door

Welcoming First Gen Law Students with 1L Intake Meetings

Jennifer Cerny, Esq.*

I. Introduction

IN ORDER TO CONTINUE TO PUSH THE LEGAL PROFESSION toward a more diverse and equitable place, it is critical that law schools seek out and educate students from all backgrounds. Our profession continues, even in recent years, to look and present similarly to the way it has for so many generations—and the way it looked back when law school was an elite experience limited to those of privilege and access. Thanks to the continued hard work of law school admissions teams, financial aid offices and the recognition and support of various pipeline programs, the path is open for law schools to ensure equal access for all students.

However, since the legal profession must overcome decades of both intentional and unintentional gatekeeping, administrators should expect and prepare to see a continued increase in the number of first-gen students matriculating. Knowing that law school can be an intimidating space even for folks who are not considered first-gen, and that the impact of such pressure is often linked to significant mental health concerns, provides law schools with both the opportunity *and* responsibility to develop support services and programming to foster student success. The current statistics on attorney wellness are alarming and require law schools to retool their methodologies in order to graduate healthy and resilient students.[1] Administrators on the front lines are hopeful that the era of intense Socratic humiliation, soul-crushing academic pressure, and inaccessible ivory towers is slowly giving way to collaborative teaching models, flexible learning schedules, and engaged faculty and staff.

---

* Associate Dean of Students at Yale Law School, though this piece references my prior position as Assistant Dean of Students at UConn School of Law.

1. *Suffering in Silence: The Survey of Law Student Well-Being and the Reluctance of Law Students to Seek Help for Substance Use and Mental Health Concerns*, administered via ABA grant and published at www.americanbar.org.

Arguably the most polarizing stage of the law school climb is the first semester. In addition to learning and adjusting to a demanding academic schedule, students are also taught a new way to think and approach everyday scenarios. Moreover, legal education utilizes its own language and individuals must adapt their classroom conversation to accommodate Latin phrases and complex legal definitions. In these scenarios, first-gen students I've spoken with have often recalled feelings of frustration and overwhelm to be learning it all at once. I recall one student comparing it to starting a road race 100 yards behind his continued-gen peers. When coupled with the learning curve of developing successful time management habits, understanding curriculum requirements, and learning networking strategies, first-gen students face a steep ascent first semester to keep pace with their peers.

As a law school administrator charged with both fostering a safe and inclusive space for students and trying to keep the playing field clear of learning obstacles, the relative unfairness of first semester has bothered me for more than a decade. While not all first-gen students come from a low-income background, many do.[2] It has been difficult to see how the momentum of a competitive law school environment effortlessly separates the "haves" from the "have nots." Legal education is expensive, as are several components of the juris doctorate journey—from applying to schools, to studying and sitting for the bar exam. Moreover, students who also need to work for income during school often visit my office to seek help on finding the time for both a job and their studies.

While UConn Law has established a number of ways to assist students with their financial needs, including a wonderful Financial Aid department and a student-centered fund made up of donations from the community,[3] other resources available only to the "haves" are not as easy to quantify. Secure learning-friendly environments with quiet places to study, the support, assistance, and understanding from immediate family, consistent access to nutritious food and drink are just a few of the ways that privilege enhances student opportunity for law school success. Since I, as an administrator, am limited in my reach outside of law school, it quickly became clear that we needed to think outside the box about other ways to equalize the experience for as many students as possible.

2. The Center for First-Generation Student Success, *First Generation College Students: Demographic Characteristics and Postsecondary Enrollment*, fact sheet notes that as of 2016, the median parental income for first-gen students was $41,000.00, while the median for continuing-gen students was $90,000.00.

3. The Law Student First Fund is managed by the Office of Student Affairs at UConn Law and assists students with small grants for things like medical bills, travel for familial health issues, and even groceries. Students can nominate themselves or their peers to receive awards, and are not disqualified after receiving one grant.

II. Developing a Plan to Better Support First-Semester Law Students

In the spring of 2018, I found myself approaching burnout and needing time away to reboot before the end of the semester. My close high school friend, a busy surgeon living in Chicago, suggested I meet her in a warm setting and together we spent the long weekend at her parents' home venting about each professional field (medicine and law) and the challenges inherent to both.

My friend is part of a surgical practice that encourages its team to spend close to 50% of its time performing pro bono clinic work in low-income areas. I was surprised to hear her discuss the wellness implications developed from her witnessing the impact of everyday patient inequities. It immediately reminded me of the recently released Report for the National Task Force on Lawyer Wellbeing. The publication brought to light that the legal profession was "struggling" and generally "falling short" on attorney well-being.[4] The information contained in the 73-page *Path to Lawyer Well-Being: Practical Recommendations for Positive Change*, includes shocking data on the mental health of the legal profession, as well as concrete recommendations for law schools to create new best practices in student mental health. One related survey found that out of 13,000 working lawyers, 28% suffered from depression, 19% had severe anxiety and more than 11% had suicidal thoughts within the past year.[5] Meanwhile, at the law school level, the study found that there was a culture of secrecy at law schools resulting in students "not asking for help."[6]

During the conversation with my friend, I expressed my frustration that most law graduates received a robust legal education, but at that time, had no guidance on self-care—a critical piece to brace them for the pressure that comes with protecting a client's freedom, livelihood, and/or family. I recall my friend giving me a surprised look and asking whether law students had any type of mental health education or exposure during law school. She shared that at her medical school, each student was required to meet once a term with a mental health counselor. Because of the program, she noted that several of her peers continued to meet with the counselors after the initial consult and that mental health was quite openly discussed and accepted within their local med school community.

Later that evening, I fell asleep wondering if the med school model could be applied to law schools. If we couldn't tackle the problem of off-campus environmental equity, could we even the playing field internally by providing all our students with

---

4. American Bar Association, *Report from the National Task Force on Lawyer Wellbeing*, www.americanbar.org, November 9, 2018.

5. *"Suffering in Silence: The Survey of Law Student Well-Being and the Reluctance of Law Students to Seek Help for Substance Use and Mental Health Concerns,"* administered via ABA grant and published at www.americanbar.org.

6. American Bar Association, *New Study on Lawyer Well-Being Reveals Serious Concern for Legal Profession*, www.americanbar.org, December 2017.

an equal leg-up on mental health? After all, no matter where you live, work, or study, if mental health issues arise and go without treatment, it can be a much more debilitating obstacle to success than a student's learning environment. Moreover, I was very aware of the various challenges that stood in the way of students seeking mental health help. I had spent years working with students in distress who refused to consider speaking with a trained mental health professional for reasons including the social stigma of seeking help, heavily imparted cultural and religious beliefs, and the cost of such services. I also knew that for students with anxiety and depression, the effort it takes to find help can be enough to prevent them from pursuing it.[7] I truly believed that if we could get our students comfortable with receiving mental health help in law school, they would continue to access and benefit from such help *after* law school. In turn, this would create healthy practicing attorneys who would, in many cases, be resilient enough to withstand the pressures of an emotionally heavy caseload, long hours, and the stress of a billable workplace. The thought of possibly changing the lawyer well-being narrative at the law school level was exciting, although I knew in Connecticut we'd be up against a wall built upon decades of ingrained stigma against seeking help.[8]

To further assist the Law School's efforts to destigmatize assistance for mental health concerns, we lobbied our parent university, UConn, for support. Located in Storrs, Connecticut, almost 30 miles away from the Law School, UConn has a robust health and wellness center where undergraduate students can go to address both physical and mental health needs. However, since our law students are physically too far to easily access this resource, in addition to not paying the service fee as part of their tuition package, we knew there was a need for direct student mental health resources on our own campus in Hartford. In late 2015 and early 2016, the Law School Student Affairs team met with several members of the Provost's office and undergraduate student affairs leadership to seek financial support for hiring a mental health counselor to work with law students.

As it turned out, obtaining backing from University leadership was ultimately much easier than finding someone willing to put their private practice on hold and take a pay cut to work with law students. After being turned down by several leads, we were lucky enough to connect with one counselor, a Licensed Clinical Social Worker (LCSW) who was familiar with our school and an acquaintance of a member of our staff. She recognized the need of our student population and was willing to divert retirement plans and accept the position at UConn Law. Structuring our

7. One student once said that trying to find help while being paralyzed by depression was akin to "shoveling their driveway after a blizzard with a teaspoon."

8. Connecticut has had a sordid history of using mental health discrimination as a gatekeeper to the legal profession. It was only within the past decade that the state removed its broad and intrusive required mental health disclosures from the bar application. Because of this, and the traumatic hearings students disclosing conditions would face in their quest to be admitted to the Connecticut Bar, many students would simply not seek treatment.

agreement with the counselor also provided an unexpected challenge, as we needed to establish enough confidentiality that the content of her discussions with students would be protected from both Law School administration and the CBEC. In the end, we settled on hiring her as an independent contractor, a decision that allowed us to market her to our community as being separate from the Law School and our reporting obligations, but still enabled us to provide the service free of charge to all students. The counselor started seeing students in January 2017 and the original 10 hours per week outlined in her contract quickly ballooned to 15–20 hours, given the student need. That said, by 2018, when I had the conversation with my surgeon friend, I still knew of a number of students who would not seek help both because it had been shunned for so long by the local legal community and out of fear of disclosure to the bar examining committee.

As I returned to Connecticut post-trip, I kept thinking about how a requirement for students to meet with a mental health counselor would benefit our community. Still, it felt like this alone would not do enough to even out the equity concerns for our first-gen and other diverse populations. Back in the office, I counseled a first-gen student on how the Law School might offer programming and resources to minimize the learning curve that students without college or law school-educated parents experience. I distinctly remember the student looking at me and saying, "Just tell us what a journal is. Encourage us to speak to our professors out of class. Give us a roadmap." Hearing this connected the dots as to what was missing: I knew my office had the resources that first-gen students could use to take advantage of their time on campus, but that seeking out student affairs might not be an obvious option, especially if they didn't engage with their undergraduate student affairs office. It was clear that requiring students to meet with a campus mental health counselor—complemented by a required meeting with student affairs, would give all students, especially first-gen, the knowledge of where to find support.

In figuring out the details of the proposal, it was important to be mindful of time. Student time in the first semester is a precious commodity for all the reasons listed in the first section of this chapter. Through trial and error, our team knew that it was tough enough to get students to read an email more than a paragraph long in the midst of a busy first semester week. We didn't email our community on Fridays unless it was an emergency, and departments usually provided long periods of time between when something was assigned outside of class and when something was due. At the same time, staff time first semester was equally valuable. Test-running this program meant that I would be pulled away from the already-pressing student issues that arose on a daily and weekly basis. Alas, student affairs professionals know that most of the year is considered "go time," but there is a special sort of chaos and work that materializes each fall.

For the required 1L intake meeting plan to be successful, it was apparent that the meetings needed to be succinct and easy to schedule. Together with the mental health counselor, we settled on 15-minute sessions for each meeting. For her, the goal was to destigmatize mental health, screen for folks with concerns and open the door to further conversations. For me, it was to put names with faces, create connections on campus and demonstrate our value as a daily student resource. With the plan fleshed out, we prepared to market and announce the new requirement at orientation the following month.

III. The First 73 Hours: OUR Learning Curve

In August 2018, the counselor and I addressed the incoming class during our panel presentation on campus life. In addition to introducing members of our team and reminding students about professionalism and healthy study habits, we let them know that each student was required to complete a 15-minute 1L intake meeting with both offices before October 1. By the next day we each were both overwhelmed with emails from students asking to get on our schedules. I recall spending inordinate amounts of time replying to emails and filling up space on my schedule. When students wouldn't show, or would ask to reschedule, it would wobble the house of cards that my calendar had become.

Carrying out the meetings, I had pages of handwritten notes scattered about my desk documenting what I learned about each student and highlighted with reminders of resources I had promised to provide. I ran out of business cards as I would grab them hastily and write names of professors or networking tips for students along with my cell phone number and hand them out as the meetings ended. The counselor and I met every two to three weeks to share general notes, concerns, and trends we saw. It was clear she was also overwhelmed as we both tried to carve out space for time we could offer to students that weren't in the 1L class. Already accustomed to Student Affairs not being a traditional 9–5 job, I hadn't considered the nearly 40 after-hours meetings I'd need to make myself available for our evening and part-time students.

The October 1 deadline melded into a "pre-Thanksgiving" deadline, and ultimately a February 1 deadline. While there weren't many students to chase down, there were a handful that we both proactively reached out to when our schedule allowed time to tally up who we'd seen. Generally, we were both pleased to see how receptive the students were to the mandatory nature of these meetings. At the time, my seven to eight years of experience in law school student affairs had taught me many things, a significant one being that law students didn't like to be told what to do. They were mostly independent adults by the time they set foot on our campus and would often push back on things that felt obligatory. That said, I remember being surprised by the number of grateful emails I received following the meetings.[9] While there were

9. One email read, "... Also, thank you again for taking the time today. I am very excited for everything that UConn Law has to offer and I can already tell how valuable a resource you and your office will be. I look forward to seeing you soon." Another said, "Just want to make sure you know

so many elements we got wrong with the program that first year, demonstrating the value of a short 15-minute meeting was one thing we managed to get right. The counselor accomplished this with cozy chairs, privacy, hot tea, chocolate, and good conversation, while I was intent on making students feel like they left my office knowing where to look for help and, as often as possible, a name or two of hand-selected campus allies or mentor possibilities.

Being a forced extrovert myself, I felt mental exhaustion from the meetings within the first few weeks. As the intakes became more routine, I combated this by developing a fluid script for the interactions. My questions evolved as the semester moved on, but generally remained along the same themes and were tailored somewhat based on each student's receptivity to our face-to-face time:

> Me: "Thank you so much for taking the time to meet with me today. As we mentioned during orientation, the goal of this brief conversation is to help connect you with resources and people on campus and to answer any questions you might have. I like to start out with generally getting to know what brought you here, so if you don't mind sharing, I'd love to know where you're from, where you went to undergraduate school and why you picked UConn Law."

From there, I'd ask students about what area of law they were interested in and try to find common ground in either their background or the type of practice they hoped to pursue. When students self-disclosed as being first-gen, I'd make sure to let them know about the ways in which our school could help fill gaps and answer questions they had along the way. I told them to think of student affairs as a liaison within the school and to use us as a starting point when they needed something but weren't sure where to look. One student used the time in our meeting to express their desire to create a student organization specifically for first-gen students. She left with resources on how to form student organizations and a list of potential faculty and staff advisors.

That first year, both our counselor and I found that the majority of meetings ended around the 10- to 12-minute mark, and we were intentional about never keeping the students beyond the 15 minutes of allotted time. Even so, I don't think either of us was fully prepared for the time commitment the initiative entailed. Despite the meetings staying relatively short, holding follow-up meetings and even trying to organize the data we collected on each student—it all took up time in our already-packed schedules. We knew that for the program to be viable long-term, it was imperative to reassess the process the following spring and make changes before the next class arrived in the summer of 2019.

---

how amazing [Student Affairs] is, both at being a resource for students, and as advocates. I really just wanted to express my gratitude for everything [Student Affairs] does, and for meeting with me. You [all] handle a lot of complicated and heavy issues and topics, and should be recognized!"

IV. Assess. Assess. Assess.

When the time came in May when things slowed down enough for our counselor and I to sit down and debrief on the intake program, we knew two things: the value of the meetings was undeniable, but the process, as it currently stood, was unsustainable. Value-wise, the meetings provided us with extraordinary insight into our 1L class. We knew what brought them here (stellar faculty and reasonable tuition), we knew what worried them (the bar exam ... already!) and we knew what opportunities we could offer to round out their time on our campus (more networking practice and outside activities). We received intel on our academic programs (our new winter term was unintentionally cutting time with their families short), what was happening in the classroom (two 1L professors hadn't been teaching in person that fall—and this was *pre*-COVID-19) and how students were spending their free time (watching Netflix or frequenting the local coffee house/bar). Our counselor immediately noticed the uptick in students needing disability accommodations, but that many of them had no idea on how to obtain a professional assessment to determine whether they'd qualify. Additionally, she quickly flagged me to the staggering number of students carrying extreme cold-calling anxiety and let me know of two areas on campus where equal access was being quietly impeded.[10]

On the Student Affairs side of the house, I used the candid feedback and information received from the intake meetings to add programming and increase student resources. Having raw data from nearly 150 new members of the UConn Law community meant it was easier to lobby for financial support from the institution.[11] When combining that information with the data collected in our biannual participation in the Law School Survey on Student Engagement (LSSSE), we suddenly had a robust assessment of our student body needs and could be more strategic about how to resolve shortfalls.[12]

Beyond that, there was surprising value in using the meetings as the first layer of our student safety net. Keeping all identifiable student information anonymous, the counselor and I culled data and statistics and compiled a presentation for the facul-

---

10. The intake meetings were a disappointing way to learn that the School could do better in fostering safe spaces around campus. Because of the feedback we received, and in addition to subsequent conversations, the School tackled tough topics such as the use of honorifics in class and ways in which certain student organizations felt marginalized for their beliefs and backgrounds.

11. One way we used the feedback collected from the first year of intakes was to seek out a second, part-time (nights and weekend) mental health counselor.

12. LSSSE was developed through the Indiana University Center of Postsecondary Research and is a multipart, 34-question survey provided to students via a confidential and unique online link. Since it is administered independently from each law school, students are able to provide honest feedback that is fully anonymous to the participating institution. Typically UConn Law students have a strong 60%+ response rate, offering the School an invaluable snapshot of our student engagement. Moreover, the survey offers a freeform "Comments" section at the end where students can write as little or as much as they'd like and address topics not included in the multiple-choice section of the survey. Since the survey is offered to all our students, regardless of their enrollment status (day, evening, part-time, international) it provides a thorough bundle of unbiased and usable feedback.

ty about the challenges facing the new class. Because UConn Law employs a confidential accommodations program, it surprised the faculty to learn that approximately 14% of incoming students planned to utilize the Disability Services office their first year.[13] Moreover, we shared ways in which students hoped their professors would address issues in the classroom and identified what to look for when a student was in distress. These presentations increased faculty engagement with our office—a critical piece of the campus support network that had been slipping in the years prior. Because the counselor and I were now familiar at a baseline capacity with almost every student in the class, when professors noticed a student had missed a few classes, we could quickly consult our notes and see if we shared engagement concerns or were aware of external issues impacting that student. It also caused our "wellness check-ins" with students who had gone AWOL to generate a higher response rate as the students each already knew who we were and that our intention was to offer support and resources in times when "life happened."[14]

The other significant and undeniable return on our time investment was the way in which the meetings reduced the stigma of seeking help for mental health issues. While this was something we had hoped and predicted would happen, to see the change evolve was simply remarkable. One student from that first class noted that, "I never worried about seeing the counselor because we've all waited outside her office at least once." The 1L intakes with the counselor offered students the chance to speak freely and without fear of negative repercussions. For students who did not need support for mental health issues, they were simply a 15-minute chance to grab a cup of tea and slow down for a bit. For those knowing they needed help, they were a way to seek it easily with an excuse to do so. This was particularly helpful for international students or those coming from backgrounds resistant to addressing mental health problems. Should they choose to share with their families, they could simply say "the school made them do it." Finally, the meetings with the mental health counselor were a way for students who didn't realize they needed help to be identified and offered support. As a result, approximately 1 in 4–5 of our students left their intake with the counselor having made a second appointment.[15]

---

13. At UConn Law, Disability Services falls under the Student Affairs umbrella.

14. I will never forget during that first year of intakes, meeting with a student who by all accounts did not want to be sitting in my office. We struggled through the meeting and later, our counselor admitted she had the same experience. A week later, the student returned to me and said that because of the meeting, I was the only person on campus they felt comfortable coming to after being the victim of an assault two days earlier. The student shared that they never would have come forward had it not been for knowing there was someone on campus that cared to get to know more about them and that they felt they could trust. We went on to become close during their three years on campus and they regularly stopped by just to say hello or drop off baked goods when they knew we were particularly stressed. Watching the student graduate last spring was one of the most fulfilling moments of my career to date.

15. While my office did not see that type of immediate engagement, general use and reliance upon Student Affairs increased exponentially in the three years following the initial student meetings.

One of the most eye-opening demonstrations of the reduction in stigma came when we witnessed a 1L walk a 3L peer over to the counselor's office to get help during a particularly grueling anxiety attack. The 1L had met with the counselor the month before for their intake and was familiar with the resources and expertise she offered. The experience left them knowing exactly where to go to get help for their colleague. We realized that the grassroots impact of our program would stretch farther than we originally expected—a big win for student wellness.

In the four years since the program was launched, we have continued to benefit from the positive impact of having early and attentive conversations with all of our first-year students. Several new student organizations formed after students expressed interest in a topic or activity and the door was opened for them to explore it following the meeting. In a number of meetings, students asked to be kept in mind as mentors for students matriculating in the years following their arrival. Mental health issues have become fairly comfortable to speak about and our students started a collective that provides peer-to-peer support and runs programming during stressful times throughout the semester.

As we review the topics that arise during these meetings each year—with both the Student Affairs team and our mental health counselors, it is easy to identify trends and, if necessary, act accordingly. A recent example occurred when concerns and complaints about a newly hired professor kept cropping up during our intake conversations. Several 1L students made comments along the lines of, "I'm not sure if you're the right person to speak to about this…" or "I don't have much to compare this to…" Their disclaimers were followed by detailed information about inappropriate statements made in class and ways in which they felt their classroom experience was unlike their peers' in other sections. In addition to not fulfilling basic teaching duties, the professor was also routinely making glib and offensive remarks about gender, race, and substance use. Moreover, 1L students were concerned that they just weren't learning legal writing, a subject that typically provides a critical foundation for both a law degree and future career opportunities. Notably, in addition to their continued-gen peers, two first-gen students shared freely on this issue, noting that having the early open forum with Student Affairs made them feel like they had a place they could go with concerns.

In the end, the Student Affairs and mental health teams compiled enough information to go directly to the Dean of the Law School and the Associate Dean of Academics on the issue. Having all of the evidence needed, campus leadership made a swift decision to remove the professor from the classroom and replace them with tenured faculty who could catch the class up academically.

Prior to the intake meetings and providing 1Ls a forum for administrator discussions, a situation such as this might have continued on until it either imploded or until students finished out the semester, unhappy with their experience—either of which would have been destructive to student morale, learning objectives, and their general opinions of the school. Instead, with the help of the intake meetings, the institution was able to validate their concerns, act promptly, and generate the trust and reassurance that their experiences matter to us.

V. Challenges and Considerations

It's easy, in theory, to observe all the positives about the 1L intake program and, in turn, not question the costs. However, as noted earlier, after the first year it was clear that the program needed adjustments to sustain itself in a manageable way. It was important for us to evaluate the sacrifices that resulted from its implementation, and realistically contrast those against the benefits. Without a doubt, the most significant challenge was time. Student affairs professionals know that the first three months of the first semester are demanding—in a good year. To add in a program that, at a minimum, would occupy 70+ hours of staff time, was a big risk. Finding a balance to produce other important events and maintain student outreach was nearly impossible. Couple all of that with the additional evening and weekend hours needed for part-time students and those with families at home, and the initiative's future was questionable.

In addition to the impact on staff time, there was an unanticipated amount of stress that also materialized in the wake of the meetings. While there was the expected stress of trying to squeeze more hours into an already busy day, there was a covert mental health tax that snuck up after hearing 150+ stories, worries, and backgrounds. Getting to know our students on a more personal level offers an exponential amount of opportunity for customized programming and support options. However, there is also an added amount of responsibility one feels for the students who are in distress or struggling to make it through—especially when you know why they are enrolled and how their lives might be impacted by walking away.

Specific to that point, another unexpected challenge the program created was a lack of referral options for students needing long-term counseling services. Our mental health counselor originally arrived on campus with an impressive Rolodex of local service providers to use in our "catch and release" counseling model.[16] The plan was for our counselor see students for a certain period of time, but in order to cast a big net of student support, after that period, the students would be referred out. However, given the number of 1L students seeking subsequent appointments after their required intake meetings, our counselor's time was tapped quickly and their options for student referrals were quickly exhausted. This created quite a back-

---

16. Because our counselor was limited to a part-time schedule, the hiring plan was to use her as a stopgap for students in immediate distress, before effectively handing them off to an outside counselor who could continue to see and treat them via private pay or their own insurance. In general, our counselor sees students 5–6 times before releasing them to another provider and facilitates the transition to ensure students continue receiving uninterrupted help, whenever possible.

log for 2L and 3L students needing mental health support and led to our counselor working well beyond the originally contracted hours.

Finally, there was the extremely prohibitive issue of scheduling. That first year, I estimate that the actual scheduling and rescheduling of the intake meetings took an additional 15–20 hours of time, not including the toll of interrupting alternate project momentum. On top of the initial scheduling burdens, there was also the frustration that came with students not showing up (nearly 9%). The time and energy spent chasing those folks down to reengage and reschedule compounded the problem and pulled us further away from normal first semester planning and programming.

Despite these valid challenges to repeat implementation of the program, we decided that the return on investment outweighed the obstacles. One tipping point for us was the way in which the meetings started an important dialogue on inclusivity and access for our first-gen students and those from marginalized backgrounds. Letting all our students know that they mattered and there were at least two familiar places on campus where they (hopefully) felt comfortable bringing problems or concerns was something from which we just couldn't walk away.

VI. Solutions to Program Sustainability

After brainstorming about the four main challenges, we were able to identify ways in which we could adjust the program the following year and reduce many of the negative impacts. On the concerns about the extreme time commitment, we decided to split the incoming classes by last name and share the intake meetings between both the Assistant Dean of Students and the Assistant Director of Student Affairs, who also oversees daily Disability Services operations. Our mental health counselor split the new incoming class with our newly hired evening and weekend counselor. Taking on half the students each, as opposed to all 1Ls, alleviated much of the time burden and, in turn, helped address the second challenge: staff stress.

While not carrying work stress is nearly impossible for many in student affairs, the combination of reducing the number of student intakes by half and creating more opportunities for self-care first semester each cut back on the wellness impact of the intakes. Moreover, with a split caseload, having a colleague in the department to share concerns with and debrief regularly also helped—a habit that we carved time for over lunches in year two. That said, one of the most significant ways in which we minimized staff stress in subsequent years was by working with IT to purchase calendaring software that allows students to self-schedule during staff-selected windows of time.[17] Appointments automatically populate on our internal email and calendar program and students receive a text or email message to remind

17. Though home-grown options existed, it was relatively inexpensive to purchase institutional licenses through Calendly. While I have no personal affiliation with this company and any opinions on it are my own, and not UConn Law, I will note its applicability was so well-tailored to student-fac-

them of the appointment with reasonable notice.[18] Another time-saver is that intake meetings can be scheduled with 5–10 minute breaks between appointments to provide staff time to update their notes on each student or flag them for follow-up. Simply put, this one development was a significant game-changer for the longevity of the program.

For fall 2019, we knew the issue of referrals and mental health counseling availability would continue to be a challenge, despite increasing the counselor staffing. One small way we addressed this was to seek support from our local Lawyers Concerned for Lawyers chapter, which provides law students with six free confidential sessions with a local counselor. By making them aware of the 1L meetings, we used them as a partner for non-emergency student counseling needs. This addition worked well until fall 2020, when the impact of COVID-19 and remote learning turned all of our mental health initiatives upside down.

VII. The Next Chapter

The changes made leading up to our fall 2019 required intakes tipped the scale in favor of continuing the program. By late 2019, we enjoyed the benefits of two classes of students with direct experience with student affairs and mental health counseling. Calendly eliminated virtually all of the staff time associated with scheduling and student outreach, while splitting the caseload diversified the meetings and reduced program-related stress. Unfortunately, UConn Law, like many other law schools, ceased on-campus operations in March 2020 due to the unfolding COVID-19 pandemic. Unlike many other law schools, however, UConn Law elected to remain remote for spring and summer 2020, as well as the entirety of the 2020–2021 academic year. While the demands of supporting the student body through the pandemic's ill effects on academic, financial, and wellness challenges could have easily eliminated auxiliary programs such as the 1L intakes, Student Affairs and the mental health counseling team determined that the intakes were more important than ever. During the fall of 2020, the team met with the incoming class in a virtual setting and shifted the meeting scripts to discussing remote campus culture and offering resources for isolation and tech fatigue, among other things. With the opportunity for casual conversation before and after classes effectively eliminated in the online setting, we knew that creating meaningful connections among our students—especially our first-gen and international students, was critical. While UConn Law reopened campus for in-person learning in the fall of 2021, we've continued to check in with our "remote" class and build upon the relationships formed virtually.

---

ing offices that in the time since our implementation, several other UConn Law departments have switched their calendaring to Calendly.

18. Since using Calendly, our no-show percent dropped from approximately 9% to 2%.

Sadly, recent studies indicate that approximately 71% of college students indicate their stress and anxiety has increased as a result of the pandemic, yet only 5% of those students see a mental health counselor.[19] Additionally, it has been well-documented that in many cases, first-gen students have been disparately impacted by the pandemic. [20] For these reasons, and the value-add discussed in Section IV, our team is more committed than ever to continuing the 1L intake program. That said, we plan to once again modify our meeting scripts to better address the changing needs of our student body. While we incorporated an introductory question in fall of 2020 to address student pronouns and culturally correct name pronunciation, we have since decided to ask students if they are the first in their families to attend law school and/or receive an undergraduate degree.[21] As it currently stands, first-gen students self-identify in conversation or through their involvement with our First-Generation Law Student Association, but it is important to empower students to do so early on so that we can offer additional campus connections and, once the COVID-19 demands slow down, implement a first-gen student mentoring program.

Looking forward, we also have discussed the appropriateness of a more structured approach to following up with students post-intake meeting. The original handwritten notes scattered across the back of business cards has thankfully been replaced with preprinted intake sheets, similar in style to a doctor's prescription pad, which makes next steps easy to identify. While we remain hopeful that the future will allow implementation of scheduled follow-up meetings, but are still debating the best timing related to student coursework. We considered initially rolling out follow-up meetings out to our first-gen, international, and disability services students; however, we are currently constricted by the ongoing demands of student support during the pandemic and want to be sure that efforts to do so don't become an additional burden for those communities.

---

19. C. Son, S. Hegde, A. Smith, X. Wang & F. Sasangohar, *Effects of COVID-19 on College Students' Mental Health in the United States: Interview Survey Study*, J. Med. Internet Rsch., 2020 Sep; 22(9): e21279, 9/3/2020.

20. *Supporting First-Generation Students through a New COVID-19 Environment*, Hunt Inst., www.hunt-institute.org; February 26, 2021; M. Garces-Jimenez, *The Coronavirus Crisis Has Been Extremely Challenging for Many First-Gen College Students*, cnbc.com, July 29, 2020.

21. In fall 2020, we began opening intake meetings by welcoming the student and asking, "Do you mind pronouncing your name and sharing what pronouns you use?" The positive reception to this addition led us to purchase an upgrade to our student classroom management software that allows students to input their pronouns and record themselves pronouncing their full name. The files are available to both staff and faculty and can be referenced before meetings and classes to increase inclusivity on campus.

VIII. Conclusion

Our unconventional approach to welcoming 1L law students to campus has been a tug-of-war between the return on our investment of time, stress, and resources, and the overall value we observe year after year. We've witnessed some of the most reluctant students become engaged frequent fliers in our offices and on many occasions the meetings opened the door for relationships that foster success for our first-gen students and those from marginalized backgrounds. In preparation for writing this chapter, I asked a number of first-gen students what their biggest challenge was in law school and, unequivocally, most all of them said the first semester learning curve outside of the classroom proved the most difficult. Across the board, the response was, "I didn't even know what I didn't know," and "I had no idea where to go for help—especially when didn't even know what to ask for."[22]

After carrying out almost 350 15-minute 1L intake meetings over the past four years, my favorite dialogue comes toward the end of the conversation when I ask students, "Do you have any questions for me?" I am always intentional about stating that they can ask me anything—student affairs-related or otherwise, and that even if they aren't sure how to articulate the question, we'll figure out the answer together. I truly think that summarizes the purpose and benefit of these meetings, despite the various costs associated with them. The ultimate goal is to open the door for all of our students, no matter their background, age, race, gender, etc., and find common ground and connection that reminds them that they belong on our campus (virtually, or in person, of course). Doing so with a brief and friendly meet-and-greet not only opens the door and makes their 1L experience a bit more personal, it's a daily reminder to us, as administrators, why we come to work each day.

22. Lauren M., a 2013 graduate of New York Law School; and Tracie G., UConn Law Class of '20.

PART V Academic Success, Diversity Initiatives, and the Library

Seventeen

A Sense of Belonging from the Beginning Equals Success from the Start

Using Academic Support Techniques to Ensure First Gen Students Thrive in their 1L Year

Haley A. Meade* and Courtney Richardson**

OFFICES OF ACADEMIC SUPPORT (OAS) ARE A COMMON FIXTURE in law schools across America. These offices should strive to be visible to students and be proactive from the beginning of the law school journey and remain that way through graduation.

Regardless of the specific setup of the offices among law schools, OAS at their core support law student learning. Offices of Academic Support offer assistance and support to students in various ways and at various times throughout their law school matriculation. As it relates to first-generation students, they are not exempt from needing support from the OAS. In fact, they spend less time studying and creating social interactions with faculty members and their peers[1] than their continuing education counterparts. As a result, first-generation students may need a greater level of support than their continuing education counterparts. Offices of Academic Support have a unique opportunity to support first-generation students throughout their law school matriculation. Creating pathways for interacting with faculty and sharing information and tips on studying can help OAS to be proactive in addressing the needs of first-generation students.

* Director, Irene Diamond Professional Skills Center, City University of New York School of Law.

** Academic Counselor and Instructor, Southern University Law Center.

1. Kerry J. Strand, *Making Sure They Make It!: Best Practices for Ensuring The Academic Success of First-Generation College Students*, 3, Council of Indep. Colls. (2013).

Intrusive Advising Method

Law schools should assume that first-generation students will need help instead of waiting for them to seek out assistance. One way to accomplish this is to utilize an intrusive advising method.[2]

In general, human nature teaches us not to be intrusive. When following societal norms, we tend to offer guidance, advice, etc. only when we are asked for our opinions. It is not commonly accepted to offer unsolicited advice on someone else's life or personal situation. However, in the law school environment, OAS teams need to be intrusive. We cannot always wait for our students to seek out assistance from us. Often when students are left to their own devices, they will struggle in silence or they will share their struggles with their peer group. The peer group likely does not have any more law school experience than the first-generation student does. In both scenarios, the first-generation student is not gaining any positive assistance or insight.

An intrusive advising model requires that an advisor be active in initiating contact with students and active in maintaining the subsequent contacts. Offices of Academic Support will find more success reaching first-generation students by using the intrusive advising method as opposed to a general open invitation for students to schedule an appointment. An intrusive advisor will not only be present at 1L orientation, but will remain present throughout 1L year, and will also maintain an open line of communication with students. The following suggests ways in which OAS can introduce an intrusive advising model for their students.

Academic Counseling Page. Creating an OAS or academic counseling page on the institution's learning management system will help advisors make their initial contacts with students and also drive the subsequent contacts. Establishing a page that is exclusively for OAS will go a long way in creating a welcoming and comfortable environment for students. When students feel comfortable and feel that the support and assistance that is being offered is genuine, they will be more likely to utilize the services provided. Using a learning management system, Academic Counselors can keep track of their advisees and quickly send a variety of information, such as: study tips, reminders of important dates, invitations for meetings, and emails to the entire group or individual students.

Welcome Emails. A welcome email that introduces first-year students to their Academic Counselor or an email reminding students that their Academic Counselor is available to them are great first steps toward intrusive advising. The email will entice some students to reach out and start the initial conversation with their Academic Counselor. There will be students who may need assistance but fail to respond to the initial communication. The failure to

---

2. Walter R. Earl, *Intrusive Advising of Freshmen in Academic Difficulty*, NACADA J. 8, 27–33 (1988).

respond may result from an overestimation of their understanding of the material. These students should not be allowed to muddle through the semester without assistance from OAS.

Track Student Performance. Another way to utilize the intrusive advising model is to proactively monitor student grades.[3] Tracking student performance will provide Academic Counselors with an opportunity to see which students will fall into that category and require an intervention. Institutions with a small OAS staff may find it difficult to track and manage a group of students that far outnumber them. This can be overcome with the use of technology. A member of the IT department or the student information system that houses student grades and transcripts will be a great place to start in receiving a document or report that provides a list of students that are in or approaching academic distress. Additionally, in institutions that use formative assessments, OAS team members can analyze the collected data to ascertain which students need assistance. Once identified, those students will benefit from receiving a meeting request to sit down with their Academic Counselor to discuss what assistance the student will benefit from.

Maintain Contact. An important part of advising students is maintaining contact. One hello at 1L orientation is likely not sufficient contact between OAS and a first-generation student. Office of Academic Support teams often find it difficult to maintain and organize contact with their students. This can be overcome easily when the advisor sets a student contact goal and makes an effort to track the contacts that are being made with each student. A spreadsheet showing when communication was made is a simple way to bring a sense of organization to the intrusive advising. A more complex way of tracking and organizing contacts may be to create a database that includes a listing of all students along with their contact information, GPA, notations on when contact was made, and a place for notes from meetings or conversation with the student.

While initiating and maintaining contact with students, OAS team members must understand that there will be times that students will struggle in law school. Throughout their lives students experience various levels of struggles, both personal and academic. They are always able to find the strength to push through those struggles and the tough times. Some of the most valuable lessons are learned amid struggles, and students come out better for having gone through that tough time. Law school is no exception—our students will experience academic struggles, stress, and tough times.

Normalize Difficulty. Academic difficulties not only affect academic performance, but can affect student wellness. As a result, law schools must work to normalize struggle among students. First-generation students would benefit

3. Jennifer Varney, *Academic Advising Today*, INTRUSIVE ADVISING, 30, 11 (2007).

from a constant reminder that challenges and setbacks are normal when learning something new. Academic struggles should be looked at as signs of effort and not of failure.

Since law schools are aware that at some point students will deal with challenges, OAS should make a conscious effort to normalize struggle in the law school environment. Learning is sometimes hard, and as a result struggle will follow. Institutions should let students know up front that there may come a time during their matriculation when they may grapple with issues. An OAS should be tasked with letting students know that trials are normal and that they are not in it alone. This can be accomplished when OAS makes an effort to reshape the idea that academic struggles are bad.

First-generation students are not always able to lean on their families and friends for support in all their academic challenges. Their families are not always able to relate to their situations. as it is not something that they have experienced in the past. As a result, they may not be able to provide the best support for first-generation students. The gap between the support that first-generation students need, and the level of support offered by their families, presents a unique opportunity for OAS. The gap can be filled when OAS provides students with resources and advice on how to best navigate law school. Academic Counselors are in a position where they can have conversations with first-generation students that may provide clarity on many situations, including things as specific as time management or as general as the transition to the law school environment.

Offering continued support for first-generation students will help OAS normalize struggles and remind students that academic struggle and failure are not the same thing. Examples of that support include hosting a first-generation meet-and-greet, providing mentors, creating student support groups for first-generation students, and creating a resource bank.

First Gen Meet-and-Greet with OAS

It is no secret that OAS teams provide a wide variety of services and support for law students and can be an amazing resource when students utilize the services. When students are in a new environment, they sometimes find it difficult to ask for help when they are faced with unfamiliar situations. In general, people tend to be more willing to seek out support and assistance when they feel comfortable with the source, and first-generation students are no different. When OAS seeks to develop relationships with first-generation students as early as possible, they will begin to develop relationships and create a level of comfort for students. When students feel comfortable, then OAS can begin fostering relationships. This allows OAS an opportunity to provide a wide array of support such as bridging gaps between undergraduate school and law school.

One step OAS can take to ensure that first-generation students utilize the resources available is to host a meet-and-greet. The OAS meet-and-greet can be an annual event that is held at the beginning of each fall semester. A meet-and-greet is the perfect way to create a casual and relaxed environment for first-generation students. In this space students will feel comfortable interacting with each other and the OAS. This activity will provide students with an opportunity to get to know the OAS team and learn about the services they offer. Hosting a meet-and-greet with OAS will be a great first step to ensuring that students feel comfortable using the resources available to them from OAS.

Mentors

The benefits of a mentoring program are numerous. Mentors can provide guidance, answer questions, and help increase a student's confidence and self-esteem. With more and more first-generation students attending law school, it only makes sense to offer them a specialized mentoring program that pairs them with a first-generation lawyer, faculty member, and/or 2L or 3L student. This is a great opportunity to get your alumni involved too. The mentorship program doesn't have to be elaborate. Simply pairing a first-generation student with a former first-generation student who has successfully navigated law school, internships, the bar exam, and legal practice can be invaluable to the student. The OAS or Office of Student Affairs could be responsible for creating and maintaining these pairings.

If you want to implement a mentorship program at your school, consider who you will pair students with—other students, faculty, and/or alumni. Think about the length and frequency of the program. Will the mentorship be for the first year or extend to after graduation? Will the meetings happen weekly or monthly? Perhaps you can survey the mentors and mentees to attempt to match areas of practice and/or interest. In addition to providing a mentor, you may decide to include an exclusive speaker series, personalized professional development, and post-graduation executive coaching.

First Gen Student Group

Law schools are filled with student organizations for all sorts of practice areas, cultural groups, and student interests. Creating and supporting a first-generation student group can provide the space and time for first-generation students to share their experiences, questions, and concerns. The group can also be a place to recognize, empower, and celebrate first-generation students. Law schools might ask members of the administration or faculty who were first-gen to be the point person for the group to show solidarity with the students.

Resource Bank

While providing resources and services to students, OAS should meet first-generation students where they are and help them grow to where they need to be. It is generally understood that first-generation students may enter law school with less understanding about the law school experience than their continuing generation counterparts. This provides OAS with yet another opportunity to serve first-generation students. In helping students have a better understanding of what to expect as it relates to their law school experience, the OAS will foster relationships with first-generation students that will last throughout their law school matriculation.

First-generation students would be greatly benefited by being presented with a resource bank containing information relative to their law school experience. Granting students access to a list of resources on or before day one of law school will help them to get acclimated to the law school environment and provide answers to some of the questions that they will inevitably have. The resource bank should be organized in a manner that best represents the programs and services available at each individual institution. For illustrative purposes, our resource bank will be organized by skills resources and campus resources, and details on the resources to be included within the resource bank are discussed below.

The skills resources section can provide a variety of information and is a great opportunity for an OAS to highlight its office and team members. A starting point for this section could be the location, contact information, and services provided by the OAS. Information on the location and best practices of using practice hypos and previous exams would be invaluable to students. Additionally, information on self-directed learning skills such as study routines, time management, and self-reflection would be beneficial in the skills resources section.

Like the skills resources section, the campus resources section can provide lots of different information to students. The focus of the section should be on the various services available at each individual institution. All institutions provide their students with excellent resources, and unfortunately students are sometimes unaware of these resources. Each OAS should tailor the campus resources section to show the resources provided by their institution. The creation of subsections such as technology, student health, and books can be a starting point for this section.

Students and institutions alike find themselves surrounded by technology, so it should come as no surprise that students would want to know about the technology available to them at their institution. Most students come to law school with a wealth of knowledge and experience using technology, and many students have several portable technology devices like laptops, tablets, and smartphones when they enter law school. The location and contact information of the Information Technology (IT) Department, the location and hours of computer labs, the costs of printing, and information on access to computer programs and software would all be valuable additions to the technology subsection.

It is sometimes easy to view our students as just students or scholars, when in reality our students are whole and complete people, and they should be treated as such. We must acknowledge that there are factors beyond the educational abilities of our students that can impact their matriculation through law school. Among those factors impacting our students are health and wellness, which has become an increasingly important concern for students. As a result, the location and contact information of: campus health centers and both on- and off-campus counseling services would be beneficial. Additionally, information and tips on self-care and stress management would benefit first-generation students.

The final subcategory of the campus resource section is books. From an early age, our students have been told that reading is fundamental. In the most general terms, this statement is true, and there is no exception for law school. Reading is something that our students are expected to do from day one throughout their law school journey. As a result, it is natural to include a subcategory in the resource bank that relates to reading and books. The location and hours of the library, digital library resources, eBooks, information on study aids, and information on both on- and off-campus bookstores will all be great information to include in the resource bank.

In addition to providing direct support for first-generation students, OAS professionals have the opportunity to use, and encourage faculty to use, plenty of pedagogical techniques and strategies to create and foster an inclusive learning experience for all students, including first-generation students. To the extent that OAS professionals teach any academic support classes themselves, they can model for other faculty how to incorporate a more inclusive approach to teaching. These techniques and strategies can range from quick and simple to more thoughtful and robust.

Simple Techniques

Creating a sense of belonging for first-generation students doesn't have to be onerous or time-consuming. In fact, there are several quick and easy practices that you can incorporate into your pedagogy.

First, use inspirational passwords for class websites, such as "youbelonghere" or "screwimpostersyndrome" to easily show students that you are thinking about them and their potential insecurities around being a first-generation law student. This simple gesture can speak volumes and takes little to no time.

Second, if you were a first-generation student, tell your students. Say it loud and proud. Sharing your own experience as a first-generation student can normalize a student's feelings and provide an example of attainable success.

Third, make it a point to get to know and use your students' names. Knowing and using someone's name can have a profound impact because the person will feel respected and important. It can make the person feel like they belong. According to Dale Carnegie, "a person's name is to that person, the sweetest and most important sound in any language."[4] In addition to knowing and using students' names, be sure you learn to pronounce them correctly. Many times, we avoid saying a student's name that we think we may mispronounce, which can lead to that student feeling excluded. Instead, ask the student to pronounce it for you, make a note for yourself, and practice saying it. Don't forget that pronouns matter too. Share your pronouns in your syllabus and on the first day of class. Invite students to share their pronouns too, whether on the class webpage, on their name tents, in their Zoom names, or through a Google Form before classes begin. You can even incorporate the pronouns into the class roster you bring to class for quick reference.

Next, admit when a topic or concept you are teaching is challenging. When you acknowledge how difficult law school can be, you are showing all students compassion, but especially first-generation students who might internalize the difficulty they are experiencing as a result of their own inadequacies. You can also regularly encourage students to show themselves grace as they travel law school's steep learning curve.

Finally, ask your students what makes them feel included in a class and what makes them feel excluded. You can quickly gather this information using an index card or Google form. Simply asking the question can show your students that you care about their sense of belonging in your class and can also provide you with invaluable information about your students.[5]

Pedagogical Strategies

In addition to the simple techniques listed above, there are pedagogical decisions that you can make to provide a more inclusive classroom for not only first-generation students, but all students.

First, be structured. Be explicit and transparent in your syllabus about your expectations for your class. Your students will not only appreciate the structure but will most likely thrive as well. While you're working on your syllabus, you can also find ways for it to be more inclusive by including a statement of diversity, inclusion, and belonging and paying attention to the words and tone you use. Consider expressing respect, support, and confidence in the students. For example, you may find ways to incorporate a warmer and more empathic approach to your attendance policy. Instead of saying, "Students are required to attend all classes," you might say, "Attending class is an integral part of the learning process. When you miss class, you not only miss out on important details or possible changes to the syllabus, but more importantly you miss out on the opportunity to develop a deeper understanding of the material. You miss the chance to ask questions, learn from your peers, and show

4. Dale Carnegie, How to Win Friends and Influence People (2009).

5. *See* Jane Grise's 2022 AALS Presentation, *Teaching Strategies to Promote Equity and Inclusion in the Classroom.*

me where I may need to slow down, speed up, or review particular areas of the doctrine. Therefore, I strongly encourage you to attend every class. I understand that extenuating circumstances can arise, so you may need to miss a class or two. If you will need to miss multiple classes, please contact me or the Office of Student Affairs." By clearly stating what you hope students will gain and why your policies will help them, you will most likely increase their motivation to do well in your class.

Second, create flexibility around participation. Traditional law school teaching methods, including cold-calling, are not inclusive and will leave students feeling unnerved. Anxiety stemming from classroom participation can certainly lead to barriers in learning. Therefore, consider allowing different forms of participation, such as anonymous participation using index cards, clickers, or Google forms.

Third, don't assume that your students know Latin, legalese, or even the court system. Take the time to define and quickly explain archaic words or phrases and complicated procedural issues that arise in the cases you assign. This will help all students, not just first-generation students.

Next, consider using non-legal contexts to teach concepts such as analogic reasoning or rule synthesis. By using non-legal contexts, you demystify the law and make it accessible to just about anyone. Charles Calleros has created these types of exercises using music, tomatoes, apples, and carrots, as well as a teenager's curfew.[6] One of the exercises uses the universally familiar context of a grocery store to illustrate the concepts of precedent, analogic reasoning, and uncertainty.[7] This simple exercise begins by setting a scene at the grocery store where an employee has boxes of large bright red apples, some unwashed and unpeeled carrots, and some tomatoes. The employer tells the employee to put the apples in the window display case outside because they are likely to attract impulse shoppers. The employer tells the employee that the carrots will not draw customers into the store, so the carrots should go in the produce section inside the store. The employer then leaves to go to the bank. The employee realizes that they forgot to ask where the employer wanted the tomatoes to go. The question the students must grapple with is where should the employee put the tomatoes?[8] Without the employer there, the employee must predict where the employer would place them.

---

6. Charles R. Calleros, *Using Classroom Demonstrations in Familiar Nonlegal Contexts to Teach Unfamiliar Concepts of Legal Method to New Students*, LEGAL WRITING, Vol. 7, p. 37, 2001, *available at* SSRN: https://ssrn.com/abstract=1464820 and Charles R. Calleros, *Reading, Writing, and Rhythm: A Whimsical, Musical Way of Thinking About Teaching Legal Method and Writing*, LEGAL WRITING, Vol. 5, p. 1, 1999, *available at* SSRN: https://ssrn.com/abstract=1464814.

7. Charles R. Calleros, *Using Classroom Demonstrations in Familiar Nonlegal Contexts to Teach Unfamiliar Concepts of Legal Method to New Students*, LEGAL WRITING, Vol. 7, p. 37, 2001, *available at* SSRN: https://ssrn.com/abstract=1464820.

8. *Id.*

The employee can look to previous "cases," or precedent, for guidance in making that prediction. By using non-legal contexts to teach students, we level the playing field, which is exactly what first-generation students can benefit from.

Finally, rethink how you assess your students' performance and grade in your class. Traditionally, the law school final exam has carried so much weight that students risk probation or dismissal with one bad final exam grade. Reduce the risk involved for any one assessment. Consider giving smaller, more frequent, low-stakes assessments. Again, this will benefit all students, not just first-generation students.

The beauty of striving to create a learning environment that fosters a sense of belonging for first-generation students is that when we take steps to help first-generation students feel more confident and connected, we inevitably make the learning experience better for all students. We must implore our faculty to employ this curb-cut thinking. The curb-cut effect is a concept rooted in years of disability activism. Cuts were originally installed in curbs in an effort to be more inclusive of wheelchair users, but this change benefited society at large—travelers with wheeled luggage, bike riders, parents with strollers, and those learning to walk.[9] Using this simple example to illustrate how all law students can benefit from fostering inclusion in the classroom should hopefully get the buy-in you're looking for from other faculty.

In addition, you may appeal to faculty with evidence of how changes you have made in the classroom have positively impacted your students. Perhaps share evaluations that mention how specific changes you made have fostered a sense of inclusion and belonging.

If you encounter faculty set in their ways, you may suggest some of the simple techniques mentioned in this chapter. Perhaps you could create and distribute to faculty a short checklist of easy ideas to incorporate.[10] As the saying goes, small steps can lead to big changes.

---

9. Angela Glover Blackwell, *The Curb-Cut Effect*, Stanford Soc. Innovation Rev., Winter 2017, https://ssir.org/articles/entry/the_curb_cut_effect#.

10. For example: https://bioethicsresearch.org/wp-content/uploads/2019/02/Handout-21-Strategies-for-Promoting-Student-Success.pdf.

The following is an example of a checklist where students can locate resources.*

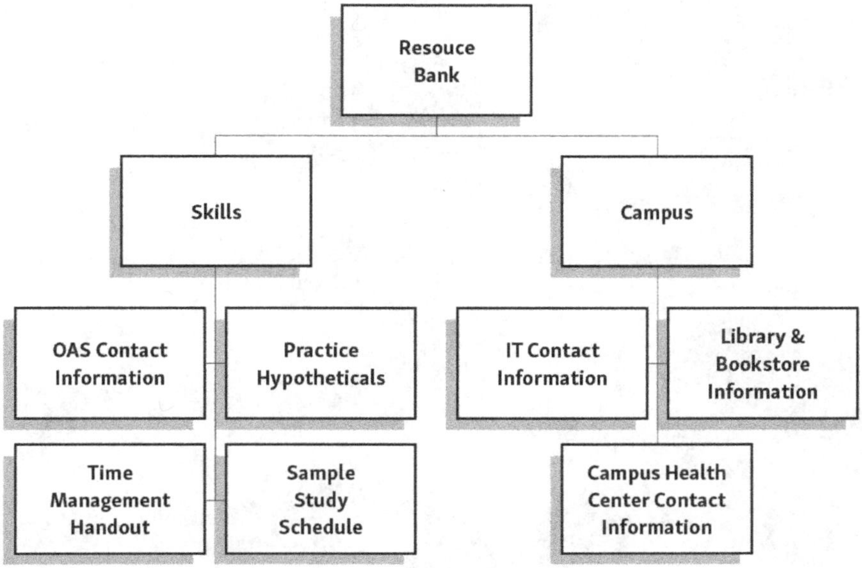

Sample Inclusion Statement for Syllabus

Commitment to an Inclusive Learning Environment

I am committed to creating an inclusive learning environment where diverse perspectives are recognized, respected, and seen as a source of strength, and foster an exchange of views and ideas that may often be impassioned, but should never be hostile or disrespectful. It is my intention that students from all diverse backgrounds and perspectives be well served by this course, that students' learning needs be addressed both in and out of class, and that the diversity that students bring to this class be viewed as a resource, strength, and benefit. It is my intention to present materials and activities that are respectful of diversity: gender, sexuality, disability, age, socioeconomic status, ethnicity, race, and culture.

* When using the Resources as a PDF, it can be helpful to include hyperlinks to referenced documents like a time management handout, a sample study schedule, or practice hypotheticals. The use of hyperlinks allows the document to remain a quick one-page reference sheet.

Eighteen

Supporting First Gen Students Through Academic Law Library Collections, Programs, and Spaces

Kelly M. Leong* and Joseph D. Lawson**

Introduction

THE FIRST DEAN OF HARVARD LAW SCHOOL, Christopher C. Langdell, described the law library as a laboratory of the law school.[1] Through the exploration of legal resources, law students measure and challenge their understanding of legal principles by analyzing hypotheticals and exploring precedent. In modern law schools, much of this is done through database subscriptions maintained by academic law libraries, and the basic process of finding cases, statutes, and regulations is taught through a combination of legal research and writing courses, vendor training sessions, and other informal learning opportunities offered by law librarians. However, growth beyond the basics of legal research requires resources in one form or another.

For many law students, social networks provide the opportunity for growth. Endless discussions with classmates about legal principles and where information about them may be found help hone many students' understanding of the law and the tools used in legal practice. For example, suppose a law student in a social group shares with her network that a better understanding of topics in a casebook may be gleaned from a hornbook, a study aid, and a practice guide. In that case, other members of the network now have a better understanding of time-saving tools that can help them excel. Perhaps the helpful student discovered all of these resources on her own, or maybe she is sharing information obtained from a family member who either works in the legal field or has a connection with someone in the legal field. If the information is obtained from and passed through family or social connections, it represents information of value available only to students who have those connec-

* Associate Dean for Library Services, Benjamin N. Cardozo School of Law.

** Assistant Director for Public Services, University of Michigan Law School.

1. *See* Richard A. Danner, *Law Libraries and Laboratories: The Legacies of Langdell and His Metaphor*, 107 LAW LIB. J. 7, 8 (2015).

tions and may not be available to a first-generation law student. Without social access to helpful information about the mechanics of legal studies, including how to use and where to find legal information, many first-generation students are left to rely on personal effort to obtain similar knowledge. Although first-generation students frequently exhibit qualities, such as grit and resilience, that may help them overcome these obstacles, their capacity to use personal effort for topics outside of required coursework may be diminished due to strains of family responsibilities, work, and unfamiliarity with campus resources, including library services.[2] Additionally, first-generation students face financial constraints that other law students do not, which means that even if they have the time and energy to put in the personal effort to obtain the required knowledge, they may not have the means to pay for resources or collateral expenses, such as training fees, technology costs necessary to access services, and travel to attend training and access resources. A well-provisioned law library located on campus can help first-generation law students overcome many hurdles that are unique to their experiences.

Collections

Law library collections play an essential role in supporting first-generation students. First, core collections, study aids, and expansive research collections can help under-resourced students fully participate in coursework and extracurricular activities necessary to compete in the job market, such as law review, moot court, and research assistant positions. Second, collections that address lawyering skills, soft skills, and career exploration can help first-generation students overcome hurdles that stem from a lack of social connections in the legal field.

Core collections, including primary law and prominent practice materials, help ensure that first-generation students have the threshold understanding of resources required to engage in the practice of law without relying on a social network to supplement their understanding of those resources. Core collections generally include primary sources of law and curated collections of traditional secondary sources such as legal encyclopedias and treatises and materials that support faculty scholarship, including legal and non-legal journals and books. The preferred formats of these materials are switching from print to digital, but print materials continue to be collected. In recent years, primary source collections have been whittled down to include the state where the school is located, federal jurisdictions with an emphasis on the jurisdiction in which the school resides, and sometimes surrounding state jurisdictions or jurisdictions where the majority of graduates begin their legal work.

Study aids often provide access to crucial information usually shared between law students through social networks. Data shows that first-generation students may

---

2. *See* Jacqueline M. O'Bryant & Katharine Traylor Schaffzin, *First-Generation Students in Law School: A Proven Success Model*, 70 Ark. L. Rev. 913 (2018).

experience different social networks than their non-first-generation peers.[3] At the end of each semester, students huddle together to share outlines of class content in preparation for final exams. Outlines may be gleaned from study aids or social connections, but whatever the source, these resources are part of law school's hidden curriculum, and first-generation students may be left out if they do not have access. Study aids also expose first-generation students to the unique aspects of law school exams by providing examples and practice. Historically, law libraries have purchased print study aids, such as Examples and Explanations, Hornbooks, Nutshells, and the Understanding Series. While digital access to study aids had been available for quite some time, their cost had forced many libraries to eschew them in favor of the print. When the pandemic began and schools moved to fully remote instruction in March 2020, law libraries scrambled to move from print to digital study aids just before spring exams. Once law libraries provided digital access to students, there was no turning back and many law students have continued to purchase digital access.

Digital access to study aids has improved access to study aids for first-generation students. Study aids are supplemental texts that are not mandatory. Since first-generation students are more likely to receive financial aid, and in greater amounts, and have other financial responsibilities beyond school, providing universal access to study aids through the library relieves an area of financial strain. With digital access, students have access to study aids for most of their classes. It also means that multiple students can simultaneously use study aids, something not possible with print. These digital study aid packages are expensive and billed by full-time enrolled student counts. Law schools and their libraries should be looking closely at if and how they can make purchasing digital study aids a priority.

First-generation law students should be supported in their extracurricular activities, such as law review, moot court, and research assistantships. These activities are vital to their law school experience and employment opportunities. Each of these programs requires access to and familiarity with library research materials. Law libraries generally collect in areas that support the school's journals and moot court. Still, we must convey that information to students and train them in the skills necessary to access those resources; this can be achieved through proactive training programs for extracurricular activities; many law libraries already have these training programs in place. However, to better serve our first-generation students, the training should focus on skills often gained through networks that they may not have access to and create a welcoming environment for questions. The law library can be intimidating, and creating a connection with a librarian where students are encouraged to ask questions can ease the intimidation.

Many law students acquire the soft skills and business skills necessary for law practice through family connections and other networks. The mechanics of net-

---

3. *See* Sarah O'Shea, *Avoiding the Manufacture of 'Sameness': First-in-Family Students, Cultural Capital and the Higher Education Environment*, 72 Higher Educ. 59 (2016).

working—setting up an office, finding your "fit" in a white-collar work environment, and managing finances—are all topics that fall outside of standard law school coursework. These soft skills may be unfamiliar to a first-generation law student whose family and social connections lack experience in corporate settings. Law libraries frequently maintain collections outside of their core collections with titles that can help all students develop these skills. However, intentionally developing these collections and sharing their value with first-generation students can help overcome unique hurdles. Before developing these collections, law libraries should seek to understand the needs of their law school graduates. For example, if graduates of your school often hang their own shingle after graduation, curating a robust collection of solo and small practice management materials will be a necessity.

There are, of course, general areas of legal practice that all libraries can collect at some level. For example, the law profession has always struggled with mental health issues and substance abuse issues, and there are many books and articles written on the topic.[4] Law libraries can collect materials that address well-being in the profession.[5] In the absence of a social network in which a first-generation student can explore these topics, curating a robust collection to support the soft skills and business skills to be a successful attorney can support students as they seek to find their place in the legal profession.

We have mentioned training and connecting students to useful library materials and services throughout this section. These are crucial elements to making a library collection of value to law students. In building a collection, we must also determine how we will best convey the benefits of library materials to students. Training and marketing materials are essential. While this often happens through formal legal research courses, informal instruction at the reference desk, or as a guest lecture in a doctrinal class, law librarians must seek additional opportunities to market their materials, services, and training to ensure that we are reaching our first-generation students.

The Library Space

The concept of the library as "place" is relatively new in the lifetime of libraries. It is born from the changing way we access information, shifting from print to digital, the changing roles that libraries play in accessing information, and how those changes impact the library space, among other things. We should also examine whether

4. Search Query for Mental Health Materials, WORLDCAT, https://www.worldcat.org/search?q=su%3ALawyers+Mental+health+united+states.&qt=results_page (search, "su:Lawyers Mental health united states.").

5. American Bar Association, ABA Publishing, https://www.americanbar.org/groups/departments_offices/publishing/. (For example, the American Bar Association publishes a series of works on lawyering both from a business and a personal perspective. Titles cover topics from setting up a paperless office and marketing a small firm to the basics of networking and practicing law as an introvert.)

our library spaces welcome students and provide a sense of belonging that can be difficult for first-generation students to find in the law school setting initially.[6]

In surveys of undergraduate students, we see varied views of the library.[7] Initially, first-generation students may be intimidated by the library.[8] This feeling may subside for some students as they progress through their schooling. There needs to be more study of first-generation students and their law school experience with the law library, but these trends should be assumed to follow through to the law school experience where students are working with new types of materials—treatises, cases, statutes, regulations, etc.—and the more professional setting of the law school.

The "library as place" concept has and will continue to allow libraries to rethink and redesign their spaces. Within that shift, libraries can better support the needs of first-generation students. First-generation students are more likely to live in multi-generational homes, commute to school, and work while attending school. These characteristics lead to different needs, including spaces outside the home to study, spend time between classes, and complete work other than studying. Many of these needs are met in the defined spaces being included in newly designed and redesigned academic libraries. A recent example is the newly constructed University of Houston Law Center. During the initial design phases of the construction process, study space in the law library was limited in favor of allocating the space to private offices for other departments. A coalition of students and library staff presented data to show that most students commuted to campus and that many were nontraditional students who do not have quiet study spaces at home. Considerations of such factors that typically impact first-generation law students led to the development of robust study spaces in the law library to support the students' needs.

Study rooms have become very popular among students. These are usually small rooms that facilitate small group study but can be large enough to accommodate groups of 10–15 students. For first-generation students who commute or reside in a family home, having a place for group study outside of their residence is essential. In addition to study rooms, we see libraries carving out defined spaces for different noise levels—silent, quiet, and common areas with conversational noise. For first-generation students or any student who seeks a quiet study space but cannot find this at home or elsewhere, these spaces are essential. It is also essential for stu-

---

6. Juliann Couture et al., *"We're Gonna Figure This Out": First-generation Students and Academic Libraries*, 21 LIBRARIES AND THE ACADEMY 127 (2021).

7. *See* Anne Jumonville Graf, *First-Generation Students and Libraries: Beyond the Deficit Narrative*, *in* SUPPORTING TODAY'S STUDENTS IN THE LIBRARY: STRATEGIES FOR RETAINING AND GRADUATING INTERNATIONAL, TRANSFER, FIRST-GENERATION, AND RE-ENTRY STUDENTS (Ngoc-Yen Tran & Silke Higgins eds., 2019); *See* Darren Ilett, *First-Generation Students' Information Literacy in Everyday Contexts*, 13 J. INFO. LITERACY 79 (2019).

8. *See* Xan Arch & Isaac Gilman, *First Principles: Designing Services for First-generation Students*, 80 COLL. & RSCH. LIBR. 996 (2019).

dents looking for a study space outside the family home with conversational noise where they can study uninterrupted by family members.

Equipment and Technology

Law libraries can help level the playing field by providing access to threshold technologies required for legal studies. Participation in law school requires specific equipment and technology. For example, most law schools explicitly require students to have laptops and provide free access to legal databases, such as Lexis and Westlaw. This means that students also need a stable internet connection to access free database subscriptions, a charger to power the laptop, and basic software, such as word processing software, to draft required documents. Ensuring access to all of the equipment needed to allow a student to participate can increase the chances that the student's talent and grit will shine through, rather than being excluded due to a lack of resources. Many law libraries already provide access to computers, printers, scanners, and other technologies but may need to reassess whether the software and peripheral equipment continue to support advancing curriculum needs. For instance, if a course requires the creation of video content, a law library may consider investing in video-editing software and recording equipment to ensure under-resourced students can participate with the rest of the student body.

Law libraries may also consider opportunities to lend equipment, such as WiFi hotspots and laptop chargers, to help students overcome temporary or long-term financial issues that can interfere with their studies. First-generation students are more likely than other students to have to work, support families, and face financial hardship during law school.[9] If a student loses a laptop charger or internet access due to financial issues, building up funds to replace the equipment or service may take weeks. The time lost is a hardship that has nothing to do with the student's commitment to her studies. Law libraries can follow a service model implemented at academic and public libraries throughout the country and loan equipment needed to participate in law school the same way libraries circulate books. The advantage of loaning the equipment through the library rather than IT or another department is that the library has established workflows and equipment to loan resources, so there is no need to reinvent the wheel. By leveraging the law library's existing services, the law school can ensure first-generation students are not excluded by basic technology and equipment needs.

9. *See* O'Bryant & Schaffzin, *supra* note 2, at 933.

Employment During Law School

A common hurdle for first-generation law students is employment. Many first-generation students have to work during law school to support themselves and their family members. Unlike peers who enter law school with the financial support of their families, first-generation students often do not have the privilege of devoting their full time and attention to their studies. They are often burdened with constraints on their time and attention that other law students do not experience. At the same time, many law schools discourage student employment, whether explicitly or by perpetuating a stigma that prevents law school departments from hiring students. The result is that students who must seek employment to support themselves or their families are pulled away from campus, which limits their opportunity to participate fully in campus culture, gain familiarity with campus services, and build networks with peers and professors.

Overcoming the stigma and providing student employment opportunities through law libraries offers an option to simultaneously solve several first-generation issues. Many law libraries provide student employment opportunities as library research assistants and staff library information and circulation desks. Employment at the law library increases the amount of time the employed student is on campus. Time spent on campus correlates with connectedness to campus culture, more use of campus services, and increased networking with fellow students, all of which promote first-generation success. Additionally, employment in the law library increases interaction with legal research materials. Current scholarship suggests that first-generation students participate in law review, moot court, and research assistantships at lower rates than continuing-generation law students. First-generation students may lose out on exposure to research opportunities beyond legal research and writing classes. Employment in the law library can supplement exposure to resources. Assisting faculty with research queries can increase the student's interaction with potential social connections and help the student build social capital. Building connections can help the student navigate law school and help improve success in finding employment and developing as a professional after law school.

Library fellowships or research assistant positions offer unique opportunities for first-generation students to build cultural and social capital while also meeting financial needs. The paid positions often offer students the ability to work closely with librarians and faculty on research projects that require high engagement with legal materials. First-generation students, who are often excluded from law review, moot court, and research assistantships due to a lack of social network and lower grades precipitated by employment and family duties, could gain exposure to in-depth research tasks they might not otherwise experience. Finally, because the law library receives requests from various sources, including professors, other law school departments, and legal clinics, fellows have more chances to interact with potential connections in an employment context, which can be a more comfortable method for many first-generation students to build relationships. At each turn, the first-generation student would have opportunities to learn skills and connect with potential references and mentors, including the law librarians who oversee such a fellowship program.

Collaboration and Outreach

One of the biggest challenges in libraries is educating students about the vital role the library can play in their legal education. For first-generation students, there may be an added barrier of intimidation or not wanting to let on that they do not know something that others see as common knowledge due to stereotype threat or self-stigma.[10] Collaboration and relationship building with other law school departments and student groups is essential to encouraging a meaningful relationship between students and the library.

The law library supports the mission of the entire law school community, including other departments. Building collaborative relationships with other law school departments, such as student affairs, career services, and professionalism programs, can extend the library's reach outside the space while also sharing the responsibility of programming with another department. It can also inform library collection policies and help identify the needs of first-generation students that have come up in the context of another department's services and can be collaboratively supported by both the library and another department. For example, cost-sharing for expensive databases is sometimes shared between the library and another department or program where there may be minimal interest from the general legal community but high interest within the library. An example where building a relationship supports sharing information is communication with student affairs personnel. Student affairs is actively seeking to support first-generation students. For instance, during the pandemic, many law libraries were triaging remote access to materials and communicating with other law school departments, such as Student Affairs, about what essential resources were necessary to support students. For some law libraries that were, in the past, hesitant to spend funds on electronic study aid packages, the pandemic was a huge catalyst. Even though a tangible collaborative project may not develop, opening the dialogue is the most important aspect. Just like students, other departments do not always know how the library can assist them and the student needs they seek to address.

First-generation students are more likely to be from an underrepresented group. One way individuals from underrepresented groups find community is through student affinity groups and student groups in general. Many libraries already have programs for student groups, particularly journals, serving first-generation students.

10. Graf, *supra* note 7, at 10.

Historically, libraries have been resistant to marketing their programs, believing that students should be intrinsically motivated to seek out library services. While that has changed in recent years, it is important to target marketing broadly; this includes reaching out to student groups that may have an interest. While affinity groups may not have members writing scholarly articles, those students are members of journals or taking seminar courses that write papers, so reaching out to them should be a natural target for marketing programs.

You may be thinking something along the lines of, "I market my library's program in the weekly email newsletter sent to the entire school." Do you read that entire email every week? Reaching out to the student groups directly sends the message: "We see you and would like you to come to the library. You are welcome in our programs."

Library Programs and Services

Most academic libraries are staffed with librarians who hold both a J.D. and an M.L.S. degree and are experts in researching legal materials for scholarly pursuits and legal practice. Librarians are excellent resources and generally seek to support students through legal research programming that focuses on research skills necessary to complete coursework, summer legal work, and, of course, support their professional legal pursuits upon graduation.

Library programming benefits all students, but for first-generation students, it may help overcome some of the obstacles related to a lack of cultural and social capital that arise in law school.[11] Law school and the legal profession operate with cultural and social norms that first-generation students may be unfamiliar with. First-generation students may also not have access to familial resources to assist in navigating the cultural and social norms of the legal profession. Libraries, and the programs and services they offer, allow students to receive training in areas that are often deemed basic where students are assumed to have the knowledge.

In the academic law library, programming will usually focus on research skills. We can break down library programs into two broad categories: law school-focused and practice-focused. These categories will often overlap and skills learned in one area will benefit the other. Law school skills encompass those needed to complete the research necessary for law school-related tasks, including first-year legal writing, seminar papers, journal notes and comments, and faculty research assistant duties. Library programming centered around law school skills may include a first-year legal research course that may or may not be mandatory and various optional workshops and training, including extracurricular activities, such as moot court and law review. Practice-focused library programming addresses skills needed in

11. *See* Graf, *supra* note 7; Arch & Gilman, *supra* note 8.

the practice of law. Library programming supporting practice skills varies significantly from institution to institution. It may include a "Prepare to Practice" series offered before summer associateships begin, law practice technology training, and legal research certificates.

Law school-focused and practice-focused research skills are often low-stakes entry points to cultural and social capital. While teaching students the skills necessary to meet a specific goal (i.e., researching for a seminar paper), library programming can compensate for lack of familial or social capital. Where some students may have family or social connections to ask questions about writing a seminar paper, workshops open to all students can provide the capital for those who may not have access. Library programming may also cover, some would say, mundane subjects, but research is an essential skill that is often overlooked, particularly with the rise of the internet and almost immediate access to information. It is often wrongly assumed that students enter law school with the research skills necessary to be successful lawyers. Training sessions led by law librarians can help bridge the research gaps for all students and are particularly useful for under-resourced students.

The structure of a library research skills program is unique to each law school and law library. It should focus on the expertise of the law librarians. Many law schools are already teaching legal research in formal courses for first-year and upper-level students. These programs are critical to exposing all students to legal research and serve as an entry point for first-generation students. Building a relationship with a librarian early in their law school careers provides a connection to the library that may overcome first-generation barriers to asking questions that they believe may demonstrate a lack of understanding and negatively distinguish them from other law students. But, for schools where for-credit courses are not possible, holding ad hoc workshops on basic legal research skills should be a priority. Librarians should consider using outside resources, particularly when teaching practice-related skills, including bringing in trainers from major vendors, practitioners, and law librarians who work with practicing attorneys. For example, if you would like to hold a program on the role of legal analytics in litigation, consider a panel consisting of vendor representatives, practicing attorneys, and law firm or court librarians to discuss where they find legal analytics and how they use them in practice.

Alumni Services

If the goal of pipeline and success programs for first-generation law students is to encourage individuals from marginalized communities to become successful attorneys, support beyond the law school years may be necessary. Law libraries can provide resources that first-generation graduates may need due to specific challenges they face in law school. Research suggests that first-generation students tend to earn lower grades due to various factors.[12] Many do not have the privilege of focusing on

12. *See* O'Bryant and Schaffzin, *supra* note 2, at 932.

their studies full time and need to work or help their family while attending classes. Some do not have the tools to build social capital with professors and administrators, negatively impacting academic performance. Regardless of the cause, the effect is a compounding negative impact on first-generation students' ability to interview for the most lucrative positions through on-campus recruiting. Directly, a lower GPA increases the likelihood of being passed over. Less directly, GPA is used to determine placement for law review, moot court, and research assistantships,[13] all of which recruiters consider when making hiring decisions. Considering additional factors that present hurdles for first-generation law students, such as the soft skills necessary to navigate the social obligations of the interviewing process, it is likely that many work in mid-sized and small-firm settings rather than the resource-rich environments present at large firms.

Access to legal research resources is necessary for all legal professionals, especially recent graduates. New associates spend up to 60% of their time performing research.[14] First-generation students who do not obtain employment at a large firm and start in a small firm setting may do even more research, including non-billable research concerning practice management. Legal research database subscriptions represent a substantial portion of overhead costs for many lawyers. Firms of all sizes frequently have to choose between subscriptions due to cost or rely heavily on free database access, limiting access to the copyrighted and proprietary resources available through the database that is not selected. While basic access to primary law can be free or inexpensive, practicing lawyers know that necessary insights and practice tips that bolster success and support professional development are found in practice guides, treatises, and continuing legal education coursebooks, most of which are exclusive to a single vendor. First-generation students who begin their career without access to these valuable resources may fall into a familiar gap of being excluded due to a lack of resources, regardless of their talent and determination.

Academic law libraries can help bridge the gap. By providing access to major databases and practice materials for alumni, law libraries can support all graduates struggling to access needed resources. In some jurisdictions, such access is already provided by public law libraries or academic libraries, which have established a "patron access" model with most major legal database vendors. Free, open access to databases like Westlaw, Lexis, Fastcase, HeinOnline, and more, ensures that all patrons have access to needed resources, such as citators, digests, practice guides, and treatises. However, access is limited to in-library use, often enforced by IP authentication. In jurisdictions where public law libraries are not available, academic law libraries can promote the success of first-generation graduates by ensuring access

---

13. Decreased participation in extracurricular activities, such as law review, moot court, and research assistantships, among first-generation professionals may also be because "first generation students miscalculate the importance that these activities play on their future career and employment opportunities." Alison Lintal, *Supporting First Generation Professionals*, NALP Bull. (July 2017).

14. LexisNexis, White Paper: Hiring Partners Reveal New Attorney Readiness for Real World Practice, https://www.lexisnexis.com/documents/pdf/20150325064926_large.pdf.

to practice materials for everyone at the library. In other jurisdictions, academic law libraries can coordinate with public law library colleagues to promote access to first-generation alumni and fill gaps by collecting missing resources (e.g., if the public law library offers Westlaw under a patron-access model, an academic law library might offer Lexis to alumni). By promoting access for all, law libraries can help level the playing field for first-generation practitioners and ensure that the lack of resources does not undo the previous work of programs meant to support first-generation students.

Another area ripe for law library support of first-generation alumni is continuing legal education ("CLE"). CLE is another significant overhead expense for practicing lawyers, which is necessary to maintain a law license and develop professionally. Many law libraries offer educational opportunities for law students who qualify for CLE credit and focus on practical skills needed to practice law. Additionally, law libraries coordinate vendor-led training sessions that could be extended to alumni, especially those at smaller firms who may not have a dedicated trainer for each vendor or are interested in learning about new resources. Classes on legal research skills and legal technology support lawyer success early in their careers and on a continuing basis as the technology evolves. Law libraries can directly impact the success of under-resourced attorneys by alleviating some of their CLE costs and by offering practical skills training they need to practice.

Conclusion

Law libraries can serve first-generation students through identifying the needs of their unique student population, reviewing and revising collections, lending essential items that support learning, creating relationships with other law school departments, and creating varied types of spaces where students can learn. When thinking about the takeaways from this chapter, they are different for different audiences. For the non-library audience, including law school administrations and other law school departments, the primary takeaway should be communication. Reach out to the library. Relationships require communication from both parties. If you are not sure if the library can assist, ask. Libraries are in the business of answering questions. By building a relationship with your law library, they can better identify and support the needs of first-generation students that your department finds most pressing. You can create a cohesive plan to assist your first-generation students by working together.

For law library administrations reading this chapter, the takeaways are different. Of course, being open to communication with the law school administration and other law school departments is one takeaway; the others emphasize change, primarily small changes, but sometimes more significant change. The most significant change is assessing library collections to determine if they support student learning, particularly first-generation students, through robust collections, including study aids. While the overall assessment process can be daunting, targeted incremental change will make a difference. For example, purchasing online study aids can be costly, but they serve a paramount need for first-generation students and provide broad access both on and off campus. Minor changes can be made to library spaces to meet the change needs of first-generation students. Perhaps you need more quiet spaces, group study space, or a space for students to take personal and professional calls. Space discussions are also an opportunity to build relationships with other departments as you work to identify the needs of first-generation students and, as anyone who has worked in an academic setting can tell you, space issues are universal.

The law library has constantly evolved to meet the differing needs of the changing and diverse populations it serves. As we learn more about the specific experience of first-generation students, there is an opportunity to build a better and more inclusive library through collections, lending, opportunity, and spaces.

PART VI Supporting First Gen Students in the Classroom

Nineteen

Demystifying the Lawyering Skills Classroom for First Gen Students

Sara J. Berman* Rachel Croskery-Roberts** Olympia Duhart***
Alison Mikkor†

THE 1L YEAR IS OVERWHELMING FOR MOST. For first-generation law students, the barriers to success may seem insurmountable. Two critical barriers first-generation students often face is a feeling that they do not belong and a lack of access to formal and informal guidance as to *how* to succeed in law school. This feeling may be particularly acute in the lawyering skills[1] classroom, where students may fear that their lack of access to family members and friends in the legal profession has left them ill-prepared for tackling the rigorous writing, research, analysis, oral advocacy, and other aspects of the skills course. This chapter addresses strategies for demystifying the lawyering skills classroom for first-generation students and cultivating an environment that supports all students' success. Broadly, this chapter covers the following critical topics, beginning with big-picture issues and concluding with some concrete exercises to employ in the classroom:

a. Minimizing stereotype threat for nontraditional students in the lawyering skills classroom;
b. Adopting techniques for curriculum design and teaching strategies that empower and engage first-generation law students;
c. Leveraging technology to even the playing field, including using asynchronous videos and providing individualized support; and
d. Employing non-lawyer translation exercises to enhance legal language mastery, bolster confidence, and promote belonging in first-generation law students.

* Professor of Lawyering Skills and Director of the Academic Success Program, USC Gould School of Law.

** Associate Dean for Lawyering Skills, UC Irvine School of Law.

*** Associate Dean for Academic Affairs & Strategic Initiatives and Professor of Law, Nova Southeastern Shepard Broad College of Law.

† Professor of Lawyering Skills, UC Irvine School of Law.

1. The term *lawyering skills* is used here to refer to classes also known as legal research and writing, lawyering skills and values, legal writing, and other similar classes that focus on analysis and legal research and writing in the first-year law school curriculum.

A. Counteracting Stereotype Threat[2]

First-generation students are at risk of experiencing both imposter syndrome[3] and stereotype threat in the lawyering skills classroom. Both phenomena make it difficult for a student to accurately gauge how they are doing in law school and impede student achievement. Like imposter syndrome, stereotype threat stems from perceptions of a student not being up to the task. But unlike imposter syndrome, in which a person may hold negative perceptions about themselves, stereotype threat is born of a student's awareness of negative stereotypes that have currency in society as a whole.

Stereotype threat is a cognitive barrier to performance that a person experiences because of her awareness that she is part of a group about whom there are commonly held negative stereotypes about group members' ability to perform in a particular sphere.[4] Cognitive scientists have repeatedly found that the weight of this awareness creates a measurable drag on stereotype-affected students' performance.[5] Stereotype-affected students reasonably perceive that if they do not perform well in the sphere, it will confirm the negative stereotypes about the group.[6] Students' awareness of the stereotype also creates "attributional ambiguities" that disrupt the feedback process—meaning that students are uncertain whether negative feedback is a product of the instructor's bias or an honest assessment of their performance.[7] In addition, there is the risk that stereotype-affected students may diminish the importance of a project or exercise or reduce their efforts in the course when they receive negative feedback.[8] In some cases, students may disengage entirely by dropping the course or even out of law school itself.[9]

Stereotype threat, thus, directly interferes with all law professors' efforts to teach our students, and it clouds students' understanding of what is required to excel in our courses. It is especially a concern in writing and lawyering skills courses because of how closely professors interact with their students' work and how often we give

---

2. This section was written by Alison Mikkor, Assistant Professor of Lawyering Skills at University of California, Irvine School of Law. She is the proud daughter of two first-generation students and herself a first-generation law student.

3. *See* Chapter I.D, R. Allyce Bailey.

4. *See* Paula J. Manning, *Word to the Wise: Feedback Intervention to Moderate the Effects of Stereotype Threat and Attributional Ambiguity on Law Students*, 18 U. Md. L.J. Race, Religion, Gender & Class 99 (2018).

5. *See id.*; Russell A. McClain, *Bottled at the Source: Recapturing the Essence of Academic Support as a Primary Tool of Education Equity for Minority Law Students*, 18 U. Md. L.J. Race, Religion, Gender & Class 139, 168–170 (2018).

6. *See* Manning, *supra* note 4, at 99–100; McClain, *supra* note 5, at 168–170.

7. For a more complete discussion of attributional ambiguity, see Manning, *supra* note 4, at 110–115.

8. *See* Geoffrey L. Cohen, Claude M. Steele & Lee D. Ross, *The Mentor's Dilemma: Providing Critical Feedback Across the Racial Divide*, 25 Personality & Soc. Psych. Bull., 1302, 1304 (1999).

9. *See id.*; McClain, *supra* note 5, at 178.

our students feedback. Counteracting stereotype threat is essential to demystifying legal education for first-generation students, who are among the groups of law students who are stereotype-affected[10] and who, in many cases, also hold another social identity that is stereotype-affected, such as being a BIPOC student.[11]

The imperative to counter stereotype threat applies to all professors, regardless of their personal views or how well-meaning they are. Even the students of a superhuman professor who was free of any conscious or unconscious biases would be at risk. Only two factors are salient to whether a student is at risk of experiencing stereotype threat. First, a negative stereotype must exist, and second, the student must be aware of the stereotype.[12] It is the stereotype itself, not the individual views of the instructor, that matter when it comes to stereotype threat.

Fortunately, law professors can counteract the threat. The same cognitive science research that first identified stereotype threat in the 1990s[13] also found that when an instructor provides "wise feedback," that interaction can serve as a bulwark against the threat.[14] There are four core pillars to wise feedback:

- **It aims high.** It invokes the high standards of the person delivering the feedback.[15]
- **It is candid.** It is honest about the ways in which a student's work falls short of meeting those high standards.[16]
- **It expresses confidence.** It expresses the deliverer's confidence in the student's ability to meet the high standard with further work and effort.[17]
- **It is constructive.** It offers specific guidance to the student as to how to meet the course's high standards and is equally specific about what a student did well.[18]

---

10. *See* Tara Dennehy, Jacqueline Smith, Chelesea Moore & Nilajana Dasgupta, *Stereotype Threat and Stereotype Inoculation for Underrepresented Students in the First Year of College*, *in* THE FIRST YEAR OF COLLEGE: RESEARCH, THEORY, AND PRACTICE ON IMPROVING THE STUDENT EXPERIENCE AND INCREASING RETENTION (R. Feldman ed., (2017).

11. *See* Russell A. McClain, *Helping Our Students Reach Their Full Potential: The Insidious Consequences of Ignoring Stereotype Threat*, 17 RUTGERS RACE & L. REV. 1, 13–20 (2016).

12. Manning, *supra* note 5, at 104.

13. Claude Steele and Joshua Aronson first identified the phenomenon and coined the term *stereotype threat* in 1995. *See* Claude Steele & Joshua Aronson, *Stereotype Threat and the Intellectual Test Performance of African Americans*, 69 J PERS. SOC. PSYCH. 797 (1995).

14. *See* David Scott Yaeger et al., *Breaking the Cycle of Mistrust: Wise Interventions to Provide Critical Feedback Across the Racial Divide*, 143 J. EXPERIMENTAL PSYCH. 804, 806 (2014); *See* Cohen et al., *supra* note 8, at 1303–04.

15. *Id.*

16. *Id.*

17. *Id.*

18. *Id.*

The foundation of each of these four pillars of wise feedback is the professor's credibility with students. The professor using the right words while delivering otherwise wise feedback will have little positive impact if students do not trust that the professor believes what she is saying. This section of the essay provides guidance as to how law professors can deliver wise feedback in the lawyering skills classroom that clearly, candidly, and credibly conveys a professor's expectations to all students. It draws on the techniques that I have used in my own classes as a professor at the University of California, Irvine.

Set a High Bar from the Beginning

The process of providing wise feedback begins long before the first assignment is even handed out through the professor's introduction to the course and its learning objectives. It is important to highlight from the outset that students are being held to a high standard and that the professor believes in each student's ability to meet that standard. If the first and only time a professor's high standards come up is in the context of delivering negative feedback to a stereotype-affected student, the risk is that students will perceive that the "high standards" are being used as a cover for a bias-based assessment.

Law professors are at an advantage when it comes to credibly establishing their high standards. First, the popular imagination thinks of law school as difficult—an impression that is amplified by media depictions such as those in *Legally Blonde*, *How to Get Away with Murder*, and *The Paper Chase*.

Second, every student who enters a law school classroom has already been steeped in the competitive process of applying and gaining admittance to law school.[19] This is a boon to law professors because it allows us to convey both that the work that students engage in is not easy and that they have demonstrated that they are up to the task, or else they would not have earned a spot in the class.

Third, just as it is not easy to get into law school, it is not easy to become a law professor. The typical law professor has excelled in multiple arenas. For example, a professor may have done some or all of the following things: clerked for a judge, published a piece of scholarship, represented a party in a high-profile matter; or worked for a highly selective employer. Professors' experiences at the highest levels of practice and legal scholarship allow them to base their standards for students on the standards that they personally encountered in these arenas. The typical law student who wishes to be successful in the profession can both appreciate how exacting such standards are and recognize their relevance to their own development. The other advantage of tying course standards to professional standards for the purpos-

---

19. This too is a message that is reinforced by popular culture, as evidenced by the scene in the film *Legally Blonde* in which Elle Woods' incredulous love interest implies to her on the first day of classes, "It's, like, hard" to get into law school. *See also* McClain, *supra* note 11.

es of countering stereotype threat is that professional standards are an external metric, independent of the professor and any perceived biases the professor may hold.

There are a host of ways to harness these three advantages to effectively establish high but achievable standards for students. Professors must find a way of framing their standards that is authentic to their own voice and tailored to the particular courses that they teach. By way of example, this is how I frame my first-year Lawyering Skills course[20] and my expectations. I begin the first class of the year by welcoming students to law school and then almost instantly mentioning how impressed I am by everything I have heard about the matriculating class as a whole, and the care with which the law school's admissions staff and committee go about selecting and recruiting each class. I have served on the law school's admission committee several times, and I often mention that experience explicitly to enhance the credibility of these comments. I then say how excited I am to get to know the students and to learn more about the experiences and expertise they each bring with them to the course. I highlight students' experiences before law school to help convey that each of them is capable of succeeding in law school. Next, I go on to introduce the course itself in the following way:

> My goal is for this course to set you up to be a successful and effective lawyer at the very top of the profession in whatever type of law you choose to practice. I am aiming high for you. I suspect many of you will practice in California, which is one of the most demanding places to practice in the country. I practiced in New York City, another place with a competitive, high level of practice. My standards in this course are informed by what it takes to succeed in these types of practice arenas.
>
> As I set these high standards for you, I also want to stress that I said my goal is to "set you up" to be at the top of the profession. I am not expecting you to reach these lofty heights tomorrow or even by the end of the year. Rather, that's the long-term goal. My short-term goal is to give you a foundation that you can continue to build on in your upper division clinics here at the law school and once you have graduated and are in practice.

My fall syllabus reinforces this message in more summary terms. The Learning Objectives section of the syllabus explains:

> Lawyering Skills is intended to introduce you to the foundational legal skills that you will need in practice. The ultimate goal is to set you up to become

20. UCI Law's Lawyering Skills course is a year-long program for first-year students that focuses on teaching skills that all lawyers use in practice, such as fact investigation, client interviewing and counseling, professionalism and problem solving, legal writing and analysis, extensive legal research, negotiation, contract drafting, and oral advocacy. I use a simulation-based, experiential approach to teach the course, in order to allow my students to practice core legal skills and develop professional judgment and problem-solving skills in as close to real-world conditions as possible.

an outstanding practitioner in the future. The goal for this year is that by the end of it you will be a proficient beginner in these skills and well-equipped to further refine them in clinic and later as attorneys. In addition to invoking my high standards, I provide students with concrete guidance as to how to meet those standards from the outset. My syllabus includes a section on "Professionalism Expectations." It advises students that professional lawyers are (i) collegial and respectful in dealings with others; (ii) prepared; (iii) engaged; (iv) precise; (v) on time; and (vi) takes ownership of their work and their professional development. For each of these habits or competencies, I describe the specific behavior that is associated with each of these habits or competencies. The syllabus entry on being prepared reads as follows:

> **Prepared.** Class members are expected to come prepared to all classes, meetings, simulations, and conferences. This means they have read all assigned materials and brought everything needed for the session. "Everything needed" includes any materials (e.g., the matter file, self-edit worksheet, or research notes) that a person could reasonably expect to use for the session's activity, even if the professor did not specifically tell class members to bring those materials with them. Paper and a pen are essentials for every session—this is especially true for online learning, during which your computer will likely be occupied with hosting the Zoom session.

Similarly, I explain what it means to take ownership of one's work and development as a lawyer in an entry that reads:

> Class members are responsible for managing their workload and schedule with respect to this class. It is class members' responsibility to regularly check their UCI email account and the course's Canvas page.
>
> More broadly, "taking ownership of one's work" involves two things at a minimum. First, attempting to resolve an issue independently before reaching out to the professor (for example, by checking the Syllabus and assigning memo). Second, presenting a proposed course of action when asking a question or making a request.
>
> Students are responsible for clarifying any uncertainty they have as to an assignment, including the scope of the work required, well in advance of its deadline. Questions (and lots of them) are very welcome early in a project. However, I and the Research Fellows will not answer any questions posed within 24 hours of the deadline for an assignment, unless they are follow-up on an issue raised in advance of the 24-hour deadline. Please also take note that an inquiry made at the very end of or after business hours (9 a.m.–6 p.m., Monday–Friday) likely will not be addressed until the next business day.

In this framing of the course, I very intentionally and explicitly set a high bar for students. These high standards are based on an extrinsic metric, the standards for excellence in two of the most competitive legal markets in the country, California and New York. These extrinsic metrics are particularly relevant to the course, which is focused on fundamental practice skills, and students' own career paths, since most UC Irvine students' first professional experience is as a legal intern in California, and many of them ultimately practice there. Furthermore, in the case of New York, my practice-based standards have the added benefit of being ones I can speak on with authority because of my own practice experience—which I consciously emphasize.

Normalize Imperfection and Critique

Another important step professors can take to facilitate wise feedback is to emphasize that initial missteps and even failure are a part of the learning process and of being a lawyer. It is also beneficial to emphasize that critique—receiving feedback on one's work and using it to make the work better—is a constant part of professional life. In my experience, it is also helpful in combating stereotype threat by priming students to understand that negative feedback that they receive from me is not an indication that I think they lack the ability to do the work. To the contrary, I am offering my feedback to every student precisely because I have faith in them and want to help their work achieve its potential.

To normalize critique, I formally and affirmatively teach students how to deliver feedback and how to effectively receive and use critique in a classroom session devoted to the topic of critique.[21] I then have students practice giving and receiving critiques in a series of peer review and self-critiquing exercises.

I also ensure that in each of my classes there are multiple formative assessments, each of which provides students with additional experience with critiquing. Incorporating some type of formative assessment into a course aid in the fight against stereotype threat, whether that assessment takes the form of discussion questions, a midterm exam, regular classroom quizzes, or something else entirely. Formative assessments allow for professors to signal to students that everyone's work can be improved and that in critiquing a stereotype-affected student's work, the professor is not singling them out. I make this point explicitly with my students. For example, in my assigning materials for my first Lawyering Skills project of the year, in which students submit a first draft on which I give them feedback before they submit a final version for a grade, I advise students:

> Do not be surprised—or concerned—if this "revision" turns out to require wholesale redrafting of your submission. I anticipate that **everyone's** Argument, including very good First Submissions, will require substantial revision. That is simply the nature of written legal analysis. Also, this is the very first

21. I am happy to share my class plans and materials on critique with faculty who reach out to me directly.

time each of you are doing this type of writing, which naturally means that you will still be learning the form as you write your First Submission.

Help Students Clear the Bar

Of course, the most important stage of the process is actually delivering wise feedback. If the professor has set the stage by establishing clear, objective, and high standards and signaling that all students can expect some negative (but constructive) feedback on their work, the task of delivering the feedback is relatively straightforward. It is my practice to provide students with two types of feedback on their written work. The first type of feedback I provide is a short cover comment on their work, which helps me capture the first three characteristics of wise feedback, namely:

- Invoking my high standards;
- Being candid about shortcomings; and
- Expressing my confidence in the student's ability to meet those standards.

This short cover note is accompanied by more targeted comments in a mark-up of the piece itself that satisfy the fourth and final criteria of wise feedback, which is to provide constructive guidance to the student as to how to meet course standards.

For the cover comments, professors may find it helpful to prewrite templates for student work of all levels that they can then tailor to each particular student. It can be difficult for professors to give feedback to an entire class of students that satisfies all of the wise feedback criteria under the time constraints and pressures we all face. It also can feel uncomfortable or difficult to state directly and candidly that a student's work is poor. Prewriting the template does the difficult part in advance and in the abstract. Each of my cover comment templates begins with a simple and direct summary of the student's performance.[22] I tie these assessments directly to my high standards for the project and leave space to highlight some specific strengths and weaknesses of the student's work. For example, a cover comment template for a student who produced good but not great work and the one I use most often in assessing a typical class of students reads:

> This first effort is a good one, but it also falls short in some important ways. It includes some of the fundamentals of an effective memo, including [*one or two key strengths*]. However, it [*most significant weaknesses*]. It does not yet meet the high standard of being work on which the supervisor and client can confidently rely when making decisions on how to proceed. I have every confidence that the next submission can meet that standard based on the strong

22. I used the "wise feedback" language found to be effective at countering stereotype threat in a study by Cohen and his colleagues, see *supra* note 8, as a template for my own templates.

aspects of this version. The comments that follow, some of which are critical, are intended to help you fulfill this work's promise.

The template for a student whose work whose work did not meet expectations reads much the same way but begins a bit differently:

> The work you put into this piece is evident. I want to show my respect for you and that effort by being candid with you in return. This first effort falls short in fundamental ways. Although it does have some of the basics I would expect to see in a memo of this kind, in its current form it falls well below the standard of being work on which the supervisor and client can confidently rely when making decisions on how to proceed. The memo will need substantial revision to meet that high standard, and the comments that follow, some of which are quite critical, are intended to help you make those changes. I was so detailed and forthcoming in the mark-up precisely because I am confident in your ability to meet the high standards that I have set. My confidence is based on [*at least one specific example of a strong point in the work itself or of the student's performance in other aspects of the class*].

Taking proactive steps to minimize stereotype threat is essential to supporting first-generation law students. Another foundational piece in building an inclusive lawyering skills classroom is selecting curriculum and teaching methods designed to bolster engagement for first-generation students.

B. Selecting Curriculum and Teaching Methods to Create a Culture of Empowerment and Engagement[23]

In his essay, *The Learning Curve*, humorist David Sedaris details his experience as a new writing instructor at the School of the Art Institute of Chicago.[24] Like most new teachers, Sedaris agonizes over his first day of class. In typical Sedaris fashion, he spends most of his prep time looking for a briefcase and perfecting his most professorial outfit; he even got a tie for the big day. His one oversight? Lesson plans. As a result, Sedaris arrives to class on his first day, greets his students, and opens his shiny new briefcase to reveal... nothing.[25]

For law faculty teaching in the demanding lawyering skills classroom, Sedaris' experience is an important cautionary tale about the saliency of comprehensive curriculum design. Truly, curriculum is the foundation of any engaged classroom expe-

23. Section B of this essay was written by Olympia Duhart, Associate Dean for Faculty Development and Professor of Law at Nova Southeastern University Shepard Broad College of Law. She is a proud first-generation lawyer and college student.

24. David Sedaris, *The Learning Curve, in* Me Talk Pretty One Day 83–96 (2000).

25. "I opened my briefcase and realized that I'd never thought beyond this moment." *Id.* at 85.

rience. When considering the unique needs of first-generation law students, the additional responsibility of developing course material that supports a classroom where students can flourish raises the stakes. But even the most robust curriculum is handicapped by static, passive teaching methods. Taken together, curriculum design and teaching methods are potentially transformative building blocks to a dynamic classroom environment. The task must be approached with intentionality and great planning. Otherwise we run the risk of showing up to class with all style and no substance—essentially an empty briefcase. And we fall short of our goals of creating an effective, supportive learning community for all of our students—especially those who are the first in their households to attend college.

Curriculum design and teaching methods are crucial to first-generation student engagement. Student engagement impacts learning outcomes, classroom experience, and classroom culture.[26] Engagement is especially important among first-generation students, who are often dealing with isolation,[27] challenging cultural transitions, and inadequate academic preparation.[28] This portion of the essay will focus on curriculum design and teaching strategies anchored in transfer learning principles, culturally relevant pedagogy, and novelty as means to empower and engage first-generation students.

Transfer Learning Principles

Transfer learning principles suggest that the transfer of knowledge from a related subject improves learning velocity. In other words, using something familiar as a foundation to teach something new allows students to construct knowledge more efficiently and effectively. Think: I knew how to peel an apple, so it was easier for me to learn how to peel a mango.

Integrating curriculum and teaching methods that build on transfer learning principles can increase learning velocity for first-generation students. This boost is needed to help close the learning gaps that often limit first-generation students.[29] In

26. Mark Reckmeyer, *Focus on Student Engagement for Better Academic Outcomes*, GALLUP (Oct. 30, 2019), http://www.gallup.com/education/267521/focus-student-engagement-better-academic-outcomes.aspx.

27. Jessica Tomer, *First-Generation Law Students: Struggles, Solutions and Schools That Care*, NAT'L JURIST (Mar. 22, 2019, 8:39 AM), http://www.nationaljurist.com/national-jurist-magazine/first-generation-law-students-struggles-solutions-and-schools-care.

28. Michael J. Stebleton & Krista M. Soria, *Breaking Down Barriers: Academic Obstacles of First-Generation Students at Research Universities*, LEARNING ASSISTANCE REV., Fall 2012, at 10.

29. Data shows that first-generation students face significant hurdles in succeeding in post-secondary education and graduating. LISA M. NUNN, 33 SIMPLE STRATEGIES FOR FACULTY: A WEEK-BY-WEEK RESOURCE FOR TEACHING FIRST-YEAR AND FIRST-GENERATION STUDENTS 37–38 (2018). "These challenges include being less academically prepared, having children of their own; working full-time while attending college." *Id.* at 41. First-generation researchers have reminded us that "what looks like intellectual talent is likely the product of excellent academic preparation from high school and earlier." *Id.* The sad but true fact is that many first-generation law students come from academically deficient school environments. Eugene Beresin, *The Challenge of First Generation College Students*, PSYCH. TODAY (Nov. 6, 2021), http://www.psychologytoday.com/us/blog

the lawyering skills classroom, there are several steps a professor can take to build upon transfer learning. First, we can design problems that create expansive common ground for students, rather than relying on problems that shrink the shared universe. Just as testers are evaluating the implicit bias of standardized tests,[30] we should carefully consider the implicit bias in our problems that may favor more privileged students, such as continuing-generation students.

For first-generation law students, much of the new information shared in law school classes does not reflect, or is irrelevant to, the first-generation students' lives. Professors can explicitly relate new information to students' prior knowledge or experience so the students can assimilate new ideas and properly characterize them.[31] That means working deliberately to design a curriculum that is accessible to students from various socioeconomic backgrounds, students for whom English is a second language, first-generation students, and other nontraditional law students.

Furthermore, "other accommodations should be made for individuals with culturally diverse backgrounds to minimize the distortions that arise from their specific disadvantages."[32] In the lawyering skills classroom, that may mean moving torts hypos from the golf course to the playground. Beyond the lawyering skills classroom, faculty who teach in doctrinal or casebook classes can also incorporate this practice in several ways. For example, Constitutional Law professors can create fact patterns that normalize considerations for people from various socioeconomic backgrounds. A time, place, and manner IRAC, for instance, can be based on a demonstration around apartment rent increases in a community. And real property professors can explore eminent domain through a lens that considers the doctrine's impact on women, minoritized communities, and first-time home buyers. A careful, honest evaluation of class disparities that may infiltrate problem design is needed to minimize the risk of problems that unintentionally disadvantage first-generation students.

In making these accommodations, law professors must constantly interrogate our own privilege and check against bias when designing curriculum. "Designers of all types, especially novice designers, can be somewhat self-centered."[33] Law professors can also foster transfer learning through specific teaching techniques. One technique that fosters transfer learning is guiding the student through performance to-

---

/inside-out-outside-in/202111/the-challenge-first-generation-college-students. Several students are products of less rigorous secondary schools; further, well-intentioned family members without law school or college experience aren't equipped to offer proper guidance. *Id.*

30. John Rosales & Tim Walker, *The Racist Beginnings of Standardized Testing*, Nat'l Educ. Ass'n (Mar. 20, 2021), http://www.nea.org/advocating-for-change/new-from-nea/racist-beginnings-standardized-testing#:~:text=Since%20their%20inception%20almost%20a,from%20early%20childhood%20through%20college.

31. Paula Lustbader, *From Dreams to Reality: The Emerging Role of Law School Academic Support Programs*, 31 U. S.F. L. Rev. 839, 844 (1997).

32. Kyung Hee Kim & Darya Zabelina, *Cultural Bias in Assessment: Can Creative Assessment Help?*, 6 Int'l J. Critical Pedagogy 129, 130 (2015).

33. Susie L. Gronseth et al., *Designing for Diverse Learners, in* Design for Learning (2021).

ward "reflexive transfer."[34] The goal is to make the learning experience so closely reflect the targeted learning outcome that it "optimizes the likelihood of performance in similar situations."[35] Fortunately, this is a teaching technique very familiar to most lawyering skills professors. Instead of merely lecturing about effective partner briefings, for instance, we conduct simulated partner briefings. Rather than lecture about oral arguments, we stage practice rounds with our students. We should strive to create even stronger simulations; in the oral argument context, for example, this effort would include bringing in lawyers and judges to bench students at a courthouse or mock courtroom. Situated learning theory builds on learning through "purposeful, authentic activities in social contexts" that provide opportunities to observe and practice.[36]

Further, researchers have found that building a "Community of Practice" is central to the efficacy of transfer learning.[37] The Community of Practice experience facilitates transfer learning by supporting learners with similar goals and interests.[38] It also leverages the strength of collaboration through interaction that may be essential to students from diverse backgrounds who find themselves struggling with feelings of isolation in the classroom.

I have created community in the real space by assigning group projects with specific roles and responsibilities. That additional step minimizes the risk of people "hiding" in a group while others dominate. I also assign a cognitive protocol[39] so students can specifically assess their roles as group members. Online, a Community of Practice can be achieved through collaborative platforms such as Google Docs and Padlet, which allow students to evaluate each other's work in real time. Google Docs facilitates group work because students can write, edit, and collaborate together in real time. Google Docs also allows professors to assign peer editors and reviewers in the virtual space with a single link. Padlet is also very useful in allowing students to offer instant feedback on issues in a format that is immediately viewable. In the lawyering skills classroom, I have used Padlet to collect instant feedback on writing samples, identify narrative techniques, and comment on ethical issues that arise during classroom simulations. In my Constitutional Law seminar, I utilize Padlet to publish student feedback on Supreme Court oral arguments, share reactions to assigned readings and podcasts at the start of class, brainstorm prescriptive

---

34. Shiva Hajian, *Transfer of Learning and Teaching: A Review of Transfer Theories and Effective Instructional Practices*, 7 IAFOR J. EDUC. 93, 96 (2019).

35. *Id.* at 98.

36. *Id.*

37. *Id.* at 100.

38. *Id.* at 98.

39. Many thanks to Professor Sophie Sparrow for introducing me to this method to promote metacognition at the start of my teaching career. *See also* Olympia Duhart, *It's Not For a Grade: The Rewards and Risks of Low-Risk Assessment in the High-Stakes Law School Classroom*, 1 ELON L. REV. 491 (2015) (discussing the benefits of cognitive protocols in the lawyering skills classroom to promote metacognitive practices and improve performance).

reasoning for seminar papers, and highlight one take-away at the end of class. Students are excited to use their cellphones for "good." They also appreciate the ability to share their feedback with their classmates and get instant feedback from the professor. Moreover, I hope that students also feel validated seeing their responses as one part of a larger collection created by our classroom community. The same Padlet prompt can be used online, in-person, or in the blend-flex classroom; therefore, it is an excellent tool to support a cohesive classroom environment and build community. Creating a "Community of Practice" helps optimize transfer learning principles.

Near-peer mentoring also supports transfer learning. Empowering students to move from the role of "student" to "teacher" can go a long way in crushing imposter syndrome. "If a student can teach another student a skill, they have taken ownership of that skill."[40] In my class, I ask students to deconstruct each other's work and build their own rubrics. Students bring their Umbrella section of a memo to class. I then have them exchange papers and deconstruct their classmate's paper. They are asked to create a "Reverse Rubric" that identifies the function and placement of each sentence they read. This exercise has proven very effective in helping students understand the unique functions of each sentence in the compact Umbrella. It also builds self-efficacy, a potent antidote for imposter syndrome.

I also affirmatively situate collaboration as a central theme of the course. Often, professors will assign group projects with little to no guidance on how to collaborate effectively. To highlight the centrality of collaboration in my class, I assign a reading about collaboration ahead of a small joint writing assignment. I am also explicit about my view that collaboration is an important lawyering skill that we will practice in class. In fact, the first assignment on collaboration is collaborative. After completing the assigned reading, students are asked to work together to build a PowerPoint or Prezi about collaboration. I "reward" the winning team by publishing their presentation on my Canvas course. This simple assignment supports the creation of community, reinforces my collaborative stance in class, and positions all members of the group as "teachers." Therefore, this accessible, fun exercise serves both collaboration, practical skills, and near-peer mentoring strategies.

Culturally relevant pedagogy

Another pedagogical strategy that empowers first-generation students is making curriculum more integrative of the culture of students from diverse backgrounds. In lawyering skills classes, hypothetical writing problems can be drafted to reflect contemporary social justice issues that highlight the experiences of people from diverse backgrounds. Inclusive teaching techniques reflect a commitment to teach with "empathy and enthusiasm" by "embracing discussion about the type of modern po-

40. Laurie Ferry, *High Impact Strategies that Support the Three Phases of Learning*, Keep Indiana Learning (Feb. 11, 2020), http://keepindianalearning.org/high-impact-strategies-support-learning-phases/.

litical and social phenomena that attracted many students to law school in the first place."[41] Examples of possible legal issues include those that emerged around the Black Lives Matter movement, transgender students' rights, school tuition vouchers, gentrification, immigration, and the CROWN Act—which prohibits discrimination based on hairstyle and hair texture.[42]

Of course, the creation of new material—particularly material rooted in current events—is a demanding endeavor that will require a substantial commitment to build a complex, evenly-weighted case file. However, schools can incentivize this work by awarding drafters a summer stipend to develop new material for the program, awarding teaching grants for innovative teaching material, or accepting a well-developed, original case file tailored to culturally relevant pedagogy toward a "publication" credit toward review, promotion, and tenure. Institutional support is needed for this hard and important work.

Next, by responding to challenges in diverse communities, the professor signals a personal commitment to a supportive, thoughtful awareness of real challenges in the real world to first-generation students.

In addition to large-scale efforts to build culturally integrative course material, there are many ways to inject a more inclusive approach through smaller curricular changes. For instance, one small step is "taking care to refer to diverse populations in our course materials, lectures, hypothetical questions, and written problems."[43] More concretely, professors should create multiple-choice questions and hypothetical fact patterns that feature names of people from diverse backgrounds. Further, when creating fact patterns that identify people by profession, professors should include people who work in fields across the socioeconomic spectrum to foster more inclusive curriculum design. The fact pattern universe should not be limited to doctors and lawyers; instead, instructors can write some fact patterns that feature nail technicians and mechanics. Professors should, of course, be especially mindful to avoid assigning all characters with more culturally diverse names to working-class

41. *Not for Free: Exploring the Collateral Costs of Diversity in Legal Education*, 48 U. Pac. L. Rev. 887, 904 (2017); *see also* Teri A. McMurtry Chubb, Strategies and Techniques for Integrating Diversity, Equity, and Inclusion into the Core Law Curriculum, A Comprehensive Guide to DEI Pedagogy, Course Planning, and Classroom Practice (2021), *available at* https://www.aspenpublishing.com/File%20Library/Resources/Faculty/Strategies-Techniques-Teaching/STDEI_1E.pdf.

42. *See* Crown Coalition, https://www.thecrownact.com (last visited Jan. 14, 2022).

43. *See* Nancy E. Dowd et al., *Diversity Matters: Race, Gender, and Ethnicity in Legal Education*, 15 U. Fla. J.L. & Pub. Pol'y 11, 12–47 (2003). Of course, this is merely the starting point. Simply rehashing the same, inaccessible problems with "ethnic" names is not enough to move the needle on meaningful cultural integration. In addition, professors should not neglect the opportunity to teach students to approach references to diverse populations with care and attention. In a recent problem, I reminded students that a tilde was needed to ensure that the right letter—ñ versus n—was actually being used for our client's name. Modeling in the assigning memo and posting a short link was enough to inject a small but important moment of cultural inclusion into my assignment.

positions in fact patterns. In addition to building more inclusive fact patterns, professors should be intentional about making sure people from diverse backgrounds are represented in PowerPoint images, videos, and guest speaker invitations.

Through both large-scale and small-scale curricular design, lawyering skills professors can develop culturally relevant pedagogy to empower first-generation students.

Novelty

Creativity counts. Faced with trying to make *Julius Caesar* appealing to 15-year-olds, one day—as a former high school teacher—I resorted to making a Caesar salad in class. In an instant, the classroom changed. Instead of pushing my tenth-grade English students through another day of stilted discussion on Shakespeare's classic, I filled a huge salad bowl with lettuce, anchovies, Caesar dressing, and croutons. I then served little salads to the students in cheap paper bowls. As we ate our salads in class, we spoke about the ingredients. Some of my questions for the class:

- If the characters in *Julius Caesar* represented the ingredients of this salad, which ingredient would represent the Plebeians?[44]
- Who represented the slimy anchovies slithering around Rome?
- Who was the "dressing"—the one truly binding everything together?
- And who would come out on top—like the croutons?

This class generated an incredibly rich discussion. Students debated whether Cassius was the "binder" or if Brutus truly kept things together? We discussed the croutons—were the Patricians the clear winners, or did Caesar prevail even in death? Students deconstructed this play in a way that was transformative, accessible, and memorable. More importantly, I learned that the novelty had huge payoffs. It was a powerful tool for engagement and an effective way to even the playing field.[45] Now I know that novelty is also an effective brain booster.

Neuroscientists have recently begun to track the relationship between curiosity and motivation more directly.[46] The human brain's "innate biological need for novelty"[47] is fueled by curiosity. Therefore, effective course design and teaching strategies that leverage creativity can promote deep learning.

The LRW class provides ample avenues for creativity. One novel concept I have implemented with great success is the creation of the "LRW Lounge." After mandatory one-on-one conferences and about a week before the big memo is due, I host an "LRW Lounge" at the law school. The lounge is invitation only (read: limited to my

44. Answer: The romaine lettuce. It is likely to "wilt" under pressure (couldn't resist).
45. The students were all new to the experience and felt equally curious and vulnerable.
46. Joshua R. Eyler, How Humans Learn 21 (2018).
47. *Id.*

class). It is in a reception room at the school. I provide boxed sandwiches, chips, fruit, and water. And cookies. Lots of cookies. I also hang a few disco balls from the ceiling and bring my best playlist and speakers. LRW Lounge helps motivate students to do their best work during the last push of the big memorandum. It starts in the late afternoon, and often runs past midnight. Students are able to do a deep dive in the safety of a community of learners. Bonus: we also have fun. Approaching the last set of memo conferences as an "LRW Lounge" instead of additional office hours is one of several novel approaches that can be implemented to help students flourish.

Even for the most privileged student, the 1L law school classroom can feel daunting. The hyper-competitive environment—coupled with the high-stakes assessments—can leave students feeling overwhelmed and isolated. For first-generation law students, the pressures and insecurities can be crippling. However, by anchoring our lessons in transfer learning principles, culturally relevant pedagogy, and novelty, professors can create a lawyering skills classroom for 1Ls that empowers and engages. Instead of an empty briefcase, we can bring with us a briefcase filled with impactful curriculum and teaching methods that support first-generation students.

In addition to thoughtful curriculum and active teaching methods, professors committed to creating more opportunities for their first-generation students should embrace the judicious use of technology in the lawyering skills classroom. Two specific strategies discussed below help narrow the real or perceived achievement gap that impacts many first-generation students.

C. Using Technology to Provide Additional Scaffolding and Support to First Gen Students in the Lawyering Skills Classroom[48]

> ***Before law school, I had become overwhelmed by academic writing and worried a lot about whether I could feel comfortable writing for law school. By reducing every big concept into manageable elements, your class gave me more confidence in writing and eased my anxiety around receiving criticism.***
>
> —Anonymous Student

One of the most pervasive stories students tell themselves in law school is that there is some body of knowledge or some set of experiences that others have but that

48. Section C of this essay was written by Rachel Croskery-Roberts, Associate Dean for Lawyering Skills and Professor of Law at University of California Irvine School of Law.

the individual student does not. And in the past, I have typically tried to help students understand that no one has the secret inside knowledge about law school. Rather, students will all struggle at various points. And yet it is undoubtedly true that students come to law school with different levels of exposure to the legal profession and different educational backgrounds, particularly as schools actively seek to create more inclusive learning environments by recruiting and admitting more first-generation students, students for whom English is a second language, and other nontraditional law students. As we move toward a more diverse and inclusive profession, we must provide the educational scaffolding and support that each individual student needs to thrive while in law school. Scaffolding—breaking up complex concepts into more accessible "chunks," each building and expanding upon the last—demystifies the writing process and boosts student confidence.

This need for careful scaffolding may be particularly great when addressing student needs in the legal writing classroom, where in the past we might have assumed students arrived equipped with a similar set of foundational basic writing skills and that the legal writing course could, therefore, focus only on teaching the highly stylized expression of complex legal analysis in written form. But what about students whose educational backgrounds leave them ill-equipped for the rigors of the legal writing classroom? Do we simply wring our hands and lament the failures of some students' secondary and post-secondary educational experiences? Do we pretend that students' exposure to others in higher education (or lack thereof) does not matter? Or do we recognize that opening the door to the law school to a broader cohort means adjusting what we do to ensure that our most vulnerable students have the same opportunities to excel as their classmates?

It seems noncontroversial to say that the lawyering skills classroom should serve all students, regardless of the skill set those students possess on day one. But actually making that happen is a tall order, given the intensive work the lawyering skills professor already does with each individual student. Where do already overworked professors find the time? One answer, of course, is that lawyering skills professors cannot do it all. Academic skills departments and writing specialists can play a crucial role in helping to bridge the gap for students who lack certain skills. But there are many interventions possible within the lawyering skills classroom, and the lawyering skills professor who leverages technology to benefit students may find those efforts help level the playing field for students while also addressing some concerns about creating or exacerbating stereotype threat.[49]

---

49. *See* McClain, *supra* note 11, at 24 (observing that "studies show that the effects of stereotype threat can be reduced or even eliminated, through deliberate modifications of the environment for learning" and further exploring "affirmative interventions that have a measurable, reductive impact on the effects of stereotype threat").

Technology is not a solution to every problem. But judicious use of technology may allow for a more personalized educational experience for students.[50] This is useful for all students, but particularly for students who come to law school either actually lacking basic skills or perceiving that they lack such skills.

Targeted Asynchronous Videos in the Lawyering Skills Classroom

I have increasingly turned to short asynchronous videos to provide additional support and scaffolding for students with gaps in their past education or those who need reinforcement of new concepts beyond what my course typically provides. Each asynchronous video covers a very discrete topic and typically lasts less than 10 minutes. Videos provide a clear overview of a topic with detailed explanations, followed by multiple examples and an invitation to the student to try their hand at whatever skill the video introduces or reinforces. These videos begin at the beginning, meaning they assume no knowledge on the part of the student. This allows for a judgment-free zone, even when introducing basic concepts that the student thinks they "should" already know.

One example of a video that students have found quite useful is one on identifying and knowing when to avoid (or, conversely, to strategically use) the passive voice. I used to write on student papers, "unnecessary passive voice" or "edit out the passive voice here." Time and time again, rewritten papers would come back with the same errors. My feedback morphed into, "You're still struggling with passive voice" or "You haven't made the corrections I brought to your attention on the last submission." There are at least three underlying assumptions in the first set of comments. First, the comments assume the student knows what the passive voice is. Second, the comments assume the student knows when the passive voice might actually be useful. And finally, the comments assume the student knows how to identify and eradicate improper use of the passive voice. For a student who does not know one or more of these things, the likely result is a feeling of embarrassment or shame; who wants to admit to their professor that not only did they do something wrong, but they also do not even understand the feedback? And the second set of comments may be even worse. They imply one of two things: (1) the student is not capable enough to address even basic writing issues; or (2) the student is lazy and is not even trying.

For many students, these assumptions are simply wrong. And for students already suffering from some level of imposter syndrome or entering college as the first in their families to do so, such comments may break the tenuous bonds of trust necessary between writing professor and student. The videos help me meet students where they are, and they also allow students who may have gaps in their basic knowledge to address those gaps in a way that allows them to take ownership over their own education and feel empowered by their ability to do so.

---

50. It is also a tool that may be particularly useful for professors who already spend hours of individualized time with each student and discover that some students need still more support.

D. Teaching Students to Make Effective Use of Asynchronous Video Content

However, even if you create outstanding content perfectly tailored to meet individual students where they are, many students will not know what to do with that content. Simply uploading a series of videos to a learning management system for the course is arguably the digital equivalent of a recommended reading list. And it is not much better to direct the student to "watch the video on deconstructing a rule statement" (or whatever concept they might be struggling with). First explain why you think a student needs a particular video. What particular challenges are you noticing in their writing or analytical approach to the material that a given video could help the student address? Then teach the student how to interact effectively with the course content.[51] Students are likely to view asynchronous video content as something to interact with passively and may also assume they will learn simply by playing the video over and over again.[52] Provide guidance on active note-taking techniques, and discourage re-watching videos. Instead, build in active learning exercises to the asynchronous experience.

Creating Effective Video Content

As I alluded to in the previous section, the best videos will not simply lecture at students. They will involve short explanatory sections followed by clear, precise examples. They will also prompt students to actively use the information they are learning in an interactive way.[53] Depending upon the subject matter, that may involve exercises, short reflections, or, for the more tech-savvy professor, embedded quizzes. But you need not be a tech wizard to create effective asynchronous video content. You can ask students to pause the video to work on a problem and then come back to work through that problem on the video. Or you can require students to complete a short quiz or reflection after the video that they submit to you (or, if you do not have the time, that they self-grade with an answer key you provide). Or

---

51. Rachel Croskery-Roberts & Queena Mewers, *Helping Traditional Students Become Effective Online Learners, in* Law Teaching Strategies for a New Era (Tessa Dysart & Tracy Norton eds., 2021).

52. *See id.* (citing Celeste Pilegard, *So Your Classes Are All Online Now: 3 Keys to Success,* YouTube (March 26, 2020), https://www.youtube.com/watch?v=1IIUVU-d1DM&t; Henk G. Schmidt et al., *On the Use and Misuse of Lectures in Higher Education,* 1 Health Profs. Educ. 12, 14 (2015); Diane F. Halpern & Milton D. Hakel, *Applying the Science of Learning to the University and Beyond: Teaching for Long-Term Retention and Transfer,* Change: Mag. Higher Learning, Jul./Aug. 2003, at 36, 40).

53. *See, e.g.*, Alice Y. Kolb & David A. Kolb, *Experiential Learning Theory as a Guide for Experiential Educators in Higher Education*, *in* Experiential Learning & Teaching in Higher Education: Vol. 1: No. 1, Article 7 (2017), *available at* https://nsuworks.nova.edu/elthe/vol1/iss1/7) (identifying steps of the Kolb Experiential Learning Cycle as including (1) concrete experience; (2) reflective observation; (3) abstract conceptualization; and (4) active experimentation.

you can have students take a paragraph of something they have recently written and apply what they learned in the video. It is not high production value that makes an asynchronous video effective. The key is simply to ensure that the student gets clear information and has to actively engage with the material and apply that information to solidify their understanding of the course material.

Humanizing Critiquing Through Personalized Audio Commentary

Another way to use technology to reduce anxiety for first-generation students is to use audio commenting to humanize critiquing.[54] A mentor once told me to avoid using a red pen when providing written feedback on students' legal writing assignments, as comments in red ink may convey a harsh or aggressive tone. I tried a green pen instead, hoping that a more calming, natural color would ease the sting of harsh critique.[55] Instead, it only caused students to hate the color green. As technology developed and I moved to electronic commenting, I thought I could convey an encouraging, though demanding tone through simply typing more personal, detailed comments. I greatly underestimated, however, the negative effect on many students of a wall of comments in the margins of a paper, no matter how useful those comments were. Of course students need to know what they have done wrong and how to fix it. But they also need to truly feel that their professor is a partner in their education and that their professor trusts that they have the ability to improve. Students described being overwhelmed by the amount of feedback, and I was unable to convey the sort of tone I wanted in written comments, something that seemed most harmful to the most struggling and vulnerable students.

It might be tempting, then, to try to temper critiques by watering them down or by heaping praise on the smallest of victories in order to avoid further damaging overwhelmed students. But that is not what the studies show is helpful. Rather, "the best feedback—meaning the kind... trusted by students and [able to] motivate[] them to improve—both h[olds] students to a high standard and also affirm[s] a belief that the students ha[ve] the capacity to meet that standard."[56]

Audio feedback (via recorded Zoom sessions or voice recording apps) allows you to figuratively be in the room with the student while that student receives your feedback. You can craft detailed, thoughtful commentary that does precisely what you need it to do: set the standards high, explain precisely how to meet those standards, and genuinely convey with both your words and tone that you have faith that the

54. I am grateful to my colleague and friend, Professor Leslie Culver, for convincing me to try audio critiquing. It has become an important tool for reaching students where they are and providing truly individualized feedback.

55. *See, e.g.*, Sevinc Kurt & Kelechi Kingsley Osueke, *The Effects of Color on the Moods of College Students*, SAGE OPEN 4, *available at* https://journals.sagepub.com/doi/pdf/10.1177/2158244014525423 (noting that "[g]reen is considered an emotionally calming color").

56. *See supra* n.1, at 25 (citing Geoffrey L. Cohen et al., *The Mentor's Dilemma: Providing Critical Feedback Across the Racial Divide*, 25 PERSONALITY & SOC. PSYCH. BULL. 1302 (1999)).

student is capable of meeting and even exceeding your expectations. I, like Professor Mikkor, have some templates prepared to ensure consistency in feedback across students, but the audio feedback also involves significant customization to reach each student where they are.

Conclusion

Asynchronous videos and personalized audio commentary are just two examples of ways to leverage technology to reach and teach students where they are in the legal writing classroom. These techniques are likely to help all students, but they are particularly likely to help those who may come to law school without the outside support or foundational skills that some of their peers have.[57]

Used wisely, technology can be a potent tool to close achievement gaps and humanize the critical feedback loop that can often contribute to struggles in the lawyering skills classroom. But teaching students to embrace struggle in their move toward fluency is another essential step to empower first-generation law students. Specifically, non-lawyer translations are important techniques to attain and maintain language mastery for lawyering.

E. Empowering First Gen Law Students with Exercises that Ask Students to "*Explain that to a Non-Lawyer!*"[58]

> ... In reading cases, I soon discovered that most judges and lawyers did not like to sound like ordinary people. Few said, "I." Most did not write in simple declarative sentences. They wanted their opinions to seem the work of the law, rather than of any individual. To make their writing less personal and more impressive, they resorted to all kinds of devices, "whences" and "heretofores," roundabout phrasings, sentences of interminable length.[59]

Written nearly 50 years ago, the excerpt above, in which the author likens law school to learning a new language still resonates, especially for first-gen students:

> Suddenly [I'm] immersed in a foreign land with its own language, history, customs, and laws—all of which I don't understand. That's how I feel in law school. That and fear. Fear that professors will live up to the terrorizing legends portrayed in books and movies. And damn, how will I do here if Elle Woods

57. Faculty members seeking to add effective asynchronous video and audio content to their courses should feel free to reach out to me directly with questions about my materials and approach.

58. This section of the essay was written by Sara J. Berman, Professor of Law and Assistant Dean of Academic Excellence & Bar Success at Touro Law.

59. Scott Turow, One L (1977).

who at least looked like she fit in had such a hard time? Why did I do this to myself? Everyone is smarter than me. Maybe I should quit...[60]

For our professional population to mirror society's diversity, we must do more than help students avoid quitting. We must help them embrace struggle, working so that language, culture, financial, and other barriers do not prevent the deep learning necessary to become great lawyers. Our part is teaching with inclusivity and inspiration, providing transparency in our *whys* and creativity with our *hows*.

This section of this essay builds on the premise that law school learning depends on fluency. Successful lawyers pursue a lifelong quest to *maintain* fluency (rather than *attain*, because terms evolve) in English and legal terminology. Some also maintain fluency in other languages and their legal counterparts. Many of us are first exposed to legal terms in law school; others, including those whose parents are lawyers, hear their first legal words as toddlers. "*Explain that to a non-lawyer*" exercises help all students and are particularly empowering for those who have had little experience with lawyers or legal settings.

Words Matter

Students embrace learning techniques when their purpose is clear. So, before describing the *how* (actual lessons), let's consider the *why*. Obvious to us, but not necessarily to students, words matter. Words to lawyers are like food to chefs. We choose terms and phrasings as ingredients to wield power, explain, persuade, intimidate, and impress. We skillfully use laptops and tablets as our chef's knives in drafting and editing documents; we determine just which seasonings to include or exclude to achieve our client's goals. And we compose carefully planned menus of detailed strategies as we negotiate or litigate.

In discussing the *why*, let's be transparent and direct with students. Let's tell them that exam answers demonstrating limited legal vocabularies or superficial understanding of legal terms often receive lower grades than those who demonstrate fluency. The same is true on bar exams.

It is particularly important in skills classes to make clear that lawyers who fail to learn well can cause severe harm to clients—real people, not anonymous plaintiffs and defendants on ancient pages—who can lose their homes, custody of their children, or even their lives. Sufficient command of our professional tools, including our vocabulary, is not optional.

Students sometimes relate to comparisons of legal terminology with clothing. Certain clothing, such as particular terms of art, are essential. In contrast, accessories, like gratuitous jargon, may serve as mere decoration. We wear different outfits depending on the weather, the occasion, cultural norms, and our budgets and per-

60. Anonymous student.

sonal styles. Sometimes, the only consequence of wearing "the wrong" clothing is feeling hot, cold, or slightly out of place. Other times, without the right attire, doors slam in our faces.

I used to say, "*Taking the bar exam without a reputable bar review course is like going to Chicago in winter without a coat.*"[61] I now add, "*And, it's more than just having a coat. You need the right coat, you need to know how to wear it, and you need a scarf, hat, and gloves.*" (Some accessories are necessary!) This may be self-evident to a Windy City native, but not for a Southern Californian or South Floridian. Law school for many *is* Chicago in February. Do we as faculty do enough to make sure everyone not only has a coat but knows how to wear it?

Using a "foreign language of law" theme, we can make clear how important and how alienating legal words can be by thinking about difficulties non-fluent English speakers, or those with thick accents, face with everyday tasks such as navigating banks, utilities, landlords—even Siri. At a FedEx store recently, another customer asked me to talk to an automated system for him. "My phone doesn't understand me," he said. The system wasn't made for him.

As professors, we can validate concerns and allay fears by acknowledging that, for many of our students, becoming a lawyer means fighting their way into a system that wasn't built for them. Hearing this from a professor can help empower students, especially when followed by: "*You belong. You can and will wield great power within the system, and have opportunities to make important changes, once you are in. Getting "in" starts with a thorough understanding of what you read, say, and write.*"

Why Law School?

A quick but essential digression. The *why master language* has a prerequisite, a bigger, foundational "why"—"W*hy law school*?"[62] Formulating, declaring, and holding fast to a personal "*why law school*" helps students facing stereotype threat and/or when imposter syndrome rages. Feeling driven and supported by a greater purpose helps them face the inevitable stresses and frustrations of an educational process designed to be challenging even for insiders, (particularly privileged or multigener-

---

61. Enrolling in bar review without completing the assigned work is like buying a coat and not wearing it.

62. Sample personal mission statements from my January 2022 *ABA Student Lawyer* column include: (1) My goal is to do my best and work my hardest as I prepare to become an advocate for my future clients; (2) I'm studying to be a smart, savvy, ethical lawyer capable of supporting my family and myself and doing work that helps others; (3) I'm driven to learn how the law can serve historically underrepresented people and to train so that I'm best prepared to help steer society toward an equitable and inclusive future; (4) I'm working to be part of a profession that will allow me the financial security I never had when I was growing up; (5) I'm dedicating myself to detail-oriented deep learning as I work to achieve a respected position within the legal community; (6) I'm committed to developing the knowledge and skills to help and inspire others while being true to myself and making my family proud of my accomplishments.

ation law students). The curve and the mythologies around law school create winners and losers. A purpose-driven perspective and focus on the future will help minimize the deleterious effects of this culture of exclusionary competitiveness.[63]

Spending even a few minutes on the big *why* puts more discrete *whys*, the why learn particular skills, into context. So, with *why law school* and *why words* in place, let's move to the *how:* first, encourage students to look up terms so their meanings are clear, then engage with active learning, including translation exercises.

To translate legal terms into plain English, students must first understand them

Law professors can encourage students to look up words they don't know *and* common words that have different legal meanings. To highlight the importance of the latter, pause and give the class 30 seconds to write 10 English words that have entirely different meanings as legal terms, then share aloud. (Mine are party, judgment, decision, opinion, information, stay, issue, argument, opinion, and brief.)

For professors who lugged around a *Black's Law Dictionary*, it's tempting to think that because dictionaries are accessible on phones, students use them. They do not, or not as often as necessary. Looking up words requires awareness of their importance (that *why* again), motivation, and habit. Many students never developed the habit, in part because dictionaries fell out of pedagogical vogue. They were taught to pick up meanings from context clues. So, we must (1) admit that looking up words *does* take time; (2) clearly explain why it is worth the time and effort ("Getting the gist" is fine for leisure reading but not in a profession where lives and livelihoods depend on verbal precision.); (3) help build motivation; and (4) help train habits, starting in class.

Growth mindset applies to motivation. We can become more motivated as we find meaning, employ effective motivational strategies, and practice. As with all habits, looking up words becomes easier and takes less time if we do it routinely. Simple, tangible nudges include stopping class and asking students to read definitions aloud from casebooks, statutory supplements, or dictionary apps on their phones; reading aloud from our own dictionaries; and perhaps sharing a story about an occasion when not taking time to look up a word backfired.

We can also teach students to prompt themselves by picturing either a "critic" or "cheerleader" on their shoulders—an imaginary meme that pops up to rally them to get out the dictionary when they see unfamiliar words or when seemingly familiar words don't make sense. For students who respond to fear-based motivation, they

---

63. Competitiveness does not have to be exclusionary as I describe in post about how John Wooden's philosophies might be adopted in law schools. Sara J. Berman, *Best Practices: What Law Schools Might Learn from One of Basketball's Greatest Coaches, John Wooden*, Best Practices for Legal Education Blog (last visited Jan. 20, 2022), https://bestpracticeslegaled.com/2018/11/16/best-practices-what-law-schools-might-learn-from-one-of-basketballs-greatest-coaches-john-wooden/.

might conjure a robed judge calling them out for not making their client's case clear. Or, if they prefer the words as clothing analogy, they might picture a "word bouncer." Like the big, burly bouncer at the trendy night club who won't let them in without the right clothes, their "word bouncer" won't let them move to the next page without knowing the meaning of particular words. When students who respond to positive motivators encounter unfamiliar words, they might imagine a tiny cheerleader calling out, *Big G, Little O, Go team!* Cheers don't interrupt; they encourage players to play well. An internal cheerleader can help a student move from concerns about taking too much time or interrupting their flow to the empowerment and efficiency that comes from reading with full understanding.

Looking up words is thus an important tool in the fluency toolkit. But tools are only useful if we use them. As professors, we can help students train legal fluency by creating non-lawyer translation opportunities.

The cover of jargon, or, faking it

When lawyers or law students talk with each other, many are tempted to stay in "jargon land." Sometimes, terminology provides a convenient shorthand that everyone in the club understands. But we can remind students that even some licensed lawyers are faking it when they use fancy terms. And, far too often, our students pretend to have a command of concepts they really don't fully grasp. Non-lawyer translation forces understanding. To illustrate, you might ask students to picture themselves in this scenario:

Following hours of library study, you return from a bathroom break to chocolate smells, the sight of brown stains on your classmate's shirt, and crumbs near your backpack. You open it and see your cookie stash is gone. "*Res ipsa!*" you exclaim. Presumably, *without any additional explanation*, your classmate would know both the literal Latin meaning, "the thing speaks for itself," and the contextual meaning: *"Even without witnesses, I know you ate my cookies. Stains and crumbs don't appear at the same time cookies disappear without someone eating them. We were studying alone and no one else was near my backpack, so, busted.* Now, if you both left and returned to find the child of a library employee in your study room, covered with stains and crumbs, what would the child think if you said, *res ipsa*?

Beyond the obvious need to facilitate the hearer's understanding, the act of translating helps speakers improve their own understanding. And, with *explain that to a non-lawyer* exercises, students who are unfamiliar with terms do not have to out themselves because everyone is taking time together to understand well enough to then translate effectively.

Non-lawyer translation exercises in skills classes

There are many ways to incorporate non-lawyer translation into skills and doctrinal classes. Some professors refer to a fictional non-lawyer relative, perhaps "Uncle Mike" or "Aunt Isabella," and regularly call on students to, "Explain that to

Aunt Isabella."[64] Other professors pause class and ask students to write a short letter to a client explaining the legal doctrine covered that day or in required readings.[65] Still others assign three-part flashcard exercises: the legal term on the front, the formal definition (that would go in an essay exam) on the back, and, below that, an explanation in the students' own words. Students can create the cards alone or in pairs/groups.[66]

I add this twist: explain it to a "very smart 16-year-old." This keeps students aware that the listener is a non-lawyer, but it stops them from being condescending. And smart teenagers are usually persistent enough to ask follow-up questions until an explanation makes complete sense.[67] After discussing a case or series of cases, a professor might ask the students to explain the rule and its significance as if they are delivering a three- to five-minute talk at a high school Law Day.

Whatever teaching techniques professors choose, it helps to close the learning loop with group and individual reflections that prompt students to think about what they gained from translation exercises. Did they start to see themselves more as lawyers than law students? Did they become aware of knowledge gaps in material they thought they understood?

F. Conclusion

Non-lawyer translation exercises help promote fluency, giving students permission to take time both to look up terms and to think about their meaning. These exercises also help students form professional identities and prepare for practice in that they:

- Instill confidence that students are using terms appropriately in written and oral presentations, including when called on in class;
- Help combat aspects of imposter syndrome that arise from fear of not using a word correctly, not employing the right words, or not understanding others' jargon usage;
- Facilitate clearer responses in job interviews and on law school and bar exam essays and Multistate Performance Test (MPT)[68] exams; and

64. For inclusivity, you might ask students to tape a picture of a non-lawyer friend or relative on the inside of their casebook, and simply say, "Explain that to your non-lawyer."

65. You can emphasize cultural humility by asking students to write first to Client A, described as having one background and education level, then rewrite the letter or discuss how the letter might change for a client with a very different background.

66. Again, hearing each other's "own words" can help them appreciate that different words make sense to different people, in turn making clear that future clients will need varying explanations.

67. Taking Street Law courses can have a similarly empowering effect on law students.

68. Information about the MPT, the practical skills portion of the Uniform Bar Exam, can be found at https://ncbex.org/exams/mpt/. The skills tested on the MPT, based in part on the "State-

- Equip students to serve future clients by instilling effective communication skills for interactions with non-lawyer clients, office staff, court personnel, or jurors, and non-lawyer collaborators such as accountants and IT professionals.

As professors, we can lecture *at* our students; we can weaponize words that intentionally or inadvertently make students feel they don't belong. We can also empower them with engaging, active, and simple lessons, including *Explain that to a non-lawyer* exercises. In doing so, we can help them self-assess their knowledge and communication skills without shame, and give them tools to attain and maintain language mastery for a lifetime of successful learning and lawyering.

As this essay reveals, there are several concrete strategies professors can employ in the lawyering skills classroom to help first-generation students cultivate a sense of belonging and empowerment. First, stereotype threat can derail even the most promising law student; therefore, professors must commit to countering stereotype threat throughout the course. Selecting curriculum and active teaching methods that specifically engage first-generation students will provide the framework for success. Using technology thoughtfully to address achievement gaps and humanize the feedback loop is also an effective tool to leverage the playing field. Further, non-lawyer translation exercises help students because fluency in the language of lawyering and bolster self-efficacy. Through deliberate efforts that deal directly with the special barriers that first-generation students must overcome to succeed, professors can help demystify the lawyering skills classroom. The result will make the classroom a more engaging, productive, supportive, and enjoyable experience for the entire community.

---

ment of Fundamental Lawyering Skills" from Legal Education and Professional Development: An Educational Continuum, *Report of the Task Force on Law Schools and the Profession: Narrowing the Gap* (Known as the MacCrate Report (ABA 1992)), include problem solving, legal analysis and reasoning, factual analysis, communication, organization and management of a legal task, and recognizing and resolving ethical dilemmas.

Twenty

Don't Stop After 1L Year

Incorporating Skills Teaching in Upper-Level Doctrinal Courses

Brittany L. Raposa

WHEN SKILLS TEACHING HAPPENS IN DOCTRINAL COURSES, it predominantly happens in the 1L classroom. Students are coming in and learning how to read and brief cases, learning how to outline, learning how to legally write, and learning how to take exams. First-generation students benefit from this instruction because this world is new to them. However, first-generation students also benefit from repetition and exposure to strengthen their skills. I've found that many first-generation students still need work and assistance in these skills when they get to their second or even their third year. This section discusses how I, through teaching the upper-level doctrinal course of Family Law, incorporate skills teaching into the classroom. It is my hope that faculty can then use similar teaching examples in their upper-level doctrinal courses.

I. Incorporating Doctrine and Skills: A Family Law Example

Like any doctrinal course, my family law course does focus on doctrine. Specifically, the course is a general survey class covering major topics like the statutory and constitutional regulation of marital and non-marital family relationships, the restructuring of parent-child relationships at divorce or dissolution of a non-marital family relationship, financial support for spouses and children at divorce or dissolution of a non-marital relationship, and distribution of property at divorce or dissolution of a non-marital family relationship. Substantively, the course also emphasizes the inequities and social injustice within family law.

However, teaching and doctrine and skills does not need to be a separate endeavor. Teaching both can exist quite successfully in one class. Teaching skills in the doctrinal classroom "provides an offsetting benefit because it greatly enhances the students' understanding of substantive theories by placing them in a practical, hands-on context."[1] It is important for all our students, but especially our first-generation students, that these skills be enhanced and taught throughout their curriculum, including in their upper-level doctrinal courses. We cannot assume that every student, after completing one year of law school, has all the same skills necessary to succeed academically and as a lawyer. As established earlier in this book, first-generation students do not enter their law school class on an even playing field—they do not have a lot of the skills their peers have. Therefore, incorporating this teaching in upper-level courses consistently throughout their educational careers is critical. The rest of this section will outline how I incorporate teaching various skills into my doctrinal family law course.

A. Rule Synthesis

Many students struggle with clear, concise writing. This translates into students having difficulty simply stating a rule that is unambiguous and can be readily applied to a set of facts. In one of our first classes, I discuss how it's critical that when reading cases in this course, students should be able to synthesize rules in a way to predict the outcome of a legal problem they may be asked to address. In this class, we read *Griswold v. Connecticut* and *Eisenstadt v. Baird* as we address the constitutional foundations of family privacy in the law. We work on synthesizing the rules from both cases. We then look at examples of what is a rule synthesis and what is not a rule synthesis. I use the following examples:

> ***Not Synthesized***: In *Griswold v. Connecticut*, the Court held that privacy denotes not merely freedom from bodily restraint but also the right of the individual to contract, to engage in any of the common occupations of life, to acquire useful knowledge, to marry, to establish a home and bring up children, to worship God according to the dictates of his own conscience, and to enjoy those privileges as essential to the orderly pursuit of happiness by free men. The court held that the intimate relation of husband and wife is a privacy right, and laws that provide that husbands and wives cannot use contraceptives violates that right and the Constitution.
>
> ***Synthesized***: In *Griswold v. Connecticut*, the Court established that various guarantees of the Constitution contain zones of privacy. The Court further held that the right to marry, and the right of married persons to obtain contraceptives, falls within that right of privacy that is fundamental. Therefore, a law that infringes on this privacy right cannot be arbitrary or without reasonable relation to a compelling purpose for the law.

1. Alice M. Noble-Allgire, *Desegregating the Law School Curriculum: How to Integrate More of the Skills and Values Identified by the MacCrate Report Into a Doctrinal Course*, NEVADA L.J. 32, 34 (2002).

After this class, many of the students find themselves writing rule statements that are not synthesized. After doing the activity with *Griswold*, we then do it with *Eisenstadt*, and the students then have an example of a synthesized rule to use when writing their own. After this first class, throughout the semester, I ask students to not brief cases, but to instead synthesize the rules from each case we read throughout the semester. We go over these for many of the cases we discuss, and by the end of the class, students indicate that they feel much more confident in pulling out the relevant rules from the cases and writing them.

B. Analysis Writing

Analysis writing is also very challenging to students, and many first-generation students have expressed that they have difficulty with it. One of my first-generation students said, "I know how to analyze it in my head, but it's completely different when I'm trying to put it on paper. It's frustrating because I get lower grades on exams and I know my stuff, I just don't know how to show my professor I do." As many students feel like this after they complete their first year, it's critical that upper-level classes reinforce and teach how to write an analysis.

We work on analysis writing in our live classroom setting with a series of hypotheticals throughout the semester. I use the first class where we do this to teach analysis writing. I explain that students fall within two extremes when writing an analysis. First, students tend to be too conclusory, where they make legal conclusions and do not explain how they reached that conclusion. Essentially, the students do not use enough facts to make connections with the law to illustrate a strong analysis. Alternatively, in the other extreme, students simply just restate facts from the fact pattern without connecting those facts to their legal significance. These students simply summarize the facts and force their professors, the reader, to make the legal connections themselves.

I then give students a hypothetical as well as the rule statement needed to answer that hypothetical. I give them the rule statement because the purpose of the exercise is to help them with their analysis—using the rule in front of them to focus solely on how to write strong and clear analysis sentences. Then, I tell students to write an analysis on that hypothetical, giving them about 15 to 20 minutes to do so. Below, see an example hypothetical and rule used in the class where we discuss child support.

***Hypothetical*:**

Husband and Wife were divorced in 2017. Under the terms of their divorce decree, in relevant part, Husband and Wife are to share legal and physical custody of their daughter, and Husband must pay Wife $1,000 per month in child support until their daughter reaches the age of 18. Six months ago, Husband was offered a job in State A that pays significantly less than his job in State B but provides him with more responsibilities and much better promotion opportunities. Husband accepted the job in State A and moved from State B to State A for this job. Husband is now seeking to modify his child support obligation to pay less than $1,000 per month due to his reduction in pay. What would be the likely result?

To modify child support, there must be a substantial and material change of circumstances since the entry of the original decree. In determining whether there is a substantial and material change in circumstances, the court considers the following factors: (1) voluntary change in the payor's occupation; (2) payor's remarriage and resulting increased family responsibilities; (3) payor's increased resources; (4) payor's deteriorating health; and (5) payee's remarriage or cohabitation. If the payor experienced an involuntary change in circumstances, this will likely justify a reduction in the support obligation. However, if the payor voluntarily changed employment, child support may only be reduced if (1) the change was in good faith and (2) the action will not deprive the child of reasonable financial support.

After giving students the time to write the analysis for this hypothetical, I then provide students with analysis examples of what to write and what not to write. For instance, I provide them with the examples below:

What *Not* to Write—Too Conclusory: Husband's job change is a significant change in circumstances. Husband made a voluntary job change in good faith and therefore will likely be able to reduce his child support obligation. Depending upon the reduction, the reduction also would likely not deprive his daughter of reasonable financial support.

What *Not* to Write—Fact Restatement: Under the divorce decree, Husband was to pay $1,000 per month in child support. However, Husband took a new job that paid significantly less than his job in State B but it had better promotion opportunities. Therefore, there was a significant change in circumstances and the court will likely reduce his child support even though he voluntarily reduced his income.

What *to* Write—A Mix of Law and Fact: Husband may demonstrate a significant change in circumstance since the divorce decree was entered because at the time of the divorce decree, he was making a certain salary, and now was working in a job making significantly less. Although Husband's reduction in salary was due to a voluntary job switch, it was likely made in good faith because it gave him more responsibilities and better promotion opportunities, and nothing in the facts suggest he had any intention of bad faith.

Through these examples, I explain how students write too conclusory and students restate facts, and that we should instead interweave law and fact, making connections in their analysis. I then provide students with a sample answer to this hypothetical, and we engage in self-assessment of their analysis writing. We complete exercises like this throughout the semester to strengthen their analytical skills, which also has the benefit of assisting the students in better understanding the topic we are covering in class.

C. Bar Exam Exposure

The graded assessments I give in this class consist of multistate essay examination (MEE) questions and multistate performance test (MPT) questions. Apart from the final exam, students have three written formative assessments in the semester, which consists of one MPT question and two MEE questions. There are many benefits to using these questions. With using an MPT, students can really focus on their analysis writing, as the library in the MPT gives them the rules they need to use. I begin with this as my first assessment in the class, so students can continue to strengthen their analysis writing. The MPT during bar preparation and on the bar exam is also incredibly challenging due to time constraints and the overall process of legal writing under test-taking pressure. Therefore, the more exposure students can get to bar exam writing, the better prepared they will be when they are studying for and taking the bar exam.

I use the MPT question *Butler v. Hill* (MPT 1) from the February 2011 bar exam. In this MPT, students analyze the issues of a valid ceremonial marriage, the creation of a common law marriage, and property distribution. I create a detailed rubric when grading this assessment, which not only contains the substantive points the student should hit, but also gives points for rule synthesis, analysis writing, and structure and organization. Many faculty can incorporate MPTs into their courses for assessments or student practice, as there are a vast number of subjects and topics covered on the MPT. Further, there are resources that organize MPTs into subject matter that faculty can utilize to quickly find a relevant MPT for class.[2]

In addition to using MPTs, my final two assessments are MEE questions. Many schools license the prior bar exam essay questions, which are incredibly useful for assessments. I take the opportunity in one of my classes to teach how students should write essays on the bar exam – using the same rule synthesis and analysis principles we have already been discussing in class. These exercises expose students to MEE questions and writing, and they can also practice rule-recall and issue spotting in family law. Students also receive a detailed rubric with my feedback on these assessments.

2. *See* Sara J. Berman, Bar Exam MPT Preparation & Experiential Learning for Law Students (2021).

II. You Can Incorporate This, Too

While it sometimes may feel like incorporating these exercises into our classes is taking away time from the substantive law we teach, it is only helping our students, and especially our first-generation students who need repetition of these skills. This piece discusses three techniques for doing so, but you can also edit these lessons and create new ones based on the specific skills you are trying to reinforce for your students.

Twenty-One

Cognitive Load and the First Gen Law Student

Alyson Drake*

THE FIRST-YEAR LAW SCHOOL EXPERIENCE IS COGNITIVELY TAXING on all law students. The limits of students' cognitive capacity are tested constantly, as they encounter a huge amount of new information in their courses while acclimating to new environments, making new friends, and dealing with other stressors. While most, if not all, law students experience cognitive overload at some point in their legal education, first-generation students in particular often have more cognitive burdens, including dealing with stereotype threat and imposter syndrome, than many of their non-first-generation counterparts. These burdens may exceed the limits of students' cognitive load, which makes learning more difficult. This chapter will introduce the concept and limits of cognitive load, discuss ways that first-generation students experience cognitive disruptions, and provide universal strategies for instruction that will benefit all learners experiencing cognitive overload—but that will be particularly beneficial to first-generation learners.

A Brief Intro to Cognitive Load

The goal of learning is to move new information into long-term memory so learners can then draw on this information as needed. Unfortunately, it is not as simple as being in the room where new information is presented; instead, we must overcome many barriers for information to make its way into a student's long-term memory. One signifiicant barrier is cognitive load, the mental challenge working memory imposes on a human's learning. As described by cognitive psychologist Frederick Reif, a task's cognitive load is the cognitive effort—the amount of information processing—a person must use to perform a particular task.[1] Cognitive load

* Interim Director of the Law Library & Lecturer, University of Houston Law Center.

1. *See generally* FREDERICK REIF, APPLYING COGNITIVE SCIENCE TO EDUCATION: THINKING AND LEARNING IN SCIENTIFIC AND OTHER COMPLEX DOMAINS (2010).

is grounded on the model of human information processing that divides memory into three parts: sensory memory, working memory, and long-term memory.[2]

Sensory memory comes from the impressions humans receive of everything surrounding them. As we encounter the world, sensory memory processes certain pieces of information humans receive through their senses into working memory. Most often, the information processed consists of things people are actively paying attention to or sensory impressions that surprise them. Once this sensory information passes into working memory, it is either processed there or discarded.

Working memory is "the limited mental 'space' " in which humans think."[3] During this stage of memory, humans are conscious of their information processing.[4] Working memory is hampered by both its limited duration and the amount of information that can be held within it. When humans process new information in their working memory, most information vanishes within 30 seconds if it is not rehearsed in some way.[5] This is why students can fail to perform a skill or remember something they were told early in a lecture if there is too much time between the relay of the content and them being asked to use that information.

Working memory is also impeded by how much information can be held within it. The most recent studies show that humans can only hold on to approximately four "chunks" of information at any one time.[6] What constitutes a chunk of information will vary based on how ingrained the information being used is in the knowledge structures of the learner's long-term memory.[7] Chunks can be groups of items collected together in the long-term memory and treated by the brain as a single item, but for new information without a knowledge structure in the brain to fit within, a small bit of information may be treated as a single chunk.[8] In other words, an expert

---

2. Fred Pass et al., *Cognitive Load Theory and Instructional Design: Recent Developments*, 38 EDUC. PSYCH. 1, 2 (2003); John Sweller, *Cognitive Load Theory, Learning Difficulty, and Instructional Design*, in 4 LEARNING & INSTRUCTION 295, 299 (1994). Our understanding of memory continues to evolve; while studies have shown that memory doesn't work in the linear fashion described in classic memory theory—from sensory to working to long-term in a straight line, it holds true that the working memory has the limits discussed in this chapter. See MICHELLE D. MILLER, REMEMBERING AND FORGETTING IN THE AGE OF TECHNOLOGY: TEACHING, LEARNING, AND THE SCIENCE OF MEMORY IN A WIRED WORLD 52–54 (2022).

3. Richard E. Clark et al., *Putting Students on the Path to Learning: The Case for Fully Guided Instruction*, AM. EDUCATOR (Spring 2012), at 8.

4. *Id.*

5. *Id.* at 9.

6. MILLER, *supra* note 2, at 58.

7. *See id.* at 59; Inbar Levy, *Simplifying Legal Decisions: Factor Overload in Civil Procedure Rules*, 41 MELB. U. L. REV. 727, 756 (2017). Knowledge structures, or schemata, are the mental structures that act as the framework through which humans organize information and interpret the world around them. *See generally* SHARAN B. MERRIAM & LISA M. BAUMGARTNER, LEARNING IN ADULTHOOD: A COMPREHENSIVE GUIDE 347–50 (4th ed. 2020).

8. *See* Amanda L. Gilchrist, *How Should We Measure Chunks? A Continuing Issue in Chunking Research and a Way Forward*, 6 FRONT PSYCHOL. 1456 (2015).

may be able to hold a great deal of information in their working memory because the information in the knowledge structure of their brains are well-connected and treated as a single chunk, while a novice may be able to hold considerably less in their working memory as each piece of new information is a single chunk. Interestingly, people's visual working memory and auditory working memory are on two separate, but interconnected channels, so working memory can be extended when information is introduced through visual and audial methods working in concert.[9] Even with both channels processing information, however, learners can only hold on to a limited amount of information.

Working memory that is not discarded is processed and categorized into the brain as long-term memory. Long-term memory is stored in knowledge structures called *schema*, which organize information according to how the person uses it.[10] Long-term memory is thought to be infinite, but it can be challenging to pull infrequently used information or information without strongly connected schema out of long-term memory into working memory.[11] The more practiced a person is at using any given schema, the more automated it becomes.[12] Eventually, schema that have been retrieved from the long-term memory and used frequently barely register as a chunk of information in working memory because that information is so deeply ingrained in the long-term memory, leaving more space in the working memory for the new information being processed.[13]

Cognitive load theorists explain that learning complex, novel information exhausts students' finite working memory and argue that there is a limit to how much information learners are able to absorb at any one time.[14] Cognitive load is broken down into three types. The first is *intrinsic cognitive load*, which refers to the inherent difficulty of the material students are learning.[15] For example, a complex calculus problem is much more difficult than a basic mathematical calculation like 10+10. Instructors have no control over this inherent difficulty; they can only limit the amount of material they choose to cover. The second type of cognitive load is *germane cognitive load*, which is a subset of intrinsic load that refers to the amount of cognitive capacity the working memory must use to develop the schema in long-term memory.[16] Germane cognitive load refers to the work or strategies one uses to systematically organize information to make it easier to learn and remember; typical

---

9. *See generally* Richard E. Mayer & Roxana Moreno, *A Split-Attention Effect in Multimedia Learning: Evidence for Dual Processing Systems in Working Memory*, 90 J. EDUC. PSYCH. 312 (1998).

10. *See* Levy, *supra* note 7, at 756.

11. Clark, *supra* note 3, at 9.

12. *Id.*

13. MICHELLE D. MILLER, MINDS ONLINE: TEACHING EFFECTIVELY WITH TECHNOLOGY 79–80 (2014).

14. Pass, *supra* note 2, at 2; Sweller, *supra* note 2, at 299.

15. John Sweller, *Cognitive Load Theory: Recent Theoretical Advances*, in COGNITIVE LOAD THEORY 29, 40–41 (Jan L. Plass et al. eds., 2010).

16. *Id.* at 42–43.

examples include instructional design strategies used to help integrate new learning, such as interleaving, reflective exercises, worked examples, and flowcharts.[17]

The last type of cognitive load is *extraneous cognitive load*, which is information unnecessary to the current learning objectives.[18] Extraneous cognitive load interferes with student learning by taking up attention and space in working memory that could otherwise be spent on the immediate learning goals.[19] Typically, extraneous cognitive load is a result of ineffectual instructional design and can be reduced with strong course planning based in evidence-based learning strategies.[20] Examples of extraneous load include unclear examples, PowerPoint presentations with too much text or that are hard to read, and instructions or technology that are difficult to navigate.[21] Because first-generation law students have cognitive burdens that take up the limited space in their working memory, it is critical to reduce extraneous cognitive load so that as much room as possible is left in the working memory for the intrinsic difficulty of the material they are learning.

Cognitive Load and the First Gen Law Student

All law students experience cognitive overload during their legal education, as they are being introduced to high volumes of new information in a very short period, and with minimal opportunity to rehearse the information they receive. Even for students with some familiarity with the law and some existing knowledge structures for legal concepts, it is challenging to hold on to the large volume of new information they are encountering daily. The limits of working memory are likely surpassed more quickly for first-generation law students than their non-first-generation classmates for two primary reasons.

First, many first-generation students have little to no exposure to the law or legal professionals. Some first-generation law students have never met an attorney, while some of their multi-generation classmates grew up in a household where they were exposed to vocabulary and discussions about the law and navigating the law school experience at an earlier age.[22] As such, words used in class may be firmly integrated

17. Jesse Fuhrman, *Cognitive Load Theory: Helping Students' Learning Systems Function More Efficiently*, Int'l Inst. for Innovative Instruction (June 6, 2017), https://www.franklin.edu/institute/blog/cognitive-load-theory-helping-students-learning-systems-function-more-efficiently.

18. Terri L. Enns & Monte Smith, *Take a (Cognitive) Load Off: Creating Space to Allow First-Year Legal Writing Students to Focus on Analytical and Writing Processes*, 20 J. Legal Writing Inst. 109, 111 (2015).

19. Julie Dirksen, Design for How People Learn 167 (2016).

20. Roxana Moreno & Babette Park, *Cognitive Load Theory: Historical Development and Relation to Other Theories*, in Cognitive Load Theory, *supra* note 15, at 9, 11.

21. Dirksen, *supra* note 19, at 167.

22. *See, e.g.*, A. Benjamin Spencer & Charleigh Kondas, *Law Schools Must Do More to Retain First-Generation Students*, U.S. Law Week (Feb. 15, 2022), https://news.bloomberglaw.com/us

into the schema in some students' long-term memories and can more easily be used in combination with new learning. For first-generation students, grappling with new vocabulary can take up significant space in their working memory. This leaves less room for other new information conveyed in class; there's not as much remaining space in their working memory to work with and begin retaining more complex new learning. While they may be able to make up for these gaps with added study before and after class, this may be difficult, as many first-generation students must work part-time jobs to afford their education.[23]

The second is that first-generation law students may have extra cognitive burdens taking up precious limited space in their working memories. With large percentages of first-generation law students coming from lower socioeconomic and historically underrepresented backgrounds,[24] many may experience cognitive disruptions that can make learning more challenging, including stereotype threat and imposter syndrome. These cognitive burdens take up space in their working memory, leaving less space for the new learning.

Stereotype Threat and Cognitive Capacity

Stereotype threat is the socially premised psychological threat members of a stereotyped group feel when they are in situations or performing acts for which a negative stereotype about their group applies.[25] Those experiencing these threats demonstrate significant apprehension of confirming or being judged by the stereotype.[26] For first-generation law students, there are multiple stereotype threats that could arise in their law school experience—stereotypes based on gender, race, socioeconomic status, and more—with many first-generation students potentially falling into more than one stereotyped group. Sensitive subjects covered in many law school classes can trigger stereotype threats, as can interactions with other people in the law school and societal events.[27]

-law-week/law-schools-must-do-more-to-retain-first-generation-students (describing some of the differences between first-generation law students and their classmates with lawyers in the family).

23. Melissa Jones, *First Generation Law Students: Barriers to Success* 40 (Aug. 2021) (Ed.D. Dissertation, University of Mississippi), available at https://egrove.olemiss.edu/etd/2110 (explaining that all first-generation law student participants in her study worked part-time jobs).

24. Jacqueline M. Bryant & Katharine Traylor Schaffzin, *First-Generation Law Students in Law School: A Proven Success Model*, 70 Ark. L. Rev. 913, 931–32 (2018) (citing Law Sch. Survey of Student Engagement, Looking Ahead: Assessment in Legal Education 8, 10–11 (2014)).

25. *See* Claude M. Steele & Joshua Aronson, *Stereotype Threat and the Intellectual Test Performance of African Americans*, 69 J. Personality & Soc. Psych. 797, 797 (1995).

26. *Id.*

27. *See* Michael Inzlicht & Talia Ben-Zeev, *A Threatening Intellectual Environment: Why Females Are Susceptible to Experiencing Problem-Solving Deficits in the Presence of Males*, 11 Psych. Sci. 365, 369 (2000) (demonstrating that even situations that bring one's negatively stereotyped identity to

Negative stereotypes about one's abilities and intelligence create additional stressors that impact one's cognitive capacity. Complex cognitive tasks require extended and focused attention and processing, as well as effective self-regulation.[28] Stereotype threat disrupts each of these. In their study on how stereotypes affect student performance, Toni Schmader, Michael Johns, and Chad Forbes describe three ways in which stereotype threat disrupts students' cognitive performance; (1) stereotype threat acts as a physiological stressor splitting students' attention; (2) stereotype threat leads to a tendency to actively monitor performance, rather than focusing on course content; and (3) students' efforts to self-regulate and push down their negative thoughts and emotions act as a barrier to learning.[29]

First, regardless of how stereotypes are triggered, the attention of students whose identities are under threat is immediately split.[30] With attention necessary for sensory impressions to enter working memory,[31] this split focus will have a direct impact on what new information students are able to absorb. With the anxiety these students feel about their performance confirming a stereotype taking up some of the space in their working memory, they can have less room in their working memory to process their learning.[32] Since new information can only be held in the working memory for a limited time,[33] interrupting thoughts about confirming stereotypes may result in first-generation students failing to retain important pieces of information. This may result in this information not being transferred into the knowledge structures in their long-term memories for later use.

Second, when negative stereotypes about a student's social identity arise, they are motivated to combat that stereotype, causing an extra situational burden that can interfere with the ability to perform as well at a task as they might otherwise be able.[34] Instead of focusing solely on the content they are learning in class, that student's hyper-alertness for signs of threats and for evidence of how successfully they are completing the task leads to "more cautious and systematic performance as opposed to the eager and creative performance seen by those who are positively stereotyped."[35] The process of monitoring one's performance likely relies on the same working memory resources necessary to complete the task one is working on to the

---

mind can trigger stereotype threat); *see generally* CLAUDE M. STEELE, WHISTLING VIVALDI: HOW STEREOTYPES AFFECT US AND WHAT WE CAN DO (2010).

28. Toni Schmader, Michael Johns & Chad Forbes, *An Integrated Process Model of Stereotype Threat Effects on Performance*, 115 PSYCH. REV. 336, 340 (2008).

29. *See generally id.*

30. *Id.* at 342–43 (2008).

31. JAMES M. LANG, DISTRACTED: WHY STUDENTS CAN'T FOCUS AND WHAT YOU CAN DO ABOUT IT 46 (2020).

32. Schmader, *supra* note 28, at 342.

33. *See supra* text accompanying notes 3–5.

34. Schmader, *supra* note 28, at 337.

35. *Id.* at 343.

best of one's ability.[36] Split attention from self-monitoring and the limited space and duration of working memory could result in important information vanishing before making it to long-term memory.

Finally, regulating negative thoughts and feelings that arise because of stereotype threat further contributes to cognitive inefficiency.[37] Students who experience the burden of negative stereotypes understandably suffer from thoughts of self-doubt, task-related concerns, and feelings of dejection. Students' efforts to suppress these natural emotional reactions impair working memory. The same cognitive functioning needed for successful performance may instead be used up trying to perform self-regulation and control one's emotions during class, to the detriment of learning.[38]

First-generation law students experiencing stereotype threat have burdens to their cognitive capacity that other students do not share, making learning more difficult. Unfortunately, stereotype threat is not the only cognitive burden that first-generation students may experience.

Imposter Syndrome and Cognitive Capacity

Many first-generation law students also experience imposter syndrome.[39] People suffering from imposter syndrome attribute their successes to external factors, such as luck or good timing, rather than their own abilities, despite their history of high achievement.[40] Those with imposter syndrome fear that those around them will discover they are imposters and confirm their beliefs that they do not belong.[41]

Imposter syndrome is well documented in higher education and has been found in minoritized students, women, and first-generation students.[42] For those with imposter syndrome, it is easy to mix up being inexperienced with being unqualified if they struggle to grasp material that is new to them.[43] Students with imposter syndrome may distort the normal desirable difficulties of the learning process with the

---

36. *Id.* at 343–44.

37. *Id.* at 345.

38. *Id.* at 346–47.

39. *See* Dawn Young & Ricardo Santiago, *Looking at the Challenges Facing First-Generation Law Students (And How to Address Them)*, Student Law. (Oct. 14, 2021), *available at* https://abaforlawstudents.com/2021/10/14/the-challenges-facing-first-generation-law-students/.

40. Chelsey L. Holden et al., *Imposter Syndrome Among First- and Continuing-Generation College Students: The Role of Perfectionism and Stress*, J. Coll. Student Retention: Rsch., Theory & Prac. (2021), chrome-extension://efaidnbmnnnibpcajpcglclefindmkaj/https://journals.sagepub.com/doi/pdf/10.1177/15210251211019379.

41. David A. Grenardo, *The Phantom Menace to Professional Identity Formation and Law Success: Imposter Syndrome*, 47 U. Dayton L. Rev. 369, 371 (2022).

42. Holden, *supra* note 41.

43. Lacy Rakestraw, *How to Stop Feeling Like a Phony in Your Library: Recognizing the Causes of the Imposter Syndrome, and How to Put a Stop to the Cycle*, 109 L. Libr. J. 465, 473 (2017).

idea that they are not smart enough to be in law school and seemingly confirm their misconceptions about themselves. Those experiencing imposter syndrome see successes as accidental or lucky and failures as inevitable.[44]

Feelings of imposter syndrome in first-generation law students are impacted by pressures to be the first person in their family to succeed and by the growing distance many first-generation students begin to feel with their families as they work to fit in with their new world.[45] They may feel like they have their feet in two worlds, no longer fitting in with their family units—as many families are unable to understand all that it takes to succeed in law school—and feeling alien from classmates who do not share the same pressures they do.[46] This can result in them feeling like an outsider both at school and at home.

The competitive environment of law school exacerbates these feelings. For first-generation law students who overcame significant barriers to succeed in their undergraduate education, realizing that techniques that worked earlier in their college careers are not enough to thrive in law school can also be debilitating. Studies have shown that classroom experiences that are competitive may increase feelings of imposter syndrome in first-generation students.[47] Competitive classroom environments like law school, with curves, class rankings, and competition for jobs, can have detrimental impacts on all students' confidence, motivation, and overall learning, but these environments have a particular impact on first-generation students.[48] For some students, this may be due to a cultural mismatch between the communal values many first-generation students are used to, in which working with and relying on others is common, and the individualist values emphasized in competitive educational environments.[49]

These feelings—fear of alienation from their families and not fitting in at school and worries that they cannot compete with their classmates—breed anxiety. When humans are stressed, the brain "overrides cognitive sources of energy deemed less of a priority," including learning.[50] The feelings of anxiety that accompany imposter syndrome can take up important space in students' limited working memory.[51] Stu-

44. Grenardo, *supra* note 42, at 372.

45. Holden, *supra* note 41, at (describing the tension between first-generation students' awareness of being the first in their family to attend colleges and succeeding for their families and those to come behind them, and their families not requiring all that is needed to succeed).

46. Mark P. Orbe, *Negotiating Multiple Identities Within Multiple Frames: An Analysis of First-Generation College Students*, 53 Commc'n Educ. 131, 133 (2004).

47. *See generally* Elizabeth A. Canning et al., *Feeling Like an Imposter: The Effect of Perceived Classroom Competition on the Daily Psychological Experiences of First-Generation College Students*, 11 Soc. Psych. & Personality Sci. 647 (2020).

48. *See id.*

49. *Id.* at 652.

50. Jackie E. Shay & Cathy Pohan, *Resilient Instructional Strategies: Helping Students Cope and Thrive in Crisis*, 22 J. Microbiology & Biology Educ. 1, 1 (2021).

51. *See id.* (describing how anxiety can add to students' cognitive load).

dents' attention—similar to students experiencing stereotype threat—is split. This divided attention can result in students missing important information during sensory impression phase. Stress associated with imposter syndrome can also disrupt students' cognitive processing while using new learning, resulting in it not making it to their long-term memories. First-generation students' concerns that someone will find them out if they answer a question poorly or struggle with some aspect of their coursework will be on their minds, taking up space that needs to be free for the most successful learning.

In addition, the student with imposter syndrome may either overwork—to the point of exhaustion, another cognitive disruptor—to try to keep their imposter status a secret, or may become disengaged, believing that they will fail no matter how hard they work.[52] Even those motivated to act the part to make sure they are not "found out" will find themselves not focusing solely on the task at hand.[53] Like the student with stereotype threat monitoring their performance to ensure they do not confirm their stereotype, the student with imposter syndrome will often engage in self-monitoring to ensure they don't give themselves away.[54] This self-monitoring can take up space that would ideally be reserved for focusing on their class materials.[55] Finally, distracting thoughts, such as alienation between themselves and their communities and fear of failure, can overload first-generation students' cognitive capacity. The mental space needed to regulate their emotions impairs working memory.

Reducing Cognitive Load for All Students

While cognitive capacity will never be equal for everyone, there are steps law professors can take to reduce extraneous cognitive load for their students. While these strategies will help all students, they may be particularly helpful for first-generation students.

The first step instructors can take is to provide a list of important terminology to all their students at the start of the semester. Low-stakes quizzing of the students on this vocabulary will help ensure it becomes well-ingrained in all students' long-term memory. Demystifying this vocabulary early on helps students prepare to hear and understand the language that will be used in lectures during the remainder of the semester and sets the tone that there will be terminology that is new to students. Normalizing that there is terminology that will be new to many students can help reduce feelings of imposter syndrome that may arise when a term is used, and stu-

---

52. Elizabeth Ramsey & Deana Brown, F*eeling Like a Fraud: Helping Students Renegotiate Their Academic Identities*, 25 COLL. & UNDERGRADUATE LIBRS. 86, 87 (2018).

53. Rakestraw, *supra* note 43, at 467.

54. *See supra* notes 50 through 53 and accompanying text.

55. *Id.*

dents assume everyone else knows what it means.[56] This pre-training help reduce cognitive overload when the class later engages in important learning using that terminology, since students are no longer having to grapple with unfamiliar vocabulary and concepts.[57]

Second, instructors should use transparently designed assignments, based on the Transparency in Learning and Teaching in Higher Education (TILT) framework.[58] The TILT framework explicitly focuses on how students are learning, why instructors are asking students to learn the way they are, and how they will use this learning in their lives after school.[59] Transparency is an important equity issue for learners. As Mary-Ann Winkelmes, the lead investigator at the TILT Project, describes:

> not all college students figure out on their own the reasons why assignments and homework are structured as they are, how to approach the required work, how the work benefits their learning, how to monitor if they are working effectively, and if they are working in a way that will meet the teacher's goals. This is knowledge that all students should possess *before* they start working on a project, but first-generation, underrepresented, and low-income students often don't start with this knowledge. They'll spend valuable work time struggling to figure out the whys and hows of an assignment before they can get to work on it.[60]

When using transparently designed assignments, instructors communicate with their students the purpose, task, and criteria for success of an assignment.[61] The purpose should explain the skills that will be practiced and the knowledge that will be gained by doing the assignment, including long-term relevance to students' lives.[62] The task should explain what students will do and the steps for how to do it.[63]

---

56. *See* Amy H. Soled & Barbara Hoffman, *Identifying the Imposters in Your Legal Writing Classroom*, 26 Legal Writing: J. Legal Writing Inst. 181, 184 (2022) (describing how normalizing the feelings of imposter syndromes as one way to address imposter syndrome in the classroom).

57. Richard E. Meyer and Roxana Moreno, *Nine Ways to Reduce Cognitive Load in Multimedia Learning*, 38 Educ. Psych. 43, 47 (2003); Richard E. Meyer, *Applying the Science of Learning to Medical Education*, 44 Med. Educ. 543, 548 (2010) (describing how receiving pre-training in key concepts can help people better learn concepts in some educational contexts).

58. Mary-Ann Winkelmes, *Transparency and Problem-centered Learning*, YouTube (May 8, 2017), https://www.youtube.com/watch?v=xqUQhSKmD9U&feature=youtu.be.

59. *Id.*

60. Mary-Ann Winkelmes, *Transparency in Teaching and Learning, Project Information Literacy*, Smart Talk Interview, no. 25 (2015), projectinfolit.org/smart-talk-interviews/transparency-in-teaching-and-learning.

61. Laurel Willingham-McClain, *Just a TAD—Transparent Assignment Design*, Flourishing Academic (Dec. 8, 2017), flourishingacademic.wordpress.com/2017/12/08/just-a-tad-assignment-design/.

62. Mary-Ann Winkelmes, *Transparency Framework 1 Purpose*, YouTube (Mar. 14, 2017), https://www.youtube.com/watch?v=PxndXE5_qMc&feature=youtu.be.

63. Mary-Ann Winkelmes, *Transparency Framework 2 Task*, YouTube (Mar. 14. 2017), https://www.youtube.com/watch?v=c_DMDRUSedU&feature=youtu.be.

Finally, the criteria for success make it clear what excellence looks like, often in the form of a checklist or rubric.[64] All three are given to the student in advance of completing the assignment so students can self-evaluate their work before turning it in.[65] "TILTing" assignments provides structure to students so that they know what is expected and helps them measure whether they are meeting the anticipated standards. While the TILT framework has not been studied in law students, its results in helping underserved students succeed have been shown across all different subject areas and college types at the undergraduate level.[66] With first-generation law students struggling with many of the same obstacles as undergraduate learners, using transparency in designing assessments would likely make a significant impact.

With the American Bar Association emphasizing the importance of formative assessments in legal education,[67] using the TILT framework can ensure law students have the tools to get the most out of and succeed on assignments. TILT methods show an impact for all students, with even greater benefits for underserved students, including first-generation students.[68] Transparent assignment design has shown increased academic confidence and sense of belonging for these underserved populations, which may help mitigate stereotype threat and imposter syndrome. Instructors interested in using the TILT framework can find a substantial set of examples across many subject matters, as well as a template and checklist for creating transparent assignments on the Transparency in Learning and Teaching Project website.[69]

Finally, instructors should minimize choices that result in more extraneous cognitive load. There are two primary ways to do so: (1) reducing instructional design choices that lead to extraneous load; and (2) designing their courses relying on existing schema in the knowledge structures of students' long-term memories.[70]

Regarding reducing extraneous load that comes from poor instructional design choices, one important step is ensuring that all visual materials (slides, handouts) and verbal content (written text and spoken word) are clear and concise and do not compete. When you have multiple sources of information, learners' attention can

---

64. Mary-Ann Winkelmes, *Transparency Framework 3 Criteria*, YouTube (Mar. 14, 2017), https://www.youtube.com/watch?v=DXjR9qbvzF8&feature=youtu.be.

65. Winkelmes, *supra* note 58.

66. *See, e.g.*, *Tilt Higher Ed Examples and Resources*, TILT HIGHER ED, https://tilthighered.com/tiltexamplesandresources (last visited Nov. 1, 2022) (see resources under Talking About Transparent Instruction dropdown).

67. American Bar Association, *ABA Standards and Rules of Procedure for Approval of Law Schools 2022–2023*, at 26 (2022) (Standard 314) (requiring law schools to use formative assessment in their curriculum to "measure and improve student learning and provide meaningful feedback to students").

68. Winkelmes, *supra* note 58.

69. TILT *Higher Ed Examples and Resources, supra* note 66.

70. *See generally* Richard E. Meyer, *Techniques That Reduce Extraneous Cognitive Load and Manage Intrinsic Load During Multimedia Learning*, in COGNITIVE LOAD THEORY, *supra* note 15, at 131.

become split between them, adding to cognitive load.[71] For example, slides used during course lectures should limit text, as seen in Image 21.1 below, as trying to listen to the instructor while reading can overwhelm students' cognitive capacity, especially if the language being used is not identical.[72] Because spoken language—the lecture—and written text—the slides—both rely on the verbal channel in the working memory, it can be easy to overload that channel.[73] In addition, instructors must use images carefully. While images are helpful, they should be related to the material at hand; pictures that are not related to the teaching and learning objectives serve as a distraction and take up space in students' working memory that could better be reserved for the concepts being discussed.

Research has shown that using images and text in concert with one another can actually be immensely helpful to students if done properly.[74] When the same information is presented in two formats—audial and visual, there is more space in the working memory because of its two separate processing channels.[75] Using this dual coding gives novice learners two ways to remember the information later on, making it easier to retrieve from long-term memory.[76] However, it is critical that any textual information that describes the visual be situated so that it can be absorbed easily by learners, as in Image 21.1 below; placing textual explanations of visual away from the diagram requires students to waste mental energy switching back and forth between the visuals and the diagram, as seen in Image 21.2. [77] Cognitive overload is reduced when the visual incorporates labels or other text into diagrams, rather than placing them below or to the side, as in Image 21.2.[78]

---

71. Meyer & Moreno, *supra* note 57, at 45.
72. *See id.* at 46 (recommending offloading some materials from the visual channel to the auditory channel).
73. *Id.*
74. Oliver Caviglioli, Dual Coding with Teachers 22–23 (2019).
75. *Id.*
76. *Id.* at 23. Studies show that this technique may actually be detrimental to learners with high prior knowledge due to redundancy effect, but this should not apply to most law students. *See* John Sweller et al., *Cognitive Architecture and Instructional Design*, 10 Educ. Psych. Rev. 251, 283–86 (1998).
77. Caviglioli, *supra* note 75, at 30.
78. *Id.*

Image 21.1

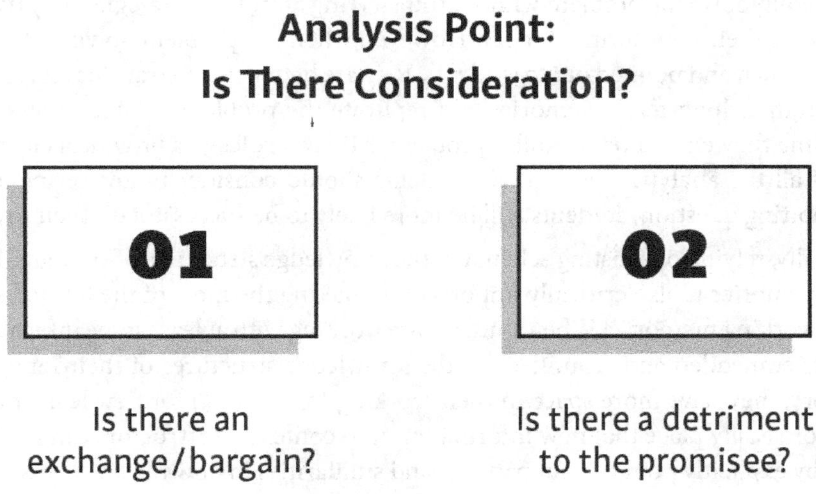

Image 21.2

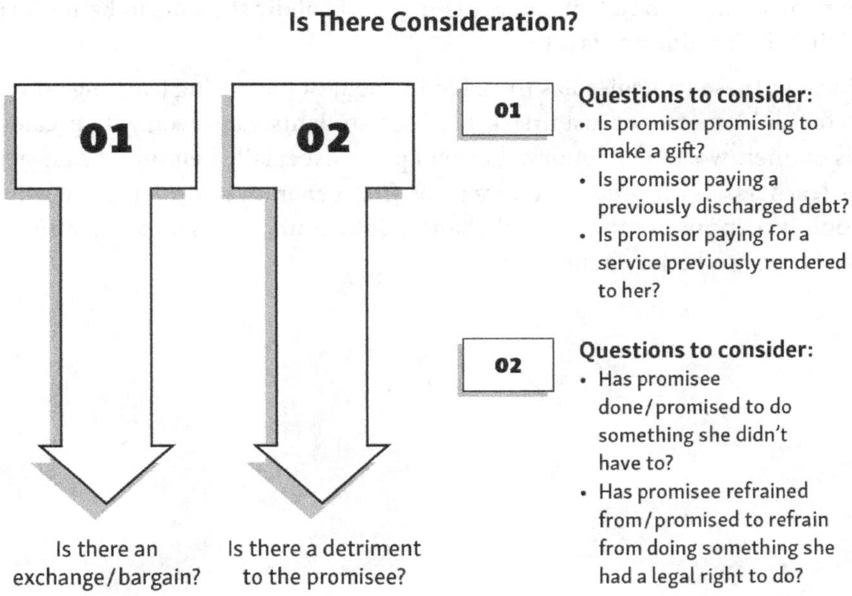

Clear worked examples can also help reduce cognitive overload. Worked examples give learners step-by-step demonstrations of how to complete a task or solve a problem, with each stage thoroughly explained. Research shows that when students are working on solving a problem, most, if not all, of their cognitive capacity is focused on solving the problem, leaving little room in the working memory to remember what methodologies they used to solve it after completing it.[79] Students may successfully solve the problem without transferring any of the strategies they used to do so into their long-term memory. However, when the problem-solving steps are broken down and pointed out to students, they are better able to transfer that knowledge to their long-term memories and replicate the problem-solving strategy the next time they encounter a similar problem.[80] If law professors provide a clear outline of all the analytical steps their students should consider in answering an issue-spotting question, students will be more likely to be successful on their exams.

Finally, relying on existing schema in the knowledge structures of students' long-term memories is also critically important in making the most of the limited space in the working memory.[81] When students are working with at least some information already embedded and "chunked" in the knowledge structures of their long-term memory, they have more space in their working information for new learning and can more easily place that new information into context.[82] Instructors can help students by explicitly pointing out patterns and similarities in how the law treats different topics. It can also be helpful to use the same fact pattern where possible, as a familiar scenario will not take up as much space in the working memory. Even giving students the fact scenario they will be engaging with during class as a pre-class assignment so they can read it and get familiar will allow students to better focus on applying the law during class time.

Each of these strategies has the added benefit of increasing learning and retention for all learners, not just first-generation students. However, with greater burdens on their working memory, they will prove especially helpful for first-generation learners. With greater numbers of first-generation students entering law school, incorporating these small changes into course design can ensure that all students have a better chance at success.

---

79. *Cognitive Load Theory in Practice: Examples for the Classroom*, Center for Educ. Stat. & Evaluation (2018), at 11.

80. *Id.*

81. Alyson M. Drake, *Building on CREAC: Reimagining the Research Log as a Tool for Legal Analysis*, 52 U. Memphis L. Rev. 57, 69 (2021)

82. *Cognitive Load Theory in Practice: Examples for the Classroom*, *supra* note 79, at 11.

PART VII A New Language: Legal Research and Writing

Twenty-Two

First Gen Students and Legal Research

Dajiang Nie*

I. Introduction

FIRST-GENERATION LAW STUDENTS (FGLS) MAKE UP A LARGE PORTION of the law student population.[1] They have many unique challenges, many of which extend to the legal research courses as well. Therefore, legal research instructors are responsible for structuring legal research courses to help FGLS mitigate these challenges. This essay discusses some of the techniques that legal research instructors can use to support the success of FGLS. For the purposes of this article, a law student is a member of FGLS if "neither parent had received a bachelor's degree or higher."[2]

II. Course Preparation

A. Supporting Students with Equipment

Unlike doctrinal courses in law school, legal research courses now require students to use computers. Two-thirds of lawyers regularly use fee-based databases for legal research.[3] Consequently, while faculty in legal research courses still teach students to use print resources,[4] they mostly emphasize databases like Westlaw and

---

* Associate Librarian of Law, Electronic & Digital Services Librarian, Texas Tech University School of Law. The author wishes to thank Jamie J. Baker, Catherine Christopher, Brie Sherwin, and Brittany Morris for their comments.

1. Law Sch. Survey of Student Engagement, Looking Ahead: Assessment in Legal Education 10 (2014), http://lssse.indiana.edu/wp-content/uploads/2016/01/LSSSE_2014_Annual Report.pdf (hereinafter Law Sch. Survey).

2. *Id.*

3. A Study of Attorneys' Legal Research Practices and Opinions of New Associates' Research Skills 33 (2013), https://www.aallnet.org/allsis/wp-content/uploads /sites/4/2018/01/final_report_07102013.pdf.

4. ALL-SIS Legal Research & Sourcebook Committee, *2010–2011 Legal Research Survey Results & Report* 10, https://www.aallnet.org/allsis/wp-content/uploads/sites/4/2018/01/ALL-SISLegal ResearchReport-final-with-attmts5.pdf (hereinafter ALL-SIS Survey).

LexisNexis.[5] Without a suitable electronic device with internet access, students cannot access these databases.

However, many FGLS heavily rely on student loans. They need student loans more than continuing-generation law students (CGLS),[6] and they borrow more.[7] Even the most affordable laptop may still cost a student two or three hundred dollars, so it is indeed a financial burden for FGLS. Legal research instructors may have seen students using their cellphones in class instead of computers to use the legal research database. Still, the research experience with a phone is awful compared to using a computer, even if the phone is more affordable. Because the database's user interface is different on a cell phone than on a laptop, and the instructor's database demonstration is delivered on a computer, it is more challenging for students to use the database on a cell phone.

Consequently, legal research faculty need to utilize the resources of law schools to ensure that FGLS have a viable device to practice legal research and complete research assignments. While some law schools mandate a laptop for law students,[8] many law schools are prepared to support students with this special need. Some academic law libraries offer loaner laptops to students at the circulation desk,[9] and some law school IT departments provide the same service.[10] While policies on loaning laptops vary among law schools, students can at least get a functioning device for the period of a legal research session. Even if students cannot keep their laptops after the loan period, they can still use the law library's computer lab, which is always open to students. Legal research faculty should collect this information and update it regularly to instruct students how to use these resources.

B. Transparent Course Design

When designing legal research courses, faculty should assume that students do not have a background in legal research, even when teaching upper-level legal research courses. More specifically, faculty should not presume that students have previously learned such skills or that they understand the educational purposes of each component in the course.[11] FGLS are less likely to engage in legal-related ex-

---

5. *Id.* at 9.

6. Law Sch. Survey, *supra* note 2.

7. *Id.* at 11.

8. *E.g.*, Laptop Requirement of University of Denver, https://www.law.du.edu/technology/laptop-requirement.

9. *E.g.*, Borrowing Technology of Tarlton Law Library, https://tarlton.law.utexas.edu/access-materials/borrowing#s-lg-box-10280426.

10. *E.g.*, Loaner Laptops and Miscellaneous Devices of Yale Law School, https://law.yale.edu/information-technology-services/computing-equipment-software-printing-and-support/it-loaner-equipment.

11. Lisa M Nunn, 33 Simple Strategies for Faculty: A Week-By-Week Resource for Teaching First-Year and First-Generation Students 25–26 (2018).

periences before entering law school, such as taking pre-law courses in college, working in a law firm, or having family members who work in the legal field. Because everything in a legal research course is new to FGLS, they are less confident of academic success than CGLS, who have had such relevant experiences. Or, worse, FGLS may be intimidated and confused by complex legal research databases. As a result, the more information they have about the course, the more confident they will feel about learning legal research.[12] Therefore, it is incumbent upon the legal research faculty to improve the transparency of the course to support FGLS.[13]

Transparent course design extends to each class and each assignment throughout the semester,[14] and it focuses on two major elements at this stage: detailed learning outcomes and expectations, and explanations of the course structure. Legal research faculty are expected to provide students with a detailed and transparent syllabus. FGLS are intellectually equivalent to CGLS, but they have to spend more time at work for pay due to financial pressures.[15] Although they are eager to learn, they generally have to spend more time studying than CGLS.[16] However, studying hard does not mean that they are studying efficiently. Therefore, legal research faculty should clearly let students know their overall expectations for student performance and the most effective ways to learn in a legal research course.[17] For example, the instructor could make it clear in the syllabus whether *Bluebook* citations are required in assignments; and, if so, what weighting is given to *Bluebook* citations. In short, faculty should not leave students to guess.

It is worthwhile for faculty to take the time to explain to students the rationale for the structure of the course and the necessity for each course element.[18] In legal research courses, students learn both the "jurisprudential influence" aspect (why) and the mechanical aspect (how) of legal research.[19] Even though some scholars suggested the inclusion of Socratic pedagogy in legal research courses,[20] the pedagogical structure of legal research courses is fundamentally different from doctrinal courses. Many legal research courses consist of lectures, demonstrations, and in-

---

12. Jeff Davis, The First-Generation Student Experience: Implications for Practice, and Strategies for Improving Persistence and Success 186–87 (2010) (hereinafter Davis, Experience).

13. *See generally* Mary-Ann Winkelmes et al., *A Teaching Intervention That Increases Underserved College Students' Success*, 18 Peer Review 31 (2016).

14. *See* discussion *infra* Part IV.C.

15. Law Sch. Survey, *supra* note 2 at 11.

16. *Id.* at 11.

17. Barbara Gross Davis, Tools for Teaching 182–83 (1st ed. 1993) (hereinafter Davis, Teaching); Davis, Experience, *supra* note 13, at 182–184.

18. *See* Michael Hunter Schwartz et al., Teaching Law by Design 54 (2d ed. 2017).

19. Robert Berring & Kathleen Heuvel, *Teaching Advanced Legal Research: Philosophy and Context*, in Teaching Legal Research 57 (Barbra Bintliff & Duncan Alford eds., 2013).

20. Yasmin Sokkar Harker, *"Information Is Cheap, but Meaning Is Expensive": Building Analytical Skill into Legal Research Instruction*, 105 Law Libr. J. 79, 92 (2013).

class exercises.[21] Some legal research courses even apply a more unconventional model of instruction, flipped classroom.[22] Therefore, FGLS may not be comfortable with a legal research course focusing on practical experiences and simulating a professional legal research environment.[23] Explanations of the pedagogical benefit of each course element do not have to be on the syllabus; faculty can introduce them to students early in the semester. These explanations may not be as crucial to CGLS, but FGLS will benefit significantly.

III. Classroom Activities

It is the instructors' responsibility to adapt activities in the classroom to support FGLS learning legal research, as the classroom environment affects student learning.[24] A structured class creates a collaborative relationship among students, which is helpful for FGLS.[25] The following in-class activities generally serve two purposes: to enhance students' learning skills with pedagogical methods and help them overcome "imposter phenomenon,"[26] by creating an inclusive classroom that is transparent, mutually respectful,[27] supportive,[28] and non-intimidating.[29] While FGLS are the primary beneficiaries of these activities, CGLS can also enjoy the same advantages.

A. Group Exercises

Although all students can learn through in-class exercises individually, group exercises provide FGLS with extra learning support. In-class exercises are common in legal research classes because they are the best way to learn legal research.[30] Stu-

---

21. *See* Joe Atlas et al., A Guide to Teaching Lawyer Skills 100 (2012); *See also Kris Gilliland, A Motivational Perspective on First-Year Legal Research Instruction*, in Teaching Advanced Legal Research 66–67 (Barbra Bintliff & Duncan Alford eds., 2013).

22. *See generally* Laurel Davis et al., *Teaching Advanced Legal Research in a Flipped Classroom*, Perspectives: Teaching Legal Research & Writing 22, 13 (2013).

23. Susan Phillips, *"Like Sands Through the Hourglass...": How to Develop a Good Legal Research Problem*, in Teaching Advanced Legal Research 209 (Barbra Bintliff & Duncan Alford eds., 2013).

24. Sarah L. Eddy & Kelly A. Hogan, *Getting Under The Hood: How and for Whom Does Increasing Course Structure Work?*, 13 CBE Life Sci. Educ. 453, 454 (2014).

25. *See Id.* at 464–65.

26. Davis, Experience, *supra* note 13, at 186 (imposter phenomenon is "a special kind of self-esteem challenge that can impede the academic progress of first-generation college students more than it can other kinds of students).

27. Roy T. Stuckey et al., Best Practices for Legal Education: A Vision and a Road Map 114–116 (1st ed. 2007).

28. *Id.* at 118–119.

29. *Id.* at 122.

30. James B. Levy, *Escape to Alcatraz: What Self-Guided Museum Tours Can Show Us About Teaching Legal Research*, 44 N.Y.L. Sch. L. Rev. 387, 406 (2001).

dents cannot learn legal research simply by reading a textbook, listening to an instructor's lecture, or watching an instructor's demonstration.[31] Instead, students need hands-on experience to exercise what they have just learned after the instructor shows students how to perform a specific type of legal research. Group practices are a typical formative assessment method that focuses on improving students' learning as they go along.[32] Students participating in practice groups can receive immediate and targeted feedback from their peers to improve their learning,[33] and, ultimately, their academic performance on subsequent summative assessments.[34] In addition, law school study groups are undoubtedly helpful for FGLS, but they usually study alone, and faculty cannot force them to participate in these study groups.[35] In-class exercises can encourage FLGS to participate in extracurricular study groups with other students, which will benefit FGLS in the long run.

Small group exercises can alleviate student anxiety.[36] Law school is a stressful environment, which puts many students under stress,[37] but FGLS are more susceptible. While FGLS generally spend more time studying,[38] they also devote more time working for pay and are less engaged in law school co-curricular activities.[39] As a result, FGLS are more like to suffer from the stress of isolation and loneliness when they do not have enough opportunities to interact with their peers in law school. The financial burden of attending law school and an uncertain future can also lead to academic stress for FGLS. When law school grades determine a student's present and future,[40] coupled with the lack of academic advising from FGLS' families, academic stress further extends to every course of FGLS. Therefore, although faculty are not responsible for ensuring FGLS have friends in class, they can use in-class exercises to "encourage student interaction and the development of relationships."[41]

As a result, group in-class exercises can not only optimize FGLS's engagement in the classroom,[42] but also help them to enjoy and expand their social support

---

31. Phillips, *supra* note 24.

32. ABA, ABA STANDARDS & RULES OF PROCEDURE FOR APPROVAL OF LAW SCHOOLS 2020–2021, 26 (2021) (hereinafter ABA STANDARDS).

33. Thomas Michael McDonnell, *Joining Hands and Smarts: Teaching Manual Legal Research through Collaborative Learning Groups*, 40 J. LEGAL EDUC. 363, 366 (1990).

34. Eddy & Hogan, *supra* note 25 at 463.

35. DAVIS, EXPERIENCE, *supra* note 13, at 184–85; STUCKEY ET AL., *supra* note 28, at 120.

36. ATLAS ET AL., *supra* note 22.

37. Nancy J. Soonpaa, *Stress in Law Students: A Comparative Study of First-Year, Second-Year, and Third-Year Students*, 36 CONN. L. REV. 353, 378 (2004).

38. LAW SCH. SURVEY, *supra* note 2 at 11.

39. *Id.* at 11.

40. Steve H. Nickle, *Examining and Grading in American Law Schools*, 30 ARK. L. REV. 411, 411 (1977).

41. Christie Hand & Emily Miller Payne, *First-Generation College Students: A Study of Appalachian Student Success*, 32 J. DEV. EDUC. 4, 14 (2008).

42. Robin A. Boyle, *Employing Active-Learning Techniques and Metacognition in Law School: Shifting Energy from Professor to Student*, 81 U. DET. MERCY L. REV. 1, 24 (2003).

network to interact with other students.[43] This stress-free learning activity tells FGLS that faculty believe they have the potential to actively learn legal research in small and interactive groups,[44] so it reduces FGLS' academic stress.[45] More importantly, it helps FGLS make new friends and build social support networks in law school.[46] Such engagement in law school life may also contribute to the academic success of FGLS.[47]

B. Sharing Personal Experience in Legal Research

One of the in-class activities that legal research faculty can do is to share personal legal research experiences with students. Teachers should take action to help FGLS overcome their disdain for,[48] and lack of confidence in, legal research. Legal research is "highly complex,"[49] making it more challenging than many students expect. FGLS may spend more time on an assignment than they anticipate. When their research is unstructured, they may lose themselves. Or they may become frustrated when they spend a considerable amount of time studying and preparing for a high-stakes exam but do not do well on it. Reassurance from faculty is undoubtedly important for FGLS to gain confidence in their legal research, but simply telling them to "buck up" or "study harder" is not enough. Sharing personal experiences gives students "a sense of comfort and information" of legal research,[50] because it is beneficial to FGLS by putting the instructors themselves in the shoes of FGLS and creating a deep sense of empathy.[51] As a result, faculty should share personal narrative stories of difficulties and challenges they encountered in real legal search projects and how they eventually overcame them.[52] It is an excellent comfort to FGLS when they know even faculty struggled with the same concepts or skills as a law student.[53] Sharing these personal struggles does not stigmatize the instructor's reputation among FGLS. On the contrary, they will see their potential through the instructor's experiences: "if she can do it, so can I."

---

43. *See* McDonnell, *supra* note 34.

44. Clifford S. Zimmerman, *"Thinking Beyond My Own Interpretation:" Reflections on Collaborative and Cooperative Learning Theory in the Law School Curriculum*, 31 Ariz. St. L.J. 957, 959 (1999).

45. *Id.*

46. *See* Pamela Pierson et al., *Stress Hardiness and Lawyers*, 42 J. Legal Prof. 1, 57 (2017).

47. *See* Davis, Experience, *supra* note 13, at 193.

48. *See* American Association of Law Libraries, AALL State of the Profession, 32 (2019) (61.4% academic law librarians believe student overconfidence is a challenge in teaching legal research); *See* Michael J. Lynch, *An Impossible Task but Everybody Has to Do It—Teaching Legal Research in Law Schools*, 89 Law Libr. J. 415, 441 (1997).

49. Brooke J. Bowman, *Researching Across the Curriculum: The Road Must Continue Beyond the First Year*, 61 Okla. L. Rev. 503, 538 (2008).

50. Michael A. Mogill, *Our Students, Our Selves: The Mirror Reflects Back*, 32 Cap. U. L. Rev. 317, 326 (2003).

51. *See* M.K.B. Darmer, *Teaching Whren to White Kids*, 15 Mich. J. Race & L. 109, 125 (2009).

52. Schwartz et al., *supra* note 19, at 121

53. Davis, Experience, *supra* note 13, at 187.

Legal research taught in law school may still be disconnected or abstract to FGLS, even though legal research courses are skills-based courses.[54] An instructor's personal stories about legal research can fill the gap between courses and the real world. Of course, different faculty may have different interesting stories about legal research in their practice. For example, students enrolled in an advanced legal research course may learn about the cost factors of legal research databases, one of which is out-of-plan costs. Here is a story that faculty can use to emphasize the importance of being familiar with database licensing agreements. An attorney received a bill for thousands of dollars in database charges because he forgot to log out of database X last night, which charges Y dollars per minute. This vivid story captures students' attention and highlights the critical abstract point the instructor wants students to focus on.[55]

C. Recording the Class

Recording class is common practice in online legal research courses. However, even if a legal research course is a face-to-face course, as permitted by law school policy,[56] faculty should still record classrooms to make this course inclusive and supportive. First, law students come from diverse backgrounds and have varying degrees of learning ability. Some prefer to use books, while others prefer to use databases. Some can absorb new skills more quickly because of previously acquired knowledge or learned skills, whereas others may need to review the course material and practice newly acquired skills later to fully master them. Some of FGLS who are weaker learners need additional study assistance to improve their legal search learning,[57] because inaccurate, inappropriate, or insufficient prior learning strategies may hinder future learning.[58] To mitigate such an inequity, legal research faculty should provide additional assistance to FGLS for academic success.

Second, it is easy for students to get lost when instructors demonstrate research tools to tackle research questions, whether using print collections or digital databases. As one of the skills-based courses, legal research focuses on the legal research process.[59] However, no matter how hard instructors try to slow down the pace of

---

54. David L. Armond & Shawn G. Nevers, *The Practitioners' Council: Connecting Legal Research Instruction and Current Legal Research Practice*, 103 Law Libr. J. 575 (2011).

55. *See* Schwartz et al., *supra* note 19, at 82.

56. Law schools' current policy of recording in-person class varies. *See generally* Alexis Anderson, *Classroom Taping Under Legal Scrutiny—A Road Map for a Law School Policy*, 66 J. Legal Educ. 372 (2017).

57. Law Sch. Survey, *supra* note 2. (FGLS entered law school with lower average LSAT scores and lower UGPA than CGLS. Also, FGLS have a lower average grade than CGLS in law school).

58. Susan A. Ambrose et al., How Learning Works: Seven Research-Based Principles For Smart Teaching, 10–27 (2010).

59. Anthony Niedwiecki, *Teaching for Lifelong Learning: Improving the Metacognitive Skills of Law Students Through More Effective Formative Assessment Techniques*, 40 Cap. U. L. Rev. 149, 163 (2012).

demonstration, some students still experience disorientation. When confused students work on in-class exercises in small groups, their peers can help them; but they have nothing available except for the PowerPoint slides when they work on homework. Unfortunately, the slides do not include the vital research tool demonstration or subsequent in-class exercise demonstrations.

Third, not every student is ready to interact with the instructor.[60] Some students are reluctant to ask questions in class, fearing that they will interrupt the class.[61] Some are hesitant to ask instructor questions during office hours because they are intimidated by the professor or feel foolish for asking questions.[62] While not asking questions is certainly not an effective way to learn, there is no reason for instructors to leave these students behind.

Because of the pandemic, legal research faculty are quite familiar with classroom recording technologies, such as Panopto and Kaltura. Classroom recordings do not add a heavy burden to faculty,[63] but they do mean a lot to students. Students can review the recordings after face-to-face instruction to help them catch up on research steps they lost during the class. The recordings are also self-explanatory about research steps and techniques for the students, so they do not have to force themselves to leave their comfort zone by asking the instructor for help.

It is important to note that a face-to-face legal research course is recorded only to help students learn. It is not a substitute for student absence from in-person class,[64] whose nature is different from an online course. Also, since the most valuable part of the recordings is demonstrations, faculty can record only the portion of the demonstration, rather than the presentation and in-class exercises, when faculty have concerns about recording the entire class, such as the inappropriate use of the recording.[65]

---

60. Cortney Elizabeth Holles, *Faculty-Student Interaction and Impact on Well-Being in Higher Education* 135 (May, 2021) (Ph.D. dissertation, University of Northern Colorado), https://digscholarship.unco.edu/cgi/viewcontent.cgi?article=1745&context=dissertations.

61. *See, e.g.*, Andrea Flores, *A Family First: Adversity Doesn't Limit First-Generation Students*, The Daily Illini (Mar. 15, 2017), https://dailyillini.com/news-stories/2017/03/16/family-first-adversity-doesnt-limit-first-generation-students/.

62. *See, e.g.*, Chris Chester, *6 Tips for Low-Income and First-Generation College Students to Live By*, Am. Univ. Radio (Sept. 8, 2015), https://wamu.org/story/15/09/08/6-tips-for-low-income-first-gen-students/.

63. In fact, some law schools grant faculty the discretion to record the whole class by default. *E.g.*, Geo. Wash. L. Sch., Class Recording Policy (Sept. 3, 2021), https://www.law.gwu.edu/class-recording-policy.

64. Because of this, some law schools' policies set strict limitations when students can request a class to be recorded. E.g., U. Chi. L. Sch., Class Recording Policy, https://www.law.uchicago.edu/students/handbook/academicmatters/classrecording.

65. John Villasenor, *Why I Won't Let My Classes Be Recorded*, Chron. Higher Educ. (Jan. 10, 2020), https://www.chronicle.com/article/why-i-wont-let-my-classes-be-recorded/.

IV. Functioning Assignments

A. Formative Assessment Methods

Practice makes perfect. Learning legal research is no exception. Therefore, in addition to in-class exercises, both FGLS and CGLS need after-class assignments to learn. These assignments should be formative assessment methods. FGLS are always intrinsically motivated to learn,[66] but some lack effective study skills, which can negatively impact their academic performance.[67] An excellent way to help them overcome this challenge is to implement formative assessment methods in legal research courses. Formative assessments focus on using low-stakes assessments,[68] in students' learning process to "improve student learning" by "provid[ing] meaningful feedback,"[69] as recommended by the ABA.[70]

Formative assessments are different from traditional summative assessments. The goal of formative assessment is to improve student learning, not to "measure the degree of student learning."[71] Therefore, formative assessments always take the form of frequent, low-stakes tests rather than one-time, high-stakes final exams.[72] Ideally, formative assessments are structured so that an independent homework assignment follows each class. Fortunately, homework is the most common assessment tool in legal research courses,[73] and most homework assignments are low stakes.[74] However, these characteristics do not guarantee that homework is a formative assessment method. The key to a successful formative assessment method depends on timely and meaningful feedback from the legal research instructor.[75] In addition, the quality of the assignments themselves and the feedback provided by the instructor depend on many factors. Therefore, legal research faculty should carefully plan such

---

66. *See* Hand & Payne, *supra* note 42, at 8.

67. Jeanne Reid & James Moore, *College Readiness and Academic Preparation for Postsecondary Education*, 42 Urb. Educ. 240, 257 (2008).

68. *See generally* Olympia Duhart, "*It's Not for a Grade*": *The Rewards and Risks of Low-Risk Assessment in the High-Stakes Law School Classroom*, 7 Elon L. Rev. 491 (2015).

69. Aba Standards, *supra* note 33.

70. *Id.*

71. *Id.*

72. *See* Paul Black & Dylan Wiliam, *Assessment and Classroom Learning*, 5 Assessment Educ.: Principles, Pol'y & Prac. 7 (1998).

73. ALL-SIS Survey, *supra* note 5 at 15, 24-25; Christopher A. Knott, *On Teaching Advanced Legal Research*, in Teaching Advanced Legal Research 112 (Barbra Bintliff & Duncan Alford eds., 2013).

74. Advanced Legal Research Web Sourcebook Subcommittee, Report: ALL-SIS Committee on Legal Research: Advanced Legal Research Web Sourcebook Subcommittee 10, https://www.aallnet.org/allsis/wp-content/uploads/sites/4/2018/01/all-sisalrwebsource bookreport.pdf.

75. Regina Panasuk & John LeBaron, *Student Feedback: A Tool for Improving Instruction in Graduate Education*, 120 Educ. 356, 359 (2000).

formative assignments. This part will discuss some key elements of formative assessment in legal research courses to support FGLS.

B. Contextual Assignments, No Treasure Hunt

Faculty should use contextual assignments rather than treasure hunt assignments. Although most legal research courses use context-based research assignments,[76] many still use treasure hunt assignments.[77] Treasure hunt assignments are the primary assignments for teaching legal research in the bibliographic approach,[78] where "the student researcher is given a problem with a clear and correct answer, enabling the researcher to self-check the accuracy of the research process."[79]

The main disadvantage of the treasure hunt assignment is that it does not simulate the research of a real attorney,[80] because treasure hunt assignments isolate legal research skills from reading, analytical, and writing skills.[81] In addition, treasure hunt assignments require narrow and detailed instructions so that students can find the answers faculty expect.[82] Such instructions not only "spoon feed" students,[83] but also further break down the process of legal research. More importantly, such assignments ignore the research process by focusing only on answering questions with short and precise answers.[84]

The non-simulated learning experience may induce FGLS to develop false overconfidence in legal research. In contrast, simulation learning in a skills-oriented course should improve the academic and leadership skills of FGLS.[85] In contextual assignments, students are expected to use multiple skills simultaneously.[86] They need to examine a fact pattern through a research process guided by each ques-

---

76. Caroline L. Osborne, *The State of Legal Research Education: A Survey of First-Year Legal Research Programs, or "Why Johnny and Jane Cannot Research"*, 108 Law Libr. J. 403, 414 (2016) (57% of first-year legal research courses use integrated research-writing assignment and 37% of them use factual-based research hypotheticals).

77. *Id.*

78. *See* Lynch, *supra* note 49, at 430.

79. Margaret Butler, *Resource-Based Learning and Course Design: A Brief Theoretical Overview and Practical Suggestions*, 104 Law Libr. J. 219, 244 n.90 (2012).

80. Terry Jean Seligmann, *Beyond "Bingo!": Educating Legal Researchers As Problem Solvers*, 26 Wm. Mitchell L. Rev. 179, 191 (2000).

81. Frederick B. Jonassen, *On-Line Legal Research Workshops*, 22 St. Thomas L. Rev. 470, 483 (2010).

82. Phillips, *supra* note 24, at 211–12.

83. *Id.* at 212.

84. Jonassen, *supra* note 82.

85. *See* Emily Acevedo & Alexandra J Lazar, *Active Learning and Interpersonal Skills Development Among First-Generation College Students*, 19 Int'l Stud. Persp. 1, 17 (2021).

86. Simon Canick, Legal Research Assessment, in Teaching Legal Research 197 (Barbra Bintliff & Duncan Alford eds., 2013).

tion,[87] and such assignments "stimulate the real life research."[88] It means that assignments should guide students through a macro-research process to address a broad research question that brings together fragmented issues.[89] Process-based legal research frameworks are widely used in legal research instruction.[90] Some popular frameworks include Rombauer's five-step framework and Wren's three-step framework.[91]

Contextual assignments should also require students to document their research steps in detail, maybe on a research log,[92] to balance the learning of micro-research,[93] and to ensure that students understand how to properly use each research tool. While it is essential to focus on the big picture of legal research, students still need opportunities to exercise specific legal research tools. Without observing students' research steps, an instructor cannot detect whether students are using legal research tools effectively.[94] In addition, instructors' feedback is important to improve student learning, which is at the heart of formative assessment.[95] However, faculty are unlikely to provide meaningful feedback to students when their answers are only a few words long.[96] The more detailed students document their research process on a particular question, the more targeted feedback faculty can offer.[97] Only then will students enjoy the benefits of feedback that will improve their learning.

For example, two students find the same governing case for a research question that the instructor expects. However, one uses a leading secondary source as a starting point and finds the case using organized terms and connectors with appropriate filters. The other one simply searches for some natural language without limiting any jurisdictions. Although the second student gets thousands of search results, she finds the designated case after reading the top 10 cases in the search results. They both provide the faculty with the expected correct answer in terms of case citations without the need for research steps. However, there are severe problems with the second student's approach, but both the instructor and the student herself feel that

---

87. Phillips, *supra* note 24, at 212.

88. *Id.*

89. *See* Kristin B. Gerdy, *Teacher, Coach, Cheerleader, and Judge: Promoting Learning through Learner-Centered Assessment*, 94 LAW LIBR. J. 59, 72 (2002).

90. *See* Lynch, *supra* note 49, at 432; Nancy Vettorello, *Resurrecting (and Modernizing) the Research Treasure Hunt*, 109 LAW LIBR. J. 205, 210 (2017); See also ATLAS ET AL., *supra* note 22, at 99.

91. MARJORIE ROMBAUER, LEGAL PROBLEM SOLVING: ANALYSIS, RESEARCH, AND WRITING 145–146 (5th ed. 1991); CHRISTOPHER WREN & JILL ROBINSON WREN, THE LEGAL RESEARCH MANUAL: A GAME PLAN FOR LEGAL RESEARCH AND ANALYSIS 41–122 (2d ed. 1986).

92. *See generally* James B. Levy, *Better Research Instruction Through "Point of Need" Library Exercises*, 7 LEGAL WRITING: J. LEGAL WRITING INST. 87 (2001); See also ATLAS ET AL., *supra* note 22, at 101.

93. *See* Phillips, *supra* note 24, at 213.

94. Canick, *supra* note 87.

95. Panasuk & LeBaron, *supra* note 76.

96. Vettorello, *supra* note 91, at 217.

97. ATLAS ET AL., *supra* note 22, at 101.

the student is capable of finding cases effectively.[98] This erroneous signaling hurts both sides, undermining the teaching value of the instructor and the legal research competence of the student.

With the goal of emphasizing that legal research includes assessing legal resources and analyzing applicable law,[99] faculty should further hone their assignments for each question to avoid answers by copying text from resources or writing short answers without explanation.[100] In general, legal research faculty should avoid questions that ask students to "retrieve some factual information from the face of the source,"[101] because this approach focuses only on finding material and ignores the importance of analyzing the material found.[102] This approach is dangerous for FGLS who lack exposure to law practice.

The assignments should balance cognitive research skills, which are the ability to use a research source, with metacognitive research skills, which are the ability to understand when and why to use such a source.[103] With the help of the legal research database, students can easily find many materials on a legal issue on a research question, but they need to evaluate these materials to decide which one to use. The reality is that analyzing legal texts takes up most of the time in the legal research process,[104] and the complex nature of legal research demands a high level of thinking.[105] Understanding the material found during the research process can determine the direction of the research, but not vice versa.[106] If a question does not ask students to explain why they chose to use a found legal material or how they intend to use it, the legal research faculty cannot assess whether the students are capable of evaluating the found material. For example, what if a student chooses, without any explanation, to use a nonbinding case when several binding cases are available? Or, what if a student decides to use a binding case that has only one paragraph discussing the pertinent legal issue and does not provide the logic of choosing this case, while other cases not only bind the particular court, but also discuss the same legal issue in greater depth?

---

98. Vettorello, *supra* note 91, at 218.

99. Helene S. Shapo, *The Frontiers of Legal Writing: Challenges for Teaching Research*, 78 LAW LIBR. J. 719, 726 (1986).

100. For example, "Yes, the defendant has an affirmative defense." This answer fails to explain how the student reached this conclusion, which amounts to a treasure hunt where the student can copy language from the primary source without any explanation.

101. *See* Jonassen, *supra* note 82, at 482.

102. *See* Lynch, *supra* note 49, at 425.

103. ATLAS ET AL., *supra* note 22 (quoting Anthony S. Niedwiecki, *Lawyers and Learning: A Metacognitive Approach to Legal Education*, 13 WIDENER L. REV. 33, 43 (2006)).

104. *See* Lynch, *supra* note 49, at 429.

105. Vettorello, *supra* note 91, at 218.

106. *See* Lynch, *supra* note 49, at 425.

C. Rubrics

The rubric is part of the legal research faculty's ongoing commitment to transparency in course design. FGLS need to know what they can get out of a class and, more importantly, whether they actually learn as much as the instructor expects them to. Rubrics provide students with measurable learning goals because they tell students what they can expect to achieve by completing an assignment.[107] They further give the students norms for assignments at different levels of quality,[108] and therefore illustrate abstract learning outcomes. Third, rubrics give students additional transparency about assignments, to ensure the validity and reliability of grades,[109] because these learning outcomes are precisely "explicit guideposts about faculty expectations."[110] In this collaborative atmosphere, students are more motivated to learn because they know how to succeed in this class.[111] Rubrics also help students self-assess their performance,[112] so they help students take responsibility for "their own learning."[113] It means rubrics help FGLS to develop the cognitive process of learning.[114] Therefore, students need elaborate rubrics for each assignment that specify learning objectives and detail how to assess each learning outcome.[115]

The concrete rubrics should not "hide the ball" from students.[116] Legal research faculty should use "hot rubrics" rather than "cold rubrics."[117] Hot rubrics include both learning outcomes and observable, measurable standards to evaluate different levels of achievement for each learning outcome.[118] Cold rubrics, on the other hand, include only learning outcomes.[119] Cold rubrics are undoubtedly important because faculty can use cold rubrics as a teaching tool to design each session and each assignment,[120] with challenging but realistic learning outcomes to motivate students to

---

107. Ambrose et al., *supra* note 59, at 128–129.

108. Heidi Andrade & Anna Valtcheva, *Promoting Learning and Achievement Through Self-Assessment*, 48 Theory into Prac. 12, 13 (2009).

109. *See* Lori E. Shaw & Victoria L. VanZandt, Student Learning Outcomes and Law School Assessment: A Practical Guide to Measuring Institutional Effectiveness, 110–11 (2015).

110. Julie Ross & Diana Donahoe, *Lighting the Fires of Learning in Law School: Implementing ABA Standard 314 by Incorporating Effective Formative Assessment Techniques Across the Curriculum*, 81 U. Pitt. L. Rev. 657, 681 (2020).

111. Wilbert James McKeachie et al., McKeachie's Teaching Tips : Strategies, Research, and Theory for College and University Teachers 148 (Sue Pulvermacher-Alt et al. eds., 12th ed. 2006).

112. *Id.*

113. Alistair E. Newbern & Emily F. Suski, *Translating the Values of Clinical Pedagogy Across Generations*, 20 Clin. L. Rev. 181, 210–11 (2013).

114. Davis, Experience, *supra* note 13, at 183.

115. Atlas et al., *supra* note 22, at 116–17; Stuckey et al., *supra* note 28, at 168.

116. Gerdy, *supra* note 90 at 76.

117. Shaw & VanZandt, *supra* note 110, at118.

118. *Id.* at 142.

119. *Id.* at 141.

120. Schwartz et al., *supra* note 19, at 157–58.

learn.[121] However, without providing students with descriptions of "varying levels of quality, from excellent to poor" for each learning outcome,[122] students still do not "take the ball." As a result, they have to use their grades on assignments as the sole factor in surmising whether they have met the expectations of the instructor, rather than self-assessing the quality of their work as they work on it. Moreover, no matter how hard legal research faculty try to polish the language of learning outcomes, students will always struggle to understand abstract learning outcomes,[123] let alone self-assess them.

Transparency in course design further covers rubrics training. While it may be helpful "merely providing the rubric to student,"[124] faculty should spend time demonstrating to FLGS how to use rubrics in their assignments.[125] A ten-minute demonstration of the assignment rubric at the beginning of the semester, preferably using de-identified previous student work of varying quality,[126] is sufficient to give students a concrete foundation for using rubrics. For FGLS who have never used rubrics before and those who have not used rubrics in the best way, such brief training adds more value to rubrics than simply sharing the rubrics with students and telling them to "go ahead and use it."[127] In addition, though FGLS and CGLS have equal buy-in to homework assignment type of formative assessment method,[128] faculty should explain the pedagogical logic to students during the training.[129] It helps FGLS understand that the rubric is a powerful learning tool that deserves their extra time to use.

D. Encouraging Time Recording

Faculty should encourage, but not require, students to log time for each assignment. It is common for FGLS to lack time management skills.[130] In the case of legal search learning, it is possible for students to acquire competence and fluency in terms of holistic achievement levels, but it is difficult for them to achieve mastery

---

121. Davis, Teaching, *supra* note 18, at 195; Stuckey et al., *supra* note 28, at 116–18.

122. Andrade & Valtcheva, *supra* note 109.

123. Daniel Reinholz, *The Assessment Cycle: A Model for Learning through Peer Assessment*, 41 Assessment & Evaluation in Higher Educ. 301, 303 (2016).

124. Heather M. Field, *A Tax Professor's Guide to Formative Assessment*, 22 Fla. Tax Rev. 363, 440 (2019).

125. Ross & Donahoe, *supra* note 111.

126. 34 C.F.R. § 99.31(b)(1) (De-identified student completed assignments may be released without violating FERPA when the completed assignments are FERPA-protected educational records).

127. Stuckey et al., *supra* note 28, at 127–28.

128. Kathleen Brazeal & Brian Couch, *Student Buy-In Toward Formative Assessments: The Influence of Student Factors and Importance for Course Success*, 18 J. Microbiology & Biology Educ. 1, 5 (2017).

129. *See* Schwartz et al., *supra* note 19.

130. *See* Reid & Moore, *supra* note 68; *See also* Peter J. Collier & David L. Morgan, *"Is That Paper Really Due Today?": Differences in First-Generation and Traditional College Students' Understandings of Faculty Expectations*, 55 Higher Educ. 425, 436 (2008). See also Nunn, *supra* note 12, at 64–66.

research,[131] which leads to effective research. Besides that, students are not usually required to, nor do they spontaneously, time their legal research assignments. Therefore, it is unrealistic and unreasonable to expect students to produce accurate and time-efficient legal research while still learning new legal research skills. Moreover, for legal employers, accuracy and reliability take a higher priority than efficiency, among many good characteristics of legal researchers,[132] because accurate research is a prerequisite for effective analysis and writing.[133] Consequently, legal research faculty naturally focus on improving their students' research accuracy more than their research efficiency. In reality, however, lawyers must document their time on legal research for billable hours. In addition to accuracy, employers further expect new associates to conduct the research efficiently, thereby saving time and money.[134] This means there is a gap between the research skills students learn in law school and the research new associates need to have in their practice. Of course, legal research faculty do not want their students to be shocked by this discrepancy only after they begin their careers.

Therefore, at a minimum, legal research faculty should encourage students to keep track of the time they spend on their research assignments.[135] Not only does this simulate the legal research in practice to better prepare students for the future,[136] it also equips students with time management skills to plan and balance their studies and lives outside of the legal research course.[137] However, faculty should avoid arranging each assignment as a formal timed exam. When students learn legal research, especially databases, there will inevitably be a learning curve. Students consolidate the skills they have learned through the process of working on their formative assessment assignments, so they still need an environment where there is no time pressure to complete these assignments. Otherwise, these assignments will lose the learning improvement nature, making them less likely to be formative assessment assignments.[138] If the an instructor only introduces students to the concept of time management and time recording in legal research in the final exam at the end

---

131. Knott, *supra* note 74, at 108–111.

132. Seligmann, *supra* note 81, at 183.

133. Bowman, *supra* note 50, at 520 n.91.

134. Aliza B. Kaplan & Kathleen Darvil, *Think (and Practice) Like a Lawyer: Legal Research for the New Millennials*, 8 LEGAL COMM. & RHETORIC: JALWD 153, 158 (2011).

135. *See e.g.*, SCHWARTZ ET AL., *supra* note 19, at 93–94, 259.

136. *Id.* at 129.

137. Kathleen L. Byrd & Ginger Macdonald, *Defining College Readiness from the Inside Out: First-Generation College Student Perspectives*, 33 CMTY COLL. REV. 22, 29 (2005).

138. Different attitudes of legal research faculty toward assignments can make a difference. If an instructor uses assignments purely as an assessment tool, then this non-assessment-related element is unnecessary. However, if an instructor uses assignments as a learning improvement tool, then this additional element conveys a positive message to students that the instructor is genuinely committed to using the assignment as a tool to help their learning. Such support is exactly what FGLS needs. *See* DAVIS, TEACHING, *supra* note 18, at 195.

of the semester, it will be too late for the students to benefit from it, and it also will be an unfair surprise to students.

Time logging helps faculty know more about students' actual performance. In each assignment, legal research faculty may list a recommended time for completing each question or the entire assignment. Students will need to record the amount of time they spend on each problem or the assignment as a whole. Through this method, students can get immediate feedback on the efficiency of their research by comparing the time they spent with the time recommended by the instructor. And then they will know if they need to do something more to improve the efficiency of their research without time pressure. Faculty, in turn, can get a general idea of how efficient students are overall on a particular question or the entire assignment. In addition, faculty can further identify students who are struggling with their assignments. After all, without this time log, the only thing the instructor gets is the students' final and best research work. It does not convey any additional information to the instructor, whereas it is sometimes valuable to both faculty and students. For example, two students complete the same assignment with the same level of quality. One student spends half an hour on it, while the other takes an hour. Although this difference in time will not affect the students' grades, it can still help the instructor gain more insight into students' real performance. Also, it is necessary to explain the rationale for logging time to students.[139] It helps motivate students to track their time on each question or each assignment spontaneously.

E. Feedback

Feedback is essential to formative assessment methods,[140] as feedback is more important than assessed grades to improve student learning.[141] Simply marking incorrect answers does not help their learning because grades without any explanation mean little to students. Even if they want to improve, they have no clues about how to improve. Furthermore, correct answers do not mean that faculty should skip them without providing any positive feedback to students.[142]

Faculty should provide cognitive feedback to students,[143] which should be constructive and informative.[144] First, cognitive feedback consists of a summary of the overall performance on a given assignment,[145] which should closely align with the

139. SCHWARTZ ET AL., *supra* note 19.

140. *See* discussion *supra* pp. 7–8.

141. MCKEACHIE ET AL., *supra* note 112, at 109.

142. *See* Anne Enquist, *Critiquing Law Students' Writing: What the Students Say Is Effective*, 2 LEGAL WRITING: J. LEGAL WRITING INST. 145, 166 (1996).

143. Melissa M. Nelson & Christian D. Schunn, *The Nature of Feedback: How Different Types of Peer Feedback Affect Writing Performance*, 37 INSTRUCTIONAL SCI. 375, 377 (2009).

144. MCKEACHIE ET AL., *supra* note 112, at 149.

145. Nelson & Schunn, *supra* note 144, at 395.

learning outcomes with the rubric.[146] Such a summary informs students of their performance beyond the simple grade and re-emphasizes the importance of rubrics.[147] For each question where a student's performance is imperfect, the instructor should identify the problem and clearly let the student know whether the error comes from a lack of knowledge or confusion of knowledge.[148] It is because the more explicitly the problem is noted, the more likely the student is to implement the instructor's feedback.[149] For example, failing to use Shepard's to validate a case when a student is using Lexis is different from, and clearly more problematic than, confusing the meaning of Shepard's colored indicators. Finally, cognitive feedback needs the instructor to provide a solution to students for each "imperfect hit" identified,[150] which makes the feedback more acceptable to the students.[151]

While cognitive feedback is paramount to student improvement, feedback should also include appropriate affective language in an encouraging tone,[152] including mitigating language and praise language.[153] Learning legal research may become a struggling and frustrating experience for FGLS when learning something they have never heard of or something more complex than they expected. As a result, affective feedback should include mitigating language to address issues rather than direct criticism.[154] The feedback using mitigating language in a softer tone,[155] helps students focus on the error itself and suggested improvements. Conversely, criticism, especially demeaning language,[156] may negatively lead students to question their abilities or even personal values.[157] Praiseworthy feedback can motivate students psychologically,[158] even if it is not as important to student learning as cognitive feedback.[159] Praise gives FGLS additional encouragement to learn because it helps students build confidence in their legal research and shows the instructor's confidence in their success.[160] The additional positive feedback may not cost extra

146. *Id.*

147. *See* SCHWARTZ ET AL., *supra* note 19, at 164.

148. GERALD F. HESS ET AL., TECHNIQUES FOR TEACHING LAW 2, 263–64 (2011).

149. Nelson & Schunn, *supra* note 144, at 392, 395; SCHWARTZ ET AL., *supra* note 19, at 162–64.

150. HESS ET AL., *supra* note 149, 264–65; SCHWARTZ ET AL., *supra* note 19, at 165.

151. Nelson & Schunn, *supra* note 144, at 393.

152. ATLAS ET AL., *supra* note 22, at 117–18; HESS ET AL., *supra* note 149, 264.

153. Nelson & Schunn, *supra* note 144, at 381.

154. *Id.* at 380–81; SCHWARTZ ET AL., *supra* note 19, at 164–65.

155. MCKEACHIE ET AL., *supra* note 112, at 149.

156. DAVIS, TEACHING, *supra* note 18, at 199.

157. *Id.* at 198–99; See JAMES M. BANNER JR. ET AL., THE ELEMENTS OF TEACHING 37 (2d ed. 2017).

158. MCKEACHIE ET AL., *supra* note 112, at 111; SCHWARTZ ET AL., *supra* note 19, 164–65.

159. Avraham N. Kluger et al., The Effects of Feedback Interventions on Performance: A Historical Review, a Meta-Analysis, and a Preliminary Feedback Intervention Theory, 119 PSYCH. BULL. 254, 275 (1996).

160. DAVIS, TEACHING, *supra* note 18, at 198; ATLAS ET AL., *supra* note 22, at 120–21.

effort from the instructor,[161] but it means a great deal to students,[162] when they are consistently progressing throughout the semester,[163] excelling on an assignment, providing a creative and correct answer, or even merely offering some solid research steps as part of the answer.[164]

Feedback should also be prompt.[165] With formative assessment tools, "making mistakes and using them to gain a deeper understanding" of learned skills,[166] is the key to legal research learning. The premise is that when students receive feedback, they should easily recollect the mistakes they made,[167] and not yet be distracted by the newly learned materials. However, students commonly start to work on the legal research assignments at "the last minute."[168] Because of the inadequate time spent on assignments, these assignments are unlikely to leave a deep impression on these students.[169] In addition, most legal research assignments cover a different set of skills and topics. Receiving feedback on an assignment completed weeks ago wastes the students' opportunity to learn from mistakes, because they have been focusing on newly learned skills and have likely forgotten what they learned weeks ago.[170] These two factors make delayed feedback to students far less helpful than it is supposed to be. Consequently, only timely feedback can ensure the learning improvement nature of formative assessment,[171] which is available to students shortly after the assignment is completed,[172] or, preferably, immediately afterward.[173]

---

161. Nunn, *supra* note 12, at 93 (even one short friendly note will help).

162. Davis, Teaching, *supra* note 18, at 285 (noting the positive effect of encouragement on poorly performing students).

163. *See id.* at 283.

164. *Id.* at 199.

165. E. Scott Fruehwald, *How to Help Students from Disadvantaged Backgrounds Succeed in Law School*, 1 Tex. A & M L. Rev. 83, 98 (2013); Deborah Maranville, Infusing Passion and Context into the Traditional Law Curriculum Through Experiential Learning, 51 J. Legal Educ. 51, 73 (2001).

166. *See* Ross & Donahoe, *supra* note 111, at 666.

167. *See* Schwartz et al., *supra* note 19, at 166.

168. Decarlous Y. Spearman, *Citing Sources or Mitigating Plagiarism: Teaching Law Students the Proper Use of Authority Attribution in the Digital Age*, 42 Int'l J. Legal Info. 177, 196 (2014).

169. Atlas et al., *supra* note 22, at 141.

170. Hess et al., *supra* note 149, 265.

171. *See* Herbert N. Ramy, *Moving Students from Hearing and Forgetting to Doing and Understanding: A Manual for Assessment in Law School*, 41 Cap. U. L. Rev. 837, 840 (2013).

172. Rogelio A. Lasso, *Is Our Students Learning? Using Assessments to Measure and Improve Law School Learning and Performance*, 15 Barry L. Rev. 75, 89 (2010).

173. Schwartz et al., *supra* note 19, at 166.

V. Encouraging Questions

Legal research faculty should make special efforts to encourage FGLS to ask questions. A good learner asks questions.[174] Qualitative questions can help students clarify their confusion, foster new knowledge, and develop problem-solving skills.[175] Asking precise questions is not easy since students need to identify what they know and what they do not know. Once faculty fill the students' knowledge gap by answering questions, the newly acquired knowledge is highlighted, thus helping students learn. The ability to ask qualitative questions about coursework is an indicator of academic success.[176] Legal research focuses on micro-process and macro-process, and asking questions helps students from both cognitive and metacognitive perspectives.[177] When students miss one step in the research process, asking for help from faculty or colleagues can fairly quickly move them through that learning barrier rather than being stuck at that step for a long period.

Compared to CGLS, FGLS are less likely to spontaneously interact with legal research faculty.[178] Because of the imposter phenomenon,[179] FGLS may be apprehensive about standing in the spotlight.[180] Another reason is that FGLS tend to keep instructors from knowing that they are being challenged intellectually.[181] FGLS may get the false impression that they understand the research techniques well and are capable of applying them in research problems based on their substantive feelings, not the objective criterion on the rubrics.[182]

While it is important to ask questions, faculty should not require students to ask questions because this will only cause them to resist asking questions.[183] Instead, faculty should encourage students to "rediscovery of enjoyment, meaning, and value" by asking questions.[184] Faculty need to ensure that students feel safe and free when asking questions, both in the classroom and during office hours, rather than being overwhelmed or distracted by other factors.[185] It means faculty should clearly let students know they can and are expected to ask questions. Faculty should explain the rationale for asking questions, such as to learn more efficiently and to help other

---

174. Patrícia Albergaria Almeida, *Can I Ask a Question? The Importance of Classroom Questioning*, 31 Procedia, Soc. Behav. Sci. 634, 635 (2012).

175. *Id.*

176. *See id.*

177. Barak Rosenshine et al., T*eaching Students to Generate Questions: A Review of the Intervention Studies*, 166 Rev. Educ. Rsch.181, 183 (1996).

178. Acevedo & Lazar, *supra* note 86, at 4.

179. *See supra* note 27.

180. McKeachie et al., *supra* note 112, at 156.

181. *See* Acevedo & Lazar, *supra* note 86, at 16.

182. *See id.* at 17.

183. Matthew H. Bowker, *Teaching Students to Ask Questions Instead of Answering Them*, Thought & Action, Fall 2010, at 130; Stuckey et al., *supra* note 28, at 115.

184. Bowker, *supra* note 184.

185. *Id.* at 132.

classmates who may be experiencing the same problems. The goal is to make FGLS feel comfortable being in the spotlight and temporarily "dominating" the classroom.[186] After all, the ability to ask questions will benefit FGLS in the future, not just in the legal research class.[187]

VI. Office Hours

Office hours help FGLS learn legal research, and FGLS should enjoy the pedagogical benefits of office hours as a "hidden curriculum."[188] However, some FGLS are intimidated by office hours.[189] Therefore, faculty need to clearly let students know the purpose of office hours as part of the overall course transparency design.[190] After all, FGLS need to know that they can ask questions in a more private and comfortable informal setting than a formal classroom,[191] and they can ask the instructor for a more detailed explanation of the research process or assignment without peer pressure. Such direct interaction is very helpful to FGLS because they are no longer the "imagined ideal student[s]" in the classroom, where they quickly feel isolated.[192]

In addition, office hours allow FGLS to develop a personal relationship with legal research faculty.[193] The more students get to know faculty, the more effort they will invest in learning.[194] Such relationships directly contribute to the academic success of FGLS.[195] To facilitate this relationship, faculty should make office hour communication less formal so that students do not feel intimidated.[196] There are many things faculty can do to create such a relaxed environment. For example, faculty can start the conversation with small talk.[197] Keeping the door open also helps.[198] Faculty should also be open to non-course related visits,[199] such as concerns about family, stress, and job searches, as these experiences may negatively impact the learning FGLS.[200] Of course, it is not the faculty's responsibility to solve these non-curricu-

186. Davis, Experience, *supra* note 13, at 186.

187. Julia Brodsky, *Why Questioning Is the Ultimate Learning Skill*, Forbes (Dec. 29, 2020), https://www.forbes.com/sites/juliabrodsky/2021/12/29/why-questioning-is-the-ultimate-learning-skill/?sh=5ad5f7a8399f.

188. *See Mastering the "Hidden Curriculum,"* Harv. Mag., Nov.–Dec. 2017, at 19–20.

189. Nunn, *supra* note 12, at 79.

190. Atlas et al., *supra* note 22, at 60.

191. Davis, Teaching, *supra* note 18, at 269.

192. Davis, Experience, *supra* note 13, at 197.

193. *See id.* at 196.

194. Davis, Teaching, *supra* note 18, at 269.

195. Davis, Experience, *supra* note 13, at 196–97.

196. Davis, Teaching, *supra* note 18, at 372.

197. Nunn, *supra* note 12, at 42–44.

198. Davis, Teaching, *supra* note 18, at 372.

199. Atlas et al., *supra* note 22, at 61.

200. Davis, Experience, *supra* note 13, at 199.

lum-related concerns, but simply listening can mean a lot to students, because they will recognize that the faculty value their growth by investing time outside of class to help them.[201]

VII. Monthly Polls

In order to give students a better learning experience,[202] legal research faculty should conduct at least two monthly surveys during the course to receive students' feedback. There will be informal surveys in week five and week ten for a fifteen-week class. And then, in the final two weeks, students will have the traditional formal course evaluation, which is the most common method to get student feedback on the course in law schools.[203] Such a conventional assessment approach is a great way to improve teaching, as faculty can receive meaningful feedback and helpful suggestions to polish future courses.[204] However, only the prospective students of this class will enjoy the benefits from these end-of-semester course evaluations, not the current students in the course. As previously discussed, FGLS may have unique challenges in a legal research course, and some of them may struggle with different course elements. For example, some may find the research demonstration is too fast, while others may need more time for research exercises. Some may have a special interest in some uncovered research skills,[205] and others may have unique concerns about assignments, tests, and the course policy.[206] Simple surveys throughout the course help legal research faculty identify these special concerns.[207] Of course, to encourage students to provide meaningful feedback, these surveys should remain anonymous.[208]

Legal research faculty should be ready to adjust the course structure as necessary because it is pointless to merely collect student feedback without any course modifications. Implementing sound recommendations demonstrates that the legal research faculty is genuinely committed to improving student learning and sincerely respect them.[209] Even if some course elements are well received by most students, there is no reason to ignore the experiences of students who struggle with popular course content. A few small changes in the classroom can make a difference to them.

---

201. Atlas et al., *supra* note 22, at 191.

202. Schwartz et al., *supra* note 19, at 209.

203. *Id.* at 208.

204. *Id.*

205. *See* Davis, Teaching, *supra* note 18, at 196.

206. *Id.* at 257–58.

207. For example, a sample of simple informal surveys during the course. Schwartz et al., *supra* note 19, at 210.

208. Pamela Gravestock & Emily Gregor-Greenleaf, Student Course Evaluations: Research, Models and Trends 13 (2008).

209. Schwartz et al., *supra* note 19, at 210.

VIII. Conclusion

FGLS may have unique challenges in learning legal research. Therefore, legal research faculty should provide additional support to FGLS in order to improve their learning. Many of the techniques discussed in this essay that benefit FLGS can also help CGLS, which can further contribute to students' long-term development.

Twenty-Three

Staying on TRAC

Simplifying the Paradigms for Law School

Jason A. Paskan*

TEACHING THE CONCEPTS OF LEGAL WRITING to first-year law students poses significant challenges even in the best of circumstances. However, with changing emphasis on educational goals at the high school and college level, written communication skills, including grammar and punctuation, are diminishing in today's society across the board.[1] While some law students with lawyers in the family or their immediate orbit may have a better understanding on the importance of writing in the profession, first-generation students may not have that same base level or access to resources to assist in this process at the advent of law school, when the appropriate foundations are laid, and good habits are learned.[2]

While it may be impossible to bridge the knowledge gap created by 20-plus years of potential educational inequity, diminishing the severity of the learning curve can improve the buy-in from students prior to the onset of bad writing habits. Moreover, emphasizing the need for students to clearly articulate their understanding of the material in their doctrinal classes can help reinforce the need for improving their writing skills. Simplifying the process and relating the material to something that students feel comfortable navigating can save students a significant struggle in their early careers and, hopefully, improve their communication skills, leading to better job prospects, bar passage, and increasing the academic profile for the institution as a whole. If the core concept of the legal profession is communication, there is no better first-year class on which to focus a student's, or an institution's, attention than legal writing.[3]

---

* Visiting Professor at University of Cincinnati College of Law. I dedicate this chapter to Dyann for getting me back to legal education.

1. Tenielle Fordyce-Ruff, *Research Across the Curriculum: Using Cognitive Science to Answer the Call for Better Legal Research Instruction*, 125 Dick. L. Rev. 1, 35–36 (2020) (citing Karen McDonald Henning & Julia Belian, *If You Give a Mouse a Cookie: Increasing Assessments and Individualized Feedback in Law School Classes*, 95 U. Det. Mercy L. Rev. 35, 40 (2017) and Rebecca Flanagan, *Better by Design: Implementing Meaningful Change for the Next Generation of Law Students*, 71 Me. L. Rev. 103, 115 (2018)).

2. Fordyce-Ruff, *supra* at 16–18.

3. *See* Nicholas W. Allard & Heidi K. Brown, *Training Powerful Legal Communicators: What Does the Future Hold?*, 90-Sep. N.Y. St. B.J. 10, 10, 13–14 (2018).

The recommendations contained in this chapter are derived from teaching first-generation law students the fundamentals and concepts in a legal research, analysis, and writing curriculum, as well as my personal experience as a first-generation law student. Making legal writing more approachable to all students is the overarching goal and demystifying the purpose and the process of the component parts is the one way of trying to put all students on equal footing at the outset of law school. Instead of creating a shortcut that diminishes effort, playing on preexisting pathways, at the expense of convoluted lingo, can help students recognize that legal writing need not be difficult or fear-inducing. Reminding students that they are not on their own and that they have resources at their disposal on a regular basis can help bring first-generation students into a new community.

Emphasizing the practicality of effective communication skills, coupled with the belief that hard work outperforms undeveloped talent, first-generation students can recognize that legal writing is the great equalizer. These students have exhibited a certain level of discipline to get where they are, and a fundamental approach to tackling legal issues will enable them to reap the benefits of their efforts. First-generation students have successfully navigated undergraduate education, the LSAT, and the law school application phase, possibly with little to no assistance. Proficient writing is the most efficient way to stay on TRAC toward improving a first-generation student's overall performance in law school.[4]

While I would never push my teaching agenda on an individual or an institution, the suggestions presented in this chapter derive from teaching many first-generation law students over the past six years. While this chapter is intended to be a resource for legal writing professors, in the age where information is becoming increasingly available and where law students are becoming more adept at electronic research, it is anticipated that the materials herein will be viewed by a broader audience, including students. With that in mind, I recommend to the legal writing experts who will be in the front of the classroom providing their insights, and what I will do for my students going forward, is to make this chapter available to them as a resource, not a substitute, to assist in the presentation of legal writing education. To the students out there who find this book, this is not intended to supplant the legal writing professor's instruction; rather, this is merely an effort to provide an additional voice and to help cut through some of the noise. To the first-generation students who find this book and have made it to law school, keep going, get your degree, and show everyone else that they were correct to expect greatness.

4. The term "first-generation law students" is not intended to oversimplify the diverse backgrounds that this population comes from. Instead, "first-generation law students" as used in this chapter is meant to call attention to the fact that as their law professor, you might be the only resource these students have who understand what it takes to be successful in this environment. Moreover, the observations pertaining to habits and behaviors of this group are anecdotal, yet instructive.

A. The Dreaded Paradigm

There is something about the constraints of a paradigm that terrifies students. Whether it be years of "creative" writing in their prior academic pursuits, the "fear" that the ball is being hidden and an ulterior motive is afoot, or the perception that a difficult and new analytical approach presented in law school is an impossible undertaking, strict adherence to a paradigm is one of the more difficult challenges legal writing professors face early on.

If you are reading this, presumably, you went to law school and had a professor who taught you that IRAC, CRAC, CREAC, TREAT, etc. was the way lawyers or judges process information.[5] Regardless of the acronym used at your institution, they are all the same at their core, with the main difference being whether the reader is provided the issue or the answer at the outset. That said, this oversimplification of the various available paradigms can only be achieved with familiarity of the contextual components each part of the applicable acronym is intended to provide. First-generation students may not be "in the know" and any additional confusion could place them at a further deficit. By referring to different paradigms in orientation and across different classes, the possibility of unintentionally creating additional obstacles exists.

Legal writing is intimidating. Legal writing should not be intimidating. But here lies the problem: without the fundamental understanding of the components, student perception can be that they learned one way of writing in high school or undergrad, another way of processing and communicating information in orientation, their legal writing professor is asking them to draft a memo using a different paradigm, and their Torts exam needs to present short answer/essay responses using a facially different structure. Short of a school adopting a uniform presentation of the paradigms or students accepting that the paradigms all seek the same level of detailed and supported analysis, an unnecessary potential for confusion exists. The idea that a mixed message is being presented hinders the learning process and undermines the practicality of the analytical process.

One of the more successful tools that I have come to appreciate as a professor is presenting material in ways students might already be familiar with at this point in their educational journey. In essence, I borrow from my days in practice and consider how I can effectively get someone to believe me when they have relatively little familiarity with the intricacies of the current issue I have toiled with for years. On the very first day of class, the students are asked how they would categorize their

5. *See* Michael D. Murray & Christine H. DeSanctis, Legal Writing and Analysis 130–33 (Robert C. Clark et al. eds., 2d ed. 2015). *See also* Gerald Lebovits, *Cracking the Code to Legal Writing Arguments: From IRAC to CRARC to Combinations in Between*, 82-Aug N.Y. St. B.J. 64, 49 (2010).

writing ability. Inevitably, students tend to believe they are somewhere toward the middle of the road, and few students claim to be "good" writers.[6]

Before I advise my classes that they are all blank canvases when it comes to legal writing, I ask if any of them like English, History, Math, Science, Sports, Cooking, or Art. They are subsequently told that legal writing at its core is nothing more than using their English skills to communicate the history of a case or cases, using a simple formula or recipe, to convey information in a meaningful and easily appreciable manner. I reiterate that like any sport or skill that they want to improve, significant practice and dedication is required. Drawing upon these universal familiarities helps students understand that they have already employed many of the necessary skills to critically analyze problems. This will further invite student participation. Casting a wider net of shared experiences ensnares more students in the process. Relying on basic math skills, important historical events, sports analogies, and simple step-by-step processes to make food as backbones to the writing process shows students that they have the requisite skills to accomplish legal analysis, regardless of their individual backgrounds.

By broaching the subject in this way and reminding the students throughout the course of the semester or year that they are already familiar with the overarching concepts at play, students seem more inclined to think that they are capable of creating acceptable work-product earlier in the semester, and they appear more willing to come to office hours to discuss some of the nuances that we cover in class because they believe they have a grasp on the underlying subject matter. The level of trust developed in the early weeks plays an important role given the impact that good communication skills can have on their overall performance in legal writing and doctrinal classes.

Building off of the familiar and trying to eliminate confusion is only half the battle. The time commitment that legal writing requires to develop into an effective communicator is a big ask, especially given the new environment the students are thrust into. Peeling back the curtain for your students with recommendations, or your "secrets" to navigating law school learned from your own experience, helps create the necessary bond and level of trust required for first-generation students to see the positives in trusting the process. Pairing this information with a practical calendar that includes benchmarks shows the students that writing assignments can best be approached in pieces and that procrastination will not suffice at this level.

---

6. McDonald Henning & Belian, *supra* at 42–43; *see also* Gerald Lebovits, *How to Succeed in Legal Writing by Really Trying*, 90-Sep N.Y. St. B.J. 61, 61 (2018) (citing Bryan A. Garner, *Why Lawyers Can't Write: Science Has Something to Do with It, and Law Schools are Partly to Blame*, 99 A.B.A. J. 24, 24–25 (2013)).

B. Improving the Initial Uptake

Picking up bad habits, unlearning them, and learning good habits is a lengthy and frustrating process.[7] Rather than try to amend understanding downstream, teaching students a uniform approach to the paradigm at the source could prove to be an effective way of instructing the students about the individual components of legal analysis. Accordingly, orientation or the first week of legal writing are as good places as any to begin the process. Frankly, including some information in an acceptance letter package would be optimal to capitalize on the students' dearth of knowledge when it pertains to legal writing. Reconceptualizing a series of long-standing paradigms might be easier said than done, but the proposal outlined below is designed to help students stay on TRAC.[8]

But throwing more "alphabet soup" into the mix helps no one if it is just another acronym in a sea of legal linguistics.[9] Also, I recognize that the long-standing paradigms will not be forgotten simply because of this chapter.[10] However, attempting to adapt legal analysis with those paradigms in mind can help a broader scope of first-year law students understand the basics of written communication skills, and lay the foundation for successful legal careers.[11] This behind-the-scenes access to the component parts of legal analysis pulls back the curtain and demonstrates that there are no secrets at play, just a solid work ethic and an attention to detail.

C. Breaking Down Barriers and Laying a Foundation

Whether the student thinks they know what they are doing or has zero confidence in their abilities, the notions surrounding legal writing, good or bad, need to be dispelled. Telling students that they likely have misconceptions about legal writing puts all of the students in the same boat and helps level the playing field at the outset of the class. An added benefit to this approach is to ward off any unfounded confidence in students' abilities to approach the high-level rational thought exercise, which could lead to students spending insufficient time internalizing the process.[12]

Additionally, taking the time to learn the structure and organization of legal analysis of everything is of greater weight than learning how to analyze one single issue that may never present itself again in the future. Moreover, the choice to remind students that they are all at same starting block helps reinforce that how one starts is

---

7. *See* Karen Erger, *Teach Your Newbies Well*, 93 Ill. B.J. 542, 542 (2005).
8. Pun intended.
9. *See* Lebovits, 82-Aug N.Y. St. B.J. at 50.
10. *See* Diane B. Kraft, *CREAC in the Real World*, 63 Clev. St. L. Rev. 567, 567–70 (2015).
11. *See* Erger, *supra*.
12. *See* Lebovits, 90-Sep N.Y. St. B.J. 61.

less important than how one finishes. This is where the concept of TRAC originated; the race itself can be influenced on the start, but it never dictates who crosses the finish line with the best result.

Legal writing from an objective position is predicting an outcome based on reasoning, whereas persuasive legal writing is an attempt to influence a decision based on reasoning. Having students recognize that they have predicted outcomes and made arguments in the past helps put them at ease with respect to the purpose. Reminding students that they can improve on their rationale using the concepts of legal writing piques their interest. Showing students that the process can unlock any door in front of them from an analytical standpoint is what keeps them engaged.

One specific example used to emphasize the students' familiarity with these concepts is to answer the pop culture question of whether a hotdog is a sandwich. This conundrum works to enforce the lessons of analyzing matters both objectively and persuasively, and it has the benefit of being a fairly divisive issue. To set up the example, present the students with three pictures of different sandwiches. Without telling them that they will be applying a legal analysis, or tip them off to the hotdog aspect of the question, have them identify the components of each sandwich, i.e., type of meat, bread, condiments, fillings, vegetables, etc. As the students describe the individual sandwiches, keep a running list while noting the subtle differences in each sandwich, so that a synthesized rule can be crafted from the base similarities of the examples. After the generally agreed-upon ingredients of what constitutes a sandwich have been identified, provide the specifics for each of the example sandwiches as explanations as to how the synthesized "sandwich rule" was created. Now that the general parameters have been agreed upon, introduce an image of a Chicago-style hotdog, and ask the students to identify observable components, just as they did for the sandwiches.

For objective writing, students will note that meat, bread, and condiments comprise a hotdog, thereby falling within the synthesized "sandwich rule" and definitively answering the question. For persuasive writing, asking students to articulate a response as to why a hotdog is not a sandwich will help them note that the subtle differences may play a large role in determining how the issue can be framed to best reach the intended result. The exercise as a whole works because it is simple, but it is unexpected, and something that they can analyze on the very first day of their law school careers. Even when the objective and persuasive tones are separated by a semester, the students will inevitably remember when they objectively agreed that a hotdog is, in fact, a sandwich. These analytical exercises can be extrapolated to authorities, especially when done in quick succession. Specifically, it is my practice to go from the hotdog exercise to the analysis of a negligent infliction of emotional distress element. Drawing upon the similarities in the processes shows the students that legal analysis, while more complicated given the number of resources at their fingertips, at its base is not as daunting as it may appear at the outset.

Instructing students that they will embark on a quest to train their brains to better process information and distill what the information means tends to get the vast majority on board. Advising students that legal writing skills are the foundation upon which their careers will be developed ensnares the remainder. Rebranding legal writing as effective communication skills reorients students' perception from an insurmountable task to a necessary evil establishes the requisite level of trust that students need to have when the process inevitably becomes frustrating, if simply because it is different.

Being honest with your students, regularly asking them what questions they have, and working toward an environment that fosters participation is the best tool in a legal writing professor's arsenal.[13] Nothing in class can be fake because the savvy student of the twenty-first century has a well-honed "BS" meter and first-generation students are no different.[14] Genuine efforts are appreciated, and the enthusiasm required to teach legal writing cannot be forced. Students will feed off the passion if it is authentic, but they will transition to merely enduring the class at the first appearance of insincerity.[15]

Rely on universal familiarities, e.g., the list of subjects or activities they would have covered during the course of their educational careers or upbringing and outlined above, to encourage the use of language that targets the layperson instead of the lawyer and remind students that their understanding of the law is a better starting point than a hyper technical statutory quote. Convey that the students already possess many of these skills and that there is no failure in trying. Circle back to what you know, how you learned legal analysis, and the things that you wish you had known when you were in their seat to help establish a rapport.[16] Being objective and fair will better prepare students for practice, as will establishing an expectation of accountability.

Like the "hotdog sandwich" example above, using other common experiences can serve as additional means to build skills. This year, I used the remix of "Old Town Road"[17] to prompt an analysis as to whether the song would be better sorted in the country or hip-hop genre. While I recognized that the song no longer appeared on the charts, I provided some additional evenhanded facts to help students argue for their respective position to set them on a path to convince a fictional character that their side's argument was most persuasive. To further tap into the collective shared experience, the song was played, and the lyrics were provided, to fairly establish the starting blocks for each team. Even though the exercise might appear silly on its face, it clearly articulates that there are different opinions or beliefs as to the correct answer, and more

---

13. *See* Heidi K. Brown, *The Emotionally Intelligent Law Professor: A Lesson from* The Breakfast Club, 26 U. Ark. Little Rock L. Rev. 273, 275–76 (2013).

14. *See* McDonald Henning & Belian, *supra* at 43–44 (today's students' consumer mentality contributes to view of professors as service providers).

15. *Id.*

16. *See* Brown, *supra* at 275.

17. Lil Nas X ft. Billy Ray Cyrus, "Old Town Road" (Columbia Records 2019).

importantly, even if they do not necessarily believe that their position is correct, it is their job as an advocate to convince the third party that what they want is the only reasonable outcome through the use of relevant supporting authority; this is further reinforced by randomly assigning teams. Moreover, if the goal is to present legal analysis in a fun and engaging manner, setting up a no-stakes assessment that can be subject to moderation and concurrent feedback accomplishes that goal, and similar exercises have their place in the classroom because they can reach a broad audience.

This environment, along with the mechanical process outlined below for legal analysis, can alleviate some self-induced pressure to succeed that is common with first-generation students. If there are no favorites and every student is truly subject to the same demanding standard, there is no educational advantage gained solely through one's surname. The faster that all students, first-generation included, learn this, the better each individual student will be prepared for a wonderful career of billable hours (sarcasm in original), client development, and the analytical approach lawyers take to every facet of their daily lives.

D. TRAC: The Paradigm for Paradigms

By nature, the letters in an acronym must stand for something. In this case, TRAC breaks out into the following component parts: (1) Thesis Statement/Thesis Question; (2) Rule Identification, Statement, and Explanation; (3) Applying the Law to the Facts; and (4) Conclusion. The utility of this acronym is that it doubles as a writing paradigm as well as a Rosetta Stone for deciphering how the other common paradigms function; this multifunctional aspect of TRAC is what helps simplify it for students and law schools alike.

Applying the paradigm to an initial three- or four-element statute, crime, or legal concept, is a good way to introduce the students to legal analysis. This multiple element or factor analysis that goes to answering a single legal issue establishes the need for an umbrella paragraph to give the students a plan to work through. First-generation students can appreciate the need to systematically work through a checklist toward a greater goal, i.e., answering the question raised in a task memo in this case, because that is what got them to law school, despite a lack of outside assistance. Moreover, if students can work through one element as part of a conjunctive test, they can similarly work through multiple elements and issues alike. The fundamental approach is no different from demonstrating any step-by-step task associated with any sports practice, musical piece, choreography, or any other attempt to learn a basic skill.

Adding the layers bit by bit eases the students into the transition from undergraduate writing to predictive or persuasive writing. Working with the students to isolate the individual variables at issue helps the students embrace the process and feel a sense of accomplishment. The little victories that can be provided early in the semester can go a long way in encouraging students and helping them see that they are capable of providing professional legal analysis.

1. Thesis Statement/Thesis Question

As noted above, the confusion often lies in the beginning of the paradigm because the acronyms are used interchangeably and thinking the analysis "differently" with each can be problematic for students. With IRAC (Issue, Rule, Application, Conclusion) the writer is tasked with identifying the issue and it often starts with "Whether," whereas CRAC (Conclusion, Rule, Application, Conclusion), TREAT (Thesis, Rule, Explanation, Application, Thesis), and CREAC (Conclusion, Rule, Explanation, Application, Conclusion) begin the writing with the answer and the statement ends with a period. Rather than introduce variables and individual preference, if the students are advised at the outset that they can lead with a question *or* an answer, a potential source of confusion can be eliminated.

Armed with the information that the beginning can start one of two ways and is simply a matter of preference for the reader (professor/boss/externship supervisor, etc.) or the writer, helping the students craft an appropriate Thesis Statement/Thesis Question becomes the next hurdle. As a first-generation law student, I assumed that the more verbose the Thesis, the more likely the reader was to follow the rationale.[18] As a practitioner, and now as a legal writing professor, I do my best to establish early that the opposite is true. Clear and succinct statements geared toward a simple answer or identification of the issue articulate the matter to be discussed in the section better than attempts to summarize the problem. Additionally, bookending the issue with Theses helps students see clear boundaries for the individual element/factor being analyzed, further simplifying the process.

By way of example, the analysis of three elements may assist in demonstrating the utility of a simple Thesis. If the students are tasked with determining whether the State can establish the *corpus delicti* of driving under the influence, that can be posed as an interrogatory (Can the State establish the *corpus delicti* of driving under the influence?) or in the affirmative (The State can establish the *corpus delicti* of driving under the influence.). A simple alteration to the phrasing can adapt to the individual professor's preference, and advising students of this simple trick can effectively eliminate confusion out of the gate. Presenting the format as an option, instead of an absolute, can streamline the message and help first-year students better conceptualize the purpose of a simple Thesis.

Example: The State can establish the "driving" element.

OR

Example: Can the State establish the "driving element?

Whether the State can establish the "driving" element.

18. Sincerest of apologies to Prof. Sandra Kerber at Cleveland State University College of Law.

2. Rule Identification, Statement, and Explanation

Having successfully navigated the interrogatory/affirmative statement confusion, legal analysis then shifts to its next source of consternation. The benefit of the longer acronym paradigms is that they are intended to show students that the overarching rule on its own is insufficient in legal analysis. Using the driving under the influence example, providing the prohibition as set forth in a statute would not provide the reader with enough information, and statutes are often unclearly worded. Moreover, simply stating that it is against the law to drive under the influence does not provide an example for what that actually means. The additional explanation, through effective discussion of case law, is required in order to adequately answer the interrogatory, or supplement the affirmative conclusion, above.

Even though TRAC is one of the shorter acronyms, not specifically parsing out Rule Explanation as a separate component to legal analysis, the need for case law still exists. As tempting as it may be for a student to believe that the law is the law regardless of the source, conveying the need for organized legal analysis, from broad concepts to nuanced specifics, can help them see how each authority is best integrated into the paradigm. Also, reiterating to the students that the Rule is comprised of its three component parts helps establish that the initial step into analysis is not nearly as intimidating as may be perceived.

a. Rule Identification

Identifying the overarching rule is one of the most important parts of the analytical process because it opens the doors to breaking down the entire issue. Regardless of whether the universe is open or closed, the first step is the most difficult, even when the hypothetical is crafted to make the answer apparent. The open universe poses an additional challenge because without the initial bearing, the students can be set adrift in a sea of legal authority, not knowing where they should begin looking. Thus, narrowing the scope for first-year law students, especially first-generation students, is paramount.

Helping students identify where to begin will depend on the task at hand, but certain authorities lend themselves to be natural starting points. Constitutional provisions or statutory elements are typical starting points in the analytical structure. The citation for the overarching rule carries a significant authority, and that broad base can help students accurately and concisely identify the source of the Rule at play.

Continuing with the driving under the influence example from prior sections, if the first element of driving under the influence requires the State to establish "driving" then the students must focus on this element. Clearly identifying the Rule, and where it comes from, allows the students to embark on a narrow analysis.

> *Example*: Pursuant to (DUI Statute Citation), the State must establish the driving element.

b. Rule Statement

Once the Rule has been identified, analysis can begin. There is no better starting point than actually providing the Rule for the reader. A succinct statement of the Rule invariably requires some discussion of what the law actually is, what it is not, and the general parameters of the core legal principle. However, the Rule Statement is more often than not a collection of statements that define the law using broad terms to encompass a wide swath of authorities that distill confusing constitutional or statutory language.

When addressing the differences between Rule Statement and Rule Explanation, I instruct my students to consider a funnel. The funnel itself is the Rule Identification and it can be appropriately identified. The Rule Statement is the top of the funnel, i.e., the broad opening that gets us started on the journey. As students advance through the Rule section, the discussion goes from the wider base (general concepts) toward a progressively more specific discussion of the law (exceptions, nuance, etc.). The students are reminded that the broad base is important because it catches more of the subject matter than the narrow end, and they cannot approach the funnel from a different direction if they are trying to distill their analysis. The natural starting point for the law, as well as the funnel, is the most basic concept that students are trying to analyze.

With respect to generating a well-crafted and appropriately synthesized Rule Statement, the focus needs to rest on the synthesis, a difficult concept for any student to grasp at the beginning. Rule synthesis is simply braiding source material to form a cohesive statement of the law like a rope. On their own, the individual strands might not be strong enough to address the issue, but together, the sentences in the Rule Statement create an encompassing discussion of the broader concepts at play in the overall issue.

Using the driving under the influence example, the Rule Statement would simply discuss what "driving" is or is not. Is there a definition of what constitutes driving in the jurisdiction? What have courts in the jurisdiction decided in determining whether the statutory prohibition qualifies as driving? Is there a test for determining whether a defendant drove? The benefit of rule synthesis is that this elemental discussion can come from a variety of authorities, but the source material should be of significant weight. This broad construct simply addresses the law at issue in the cases to be discussed in the following section.

> *Example*: Driving requires the vehicle be in motion and under the control of the driver. Citation. "Driving" is not synonymous with "operating" because operating simply requires that the mechanisms of the vehicle be engaged, e.g., the engine running or the car in gear, whereas driving requires intentional movement of the vehicle by the driver. Citation. Accidental or incidental movement of the vehicle will not satisfy the driving element of (DUI Statute Citation). Citation.

c. Rule Explanation

After the Rule has been stated and synthesized, the next step is to work through the cases that apply the law to a finite set of facts. In this section, the law is no longer hypothetical, it has been put through a stress test in one or more cases. The Rule Explanation section carefully identifies the facts, outcome, and rationale of the court utilizing the law.

Although the reference would be better appreciated by toddlers or geriatrics, the Rule Explanation section is one half of what makes Velcro work; it is either the hooks or the loops that keep the bond strong.[19] Students are tasked with pulling enough information out of the cases (the hooks) so that there is something to adhere to when walking through the Application section that immediately follows (the loops). The more information that is pulled, the more hooks that can attach to the loops, enabling a better prediction or a more persuasive argument.

The students have been tasked with "solving" for the outcome, either predicting how a court will decide an issue or steering the decision toward the ideal outcome for the client. This becomes a relatively simple equation to decide once the students realize that they have been provided (closed universe) or can locate (open universe) the necessary information. In fact, if the students are given a set of facts, whether through a memorandum or a client interview, they know what they need to pull out of the cases for a useful comparison. Similarly, the rationale derived from the cases, through the court's logical process, permitted the court to reach a conclusion on the issue, i.e., the outcome of the underlying authority.

Accordingly, the students can compare the facts of their case and the cases they discussed in the Rule Explanation section, using the rationale of the courts as a constant, to arrive at the outcome in their scenario. This is why, when working through the Rule Explanation section, the emphasis is directed toward highlighting the facts, outcome, and rationale of the cases provided or located in their research to answer the question posed.

Other considerations for this section focus on students working toward documents that are professional in appearance. Specifically, case introduction appears to be a more difficult concept to grasp amongst first-generation students. Whether it be uncertainty with respect to citation's effect on the flow of a sentence, or a concern that the repetition is unappealingly robotic, students are wary of mimicking the style provided in the cases used as examples. One beneficial piece of advice that I have found helpful for first-generation students is to remind them they are writing for a job they want, not a job they have. Not only does this put becoming a lawyer well

---

19. For the technical discussion of how Velcro works, visit VELCRO, https://www.velcro.co.uk/blog/2018/06/how-do-velcro-brand-fasteners-work/ (last visited November 16, 2021).

within reach, but it also opens up the real possibility that they too can become judges someday. Having something to aspire to can only help students see the importance of legal writing in law school and beyond.

Parenthetical citations and signals also cause students issues in the Rule Explanation. The utility of parentheticals and signals is that each allows for high-density information in the Rule Explanation and precludes the need for duplicative efforts when cases are overtly similar to one another. Coupling these tools with case-by-case analysis enables students to fully encapsulate the law and succinctly discuss how it actually works under a certain set of circumstances. Done right, the Rule Explanation section is the most difficult section to draft, or at least the most time-consuming, because it takes into account the applicable law and sets up the next section of the analysis.

For purposes of the ongoing example, the Rule Explanation section would simply run through cases wherein the driving element was at issue, and presenting the facts, outcomes, and rationales of those cases. The purpose of the Rule Explanation section is to provide palpable examples of situations where the element at issue satisfied the court, or the circumstances prevented a court from concluding that a defendant drove a vehicle for purposes of the statute.

Importantly, one thing that first-generation students might not recognize on the face of the cases is that when a conjunctive test is at issue, if the test is satisfied or all prongs of the test are met, even the most passing reference to an individual element by the court may be instructive in a student's analysis. Thus, if driving is a conjunctive element, then any conviction that is affirmed renders the driving element present.

> *Example*: In (Case Citation), the Supreme Court of (Jurisdiction) reversed the decision of the court of appeals and vacated the defendant's driving under the influence conviction. When the officer arrived, the car was running with the defendant asleep in the driver's seat. Citation. Even though the car was in drive, the defendant had his foot on the brake, preventing any forward movement. Citation. The Court held that the State failed to establish the driving element of (DUI Statute Citation) because the only evidence presented at trial indicated the vehicle moved only after the defendant exited the car in compliance with the officer's command. Citation. The incidental movement of the vehicle lacked the requisite degree of purposeful control by the driver, and the mere operation of the vehicle did not amount to driving as contemplated by (DUI Statute Citation). Citation; *see contra* Case Citation 2 (brief discussion of what happened in the case where a different result occurred based on a different fact pattern).

3. Application

This is where it all comes together, so naturally, it is the most difficult concept for students to grasp, and Application can be particularly troublesome for first-generation students. The biggest hurdle is overcoming the realization that identifying similarities between their research and their fact patterns and placing them in proximity is insufficient. Up to this point, responding to test questions or writing prompts have largely been driven by regurgitation. In law school, simply placing the factual information in proximity to the legal authorities is not applying the law. Without any indication otherwise, whether it be from a mentor or being introduced to legal analysis before law school, first-generation students tend to get stuck in the belief that identification equates to analysis, whereas students with prior exposure recognize the need to "do something" with the information to provide the answer for the reader that demonstrates a mastery of the material.

Walking the students through the process and providing examples will provide an idea for what Application should look like, and this sounds simple enough. However, until students take the facts of their case and use the rationale from the cases in the Rule Explanation section to provide examples of how a case was decided under similar or different circumstances, this section of the analysis can be perceived as arduous and imposing. To further complicate matters, the need for citations in this section to specific authorities, like subsections, page numbers, or paragraphs, does not make this section any more inviting. Nevertheless, if the students are reminded they have already laid the tracks for the Application in the prior sections, drafting a competent Application section should be nothing more than applying pen to paper.

A common suggestion to students when discussing the Application section of their analysis is to draft their Explanation section with the Application section in mind. If the facts of the cases that the students are relying on are on point, they should use the same vernacular to lessen the logical gymnastics on the part of the reader, who may be reading the information without prior knowledge of the subject matter. The more the information is presented in the same, or completely opposite language, the easier it is for the reader to see the connection between the authorities and why the answer must be what it is to follow binding precedent. Moreover, telling the reader why the specific information from the cases used in the Rule Explanation section is important is reinforced in the Application section; if it was important to a prior reviewing court, it will be instructive in the current matter as well.

The warning that must be provided prior to sending students off to draft an Application section is that proximity alone is insufficient for analysis. First-generation students specifically tend to rely on the misconception that because the Application immediately follows the Explanation section, the reader will have retained all of the information and a simple factual discussion is all that is required. This assumption is incorrect because it defeats the purpose of the assignment. If the task is to predict the outcome, it effectively leaves the reader with a "choose your own adventure" story: I have provided the law, here are the facts as a reminder, and the reader should be able to see the connection.

However, this style of crafting legal analysis does not account for the original assignment and the students are relying on hope, rather than objective analysis, that the "correct" conclusion will be reached by anyone reading the document. The problem is exacerbated with persuasive writing because it leaves too many openings for the opposition to convince the reader. If the correct decision for the assignment is one that benefits the client, leaving the decision up to chance, as opposed to telling the reader why this is the only reasonable outcome given the law and facts, is non-responsive and unconvincing.

Shifting from what would essentially be a law dump next to a repetition of select facts toward actual analysis is not all that complicated. The Application section in most instances is nothing more than a direct comparison of the law the student just told the reader about, to the facts of the hypothetical they were provided. If the student provided the facts, outcome, and rationale of the cases in the Rule Explanation section, the comparison of the facts from the hypothetical, using the same rationale, allows the reader to solve for the outcome. Stated differently, the students use precedent to arrive at a prediction or persuasive argument for the case that has landed before them. There are more nuanced ways to construct Application sections, but this basic structure will allow students to see how and why some type of comparison is necessary for good analysis. Further, the structure emphasizes the mechanics that can be applied elsewhere over the specific answer for the given hypothetical.

Returning to the driving under the influence example for the last time, the tips and warnings provided above are taken into account. The explicit comparisons in the Application, with appropriate citations, will show the reader the answer that follows in the Conclusion is supported and consistent with precedent. Using the facts, outcome, and rationale of the supporting cases, in conjunction with substantive vernacular, there can only be one outcome, and the reader only needs to examine the words on the page to learn the answer.

> *Example*: Unlike the defendant in (Case Citation), Defendant in this case controlled the direction of the vehicle, ultimately colliding with the fire hydrant. Citation. The movement of the vehicle in this case was not incidental because Defendant's foot was on the gas, not the brake, and Defendant controlled the movement of the vehicle with the steering wheel. *See contra* Case Citation. Although the vehicle in this case and the vehicle in (Case Citation) were both in drive, Defendant purposefully controlled the motion of the golf cart, even if the collision was unintentional. *See* Citation.

4. Conclusion

Coming from the most difficult part of legal analysis, drafting the Conclusion is relatively simple. In the event that any confusion might be present, the student need only examine the Thesis Statement/Thesis Question above and ensure that the Conclusion consistent with the immediately preceding Application. The benefit of the paradigm is that it prevents the student and the reader from getting lost and ensures that all oars row in the same direction. Double- or even triple-checking their own writing is an important part of the learning process and forces the student to make adjustments prior to submission.

Unlike other sections of the analysis, the Conclusion needs to be a simple statement that serves as its own paragraph. The purpose of the single-sentence paragraph for the Conclusion is twofold, the first being consistency as noted above. The second, and the more important of the two, is that the Conclusion tells the reader that the section is over, and it is on to the next subject of the analysis. The culmination of the analysis needs to be clear and explicit to ensure that the reader understands the answer.

Using a transition word for the single-sentence paragraph, the reader can see that the analysis for this element/factor is now complete, and the next issue will be subjected to TRAC. These subtle reminders aid the students and readers in keeping track of where they are in the paradigm. A restatement of the Thesis Statement/Thesis Question, even if it is to simply add the conclusory transition word/phrase, is all that is needed to finish the section.

Example: Accordingly, the State can establish the "driving" element.

E. TRAC in Action

The benefit of this simplistic approach is that it is easy for first-generation students to pick up, and they are not tasked with learning the subtle differences of multiple paradigms or risking potential confusion that their individual professors are looking for different styles of analysis. The mechanical approach of TRAC can be replicated across every legal writing assignment, midterm, final, or bar question. Moreover, as seen from the example above, TRAC attempts to demystify the stigma that legal writing is complicated or that it requires first-generation students to sound like lawyers. Compiling the examples above together for convenience, this is what the students will be expected to produce:

A. ***The State can establish the "driving" element.*** **(Thesis Statement/Thesis Question).**

OR

A. ***Can the State establish the "driving" element?/Whether the State can establish the "driving" element.*** **(Thesis Statement/Thesis Question).**

Pursuant to (DUI Statute Citation), the State must establish the driving element. **(Rule Identification).** *Driving requires the vehicle to be in motion and under the control of the driver. Citation. "Driving" is not synonymous with "operating" because operating simply requires that the mechanisms of the vehicle be engaged, i.e., the engine running, whereas driving requires intentional movement of the vehicle by the driver. Citation. Accidental or incidental movement of the vehicle will not satisfy the driving element of (DUI Statute Citation). Citation.* **(Rule Statement).**

In (Case Citation), the Supreme Court of (Jurisdiction) reversed the decision of the court of appeals and vacated the defendant's driving under the influence conviction. When the officer arrived, the car was running with the defendant asleep in the driver's seat. Citation. Even though the car was in drive, the defendant had his foot on the brake, preventing any forward movement. Citation. The Court held that the State failed to establish the driving element of (DUI Statute Citation) because the only evidence presented at trial indicated the vehicle moved only after the defendant exited the car in compliance with the officer's command. Citation. The incidental movement of the vehicle lacked the requisite degree of purposeful control by the driver, and the mere operation of the vehicle did not amount to driving as contemplated by (DUI Statute Citation). Citation; see contra Case Citation 2 (brief discussion of what happened in the case where a different result occurred based on a different fact pattern). **(Rule Explanation).**

Unlike the defendant in (Case Citation), Defendant in this case controlled the direction of the vehicle, ultimately colliding with the fire hydrant. Citation. The movement of the vehicle in this case was not incidental because Defendant's foot was on the gas, not the brake, and Defendant controlled the movement of the vehicle with the steering wheel. See contra Case Citation. Although the vehicle in this case and the vehicle in (Case Citation) were both in drive, Defendant purposefully controlled the motion of the golf cart, even if the collision was unintentional. See Citation. **(Application).**

Accordingly, the State can establish the "driving" element. **(Conclusion).**

The analytical template that TRAC provides is intended to be replicated as many times as needed to answer the intermediate questions before answering the ultimate issue. This "wash, rinse, and repeat" type of approach enables the student to provide well-supported analysis for each section and gain additional comfort with the paradigm the more they go through the process. Good legal analysis can be gained by staying on TRAC, and the simplistic approach benefits both the student and the reader. Making the process simple for both parties reinforces that legal writing is nothing more than communicating and reaching the broadest audience possible is effective and optimal given the most common recipients of a lawyer's message.

F. Maximizing the Utility of TRAC

After working through the process and seeing TRAC break down an issue, the focus can shift to other avenues to improve a student's legal writing. Although this chapter focuses primarily on simplifying the paradigm for legal analysis, an opportunity to provide additional tips and strategies would be lost if the same were not conveniently included in this resource. There are plenty of traps that can undermine proficient legal writing—identifying them ahead of time is the best way to help first-generation students navigate these hazards.

1. For the Professor

The legal writing equivalent of "training wheels" is a simple multiple element/factor objective memorandum assignment. This is not to insult the students' intelligence, but rather is intended to show them the most basic aspect of breaking things down to analyze singular issues in a systematic fashion.

I recommend starting with a closed-universe problem, preferably in a subject that the students do not have as part of their first-year curriculum. This will limit the variables and allow the instructor to focus on the writing and there will not be a perceived disconnect from the blackletter or generalized law being learned in the doctrinal class and the jurisdictional specific cases provided for the assignment. With the research that you provide to the students, provide some cases, secondary sources, and a couple of red herrings to help them realize that not everything is helpful or worthy of inclusion. Provide substantive feedback along the way to help the students see where they are excelling and where they are falling short. Remembering that the point of the first assignment is to not provide the correct answer, but rather, to learn the correct format and attention to detail necessary to succeed in law school and as a lawyer, will help focus attention when providing constructive feedback.

This first assignment is also an assessment for the professor because it allows for an objective checklist of on-going issues. If there are things that require additional explanation or clarity, this is an appropriate time to tackle the matter as a class to identify common problems. Every section of legal writing is different, and examples that may have landed in the past might not land with your current group. Use the opportunities for student feedback as a moment for self-reflection to better ascertain the connection between the students' issues and the materials that were covered. If it is a one-off problem with an individual student, the tailored feedback you provide should address the issue privately, but if it is a widespread problem, a refresher on the subject matter in a group setting could prove useful. This strategy is particularly helpful for first-generation students because it identifies the consistent issues of the group and places them on equal footing with their peers.

After the simple objective memorandum is submitted, transition to a multiple-issue, multiple-element, open-universe problem to better place the student in the position of a law clerk. The training wheels are off, and the students will use all of the tips and tricks that you provided thus far to obtain binding authorities and craft a responsive memorandum. Again, in favor of limiting the variables, stick with the objective tone for this assignment. The students have a lot on their plate, especially with finals on the horizon, so tension will be high. Mastering the building blocks is imperative toward efficient writing in all aspects of law school and beyond. If students perceive that they are not being thrown too many curveballs at one time, the systematic benefits of the structure and organization are more likely to be realized. Moreover, the "peeks behind the curtain" that you provide can help foster positive relationships with students.

There is also a very real possibility that this will be the first time that these historically high-performing students earn grades they are unaccustomed to receiving on assignments. In an effort to bridge the gap, selected submissions from the first assignment can be used as part of a group peer-review exercise. Show the students actual submissions as a means to demonstrate how their work will be perceived by a neutral third party. This group discussion is an additional opportunity to demonstrate to students that they are not the only one struggling with the finer details of legal writing, and the students can also benefit by working through solutions to common issues. This modality further instills that the first-generation students are well within the delta at this stage in their legal careers.

To fully immerse students into their future career paths, a persuasive writing assignment can help show the tonal differences, but that the structure of an argument is the same as the structure for predictive writing. Using common filings at the trial and appellate levels will provide students with insight as to how writing will shape their practice and give them a great starting point for their brief banks.[20] Coupled with oral arguments, this part of the curriculum helps first-generation students develop the confidence to stand and deliver, but also appreciate that writing is the foundation.

As part of helping students develop their ability to be persuasive with facts, I present a series of statements that must be incorporated by both sides as part of their fact pattern. This exercise is not simply looking for a parroting of the information back; rather, the importance on the placement and emphasis on certain aspects of the facts helps enforce the need for candor and the utility of confronting imperfections in a case. The students could construct their narrative in whatever way they felt best prefaced the underlying facts of an actual dispute, but they could not hide from the "bad facts" that they would eventually have to address.

For example, I provided this series of facts to have students draft a Statement of Facts for a persuasive argument:

- Bob built a robot for a robot fighting show.
- The robot has a saw blade and a flame thrower.

---

20. *See* Erger, *supra* at 543.

- Bob let his nine-year-old "play" with the robot.
- The nine-year-old was playing with the robot in the street.
- Bob's neighbor turned onto the street, became impatient, and honked at the child.
- Bob's nine-year-old got scared, hit a few buttons, and in the process, the robot destroyed the neighbor's vehicle.
- The neighbor is suing Bob for negligent entrustment.

Additionally, I present the students with a series of rhetorical questions to help probe whether the facts are most helpful to their objective. The students are tasked with answering the following, from the point of view of a disinterested person: (1) Which side do I represent? (2) Do you understand what the case is about? (3) Based on this information alone, what do you want the outcome to be? (4) Do you like one side more than the other? (5) If you had to pick, which side do you think has the better case?

Alternating sides and different types of underlying applicable law with each fact pattern, the students are exposed to different voices that can help best drive the answers to the aforementioned questions.[21] Accordingly, the end products from the exercise above can lead the students to create narratives that discuss the lack of reasonableness by the parent to unleash a young child controlling a destructive robot in public, or an unforeseen lack of patience from a neighbor unexpectedly scared a nine-year-old, and the neighbor is at least partly at fault. There is no "correct" answer

21. Other fact patterns used as a part of this exercise include: **Criminal Law** (Bob makes a living stealing cars and selling them for parts; Bob stole a vehicle from a parking lot on a hot summer day; the owner of the vehicle left their child in the backseat of the car while they were in the store; Bob drove the vehicle approximately five miles before noticing the sleeping child; Bob saw the child while in front of the fire department; Bob dropped the child off at the fire department, and after doing a vitals sign check, EMTS provided an IV for dehydration, and took the child to the hospital; Bob left in the vehicle; Bob is being charged with kidnapping); **Contracts** (Bob entered into a contract with his neighbor to paint neighbor's house on February 1, 2024; Bob's neighbor wanted the house painted by April 1, 2024, so that his daughter could get married at thehouse; Bob did not get the painting done in accordance with the contract; Bob did not order paint until March 17, 2024; Bob intended to paint the house the following week; it rained from March18, 2024 through March 29, 2024; the jurisdiction recognizes "acts of god" as a defense to contracts; and Bob's neighbor sued Bob for breach of contract); and **Wrongful Death** (Bob is a pledge master at a fraternity; a pledge died during a charity event; the jurisdiction does not permit hazing and defines "hazing" as "any event where an individual exerts peer pressure on a fellow student to belong or become associated with a group" and includes, but is not limited to, "activities such as binge drinking or eating, acts of physical exertion, or sleep deprivation"; Bob hosted the charity event called "Dance Till You Drop" and invited the pledges to use it as a fundraising opportunity; the deceased pledge had an unknown heart condition; the event was not a mandatory fraternity event, but it was held at the fraternity house and pledges felt obligated to attend; the school kicked Bob out after an investigation, citing the hazing statute, but the local jurisdiction refused to press criminal charges, also available under the statute; and the deceased pledge's parents filed a wrongful death claim against Bob under the statute).

for either position, but the different persuasive effects of each statement of facts can be judged by the class as a whole, and the students can see that borrowing and employing different techniques can be beneficial under the right set of circumstances.

Above all, remember that you are a resource and a mentor capable of being a positive example for how an attorney functions on a day-to-day basis.[22] There will be questions, and the best thing that you can do is to be available and approachable; this is an entirely new environment, one that you have navigated in the past.[23] Regardless of whether the questions seem simple, unrelated to the matter at hand, or incredibly pointed, providing an answer will help build the type of mentor-mentee relationship that can guide students toward successful careers in law.

In a sense, you are the first line of offense. Teaching students how to parse out legal issues and analyze them in a clear and effective manner will enable them to succeed on their midterms and finals. Any assistance that you can provide them along this path, even if not met with outright appreciation, helps you shape the future of the legal community and allows you to put your stamp on this profession more than practice could on its own.[24] This is a lasting legacy that impacts generations, and it is an immeasurable return on your investment in teaching students how to write effectively and with a plan.

2. Advising the First Gen Student

As a first-generation law student, there should be a sense of pride in everything they have accomplished to this point. However, pride can get in the way of success. Asking for help can be intimidating, but it should not impede a student's road toward maximizing their potential. One of the best things that you can do is consistently remind your students to seek help from anyone who is willing to provide a better understanding of how to get through their first semester, first year, and law school in general.

One of the primary areas where students will want to seek whatever help is available is citation. The *Bluebook* is the subject of plenty of memes depicting it not as a uniform system of citation, but an unholy source of intimidation and torture. Eventually, the *Bluebook* must be confronted, but like the rest of this chapter, this suggestion is to help students work smarter, not harder. The most useful part of the *Bluebook* is the index and that is where one should start when there are questions. The index does a good job of using clear terms to help identify the subjects that commonly arise with citation, so do not be afraid to show the students that you also use the index as a resource when fielding citation questions.

---

22. *See* Brown, *supra* at 314–16.

23. *Id.*

24. *See* Brown, *supra* at 316 ("I would choose a personable, value-centered professor over an expert who is a jerk any day of the week.") (quoting James Levy, *As a Last Resort Ask the Students: What They Say Makes Someone an Effective Teacher*, 58 ME. L. REV. 49 (2006)).

A misconception among law students is that the *Bluebook* is just another device used to nitpick writing. Instead, the *Bluebook* is the writer's tool to establish credibility and that is how it should be viewed to give them an advantage among their peers.[25] The purpose of the *Bluebook* is to provide clear articulation of where the authority the writer relies on can be found, down to the specific page or paragraph, depending on the jurisdiction. In objective writing, proper citation shows a supervisor that the writer can be trusted. In persuasive writing, it limits the daylight for opposing counsel to provide a counterargument. In the world of academics, it is a chance to demonstrate that a student is detail oriented and well-suited for a profession that requires precise attention. Any time spent mastering this tool will be well spent and the benefits are boundless.[26]

Citation to authority first requires students locate the materials, which is why research is an additional area where help should be sought. The standard of practice in most firms is shifting entirely toward electronic research, but these services can be cost-prohibitive for small firms or solo practitioners. Accordingly, recommend that students spend time exploring the electronic databases and the law library to discover what is available and how to maximize their research skills.

When it comes to research, proficiency alone is not enough; efficiency is also required. In helping students develop a research plan, advise them to start broadly and narrow the scope, so the universe of information is limited to more pertinent authorities instead of everything. Use more recent cases, and those coming from the highest court, to help them get a better understanding of how the law has evolved over time. Remind them to not ignore secondary sources at the outset, even if they cannot be cited, because these resources attempt to explain the law and direct practitioners/students to useful primary authorities. Secondary sources help explain the primary authority, providing a natural starting point for the base-level knowledge that will help refine research queries.

One final area where first-generation students benefit from seeking additional assistance is editing and proofreading documents. All of the forgotten grammar lessons from grade school might not come flooding back to them, or bad habits might have buried them.[27] Reminders on comma usage, subject-verb agreement, singular-plural agreement, active voice sentence structures, and apostrophes will be incredibly useful.[28] Reiterate that in this profession, words matter, and if there is any doubt with respect to homonyms or tricky words, consulting a dictionary, thesaurus, or even the internet, is a necessary step. Even if it is not required for your legal writing class, suggest that students get or find a copy of the *Redbook* and really dive into

---

25. Beth McCormack, *Making Your Writing Out of Cite: Using the Bluebook to Improve your Writing and Credibility*, 41-WTR VT. B. J. 30, 30 (2016).

26. *Id.*

27. *See* John H. Ridge, *Writing with Integrity*, 37-Oct. WYO. LAW 56 (2014).

28. Ann Nowak, *The Struggle with Basic Writing Skills*, 25 LEGAL WRITING: J. LEGAL WRITING INST. 117 (2021).

it, starting with the index.[29] The whole purpose of legal writing, as well as this chapter, is to assist students learn how to provide or improve clear and effective communication. Time spent with the *Redbook* to improve students' understanding of the language will provide a solid foundation toward achieving that goal.

In working through editing and proofreading lessons, I identify specific pet peeves that I have in writing. The intent of the list is to articulate common issues in legal writing, but this list will also spark questions and examples that we can work through as a class. While my list of issues is subjective to an extent, things such as subject/verb agreement, singular/plural consistency, proper noun/specific court names, tense agreement, passive versus active voice usage, and punctuation are all objective issues subject to correction. When layered with other concepts that I am trying to get students to focus on, e.g., formatting issues, structure, and citation, the students tend to ask additional questions and we can work through the solutions together. By being collaborative and not condescending, the students come see me during office hours, submit excerpts, or seek additional instruction in class. In fact, the subjectivity of the pet peeves list invites additional explanation as to why I do not like certain sentence structures, formats, etc., and we work through ways to rework how the information is conveyed to meet what would be expected of a new attorney.

Further, by providing timely, substantive feedback that provides exemplars of practical writing, the students are able to identify baseline issues and can monitor their own improvement over the course of instruction. This approach has been helpful to both first-generation and international students because it focuses on the message the student is attempting to convey at the outset, then polishing to the best possible product that they are capable of at that given moment. To that last point, I consistently remind students that much like the practice of law, writing also requires time and experience to hone the craft. As part of driving this message home, I provide practical examples that show citation issues or other mistakes to show them that the pursuit of perfection on a given day may yield varying results, and there are always opportunities for improvement, especially when providing adequate time for careful proofreading and editing. Working through purposefully bad writing (created by me) also helps students identify issues, especially when read out loud. To the latter point, sometimes the ear is better at identifying issues in syntax and punctuation than the eye. Reminding students that they have multiple senses to ascertain whether the sentence is saying what students actually want to say helps with the editing and proofreading process.

Although it might seem out of place in a chapter dedicated to legal writing, convey to your students that lawyers do not try to communicate like the actors who portray lawyers in television or movie dramas.[30] If the trier of fact is a jury com-

---

29. K.K. DuVivier, *You Can Judge a Book by Its Cover: The Redbook*, 31-Sep. COLO. LAW. 51 (2002).

30. Jim McElhaney, *Stop Sounding Like a Lawyer*, 94-Nov. A.B.A. J. 34 (2008).

prised of average people, trying to "sound like a lawyer" will only result in talking over the jury's head and confusing them; this is the exact opposite of what a good attorney wants to do. Tell students to use the language that they are familiar with while adopting the vernacular of the cases to reach an appropriate middle ground.[31] If the written materials sound like it could be written by a court, coupled with the thoughtful analysis provided by the students, there is no need to enter into a field of complex words that, if used incorrectly, demonstrate a lack of understanding of the subject matter. Be sure to remind the students that they should not feel the need to "fake it" because they have already arrived.

After all of the research is compiled, cited, and the analysis is provided, students need to review their work prior to submission; this bit of student advice is somewhat self-serving and ensures that the best possible product will be submitted for grading.[32] Remind students that legal writing requires significant time to edit and proofread. The most effective way to ensure that multiple reviews are possible is to have students create a calendar by working backward from the final due date. One week before the due date should be their personal deadline for the final draft, giving students seven days to perfect the document and allow them to take breaks in between each review, each one focusing on a specific task.[33]

For example, ensuring that their submission stays on TRAC can be one review, and citations can be another. Editing with a singular purpose with each review enables students to employ the overarching lessons of this chapter—isolate and analyze one thing at a time. This tried-and-tested strategy can help students work through the most complicated issues and communicate their understanding to a broad audience, ultimately preparing them for a successful career as a practicing attorney. Fresh eyes and a clear focus on a precise task will yield better results than trying to catch every issue at one time.

G. TRAC Meets Real World

The legal writing paradigms used in law school are not intended to have a three-year work life.[34] Instead, the foundational tools that are learned in the legal writing class will help shape your students' careers. Identifying the issue, breaking it down into manageable parts, and taking a systematic approach toward answering the ultimate question are steps that are equally applicable in law school and the real world. Much like time with the *Bluebook* and the *Redbook*, the time investment in learning the systematic and mechanical approach early, and perfecting it over years of prac-

---

31. *Id.*

32. Ridge, *supra* at 57.

33. *Id.*

34. Meagan McAlpin, *Transferring Writing Skills from Law School to Law Practice*, 76-Oct. Or. St. B. Bull. 13 (2015).

tice, will allow legal analysis to become second nature and the default manner in which problems are dissected.[35] By adopting this uniform approach, analytical structure is not an additional variable, but a solution.

An unsung benefit to teaching legal writing is that your own writing will improve. Revisiting the basics, helping students understand the materials and the core principles of writing, and reminding yourself of where you were as a writer will each help you appreciate that improving communication is an ongoing process. Regardless of whether you have been practicing for years or decades, an occasional reminder to "keep it simple" never hurts.

H. Final Thoughts on TRAC

Legal analysis needs to follow a paradigm to ensure that all of the requisite components are provided. This de facto checklist is not a new concept, but TRAC is intended to simplify the message for a new crop of recipients, especially first-generation students who might lack any preexisting guidance as to how this analysis is accomplished.

Hopefully, this chapter has made legal communication more approachable and relatable, even if only to distill and streamline long-standing writing methods into a more straightforward manner. Whether the information contained herein is effective is subjective and up to the recipient. However, if this helps one first-generation student stay on TRAC and allows them to achieve their goal of becoming a lawyer, it was well worth the effort.

---

35. *Id.*

Twenty-Four

The Silencing Power of Expectation

The Need for Law Schools to Amplify Diverse Voices in Legal Scholarship

Brittany L. Raposa*

WRITING IS A WAY OF THINKING. It not only allows us to feel but also allows us to think about things that are unjust, unresolved, or problematic. Writing carries our history, our story, and our voice. When something is not written about, the answer is to write it. To share our perspective with the world. To influence the reader to feel, to hurt, and to see our perspectives. There is power in allowing yourself to be heard—to tell the story of your authentic perspective. However, there is a place, among many, where individuals are not given the opportunity to exercise that power: *law schools and the legal profession.*

In 2019, I met a student of color who was passionate about women's access to quality reproductive healthcare. We sat in my office talking about such important issues for nearly three hours when I finally said, "In your time here, you should share your ideas in a law review journal." The student immediately responded by saying, "People like me do not get on law review. Plus, I can't really write." *People like me.* I thought about the final minutes of our conversation for months. Important and critical voices are left out of the legal conversation. The nature of legal education, and the system it is built upon, oppress those voices.

The silence of diverse voices in the legal profession can be oppressive and thick. Silence has power. The dominant cultures and perspectives define what is spoken about and decide who gets to speak. The effect on the non-dominant cultures is to learn the language of pure camouflage. They learn to dissociate from their own knowing and their own voice. Cue law schools. The dominant culture of law schools is whiteness. Whiteness is the very thing that built the system of law schools, with the expectations of elite white males carved into its very structure. Now, to this day, we have those learned expectations. The expectation that our students know how to write. That they know how to research. That they are comfortable with legal dis-

* Professor, Legal Editor, and Attorney. I would like to thank my students. Sometimes, you have to make a lot of noise, and the world's silence can be oppressive. But if you want them to hear you, then they will. So do not, not even for one second, ever stop making noise.

course. Those very expectations hold the power to silence our students of color and our diverse voices in legal writing. And unfortunately, the complaints that our students do not meet legal education expectations are far louder than the voices advocating for change to the system.

This chapter argues that by not teaching basic writing skills in our curriculum, we are oppressing the voices of our students of color and marginalized students as the unequal playing field created by the institution makes it harder for these students to publish. This chapter will first discuss how prior educational experiences disproportionately impact the writing skills of certain students. The chapter will then discuss the challenges that these students experience with legal writing, which make it more difficult for them to compete with their white counterparts for publication opportunities. Finally, this chapter will suggest programming outside of the traditional curriculum that law schools can put into place to assist and strengthen diverse voices in traditional legal scholarship.

I. The Problem: Legal Scholarship Lacks Diverse Voices

The lack of diverse voices in legal scholarship is, of course, tied to the lack of representation of a variety of races and ethnicities in law schools. According to the American Bar Association (ABA), 85% of all lawyers are white.[1] To be more specific, the ABA reports that 5% of lawyers are Black, 5% are Hispanic, and 2% are Asian.[2] Naturally, this data is mimicked in law schools, with students of color tremendously underrepresented in legal education.[3] White students represent approximately 62% of law students, while Black students represent 8%, Latinx students represent 13%, and Asian students represent 6%.[4] Students of color often feel that they are socially isolated in law schools, that they are invisible, and that their concerns are not valued.[5] Consequently, this has a negative impact on students' acclimation to law school, their confidence in their abilities, and their academic performance.[6] Most

---

1. Am. Bar Ass'n, ABA National Lawyer Population Survey: 10-Year Trend in Lawyer Demographics (2019), http://www.americanbar.org/content/dam/aba/administrative/market_research/national-lawyer-population-demographics-2009-2019.pdf [https://perma.cc/EQ7D-4NN4].

2. *Id.*

3. Aaron N. Taylor, *The Marginalization of Black Aspiring Lawyers*, 13 FIU L. Rev. 489, 508 (2019).

4. *See Statistics: 2019 1L Enrollment by Gender & Race/Ethnicity (Aggregate)*, Am. Bar Ass'n, http://www.americanbar.org/groups/legal_education/resources/statistics.html (last visited Mar. 1, 2021) (noting 23,761 white men, women, and others enrolled in law school in 2019 out of 38,283 total).

5. Pamela Edwards, *The Culture of Success: Improving the Academic Success Opportunities for Multicultural Students in Law School*, 31 New Eng. L. Rev. 739, 757–59 (1997).

6. *Id.* at 759.

pertinent to this chapter, one of the manifestations of this isolation is the silencing of diverse voices.[7]

Publishing law review articles or alternative types of legal writing offers a strong pathway to share your voice on legal issues and problems. Unfortunately, publication opportunities are limited for certain students based on ingrained expectations of writing in the law school system. Law review is one opportunity where students can share their voices, ideas, and perspectives with the legal community. However, biases typically deter students of color from participating in law review[8] and law schools reward students who "write White."[9]

The history of law review and journal publications illustrates an abundance of white male authors.[10] When looking at the top 250 authors in HeinOnline, an overwhelming amount of them are white.[11] Prior to the Civil Rights Movement, only "a few handfuls of Blacks made law review at the prestigious law schools."[12] Although there have been more Black law students admitted to law schools in recent years, these students have a minimal presence on the editorial boards of many law reviews.[13] In a 1998 study conducted by the *Journal of Blacks in Higher Education*, Black students made up 4.8% of the 1,038 law review editors at the 12 most prestigious law schools.[14] Another study from that period analyzed all of the law reviews in the United States and found that 75% of schools had no Black members at all.[15] Although law schools are not required to report the student demographics of their law reviews, it appears that Black students remain significantly underrepresented. For example, it was not until the year 2021 that the *Virginia Law Review* named its first Black editor-in-chief.[16] This lack of representation in the legal publication sphere undoubtedly makes students of color feel like they do not belong in legal scholarship. Consequently, many students of color see publishing or participating on a journal as an unattainable or unrealistic goal.

---

7. *Id.*

8. Christopher Williams, *Gatekeeping the Profession*, 26 CARDOZO J. EQUAL RTS. & SOC. JUST. 171, 191 (2020).

9. Talibah-mawusi Smith, *The Law and Educational Inequities: In Other Words, the Dilemma of Writing While Black*, 4 CRIT: CRITICAL STUD. J. 73, 74 (2011).

10. Cynthia Grant Bowman, Dorothy Roberts & Leonard S. Rubinowitz., *Race and Gender in the Law Review*, 100 NW. U. L. REV. 27, 27 (2007).

11. *ScholarRank's Top 250 Authors in HeinOnline*, HEINONLINE, https://home.heinonline.org/top_authors/ (last visited Mar. 6, 2021).

12. *See* Many of the Nation's Most Prestigious Law Reviews Have Lily-White Editorial Boards, 19 J. BLACKS HIGHER EDUC. 55, 55 (1998).

13. *Id.* at 56.

14. *Id.*

15. *Id.*

16. Mike Fox, *Virginia Law Review Names First Black Editor-in-Chief*, UNIVERSITY OF VIRGINIA SCHOOL OF LAW, https://www.law.virginia.edu/news/202102/virginia-law-review-names-first-black-editor-chief (Feb. 1, 2021).

Students of color often lack a sense of belonging when it comes to academic scholarship. In a series of conversations with students, I asked them various questions about their desire to be on law review and write legal scholarship. One student from Nigeria responded, "English is not my first language, and you have to write well to be on law review."[17] Another Black student replied, "I already had to work so hard to prove that I should be in law school. I don't have energy left to prove myself again.[18] Similarly, a Black female student indicated, "I want to write about so much. I want to write about how Black women are treated in law school and about how police treat Black people. But I will just be seen as angry.[19] When reflecting on the above statistics and views of students of color, it is clear that the white privilege exuded by law review journals contributes to invisibility and silencing. This inequity has tremendous consequences for students of color and marginalized populations, affecting their educational and future career opportunities.

II. The Expectations: Continued Silencing of Diverse Voices in Legal Scholarship

The lack of diversity in legal scholarship is a problem, and students of color are further silenced by expectations rooted in traditional law school structure and pedagogy. This section will highlight three expectations law schools have of their students and why these expectations silence our students voices.

A. Expectation One: All Students Receive the Same Skill Training Before Coming to Law School

Over the past decades, more and more minoritized students are attending undergraduate universities and law schools. Diversity has been written into the mission of almost every law school across the country with the intention to "eliminate bias in the legal profession" by bringing individuals together from different backgrounds.[20] Naturally, due to these varied backgrounds, differences in writing development are expected and should be understood by those teaching in law schools. Learning to write is a complex undertaking, and a student's personal and cultural identities tremendously impact their relationship with writing.[21]

---

17. Telephone interview with anonymous student 1 (Dec. 14, 2020).

18. Telephone interview with anonymous student 2 (Jan. 4, 2021).

19. Telephone interview with anonymous student 3 (Jan. 19, 2021).

20. *See, e.g.*, Diversity Plan, Am. Bar Ass'n, 1 (May 2011), https://www.americanbar.org/content/dam/aba/global/ABA_Diversity_Plan_May_2011.pdf.

21. Dana Lynn Driscoll & Jennifer Wells, *Beyond Knowledge and Skills: Writing Transfer and the Role of Student Dispositions*, 26 Composition Forum, https://compositionforum.com/issue/26/beyond-knowledge-skills.php.

High school students are not engaging in meaningful writing activity in order to be prepared for college.[22] A study by George Washington University revealed that high school writing assignments rarely required students to "criticize an argument, define a problem and propose a solution, shape their writing to meet their readers' needs, or revise based on feedback."[23] Further, in another study conducted by *The Chronicle of Higher Education*, 61% of high school teachers said their students have not written a paper longer than five pages.[24] Consequently, more than one-third of admitted college students have insufficient writing skills.[25]

Second, many studies reveal that there has been a significant decline in learning basic skills in undergraduate education.[26] Liberal arts education, which predominantly focuses on writing, has particularly declined over the years. According to a Primary Research Group study, nearly one-third of college students have never written a paper longer than 10 pages.[27] "I didn't really have to write in college"[28] is a common phrase we hear from law students. A study following 2,300 students throughout their four college years found that half of their courses required less than 20 pages of writing over the entire semester.[29] Further, writing skills are often graded minimally or not at all in college. One professor commented on how "faculty members are content merely to jot down a brief comment or two about a paper and hardly go through a paper line by line to correct writing mistakes."[30] Faculty may "justify their indifference to dreadful student writing by saying that when reading a paper, they mainly want to ascertain whether the student understands the ideas in the course.... Content alone matters, not how well the student has expressed it."[31]

---

22. *Why Are Students Coming Into College Poorly Prepared to Write?*, Carnegie Mellon University, https://www.cmu.edu/teaching/designteach/teach/instructionalstrategies/writing/poorlyprepared.html.

23. *Id.*

24. *Id.*

25. Debbie Morrison, *The Decline of Student Writing and What Instructors Can Do About It*, Online Learning Insights, https://onlinelearninginsights.wordpress.com/2012/09/11/the-decline-of-student-writing-and-what-instructors-can-do-about-it/ (Sept. 11, 2012).

26. Rebecca Flannagan, *The Kids Aren't All Right: Rethinking the Law Student Skills Deficit*, 2015 BYU Educ. & L.J. 135, 141 (2015).

27. *Report: Long Writing Assignments Now Less Common at US Colleges*, Learning English (Sept. 22, 2018), https://learningenglish.voanews.com/a/long-writing-assignments-not-so-common-at-us-colleges/4580476.html.

28. Delece Smith-Barrow, *Learn to Read, Write Like a Law Student Before Classes Start*, U.S. News & World Report (Aug. 1, 2013), https://www.usnews.com/education/best-graduate-schools/top-law-schools/articles/2013/08/01/learn-to-read-write-like-a-law-student-before-classes-start.

29. Doug Lederman, *Less Academically Adrift?*, Inside Higher Ed (May 20, 2013), https://www.insidehighered.com/news/2013/05/20/studies-challenge-findings-academically-adrift; see Richard Arum, Academically Adrift: Limited Learning on College Campuses (2010).

30. George Leef, *For $100K, You Would at Least Think That College Grads Could Write*, Forbes (Dec. 11, 2013), https://www.forbes.com/sites/georgeleef/2013/12/11/for-100k-you-would-at-least-think-that-college-grads-could-write/?sh=6c2608e31c99.

31. *Id.*

This writing decline in undergraduate education has disproportionately impacted students in low socioeconomic areas and the most marginalized students.[32] Even apart from this decline, writing in law school is significantly different from undergraduate education. Writing in undergraduate education is about using an "expansive vocabulary," while legal writing is "about being concise and to the point."[33] Despite this reality, there is an expectation that students should *know how to write when they walk through the door*.[34] Law schools assume that students just need to build upon their current writing skills and can simply transition into legal writing.[35] Foundational writing is not necessarily incorporated into the law school curriculum, and the current pedagogy "teaches law as a language, and thereby both reflects and perpetuates the biases in legal language and reasoning."[36] Therefore, the expectation that all students have the same writing abilities both harms students and perpetuates disparities that exist in legal writing.

B. Expectation Two: Faculty Should Grade According to Notions of Traditional Legal Writing

There are racially based perceptions about writing ability that unconsciously impact our ability to evaluate student writing objectively. There is a direct relationship between student achievement and teacher expectation.[37] Research has demonstrated that professors' expectations about writing, and how they grade based on those expectations, relate to student speech style, race, and social class.[38] Legal writing is rooted in tradition—a tradition created by white men. The standard for "good" legal writing is influenced by an age-old cultural bias, favoring a writing style handed down to us from white appellate judges. When our students do not meet this expectation, they are ultimately graded down. Indeed, "[t]he better legal writing is at teaching the language of the law, the more effective it is at muting those individuals whose voices are not included in the language of the law, and the more effective legal writing is at ensuring those voices will continue not to be heard in the legal context."[39]

---

32. Kathryn M. Stanchi, *Resistance Is Futile: How Legal Writing Pedagogy Contributes to the Law's Marginalization of Outsider Voices*, 103 Dickinson L. Rev. 7, 20 (1998).

33. Leef, *supra* note 30.

34. *Ten Tips for Transitioning to Legal Writing*, Georgetown Univ. L. Ctr. (2017), https://www.law.georgetown.edu/wp-content/uploads/2018/07/Ten-Tips-for-Transitioning-to-Legal-Writing-Final.pdf.

35. *See id.*

36. *See* Stanchi, *supra* note 32.

37. Cecilia E. Ford, *The Influence of Speech Variety on Teachers' Evaluations of Students with Comparable Academic Ability*, 18 TESOL Q. 25, 26–27 (1984).

38. *Id.*

39. Stanchi, *supra* note 32, at 20.

Not all individuals entering law school were exposed to traditional notions of writing. Some individuals speak in a dialect of English known as African American Vernacular English (AAVE).[40] There are two key features of AAVE that impact the ability of Black students to write in accordance with their professor's expectation of standard English. First, "certain phonetic elements of AAVE contrast with standard English.... In AAVE, certain sounds, or phonemes, do not exist and are replaced, and other phonemes are omitted."[41] Second, "AAVE is marked by negative concord; ain't in negation; irregular or bare past tense forms (e.g., jump for jumped); preterite/participle variations; the habitual be and steady (e.g., he be at work); and remote perfect been/bin (e.g., she bin had that car)."[42] In addition, "the absence of the copula and auxiliary *is* and *are* do not conform with the grammar of standard English."[43] The use of this dialect is stigmatized, which then leads to biased grading.[44]

In addition, legal education employs an analytical style of writing that may be unfamiliar to the culture of Black students.[45] Essentially, "[l]earning to write like a lawyer means to stop Writing While Black and to write like Whites. This impact may be felt in the shortage of Blacks ranked high in their classes, and the shortage of Blacks on law review."[46] Consequently, students of color must also navigate legal writing, which in many instances pretends to be colorblind. Colorblindness is a way of avoiding the complexities of racial history by ignoring the fact that racial differences exist.[47] Our law students are expected to write as though their color does not matter. Ignoring race when grading perpetuates the denial of racism and the perception that white racial frames are both objective and accurate.[48]

Further, many law students speak English as a second language (ESL).[49] ESL students face difficulties with "language fluency, comprehension, organization, and familiarity with rhetorical patterns of academic writing in English."[50] ESL students struggle the most with writing assignments due to the complexities of the American

---

40. For a detailed discussion of the linguistic origins of AAVE, *see* Gelsey G. Beasubrun, *Talking Black: Destigmatizing Black English and Funding Bi-Dialectal Education*, 10 COLUM. J. RACE & L. 196, 199 (2020).

41. *Id.* An example of this is "replacing the voiceless dental [q] with [f] (e.g., earth becomes earf)." *Id.*

42. *Id.*

43. *Id.*

44. *Id.* at 224.

45. *Id.*

46. Smith, *supra* note 9, at 85.

47. Nancy Barron & Nancy Grimm, *Addressing Racial Diversity in a Writing Center: Stories and Lessons from Two Beginners*, 22 WRITING CENTER J. 55, 59 (2002).

48. Bethany Davila, *Standard English and Colorblindness in Composition Studies: Rhetorical Constructions of Racial and Linguistic Neutrality*, 40 WRITING PROGRAM ADMIN. 154, 168 (2017).

49. Jennifer Jolly-Ryan, *Bridging the Law School Learning Gap Through Universal Design*, 28 TOURO L. REV. 1393, 1394 (2012).

50. Jane Hirschhorn, *ESL and LD Students: Diverse Populations, Common Concerns*, 5 PRAXIS: A WRITING CTR. J. (2007), https://repositories.lib.utexas.edu/handle/2152/62250.

legal writing system.[51] English "rhetorical patterns [are] shaped by western culture, politics, and values," and because ESL students may lack this background, they may not write in the way their professors expect them to write.[52] For example, certain cultures do not use thesis statements. In some cultures, a statement is strengthened by "repetition or citing proverbs; elaboration and decoration of ideas may be valued more highly than conciseness and specificity."[53] Unfortunately, ESL students, or students coming from multicultural backgrounds, are graded against students who can understand and write in clear, westernized English.

Ultimately, we all carry implicit biases and it can affect how we grade legal writing.[54] If a professor holds a bias that writing rooted in white Western culture is good writing, that bias could cause the professor to view her students who don't conform to that writing style as less capable. In turn, this could affect the students' grades, their ability to get on law review, and the students' view of their own capabilities. When a student does not write a certain way and is graded in relation to a professor's bias on how that writing should sound, the impact is much greater than a low GPA. Ultimately, the student is silenced.

C. Expectation Three: All Students Feel Like They Belong in Law School

Due to issues of belonging, not every student comes to law school with the same levels of engagement. There are certain barriers to engagement, academic success, and psychological well-being that impact select students. One study concluded that while there were no differences in academic preparation, students of color reported significantly higher levels of alienation and discomfort by the end of their first semester compared to their white student colleagues.[55]

Many of our marginalized law students experience stereotype threat. Stereotype threat refers to the risk of confirming negative stereotypes about an individual's racial, ethnic, gender, sexual orientation, or cultural group.[56] "Normal" law school experiences are different for students subjected to stereotype threat. For example, students of color who experience frustration are also likely to experience "the fear of

51. Jolly-Ryan, *supra* note 49, at 1394.

52. Hirschhorn, *supra* note 50.

53. Nancy Kreml, Laurie Berry & Jan Jake, *Working with ESL Students in the Composition Classroom*, Midlands Technical Coll., https://web.archive.org/web/20100529185103/www.midlandstech.edu/esl/eslmanual.pdf (last visited Mar. 16, 2021).

54. Russell A. McClain, *Bottled at the Source: Recapturing the Essence of Academic Support as a Primary Tool of Education Equity for Minority Law Students*, 18 U. Md. L.J. Race, Religion Gender & Class 139, 160 (2018).

55. Bonita London, Geraldine Downey & Shauna Mace, *Psychological Theories of Educational Engagement: A Multi-Method Approach to Studying Individual Engagement and Institutional Change*, 60 Vand. L. Rev 455, 469 (2007).

56. McClain, *supra* note 54, at 163.

confirming a negative group stereotype that they are not as bright as their peers."[57] If we put this into the context of writing, we can see two scenarios. If a white student is struggling with how to write a statement of an argument, they may think, "This is really challenging. I will have to work on this and ask my professor how I can improve." Faced with the same situation, the Black student may think, "This is really challenging. I cannot turn this in or ask my professor about it until I get it perfect because I don't want my professor to see me as the dumb Black student who can't write and doesn't get it." Therefore, the Black student may be further impacted by increased anxiety and a reduced ability to focus, which could affect their writing performance and their law school grades.

In addition, students of color are more likely to have a fixed mindset in law school. A growth mindset essentially views intelligence and abilities as things that are capable of improvement and growth.[58] According to psychologist Carol Dweck:

> In this mindset, the hand you're dealt is just the starting point for development. The growth mindset is based on the belief that your basic qualities are things you can cultivate through your efforts, your strategies, and help from others. Although people may differ in every which way—in their initial talents and aptitudes, interests, or temperaments—everyone can change and grow through application and experience.[59]

If a student's mindset is fixed, it means they believe they have limited ability.[60] No matter the amount of work they put in, the student will not be able to exceed their predetermined performance. Having a fixed mindset has two consequences within legal writing. First, if the student has a fixed mindset, they are likely to view negative feedback and setbacks as evidence of their limitations.[61] Consequently, the student's fixed mindset becomes a self-fulfilling prophecy: I think I cannot write, so I will never be a good writer.

Second, a professor may have a fixed mindset.[62] If a professor has a fixed mindset about their students, they are bound to be pessimistic about a struggling student's ability to succeed. Dweck specifically indicates that "[t]eachers with the fixed mindset create an atmosphere of judging. These teachers look at students' beginning performance and decide who's smart and who's dumb. Then they give up on the 'dumb' ones."[63] This brings us full circle, doesn't it? In law schools, a fixed mindset professor will believe that certain students are cut out for law school while others are not. The students cut out for law school likely fall within the traditional view of what a law

---

57. *Id.* at 172.
58. Carol S. Dweck, Mindset: The New Psychology of Success (2016).
59. *Id.* at 7.
60. *Id.* at 9.
61. *Id.* at 39–44.
62. *Id.* at 196–205.
63. *Id.* at 200.

student looks like—white. Further, if a student's writing strays away from white, Western European dialect, the professor may be less likely to expend the effort needed to assist the writing development of that student. Consequently, students who are non-native speakers may revert back to their native language when their anxiety is increased. A fixed mindset is problematic for both professors and students and creates a self-fulfilling prophecy: the writing will never improve and the student will never publish.

III. Suggestions for Moving Forward

Although we cannot instantly change these problems in law schools, we can absolutely take active steps to address these issues. Law schools have an obligation to give all students an equal opportunity to be on the law review. The following are suggestions on what we should consider and what programming we can create to allow our diverse students to have a voice in legal publications.

A. Rethink the Way We Introduce Legal Writing to Our First-Year Students

Many first-year legal writing courses focus on case development, analysis writing, and objective writing, but we should also consider adding basic writing instruction in the first semester. Teaching sentence structure, paragraph structure, and similar skills could help ensure that all students walking through the law school door have a baseline competency in writing. A student's first semester legal writing course is the proper place to teach students the basic writing skills they need to succeed.

Law schools have a variety of required legal writing courses for students in their first year. Virtually every law school requires a legal writing and research course for students in their first semester of their first year.[64] The first semester legal writing course typically focuses on case reading, briefing, researching, and memorandum writing. However, in order to address the needs of our current students, a significant portion of the course should focus on basic writing before transitioning to *legal* writing. Prior to moving onto memorandum writing and research, a legal writing course should cover the following: (1) grammar and syntax; (2) active and passive voice; (3) audience; (4) sentence and paragraph structure; (5) organization; and (6) basic argument writing. By teaching these writing skills, law schools will create an equitable space for students to transition into legal writing together.

Alternatively, or in addition to the above proposal, law schools can utilize the summer prior to students' first year of law school to teach foundational writing principles. These workshops can be available and free for all students, or for students

64. At my law school, students are required to take Legal Practice I in their first semester, and Legal Practice II in their second semester.

who are identified as needing additional writing support. In this way, we can help create a more equitable writing environment for all students.

B. Evaluate The Expectations We Bring to Legal Writing Instruction and Rethink Our Grading and Feedback

In order to be more inclusive and to facilitate publishing by students of color, we must change the way we think about teaching and responding to student writing in law school. In order to assist students with their writing, it is not enough to simply grade and then move on. We must assess our assignments. What do we do when we find that some students do not perform as well as other students? What do we do when performance seems to be linked to race? Instead of explaining the outcome of assessments in terms of identity groupings, we should consider what expectations law professors and students bring to writing. The assumption cannot be that students come to law school with different motivations to learn and different ability levels. It is not that simple. A serious problem arises with this assumption: our own biases lead to incorrect conclusions about race and writing ability. As a result, racial stereotypes often lead to performance differences even though race itself does not cause individuals to perform differently.

Students of color often respond best to feedback that holds them to a high standard but also affirms a belief that they have the capacity to meet the standard.[65] This type of feedback "reduced the effects of stereotype threat in that by holding the students to a higher standard, rather than a lower standard, and by affirming students' ability to meet the standard" professors were able to eliminate "the internal narrative suggesting that poor initial performance was confirming a negative stereotype."[66]

When grading legal writing papers, there are some other important issues to consider:

- When making corrections, use consistency and indicate the type of error made, rather than simply making the correction.[67]
- Ask questions when leaving feedback on papers to clarify what the student intended to say, as a correction may change the student's intended meaning.[68]

---

65. Geoffrey L. Cohen, Claude M. Steele & Lee D. Ross, *The Mentor's Dilemma: Providing Critical Feedback Across the Racial Divide*, 25 Personality & Soc. Psychol. Bull. 1302, 1304 (1999).

66. *Id.*

67. Laureen A. Fregeau, *Preparing ESL Students for College Writing: Two Case Studies*, Internet TESL J. (Oct. 1999), http://iteslj.org/Articles/Fregeau-CollegeWriting.html.

68. *Id.*

- In any law school classroom where writing is involved, provide model or sample answers to assist students in understanding the type of writing they are expected to mimic.[69]
- Allow students to work with a writing specialist or an academic success professor on their writing.
- When giving students readings on legal writing, utilize diverse voices and authors. Do not simply provide students with more writing instructions from white men.

C. Incorporate Diversity and Social Justice Issues Into Legal Writing Courses

Incorporating social justice issues into legal writing courses can associate legal writing with a sense of belonging.[70] Teaching issues involving race, gender, and ethnicity through legal writing can provide an outlet for students who feel silenced by traditional legal education. Using a social justice approach in legal writing classes can teach the value of both a legal voice and a personal voice, which can be especially helpful for marginalized students who feel like "outsiders" in the legal writing arena. Incorporating issues of social justice will not only encourage white students to examine the law from different perspectives, but it will also encourage students who feel like outsiders to express their ideas and share their experiences in writing.

D. Reevaluate the Law Review Admissions and Journal Selection Process

Law schools in which law review membership depends upon grades should reevaluate their policies in order to expand student access. Law students of color tend to have lower GPAs than their white counterparts.[71] As discussed above, these statistics have nothing to do with ability, but instead are attributed to implicit bias, stereotype threat, and mindset.[72] Therefore, basing law review membership on grades disproportionately impacts students of color, ESL students, first-generation students, and many other marginalized populations.

Instead, law schools can implement writing competitions for law students in which students are given a reasonable and fair amount of time to complete a writing assignment for consideration. Students should be able to seek the help of faculty, a writing specialist, or an academic success professor when working on this assignment. Disallowing student assistance in a writing competition not only stifles the

69. Kreml, *supra* note 53.

70. *See* Pamela Edwards, *Teaching Social Justice Through Legal Writing*, 7 Legal Writing: J. Legal Writing Inst. 63 (2001).

71. McClain, *supra* note 54, at 154.

72. *Id.* at 175–177.

opportunity for students to improve their writing, but further widens the gap between students who arrived at law school with strong writing skills and those who did not. All student writing submissions should be considered without considering student grades in order to remedy the different experiences of these populations in law school.

In addition, creating a journal devoted solely to race or social justice issues may also create a sense of belonging for students of color, as issues of race are not a predominant focus in the law school classroom or in legal publications. It could possibly give students of color the confidence to submit a piece of writing for publication. If law schools are unable to incorporate an entirely new journal (for financial reasons or otherwise), law reviews should commit to publishing social justice pieces in every issue in order to foster belonging and inclusion.

E. Teach Stereotype Threat and Mindset to Students in Their First Year of Law School

If we directly acknowledge the existence of stereotype threat, we can potentially neutralize its existence.[73] In the first year, law schools should teach stereotype threat and mindset to their students to both acknowledge these feelings and come up with ways for students to overcome them. All law school faculty should also receive training on stereotype threat. A great way to incorporate this is during law school orientation for all first-year students, where there can be a presentation on (1) what these concepts are, (2) how to identify feeling these concepts, and (3) ways in which we can combat them as a community.

F. Other Ideas to Foster Diverse Student Voices

- ***Partnerships with affinity groups***. Work with student affinity groups to conduct legal writing and law review article writing workshops.
- ***Faculty scholarship mentors***. Assign students of color a faculty scholarship mentor. This is especially important for students who did not make it onto law review. These students should be assigned a faculty mentor in order to help them with their upper-level writing requirement in law school. In this way, students get the same mentorship they would receive as those on law review.
- ***Panels or roundtables***. Law schools should host a variety of panels or roundtables in which diverse voices can talk to law students about their publications. This would allow students of color or marginalized students to see others like them publishing in the field, instilling a sense of confidence and motivation for their own legal writing futures and their ability to publish.

---

73. *Id.* at 177.

IV. Conclusion

No one voice needs to be the loudest, but every voice needs to be used and heard. The history and tradition of white voices dominating law reviews and legal scholarship is an unfortunate product of systemic racism. Law schools are obligated to give all students an equal opportunity to succeed both inside and outside of the classroom. Failing to do so is an injustice to our students and to the legal community as a whole.

Diverse voices in legal scholarship are critical to fostering a culture of respect and understanding. However, our law schools perpetuate oppression and silence our students' voices by denying them an equal opportunity to strengthen their writing and to ultimately publish. There are so many unwritten stories, and it is our duty as legal educators to give all of our students the tools needed to write them.

PART VIII Personal and Professional Development

Twenty-Five

Leveraging the Efforts of Law Schools and University-Wide First Gen Programs for First Gen Law Students' Success

Maria Dykema Erb* and Geraldine M. Muir**

Introduction

HISTORICALLY, SUPPORT FOR FIRST-GENERATION COLLEGE STUDENTS has been limited to the undergraduate experience. In addition, law schools situated within a larger institutional context, i.e., a university, have operated as individual entities; and graduate/professional programs have not typically collaborated with university first-generation resource centers. While some law schools offer specific, targeted support to their first-generation students, by not collaborating with the broader university first-generation student services, equity and access to specialized knowledge can be limited for first-generation law students.

* Maria Dykema Erb is the Inaugural Executive Director of the Boston University Newbury Center which was established in 2021 to foster the holistic development and success of first-generation undergraduate, graduate, and professional students. Maria has over three decades of higher education and student affairs experience having previously worked at the University of Vermont, Elon University, Duke University, and the University of North Carolina at Chapel Hill. As a proud first-generation college graduate, Maria holds a Bachelor of Science degree from the University of New Hampshire and a Master of Education degree from The University of Vermont.

** Geraldine "Gerry" Muir serves as the Associate Dean for Academic Engagement at Boston University School of Law, where she fosters a dynamic and equitable academic environment for JD students through comprehensive advising and strategic partnerships. With a rich background in higher education administration and regulatory education law, Associate Dean Muir has held progressive leadership roles in residence life, student conduct, academic affairs and central administration. She earned her JD from Georgetown University and an MS in College Student Personnel Administration from Canisius University. In addition to her administrative responsibilities in the School of Law, Dean Muir teaches the Legal Issues in Higher Education course for the Boston University Wheelock College of Education & Human Development's Educational Leadership & Policy Studies program for Higher Education Administration.

This chapter focuses on Boston University School of Law's efforts to, first, identify the unique needs of our first-generation law students, and second, meet those needs. And then, with the founding of the Newbury Center in January 2021, explains how the building of a collaborative model between a law school and a university's first-generation student center that supports undergraduate *as well as* graduate and professional students, facilitates greater success and equity for first-generation law students.

Boston University School of Law

During the 2013–2014 academic year, Boston University School of Law ("BU Law") initiated a review of its graduates' success on the bar exam, exploring a myriad of potential predictors for first-attempt graduate success, such as 1L GPA, 3L GPA, undergraduate GPA, course of study, and number of experiential credits completed. This faculty-led initiative opened discussions between administrators and faculty as to whether or not we were missing a potential factor, or demographic, in our assessment of who was overrepresented among those not successful on their initial attempt of the bar exam. Specifically, questions were raised about first-generation students and how best to identify and support their academic and professional success, both during their enrollment and as alumni.

Prior to 2014, BU Law did not have a centralized practice for gathering information on, or even defining who qualified as a first-generation law student. Questions arose as to whether this group identifier should be applied to students who were the first in their immediate family to attempt a college degree; the first in their extended family to attempt a college degree; the first in their family to attempt a professional degree; or whether the definition should be limited to only those who were first in their family to attempt a law degree.

The administration initiated a peer review of institutional and law school websites but found little public information on first-generation law student programs at the time, though there was significant information on the needs of undergraduate students.[1] The greatest presence of first-generation support services found documented individual events or academic support initiatives for first-generation students.[2] Having not found models external to the School, the administration looked inward, first implementing a survey of the then-returning J.D. classes, and then assessing these initial findings through a focus group of first-generation students. The administration sought to create a definition for first-generation *law* students, specific to our community, and to identify those students' unique challenges and needs through

1. Memorandum from Student Affairs to Associate Dean Geraldine Muir (May 1, 2015) (on file with the Boston University School of Law Student Affairs Office).

2. *Id.*

the survey, while checking our understanding and soliciting ideas for solutions through the focus groups.

From May 27–June 9, 2015, an electronic survey of five qualitative questions was emailed to the rising 2L and 3L JD students (approximately 430 students). The questions were:

> *"Are there challenges that you face in law school that are related to your identity or experience as a first-generation professional school student?"*
>
> *"Is there, or has there been, BU Law programming that you found particularly helpful in navigating law school thus far?"*
>
> *"In what areas do you think BU Law could better support first-generation professional students?"*
>
> *"Are there any specific program(s) that you feel would be most effective in supporting first-generation professional students?"*
>
> *"Please leave any additional comments here."*

Thirty-five students responded to the mailing, of which 31 identified themselves as first-generation students.[3] Of the 31 students who identified themselves as first-generation students, 12 were the first in their family to attend college, and 19 were the first in their family to attempt a professional school degree. From that initial survey several themes emerged as to the unique needs of these Boston University School of Law first-generation law students: (i) a need for support in building professional contacts; (ii) a need to understand the culture, as well as the breadth of different professional opportunities in the legal profession, beyond trial and transactional work; (iii) a need to find others with similar experiences and backgrounds; (iv) a need for mentors, champions, advisors, and role models; (iv) a need to work through imposter syndrome and/or questions of self-doubt; (v) a need to learn otherwise "hidden" aspects of law school—the costs of interviewing, financial planning, and casebooks, as well as social expectations for networking; and (vi) guidance with navigating difference; whether cultural, financial, religious, or other from the majority culture of the school, which is predominantly white and multigenerational professional/college graduates.[4]

The survey respondents made clear that they used a variety of resources to address the challenges they identified by the initial survey question. For our LGBTQIA+ and first-generation students of color, participation in an optional "Be Yourself" Orientation program, created for students of populations underrepresented in the legal profession, offered early strategies for academic success; introductions to 2L and 3L students, who could become experienced guides, if not mentors; and an

---

3. Memorandum from Student Affairs to Associate Deans Muir and Hornblower (June 10, 2015) (on file with the Boston University School of Law Student Affairs Office).

4. *Id.*

overview of the School of Law's resources to support student success. This optional program provided insights beneficial for the first-generation student, though it was not originally designed with first-generation students as a target participant group.[5] The first-generation students who were active members in the School's affinity groups (such as the Black Law Students Association, OUTLaw, and/or the Jewish Law Students Association), reported greater community, affirmation, and direction among their peers with whom they shared identity and experiences.[6] Multiple students noted the guidance of the Career Development Office and Student Affairs programs as beneficial for addressing questions around the professional expectations and culture of the law, as well as resources for personal decision-making and well-being. Yet, with all of these resources in place, there were still deficiencies that the students felt had to be addressed for them to have an equitable experience with their multigenerational professional student peers.[7]

Among the deficiencies identified in the School of Law's programming and support for students who were the first in their families to seek a professional degree, were safe spaces where a first-generation student could ask the "stupid" or "obvious" questions without fear of judgment or the distress of imposter syndrome. Networking with alumni who had shared their experience and could talk about the changes required—and not required—when entering a professional realm unfamiliar to their families, and how they navigated the transition was a request from the respondents. Earlier guidance, if not intervention, on exam preparation, and how the study of law differed from their undergraduate experience. There was also a request to connect with first-generation students at other law schools and graduate programs. And, repeatedly, the need for financial support and financial advising was expressed. Several students noted that their family could not offer the financial support or guidance that seemed to be assumed by others. Comments in class, such as a Property faculty member indicating that the students' parents would give them funds for a home deposit, could be alienating for some of the first-generation students whose experience, and opportunities, would be quite different from that assumption.[8]

After completing and summarizing the survey's findings, members of the Boston University School of Law faculty and administration outlined possible programs and initiatives that could be responsive to the students' feedback. Yet, before engaging these programs, representatives from the Career Development Office and Student Affairs team hosted a focus group with students who had identified themselves as first-generation professional students in the May–June, 2015 survey, and were available for the follow-up. In July 2015, feedback from the focus group allowed for the School of Law to set priorities and define action items to meet those priorities. The three priorities that came forward were: (i) access to practitioners for job counseling,

5. *Id.*
6. *Id.*
7. *Id.*
8. *Id.*

job access and knowledge of the profession; (ii) clarity on the unforeseen costs of legal education; and (iii) a first-generation student community.[9] Having set the priorities, members of the faculty, staff, and student body outlined, and implemented, a plan of action.

In the fall of 2016, the Admissions team modified the School's application to include the following question: "Did any of your parents or legal guardians receive a degree from a four-year college or university?"[10] This determination as to the scope of the group BU Law would include as "first-generation law students," was the first in a multi-pronged effort to identify the first-generation law students, determine what resources were needed to provide an equitable experience to that of our multigenerational professional students; and then to incorporate the first-generation students into our diversity, equity, and inclusion strategic planning such that their needs would be regularly considered when developing new programs. With the foundation of the Admissions team adding this question to our applications, BU Law was able to identify the cohort of first-generation students in each entering class and sought to connect incoming students with returning first-generation students.

In 2017, the students took a leadership role, forming a peer-to-peer student group for support, community, and education: the Boston University First Generation Professionals (FGP). FGP was founded by then first-year law student Miosotti Tenecora with a goal of creating a community where first-generation professionals could share their struggles and successes.[11] FGP defined, and still does today, "first generation professional" as "a law student who has attained or is pursuing a level of education beyond that of their families,"[12] and over the past few years, FGP has offered "mentoring, support, and the occasional class on the [law] profession's sometimes arcane rules of decorum."[13] Law students engaged in the group believe it has been invaluable in alleviating some of their imposter syndrome and informing them of the "esoteric customs"[14] expected in both law school and the profession at large.

Administrators at BU Law note that FGP has been a great support for the increasing number of first-generation college students enrolled at the school, from 39 in

---

9. Memorandum from Boston University School of Law Career Development and Student Affairs Offices to the Law Dean (August 3, 2015) (on file with the Boston University School of Law Student Affairs Office).

10. E-mail from Assistant Dean Alissa Leonard to Associate Dean Geraldine Muir (January 11, 2022, 2:20 EST) (on file with author).

11. Megan Woolhouse, *First Generation Law Students Bond Through Shared Backgrounds*, BU TODAY (April 23, 2019). https://www.bu.edu/today/2019/first-generation-law-students-bond-through-shared-backgrounds/.

12. Jessica Tomer, *First-Generation Law Students: Struggles, Solutions, and Schools That Care*, NAT'L JURIST (March 2019) http://www.nationaljurist.com/national-jurist-magazine/first-generation-law-students-struggles-solutions-and-schools-care.

13. Woolhouse, *supra*.

14. *Id.*

2018 to 55 in 2019, roughly 14–16% of each admitted class.[15] The FGP organization is not unique to BU; in fact, similar FGP groups can be found at law schools such as New England College, New York University, Stanford University, University of California, Berkeley, University of Georgia, University of Southern California, Yale,[16] and University of Pennsylvania.[17]

The BU FGP received funding for events and resources from the Student Government Association, empowering the students to advocate for their needs. The FGP has arranged trips to area sites, partnered with the Financial Aid team for financial responsibility and budget training beyond that already provided at the J.D. Orientation. They created a website, and included resources where prospective students could submit questions and, in partnership with the Career Development and Alumni offices, initiated a first-generation alumni network. Also, the group, working with the Career Development team and alumni mentors, developed a programming series addressing adaptive, or "soft" skills, how to network in large groups versus small groups, and how to make the "ask" for informational interviews without shame or self-doubt. Quickly, the FGP has established itself as one of the most dynamic and engaged student groups at Boston University School of Law.

One of the great successes from the creation of the BU FGP was that the group became better aware of university resources earlier in their enrollment process. The group maximized the skills of a few of the administrative offices and encouraged the offices to adopt new programs and initiatives. To address the priority of alumni advising and provide even more guidance on the "hidden curriculum" of the School of Law, the Student Affairs office created a series of pre-orientation modules, available to all students, containing information on the cadence of law school, the resources of Boston University, and opportunities for the students. The Student Affairs team also created the First-Generation Convening (FGC) as an optional part of the School's orientation program. The FGC brings first-generation students—new and returning—together with first-generation faculty, staff, and alumni for a welcome with the Dean and a social. This is then supplemented with an informational round-robin of academic, social and university resources for them to explore, effectively creating a safe space for new students to ask anything of the community. By bringing the breadth of resources forward to the first-generation students sooner, the students were able to dissolve the previous "invisibility" of the community, connect across class years, initiate mentor relationships, and know that their experience was seen, and valued, within the community. While this FGC is only one, optional,

15. *Id.*

16. Jessica Tomer, *First-Generation Law Students: Struggles, Solutions, and Schools That Care*, NAT'L JURIST (March 2019). http://www.nationaljurist.com/national-jurist-magazine/first-generation-law-students-struggles-solutions-and-schools-care.

17. Carmina Hachenburg, *Penn Law Initiative to Provide Mentorship for First-Generation Law Student*, DAILY PENNSYLVANIAN (March 25, 2019), https://www.thedp.com/article/2019/03/penn-law-first-generation-fellows-fgli-upenn-program.

half-day in the orientation week, it provides a foundation for some students that carries them for the next three-years.

Part of the FGC, but supplemented in additional programming, is an overview of the "surprise" costs of law school, and examples of how other first-generation students manage them. During the COVID-19 pandemic of 2020–2021, the strain on student and family finances became increasingly evident, especially when first-generation students were forced into remote learning. While many first-generation students were in areas with reliable internet, some were not, and new costs and challenges had to be addressed quickly. During this time, the School of Law, with generous alumni support, created an Access Fund: a development fund to be distributed by the Dean or her designee to currently enrolled students addressing unforeseen costs that could, without financial support, prevent the student(s) from continuing with their studies. The Access Fund, while available to first-generation and multigenerational students, enabled several first-generation students to continue their studies when they needed to buy better internet for their homes, had to relocate unexpectedly, faced food insecurity, or had to pay their own way for interviews or other professional development opportunities.

While the Access Fund was a vital emergency financial support, the School also created other, targeted funds to meet student needs. One program facilitates the purchase of interview clothes by students with limited means; another utilizes institutional travel points to support required travel for students; a third supports student attendance at conferences and networking events; and another provided information and training on topics such as renter's insurance, application waivers for bar admission and testing, and scholarships. Upon the solicitation of the FGP, the School of Law's Student Government Association created "equity tickets" for its signature annual events, making a limited number of tickets available for free or at a deeply discounted rate, so that students of all levels of means could participate in the memory-making events, such as the September Boat Cruise, the October Halloween Party, November Apple Picking, January Ski Trip, or late spring Barristers' Ball (aka "Law Prom"). Just as the source of financial need can differ, so too must the proposed solutions. Both the School of Law and the University have continued to invest in financial support for students with limited means to address an unforeseen or unexpected expense. It was exciting to see how the law school community responded to the needs and challenges of our first-generation law students once we had clearly identified them through the survey and focus group.

Yet even though first-generation students began reporting better experiences in 2017 through 2020, the School of Law noted a few needs that the law school administration could not fulfill without either greater training for the faculty and staff on first-generation student development, or access to a greater network of resources. While wanting to provide connection for first-generation law students to the other first-generation graduate and professional students within the broader Boston University community, the law school administration struggled to coordinate this effort.

Also, questions arose around the intersectionality of identity within the group, and how best to create a larger community of support seemed insurmountable with other competing demands on the diversity and student affairs professionals. There was an awareness of limited research on the needs of first-generation law students, or a limited knowledge of where to find such research. Serendipitously, in 2020–2021, Boston University was in the process of opening its inaugural center for first-generation students, the Newbury Center. This university-wide center was staffed with professionals trained in the needs and services required for first-generation student success and had the experience to implement programs both for undergraduate and graduate/professional student populations.

The Newbury Center

There has been very little research and scholarship conducted on graduate and professional students from marginalized backgrounds, including those who are first-generation, leading to a limited understanding of these populations' needs, especially when they are part of a larger institution with a primary enrollment of undergraduate students. However, in recent years, a shift has begun in graduate and professional schools across the country to better serve their diverse students, including first-generation students. In *A Diversity, Equity, and Inclusion Approach to Graduate Student Success and Outcomes*,[18] the co-authors recommend five suggestions for practice: (1) identify the unique needs of your diverse graduate populations; (2) create a sustainable infrastructure and build capacity; (3) conduct assessment of your programs/initiatives; (4) understand current issues and challenges facing your students; and (5) create a sense of belonging. By truly paying attention to the specific needs of students, colleges and schools can start moving away from the "one-size-fits-all" approach. Knowingly or not, the Boston University School of Law faculty and administration had taken steps that aligned with these recommended practices through seeking a deeper understanding of the varied needs of first-generation students, a highly intersectional population.

In *First-Generation Graduate Students: Reducing Barriers with Support Mechanisms*, Ardoin and Erb discuss the different types of supports available to first-generation graduate and professional students: peer-to-peer and institutionalized. With most first-generation student initiatives on college campuses focusing on the undergraduate student experience, more first-generation graduate/professional students are advocating for themselves by establishing their own organizations or clubs, as discussed with the BU First Generation Professionals. Some other institutions that offer peer-to-peer models are the Duke F1RSTS at Duke University, the First-gener-

18. Maria Dykema Erb, Kathy Wood & Matt Newlin, *A Diversity, Equity, and Inclusion Approach to Graduate Student Success and Outcomes*, in A PRACTITIONER'S GUIDE TO SUPPORTING GRADUATE AND PROFESSIONAL STUDENTS, 155–157 (V. Shepard & A. Perry eds., February 2022).

ation Graduate Student Coalition at the University of Virginia, and the First Generation and Low-Income Graduate Student Organization at Cornell University.[19]

Through the institutionalized approach, universities have come to know the needs of their first-gen graduate/professional students by establishing initiatives or programs that include dedicated professional staff and resources with expertise in working with these populations. Some examples of the institutionalized approach include the Carolina F1RSTS in The University of North Carolina at Chapel Hill (UNC) Graduate School, First Generation Support Services in the University of California San Francisco Student Success Center, the First-Generation Graduate Students Core Programs in the University of Washington Graduate School, and First-gen Connect in the University of Minnesota Graduate School. The distinctive feature of all these programs is that the responsibility for support resides with full-time staff, rather than the students having to be the catalyst. Some of the unique aspects of these programs include workshops that are focused on both the professional and personal development of first-generation graduate students; social events to build community; mentoring programs with peer, faculty/staff, or alumni mentors; and online directories of first-generation faculty, staff, and allies.[20]

At Boston University (BU), the institutionalized approach was initiated with the opening of the Newbury Center in January 2021, to celebrate and support the holistic development of first-generation students. The Center defines a first-generation graduate/professional student as someone whose parents/guardians/caregivers have not completed an advanced degree, e.g., master's, doctoral, or professional degree.[21] The Center is positioned within BU Community and Inclusion, which also includes Diversity and Inclusion, and reports to the provost.[22] Because of this unique reporting structure, the Newbury Center has the ability and flexibility to break down the silos across campus and collaborate with all the colleges and schools to support their first-generation student populations. With three full-time staff members, a dedicated physical space, and an operating budget, the Newbury Center serves the entire first-generation student community. The Newbury Center is

---

19. Information on these programs is available at: Duke F1RSTS at Duke University, https://sites.duke.edu/dukef1rsts/; First-generation Graduate Student Coalition at the University of Virginia, https://graddiversity.virginia.edu/student-affinity-groups/first-generation-graduate-student-coalition; First Generation and Low-Income Graduate Student Organization at Cornell University, https://cornell.campusgroups.com/figli/home/.

20. Information on these programs is available at: Carolina F1RSTS at The University of North Carolina at Chapel Hill, https://graddiversity.unc.edu/initiatives/1st-gen-grads/; First Generation Support Services in the University of California San Francisco Student Success Center, https://firstgen.ucsf.edu/; First-generation Graduate Students Core Programs in the University of Washington Graduate School, https://https://grad.uw.edu/current-students/student-success/first-generation-graduate-students/; and First-gen Connect in the University of Minnesota Graduate School, https://firstgen.dev.umn.edu/grad/being-a-graduate-student.

21. Newbury Center, https://www.bu.edu/newbury-center/.

22. Boston University Diversity & Inclusion, https://www.bu.edu/diversity/.

one of the few, if only, university-wide first-generation student centers that supports all who identify as first-generation—undergraduate, graduate, and professional students.

In February 2021, the Newbury Center director conducted focus groups with the first-generation graduate and professional students from the University's medical, dental, law, and graduate schools. Through these conversations, similar themes emerged from first-generation graduate/professional students from across disciplines: (i) establishing and expanding one's professional network; (ii) deciphering the hidden curriculum of what's expected while in graduate/professional school and then the professional world; (iii) finding mentors in faculty, staff, and alumni who might have been first-gen students themselves; (iv) building a sense of belonging and community with other first-generation students; and, (v) navigating school in general with everything, ranging from mental health and wellness, identifying and mitigating imposter syndrome, managing finances, maintaining relationships with family, to learning to say "no"/establishing boundaries.

Because BU Law Student Affairs and the Newbury Center strive to operate from a "student-centered" approach, they came together to strategize on how best to support the FGP. The connection between the FGP and Student Affairs in BU Law with the Newbury Center has gone smoothly because of early conversations and relationship building by all parties involved. Immediately engaging FGP was an important part of them knowing that they were welcome to participate in all the offerings of the Newbury Center. The programming and goals of the Newbury Center were directly aligned with the previously identified needs of BU Law students through their surveys and assessment. The physical proximity of the School of Law being immediately adjacent to the Newbury Center has been beneficial in fostering the natural connection as well.

The growth in the first year of the Newbury Center has been rapid and the FGP students have engaged enthusiastically in our offerings. Programming encompasses professional and personal development workshops, as well as social activities, to build community across campus. The law students meet other first-generation graduate and professional students from all different disciplines and build relationships with them because of their shared first-generation identity.

Signature events that bring the first-generation student community together occur regularly throughout the year. These include the Newbury Center Welcome and Orientation, the Tri-Alpha (Alpha Alpha Alpha) National Honor Society, and the First-generation Graduation Pinning Ceremony. At the beginning of the academic year, all first-generation students are invited to a Newbury Center Welcome and Orientation. This is an opportunity for the new graduate/professional students to learn how they can engage with the Newbury Center, where they can turn to find support, and start to establish their community at BU by meeting other new students. The Newbury Center staff also participates in BU Law's First-Generation Convening as another opportunity to promote collaboration.

The BU Gamma Iota Chapter of Tri-Alpha,[23] a national honor society for first-generation college students, is an opportunity to become part of a community that celebrates first-generation students' achievements. This honor society was founded in 2018 at Moravian College (now Moravian University) to recognize the academic accomplishments of first-generation college students, as well as their leadership roles, extracurricular activities, and service to community. In addition to undergraduate first-generation college students, they welcome graduate/professional students, faculty, staff, and alumni who themselves were first-generation college students as members. This honor is also an excellent addition to students' curriculum vitae or resumes that highlights the fact that they were a first-generation student.[24]

When first-generation students graduate from BU, it's important to take a moment to recognize the journey to achieving their degrees. The Newbury Center holds an annual First-Generation Graduation Pinning Ceremony during the May Commencement Weekend.[25] Family and loved ones are invited to the ceremony where the graduates will receive their Terrier F1RSTS pin from someone who has played a significant role in their BU journey. All graduating Tri-Alpha members will also receive their honor cords during that ceremony. The First-Generation professionals will share the common identifying markers that will unify them with all of the graduating first-generation students university-wide.

Specific programming that caters to the first-generation graduate/professional student identity is one of the key elements of the success of the Newbury Center and is shared with students via the weekly newsletter. One area is the mental health and wellness of graduate students. This has become a top priority on college campuses as evidenced in the "Supporting Graduate Student Mental Health and Well-being: Evidence Informed Recommendations for the Graduate Community" report released by the Council of Graduate Schools. We also know that students whose intersections of identity, like being first-generation, can further exacerbate their health and wellness challenges.

The Newbury Center has collaborated with campus partners like the College Mental Health Program, Student Health Promotion and Prevention, Student Wellbeing, and Marsh Chapel to offer programs like: "Family Matters: Your Relationship with Family as a First-generation Graduate Student," "It's OK to say NO: Creating and Maintaining Boundaries as a First-generation Graduate or Professional Student," "Koru Mindfulness," and "Pivot Don't Panic." The College Mental Health Program has also offered individual student wellness coaching to students. Not all students may need regular mental health counseling and, for some, counseling may hold a stigma. Coaching is a way to introduce students to the concept of counseling and offer students advice about situations that may not rise to the level of a mental

23. *Available at* https://www.bu.edu/newbury-center/category/tri-alpha/.

24. *Id.*

25. *Available at* https://www.bu.edu/newbury-center/category/graduation-pinning-ceremony/ (last accessed May 18, 2022).

health counseling appointment, especially when so many campus counseling centers are over capacity.

Another area that the Newbury Center director addresses is a four-week facilitated workshop series on Meaning-Making for First-generation Graduate/Professional Students. Through this series, students explore their core values, and the past/present/future of where they are in life and why they are pursuing their advanced degree. Understanding how they make meaning and find purpose in pursuit of their career path can help provide clarity and intentionality to their experiences while in law school.

Financial literacy is often an area that first-generation students want to learn more about while they're in school to plan ahead for life after they complete their degrees. Some of the workshops that the Newbury Center offers are: "Taking Credit—Owning Your Relationship with Money," "First-generation and Finances—Budgeting, Credit Scores," and "Tips to Save Money." Other workshops and events that fall within the area of academics and career preparation have included: "How to Negotiate When Negotiating Makes You Nervous," "Identifying and Overcoming Imposter Syndrome," "A Field Guide to Graduate School: Uncovering the Hidden Curriculum—Campus-wide talk by Jessica McCrory Calarco," and "The Unspoken Rules: Secrets to Starting Your Career Off Right—Campus-wide talk by Gorick Ng."

One of the most important parts of building a first-generation community is ensuring that the students have an opportunity to gather for social events. Some examples include "Fuel-Up Fridays," which is a weekly breakfast in the Center where all first-generation students (undergraduate, graduate, and professional students) come together for informal conversation and connection; "First-generation Fridays," a first-generation Thanksgiving Community Dinner, and opportunities to build social capital like attending the Nutcracker performed by the Boston Ballet and exploring local museums.

The First Generation Professionals are also included in the BU/Duke University/University of North Carolina at Chapel Hill First-generation Graduate and Professional Student Symposium.[26] This symposium, which was originally established in 2018 by the Carolina Grad Student F1RSTS at UNC Chapel Hill and Duke F1RSTS at Duke University incorporated BU's first-generation graduate and professional students in 2021. This half-day program brings together students from all three of these institutions and beyond to learn about issues of importance to first-generation students and provides time for them to network and share their first-generation stories with one another.

One of the most frequent comments that first-generation graduate and professional students make is that they want the faculty and staff of their institution to be

26. *Available at* https://www.bu.edu/newbury-center/2022/02/23/the-5th-annual-first-generation-graduate-student-symposium/.

aware of and sensitive to their needs. They want the faculty and staff to genuinely listen to their experiences and not diminish their first-generation identities. To create a network of support across the campus, the Newbury Center provides training that is open to all BU faculty and staff to learn about the characteristics and experiences of first-generation students, and how they might support them in their educational journey. This training, known as the Terrier F1RSTS Advocates Training, involves two parts—part 1 focuses on the undergraduate experience and part 2 focuses on the graduate/professional student experience.[27] Each training includes a live student panel where the participants can ask questions and listen to the firsthand experiences of first-generation students. Student panelists come from all different disciplines, including the School of Law. By publicly displaying the Terrier F1RSTS Advocates directory on the website, students can have an easier time searching for faculty and staff who are willing to serve as mentors to them.[28]

As the Newbury Center and BU Law Student Affairs look to the future, further initiatives will be developed to continue building on the foundation already established in year one of the Newbury Center's existence. While BU Law has created a fund for students to purchase interview clothing for students, the Newbury Center has partnered with the Center for Career Development to open the BU Professional Clothing Closet. [29] This project was an identified need by Tima Dasouki, an undergraduate first-generation student who approached the Newbury Center director with the idea. Over the course of one year, Tima did the research and legwork through the BUild Lab IDG Capital Student Innovation Center to turn this into a reality. All BU students, regardless of their income level or identity, will be eligible to choose free professional attire from this clothing closet.

The Newbury Center is also partnering with Development and Alumni Relations to not only raise funds for the specific clothing and supply needs of the Professional Clothing Closet, but also for first-generation students who need funds to assist them in attending/presenting at professional conferences and provide paid internships. These funds would be open to all first-generation students at BU, including the FGP.

Sponsoring events for the FGP with undergraduate first-generation students who are interested in pursuing a law degree will not only support the aim of diversifying the field of law, but will also build an immediate mentoring opportunity where the undergraduates will have role models who share their first-gen identity. The FGP can share their tips on how to apply for law school and things that they wished they had known throughout the process.

---

27. *Available at* https://www.bu.edu/newbury-center/faculty-staff/mentorship-training/ (last accessed May 18, 2022).

28. Terrier F1RSTS Advocates Directory, https://www.bu.edu/newbury-center/about/terrier-f1rsts/terrier-f1rsts-directory/.

29. *Available at* https://www.bu.edu/careers/networking-interviews/interviewing-the-big-picture/professional-clothing-closet/ (last accessed May 18, 2022).

Plans are also underway to create a vibrant and robust first-generation alumni network with BU Development and Alumni Relations, which has never been done before. By identifying alumni who were first-generation undergraduate or graduate/professional students themselves, current FGP will have access to an even greater alumni network that will go beyond just BU Law. No matter what area of law the FGP might pursue, they will benefit from the broader reach to alumni in all different career paths.

An important facet of this innovative model for supporting FGP within a larger university setting is the assessment of the progress, student satisfaction, and degree completion. The Newbury Center has partnered with the Assistant Provost for Academic Data and Decision Support to develop a comprehensive assessment plan that will include focus groups, surveys, and data analysis to examine the entire Center. The overall data that will be collected will be able to be broken down by college/school so the direct impact can be measured for FGP students in BU Law.

Better Together: Law School and University

In closing, law school administrators are encouraged to look beyond the walls of their own building(s) to find the resources and expertise best able to support their first-generation students' success. Taking time to identify what is needed by each institution's unique student body is a vital start to building out a substantive and equity-focused support program for first-generation students, but limiting the resources for these students to only the law school or the legal community shortchanges the experience of the first-generation students, and can overtax the law school administrators. By collaborating with the Newbury Center, the first-generation law students of Boston University are making connections with alumni and students from other University colleges, such as the Medical and Dental Schools, the Questrom School of Business, as well as other graduate programs. This offers more than a broader friend group or mentor group—which is valuable in and of itself—but also a network of fellow experts and leaders who will be progressing in their careers, enabling our students to have a broader understanding of industry, education, as well as a network of potential supports, or clients.

Law school administrators benefit by having first-generation Center professionals with broader experience and subject matter knowledge provide them with targeted options and solutions for various challenges, such as addressing interviewing clothes, financial challenges, imposter syndrome, or even food insecurity. For law schools not affiliated with a university, administrators are encouraged to seek out resources from Tri-Alpha and other national organizations. By reaching out to either university resources or broader community resources, law schools can coordinate resources to empower first-generation students and facilitate an educational experience that is equitable to that of their multigenerational peers.

References

Sonja Ardoin & Maria Dykema Erb, *First-Generation Graduate Students: Reducing Barriers with Support Mechanisms, in* A HANDBOOK FOR SUPPORTING TODAY'S GRADUATE STUDENTS (D.J. Nguyen & C. W. Yao eds., May 2022).

E-mail from Assistant Dean Alissa Leonard to Associate Dean Geraldine Muir (January 11, 2022) (on file with author).

Maria Dykema Erb, Kathy Wood & Matt Newlin, *A Diversity, Equity, and Inclusion Approach to Graduate Student Success and Outcomes, in* A PRACTITIONER'S GUIDE TO SUPPORTING GRADUATE AND PROFESSIONAL STUDENTS 155–157 (V. Shepard & A. Perry eds., February 2022).

Carmina Hachenburg, *Penn Law Initiative to Provide Mentorship for First-Generation Law Students,* DAILY PENNSYLVANIAN (March 25, 2019), *available at* https://www.thedp.com/article/2019/03/penn-law-first-generation-fellows-fgli-upenn-program.

Memorandum from Student Affairs to Associate Dean Geraldine Muir (May 1, 2015) (on file with the Boston University School of Law Student Affairs Office).

Memorandum from Student Affairs to Associate Deans Muir and Hornblower (June 10, 2015) (on file with the Boston University School of Law Student Affairs Office).

Memorandum from Boston University School of Law Career Development and Student Affairs Offices to the Law Dean (August 3, 2015) (on file with the Boston University School of Law Student Affairs Office.

Jessica Tomer, *First-Generation Law Students: Struggles, Solutions, and Schools That Care,* NAT'L JURIST (March 2019), *available at* http://www.nationaljurist.com/national-jurist-magazine/first-generation-law-students-struggles-solutions-and-schools-care.

Megan Woolhouse, *First Generation Law Students Bond Through Shared Backgrounds,* BU TODAY (April 23, 2019), a*vailable at* https://www.bu.edu/today/2019/first-generation-law-students-bond-through-shared-backgrounds/.

Council of Graduate Schools & The Jed Foundation, *Supporting Graduate Student Mental Health and Well-Being* (2022), *available at* https://cgsnet.org/wp-content/uploads/2022/01/CGS_JED_Grad-Student-Mental-Health-Report-1.pdf (last accessed May 18, 2022).

Twenty-Six

Experiential Learning

Jennifer Safstrom*

EXPERIENTIAL LEARNING—including clinics, practicums, externships, and other immersion-based courses—is an essential component of the law school experience. For some, experiential learning is integral to their student experience[1] or played a role in deciding where to attend law school.[2] Such experiential education opportunities may constitute a student's first substantive immersion into legal work and client services, or even constitute their first consequential professional immersion. Administrators, faculty, and staff should carefully consider the unique experiences of first-generation students in approaching this work, given the personal and professional significance of immersive learning for law students.

I. Defining Experiential Learning

Experiential education has been described as "a platform for hands-on learners, [that] intertwines theory and practice in ways that the classroom alone cannot, and explores problem solving, hypothesis testing, and strategic planning, among other pedagogical benefits."[3] Law schools and practitioners alike recognize the empirical importance of "practical" or "hands-on" experience.[4]

---

* Assistant Clinical Professor of Law and Director, Stanton Foundation First Amendment Clinic, Vanderbilt University Law School. All views expressed are my own and do not reflect those of any current or previous employer, client, or other entity.

1. The importance of experiential learning has even been cited as a basis for the recovery of tuition in COVID-19 litigation against colleges and universities. See e.g., Botts v. Johns Hopkins Univ., No. CV ELH-20-1335, 2021 WL 1561520, at *3 (D. Md. Apr. 21, 2021); Amable v. New Sch., No. 20-CV-3811 (KMK), 2021 WL 3173739, at *10 (S.D.N.Y. July 27, 2021).

2. *Best Clinical Training Programs,* U.S. News & World Report (2022), https://www.usnews.com/best-graduate-schools/top-law-schools/clinical-training-rankings.

3. Keith A. Findley, *Assessing Experiential Legal Education: A Response to Professor Yackee,* 2015 Wis. L. Rev. 627, 630 (2015)

4. *See* Alli Gerkman & Logan Cornett, *Foundations for Practice: Hiring the Whole Lawyer: Experience Matters* (Jan. 17, 2017) ("respondents indicated that if they wanted to hire people with the broad array of foundations they identified as important, they would rely on criteria rooted in experience, including legal employment, recommendations from practitioners or judges, legal externships, participation in a law school clinic, or other experiential education"); *see also, e.g.,* Columbia Law, Experiential Learning, https://www.law.columbia.edu/academics/experiential; George Washington University School of Law, Experiential Learning, https://www.law.gwu.edu/experiential-learning;

The American Bar Association's (ABA) Standards for Approval of Law Schools require that law students take at least six credit hours in "experiential courses."[5] A "simulation course, a law clinic, or a field placement" satisfies this requirement.[6] Experiential learning courses:

1. integrate doctrine, theory, skills, and legal ethics, and engage students in perform[ing]...professional skills, [including] "[l]egal analysis and reasoning, legal research, problem-solving, and written and oral communication in the legal context,"[7] [as well as] "interviewing, counseling, negotiation, fact development and analysis, trial practice, document drafting, conflict resolution, organization and management of legal work, collaboration, cultural competency, and self-evaluation";[8]
2. develop the concepts underlying the professional skills being taught;
3. provide multiple opportunities for performance;
4. provide opportunities for student performance, self-evaluation, and feedback from a faculty member, or, for a field placement, a site supervisor;
5. provide...a classroom instructional component, regularly scheduled tutorials, or other means of ongoing, contemporaneous, faculty-guided reflection; and
6. provide direct supervision of the student's performance by...a faculty member or a site supervisor.[9]

Under the ABA requirements, "law school[s] shall provide substantial opportunities to students for law clinics or field placement(s)."[10] While institutions generally have broad discretion in the implementation of this standard, the requirements as a whole impose some additional limitations. For instance, the standards preclude the university from allowing a single course to satisfy both the upper-class writing requirement and experiential learning requirement.[11]

Many programs engage in law-related public service activities, including: helping "protect civil rights, civil liberties, or public rights"; assisting "charitable, religious, civic, community, governmental, and educational organizations not able to afford legal representation"; "participating in activities providing information about justice, the law or the legal system to those who might not otherwise have such infor-

---

University of Wisconsin School of Law, Experiential Learning, https://law.wisc.edu/experiential learning/.

5. ABA Standard 303(a)(3).
6. *Id.*
7. ABA Standard 302.
8. ABA Standard 302, Interpretation 302-1.
9. ABA Standard 304.
10. ABA Standard 303.
11. ABA Standard 303, Interpretation 303-1.

mation"; and "engaging in activities to enhance the capacity of the law and legal institutions to do justice."[12]

A. Clinic

A legal clinic is a program that provides students with the opportunity to engage in direct legal work, providing services to clients under the guidance of a licensed attorney. In legal clinics, students are primarily responsible for engaging in legal services, often taking on first chair responsibilities as student-attorneys. Clinics can cover a wide range of subjects, including housing,[13] immigration,[14] labor,[15] technology,[16] disability,[17] gender,[18] the environment,[19] carceral issues,[20] and intellectual property,[21] among others. Student practice rules across jurisdictions facilitate such engagement, as federal and state courts authorize eligible law students to practice under the supervision of a licensed, practicing lawyer.[22] However, some clinical work focuses on policy, contractual, and other non-litigation projects outside of courts.[23]

---

12. ABA Standard 303, Interpretation 303-4; *see also* ABA Model Rules of Professional Conduct Rule 6.1.

13. *See, e.g.*, University of D.C. David A. Clarke School of Law, Housing & Consumer Law Clinic, https://law.udc.edu/?HousingClinic.

14. *See, e.g.*, Stanford Law, Immigrants' Rights Clinic, https://law.stanford.edu/immigrants-rights-clinic/.

15. *See, e.g.*, Cornell Law School, Labor Law Clinic, https://www.lawschool.cornell.edu/academics/experiential-learning/clinical-program/labor-law-clinic/.

16. *See, e.g.*, New York University School of Law, Technology & Law Clinic, https://www.law.nyu.edu/academics/clinics/tech-law-policy.

17. *See, e.g.*, Syracuse University, College of Law, Disability Rights Clinic, http://law.syr.edu/academics/clinical-experiential/clinical-legal-education/disability-rights-clinic/.

18. *See, e.g.*, Columbia Law School, Sexuality and Gender Law Clinic, https://gender-sexuality.law.columbia.edu/content/sexuality-and-gender-law-clinic.

19. *See, e.g.*, Emory Law, Environmental Law Clinic, https://law.emory.edu/academics/clinics/faculty-led-clinics/turner-environmental-law-clinic.html.

20. *See, e.g.*, Northeastern School of Law, Prisoners' Rights Clinic, https://law.northeastern.edu/experience/clinics/prisoners-rights/.

21. *See, e.g.*, University of Southern California, Gould School of Law, Intellectual Property and Technology Law Clinic (IPTLC), https://gould.usc.edu/academics/experiential/clinics/iptlc/.

22. *See, e.g.*, Georgetown University Law Center, Student Practice Rules—Clinical Research Guide, https://guides.ll.georgetown.edu/c.php?g=271042&p=1808943 (federal); https://guides.ll.georgetown.edu/c.php?g=271042&p=1808946 (federal agencies); https://guides.ll.georgetown.edu/c.php?g=271042&p=1808947 (state).

23. *See, e.g.*, American University Washington College of Law and Georgetown University Law Center, Transactional Law Clinic Collaborative, https://www.wcl.american.edu/academics/experientialedu/clinical/theclinics/elc/tlcc/.

B. Field Placement

Field placements provide supervising attorneys, or other qualified individuals, the opportunity to supervise and mentor students in the field, as well as allowing students to receive academic credit for work at internship-styled experience with a practitioner.[24] Externships are when a student works primarily with an outside organization, government, agency, or court.[25] By comparison, "practicum courses combine focused classroom instruction in a particular area of interest and fieldwork under supervising attorneys," and are subsumed in this section, whether they are based directly within legal institutions or housed within various agencies and organizations.[26] In project-based or fieldwork practicum courses, students participate in coursework by also assisting with active matters under supervision.[27] Schools may have an office or coordinator to assist with placements and navigating university academic requirements.[28] Field placements can be sought and secured in any practice area and subject matter.

C. Simulation Courses

Simulation courses permit "students [to] develop lawyering skills by participating in practice-based exercises in which they perform the legal tasks required to effectively represent a client in the type of dispute or transaction being simulated or with respect to the type of legal issue being researched," but that do not involve a real client or live litigation.[29] Simulation courses allow students to develop their skills

---

24. *See, e.g.*, Saint Louis University School of Law, Field Placement Handbook, https://www.slu.edu/law/experiential-learning/pdfs/slulaw-field-placement-handbook.pdf; University of Oregon School of Law, Field Placement Information, https://law.uoregon.edu/become-practice-ready/field-placements;

25. *See, e.g.*, American University School of Law, Externships, https://www.wcl.american.edu/academics/experientialedu/externships/students/place-credit/.

26. *See, e.g.*, University of Pittsburgh School of Law, Practicums, https://www.law.pitt.edu/academics/experiential-learning-opportunities/practicums.

27. *See, e.g.*, George Mason University Antonin Scalia Law School, Legal Practicum—Regulatory Comments, https://www.law.gmu.edu/academics/clinics/regulatory/; Northwest University School of Law, Rules for Practicum Courses, https://wwws.law.northwestern.edu/legalclinic/externships/documents/practica-rules-2014-final.pdf; Temple University School of Law, Practicums, https://law.temple.edu/academics/experiential/practicums/.

28. *See, e.g.*, Berkeley Law, Field Placement Program, https://www.law.berkeley.edu/experiential/field-placement-program/.

29. *See, e.g.*, Boston University, Simulation Courses, https://www.bu.edu/law/current-students/jd-student-resources/experiential-learning/simulation-courses/ ("Transaction Simulation: Acquisition of Urban Real Estate for Major Commercial Re-Development: This course is one of the semester-long transaction simulations offered as part of the School's Transactional Law Program and... [involves] [t]he simulated transaction involves the sale of an urban site in Cambridge, MA... to be re-developed into a high-end mixed-use multi-family and retail building. The course is intended to expose students to various transactional, regulatory, and other issues faced, and lawyering tasks undertaken.")

through "simulated negotiating exercises, document-drafting skills, and other practice-based activities under the supervision of experts in various fields."[30] In contrast to doctrinal or lecture-based classes, simulation courses can allow students to hone their skills in situations that imitate professional challenges.[31]

II. Robustness of Programming

While many factors influence the success of experiential learning opportunities, the following are several key aspects that help foster creative and inclusive programming for all students:

Range of Options and Opportunities: Having a diversity of experiential learning opportunities can help enrich the student experience. By hosting a variety of clinics, law schools allow students to have the widest range of options in finding the opportunity that will provide them with the content and skills immersion they seek, specific to their interests, experience, and career aspirations. However, clinics can be extremely expensive, primarily for two reasons. First, they are usually taught in small classes with low student-teacher ratios "of 8-1 or lower, thus making them expensive in terms of faculty cost."[32] Second, clinics may incur significant costs relative to other law school programming. For instance, it "is particularly true of more complex clinics, such as those that litigate in federal courts... [that costs] can easily exceed $100,000."[33] Additional costs, such as "summer coverage" for deadlines and ongoing work between semesters, can also be substantial.[34] Ensuring students have access to field placement in issue areas that the law school's clinics do not cover can help fill any potential such gaps in the experiences students may access. There is a concern that "law schools will pass these costs along to the students by increasing tuition," which would increase prospective students' financial burden.[35]

Quality of Supervision: The quality of the teaching and supervision that experiential learning students receive is a key determinant of a student's experience, both with respect to their learning and skills development, but also their personal feelings of engagement, support, and growth. The quality of supervision is based both on a

---

30. *See, e.g.*, Yale Law, Simulation Courses, https://law.yale.edu/studying-law-yale/clinical-and-experiential-learning/simulation-courses.

31. *See, e.g.*, Texas A&M School of Law, Simulation Courses & Workshops, https://law.tamu.edu/docs/default-source/current-students/simulation-courses-and-workshops.pdf?sfvrsn=0; University of North Dakota School of Law, Experiential Learning, https://law.und.edu/academics/experiential-learning.html; Albany Law School, Experiential Learning, https://www.albanylaw.edu/programs-centers/experiential-learning.

32. Martin J. Katz, *Facilitating Better Law Teaching*—Now, 62 Emory L.J. 823, 830–31 (2013).

33. *Id.*

34. *Id.*

35. Emily Traylor Vande Lune, *Settling for Six: Should the American Bar Association Have Done More to Promote Experiential Learning in Law Schools?*, 39 J. Legal Prof. 305, 319 (2015).

supervisor's effectiveness as a lawyer and as a teacher. Substantive experience within an area of the law, or with a particular skill (appellate litigation versus administrative law procedures), might provide the requisite practical experience needed.

A supervisor's teaching skills are also significant. "Legal educators and the legal academy have long made the mistaken assumption that new teachers have an intuitive grasp of teaching methodology based on their experiences as students, and that therefore they can begin and continue teaching throughout their careers without any understanding of teaching methodology."[36]

There are a range of pedagogical approaches that can inform both the classroom component of experiential learning as well as the day-to-day supervision.[37] For instance, "adaptive clinical teaching...is a structured method of guided analysis and reflection that applies to any clinical teaching situation, allowing a clinician to make her teaching choices based on as much knowledge and with as much intentionality as possible."[38] Such a structured, intentional approach provides a framework for maximizing learning; as such, the method "provide[s] insight into the connections between the clinical teacher's reactions, the expectations to which they relate, the context in which they occur, and the potential strategies that result."[39]

Ease of Access: Ensuring that dedicated support is available to students, both in accessing these opportunities and throughout their involvement, is especially critical for first-generation students, who are less likely to be familiar with the options available to them, how to navigate university paperwork or red tape that can create institutional barriers, or how such opportunities may align with their career goals. Meaningful support in navigating this process requires a time-intensive and student-centric approach. While advising need not exclusively target first-gen students, ensuring that advising is comprehensive and provides adequate guidance for all students is essential. "Advisors must have a comprehensive knowledge of the campus resources that could help [first-generation] students including programs geared for first-generation students," including financial and scholarship information, and "the contact information of the person who knows the procedures and paperwork needed to apply for these campus programs."[40] Where grades or other co-curricular

---

36. Wallace J. Mlyniec, *Where to Begin? Training New Teachers in the Art of Clinical Pedagogy*, 18 Clinical L. Rev. 505-591, 505 (2012) (noting "unique pedagogical challenges relating to class goals, supervisory methods, feedback, and grading... [which] are magnified by the existence of clients and by the need to engage with students regarding the ethics of legal practice and cultural difference.").

37. Barrette, *supra* note 54, at 9 ("Most of the theories on experiential learning suggest a cycle that has at least four stages: (1) articulation of a theory of action, (2) action/concrete behavior, (3) reflection, (4) formulation of new theory of action.").

38. Colleen F. Shanahan & Emily A. Befner, *Adaptive Clinical Teaching*, Clinical L. Rev. (2018), https://www.law.nyu.edu/sites/default/files/upload_documents/Shanahan-Benfer%20-%20Adaptive%20Clinical%20Teaching.pdf.

39. *Id.* at 526–27.

40. Angela Renee Sickles, NACADA Clearinghouse (2004), https://nacada.ksu.edu/Resources/Clearinghouse/View-Articles/First-generation-students.aspx.

involvement serve as prerequisites for experiential learning opportunities, advisors should provide guidance to students on how to maximize their eligibility in light of those requirements.[41]

III. Benefits of Experiential Learning

While not exhaustive, some of the most significant benefits that experiential learning programs can instill are explored briefly. Law school administrators, faculty, staff, or field supervisors may seek to use these as the cornerstones for the development of their initiatives or programming, as these are likely to enhance the first-gen student experience:

Multiple Teaching and Learning Styles: Experiential learning maximizes the educational opportunities available to students, by giving an immersive, practice-based method for learning new content and skills, although it may uniquely benefit those with particular learning styles. "[I]t serves students well to provide varied educational opportunities that meet those divergent learning needs. Some students are visual learners, others are auditory learners, and others learn best by engaging in interactive and kinesthetic activities. Clinics serve the needs of hands-on learners especially well."[42] Clinical teaching is vastly different from the case-focused, Socratic method instruction that dominates law school education, particularly doctrinal courses.

Holistic Learning: In addition to teaching practical skills and techniques, such as brief drafting or oral advocacy strategies, experiential learning provides the theoretical and strategic foundations underlying those skills. Experiential learning imparts "methods of critical analysis, planning, and decision-making which are not themselves practical skills but rather the conceptual foundations for practical skills and for much else, just as case reading and doctrinal analysis are foundations for practical skills and for much else."[43] Those skills are applied in a diverse set of advocacy situations: litigation, both trial and appellate, but also direct assist, policy, and other non-court work. This exposure to a range of new experiences can also help students determine the type of attorney they wish to become, through short-term exposure to new content areas or modalities of practice.

Promoting Diversity in Academia: Experiential learning programs are often among the most diverse teams within law school academia.[44] For instance, minori-

---

41. *See, e.g.*, University of Baltimore School of Law, Clinical Policies, https://law.ubalt.edu/clinics/policies/ (requiring students to complete an "application form and provide a resume and unofficial transcript").

42. Findley, *supra* note 3, at 630.

43. *Id.*

44. While this may provide students with opportunities for mentorship and engagement, it highlights potential barriers within academia. Robert Kuehn, *Clinical Faculty—Who Are You? Who,*

ties make up a greater percentage of clinical faculty than either legal writing or law faculties as a whole. Per one survey, "21% of full-time faculty who primarily teach in a law clinic or externship identified their race/origin as something other than white" as compared with "[o]nly 11% of legal writing faculty are non-Caucasian, while 20% of all law teachers and approximately 32% of J.D. students at ABA-approved law schools are minorities."[45] The survey also found women were also disproportionately represented in teaching clinical (62%) and externship (75%) courses.[46]

Mentorship: Experiential learning provides a guided pre-planning, supervision, and reflection framework that is dissimilar from the traditional workplace model. The targeted practice, skill-building, and individual coaching provided by experiential learning supervisors, integrated with the educational mission, synergizes the academic and professional goals. Although on-the-job training and mentorship for young attorneys are provided to some extent, "not all lawyers will have good opportunities for mentoring and on-the-job training, and all lawyers need to enter the profession with a solid foundation in essential skills."[47]

Citizen-Lawyers and the Justice Gap: Law school graduates will not only go on to become legal practitioners; they are also members (or even leaders) of their communities at large, as citizens participating in society at the local, state, and national levels. The Jeffersonian concept of the citizen-lawyer is embedded in experiential learning, as students work within and on behalf of government or legal institutions (such as courts, government agencies, and legislative or administrative bodies), and communities that have been marginalized by legal systems (nonprofits or direct pro bono assistance by law school program).[48] Services provided pro bono or low bono to those who would not otherwise receive representation allows students to use their skills in closing the access-to-justice gap.[49] Experiential learning lays the groundwork for a student's identity as a lawyer and sense of professionalism throughout the course of their career, "includ[ing] ideals such as civility, collaboration, integrity, and the notion that the role of a lawyer is to work for the betterment of society, not for

---

Who, Who, Who? (Jan. 3, 2018), https://bestpracticeslegaled.com/2018/01/03/clinical-faculty-who-are-you-who-who-who-who/ (noting only "23% of clinical faculty had tenure or were on tenure track"); Nantiya Ruan, *Papercuts: Hierarchical Microaggressions in Law Schools,* 31 Hastings Women's L.J. 3, 15 (2020) ("Skills professors experience the insidious nature of status hierarchy in many ways: by their title, their compensation, their job security, and their governance rights, ... [and] microaggression[s] in the workplace.").

45. Kuehn, *supra* n. 44.

46. *Id.*

47. Findley, *supra* note 3, at 631.

48. Ann L. Schiavone, *Writing the Law: Developing the "Citizen Lawyer" Identity Through Legislative, Statutory, and Rule Drafting Courses,* 55 Duq. L. Rev. 119, 121 (2017).

49. Lori A. Buiteweg, *Bridging the Gap: Externships Make Better Lawyers* (July 2016), http://www.michbar.org/file/barjournal/article/documents/pdf4article2900.pdf; Rayna Jackson, *Finding Purpose: Law Student Helps Close the Access to Justice Gap,* University of Oregon, https://law.uoregon.edu/finding-purpose-law-student-helps-close-access-justice-gap.

his own interest."[50] A student's "sense of professional identity" influences their "practical and prudential wisdom," "ethical conduct and integrity," and "dedication to justice and the public good."[51] This work can have a lasting legacy of change, both legally and interpersonally, for student-attorneys and clients alike.[52]

IV. Potential Challenges in Experiential Learning

Despite its critical value in legal education, experiential learning also presents challenges, which might be heightened for some groups, including first-generation students. These potential obstacles present a risk to the goals of experiential learning:

Balancing Other Commitments: "Because of the financial commitment that law school demands, first-generation law school students may also have to contend with working through law school while their peers may spend that time in" other ways, including balancing experiential learning opportunities.[53] While some experiential learning opportunities may already be encompassed in a student's tuition, the financial toll on a student may be exacerbated when an institution requires a student to choose between receiving academic credit or payment. Additional expenses, like commuting costs or the purchase of professional attire, may also be incurred by the student depending on their specific circumstances.

Pedagogical Flaws: As discussed, experiential learning models generally provide that a student must articulate their theory of action, explain their concrete actions and behavior, reflect on their course of action, and then develop a new theory of action, in an iterative manner.[54] Experiential learning perhaps is best understood "as 'whole person' learning" because it focuses on the "interaction of the learner within a lawyering context that allows for a meaningful experience and understanding."[55] However, because such a process is not formulaic and specific to the learner,

---

50. Emily Traylor Vande Lune, *Settling for Six: Should the American Bar Association Have Done More to Promote Experiential Learning in Law Schools?*, 39 J. Legal Prof. 305, 310 (2015).

51. Nantiya Ruan, *Student, Esquire?: The Practice of Law in the Collaborative Classroom*, 20 Clinical L. Rev. 429, 436 (2014).

52. *Appellate Clinic Sets Precedent with Prisoner's Case*, Vanderbilt Law (2014), https://law.vanderbilt.edu/news/appellate-clinic-sets-precedent-with-prisoners-case/; Lois Elfman, *Columbia Law School's Sexuality and Gender Law Clinic Sets a Precedent*, Diverse Issues in Higher Education (Nov. 24, 2007), https://www.diverseeducation.com/demographics/lgbtq/article/15086324/columbia-law-schools-sexuality-and-gender-law-clinic-sets-a-precedent; *Legal Clinics' Effort Results in Precedent-Setting Agreement to Benefit Children in Foster Care*, Saint Louis University School of Law (Oct. 20, 2019), https://www.slu.edu/law/news/2019/legal-clinics-settlement-missouri-foster-care.php.

53. JD Advising, Am. Bar Ass'n, *How to Overcome Challenges as a First-Generation Law Student* (Aug. 25, 2021), https://abaforlawstudents.com/2021/08/25/first-generation-law-student-challenges/.

54. Joseph A. Barrette, *Self-Awareness: The Missing Piece of the Experiential Learning Puzzle*, 5 T.M. Cooley J. Prac. & Clinical L. 1, 9 (2002).

55. *Id.* at 12.

supervising attorneys must contend with the individual thoughts, "beliefs, values, and emotions" of each learner and experience.[56] Supervision that does not require introspection of the attitudes, principles, and perspectives that drive choices and behavior is inadequate, undermining a key purpose of experiential learning. While training may be deficient in other ways, such as with respect to fundamental skill-building (e.g., inadequate feedback on writing), failure to engage the whole student is particularly detrimental.

Reinforcement of Negative Law School Concepts: The structure of law school is not always conducive to "healthy professional development and [can] foster[] student disengagement"; as such, "fixed theories of intelligence, identity threat and anxiety about rank combine in the zero-sum competition for law school rank [can] elevate stress and inhibit learning."[57] One such example is the pressure of earning good grades. While each school's grading policy differs, an institution may offer experiential learning courses for a grade or credit.[58] The imposition of traditional classroom-style grading on experiential work can affect a student's clinical experience or their perceptions of their work after the fact. Law school "[g]rades are norm-referenced (i.e., based on a curve) rather than criterion-referenced (i.e., based on mastery

---

56. *Id.* at 16 ("[B]ehavior is the product of beliefs and values that students have regarding their role as an attorney. Beliefs and values determine perception of self and others. If students have beliefs that an effective attorney is an aggressive attorney, these beliefs will drive their behavior. Students may or may not be aware of their beliefs. However, if students behave aggressively it is the teacher's responsibility to explore whether their beliefs are responsible for their behavior or whether the students consciously chose to be aggressive (articulation of theory in action).").

57. Peggy Cooper Davis, Ebony Coletu, Bonita London & Wentao Yuan, *Making Law Students Healthy, Skillful, and Wise*, 56 N.Y.L. Sch. L. Rev. 487, 495 (2012); *id.* at 488–89:

- It is inherently competitive in that it assesses students according to rank rather than according to achievement toward professional development.
- It distinguishes and segregates the process of learning law and the process of learning to practice law.
- It encourages a domain-specific, "fixed intelligence" mindset, in that it implicitly or explicitly supports the idea that legal acumen is more the result of inborn intelligence than the result of training and disciplined, thoughtful effort.
- It heightens "social identity threat"—a disabling anxiety that one's performance will confirm a disparaging or otherwise limiting stereotype about a group with which one is identified.
- It extends the phenomenon of social identity threat by using a curved grading system to create a newly stigmatized low performance group.

58. *See, e.g.*, William & Mary Law School, Mandatory Grade Policy, https://law.wm.edu/academics/whatabout/examsgradestranscripts/gradingpolicy/gradecurve/index.php (noting maximum GPA for all clinics as 3.70 and providing distribution of grades); Columbia Law School, Grading Policy for Upper-Year Offerings Academic Year 2019–2020, https://www.law.columbia.edu/sites/default/files/2020-02/2019-2020_grade_guidelines_0.pdf; George Washington School of Law, Academic Regulations, https://www.law.gwu.edu/academic-regulations ("The majority of courses are graded on a letter-grade basis, but for some courses, primarily those that are clinical or skills-oriented, the grade of Credit (*CR*) or No Credit (*NC*) is given or the following grading scale is used: Honors (*H*), Pass (*P*), Low Pass (*LP*), and No Credit (*NC*)."); Stetson Law, FAQ—Clinics and Externships, https://www.stetson.edu/law/academics/clinical-education/faq.php ("All clinic and externship programs are graded on a S+, S, S-, or U basis.").

of specific learning objectives), and... [are] summative rather than formative."[59] This grading system can conflict with clinical pedagogical interests. Whereas a "key assumption supporting curved grading is that students are naturally distributed along a continuum of ability,"[60] with grading serving a rank-and-sort function, clinical education is non-hierarchical and team-based. This can hinder a student's academic achievements and exacerbate a student's imposter syndrome.[61]

Supervision Management: The rigor and efficacy of experiential learning supervision can vary significantly, deeply impacting a student's experiences and learning. Clinics managed by law schools employ clinical educators directly to teach and are thus "free from other law practice obligations."[62] Where there is both a university supervisor and a field supervisor, "[t]he dual supervision in an externship course [can] make[] it more challenging to achieve [learning] benefits."[63] Field practitioners, in addition to navigating many professional obligations with limited time, may not have the pedagogical training to facilitate the student reflection process. Targeted efforts to support field placement supervisors may facilitate the greatest success for host organizations and students.[64] In particular, guidance on the structure, regularity, and content of feedback could provide enhanced clarity on learning objectives, student expectations, and grading.

Valuation of Non-Doctrinal Faculty: Despite increasing demand for legal education to make students employment-ready, "[l]aw skills courses are viewed as anti-intellectual, peripheral and remedial," resulting in "a wide prestige gap [] between doctrinal and lawyering-skills professors. [65] Such differentials are evident in salary and terms of employment.[66] In calculating the disparity in wages, "one study in 2003 reported that

---

59. Debra M. Schneider, *Blending Doctrine, Practice, and Purpose in Legal Education: The Case for an Integrated Pedagogy Case for an Integrated Pedagogy*, VCU Scholars Compass, Virginia Commonwealth University (2008), at 63, https://scholarscompass.vcu.edu/cgi/viewcontent.cgi?article=2105&context=etd.

60. *Id.* at 69.

61. *Imposter Syndrome? 8 Tactics to Combat the Anxiety*, Am. Bar Ass'n (Oct. 2018), https://www.americanbar.org/news/abanews/publications/youraba/2018/october-2018/tell-yourself-_yet--and-other-tips-for-overcoming-impostor-syndr/.

62. Karen A. Jordan, *Enhancing Externships to Meet Expectations for Experiential Education*, 23 CLINICAL L. REV. 338, 344 (2016).

63. *Id.*

64. *See, e.g.*, Bay Area Consortium on Externships, *Effective Feedback: To Give and How to Give, Supervising Attorney Training* (Nov. 10, 2015), https://www.law.berkeley.edu/wp-content/uploads/2018/06/BACE-Nov-2015-Materials.pdf.

65. Schneider, *supra* note 59, at 40.

66. *Abolish the Academic Caste System*, AALS President Darby Dickerson, Dean, UIC John Marshall Law School (2020), https://www.aals.org/about/publications/newsletters/aals-news-fall-2020/presidents-message-abolish-the-academic-caste-system/ ("Any caste system is insidious. But most, if not all, law schools have them. In many schools, the caste system means that many individuals are not recognized appropriately or compensated fairly for their contributions. At some schools, non-tenure-track (NTT) faculty carry a disproportionate share of the teaching and service loads so that others can focus on research.") (referencing Kent D. Syverud, *The Caste System and Best Practices in Legal Education*, 1 J. ALWD 12 (2002)).

full-time legal writing faculty on average earned $30,000 less per year than doctrinal faculty."[67] Similarly, experiential learning faculty and staff have less job security, with many positions being hired "for renewable contracts that lack the benefit of tenure" and that "the term of renewal is short—one to two years—and the number of renewals allowed for any one instructor is capped."[68] Such "renewable contracts offer no protection for teachers whose political or pedagogical positions differ from those of the administration and other faculty."[69] Even those with permanent contracts many not be tenured, which "represents the ticket into the professional and academic guild and signals acceptance by, and parity with, other law school professors."[70] Lack of tenure can also limit involvement on campus and decision-making.[71]

Complications of Working with Clients: Clinical and practice-based work often requires students to build competency in culturally responsive and trauma-informed lawyering. This requires students to develop an awareness of unconscious preconceptions and the tendency to fill in factual gaps with assumptions based on our own limited life experiences. Developing an awareness of implicit bias, learning to recognize gap-filling, and conscientious introspection allows students to consider the norms, values, ideas, experiences, customs, beliefs, and institutions that are specific to ethnic, geographic, or social groups. Clients may hold identities that are similar to or different from student-attorneys on the basis of race, ethnicity, gender, gender identity, sexual orientation, religion, disability, family status, education level, class, geographic location, or other affiliation.[72] Understanding how to work along or across lines of difference is critically important and often begins with language to facilitate respectful communication. For instance, the proper use of pronouns or the

---

67. *Id.* at 41.

68. *Id.* at 41.

69. *Id.*

70. *Id.* at 42.

71. Minna J. Kotkin, *Clinical Legal Education and the Replication of Hierarchy*, 26 CLINICAL L. REV. (2019), https://thepractice.law.harvard.edu/article/clinical-legal-education-and-the-replication-of-hierarchy/ ("Tenure status brings with it full voting rights, while long-term contract holders are typically excluded from voting on faculty hiring, and promotion and tenure matters. A 2012 study found that only 15 percent of these long-term, contract clinical faculty have voting rights on all matters of faculty governance. Sixty-nine percent are permitted to vote on all matters except the hiring and promotion of doctrinal faculty. Five percent are permitted to vote on administrative matters only, and 11 percent are not permitted to vote on anything, although they can attend faculty meetings.").

72. The need for wraparound, holistic services (or non-legal assistance) can also be a limitation for clients. While a client's housing issues may be resolved, their child's educational needs or their health issues might not be addressed through limited-scope representation. Some models are structured to provide integrated support. *See, e.g.*, Rising for Justice, https://risingforjustice.org/ ("We make justice a reality for vulnerable District residents via free, high-quality attorney and law student representation, and our wrap-around social work services create long-lasting outcomes for our clients."); Health Justice Alliance, Georgetown Law, https://www.law.georgetown.edu/experiential-learning/clinics/our-clinics/health-justice-alliance-clinic/ (provides poverty law advocacy to low-income families through a medical-legal partnership between Georgetown University's Law Center and Medical Center).

avoidance of triggering terms (like inmate or victim), can help build rapport and trust. Experiential learning requires students to consciously, systematically, explicitly, and with discipline, challenge their own assumptions—using self-assessment as a tool for growth.

Client-centered work can also deeply impact students emotionally. Students of color or first-generation students may find themselves carrying a greater emotional load or performing more emotional labor than their peers.[73] For example, students may experience secondary, or vicarious, trauma as a result of their client interactions.[74] Just as with learning about substantive legal issues or technical skills, competencies around self-care and resilience should be consciously incorporated into the learning model.[75] Doing so in ways that recognize students as individuals and respect intersectionality principles[76] can help build coping skills and avoid burnout.[77]

---

73. Jill Switzer, *On the Emotional Labor of Being a Lawyer*, ABOVE THE LAW (June 27, 2018), https://abovethelaw.com/2018/06/on-the-emotional-labor-of-being-a-lawyer/ (observing "[o]ne issue with 'emotional labor' is that not only do we modify our emotions to conform to employer and client needs, we also modify our emotions in our personal lives, which is not the way it should be.").

74. Marjorie A. Silver, Sanford Portnoy & Jean Koh Peters, *Stress, Burnout, Vicarious Trauma, and Other Emotional Realities in the Lawyer/Client Relationship: A Panel Discussion*, 19 TOURO L. REV. 847 (2004); Jeena Cho, *When Caring Costs You: Lawyers Can Experience Vicarious Trauma from Work*, A.B.A. J. (Feb. 1, 2020), https://www.abajournal.com/magazine/article/when-caring-costs-you-lawyers-can-experience-vicarious-trauma-from-work; Christina Rainville, *Understanding Secondary Trauma: A Guide for Lawyers Working with Child Victims*, AM. BAR ASS'N (Sept. 1, 2015), (https://www.americanbar.org/groups/public_interest/child_law/resources/child_law_practiceonline/child_law_practice/vol-34/september-2015/understanding-secondary-trauma--a-guide-for-lawyers-working-with/.

75. *See, e.g.*, Ronald Tyler, T*he First Thing We Do, Let's Heal All the Law Students: Incorporating Self-Care into a Criminal Defense Clinic*, 21 BERKELEY J. CRIM. L. 1 (2016).

76. Taleed El-Sabawi and Madison Fields, *The Discounted Labor of BIPOC Students & Faculty*, CALIF. L. REV. (June 2021), https://www.californialawreview.org/the-discounted-labor-of-bipoc-students-faculty/ ("Black Law Students experienced a different COVID-19 pandemic than their majority counterparts due in part to the emotional and physical toll caused by the violent, public mistreatment of Black persons at the hands of law enforcement. While some law faculty at some institutions were proactive in identifying the struggles that their Black students were facing, most law faculty and administrators did nothing—prompting Black students to take time away from their studies to organize, draft letters, gather signatures, and have very uncomfortable conversations with university administrators and faculty about the need for change. Meanwhile, Black faculty and faculty of color, who were experiencing their own trials with pandemic teaching, childcare, increased service obligations and mental fatigue from the political and racial unrest, were often called upon to contribute substantial time to the design and implementation of the 'diversity' or 'anti-racism' initiatives necessary to increase diversity and to create inclusive environments for their BIPOC students and faculty.").

77. Debra Cassens Weiss, *Surveyed Lawyers Report They Experience Burnout in Their Jobs More Than Half the Time*, A.B.A. J. (Mar. 9, 2022), https://www.americanbar.org/groups/journal/articles/2022/surveyed-lawyers-report-they-experience-burnout-in-their-jobs-mo/; *How to Avoid Burnout*, BLOG FOR THE PUBLIC GOOD (Dec. 9, 2021), https://blogforthepublicgood.com/2021/12/09/how-to-avoid-burnout/.

V. Conclusion

Experiential learning serves a critical role in legal education, providing students with formative, hands-on experiences to serve clients across a range of substantive issues in courtrooms, transactional work, and legislative advocacy.[78] Although non-exhaustive, the following critical recommendations can maximize experiential learning opportunities for first-generation students:

- To balance the inherently competitive nature of the law school environment (and in response to findings that collaboration mitigates identity threat), we engage students in collaboration and formative, non-competitive assessment.
- To counteract skill segregation, we supplement the case method formats that usually dominate the first-year curriculum by providing intensive quasi-clinical experience and critique.
- To encourage a malleable intelligence mindset with respect to legal skills, we encourage faculty and teaching assistants to measure and record professional growth rather than reward displays of talent.
- In response to theory and research suggesting that performance is boosted when students are using skills about which they feel relative confidence, or skills at which a group they belong to stereotypically excels, we design lawyering exercises to maximize collaborations around projects that draw on a full range of relevant mathematical, relational, logical, and performative skills and thereby boost the performance and esteem of the greatest number of students.
- Maximize options: recognizing different programs (clinics, externships, simulation-based courses) have their own advantages and limitations; offering a combination and range of offerings can maximize student investment and success.
- Establish academic parity: adopt policies that equalize practice-based and clinical faculty to ensure practice-based faculty representation in all parts of school operations, planning, and student engagement.[79]
- Invest in educators: support clinical staff, externship supervisors, and other experiential learning educators with training, resources, and requisite help.

---

78. Peggy Cooper Davis, Ebony Coletu, Bonita London, Wentao Yuan, *Making Law Students Healthy, Skillful, and Wise*, 56 N.Y.L. Sch. L. Rev. 487, 496 (2012).

79. Bryan L. Adamson, Bradford Colbert, Kathy Hessler, Katherine R. Kruse, Robert R. Kuehn, Mary Helen McNeal, Calvin G.C. Pang & David A. Santacroce, *The Status of Clinical Faculty in the Legal Academy: Report of the Task Force on the Status of Clinicians and the Legal Academy* 2 J. Legal Prof. 353 (2012).

- Adopt an integrated pedagogy: "cooperative and collaborative learning, using writing as an instrument for instruction, and making assessment a formative component of learning."[80]
- Encourage holistic student development: promote well-rounded and multi-faceted student development to enable success as "competent, ethical, socially responsible lawyers."[81]
- Develop effective assessment metrics: thoughtfully assess grading policies to ensure they accurately reflect performance and skill development (and especially where grades are offered, clear rubrics and guidance in how experience-based performance will be evaluated).

---

80. Schneider, *supra* note 59, at 4.

81. Stephen Wizner, *The Law School Clinic: Legal Education in the Interests of Justice*, 70 FORDHAM L. REV. 1929, 1930 (2002).

Twenty-Seven

From the Classroom to the Courtroom and Beyond

Meg Penrose*

I. Introduction — The Unknown Unknowns

FORMER SECRETARY OF DEFENSE DONALD RUMSFELD perfectly captured the dilemma first-generation law students face when seeking post-graduation employment:

> There are known knowns—there are things we know we know. We also know there are known unknowns—that is to say, we know there are some things we do not know. But there are also *unknown* unknowns, the ones we don't know we don't know.

These *unknown* unknowns, it turns out, are the hardest to prepare for. If you don't know about it, you certainly can't prepare for it. This is particularly true for first-gen students who lack the familial and social support system to help them navigate post-law school choices. The post-graduation job market presents many *unknown* unknowns for first-generation law students.

This chapter seeks to help you, the faculty liaison for judicial clerkships, to navigate the post-graduation job market for first-generation law students. You play a pivotal role in the future success of first-gen students and can literally be the difference between a student securing a judicial clerkship or losing out on an unparalleled opportunity. This chapter discusses your role in three steps: (1) informational, (2) motivational, and (3) directional. At each juncture, the first-generation student will need more guidance than others. Successful first gen students are significantly less likely to pursue, or secure, a post-graduate clerkship. They will need your help in making sure that a decision to forgo clerking is a conscious decision and not simply a missed opportunity.

* Professor of Law, Texas A&M School of Law.

II. Your Informational Role

Your first task is to inform the first-generation student of the value and importance of serving as a judicial law clerk. First-gen students need our guidance to ensure their academic success translates to long-term financial success and broad career opportunities. Many first-gen students are not equipped to look beyond their amazing summer internship jobs that pay more than their parents' current jobs. That was my experience. I made more in my second-year summer internship than my father was making after years in his profession. When first-generation law students succeed academically their focus may be on their first job—a job that likely holds previously unknown financial benefits. But most lawyers do not stay in their first job. And yet most first-gen students aren't looking any further down the road. This new experience, and previously unknown financial success, is seen as a destination rather than a temporary stopping-off point. This is where you come in.

First-generation law students often need guidance to capitalize on their law school success. Many do not realize that the most prestigious legal jobs available to successful law students are secured in the first semester of their second year. And the preparation for these positions begins in earnest during the first year. Without proper guidance and preparation, first-generation law students find themselves on the outside looking in. They are caught off guard by the *unknown* unknowns. This short chapter hopes to change that.

First-generation law students are less likely to secure a judicial clerkship than other law students. And when first-gen students do secure these highly competitive and coveted positions, they may not be aware that federal clerkships are often perceived as more prestigious than state judicial clerkships. Lack of information on where, with whom, and when to apply is partially to blame. Law school admission does not automatically translate into informational access or readily available job resources. As previous chapters note, first-gen students often lack the social and informational currency that other law students have. Familial assets are not merely monetary. Familial assets for non-first-gen students include informational advantages, particularly relatives who have already learned how to navigate the system. Navigating the post-graduate job market is incredibly difficult for first-gen students who may not realize that a lower-paying, one- to two-year clerkship position will ultimately prove more beneficial than securing the immediate payout of a six-figure big law job.

Law students are expected to know what activities best prepare them for professional success. But first-generation law students often lag behind in access to this information. If a student doesn't know what she doesn't know, then she quietly studies and diligently achieves without realizing that her less successful but "in the know" colleagues will overtake her. Further, those with familial connections—a privilege many first-gen students lack—may secure positions based on relationships rather than academic performance. Law schools should provide as much informational access as possible to help level the playing field. You must ensure that you provide adequate guidance to the first-gen student who will lack the social capital other students bring to the table.

The purpose of this chapter is to help you empower all students to achieve professional success. But as this text is focused on first-gen students, you must intentionally seek out the first-generation student to equalize the information gap. You must transform judicial clerkships from an unknown postgraduate position to a potentially life-altering opportunity. This is what I term the Informational Role.

You will need to start with clearly explaining what judicial clerkships are. Judicial clerkships are the gateway to professional success. Regardless of what a person does following their clerkship, clerkships will open more doors to more places than any other post-graduate position. But "clerkships" are also a misnomer. A judicial clerkship is not a clerical position. Instead, judicial law clerks usually serve in a one- or two-year position working directly for a judge as his or her research attorney. Judicial clerkships are highly sought-after, competitive positions generally available to only the highest achieving students. These post-graduate positions ordinarily begin shortly after the summer bar exam following graduation.

Clerkships provide individuals with unparalleled opportunities to see how law is made. Judicial law clerks have an opportunity to see "behind the curtain" and watch how judges resolve legal controversies. Judicial law clerks read briefs, motions, and other legal filings and then either prepare legal memos or draft opinions that help decide actual cases. Judicial law clerks see hundreds of legal filings. They watch trials and oral arguments. And, depending on whether they work at the trial or appellate level, law clerks observe jury selection and watch attorneys try cases or argue appeals. It is a once-in-a-lifetime opportunity to raise your legal skill set in a real-world setting under the tutelage of an experienced legal thinker.

Judicial law clerks are ordinarily selected from the most distinguished students. They are academically successful—usually in the top 10 to 15% of their class. They are editors on the law review, not merely members. And while moot court can be helpful, most judges seek students with excellent research and writing ability as demonstrated by journal membership and strong grades. Judges also like to see students that have served as a professor's research assistant, as complex research assignments mimic one task judicial law clerks will be performing in chambers. Potential law clerks must be exceptional writers, strong communicators, and able to work in a small setting. Most judges will only have between four to six individuals working in chambers. Even those with excellent academic credentials will be evaluated to see if their personality fits well in the chambers setting.

Not all judges have judicial law clerks. Many state trial and lower-level appellate judges are not budgeted for judicial law clerks. Some may be, but most are not. Each law school should shoulder the responsibility of locating available clerkships at both the state and federal level for its graduates. Most state supreme courts, civil and criminal, will have judicial law clerks. These state clerkship opportunities are ideal for those who seek to remain in state or desire a particularized experience (i.e., working for the Texas Court of Criminal Appeals, the highest court for criminal appeals in the state). State clerkships, while incredibly valuable, may be seen as less prestigious than federal clerkships. Each situation, each court, each judicial opportunity will need to be evaluated for student fit. Schools should work individually with students to determine whether a state or federal clerkship provides the best option for a given student. There is no one-size-fits-all clerkship.

Unlike state judges, nearly all federal judges have judicial law clerk positions. In fact, some federal judges opt against budgeting for a judicial assistant and instead add an additional law clerk to enhance chambers. U.S. Magistrate Judges ordinarily have one law clerk unless they have opted to hire a second law clerk rather than a judicial assistant. U.S. District Judges, or federal trial judges, will usually have two law clerks, unless they opt for a third law clerk rather than a judicial assistant or are the Chief Judge of the District. The Chief Judge in each District is entitled to three judicial law clerks. U.S. Circuit Judges, or federal appellate judges, will have three judicial clerkship spots. And active U.S. Supreme Court Justices are allotted four judicial law clerks.

Post-graduate judicial clerkships should not be confused with staff attorney or permanent clerk positions. Staff attorneys and permanent clerks are different from "term" clerks—individuals who work for a one- or two-year "term" for a given judge. When individuals speak of judicial clerkships, ordinarily they are referring to term clerkships. Staff attorneys have career positions that often involve a particular concentration, such as death penalty or *pro se* work. Permanent clerks are, as the phrase implies, law clerks hired to work permanently with the judge year after year. Judges are increasingly hiring permanent clerks to provide stability or consistency through the years. Many federal judges have both permanent clerks and term clerks. While permanent clerk positions differ in length from "term" clerkships, it is not uncommon for a previous "term" clerk to be hired as a career clerk. This chapter's focus is on term clerks who serve for one to two years immediately following graduation.

Judicial clerkships are also distinct from judicial internships. Judicial law clerks are employees. Judicial interns work temporarily for a judge, usually without pay, during a semester for school credit or over the summer to gain work experience. Judicial internships provide wonderful opportunities for students to work with a judge's current law clerks to see whether a post-graduate clerkship position is something they would like to do. Schools should carefully screen judicial internship opportunities to make sure that interning does not preclude a student from later working for that same judge. In fact, there may be instances where an internship can itself yield a post-graduate clerkship opportunity.

Judicial clerkships provide a unique professional learning opportunity. From research and writing to watching resolution of complex cases, judicial law clerks learn skills that are attainable only by serving in chambers. The lessons taught by judges extend the classroom beyond graduation. But these scarce positions require preparation beginning early in the law school experience. Law students generally do not know what they do not know. The learning curve for those without family members that have experienced law school and already navigated the post-graduate employment setting can be even more challenging. This is where your guidance becomes pivotal. You must be their informational source. Learn about clerkship opportunities in your geographical area and beyond. Familiarize yourself with the opportunities for your students. And then readily share this information.

III. Your Motivational Role

Every one of us has the potential to make a dramatic difference in the life of a first-generation student. We can fill the informational vo*id*. We can unmask opportunities that will help successful first-gen students reap the rewards of their hard-fought academic success. But information alone is insufficient. We must not only explain. We must also motivate. We need to nurture the first-gen student's opportunities by providing information *and* motivation. And that motivation needs to distinguish between short-term success and long-term achievement.

Big law jobs draw top students for at least two reasons: (1) we are led to believe that top law firms are the pinnacle of success (and they may, in fact, be), and (2) money. The modern law student graduates with a heavy debt load. Money provides quick assurance that the time and financial investment of law school was worthwhile. Six-figure incomes remain the goal of many law students. No one can deny that money is important. Yet money should not be the primary calculus when deciding whether to pursue a judicial clerkships. Clerkships, while paid positions, pay far below market value for top-tier students. Post-graduate clerkships paying between $50,000 and $70,000 dollars are a hard sell when big law firms are offering at least twice that much. We must show students, particularly first-gen students who may have just become the most financially successful individual in their family, that clerkships will do more for their career than jumping at the most immediately profitable job. We must motivate the student to consider a judicial clerkship for its immediate and long-term value.

It will be hard to convince a student that taking a lower-paying position right out of law school is an investment that will yield long-term results. This is particularly difficult for students who are heavily in debt and receive big law job opportunities promising a quick financial reward. Bypassing a six-figure job poses a difficult choice for the student that wants to parlay their academic success into monetary success. Big money offered right out of law school is hard to pass up. You must convince students that this one to two year position is worth the investment. Those without family members to explain the importance of these positions must be shown the value of a short-term lower-paying job for a more opportunity-filled future. Money is important. But long-term career success will be more readily achieved through a judicial law clerk experience.

An easy place to start when explaining the value of post-graduate clerkships is with our own Supreme Court Justices. The past five individuals appointed to the United States Supreme Court served as judicial law clerks. Justices Kagan, Gorsuch, Kavanaugh, Coney Barrett, and Jackson all clerked at the Supreme Court. Justices Gorsuch and Kavanaugh clerked during the same year for the same justice. In all, six of the current nine justices served as law clerks on the Supreme Court—adding Chief Justice Roberts and replacing Justice Breyer, who clerked, with Justice Jackson, who also clerked, to the list set forth above. Many of these Justices, and Justice Alito, also had federal appellate clerkships. When you realize that seven out of the nine Supreme Court Justices served as judicial law clerks, it makes sense to follow in their footsteps. While very few students ever ascend to the highest court in the land, many federal and state judges also have worked as judicial law clerks. Clerking appears to be the newest gateway to becoming a judge.

Even for those students who do not want to serve as judges, there are significant advantages to clerking for students who want to enter government positions or work in big law. U.S. Attorney positions may be easier to secure from federal judicial clerkships. This is largely due to the familiarity that the U.S. Attorneys have with federal judges, as they serve in their courtrooms regularly, and the clout that such judges have when making recommendations. Federal judges, particularly, are uniquely suited to know what skill sets translate to serving as a U.S. Attorney since these lawyers are the lawyers these judges see most regularly. If financial gain is the priority, advisors should clearly explain that some big law firms require clerkships and several more provide five to six figure sign-on bonuses to judicial clerks. This information matters and is otherwise unknown.

Judicial clerkships provide excellent opportunities for students on nearly every career path. While the most natural fit may be for students pursuing a litigation track, judicial clerkships provide a worthwhile experience for far more students than those focused on litigation. Many students are unsure what specialty, if any, to pursue following graduation. The extra year or two that judicial clerkships provide allows students to determine whether litigation truly is for them. Exposure to diverse types of cases ranging from federal employment and civil rights to criminal appeals and patent litigation may change a student's perspective about what specialty they want to pursue. Knowledge is power. And clerkships provide incredible knowledge about numerous areas of law. Simply put, clerkships provide unique informational value for a student's career.

Judicial clerkships are also valuable because they provide exposure to actual cases, actual motions, actual briefs, actual lawyering, and—most importantly—actual judging. While law school is filled with case opinions, cases take on a distinct perspective when you see the defendant or the victim's family or the actual plaintiff in a case. These cases involve real people you may see in court and real lawyers whose work you will evaluate. Judicial law clerks will see cases resolved in real time. They will get to see excellent lawyers try complex cases or argue nuanced appellate issues. They will see not-so-excellent lawyers fumble their arguments, weakly question a witness, or lose a case due to poor writing. Judicial law clerks learn from others' mistakes and successes. It is the best on-the-job training available.

Judicial clerkships train new lawyers in a way that no other experience can. But a clerkship's value goes far beyond the experiences learned on the job. Clerkships open doors that other fellowships and positions cannot. Whether seeking a position with the U.S. Attorney's Office, a big law position with a renowned law firm, or a path toward academia, judicial clerkships give students options that would otherwise require years of experience or a stroke of good luck. The judicial law clerk will have invested one to two years gaining critical experience, watching lawsuits resolved in real time, and making contacts that will more quickly yield results from both the training received and the mentors obtained. You must convey the value of this training to the first-gen student. It is hard, in the abstract, to appreciate the long-term value this one job provides. It is even harder when you are asking a student to wait at least one more year before cashing in on their hard-earned success.

One of the best results of working for a judge is that you will always be that judge's former clerk. Many judges consider their law clerks as extensions of themselves. Judicial law clerks become, quite literally, part of a small family that sees new members added each year. Judges will be there to witness marriages and help their clerks achieve career goals. Judges become invested in the success of their former clerks because clerks are the judge's judicial family. This relationship-building is a special part of serving in chambers. And these relationships are especially important for first-generation students who lack the family ties to yield opportunities that a judge's call or letter might help obtain. For those without familial ties to help introduce them professionally, a judicial clerkship can fill this void.

In short, students seeking judicial clerkships apply for a job but end up with a lifelong mentor and a group of extended family by way of former clerks. I have the privilege of writing this chapter because one of my judges thought I should leave my staff attorney position and move into teaching. She was a great judicial teacher and remains a treasured mentor. My fellow clerks have run for governor, served in the state legislature, become academics, become partners in nationwide law firms, become vice presidents of major corporations, written novels, and argued cases before the United States Supreme Court. The paths we have taken might not be the same. But all of us benefited from our time in chambers.

Your motivational role requires that you convince the first-gen student that clerking has value. That value is far greater than money alone. But it is worth explaining that most former clerks benefit financially following their clerkships. Clerking is often regarded by lawyers as one of their favorite jobs. The more first-person stories you can share with a student, the more likely you are to motivate them to consider this amazing opportunity. Make a list of all your faculty who have had clerkships. Determine which faculty members are willing to mentor first-gen students as they consider clerking. Find former students that have clerked and are willing to serve as mentors. The information you provide must be humanized so that your first-gen students, lacking familial sources to guide them, will be able to fully appreciate the value of clerking.

Your motivational role cannot be overstated. First-gen students rely on advisors for professional guidance. But our guidance will be tempered by family expectations and influences. You must convey the tangible and intangible benefits of clerking. You must push back against the immediate gratification desires and remind the first-gen student of the long road to success. Our careers span decades, not just years. You must motivate the student to reach their true potential. You must explain that their future career choices may literally depend on whether they secure a post-graduate judicial clerkship. In short, you may be the difference between a first-gen student becoming an Assistant U.S. Attorney or federal judge or that student coming back to you in five years asking why they haven't been able to secure a desired position at the Office of Civil Rights. Our students must sail their own ships. But we can help them chart their course. Your motivational role makes a critical difference. Don't underestimate your influence.

IV. Your Directional Role

Preparing students for clerkships begins early in law school. Some Career Services programs will begin by trying to explain what judicial clerkships are, and why they matter, during orientation. Others will wait for first semester grades and begin introducing judicial clerkships to high-achieving students. Still others wait until students have secured positions on the school's flagship law review, secondary journals, or moot court teams. Regardless of your institution's timeline, the earlier you can convey the value of judicial clerkships, the more likely you will be able to help students prepare for clerkships. Capture their attention early and advise them often. It make take several informational (and motivational) sessions to get student buy-in. But this is time well spent.

The first-generation student will need more time and more guidance than a student with lawyers in their family. Because judicial clerkships are a misnomer, first-generation students might not immediately recognize the value these positions hold. And first-generation students might not know how to best position themselves for these highly competitive jobs. Your task is to fully explain what a clerkship is and why clerkships matter.

You must convey this information that is otherwise elusive. More importantly, you must convey this information at a time when it can make a difference. The earlier students know that academic success is necessary to work in chambers, the earlier you can convince students to focus on their studies and get the requisite support they need to be academically successful. The earlier students understand that they must strive for a journal position to open future doors, the more likely they are to work toward journal membership. The more clearly you can convey the value of a student journal editorial position and serving as a professor's research assistant, the more likely the student is to secure one (or both) of these positions. You must help the student chart their course. You must provide the map. This will be particularly important for first-generation law students who often lack this guidance. Your directional role in explaining, in detailed fashion, the steps to securing a post-graduate clerkship may mean the difference between a first-generation student having access to a clerkship or not. Because clerkship applications begin in earnest in the first semester of the second year of law school, if not earlier, any delay in advice can limit the student's opportunities.

Once you have convinced a student to work toward a clerkship, you will need to help the student prioritize: (1) academics; (2) securing membership on the school's Law Review or a secondary journal; (3) striving to have their journal note or comment published; (4) working toward an editorial position on the journal; (5) securing a research assistant opportunity with a professor; (6) evaluating moot court opportunities or teaching assistant positions—with an eye toward keeping academics consistently high; and (7) securing high-value judicial internships that will provide helpful experience or potential future employment.

You must ensure that the student's primary focus is academic success. Grades are often determinative for clerkship eligibility. Whatever other opportunities the student seeks must not take value away from their academic achievement. In this regard, you also play an important role in making sure the successful first-generation law student has appropriate balance. It is hard to be academically successful in law school. It is equally hard to maintain that academic success once you add Law Review, moot court, research assistant positions, and external internship/externship opportunities. No matter what opportunity presents itself, the focus must consistently remain on academic success.

Your task is even more important for the first-gen student who may struggle to differentiate between the value of opportunities. You must help the student keep their focus. Priority one is grades. Priority two is law review or a student journal. Priority three is an editorial position on the law review, preferably a high-level position such as editor-in-chief, managing editor, articles editor, or note and comment editor. The first-generation student may gravitate toward a position that meets their interests, such as online editor or symposium editor. And while each editorial position has value, most judges are looking for students who have shown the ability to sustain academic performance while serving in high leadership positions. Judges also want to know that a judicial law clerk has strong time-management skills. Serving in one of the most time-intensive and responsibility-laden positions demonstrates good time management.

You must clearly express the value of law review and other in-building opportunities, such as faculty research assistant positions. In addition, you must explain the importance of non-paying opportunities, such as judicial internships or externships with a U.S. Attorney's Office. Law students, particularly first-generation law students, are eager to get paid while gaining experience. Paid summer internships with big law firms offer one popular example. But many law students also work during the semester for what seems like good pay and is likely good experience. You must help contextualize why a $25–30 per hour job is not as vital as sustained academic success. You must help the first-gen student navigate the value of law review versus staying on as a paid intern during the school year. You must provide direction. Encouraging students to stay focused on opportunities that may delay capitalizing on their immediate financial success will be hard. But you must be able to explain the value, both monetarily and career-building, in securing a judicial clerkship. You must encourage students to stay on the path for long-term success, which might mean delaying financial rewards.

This section focuses on your advisory role in providing direction. Once you convince students of the value of clerking, you must then provide advice to ensure they position themselves to secure a clerkship. This advice must be given as early as possible for first-generation students. Your advice may be met with resistance if family members, unfamiliar with judicial clerkships, encourage the student to begin reaping the immediate reward their academic success has provided. You must meet this advice with clarity, planning, and examples that will inform the student, and their family members, that delayed gratification in this instance will yield better long-term results. Judicial clerkships open doors that first-generation students cannot even imagine exist. The value of post-graduate clerkships is known. That knowledge, and the steps likely to yield a clerkship, must be conveyed.

Once clerkships are on the table, you must help match students with clerkships that fit their interests and needs. To do so effectively, you should familiarize yourself with the various types of available clerkships. You must also understand that the wider the student is willing, or able, to cast their search, the more likely they are to secure a post-graduate clerkship. First-gen students may feel more comfortable staying close to home. Depending on where home is, that may limit—or even curtail—clerkship opportunities. Bigger cities tend to be bigger draws for students at top law schools. Everyone, it seems, wants to spend a year living on the East or West Coast. Fewer people may be willing to spend a year in smaller places located between the coasts. But geography alone should not dictate the search. There are many talented and influential judges with chambers in smaller cities or more remote regions. You must help the student move beyond geographic barriers.

A. State Clerkship Resources

An excellent resource for researching state court clerkships is the National Center for State Courts (NCSC) website.[1] This website provides hyperlinks to every state's court systems. The depth and breadth of this resource is remarkable, including links to juvenile and probate courts. However, these links require you—or your student—to cull through each court website to determine whether a given court hires law clerks and, if so, the application process.[2] The website makes accessing a given court easier. But the hard work must still be done. You and your student will need to devise an individual application plan based on court location and clerkship opportunities.

In contrast to the NCSC website, Vermont Law School provides an unrivaled publication summarizing state clerkship opportunities. Vermont's annual publication, Vermont Law School's Guide to State Judicial Clerkship Procedures, is written for Career Services staff and students seeking clerkships.[3] It is comprehensive and user-friendly. The Guide provides a state-by-state overview of application deadlines for state supreme, appellate, and trial courts. Each state court system is individually described. The Guide indicates the number of available positions per court, required application materials, important addresses, and hyperlinks that allow individuals to directly visit court websites. This Guide should be a staple in every Career Services office throughout the country. It is an excellent reference for students seeking state court clerkships. It also allows advisors to help calendar application dates. But these dates change every year. So make sure that (1) you have the most recent version of the Guide, and (2) you or your students confirm all dates within your own and neighboring states.

B. Federal Clerkship Resources

Providing federal clerkship guidance is trickier. There is no one reference guide. And federal judges do not follow any one approach or timeline. Some judges use the federal court's online application portal—OSCAR (Online System for Clerkship Application and Review).[4] Others hire through the federal courts generic judiciary

1. The NCSC website is located at www.ncsc.org.

2. A good example is the Colorado Court of Appeals link. This link brings up a page containing a drop-down menu on the left with a link for "Law Clerk Applicants." When you click on this link, you are given an address, phone numbers, email contacts, and judge-specific information for each of the state appellate judges. While this website requires work, the ready availability of each state's—and each court's—hyperlinks allows you to work with students to create an individual clerkship application plan. Some judges still require paper applications.

3. The Guide is available from the Vermont Law School website, via subscription, at www.vermontlaw.edu/careers/judicial-clerkship-guide. The Guide, and its contents, may also be available through a simple Google search, as some schools publish a copy online.

4. The OSCAR website can be found at www.oscar.uscourts.gov.

jobs page.[5] And some still require paper applications. The one constant is that you and the student will need to invest significant time in researching which judges have open positions and whether those positions are for one or two years. If your law school has a formal clerkship program or a Career Services liaison for clerkships, a primary goal should be familiarizing your students with open clerkship positions within and around your state. For schools that attract a geographically diverse student population, more work is necessary to ensure that your students are aware of clerkship opportunities throughout the country.

Your directional role here includes reminding students that moving somewhere for a one- to two-year clerkship is worth the sacrifice. Students will often indicate unease or even unwillingness to relocate for a temporary position. Yet judicial clerkships may require creative thinking. Federal clerkships are the most competitive clerkships available. Judges in large cities may receive hundreds of applications for a single position. Judges in less populated cities generally receive fewer applications. Your directional role requires that you help students see the importance of possibly relocating for these highly coveted positions. Even if the student ultimately opts against applying broadly across the United States, the decision will have been informed and any missed opportunity known.

C. Law School Websites

Many law schools maintain webpages dedicated to judicial clerkships and how to research clerkships. One of the better guides for federal clerkships is the University of Michigan Law Library's "How to Research Judicial Clerkships: Federal Clerkship Postings." This webpage has links to OSCAR, the U.S. Courts general hiring page, individual federal court links, the U.S. Tax Court program, and the U.S. Court of Appeals for the Armed Services.[6] The Michigan page also provides excellent information for state clerkships, with hyperlinks to the state resources described above. The University of Texas Law School has a nice webpage that explains the various types of available clerkships.[7] But the Texas page is informational only and does not provide easy access to necessary links.

Your directional role is to help students search for online resources to advance their clerkship search. If your school has its own judicial clerkship program or website, this may be unnecessary. But if your school does not readily provide these resources, you must help the first-generation student create their job search by utilizing the many online resources that are available.

5. The Judiciary Jobs listings, including several non-clerkship positions, can be found at www.uscourts.gov. Those seeking to find the Judiciary Jobs listings can either good "federal clerkship listings" or use the drop-down menu at the uscourts.gov website and click on "Careers."

6. The Michigan Law Library page also has a link for state court resources that provides access to the National Center for State Courts: State Courts Website and the Vermont Law School Judicial Clerkship Guide. The Michigan Law Library page is available at www.libguides.law.umich.edu.

7. The University of Texas webpage is available at https://law.utexas.edu/judicial-clerkships/.

V. Preparing the Clerkship Application

Now that you have fulfilled your informational, motivational, and directional role, you are ready to help the first-generation law student prepare their clerkship applications. Locating clerkship opportunities may be time consuming. But the task is not difficult. In contrast, preparing the successful clerkship application will be both time-consuming and difficult. The entire application will be scrutinized for writing, structure, and grammar. A single editorial error in a clerkship application could be grounds for tossing an application. Judges need to know that their law clerks will be careful with their research and writing. If an applicant can't prepare their own materials with the utmost care, they probably won't show any greater concern when it's the judge's materials they are presenting.

You, or someone at your school, must be responsible for working with first-gen students in preparing their application materials. There are four main components to the application—an introductory letter, resume, writing sample, and recommendation letters. The introductory letter is the student's first writing sample seen by the judge. It must be accurate, brief, and clear. This letter should be three to four paragraphs, but no longer than a page. Judges will read hundreds of these letters. Rarely will a letter stand out in a positive manner. But introductory letters can easily stand out for poor grammar or editing errors. The goal of the introductory letter is to simply encourage the reviewer to move on to the remaining application materials.

If the student has either an educational or geographical tie to the judge, that should be mentioned in the introductory letter. For example, if the student went to Notre Dame and the judge also went to Notre Dame, that is a connection worth noting. But simply commenting on how much a student loves Notre Dame if there is no connection seems obsequious and may negatively impact the application. Geographical ties are also important to note. Perhaps the student has attended Texas A&M Law School but is originally from the Chicago area. The introductory letter should emphasize local and familial ties to the region. While these items will rarely be decisive in the application process, they provide some connection separating one application from others. Some judges are known for hiring students from a particular school or area. Introductory letters should be deliberate. Don't overlook connections that might influence a judge to move your student from "pass" to "further consider." Be deliberate.

To the extent possible, try to help the student personalize her introductory letter. If there is a particular reason the student selected this judge, note that reason. For example, if a judge has a high patent docket and the student has stellar intellectual property credentials, say so. The student should do as much research as possible to learn about the judge and the types of cases the judge handles. If this information is not available, then simply have the student explain why she wants to clerk. Again, the purpose of the introductory letter is to introduce the candidate. If there are no connections to a judge or her chambers, simply move the application on to the next phase—the resume review.

The resume is important for both content and presentation. Students should avoid clever email addresses and non-professional social media tags. In fact, conducting a resume review is the ideal time to remind clerkship applicants that their social media presence must be evaluated for unprofessional conduct. It is not uncommon for a judge to have her current clerks assess an applicant's social media profiles. The most impressive resume will not survive an assessment showing the individual's poor judgment or overtly political presence online. Family photos are fine. Photos of your pets and friends are fine. But alcohol-filled postings should be evaluated for their professionalism. Likewise, overly partisan postings should be avoided. Judges do not want their law clerks to ever become an issue in a pending case. Judges also want to know that their law clerks maintain an air of professionalism in all their life activities.

The resume should be no longer than one page. The resume should emphasize all law school achievements, including journal position, academic awards, scholarships, and other accomplishments. Judges want to see evidence that an individual has been academically successful while managing other activities. Time management is a crucial clerkship skill. Demonstrating sustained excellence is critical. Judges also want to see a student who is, and has been, successful and needs little oversight to maintain that success. Make certain to show all academic achievements and leadership positions.

The one item that is often overlooked on resumes is a short section titled "interests." Judges work in a small setting with their clerks. Because so many highly credentialed students seek clerkships, the key to securing a job often turns on "fit." Does your personality fit this judge? Listing your interests allows the judge to see whether you and he have anything in common. Are you both runners? Do you enjoy travel? Judges will rely on the "interests" section to match clerks. And current clerks will use the interest section for something to talk about during the clerkship interview. Be aware that any item listed as an interest needs to be a true interest or experience. Listing "travel" as an interest and then confessing during the interview that you have never left the state of Oklahoma will be seen as deceptive. In contrast, if you enjoy a particular type of travel (i.e., train travel, European travel, hiking), list this. The more you can show your personality without sacrificing formality, the better.

The next item in the application is the writing sample. Pay close attention to what is requested. Most judges desire an unedited writing sample. This means that a student's journal note or comment, a highly guided and edited writing piece, is probably not the best option. The writing sample should be relatively short (four to six pages) and contain evidence of analytical reasoning. Do not encourage the student to provide a lengthy or merely descriptive writing sample. The submitted sample will be evaluated to determine whether to grant an interview.

Judges use the writing sample to ascertain an applicant's writing and reasoning ability. Judges need clerks who can clearly express their reasoning when resolving complex legal issues. For students who have had U.S. Attorney or judicial internships, a writing sample that is approved by the former supervisor provides an ideal sample. For those who have worked on a summary judgment, motion to dismiss, or appeal while working at a law firm or prosecutor's office, this, too, makes for a nice writing sample, provided that personally identifiable materials are redacted. Be certain the student has received permission to use any real-world work product and clearly note that permission by placing a disclaimer either in a cover page for the writing sample or on the writing sample itself.

Judges are increasingly using in-chambers writing tests to ensure that the writing sample provided came from the applicant. These writing and citation tests will be taken either in chambers or overnight. Most tests are timed. Begin preparing the student for the possibility of this testing process when they select their writing sample. Providing a sample that has been edited and improved beyond the student's skill set will ultimately come out. It is better to know this up front. Be honest in presenting the student's writing ability. Even if a student manages to get a clerkship, poor writing could spell disaster once in chambers.

Finally, applicants must carefully select their references. Again, pay close attention to the number and types of references requested. Applicants that fail to follow application instructions will be seen as incapable of following directions. If a judge asks only for names, provide names. If a judge asks for letters, provide letters. If a judge asks only for law professors, provide only law professors. Read the judge's requirements and follow those requirements. The application process is a lengthy and constant evaluation process. Everything matters.

Most judges require at least two, and usually three, reference letters. Judges want to know that potential clerks have intellectual aptitude, exceptional research and writing skills, excellent time management skills, a strong work ethic, the ability to handle pressure, the ability to work well without constant oversight, and the personality to work in a small setting. You will need to work with the student to secure at least two law professor references that can speak to these traits. Choose references carefully. Having the Dean or a famous professor that doesn't know the student well write a letter is a recipe for disaster. Judges pay close attention to reference letters. These are scarce positions, and most applicants will have similar objective credentials (high GPA, Law Review editor, etc.). An impersonal letter can do more harm than good. This is true whether the letter writer is the Dean, a high-profile professor, or a named partner at a law firm. It is far better to get a genuine letter from a person who can speak to the student's positive traits than a "name-dropper" letter.

First-generation students should begin nurturing relationships with their faculty early on in law school. This is vital for ensuring academic success as well as fostering mentorship. And when it comes time to seek recommendations, it is far easier to go back to a professor a student has visited with before than to knock on a door for the first time. If a student waits until they need reference letters to begin relationship building, they may not be able to find a professor able or willing to draft a letter. You must convey the importance of nurturing faculty relationships to first generation students.

Faculty mentors are important in life. And they are especially important during the clerkship process. Some first-gen students may be reluctant to engage their professors. They shouldn't be. And you must convey this to them. Faculty members are there to support the students. This support does not stop once a student completes a class. Faculty members can, and should be, career-long resources. Help convey this message as early on as possible to the first-gen student. It will enhance both learning and future career opportunities.

There should be someone on your law school staff who is able to assist with reviewing clerkship materials. Neither the introductory letter nor resume should be submitted to a judge without passing through numerous eyes on the faculty and your Career Services office. I encourage students to share their resume with those who will be writing their recommendation letters to help edit the resume as well as inform the recommendation letter. As the faculty liaison for clerkships at my school, I go through multiple drafts of letters and resumes for each student. I tell them in advance this will be the process so that the continued return of materials is expected. I then have the student share these same materials with non-lawyer friends and family members to look for editorial errors. The student will get one chance at applying, so their application materials must be flawless. First-generation students may not have familial resources to help in this process. This is why your school must ensure that first-gen students receive the oversight needed during the application process.

Once the student has completed the application process, the waiting begins.

VI. Preparing for the Interview

Students are always excited to receive a clerkship interview. With the advent of Zoom and Skype, judges increasingly use technology to perform screening interviews. These interviews may be conducted by the judge's clerk or the judge herself. You must prepare the student for either possibility.

If a student has made it to the interview phase, the judge is now looking for fit. Students generally do not appreciate this during the process. A one-year job in a small setting requires a near-perfect fit. Judges will have their current clerks help them find suitable replacements. The judge may be very extroverted and, therefore, seek out extroverted clerks. The judge may need workhorse clerks, so the judge may need to discern a student's availability and willingness to work long hours and, possibly, weekends. The interview process helps the judge determine who among several exceptional applicants presents the best fit for her chambers.

Your role here is to help the student through the interview process by conducting mock interviews and explaining the process. As set forth above, there will likely be a writing or citation test. This information helps defuse the stress of learning—for the first time during the interview—that the student has one hour to write a closed universe memo. Preparation is key. Your job is to help eliminate surprises.

You can also aid the student by learning as much as possible about the judge's interview process. If you have former students who have clerked for the judge, contact them. If you have colleagues who have clerked for the judge, contact them. Every bit of information you can give the first-gen student will help defuse the stress of walking into the interview. Interviewing with a judge will often be an experience no family member has had before. You must help demystify the process and calm the nerves. Any student who earns an interview has already achieved an impressive feat. Preparing that student for the process will enable him to showcase his talents and personality to the judge. If an interview has been extended, the position is within reach.

In the end, the interview is truly about fit. Is this student the best fit for this judge? Some students will find that fit on their first interview. Most will not. Make sure that you have someone on staff to help the first-gen student navigate their interviews and debrief each experience. What was a surprise? What went well? Each interview adds experience to the process. Focus on helping each student present their genuine self. A one-year position, even a clerkship, can become a dreadful experience if the fit isn't there. You must help the student navigate the potential of multiple unsuccessful interviews while awaiting the right fit.

The general protocol is that a student should not apply to any judge she is not willing to work for. It is also expected that a student will accept any job offer extended. The first-gen student will need guidance on how to strategically schedule their interviews as they come in. You start by explaining that students should only apply to judges they would work for if offered a job. Do not send applications to judges you wouldn't be thrilled to interview with. This wastes their time in reviewing an unnecessary application. And it reflects poorly on your school if the proper protocol isn't followed. Having someone in the building work directly with the first-gen student is critical to ensure they *know* the protocol and *follow* the protocol.

VII. Final Thoughts

This chapter began by explaining that you play a pivotal role in helping first-generation law students secure a judicial clerkship. Your presence, and influence, throughout the process cannot be overstated. The first-gen student does not have the advantages of a familial resource to help shepherd them through post-graduate opportunities. The first-gen student may not understand that serving on the law review will open future doors in a manner that merits the sacrifice. The first-gen student may be drawn to current monetary incentives over long-term financial success. Simply put, the first-gen student needs you to play an informational, motivational, and directional role. You know the value—both short and long term—of post-graduate judicial clerkships. That knowledge must be shared. And you must work diligently to ensure that the first-gen student has the broadest long-term opportunities possible. A first-gen student may not have familial contacts to make calls and provide opportunities to further their career. But helping them secure a judicial clerkship will level the playing field. In a world of unknown unknowns, you hold the key to transforming judicial clerkships into a known known. Then—and only then—with full knowledge and understanding, will the first-gen student be equipped to decide what is best for them and their career. You may be the difference between a missed opportunity and an informed decision.

PART IX Bar Exam and Post-Graduation Support

Twenty-Eight

If You Build It, They Will Come

Using Incubator Programming to Promote First-Generation Bar Exam Success

Caitlin Dougherty

I. Introduction

ANYONE WHO WORKS AT A LAW SCHOOL CAN AGREE, that if completing course credits is the first 25.2 miles of running a marathon, passing the bar exam is the dreaded last mile that feels nearly impossible. For law students, the bar exam single-handedly determines whether the previous three to four years were a success. Which is why internal systematic bar programming is so critical in getting students across that finish line.

Preparing for arguably one of the most nerve-wracking exams is an uphill battle for anyone, but first-generation students are disadvantaged from the start, partly due to having limited familial support and experience with the exam. I am not a first-generation student, as my mother and father both attended four-year undergraduate programs. However, I can identify with many of the questions, concerns, and isolating feelings that first-generation students at UConn Law face, because I did not attend law school, and am usually the only administrator at the table without a J.D.

As I sat down to begin this chapter, I found myself in a recurring cycle of starting and stopping. It was hard not to question myself and my ability to give advice on preparing for an exam I never took. After working through the imposter syndrome I felt, I realized the unique position I'm actually in to support our students, because I can relate to the stress and worries of sitting for such an unfamiliar exam.[1] When speaking with colleagues who have sat for the bar exam, I noticed it can be challeng-

1. Imposter Syndrome: Imposter syndrome can be defined as a collection of feelings of inadequacy that persist despite evident success. "Imposters" suffer from chronic self-doubt and a sense of intellectual fraudulence that override any feelings of success or external proof of their competence. Gill Corkindale, *Overcoming Imposter Syndrome*, HARV. BUS. REV., https://hbr.org/2008/05/overcoming-imposter-syndrome#:~:text=Imposter%20syndrome%20can%20be%20defined,external%20proof%20of%20their%20competence.

ing for them to dissociate their experiences from the experiences of our students. My unbiased and unprejudiced view on the exam itself is often beneficial when assisting overwhelmed students setting out to take the exam. I am able to offer support without imparting all the ways in which I was impacted by the iconic test. When I first started working at UConn Law, I didn't have a background in the legal field, or the knowledge of what law school entails. Even though I didn't have close relations with any lawyers, I quickly learned throughout the first few months in my position, the significant impact the bar exam has on students. Now, after being in the student affairs field at a law school for almost half a decade, I understand how essential it is to implement programming to support students outside of the classroom.

This chapter explores how UConn Law turned toward institutional resources to develop a comprehensive bar exam support program called "Bar Breaks." I will discuss the ways in which this multipronged approach was successful in increasing our bar passage rate and specifically benefited our first-generation students. Anecdotally, we see several first-generation students that face financial challenges while in law school, often being forced to choose between working or studying for the bar exam. Financial issues are also responsible for reduced access to bar prep materials and lack of suitable self-care options. While developing the Bar Breaks program, we acknowledged the struggles many first-generation students face and included support services we knew would directly benefit them. The results of the program were remarkable and in implanting this bar specific programming, we provided a support system and access to resources that our first-gen students had been missing.

II. UConn's History with Bar Support Efforts

UConn Law has a vast history of supporting our graduates through the bar exam and our efforts have been apparent by a solid background of high pass rates. In an email distributed to our community in the fall of 2019, Dean Timothy Fisher stated, "... our first-time bar takers in Connecticut have traditionally had pass rate percentages in the mid-80s to low 90s. And our pass rates have almost always been above, and sometimes far above, the statewide averages." The attainment of our pass rates is owed to measures taken by our administration to ensure students have a distraction-free environment to study in, among other things.

The months leading up to the bar exam, May, June, and July, are the slowest months for the Thomas J. Meskill Law Library, when most students are out of class, thus not utilizing the library's resources. One of the main priorities of UConn Law's administration is to ensure all students have access to a quiet area to take their bar prep courses and prepare for the exam. Library hours are extended during the summer months rather than shortened. On days of especially low foot traffic, particularly nights and weekends, other buildings on campus are opened specifically for bar study.

While discussing library usage with Jessica Panella, Head of Access and Administrative Services at the Law Library, she explained how the extended library hours during the summer are used by a very small, but passionate group of students, who rely on the quiet space and library resources. Providing additional library access enables these students to create a routine. It is clear from those on campus during this time that students find their perfect study location within the library after the first week of bar prep and remain there for the rest of the three months they spend studying. After years of witnessing this, Ms. Panella can vouch for how important it is to provide space and hours for these students, even though utilization is limited during the summer. Establishing a daily study routine is critical for success on the bar.

Studies have shown that students who use the library are more successful academically. Though there is limited data correlating academic success and library utilization for law schools specifically, in a study of undergraduate students titled *Library Use and Undergraduate Student Outcomes: New Evidence for Students' Retention and Academic Success*, it was concluded that the collected data "suggests first-year students who used the library at least once in the fall semester had higher grade point averages compared to their peers who did not use the library at all during their first semester."[2] Furthermore, in a different study, a similar outcome was reached. "Two areas of academic library use were positively and significantly associated with students' academic engagement: students who used web-based services (academic journals, databases, or the libraries' website) and students who engaged in libraries instruction (workshops, classes, or course-integrated instruction) had significantly higher GPA, on average, over their peers who did not use these services."[3] We kept these studies in mind when we noted that for our students, average GPA was the greatest predictor of bar exam success, a topic I'll expand upon later in the chapter.

UConn Law and Thomas J. Meskill Law Library are unique in the sense we stand alone from our main campus. Having a community separate from other parts of the University allows law students to have direct access to resources specific to their study needs. Library staff understand what students are experiencing and can look out for potential signs of concern.

Another point of significance is that our Library houses other student-facing support departments. Having Student Affairs in the same building creates a pipeline for communication to cast a bigger net to "catch" students who may need additional support. There have been multiple situations in which a library staff member noticed a student struggling and was able to personally walk them down to our office. This

---

2. Krista M. Soria, Jan Fransen & Shane Nackerud, *Library Use and Undergraduate Student Outcomes: New Evidence for Students' Retention and Academic Success*, https://muse-jhu-edu.ezproxy.lib.uconn.edu/article/504593/pdf.

3. Jennifer Mayer, Rachel Dineen, Angela Rockwell & Jayne Blodgett, *Beyond Books: The Extended Academic Benefits of Library Use for First-Year College Students*, https://digscholarship.unco.edu/cgi/viewcontent.cgi?article=1097&context=libfacpub.

connection permits Student Affairs to step in and offer services before students fall too far behind.

Library staff also flag students who seem more confused or overwhelmed than their peers. Without self-identifying, Student Affairs and Academic Support don't have information on which students are first-generation. However, we noticed that the students who seek assistance from library staff, and ask more questions about library databases, are often first-generation students who are lacking a familial mentor to guide them. Often times, these students are receptive to our support and we can pin them as students to remain engaged with.

In the summer of 2016, a faculty member had an idea to throw a dosa party for recent graduates. While the idea initially stemmed from a diverse initiative to introduce South Indian culture and its food to our students, it ultimately served as an event to motivate our bar exam studiers. The courtyard on campus was opened and all graduates were invited to eat, socialize, and take a break from their studies. Even the Dean made an appearance, bringing along ice cream for the group, further motivating our students through sideline support.

A student affairs administrator noted how impactful this event really was. Not only did it provide an opportunity to engage with the community during a time of stress, but it allowed students to find a sense of relief, realizing they were not alone and acknowledging they weren't the only ones in a place of frustration and terror. Students began discussing study techniques, asking questions about the best study resources, and comparing notes on topics they were struggling with. "For the first time in a while, we saw students taking a breath and commiserating with each other about their studies and preparation," says Assistant Dean of Students, Jennifer Cerny. "There were students who seemed immediately more relaxed knowing they weren't the only ones feeling overwhelmed by the bar prep process."

Moreover, the administration was shocked by the turnout. During a time when graduating students were notoriously out of touch with the school, nearly 75% of the graduating class had stopped by the event. Even more impressively, the positive feedback was unanimous. In the simple act of throwing a barbecue, students saw how engaged and supportive the entire law school community was and found comfort in knowing that even if they didn't have support elsewhere, their law school family knew what they were going through and were cheering them on.

Another thing the School learned from what we later termed the "Halfway to the Bar Party," was that most students who attended utilized the library either before or after the event. And of those students, many of them returned to the library in following days. Interestingly, the outcome verified that internal programming can be used as an incentive to get students on campus. What followed was a light bulb moment for our administration as we considered using this strategy to retain student studiers on campus.

It was easy to see the benefits of throwing this event, but being a state university, there was limited funding to continue such events. It is important to note that, in this case, the "Halfway to the Bar Party" was individually funded by a faculty member. Without reoccurring donations from members of our community to subsidize the costs of such gatherings, our hands were tied, and we were not able to continue this party in the following two years.

III. Brainstorming a Support Plan

The success of this event remained in the back of our minds as we learned about the School's particularly low bar pass rate in 2018. Nationally, bar pass rates were down, but we could not help but be concerned with our own percentages dropping by nearly 10%. In a conversation with Dean Timothy Fisher regarding that rough year, he explained an immediate analysis of the July 2018 results was critical in determining the reasons for such an anomalous pass rate. It was concluded that in addition to a generally broader issue of recent changes in the exam itself, which called on skills and methods of test taking unfamiliar to this class, most of those who failed had one or more personal challenges occurring during the months leading up to the bar exam. Being during the summer months and students often studying off-campus, these challenges often were typically handled without administrator support, ultimately affecting the student's ability to dedicate the time and energy needed to pass the exam.

Next steps relied on turning to our institutional resources in order to address the problem and examine both the academic and student wellness components at the Law School. A task force was assembled, including a member of Student Affairs, the Registrar, and an Academic Support professor. The team sat down to comb through a list of students who did not pass. Fascinating to the team, the majority of students on the list were identified as individuals who the team members already had concern for. The students on this list were frequent flyers in the Student Affairs office and Academic Support office, or the students had been referred to the Registrar due to low grades.

After bringing in the mental health counselor, who shared the same knowledge on concerned students, the task force decided to meet regularly throughout the next academic year to review students eligible to take the bar exam and flag individuals of worry. Having a safety net of administrators actively seeking out students who were sticking out as struggling, helped the team develop a multipronged check-in system. Oftentimes the group would consult with me based off of the conversations I was having with students as well, and together, we figured out which students would require outreach or additional support services to prepare for the bar exam.

While the list was populated by students of all backgrounds, we noticed that a disproportionate number of students on this list were from marginalized populations, first-generation students, and students registered with our Disability Services Office. The number of students on this list made up about 15% of our eligible bar takers. This was a relatively easy number to manage between the task force, which allowed us to produce an individualized plan for each student. When deciding how best to reach out to students of concern, the group discussed who had the best relationship with them, and how to engage with the student. Assistant Dean Cerny notes that while there was not a direct association between student bar success and first-gen status or disability, "the pressures of preparing for the bar exam often compound to impact all facets of a student's life. For students carrying anything extra in their theoretical backpacks, be it financial, familial, or mental health challenges, sometimes the effort to maintain such a rigorous study schedule is simply too much."

IV. The Bar Breaks Program

To combat the pressure our students were facing, we decided to take a holistic support approach. Our three areas of concerns were: academic solutions, the individual situations that can interfere with a students' studying capacity, as well as creating engaging and entertaining sessions to retain students on campus. The team brainstormed and after considering the success we saw from the "Halfway to the Bar Party," which ultimately pulled students to study on campus, an on-campus beta "Bar Breaks" program was outlined. If we could get students to participate in our program, we could ensure students access to campus resources and support services, as well as keep a support network intact for those who needed it.

Academically, we made three major changes. We retained a member of the Legal Process faculty to work full-time specifically dedicated to academic support and bar exam prep. This was impactful because it created a point person for professors and staff members to refer students to when they were having a difficult time. This increased our already-strong chain of communication throughout the administration and gave students an easy outlet for their questions and concerns. Second, UConn Law created a three-credit Applied Analytical Skills course offered in the fall and spring semesters, as well as a one-credit version over January term. This course focused on preparing students for bar review and the bar exam process. Third, a series of four bar exam writing-skills workshops were offered starting in May to complement outside bar prep courses such as Themis and Barbri. These information sessions were free to all UConn students, even students from previous years that needed to retake the exam.

On top of the new academic initiatives, in 2019 a policy was applied to all 1Ls falling in the bottom 10% of their class. These students would be required to take an academic support course during the second semester of their 1L year. The idea was to ensure the School was providing appropriate attention for students who were having a difficult time as early as possible. While reviewing UConn's pass rate statistics, it was discovered that class rank is usually the strongest predictor of bar passage. Students falling in the bottom quintile have traditionally lagged in bar pass rates. Information from the first year of law school, even just performance in the first semester, helped to identify which students should be flagged for passing the bar exam.

A large portion of our planning consisted of research. On average, a law student spends 400 hours studying for the bar exam. Taking scheduled breaks while studying leads to increased focus, higher energy, reduced anxiety, and allows one to have something to look forward to and motivate them. Without giving the human brain a moment to digest what it has been studying, students are not able to convert newly learned information into long-term memory for the exam.[4] Bar studiers value every minute of their day. Our team knew the sessions in our program would need to be enticing to pull them away from their studies; they also had to be beneficial to their end goal—passing the bar. After researching the most impactful ways to take a break, we decided to focus 25% of our activities on each of the following four topics: stress relief, nutrition, wellness, and entertainment.

The Student Affairs department implements wellness programming throughout the academic year to keep students mentally and physically healthy. These two aspects of life often seem to fall by the wayside when trying to survive three or four years of law school. To highlight the importance of self-care during such a stressful time as preparing for the bar exam, the team made sure to center some of the Bar Breaks sessions around wellness. "Researchers theorize that mindfulness meditation promotes metacognitive awareness, decreases rumination via disengagement from perspective cognitive activities and enhances attentional capacities through gains in working memory."[5] More specifically, practicing mindfulness reduces stress, boosts working memory, and increases an individual's ability to focus and suppress distracting information.

Wellness sessions that were the most popular with our students were yoga sessions, guided meditations, art activities, community walks, and therapy dog visits. We utilized the Library for most of the activities, hoping that most students would already be in the building studying, and those who were not would be encouraged to do so. A newer addition to our library is a space called the Zen Zone, equipped with massage chairs, puzzles, art supplies, virtual reality sets, and access to the HeadSpace app. This space was a great place to host wellness events and many students returned later to take their own short breaks between study sessions. Some of the

---

4. *How to Manage Bar Exam Stress*, Kaplan, https://www.kaptest.com/study/bar/getting-mentally-prepared-for-the-bar/.

5. Daphne M. Davis & Jeffrey A. Hayes, *What Are the Benefits of Mindfulness?*, https://www.apa.org/monitor/2012/07-08/ce-corner#:~:text=Researchers%20theorize%20that%20mindfulness%20meditation,to%20effective%20emotion%2Dregulation%20strategies

activities were more expensive than others, but it is easy to create cost-effective programming and still make a positive impact. For one activity, we bought bullet journals in bulk and handed them out to students to decorate. Bullet journals are a simple tool that can help with anxiety, time management, and organization. One 3L used their journal to write down motivational quotes to read when they were feeling overwhelmed, and another used theirs as a creative outlet and colored in the pages to reduce stress.

Our mental health counselor was also involved in the programming and made herself available once a week for a de-stressing group therapy session. Mental health issues among law students is already extremely prevalent and studying for the bar increases already existent stress and anxieties. "Stress among law students is 96%, compared to 70% in med students and 43% in graduate students."[6] Knowing these statistics, our highest priority was to make sure our students had resources available. "Entering law school, law students have a psychological profile similar to that of the general public. After law school, 20–40% have a psychological dysfunction."[7] This is certainly unsettling and something that needs to be rectified. Providing access to a free and confidential mental health counselor was a significant part of our Bar Breaks planning. These sessions were deemed very beneficial to our students because it once again allowed them to take solace in the awareness that they were not alone in their bar prep journey. They also provided an opportunity for students to share the frustrations they were facing and learn coping mechanisms for dealing with the stresses and anxieties of such a daunting endeavor.

The Thomas J. Meskill Law Library has a small café with limited food choices. We noticed the main reason why students left campus was to find better food options. To keep students on campus and satiated, the Bar Breaks program offered food at least once per day. What you eat directly affects the structure and function of your brain.[8] When completing a draining task such as studying for the bar exam, a key to success is eating healthy. Many times, students go for the quick and easy option when choosing meals. Instead of focusing on health, studiers are more concerned about eating cheaply, fast, and with minimal effort. Although, "Multiple studies have found a correlation between a diet high in refined sugars and impaired brain function—and even a worsening of symptoms of mood disorders, such as depression."[9] To combat this, we provided high-quality, nutritious foods, containing vitamins, minerals, and antioxidants to nourish the brain. In doing so we provided food security for low-income students who may not have had the option to eat healthy. Once

6. Dave Nee Foundation, *Lawyers & Depression*, http://www.daveneefoundation.org/scholarship/lawyers-and-depression/.

7. *Id.*

8. Eva Selhub, *Nutritional Psychiatry: Your Brain on Food*, https://www.health.harvard.edu/blog/nutritional-psychiatry-your-brain-on-food-201511168626#:~:text=Eating%20high%2Dquality%20foods%20that,oxygen%2C%20which%20can%20damage%20cells.

9. *Id.*

again, this part of the initiative encouraged students to remain on campus and converse with others in the midst of the same process.

Finally, we also included sessions for pure entertainment. Highlighting the importance of levity and giving studiers a break, we coordinated movie and game nights. A group of staff members volunteered to design a trivia event full of non-bar-related questions and offer fun prizes for the winners. It was encouraging to see how many community members attended in support of our bar studiers, once again generating a network of people to provide practical and emotional support to our students.

V. Implementation and Technical Details

From speaking with first-generation students on our campus in 2019, they voiced concerns of not having a support network on which to rely on while studying full time for the bar exam. Some even mentioned the struggle of having to choose to stop working in the summer in order to put their full attention toward studying for the bar. The potential benefits of our Bar Breaks program for first-generation students, specifically, fueled our fire to advocate for the funding of this program. Our proposal to the university was simple: if we used reward strategies, subtle checkpoints, and accountability methods through the Bar Breaks program, we would be able to create an incubator-like environment on campus to support our bar studiers.

I was pleasantly pleased when we brought our first proposal of the program to administration for funding. Acknowledging the impact on our entire student body, the administration was immediately excited at the positive impact it would have on our first-generation population, among others. Dean Timothy Fisher noted how first-gen students are a crucial part of our mission as a Law School. When asked to explain his philosophy behind the decision to ultimately fund the program, he stated "Since the founding of the school 100 years ago, we have always been a place where first-gen students have been able to transform the trajectory of their lives by getting a law degree from a school of our quality. I was always tremendously proud of that and the first-gen students I have met. We would make the funds there for any program that would make a difference for them."

The largest component of our proposal was a detailed rundown of the projected cost. Our team put together a spreadsheet of the funds we would need to implement each session and came up with a number around $5,000. This would include all food, wellness activities, and supplies for programming during the months of June and July. In addition to funding, we would need staff support and understood that Bar Break sessions may have an impact on the Library and our campus during the normally slower summer. After all aspects were considered, we were thrilled when we received the green light to move forward with the Bar Breaks program. We were allocated our total requested amount and began to coordinate the details of the program in March 2019.

We set out to develop a marketing plan for the program. When we asked ourselves how we could obtain the greatest number of grads to participate, we considered that UConn Law is a commuter campus. Without residence halls, our students commute from all parts of our small state. Would students engage in our program sessions if it meant traveling to and from campus? We knew our target audience would be those living in the surrounding areas of campus, many of which are higher-income suburbs, but we wanted to reach students who lived in other areas of the state, and those who, for whatever reason, may not have a distraction free area to study. Another factor was varying study schedules. Some students would be keeping their full-time jobs through the summer and studying in the evenings. With multiple bar course options, students would be available for breaks at different times.

To tackle this possible complication, we settled on a Bar Breaks program that would offer three sessions a day—morning, afternoon, and evening, enabling students to have options on when they could pull themselves away from studying and utilize the resources we were providing. The other component in planning the timing of our events was making the schedule consistent. We assumed if sessions were presented at regular times each day, students might be able to adjust their personal study schedules slightly to be finished with a certain topic in time for the activity. We quickly learned the necessity of distributing weekly agendas in advance. Students provided positive feedback on the activities but asked to receive more notice on activity details to plan for which sessions would benefit them the most. For students' planning purposes, we began sending out schedules and details for each session a week prior. Doing so increased our participation numbers of those studying on campus, and even retained more students who were studying elsewhere to make the trip and take part in the program.

Similar to many programs being implemented in their first year, we used trial and error throughout the first few weeks. We determined what was working and what needed to be adapted through reviewing the attendance sheets at each event and listening to our students. While staffing a session that had a rather low turnout, I questioned the students participating on why they decided to attend and if the time of day may have been a reason for the limited number of students. Interestingly, it had nothing to do with timing, but rather the number of events. It wasn't reasonable for students to make time available for a Bar Break every day, which led us to update our program from five days a week to three. This also permitted us to utilize our funds more efficiently. "Simply put, we failed to realize how determined the students were to have uninterrupted study time," states Dean Cerny. "While we wanted to offer them as much as we could, it was the classic case of learning that, in some cases, less is more."

We staffed each Bar Break event with a Student Affairs team member. On top of receiving important feedback on how to make the program more successful, it was an opportunity for a subtle check-in with our students. Through informal and low-pressure conversations with students at these gatherings, we were able to identify students who were noticeably distressed and recommend academic resources for those who were struggling. We observed student interactions and noticed that our sessions were also the perfect point of contact for studiers to hold each other accountable and discuss which topics they had completed. The network of support created through these sessions positively impacted both study habits and the mental health of our students. The simple appreciation in knowing there are others going through the same experience encouraged them to stay motivated.

VI. Impact on Bar Passage Rate

Each July, members of our law school leadership team anxiously cheer on our students and prepare for the inevitable wait that accompanies the bar results process. July 2019 was no different, as we were all hoping our extended measures would prove to be effective in increasing our bar pass rate from the dramatic decrease the year prior. When the results came out, we were ecstatic to find out our goal was accomplished, and the pass rate increased from 72.8% in 2018 to 82.2% in 2019. Approximately 15–20 of UConn Law students fail on their first attempt, regardless of class size, and only 13 students in 2019 were unsuccessful in passing, our lowest number in six years.

The bar exam task force sat down before the 2019 bar exam and used their combined knowledge to evaluate the list of bar takers and guesstimate what the pass rate would be. Amazingly, their estimate was within 1% of the actual passage rate. At this point, it was clear how incredibly powerful collaboration can be. Creating a team environment for not only our students, but also our administration, proved victorious. One of the biggest takeaways from this experience was how beneficial a wide support net can be in strengthening communication throughout appropriate departments.

VII. UConn Law Bar Support Post-2019

Where are we now with Bar Breaks programming? Well, as every Student Affairs department across the nation knows, the COVID-19 pandemic was a serious hindrance in our ability to provide the same level of support to students from a distance. The idea of our program was centered around keeping our students on campus to monitor their progress. We needed to transition our support methods to accomplish the same goals. 2020 graduates were facing an extreme disadvantage, and one we as educators were not familiar with. There were many concerns surrounding the ability to take a remote bar exam. Additionally, the exam was delayed until October of that year, causing anxieties around study plans and return to work.

Enabling our mental health counselors to maintain availability for virtual sessions was critical. Not surprisingly, the demand for 1:1 counseling increased during our time away from campus. Students were processing a major change in their way of life, including grief from loss of family members, and the general state of society. The added pressure of preparing for the bar pushed many students to seek mental health support during the summer of 2020. We made efforts to conserve communication between the mental health counselors and our office through biweekly meetings. Any cause for concern was referred between the two offices and we kept well-informed on students who needed additional support.

Remote learning was unequivocally a learning curve for students, as well as administrators. Establishing distraction-free spaces at home, where many students coexisted with family, friends, and even children, was challenging. Students were not only isolated from campus and access to study locations, but they had also lost the support network we had worked so hard to create. Our first-gen students felt this the most as they were removed from the support of their law school peers and, while not always the case, often were in shared living spaces with individuals not aware of the high-stakes nature of law school academics and the bar exam. To try to reestablish a connection and encourage virtual engagement, we developed a weekly video podcast that ultimately addressed feelings of going through law school and preparing for the bar exam alone. We also highlighted how our safety net was still intact and students did not need to feel alone. Videos included messages from faculty, staff, and students, all sharing their experiences of lockdown, successful coping mechanisms, mental health resources, and tips for working at home.

For some students taking the remote bar exam, it was also nearly impossible to obtain a space that complied with testing protocols. For some, there were financial worries regarding a secure Wi-Fi connection. To combat this, we provided financial assistance to graduates sitting for the bar exam who were unable to take the exam at their home. During the pandemic, a support fund was created for students experiencing unanticipated hardship. We allocated a portion of this money to directly assist our bar exam efforts. The Law Student First Fund was supported by private donors, including the AccessLex Institute. A UConn Law administrator explained the impact this fund had for our students, stating, “The Law Student First Fund allowed the Student Affairs Office to demonstrate the care and concern that the UConn Law community feels for our students.” This gesture helped in maintaining our sense of community and provided guidance in serving our support net—be it academically, emotionally, or financially.

In addition to using the Law Student First fund to offset the costs of study materials, enhancing home study spaces, and basic day-to-day needs, we also rented office space for those who could not study or take the exam from home. We were fortunate to be able to provide this to our students, and those who utilized the fund were extremely grateful, having put a lot of the credit of their success to having this option.

Ultimately, we did see a positive impact on pass rates after the October 2020 bar exam. Of all UConn students who sat for the bar this year, regardless of first-time testers or not, we saw a total pass rate of 86.14%, compared to the same statistic in 2019, which was 78.75%.

VIII. 2022 and Beyond

When considering what comes next, and our plans for future bar study support, we now know that the two-pronged, on-campus programming is successful. First, collaboration between the bar exam task force helps to easily flag students and perform outreach when necessary. The second element is getting students on campus to study. Depending on the health and safety guidelines within the University, we hope our Bar Breaks program can return in 2022. At the very least, we know we can implement successful programming from a distance. So much of our program development came from simply listening to our students. We intend to move forward ensuring our community has resources and listening ears for students comfortable self-identifying as first-gen.

The First-Generation Law Students Association was founded at UConn Law in 2019. This has been tremendously helpful in making sure this student population has the resources to be supported and alleviate burdens where possible. Outside of our Bar Breaks program, the FGSA hosts additional informational sessions and connects first-gen students with others who have been in their shoes. Having a relationship with this student organization made it possible to receive feedback from personal experiences and make our campus more inclusive for all.

What might we change for future years? When we sat down to debrief in September 2019, there were many aspects of the program that were voted successful, and that we would return to the next time around. The holistic approach of tying together academic and wellness initiatives was the perfect balance to increase the bar pass rate. A goal for future years is to highlight physical health. "Physical activity can improve your cognitive health—helping you think, learn, problem-solve, and enjoy an emotional balance."[10] We realized physical movement is a key element we need to emphasize. Looking forward, we will put more attention on physical activities enabling students to get their bodies moving before going back to stagnant studying.

All in all, the Bar Breaks program has been a successful addition to our community programming. We feel confident recommending a similar program to other institutions seeking to further their support efforts to assist graduates studying for the bar exam. The Bar Breaks program is easy to individualize and adapt to fit the needs of your student body, which, among other things, allowed us to provide intentional support geared toward first-generation students.

---

10. Physical Activity Boosts Brain Health, CENTERS FOR DISEASE CONTROL AND PREVENTION, https://www.cdc.gov/physical-activity/features/boost-brain-health.html?CDC_AAref_Val=https://www.cdc.gov/nccdphp/dnpao/features/physical-activity-brain-health/index.html.

Twenty-Nine

Bar Talk

Learning from First-Generation Bar Takers to Create Bar Support Programming

Brittany L. Raposa

WHEN I FIRST BEGAN IN MY ROLE at Roger Williams University School of Law as the Associate Director of Bar Support in 2017, I knew that I wanted to create programming to help all students, but particularly first-generation law students. In 2018, I conducted an interview comprised of first-generation graduates who were both successful and unsuccessful on the bar exam on their first attempt.[1] First, this chapter will detail my interviews with the graduates and how being a first-generation student impacted their bar study and performance. Next, this chapter will describe the bar exam program I created, which was influenced in large part by feedback I received from the graduates to be sure I was supporting first-generation students and bar takers.

I. Let's Talk the Bar Exam: Insight from First Gen Students

Financial Hardship

It is no secret that preparing for and taking a bar exam is expensive. All the first-generation students interviewed identified cost as the largest barrier for them. Washburn University law professor, Marsha Griggs, found that bar exam preparation courses range from about $1,100 to more than $3,800, and graduates must pay anywhere from $2,000 to almost $10,000 in exam fees, character and fitness review costs, laptop fees, and their commercial bar review courses combined.[2] In order to increase a graduate's chances of first-time bar passage, it is also strongly recommended that they do not work in the 10 to 12 weeks while preparing for the bar exam

1. Interviews on file with author.

2. Karen Sloan, *Does The Bar Exam Cost Too Much? These Law Profs Think So*, REUTERS (Apr. 22, 2022), https://www.reuters.com/legal/legalindustry/does-bar-exam-cost-too-much-these-law-profs-think-so-2022-04-22/.

after graduation. Therefore, law school graduates are also expected to cover living expenses during this time after most being full-time students with student loans hanging over their heads.

When asked about finances, a student commented, "When I applied to law school, I had no idea that I would need an additional $12,000 after graduation to take and pass a bar exam. I had to take out an additional private bar loan on top of my federal loans. I felt suffocated by these costs and my circumstances." Similarly, another student stated, "My family did not have the money to help me with any of these costs. I remember sitting down and thinking that maybe I couldn't take the bar exam right now. Maybe I needed to save money first. But it's recommended you take the exam after graduation, to I felt like I had no choice but to take it."

Working While Studying

Related to finances, most first-generation graduates could not afford to just study—they had to work part-time jobs to financially get through their bar exam preparation period. Graduates worked in a variety of jobs, including in restaurants, bars, retail stores, law firms, or family businesses. One student commented, "It was absolutely physically impossible for me not to work during bar prep. If I didn't work, I don't think I would have been able to eat." Another student stated, "I kept hearing about students who had their families to help them financially and I had to work while studying because I didn't have that. I felt like I was starting behind and while studying I just felt like I would never catch up to my classmates." Finally, another student stated, "It's my responsibility to send money to Nigeria every month to help my family—not the other way around. I had no one to help me, so I had to work 35 hours a week while studying for the bar exam, and it contributed to my failing the bar exam the first time."

Lack of Familial Understanding

Another common theme when interviewing first-generation law student bar takers was a lack of familial understanding about the bar study process. First-generation student families have never taken the bar exam before and have never taken standardized tests or any exams at the post-high school level. Consequently, bar takers felt that while they may have had emotional support throughout their bar exam preparation journey, they couldn't speak to their families about what they were going through, and they couldn't expect them to understand the difficulties they were having.

As mentioned earlier in this book, first-generation students tend to have more family obligations and cultural expectations than other students. Therefore, when there is a lack of familial understanding about the pressures and rigor of bar exam preparation, the familial pressure, obligations, and cultural expectations do not get minimized. In fact, many first-generation students who were interviewed said those expectations heightened because they graduated and were no longer in class. Further, most of these students felt like they could not explain to their families that they would not be as available during the bar preparation period. Some told their families they had to study and could not be as responsive while studying but felt like their families did not really understand and became upset. One student stated, "My dad, over and over again, would say to me, 'you graduated law school so why are you still studying you can just take the test.'"

This is no fault of anyone. Families of first-generation students don't understand what the bar exam is and don't understand how demanding it is because they simply have not been through anything quite like it. Due to family dynamics, it can be difficult for our law students to explain this process to their families, and some students do not feel comfortable telling their families that they won't be available because of how much they are relied upon and integral to their family unit.

Feeling Isolated

Many first-generation bar takers reported feelings of isolation, which had negative consequences on their mental health. Bar study is extremely isolating for most, and without the understanding of those most close to them, first-generation students feel that isolation tremendously. Transition can be difficult for first-generation students, and they go from being in live classes to complete asynchronous bar exam preparation. One student reported, "It was hard to get out of bed most days. I was alone, studying for hours, and constantly questioning my self-worth with every question I would get wrong." Another indicated, "I think I felt what anxiety and depression was when I was studying for the bar exam. Sometimes I felt like I couldn't breathe, and that I just needed a break, but I kept going because if I didn't, I thought I would fail." Every graduate interviewed expressed similar sentiments—bar exam preparation was another thing that was completely new to them and that isolated them from their families and their peers.

Maybe This Will Be a Practice Run

Many of the first-generation students I interviewed had a fixed mindset[3] during bar preparation that they would fail the exam the first time. Many thought this because they struggled during their first year in their doctrinal courses, so they saw themselves as unable to conquer those subjects within the time frame they had to study for the bar exam. Multiple students indicated something along the lines of, "I think I will fail the first time, but at least this first time will be a practice exam before I can pass it on the second try." Much of this fixed mindset likely comes from the

3. When a student has a fixed mindset, they believe their intelligence, capabilities, talent, and other qualities are innate and unchangeable. For example, if a student thinks they are "bad at multiple-choice questions," they believe they will never be good at multiple-choice questions, no matter how much work or studying is put in.

issues identified throughout this book, including imposter syndrome, stereotype threat, and lack of feeling of belonging.

I Needed More Time

Finally, many of the first-generation graduates indicated they needed more time to study for the bar exam than the traditional nine to ten weeks they were given after graduation. One stated, "I wish I got more of a taste of what bar exam preparation was going to be like. It took me the first few weeks to just get comfortable, and once I found a routine, I felt like it was too late." Another student remarked, "I struggled in my first year because I was adjusting to this new language and curriculum. If I had more time looking at the material, I may have had a better chance of passing the exam the first time I took it."

II. Bar Support Programming to Assist First Gen Bar Takers

These graduate reflections caused me to sit and think of ways to support these specific concerns of our first-generation students into our bar exam preparation program at my institution. In this section, I will describe how our bar exam preparation program attempts to combat these challenges and assist students with the above-mentioned feedback.

Alleviating Some Financial Burden and Engaging in Financial Planning

Most law schools lack the resources to fully fund students' bar exam preparation. Although we wish we could alleviate all financial burdens of our students in need, it is almost impossible. However, there are certain initiatives law schools can take to assist students financially with the bar exam.

1. ***Bar Exam Equity Fund***. At my institution, I have created what I call the "Bar Exam Equity Fund." This fund asks commercial bar review companies, law firms, and alumni to donate bar preparation courses into the fund. In this way, the law school has bar review courses to give in full to students in financial need. To decide who gets one of these courses, law schools can either have students in need fill out an application, look to see which students have needed financial assistance throughout their time in law school, or assess a student's financial need after having one-on-one bar exam preparation meetings with students and asking them about their financial planning for the bar exam. At my institution, every third-year student is required to meet with me, and in the meeting, I ask the following questions related to finances:

a. What is your financial plan for bar exam preparation?
b. Do you need to take out a private loan to pay for your bar exam expenses?
c. Do you need to work while studying for the bar exam?
d. Do you think you may need additional financial assistance during your bar exam preparation?

These meetings take place after I have already been able to establish relationships with the students, and I find that students are quite open and honest with me about their financial situation and whether they may need help. These meetings can help law schools gauge not only who needs a bar review course from the equity fund, but also allows one to determine how many they need to get for the fund to ensure everyone in need gets one.

2. ***Financial Planning Workshop and Worksheet***. It's important that all our students not be blindsided by the cost of the bar exam when they get to their third year, but this is especially important for our first-generation students who come to law school with more financial hardship. To inform our students as early as possible about the costs of the exam, and to get them thinking about financial planning, I host a Bar Exam Informational Session each year, which all students are encouraged to attend. During this session, I discuss how much preparing for and taking the bar exam costs. Each student is then given a Financial Planning Worksheet, which is also included on our website. In this way, students (1) know how much the bar exam costs, and (2) can begin financially planning for it as early as possible. The worksheet is mimicked in the table on the following page.

Application, Preparation, and Exam-Taking Costs	
Item	**Amount**
Bar Exam Application (For Your Jurisdiction) *Include typing/ExamSoft fee if applicable	
Total Incidental Bar Exam Application Costs (If any are applicable) • Criminal Background Checks • Driving Abstract • Credit Report • Fingerprinting • Official Document Requests (birth certificate, marriage certificate, etc.) • Notary Services • Postage/Mailing	
Commercial Bar Review Course	
Additional Study Materials Cost (If Applicable)	
Travel Cost (train, plane, hotel, etc.)	
Food/Dining	
Living Expenses (10+ Week Period)	
Mortgage/Rent	
Gas/Electric	
Internet	
Phone	
Other Utilities	
Groceries/Food	
Car Payment	
Car Insurance	
Gas/Fuel	

Living Expenses (10+ Week Period)	
Other Daily Transportation Costs	
Household Supplies	
Other Personal/Misc. Bills and Costs	
Childcare Expenses	
Petcare Expenses	
Credit Card Payments	
Other Bill Costs	
Other Expenses	
[Leave blank for students]	

3. ***Housing Assistance.*** With financial insecurity oftentimes comes housing insecurity. Therefore, law schools, if they can, may play a role in assisting their students with housing. At my institution, we have dormitory and apartment housing on campus due to the fact we are attached to an undergraduate university. I work with undergraduate housing to provide winter and summer housing for our graduates studying for the bar exam at a discounted rate. This helps alleviate the stress of finding housing after graduation, provides them with a stable living environment during bar study, and assists the students financially.

Helping the Bar Taker Who Is Working

While it is ideal for graduates not to work while studying for the bar exam, some simply do not have that luxury. It's important that we do not shame or scold our graduates who tell us they must work. It is a necessity for most who do, and they do not have any other option. Therefore, law schools should provide more guidance to students who need to work while studying for the bar exam.

1. ***Group and Individual Counseling.*** In my third-year institutional bar review course called "Applied Legal Reasoning (ALR)," I utilize the first class to explain all things bar exam. In this class, I talk to the students as a group about bar exam risk factors, and the reality is that one risk factor is working while studying. However, I stress that every risk factor can be overcome with a plan. Therefore, to the class, I discuss how they should schedule a meeting with me to come up with a bar exam preparation plan when they are working. However, I also talk about

what that plan could look like. I tell students that bar exam preparation should begin earlier than the standard nine to ten weeks of study so someone who is working can make up some of the time that a full-time studier gets to utilize. I also indicate that every student situation is different, so meeting with me about an individual plan is also critical. I then share stories of alumni who were successful and worked while they were studying to normalize students having to work, and how every student can be successful on the bar exam even if they must work. Below, find sample advice I give to students who must work while studying for the bar exam.

- Increase the number of weeks you study over time to maximize your study time. If the student is taking the February bar exam, I typically recommend they begin studying in October. If the student is taking the July bar exam, I typically recommend they begin studying in March.
- Stretch out your studying over a longer period. While in your final semester, try to spend 10 to 15 hours studying for the bar exam. Then, after you graduate, increase that number (which will depend upon the number of hours the student must work).
- While working during the bar exam preparation period, a student should not study seven days per week. Rather, students should take off two study days on the days they are working and use the rest of the days in the week to study for the bar exam.

2. ***Repeat Taker Programs***. It's also critical that we help our first-generation law students who are taking the bar exam for a second or more time. It's rare when a first-generation student can study full-time for the bar exam when on their second or more attempt. These students, if they were able to not work the first time while studying, usually must work while taking the exam again due to financial burdens. To assist these students, I provide them with what I call a Repeat Taker Bar Exam Schedule that is a bit more manageable than just looking at a schedule created by a commercial bar review course.

3. ***Check In and Often***. I note all the bar takers who are working, and whether it is their first or more time taking the exam, I make sure to check in with them either weekly or bi-weekly. Due to working, they may fall behind in their studying, and likely need guidance on what to prioritize in their courses and how to catch up. These check-ins can ensure that you are helping the first-generation bar studier who is working and that they are not alone in this. Further, this helps normalize the idea that some students must work out of necessity—and having these check-ins specifically for students who are working as part of your bar exam preparation helps that messaging even further.

Assisting with Familial Understanding

1. ***Supporting Our Bar Takers Webinar***. In 2021, I created a webinar titled "Supporting Our Bar Takers." This webinar is designed not only for our students about to take the bar exam, but also for their loved ones. In this session, I explain what the bar exam is. In addition, I have first-generation alumni who were successful on the bar exam join me, to share to families what their experience of studying was like and what hardships they faced. We ultimately set what the expectation is for them—that they will be studying after graduation, and maybe a bit before, up until the end of July. We express that they study almost every day for about eight to ten hours a day. Then, both I and the alumni give suggestions to the families on how they can support their bar taker. We also explain that the process of studying for the bar exam is intensive and stressful, as there is a lot of content and a lot of practice in any given day. Many alumni on the panel describe it as exhausting, not only due to the volume of information to study each day, but also because of the brain power needed each day. Further, we have given the following advice:

    - If your bar taker has familial obligations or expectations, it may be time to step in and help them with that obligation while they are studying.
    - Help your bar taker maintain boundaries. Help them study for the bar exam by assisting them in maintaining healthy boundaries and limiting distractions.
    - Try to refrain from asking them how studying is going, because it's usually stressful to be asked that question. Instead, distract them with a funny story or something unrelated to the exam all together.
    - Although it feels natural to say, "you will be fine" and "you will pass," try to stay away from statements like that. Your bar taker already feels so much pressure to pass this exam, and these seemingly harmless statements are likely adding to the pressure. Instead, say things like 'I'm here for you" or "I believe in you."
    - Help them with other things if you can. Help out with household duties, make them some meals, or bring them their favorite snacks if you are able to. If you are not living near them, just call them and be present in their lives.
    - Don't give them a hard time for being absent. They need to focus on this exam for a couple of months, and they need you to be understanding. Instead, give them something to look forward to after the bar exam is over.
    - While allowing them to study, also try not to let them fall into a black hole and disappear. Check in on them and help them maintain some type of balance. Your bar taker needs breaks, and you can be someone who makes sure they are taking them.
    - Keep loving them, even when they are at their worst.

It's important that the advice for the families does not stress money. For example, you want to avoid advice telling them to send their bar takers money, sending them food, or taking them on vacations after the bar exam is over. Not everyone in attendance has those means, and that has been particularly true for a lot of my first-generation students.

This webinar has been tremendously successful in the two years I have done it. The students and their families are thankful, and the students report that their families are more understanding and instead of asking them for help, ask how they can help. This also takes some of the pressure off of our first-generation students of feeling like they are disappointing their families when the information is coming from a third party entrenched in the bar exam world. This one webinar can go a long way to help our first-generation students about to prepare for this exam.

2. ***Provide Study Spaces (with Snacks).*** Many first-generation students may still live at home with family or, in the alternative, live with roommates. Oftentimes these students don't have a quiet, reliable, distraction-free place to study. At my institution, I set up specific rooms throughout the law school reserved for bar takers to study in the winter and the summer. Snacks are also provided to help any bar taker struggling financially to afford some fuel. If a student is no longer in the area and has the same issues, I will reach out to someone at a law school near where they are currently located to secure a study space for them. Knowing they have a space that's distraction-free and quiet is both comforting and helps promote their success.

Combating Isolation

1. ***The Bar Excellence Program.*** Bar preparation programming during the winter and the summer for our graduates can help combat the feelings of isolation they may experience (while also helping them with their skills). My bar support programming is called our "Bar Excellence Program," which contains a series of workshops, office hours, and one-on-one meeting sign-ups. Each week during bar study, I have a check-in meeting with the bar studiers, to talk about progress, performance, and suggestions to improve performance. In some sessions, we may go over MBE questions or essay questions as well. Meeting each week in a group setting allows bar takers to interact with me and each other, to ask questions and get answers, and to know they are not in this alone. Workshops also consist of simulated practice sessions, where they will simulate MBE questions, MEE questions, or MPT questions. After the simulation, we then go over it in detail. These sessions help students, especially first-generation students, still have the experience of live instruction to go with their asynchronous bar preparation courses. Many first-generation students expressed a need for this balance due to the difficulty they have with the transition from law school to bar exam preparation.

Further, office hours and one-on-one meetings are incredibly helpful. They know they can pop in and someone will be there if they need it, or someone is there to work with them on something they are struggling with.

2. ***Incorporate Mental Health.*** We must incorporate wellness into our bar exam preparation programs. At my institution, we work with our on-campus counseling center to provide sessions for students on anxiety, stress management, self-care, and test-day anxiety management. We also have begun to work with our state's lawyer's wellness program, which many state bars also have. These partnerships can be excellent, as they provide students with support and give them a connection to the state bar.

3. ***Bar Exam Alumni Mentor Program.*** I found it incredibly helpful to establish a bar exam mentorship program. For each bar exam administration, I pair each graduate with an alumni mentor. In pairing the mentor and mentee, I look to match two individuals who performed similarly in law school, who used the same bar exam preparation course, and who sat in the same jurisdiction. I ask the mentees if they have any preferences for characteristics in a mentor, and many express preferences such as wanting a first-generation alumnus, an alumnus of color, an alumnus who speaks English as an additional language, and so on. The mentor is required to have an introductory meeting with their mentee through their medium of choice, to check in with their mentee once per week, and to be available to their mentee for any questions and support as needed. This program has been tremendously successful and has gotten much praise from our bar studiers to have someone else, in large part who they see themselves in, to also be by their side during bar exam preparation.

4. ***Create Community.*** One of the best ways to combat isolation in bar exam preparation is to create a sense of community. All the programming discussed in this section, together, contributes to a sense of community. However, we can also create community with our faculty and staff in our bar preparation programs. At my institution, we set up a series of coffee hours, which are hosted by faculty and staff each week. Some are based on doctrinal subjects. For example, a Civil Procedure professor may host a coffee hour and be available for any questions bar studiers have on the subject. Or it can be unrelated to content, where a faculty or staff member hosts one to allow students to vent or to do some meditation. Each week, the bar takers know that someone else is invested in their success within our law school community. Further, faculty have created content videos on complicated topics and subjects that are available to students to watch asynchronously. These efforts show our bar takers that we have a community at the law school, and our entire community is participating in their bar preparation and success.

They Can Do This

1. ***Institutional Bar Preparation Course.*** Students in their final semester prior to graduation take a three-credit, graded bar exam preparation course. This course exposes all students to each component of the bar exam, and allows them to practice MBE questions, essay questions, and performance tests while also reviewing heavily tested law. Offering an institutional bar exam preparation course in a student's final year of law school is significant and has been successful at many law schools.[4] The first-generation students who feel like they need more time, or wish they could begin studying earlier, get more time and begin their studying in this course. Further, with this type of course, students know what to expect. First-generation students have no one in their families who have taken the bar exam or even a big exam. This course lessens the fear of the unknown and allows students to feel more comfortable with (1) what bar study is like and (2) what they will be confronted with on the bar exam.

2. ***Kick-Start to Bar Review.*** I also offer something called Kick-Start to Bar Review in my program, which again enables students to begin early study and review for the bar exam. I offer a series of workshop sessions prior to the students graduating that covers heavily tested and sometimes confusing areas of law for students. In addition, in these sessions, I offer additional bar exam writing practice and review. Like the institutional bar preparation course, this program gives students an opportunity to begin their bar review early and lessens anxieties about the bar exam. Instead, the bar exam just becomes another set of practice questions that we have already done so many of.

3. ***Alumni Panels.*** I believe it is incredibly important to create a program in which law students, especially first-generation students, can see themselves in someone else who was successful. To do this, I have created a series of alumni panels to talk to students about their experience preparing for and taking the bar exam. The panel series includes the following:
   - First-Generation Bar Taker—A panel consisting of first-generation students discussing how they were successful on the bar exam.
   - Being a BIPOC Bar Taker—A panel consisting of BIPOC alumni discussing how they were successful on the bar exam and how to combat the statistic of lower bar passage for law graduates of color.
   - Beating First-Year Grades—A panel consisting of students who were successful on the bar exam on the first attempt but had a low law school GPA after their first year.

4. *See* C.J. Ryan & Derek T. Mueller, *The Secret Sauce: Examining Law Schools that Overperform on the Bar Exam*, 75 FLA. L. REV. 65–116 (2023).

- Accommodations and the Bar Exam—A panel consisting of alumni who received accommodations on the bar exam discussing how to approach bar study with accommodations and disabilities.

These panels have room to expand and grow into more topics, but they have been quite successful in promoting a growth rather than a fixed mindset in our first-generation students. It is no longer about "I never did this before, so I might fail," but is instead about "Someone like me did it, and I can do it, too."

III. Final Thoughts

We must support our first-generation students up until the end, which includes help with the bar exam. It's our jobs as academic success or bar success professionals to demystify the experience and give them the support that they do not have. I encourage you to also talk to your first-generation bar takers to get feedback to see how you can create specific programming for your law school to support this population. These individuals bring with them incredibly hard work, determination, and unique perspectives, and we must help them pass this exam so they can be the amazing attorneys we know they will be.